Mission
in
Dialogue

Mission
in
Dialogue

The Sedos Research Seminar
on the Future of Mission
March 8–19, 1981, Rome, Italy

EDITED BY
MARY MOTTE, F.M.M.
AND
JOSEPH R. LANG, M.M.

ORBIS BOOKS
Maryknoll, New York 10545

Design on p. ii by Eunice Cudzewicz, SCMM

The Catholic Foreign Mission Society of America (Maryknoll) recruits and trains people for overseas missionary service. Through Orbis Books Maryknoll aims to foster the international dialogue that is essential to mission. The books published, however, reflect the opinions of their authors and are not meant to represent the official position of the society.

Copyright © 1982 by Orbis Books, Maryknoll, NY 10545
All rights reserved
Manufactured in the United States of America

Manuscript editor: Lisa McGaw

Library of Congress Cataloging in Publication Data
Main entry under title:

Mission in dialogue.

Proceedings of the SEDOS Research Seminar on
the Future of Mission, held in Grottaferrata,
Rome, Mar. 8-19, 1981.
Includes bibliographical references and index.
1. Missions—Congresses. I. SEDOS (Organization)
II. SEDOS Research Seminar on the Future of
Mission (1981: Grottaferrata, Italy)
BV2160.M53   266'.2   82-2258
ISBN 0-88344-332-5   AACR2

**To Father James Loze, S.J.,
a missionary priest
who died for mission.**

Emptied for His grace to fill,
you stood briefly among us,
transparent like water for the light
and waves at sunset;
a spiraled incense we tried
to understand, growing to love
as you gently opened us to grace;
you taught us not to be afraid.

Contents

PREFACE

SEDOS is a study and documentary center at the service of forty-five member religious families, which share a common denominator and are united almost by a common charism, the mission *ad gentes,* within the unique eternal Christian mission to the world. Each of the institutes that makes up SEDOS has received from the Spirit this specific charism within the church. Since its inception after Vatican II, SEDOS has given itself to assist the member institutes in carrying out their common specific charism in the best manner possible.

When we think of mission, our first thought is of complexity and multiformity. The world today is characterized by rapid continual change. Mission is world-directed, hence it necessarily undergoes changes of perspective, choices, and priorities. This is true not only with respect to different ages, but also with regard to diverse cultural milieus.

The theological reflection, pastoral thrust, church's magisterium—so rich in research and aggiornamento in this postconciliar period—have brought about a gradual reassessment of the various elements that constitute the practical application of the sole mission that Christ entrusted to his disciples.

Agents of mission, therefore, must periodically reflect upon and evaluate the quality of their mission contribution to verify whether or not their activity goals are properly oriented, the means used apt to the end to be attained. In other words, they must determine whether or not their activity is truly a service to the work that the church has offered them and see if the human resources and means invested have been employed in the proper prospective.

Hence, in 1969 after Vatican II, SEDOS convoked a reunion in Rome of theologians and missionaries to study motives underlying mission and the commitment of the many men and women consecrated to mission activity. The questions raised were charged with weighty and concern-filled consequences.

With the passage of time and the impact of Vatican Council II, with the balance attained by the Synod of 1974 and the subsequent publication of *Evangelii Nuntiandi,* the period questioning the "why" of mission was over. In the meantime other equally pressing questions were raised, which touched the consciences of those who had consecrated their lives to mission. How is mission to be lived today? How enter into the ecclesial reality that is the monopoly of no one in particular, but the vocation of all? What are the dimensions and the priorities of mission?

The lessening number of vocations and hence of personnel engaged in mission, the changed mission areas, the new awareness that all Christians are both subject and object of mission at one and the same time, the challenge of political systems and diverse ideologies, secularization, and atheism in our day demanded a new reflection on the way of carrying out mission, or better still, of being a sign of mission, of being subject and object in a time of mission. The problem became more pressing as the churches gradually became more conscious of their mission vocation, when—at the same time—Paul VI declared that the church "keeps her missionary spirit alive, and even wishes to intensify it in the moment of history in which we are living" when there are not lacking those who think "that the time of missions is now past" (*Evangelii Nuntiandi,* no. 53).

In 1979 SEDOS, upon the request of various superiors general, decided to hold a seminar on this whole series of questions and problems. This meeting took place in the hills surrounding Rome, at Grottaferrata, March 8–19, 1981. We wish to single out two characteristics of this SEDOS Mission Seminar that seem quite significant: first, the spirit of communion and brotherhood that marked this meeting of 102 people hailing from more than thirty nations and six continents; second, the frankness with which the assembled delegates questioned themselves together. The combined wish for communion and frank research could have proved to be a difficulty, since the topic chosen for the seminar touched upon that "collective charism" of which we spoke earlier, and which constitutes the very raison d'être of the participants themselves. In this volume are offered not only the preparatory papers and conclusions of the seminar, but also a description of the way in which the work of these ten days gradually proceeded. Without this description it would seem difficult fully to comprehend the total reality that was the SEDOS Mission Seminar.

These notes of brotherhood, freedom, and openness, as well as the awareness of our own limits that were experienced during the seminar permitted us to conclude our study with renewed hope in the future of mission and left us with a more keen sense of our own smallness before the mystery of mission. Aware of this mystery, like the apostle Paul we kneel "before the Father, from whom every family, whether spiritual or natural, takes its name" (Eph. 3:14–15).

GABRIELE FERRARI, S.X.
Superior General
SEDOS President

GODELIEVE PROVÉ, S.C.M.M.-M.
Superior General
SEDOS Vice President

Acronyms and Abbreviations

AACC	All-Africa Conference of Churches
ACFOD	Asian Cultural Forum on Development
ACR	Australian Catholic Relief
ADS	AMECEA Documentation Service
ADVENIAT	German Catholic overseas relief organization
AEC	Australian Episcopal Conference
AIM	Africa Inland Mission
AMECEA	Association of the Member Episcopal Conferences of Eastern Africa
AMOR	Asian Meeting of Religious
APHD	Asia Partnership for Human Development
AWD	Action for World Development (Australia)
B.A.C.	Biblioteca de Autores Christianos (Library of Christian Authors)
BIMA	Bishops' Institute for Missionary Apostolate (Asia)
BIRA	Bishops' Institute for Interreligious Affairs (Asia)
BISA	Bishops' Institute for Social Action (Asia)
CAN	Christian Association of Nigeria
CBCI	Catholic Bishops' Conference of India
CCJP	Catholic Commission for Justice and Peace (Australia)
CEDI	Ecumenical Center for Documentation and Research
CEI	Bishops' Commission for Natives (Mexico)
CEJD	Commission for Evangelisation, Justice and Development (New Zealand)
CELAM	Latin American Bishops' Conference
CENAMI	National Center for Assistance to the Native Missions (Mexico)
CEPAC	Combined Episcopal Conferences of Australia, New Zealand, Papua New Guinea and the Pacific
CERTEX	An association for free exportation by businesses (Peru)
CIDSE	International Cooperation for Socio-Economic Development
CIED	Center for Information, Study, and Documentation (Peru)
CIM	Centre International Missionnaire (International Missionary Center)
CINCOS	Center for Social Intercommunication (Peru)
CIRM	Confederation of Mexican Religious Institutes
CLAI	Latin American Council of Churches

CMS   Church Missionary Society
CNBB   Conferência Nacional dos Bispos do Brasil
                (National Conference of Brazilian Bishops)
COCU   Consultation on Church Union
CRESA   Consultation for Religious Education in Southern Africa
CRS   Catholic Relief Services
CSC   Christian Service Committee (Malawi)
CSM   Church of Scotland Mission
CWL   Catholic Women's League
CWME   Commission on World Mission and Evangelism
CWS   Christian World Service
Denz.   H. Denzinger, *Enchiridion Symbolorum,* 32nd ed. (1963)
EA   Evangelical Alliance (Melanesia)
ESOD   Ecumenical Secretariat on Development (New Zealand)
FABC   Federation of Asian Bishops' Conferences
FABC-N   *FABC Newsletter*
FSLN   Frente Sandinista de Liberación Nacional (Nicaragua)
                (Sandinista Front for National Liberation)
HART   Halt All Racist Tours
IMMIS   Mexican Institute of Seculars
ISAL   Iglesia y Sociedad en América Latina
                (Church and Society in Latin America)
JEC   Young Christian Students
JOC   Young Christian Workers
JRSK   Joint Refugee Services of Kenya
KONGGAR   Joint Congress on Religious (Indonesia)
LAI   Indonesian Bible Society (Protestant)
LBI   Indonesian Bible Association (Catholic)
LK3I   Institute for the Welfare of Catholic Families (Indonesia)
MASRI   Religious Congregations in Indonesia
MATS   Melanesian Association of Theological Schools
MAWI   Indonesian Bishops' Conference
MCC   Melanesian Council of Churches
MEC   Student Christian Movement (Cuba)
MISEREOR   German Catholic development agency
MISSIO   Missionswissenschaftliches Institut (West Germany)
NATO   North Atlantic Treaty Organization
NCC   National Civil Council (Australia)
NCC   National Council of Churches
NCCB   National Conference of Catholic Bishops (United States)
NCCK   National Christian Council of Kenya
NMC   National Missionary Council (Australia)
NZCOA   New Zealand Catholic Overseas Aid
PERDHAKI   Association of Voluntary Health Services of Indonesia
PIME   The Pontifical Institute for Foreign Missions (Milan Fathers)

PMAS	Pontifical Mission Aid Society
PMI	Pacific Mission Institue
PPHD	Pacific Partnership for Human Development
REB	*Revista Eclesiastica Brasileira*
REPELITA	Indonesian five-year development program
SALT	Strategic Arms Limitation Treaty
SCEP	Sacred Congregation for the Evangelization of Peoples, or Propaganda Fide
SDA	Seventh-Day Adventists
SEATO	South-East Asia Treaty Organization
SEDOC	Serviço de Documentação (Documentation Service)
SEDOS	Servizio Documentazione e Studi (Rome)
SICA	Solomon Islands Christian Association
SODEPAX	Committee on Society, Development and Peace (Geneva)
TM	Transcendental Meditation
UISG	International Union of Superiors General (women)
UMCA	Universities Mission to Central Africa
UMM	United Methodist Mission
UNDA	International Association of Catholic Broadcasters
UNESCO	United Nations Educational, Scientific and Cultural Organization
UPC	Uganda Peoples Congress
USCC	United States Catholic Conference
UISG	International Union of Superiors General (women)(Rome)
USG	Union of Superiors General (men)(Rome)
WCC	World Council of Churches
WCF	World Confessional Family
WHO	World Health Organization (United Nations)

Introduction

THE SEDOS RESEARCH SEMINAR ON THE FUTURE OF MISSION

Joseph R. Lang, M.M.

The SEDOS Research Seminar on the Future of Mission was a consultation of 102 persons from six continents which met at Villa Cavalletti, Grottaferrata (Rome), from the 8th to the 19th of March, 1981. The preparations for this second major SEDOS conference were long and detailed. Rightly so, because at this point of history many missionary-sending institutes are concerned about the future of mission in that the concept of mission theology and methodology, and its application, in the modern world is changing very rapidly. It is possible that these constant changes in the world could affect the future structures of missionary institutes.

The idea for the 1981 research seminar was first presented in June 1978 when a handful of people, both clerical and lay, met in Louvain, Belgium, to discuss the possibilities of holding a rather lengthy and important research seminar on the future of mission. The ideas brought forth at this meeting were practical in nature due to the fact that the input at this stage was limited in scope. At this time the concern centered around the need for missionaries in the future and, if there would be a need for missionaries, what would be the political, social, and ecclesiastical environment for future missionary activities in the world. However, it was readily seen that a detailed research seminar on the future of mission would touch not only these practical points, but go far beyond these concepts and lead us to a completely new understanding of our missionary role as the many local churches of the world begin to take on their own identity within the mission of the universal church.

It was soon seen that the missionary institutes, with the help of consultation, needed to face such problems as the freedom to proclaim the gospel of Jesus Christ, the challenge to change present institutional structures in order to fit into the present signs of the times, a readiness to risk certain cherished traditions and methods in order to identify themselves with the People of God, the courage to denounce the violation of peoples' rights, the necessity to identify themselves with the poor, the urgency to place themselves in complete cooperation with one another and with other Christian bodies, the desire to inculturate themselves in the pluralistic culture

1

of the world, and the ability to support one another in conflicts, in isolation, and in failure.

Mission originates in God the Father, centers itself in Jesus Christ, and is carried out among peoples of the world. Its movement is that of the Holy Spirit. It involves extending the liberating and healing ministry of Christ and sharing the peace of Christ with the inhabitants of the six continents. Thus in sharing the good news of Christ, missionary institutes, according to their own charisms and competencies in specific areas, will have an important role in the future of mission of the universal church in proclaiming the kingdom of God, although this role will take on somewhat different forms from those used in the past.

Consequently the missionary institutes, faced with the uncertainty of missionary activity in the future, asked SEDOS if it could sponsor a research seminar on the future of mission. Thus a feasibility study was drawn up in February 1979 in order to give a detailed response to this question. It was concluded in the feasibility study that SEDOS could sponsor such a research seminar, which, although it might not provide clear answers and projections about mission in the future, would have the possibility of uncovering the deeper significance of what is actually happening in mission today; and, from this perspective, it could indicate needed orientations for the future. As a result of the feasibility study, at a special General Assembly of the SEDOS members held on March 27, 1979, it was voted unanimously to hold a Research Seminar on the Future of Mission.

A task force was formed and from this moment forward the realities of the research seminar began to take shape. In May 1979 the first consultation with the members of SEDOS took place with respect to the topics that should be studied during the research seminar. Through this consultation it was decided that the main theme of the research seminar would focus on the local church in its relationship to the present emerging concerns in mission, namely: the missionary dimensions of the local church, the local church in secular societies, the local church and ecumenism, the local church in relation to missionary institutes, the other religious traditions in the local church itself, religious freedom and the local church, inculturation in the local church, and, lastly, the liberation and justice dimension of the mission of the local church. In July 1979, by means of a second consultation, the members of SEDOS and certain experts were requested to critique these statements. These statements were then analyzed and reformulated, and in December 1979, by means of other ad hoc consultations, a list of pertinent experts was drawn up who would be asked to write papers on the various subjects mentioned above.

Out of fifty-five experts contacted from the six continents, fifty wrote papers that would be used as input for the research seminar. At this point, at the request of the SEDOS membership, another question was added, namely, the present situation of the local church in China. Three papers were written on the China question and forty-seven were written on the other topics. These papers represent reflections about different situations in the local churches on the six continents, written for the most part by persons who are indigenous to these situations. The reflections in the papers themselves are centered on concrete experiences in mission from the perspective of the local church within a specific context, and on the opening of these experiences through various kinds of relationships to the larger experiences of the universal church.

In July–August 1980 eighteen persons in Rome critiqued these papers in order to rate the quality of their contents, to indicate important and/or new ideas about mission/evangelization, and to specify ideas needing further clarification. With a few exceptions, each of the papers was critiqued by two persons, taking into account both the content and the geographical situations of the authors. The information gathered from this process was very important for the Steering Committee of the research seminar in order to allow them to invite the most appropriate experts who would give the right input to the research seminar.

During this time of preparation various ad hoc consultations took place concerning many of the details for the research seminar itself. It was envisioned that as many persons as possible should be involved in the process of preparation. The persons involved were usually members of SEDOS; but there were other persons who gladly collaborated in helping to overcome the many obstacles that presented themselves and to give positive input, not only for the practical preparations, but for the formulation of the future methodology that would be used.

The model chosen for the methodology for the preparation of the research seminar, and for the seminar itself, was an ongoing evaluation model. Like all research methodologies, this model is concerned with objectives and strategies to obtain its goal with reliability and validity. This ongoing evaluation model begins with a vaguely defined general objective and clarifies that objective through the actual research process. This model allows for the incorporation of new data and new participants as developments emerge in the process of doing the research. The ultimate objective is gradually modified and sharpened through the contribution of the various participants toward behavioral expressions that represent real or possible experiences on the part of the participants. If this model is carried out carefully and consistently, it can offer end-results that will reflect life in the situation about which a research seminar is concerned, because this model can assume a great deal of variance without affecting validity in a negative way.

During the SEDOS Research Seminar itself the ongoing evaluation model allowed for interaction between life experience and theory, between concreteness and abstraction, and between pastoral practice and theology. This model provided an ambience that fostered enriching relationships among persons from different cultural environments, that allowed for a sufficient balance between work and rest, and, lastly, that had sufficient structures to enable the participants to articulate a sharing in a meaningful way for the future. At the same time, it gave the participants a sufficient openness to the inspiration of the Holy Spirit.

This methodology of the ongoing evaluation model permitted the participants to do most of their work in group meetings, although there were plenary sessions. There were ten groups in all, of various languages, with approximately ten persons in each group. The working together in small units gave the participants an opportunity to have a very valuable living/liturgical/prayer experience that formed an integral part of the overall agenda. During the group meetings there was ample time to exchange and share reflections, experiences, and views about subjects being studied in order to deepen an understanding of a needed vision for future missionary activities, and to move toward a new level of insights about the subjects under consideration. This model gave the participants sufficient time for personal and prayerful reflection in order that they might discover for themselves what was emerging from the group discussions for the importance of the future of mission. Likewise this particular methodology presented an opportunity for an intensive dialogue between persons coming from different local churches on the six continents. At the end of the ten-day session a real community of confidence, trust, and faith was formed.

In order to guide the participants during their ten days of reflection, study, and discussion, four working papers were drawn up, which revolved around four clusters into which the original eight topics were divided. The four working papers dealt with the following: (1) the mission of the church in local churches on six continents, (2) elements for theological and scriptural reflection describing the mission of the church today, (3) the relationships, structures, and services that enable the church to carry out its mission, and (4) historical variables in the evolution of mission that have effected both positive and negative transformations. A fifth working paper concerning the mission of the local church in China was added.

The participants at the research seminar were from different continents, from different cultures, and from different backgrounds. The participants included administrators of the different SEDOS member institutes and those who are actually engaged in mission in the different local churches and who had contributed reflection-study papers as input for the research seminar. The participants were lay, religious, and clerical from both Catholic and other faiths. The participants were from thirty-three different nationalities and represented the six continents of the world.

The outcome of the research seminar was an Agenda for Future Planning, Study, and Research in Mission. This agenda is not a "final document" in the ordinary sense of the term, but simply an agenda that contains both the convergences and the divergences of the participants, which will serve as a plan of action for the future of mission for both the mission-sending institutes and those concerned for the future of mission. This agenda contains three major divisions: The Directions in Mission Today, The Central Role of the Local Church, and The Task for Missionary Institutes.

It is hoped that the research seminar itself and its results, along with the contents of this book, will serve as an inspiration for future missionary evangelization and will give us a renewed missionary conscience for the future. We have been sent to proclaim the kingdom to those with broken hopes who inhabit the six continents of the world. "For the Church, evangelization means bringing the Good News into all the strata of humanity, and through its influence transforming humanity from within and making it new . . ." *(Evangelii Nuntiandi,* no. 18).

Part I

PERSPECTIVES OF THE MISSION OF THE LOCAL CHURCH: THE REFLECTION-STUDY PAPERS WRITTEN FOR THE SEDOS RESEARCH SEMINAR

The reflection-study papers that were written in response to the eight principal questions developed for the SEDOS Research Seminar on the Future of Mission are presented in the following pages.* These papers, which explore the major dimensions of the way mission is being realized in various local churches on the six continents, are grouped in sections by theme. The questions pertaining to each of these themes are presented at the beginning of each section.

Various styles are found among the papers, ranging from conversational reflections to documented research. A range of views and opinions is represented, just as the authors brought among us a myriad of insights, questions, and ideas while we sought to understand the way of mission in the future during the days of the seminar. In this spirit—hoping to provoke to yet deeper depths the search that will lead into the future—these papers are presented.

* The papers written on the mission of the local church in China have not been included because of the nature of the documentation used, which did not lend itself to publication in book form.

Section 1

THE MISSIONARY DIMENSIONS OF THE LOCAL CHURCH

Statement of the Question

The process of ongoing evangelization within a local church is a principal factor determining the expression of mission. Mission is likewise determined by the openness of a local church to the universality of the church. Therefore in every local church, mission is a focal point for receiving and sending; some persons in every local church have a special call to be sent to another local church. In fact a sign of the maturity of a local church is the sending of missionaries to other local churches. Every local church has the call also to receive others to assist in its mission. Thus within every local church the universal church is present.

Elements for Reflection on the Question

- The universality of the church
- The insufficiency of a local church if left to itself
- The need for members of a local church to complete their experience of faith through sharing the experience of those who come from other local churches
- The role of missionaries, task-oriented in the past, is now moving toward a role of relationship, friendship, sharing of faith experience
- Different forms of financial dependency that prevent a local church from becoming mature
- The self-assessment required of a local church when requesting missionaries from other local churches
- The relation between sending forth missionaries and signs of maturity in a local church
- The recognition on the part of bishops of their responsibility for mission
- The process of integration in a local church on the part of those coming from other local churches
- The tensions between a local church and those coming from other local churches
- The continued presence of neocolonialism in some local churches

Related Questions

- What are the new needs and roles that are becoming the motivating force for mission in your local church?

7

- How is openness to the universal church expressed in your situation, and is this adequate?
- What is the focus of self-evangelization within the local church, and how is this being related to openness to the universal church?
- What elements are emerging in your local church to indicate a new kind of relationship with missionaries coming from other local churches, including missionary institutes?
- How could official structures of the church promote universality within your local church?
- What problems are specific to the situation in your local church?
- What orientations are emerging that would seem to have significance for the future?

1

HAITI

Paul-Antoine Bien-Aimé, O.P.

The marvelous event of our salvation is a matter of astonishment to the powers of heaven. Its form and manner is something altogether novel and unprecedented. At the appropriate moment, or so Gregory of Nyssa tells us in his explanation of Ephesians 3:10, the angels were indeed admitted to the contemplation of the divine wisdom that wrought creation. But of the *admirabile commercium* they had no idea whatever. Only through the church have the angels come to a knowledge of the awesome work of divine wisdom that thereupon ensued: the kenotic union of contraries, in which infinite and finite, indeterminate and determined, God and the human being, become one—without confusion, but without separation—in a Second Creation more marvelous than the first (Gregory of Nyssa 6:254.20–255.4).

Surely we shall not be deemed rash if, amid the wild prodigality of this miraculous incarnation, we were to add something to the angelic amazement. This church, this communion undreamed of by the professional admirers of the divine wisdom, is catholic. God becomes a human being and saves every one of his fellows. The catholicity of the church, evangelizer of all cultures—*that* is an admirable invention of this multiform divine wisdom!

The whole universe is caught up in this work of restoration accomplished in Jesus Christ. The church becomes a sign of this new creation for all peoples. In it, in the church, every knee bends, every tongue proclaims the lordship of Christ. The church is catholic. Every Christian community is a replica of the universal character of the church. And unless we restrict our concept of the missionary task of a local church to the sending of men and women to another people, we can say that a local church, by the very fact of being catholic, is missionary. The missionary impulse in a local church is not the leftovers, the residue, once the Christian community is well established and its parishes and ministerial assignments are going well. Every local

Paul-Antoine Bien-Aimé, a Dominican priest from Haiti, is presently engaged with a team composed of other religious and laity in the animation of a vast rural parish in Haiti, and the changeover of the parish structures into those of *une communauté ecclésiale de base,* or a grassroots Christian community.

9

church carries out the universal mission of the church just by existing. And every effort it makes to be a better Christian community, however little it may have to do with matters abroad, is an effort to the advantage of the universal church, as Puebla teaches.

In this view of things, every local church can send and receive missionaries. In fact it would probably be a good thing if the younger churches would send evangelizers to some part of the Western world. But, you say, only a mature church can send missionaries. Surely the "maturity" required here is not a temporal one, the one that arrives slowly in the course of history, but a maturity of solid establishment. On the deepest level a missionary vocation exists for every local church, even though a particular call can be received by one or other member of the community. A reassessment of the missionary endeavor to include bilateral exchanges between local churches would itself be a sign of the genuine maturity of the churches.

Universal salvation in Jesus Christ, yes; the church as sacrament of this total restoration, yes; the missionary call and task of every local church, yes—but there is no escaping the fact that the actual mission is more concrete than this, and that this is what poses problems for the actual missionaries, as well as for the Christians and non-Christians of the churches that receive them.

The Concrete Mission of the Haitian Church

The Afro-American missionary endeavor of the Western church during the 1940s–1960s was to a considerable extent, as is well known, a matter of brainwashing. Even apart from the frequent, unfortunate simplification (necessarily, just a simplification) of the missionary undertaking of the West as an enterprise of total colonialism—sword, cross, and plow—the evangelization of our continent has had results that tend all too clearly to confirm this analysis. It was the Black Muslims, black power, and the Black Panthers who originally popularized this view that evangelization was brainwashing, especially in the words and works of Malcolm X. Their remarkable propaganda effort constituted then, and still constitutes today, the often ignored epicenter of tremors of very broad radii.

Historical Matrix

In Haiti, too, for almost two centuries, the church doughtily participated in the brainwashing required for an integration of the black slave into the prevailing economic system. By its automatic baptisms, with the imposition of occidental names, by its concerted repression of the African religions, the Christian community of the times threw its weight to the global attempt on the part of the colonial powers, and of course of individual colonists, to de-Africanize the black slave. He or she was to be reduced to a state of servile, animal energy for work, reduced to a living tool.

The Africans' response was not long in coming. They invented the lifestyle we call *marronage,* a form of clandestinity including at first only rebel slaves, but eventually comprising and associating everything that was forbidden to the black. It was the psychological resistance of a whole people, and it gave rise to a whole politics of avoidance, the only thing possible where all frontal attack was out of the question. One of the results was a collective personality. But another was a singular climate of hypocrisy and mistrust. And so the "system Negro" was born, the black stool-pigeon, the social outcast astutely created by the white.

After nearly two centuries of superficial and repressive Christianization, of the systematic exclusion of blacks from their own universe, of their membership in two different societies according to two different mentalities, of their quasi-natural attraction for the society and religion of the master, that arbiter of social respectability, and of an undying memory (often depreciatory) of the black world—one does not need a pocket calculator to conclude that a universe like that will not automatically crumble away as a result of a genuine War of Independence (1804), the signing of a concordat (1860), campaigns against superstition, and the happy event of the Haitianization of the episcopate (1966).

The Vitality of the Haitian Church

And yet our church is a living one. The laity seem to have taken the future of the rural communities in hand perforce, long before Vatican Council II. The responsibility and determination of the laity are probably the most beautiful flower of all the missionary activity in Haiti. For around the parish complex itself, where the priest generally resides, there cluster communities of Christians from four or five different villages, and these little communities are called *chapelles* ("chapels"). Each is served by its *sacristain,* who is the actual pastoral minister, or by a lay group. More often than not the whole life of the community centers around the *chapelle.* Christians do not hesitate to undertake a two- or three-hour journey on foot to reach their chapel on Sunday. Catechesis proceeds in normal fashion, and the demand for the sacraments is enormous. To boot, the Christian message is important to a rather large part of the population. And all of this involvement and activity is often carried out with an admirable unselfishness and commitment.

At the present time our most backward Christian communities are out ahead of the secular community. In many places the most active members of the local councils and committees come from our churches and *chapelles.* It is the Christians who build the roads and the infirmaries, clean up the sources of drinking water, teach the rudiments of reading and writing, and set up cooperatives. A whole ideology of community development takes its inspiration from a biblical catechesis oriented toward the first chapter of the book of Genesis—in fact one of the catechisms is actually entitled *Jénèz 1:28.* Many among us are beginning to grasp the solidarity that exists between the endeavor of personal conversion and that of a transformation of society. And indeed the church is everywhere present. True, it has to become more a church of the people, and divest itself of a too middle-class and urban image (its boarding schools are in the cities). But thanks to its avant-garde laity, with their development projects (dispensaries and *Écoles Presbytérales* are to be found nearly everywhere), thanks to its administrative framework of parish centers and *chapelles,* the church can go where many others cannot.

In certain respects our church is even capable of self-criticism. In our own diocese especially, there has been a mighty campaign against superstition (voodoo), along with a preparation for the celebration of the sacraments, for thirty years now. On orders of the hierarchy, and by the will of the people of the church, a great effort is being made to meet the challenge of the rather aggressive North American Baptist churches by imitating their methods, and Catholics are willing to make innumerable sacrifices to this end. They have come to the realization that it is time to be done with ornamentation and syncretism and have sent into the field a whole army of apostles, which has learned to make use of the challenging, confronting tone used by the sects in their own kerygma, their proclamation of the gospel. After some instances of the conversion of practicing Catholics to the Baptist confession, the Catholic community woke up and began to convert itself.

The liturgy, too, testifies to the vitality of our church, even when it is satisfied with merely translating and accommodating what is done elsewhere. The Creole language and Haitian music have been in use for some fifteen years. Visitors from abroad are in constant admiration of the vitality of our liturgical assemblies, where a whole people sings, and sometimes dances, to the beat of the drums. In the area of religious music we have a great deal of creativity, even if its authentic liturgical inspiration is still lacking. In a true sense, which we ought to make more explicit, our people enjoy free speech in the church—or at least they speak freely. Their ease of expression is astonishing. A person who can barely read and write will often read and comment on a passage from the Bible and even give an impromptu homily. The Prayer of the Faithful often comes close to degenerating into a minor riot: people's spontaneous intentions reach a pitch where one might think it was a shouting match instead of a prayer. (Something our more proper churches only dream about!)

The Need for Auto-Evangelization

And so the ideal conditions are present for a self-evangelization. The moment has come for our church to evangelize itself while it is evangelizing the Haitian culture. We ought to remark that this auto-evangelization is not a "normal consequence" of suddenly having a native clergy. We are all familiar with Christian communities, solidly established and in the hands of a native clergy, where authoritarianism is getting stronger every day. It is often a matter of clericalism. A surprising number of pastoral ministers in the third world still seem to consider a maniacal conformity with anything and everything Roman to be the infallible sign of fidelity to Christ. But even apart from this, there are imperatives in Haiti today of an urgency well calculated to persuade one to undertake the work of self-evangelization without a moment's further delay. The main reasons are two.

The Voodoo Influence. In spite of at least three centuries of repression in various forms, voodoo continues to pervade the warp and woof of Haitian life. It is still a genuine national religion. It is most unpleasant to have to say it, but it is inescapable that all Haitian societal forms have their religious counterparts in voodoo. Even the source of wealth, the accumulation of riches—which is the problem of problems in a country where every level of society has the daily experience of what it means to be "underdeveloped"—is attributed to voodoo. Of course, a plethora of other ills as well inspire the flight to voodoo: illness, the infertility of the soil, political unrest, death, madness, racial differences. Every juncture or passage in the life of a human being is thus placed in a religious perspective of this type. And entirely apart from practice, be it habitual or occasional, voodoo theology, with its forceful attempt to legitimize the social status quo, is interiorized by at least 90 percent of the population.

We are not speaking about the past. We are describing the present situation. The persistence of voodoo is disquieting when measured against the efforts at its elimination that have been undertaken. It would be superfluous to cite once more all the efforts of the colonials to annihilate it. It is notorious that social structures of the period were altogether incompatible with anything like a unifying element in the mentality of the people, and that the overlords left no stone unturned to eradicate as mighty a unifying influence as voodoo. Nor need we rehearse the somber hours of official colonial evangelization, when the clergy employed the secular arm, or their own brawn, to burn the objects of the voodoo cult and to chastise its priests and recalcitrant devotees. Let us be content with the simple consideration of how irreverent it is to go about carelessly preaching the identity of voodoo gods with the devil. When one considers how numerous are the manifestations of the actual devil in voodoo, one has to shake one's head at the naïveté of such an identification. Voodoo is satanic, yes—but satanism attracts. Three-fourths of convinced Catholics are occasional practitioners of voodoo.

The contradiction is only apparent. Catholicism, the religion of the master, taken up by the slave, could never have offered him or her the same attraction as voodoo. It was ever a far-off world, strange and white, that was superimposed. Voodoo, on the other hand, is right there, at home, sacralizing the garden, commerce, love, the construction of a house, a voyage abroad, a dream, an accident, an important decision; sacralizing the family as well, and one's own body on occasion, for it can become the steed of the god, during the so-called seizure of possession. The *loas* are right there, they materialize. You hear them speak. They live among us. Perhaps in that tree! Then too, one is always at home: anyone who has the misfortune to be driven mad can rely upon his or her whole family to take care of the religious, then the social, purification and reinstatement.

Here we have an open letter to Christianity. Only, it has not been really read. Its reading is urgent, for even if evangelization is not simply the beatific admiration of a non-Christian culture (as more than one modern missionary, it would seem, would like to have it), neither has that word of Pentecost yet come on the scene that will do any real converting in Haiti. There is nothing ingenuous or innocent about voodoo in the exercise of its ideological function. Mental laziness, a climate of fear and mistrust, and as their corollary, mischief, charlatanism, shameless exploitation, and intimidation—all these form part of voodoo's stock in trade.

We face an immense task of evangelization. Here is a whole culture to evangelize in depth, and by the very methods that everyone applauds and no one implements. To begin, why not try a little simple respect? Why not treat voodoo as a non-Christian religion, solidly established in Haiti, practiced by many, interiorized by the great majority—and follow the conciliar recommendations for all non-Christian religion?

The second stage would be an inventory of building blocks already lying right there waiting to be used. The Christian critique, something after the manner of a transfiguration, would come later. It will require an intelligent church for all this.

The Road to Self-Understanding: The Grassroots Ecclesial Communities. Intelligence is in short supply, unfortunately, and its lack illustrates the urgency of self-evangelization. The theology of the Greek fathers ceaselessly invites us to a spiritual understanding, a "spiritual intelligence"—the sharpsightedness that permits us to unveil the Presence in a simple reading of the signs of the times. The prophets were not, after all, great clairvoyants. But in spite of all these trump cards, the church does not seem to know how to win a trick. The church does not read the signs of the times, does not help us to understand. Indeed, curiously, one of the great fruits of the presence of the church is that the church assists us in a non-narcissistic perception of things (contrast neocolonialism), helps us to open up our vision of our own selves. Where does the divine friendship dwell if not in just such transparency? The message that is striving to come through here amid all the babbling is the voice of a people that historically by its past, and still today, lives in an interior exile. The permeation of all aspects of life which voodoo enjoys is as yet unknown to Christianity. What is needed is a genuine willingness to reappropriate the Christian message. In this way, it is to be hoped, we shall gain in our intelligent understanding of our global situation.

The perspicacity in question here is not, I think, the result of a simple effort at personal or collective lucidity. The indwelling of the Spirit of Christ provokes a genuine induction of truth, as an old collect, that of Ember Wednesday after Pentecost, seems to suggest: "Mentes nostras . . . Paraclitus illuminet . . . et inducat in omnem veritatem" ("May the Paraclete enlighten our minds, and lead us to all truth"). Intelligence, in the sense of a clear grasp of the truth, is a consequence of evangelization. It seems to me that the single most important thing about the indigenization of Christianity is its quality as a signpost pointing in this direction, pointing toward this result. It is not a simple matter of ordaining the indigenous peoples, of handing over the power to the autochthonous, of translating the liturgy into the vernacular, and of letting the zither, the tom-tom, and the Indian flute be played in church. To indigenize Christianity is to allow it to participate in the enterprise of understanding and accepting a culture in itself. This normal, positive contribution of Christianity is not exactly common coin. But we do have one beautiful example of it in the phenomenon of the theology of liberation. This theology, through a process of groping, is permitting a whole continent to penetrate its reality.

Our Haitian church is still in search of such an understanding. Elsewhere, indeed not far away, a reflection on the socioeconomic and anthropological realities of evangelized peoples is being carried on, often at considerable risk, by the Christians themselves. Yet we here continue to resonate to the rhythms of a collective harmony. When the chips are down and Christianity has no response, we turn to voodoo. Our mentality has not yet been Christianized. To justify what cannot be justified, voodoo schemes are invoked. To take care of the problems of underdevelopment, we hope for a New Occupation. Still the Christian contribution can be an original one here. There is hope.

At the moment we feel the necessity of reorganizing the traditional *chapelle* into *communautés ecclésiales de base,* into grassroots communities, and several experiments have already been attempted. Here we are in the presence of a spontaneous rearticulation of religious discourse. The response on the part of the People of God is immense, and we should not be surprised. Has not one of the great advantages of voodoo been the geographical, hence existential, concentration of its devotees? In order to complete the task begun, the emphasis will have to be on the renewal of life in the sense defined at Puebla. A reflection, existential and not speculative, on everyday life helps to clear the vision. The work to be done is considerable—for although we have learned to organize prayer meetings, to preach, and to participate, our spiritual understanding is still slothful.

Furthermore there is the real danger of these new communities transforming into simple *chapelles* under the leadership of a sacristan. A study that has been carried out of the experiments already attempted shows the persistent popularity of the "group-following-a-leader's-directions" model. Concretely the battle is real and constant: preventing a member of the *communauté de base* from becoming a *sacristain,* the unchallenged leader, the priest-archetype of intra-ecclesial social relationships; likewise preventing certain other members from spontaneously accepting such a transformation, preventing them from making someone king. It is remarkable in the evolution of these communities among us that we very quickly feel the need of doing something in common—a garden, a business enterprise, a school—interesting attempts to de-intellectualize these communities.

Eventually the appearance of these communities will provoke a reflection on ministry. Presently the whole life of a church is organized by the parish center, which is for the most part urban, or semiurban. Rural communities celebrate Mass once a month at best, on the occasion of the priest's visit. For the remainder of the time liturgies of the word are held, presided over by lay persons. The urban or semiurban centers have all the advantages. On the great holy days of the liturgical year, the priest celebrates at the center. Certain *chapelles* manage to get to the parish in the suburb or the city, but they have the feeling of being away from home. And then many cannot come at all. None of this is very helpful for an appreciation of the liturgical cycle, and it is sometimes easy to understand the random occurrence of the call from the pulpit to personal conversion. Not enough manpower, you hear it said. Well, what about the *jus membrorum,* the right of Christians to celebrate Mass, to receive a decent catechesis, to have access to the sacraments? Does this right have less force than the need for ministers to be college graduates? This is a question that we shall not be able to escape in coming years.

And so we are at work, with courage and faith. We believe in the need for self-evangelization, and the success of the North American sects has provoked us to action. We have done too much talking and too little in the way of deeds until now, but things are under way, and the first stage of evangelization will have to be followed by the question of relationships between churches and between the foreign missionaries and the local church. This question will have to be resolved in a project of the self-affirmation of the local church. And this is a good thing for the foreign missionaries. Working in a local church that cannot quite get up on its feet will bring a disappointment or two to the brother or sister from another church. The local church has to be able to say that it believes it has understood something of the will of God for the present moment in its history. Otherwise what good would money, building projects, devotion, exile from one's native land, and the effort of adaptation be?

Neocolonial Residue and Relationships among Local Churches

Generally, in Haiti, foreign missionaries and the indigenous population get on well, and the animosity that seems to exist in other places is missing. However, we cannot allow ourselves to become smug. The foreigner is generally well regarded among us, and thus must not cease to be a source of uneasiness for us. For the great majority of Haitians, because of their history of neocolonialism, salvation can come only from abroad. Either we must go abroad ourselves, or welcome here the various foreigners who arrive with interesting projects in hand—cement, electricity, prefabricated factories. This is true in the church; it is true outside the church. In large part this xenophilia is the fruit of imperialism's ideological domination on a world scale—and in this it strangely resembles its counterpart, xenophobia. Every relationship between Western missionary and local person is marked in some way by the neocolonial reality.

Dependence

In such conditions, to speak of "traces" of neocolonialism is a euphemism. We live in a situation where socioeconomic conditions do an excellent job of reinforcing all the preexistent opacities. It is deplorable, then, that the opening of a local community to the universality of the church must consist in the implementation by a peripheral community of directives emanating from the center, or the even more traumatizing form of the underdeveloped community seeking financial assistance. Financial dependence is surely a sign of the power of neocolonialism.

This point deserves some consideration. I do not think that there is a satisfactory solution. Nor is there a miracle-strategy to follow. Everything is complex in this area. Can we ask every missionary to live exactly like a Haitian? To be supported by a community that is hungry? Where new building is really needed, can we require the community to do it, no matter what community it is, on grounds that the community should be independent? Should all contributions from the outside be refused? Should catechists be required to work on a purely voluntary basis? And how can the institutions be kept functioning without aid from abroad? How can a community do its own management of outside assistance without running into snags? And the list goes on. In any case, we are helpless in the face of the quantitative and qualitative reinforcement of the financial dependency of the local church—and not at all by reason of the contribution from abroad, but by reason of the medium of its receipt.

The possibilities for education, for growth and maturation, in this area would in any case doubtless be improved if one were to authorize interparochial exchanges, or "intergroups." An entire group of local churches could set out together to become acquainted with one another and offer mutual assistance. When a project presented by a single local church turned out to be too expensive to be executed by a single church, a Haitian organization would be available for mediating the presentation of the project to a sister community. In this fashion we might correct the image of the priest or missionary as a bundle of relationships, receiving aid from an international organization that in the eyes of the people is no different from an agency of the United Nations. We are not even speaking of those missionaries who, thanks to their money, have become real feudal lords. It is difficult to see what their evangelical contribution could be in the endeavor of self-understanding considered above.

Missionary Prudence

In the face of the historical neocolonial reality, and of the existential results of this reality (by and large the missionary is not a pure stranger ministering to a pure native—each one's perception of the other is marked by the altogether precise socioeconomic relationships between their two countries), the transfer of members from one local church to another is not easy and automatic. And contrary to the opinion of some, a certain naïve spirit of evangelism does not suffice here. The foreign missionary has to have a genuine and courageous understanding of the situation. If we were to chart the profile of the prospective missionary, this spiritual intelligence or understanding would occupy an important place alongside the more traditional requirements of good health, a facility for foreign languages, the ability to get along on one's own, a talent for fixing and repairing things, an outgoing personality, and so on. Self-knowledge, knowledge of one's new country, a grasp of its international context, an ability to discover the good and bad sides of its indigenous society and the courage to come right out and identify them, first for oneself and then for others, the gift of drawing the necessary and practical conclusions—this is what will really show up the missionary spirit. And the ability to accept others, even when one is not accepted oneself.

This is the first step in the apprenticeship of missionary prudence. When you first set foot on foreign soil, especially in a poor country, the temptation is strong to refuse to learn. A salutary doubt—one that does not paralyze, of course—would have spared us many a misadventure. Who is proceeding properly? Who is right, he or I? Let me explain what I mean by an example. In missionary territory there is often building to be done. Who is going to select the plan and the materials—the foreign missionary or the local people? In a sense everything would be easy if the latter were not under the domination of an ideology, that is, if they did not wish to reproduce the architecture of foreign countries. The well-intentioned missionary will want the edifice to bear an indigenous stamp. The local church will want to use the foreign model. Who is going to decide? What will you do, teach local architecture? Or let the people have their way for the present, and hope that an evangelization that is spiritually more complete will restore lost confidence some day? The example may seem theoretical, but it has a correspondent in solid reality: church decor, the presence or absence of singing in French in a Creole liturgy, the image of the priest, a certain attitude toward the sacred, the frequenting of the sacraments. These are all circumstances in which only a missionary prudence that foresees the future of the local church can make a decision.

The Situation of a Missionary Undertaking within the Framework of Established Christian Communities

Who are these foreign Christians who fall out of the sky? This question rarely receives an answer in the local churches. One sometimes has the impression that, for the local person, a missionary is a being sent by a benevolent or malevolent international organization in order to establish Christianity somewhere. Old infantryman of the Christian faith that he is, the missionary knows everything about the imported religion. The society he comes from is a beautiful one, and if you embrace his faith and cling to his words you can enjoy a whole happy social emigration through him. After all, he is in the employ of the pope, the chief of all missionaries, and it is this great Prince of the Church who provides him with his funds. He is relatively honest—so honest that he has managed to acquire a fundamentally good image for the whites. He can count on a certain amount of social mobility. For that matter, even the Haitian priest is no longer Haitian. He is a priest, a regular important person, he comes on time . . . he is no longer Haitian, he is white.

Yes, this is a caricature. But where is the mission to local, living churches by local, living churches of truly living brothers and sisters? Here again it is clear that we must restore to the missionary assignments their character as intercommunitarian exchanges. The brother or sister who arrives in the missions does not come from a "center of Christian maturity"; he or she comes from a church in its own stage of development. The missionaries do not speak to us enough about the local churches that have sent them—a hard job when the local church of one's origin is situated in an advanced, imperialist, capitalist society! In one sense, though, the challenge of openness and transparency is a challenge on all sides: the system has done its work only too well, and even the local religious (or priest) has to work hard to come out in the open as a believer!

Changes Occurring in Missionaries' Attitudes

Certain well-known changes have begun to appear in relations between local churches and missionaries in Haiti. Facing up to the challenge of voodoo—finally—some foreign Christians have revised their approach to it, and a whole new behavior in its regard is the result. Haitians are more regularly consulted for information, and more frequently challenged by way of encounter. There is a marked increase in willingness to be open, to learn. Along with a Haitian confrere, I have twice been invited by large groups of French and Belgian missionaries to make workshop presentations on problems of evangelization and culture. Perhaps this is the most spectacular behavioral change of all. And finally—we are not there quite yet—the day is coming when practitioners of voodoo will no longer be accused of being agents of the devil. In that day many things will change. And we hope that the missionaries will be true pioneers in this adventure, for they will be faced with great numbers of indigenous peoples who will not always have managed to rid themselves of the old models of authoritarianism and sectarianism.

Conclusion: Complementarity

The path a church takes in its development can never be explained by autarchy, not even when it is a local church. I have had to learn this by personal experience. I have no regrets at having spent eight years in France, in a place where, without flattering anyone, I have to say I was able to participate in the life of the local church most intensely, if somewhat cerebrally. There for the first time I came in contact with a freedom that was not afraid to question things, and with a thirst for authenticity that surpassed its own vagaries. Through contact with another church I came to know myself, and my attachment to my church and my culture is the fruit of this exile, or rather, of this emigration. As a university student at the same time, however, I was able to experience a certain form of neocolonialism. Some of my confreres, students themselves, fine and true religious, were astonished to see me reading books of philosophy or theology. With only my own good in mind they would ask me, "What good is that going to do you?"—meaning, what you ought to be doing is studying sociology, linguistics, ethnology, political economics, and agriculture, in order to be useful to your country later on. In other words, become a national expert! (To put an end to the discussion, and to be able to continue to read what I wished without being a source of concern to anyone, I actually signed up for a correspondence course in Tropical Agronomy!) That was in France; and today, as a member of our team of Dominicans working in two parishes in Haiti, I still appreciate the stimulation of being in the presence of foreigners who are desirous of contributing to the process of self-understanding, of auto-evangelization.

The faith-experience of one local church should be complemented by the faith-experience of other churches. As long as missionary exchanges among local churches were conceived in terms of an enterprise of depaganization, it was difficult to see how a young church could contribute to the auto-evangelization of an older church. The problems of understanding among peoples, the human difficulties of comprehension among local churches—difficulties both born of and fostering the divisiveness of today's world—ought to lead us to search out another *modus vivendi*. Doubtless foreign missionaries, who are well integrated into their mother church, who are open and well aware of what time it is on the world clock, can help our local churches of the third world toward a self-understanding, a self-acceptance, the evangelization of their cultures, and the transformation of their societies. But in return perhaps the moment has come for a collective understanding by the churches of the wealthy countries of the message coming to them from the South.

The Western middle classes, in their respective countries, have actually succeeded in occupying other peoples' mentalities. This occupation, frankly ideological, has organized a genuine consensus, which is a powerful and telling weapon in a vested interest's legitimation of its system. Christians, in the name of their faith and through the everyday dynamics of the Christian life, do not manage to escape this subtle subjugation very well. All consumer goods tend to become absolutely necessary articles; and what is called "advertising" is merrily engaged in, in an effort to create a demand for them. One only has to think of the advertising campaign being waged in certain advanced countries with respect to the individual household.

The need for a certain international solidarity is becoming more and more evident, in view of the world disparity of human conditions and the widening crevasse between rich and poor nations. The sensitive and aware element in the local churches of advanced countries recognizes this, and preaches it. Progress has been made in the area of practical action. We now hear that charity is no longer enough. (Of course, since charity will no longer do, certain of our brothers and sisters in the wealthy churches have stopped doing anything at all, leaving us to take care of ourselves!) Reflective people know very well that the disparity between rich nations and poor nations, between the evangelizing nations and the evangelized ones (speaking very broadly), is the result of an exploitation, and of a number of value transferences. Both sides talk of structural reform. It goes without saying that the future of Christianity is at stake here as well. After having so often been the companion of a total colonization, will the Christian religion be able to erase its trademark at the heart of a world capitalism?

Assistance, exchanges, sending technicians, accepting students from the third world—none of this will advance the issue as long as there is no means of an authentic structural reform, beginning with the West. A great reason why the West has failed to see the light is its consumer needs. These needs ought to be evangelized. How can a serious effort toward international solidarity be made while the list of unmet needs is still so long in the nations who form the center? Is not the whole climate of xenophobia in certain rich nations today the result of the world recession, in which nations are beset by a collective fear of being no longer able to satisfy their own needs? We know very well that not even the proletariat is immune from this phobia.

When monasticism was born, the Christian message was a great educator in regard to needs. Without proposing a return to our beginnings, we may be allowed to point out that the collective ideal of pilgrimage would seem to be an urgent necessity today. Brothers and sisters of ours in the rich countries have abandoned their cities and gone in search of another way of life. But it would not do to become too isolated in one's search. What an uplifting task for religious communities!

Unjust structures have been denounced long enough. Now it is time to say No to the ideological domination of money, No to the interference of advertising, No to the inexorable lengthening of the list of things we "need." As long as we feel these needs, we think we have to exploit the third world—plunder its resources, set up cheap factories, support reactionary governmental cliques, encourage a development model that generates its own markets (tractors, fertilizer, lovely cars, and experts), and corrupt the middle class, then the intelligentsia, of poor countries. But at bottom, if capitalism no longer had available, at home, an army of people crying out how much they "need," many an apparently urgent priority would collapse of itself. Will Christianity in the West then be able to propose itself a new manner of presence in those countries?

Our answer is in the affirmative, beyond the shadow of a doubt. Intelligent, understanding evangelization, powerful force of assertion that it is and worthy of faith and credence, should not find itself confronting third-world opposition and protest. The truth of Christ can set us free—can return us to our truth. We are actually experiencing here the ability of the church of Christ to transfigure, and we should like others to hear this message and have done with their defiance.

—Translated by Robert R. Barr

2

INDIA

Patrick D'Souza

The Context

We are primarily concerned with the missionary dimensions of the local church in India. When we speak of the local church, it is not to be understood merely as a sociological or administrative entity. The focal point of the local church is its theological content; it is to be understood as a living cell of the people of God, reflecting and actualizing the life and mission of the universal church in a particular context. The particular context in India as a whole is so varying in different parts of the country that it is difficult to speak of the Indian church as one local church.

Although we apply the term "local church" in a broad sense to the church in India at the national level, our considerations here are more often limited to the situation and context of the Hindi-speaking, northern region of India.

The Historical Background

Christianity reached India very early. Tradition says that the apostle Thomas came to India and died here. Certainly there has been a Christian church in Kerala, South India, since the early beginning of Christianity. The theological divisions of the early church—for example, that between Monophysites and Nestorians—took a denominational form in India at the beginning of Indian Christianity.

We know little of the missionary methods or evangelizing activity of the early Christians in India. The tradition is that, as a result of the preaching of Saint Thomas and others, a number of high-caste families became Christian. A strong Christian community was eventually established in Kerala. Until comparatively recently the Christian community there was rather introspective, living more or less as a separate caste in the Hindu milieu, and with little or no concern for evangelization. The same is true also of the other more recently formed Christian communities of India, for example, those of Goa, Mangalore, and Bombay. The Christian communities exer-

Patrick D'Souza is Bishop of Varanasi, North India.

22

cised little or no influence on the social, cultural, economic, and political life of India. The missionary awakening and interest in the evangelizing activity of the church, which we experience today in the older Christian communities, are of very recent origin, less than a century old. There were individuals from all these communities who merit the name of missionary (Father Joseph Vaz of Goa is hailed as the apostle of Mangalore and Sri Lanka), but it is difficult to see the missionary dimensions of these communities prior to the beginning of the twentieth century.

The Present Situation

Any missionary activity must start with an open and sympathetic understanding of the realities that constitute the life of the people of the place. It is the role of the local church, in fidelity to Christ, to work out its own distinctive patterns to meet the exigencies of the local situations. In other words, the mission of the local church finds its expression in an ongoing process of evangelization. This expression takes various forms in accordance with the variety of contexts in a local church. In order to understand the various missionary expressions or dimensions of the Indian church, an analysis of the present missionary situation of the Indian church is necessary. Among other things the following could be mentioned.

The Indian church faces a plurality of religions. The people of the country are deeply religious. While secularism is gaining ground, the old religious traditions are still living forces both in popular religiosity and in their appeal to the intellectual and to the mystic. Further, new religious centers, for example, Sai Baba cult, are growing in the villages and in the cities.

India is a subcontinent of teeming masses, with 660 million people, two-thirds of whom are in poverty and misery. Among these teeming millions are, perhaps, more cultural, religious, economic, political, social, and linguistic divisions than can be found in any other country of the world.

India is a country of social injustice and inequality, and it is a country in turmoil. The people here are engaged in numerous struggles, *(a)* to rise out of poverty and malnutrition into a world order based on justice; *(b)* to assert themselves and their collective identity (liberation), as a result of their growing self-awareness (conscientization); to be somebody, to be accepted and have human dignity on a par with others (the growing consciousness and assertiveness of Adivasis, witness the various movements among them, and of Harijans such as the Dalit Panthers, show this sufficiently); *(c)* to overcome natural forces and natural calamities, so as to make nature an auxiliary of humankind, as in more intensive cultivation, the green revolution, the irrigation program, the river control plans; *(d)* to reconstruct religious tradition in order to provide a new spiritual basis and motivation for modernization and humanization (many religious-minded leaders, and those searching for motivation for social reform, are working at this); *(e)* to build national solidarity (the recent election results are very revealing here). In these struggles we read the aspirations of the people.

India, like most developing countries, *is a country of the young.*

Although India is the cradle of two world religions and is still deeply religious, *today the faith in religion is being shaken* in the face of stark poverty and shameful injustice. For example, the young are moving toward secularism, materialism, and even revolutionary ideology.

India's Christian population is extremely small: 1.3 percent. Catholics form about 60 percent of the Christian population. If we consider the political and cultural situation of the country, keeping in mind this small percentage and the absolute figures, it becomes clear that the conversion of the whole of India to Christianity in the foreseeable future cannot be expected in the normal working of God's providence.

The Church in India

Apart from analyzing the Indian situation in general in which the church is active, we need to reflect also on the image of the church, projected within this situation. The following could be specially mentioned:

a. Inheriting a missionary practice and a mission theology of the past, many missionaries in the field see the fulfillment of their mission primarily in their catechetical work, aimed at the conversion of non-Christians and their formal membership in the church. The non-Christians generally resent this situation. Although often deeply religious, they have, in general, an aversion to the idea of conversion. They do not look upon conversion as metanoia, but as a mere change of external denomination, generally for ulterior, undesirable motives. Even while venerating and sometimes believing in Christ, they refuse to belong to the organized church. Many openly oppose conversion because they see in it a threat to themselves and their social setup, to their religion and culture. In this background even our developmental works are viewed with suspicion.

b. The church invests much in institutions. Through its institutions, such as hospitals, schools, and colleges, the church meets the needs of many. Though a minority community, it exercises an enormous influence in the country through its charitable, educational, and developmental works. But what is the image projected? It is seldom of the church, sign and sacrament of God's love; rather, it is of an efficient benefactor.

c. In rural areas, a goodly number of missionaries are engaged in various kinds of developmental works and projects, generally financed from abroad. Although many poor people benefit materially, it is doubtful that the people achieve an integral liberation. The image of the missionary is that of a powerful, influential, beneficent organizer. The rural people, who were once dependent on the land-owners, not rarely change their allegiance to the missionaries. It is difficult to say that our developmental works in fact have helped them to grow toward self-dependence.

d. The local Christians of North India come almost exclusively from the Harijans and the Adivasis. As a result, in the Indian caste-ridden society they have practically no place of honor. The people of higher castes, who are the bearers of Indian culture, keep themselves away from any religious influence of Christianity, which is for them a foreign religion.

e. Over 90 percent of the men and women missionaries working in North India hail from the southern part of the country, mainly from Kerala, Mangalore, and Goa. Though some serious efforts have been made, in many respects they are seldom fully integrated, especially with regard to language, customs, and lifestyle.

The Mission of the Indian Church

If the expression of the church's mission in India is to be relevant, it cannot ignore the concrete situation in India, nor can it be unmindful of the attitude and response of non-Christians to the church, which are perceivable toward the image the church projected in India during the past centuries. The missionary dimensions of the local church will be given expression in various forms corresponding to the situation. In all the various expressions, the unifying factor must be realization of the church as the sign of universal salvation. In the measure in which a local church is a sign of universal salvation with other local churches throughout the world, the universality of the church will be maintained. The universality of the church and of its mission does not consist primarily in the organizational multinationality of the church, but in the unity of faith lived and shared throughout the world. It is an organic universality as befits a church that is a mystery. Similarly when we speak of the insufficiency of a local church it is not to be understood as financial insufficiency or the small number of priests and religious, but primarily as its ineffectiveness as a sign in isolation. An overemphasis on "universality" conceived in an organizational way can only lead to the destruction of originality and creativity in the local church, preventing it from incarnating itself in its particular culture. Our primary question must be: How can our local church be an effective sign and sacrament of salvation, a sacrament of unity here on earth?

Various Forms of Mission

Different kinds of apostolate are called for, corresponding to various contexts. We are familiar with a number of missionary approaches in North India. For example:

Catechesis. This is the most commonly known practice. Our mission stations are centers of catechesis where people are instructed in our religion and are received into the church.

Dialogue. Recognition of the positive values of non-Christian religions has led the church to enter into dialogue with people of other religions, taking them as partners in dialogue. Of post-Vatican II origin, many attempts are being made in this line.

Socioeconomic Uplift. Many missionaries are engaged in the social apostolate, preaching Christ and his gospel message through various forms of social work. In many centers catechetical work and social activities go hand in hand. We also have centers with such emphasis on social work that catechetical activities are excluded.

Ashrams. In accordance with the religious tradition of India, not a few pastoral centers in the north have become "ashrams." An ashram is traditionally known to be a place of intense and sustained spiritual quest and contemplation with a simple lifestyle. In recent years the concept of ashram has been very much broadened and widely used. Now we have many examples of Catholic presbyteries, convents, centers of social work, dialogue, and conscientization being called ashrams. Essentially an ashram must be a center of prayer and silence, or of prayer and service, headed by an *acharya* (the spiritual guide), open in its hospitality, simple in its lifestyle.

Presence, Sign, and Witness. In certain difficult situations in India, the church carries out its mission by its Christian presence and witness to Christ's message of love, thereby becoming a sign of joy and hope to the people. The effectiveness of this approach is seen mainly in some ashrams, as well as in the work of charity, conducted by dedicated Christians like the Missionaries of Charity and the Little Sisters of Jesus.

Conscientization and Liberation. We have of late numerous examples in the Indian church, where many are active, generally in accordance with *Evangelii Nuntiandi,* in promoting an interior transformation of society by bringing about an awakening among the people, and trying to achieve a liberation from all kinds of evil. Unfortunately, the concepts of conscientization and liberation are ambivalent, primarily because the terms are associated with Latin American situations. On the other hand, an awareness is being created, especially among the younger clergy, that evangelization cannot be relevant unless it addresses itself to the unjust and oppressive situations of contemporary India and takes the form of liberation. Evangelization, they would say, means the progressive penetration of liberating Christian values into the thought-patterns, customs, and structures of Indian society. Hence their conclusion that only in this way can the church fulfill its evangelical mission in the concrete setup of India.

From these examples mentioned we see that the mission of the Indian church has many dimensions and forms—necessary and called for by the varying situations in India. It is not for us to emphasize any of them at the theoretical level. Specific circumstances at a given time may suggest that we adapt a particular approach. What we need today is an integral approach.

The efforts of the Indian church, its personnel, and its resources are scattered throughout the country. The Indian church does not appear as a sign of salvation. Although a number of institutions—mission stations, ashrams, and so forth—are functioning in different parts of India, their inner interrelationship, common mission, unity, and solidarity are not perceived by non-Christians. Their geographical distance from one another, their desire for institutional independence, as well as vested interests of persons and institutions, contribute to this situation where church agencies, scattered in various places, work in isolation. How can such a church become an effective sign of God's salvation and of human solidarity?

Perhaps it may now be time for concentrated action. Instead of scattering our energy and personnel in ever newer places, geographically far away from the existing centers, basic ecclesial communities from and around these existing centers could engage themselves in expressing concretely the mission of the church in one way or other, as mentioned above. That is to say, a particular grassroots community could be engaged in a particular way of missionary expression, in cooperation and solidarity with other communities engaged in other forms of evangelization. But their mutual relationship, cooperation, and solidarity must be expressive of their common mission. United among themselves, they must be able to project to non-Christians the reality of one church, the sign of salvation.

For its realization we need to restructure the present-day church. The mutual relationship of various ecclesial communities can no longer be merely task-oriented, but from a shared experience of faith they should lead to an ever growing experience of a "community in the Lord." Legal concepts of religious congregations and their institutions, parishes and their jurisdiction, even dioceses, require to be rethought where the church is so much in diaspora that it is suffocated by these concepts.

It calls for a constant self-evaluation of the missionary function of individuals and communities in response to the Living Word of God. The problems arising from such a person-oriented approach to the mission of the church can better be tackled if the Christian communities are open to a constant spiritual discernment. No evangelization of others is possible without self-evangelization.

The Local Church in Mission

What therefore is the first need of the local church to be in mission? It has to be a sign and sacrament of God's saving love to all. For this primary purpose, it must subordinate all—laws, church traditions, church institutions—remaining faithful to the Word of the Lord, keeping the necessary contact with other churches, especially with the Apostolic See as a pledge of its fidelity. It will find its own laws, its own liturgical expression, its own missionary methods. That is, it needs, along with fidelity to the Lord and his Word, an originality and creativity spoken of by Saint Peter on Pentecost—the dreams and visions that the Spirit of the Lord will inspire.

How must the local church in India, especially in the largely non-Christian north, understand and exercise its mission? This has to be in the context of religious, social, and cultural pluralism. This will require that the church be present vitally in this pluralistic milieu to act as leaven, influencing and transforming the religions from within. Obedient to its task to be the transparent witness to Christ, the church will present the gospel and its values in such a manner as to challenge and help the religions to transform themselves. The church's action can be described as an ongoing, spiritual osmosis, which purifies, heals, and elevates the values found in non-Christian religions. In the words of *Ad Gentes,* no. 9: "Whatever grace and truth are to be found in the nations as a sort of secret presence of God, this activity [mission] frees from all taint of evil and restores to Christ its maker. . . . And so, whatever good is to be found sown in the hearts and minds of men, or in the rites and cultures peculiar to various peoples, is not lost. More than that, it is healed, ennobled and perfected for the glory of God, the shame of the demon, and the bliss of men." Like all human realities the non-Christian religions are stamped by both grace and sin; grace, because of the action of the Holy Spirit in them, which the church clearly and gratefully acknowledges (cf. *Lumen Gentium,* no. 16; also *Ad Gentes* and *Nostra Aetate*); pessimism, because God's gift is enfleshed in sinful humanity, to lead people to Christ. Undoubtedly there are many persons of "goodwill" among the non-Christians, and in the words of Cardinal Newman: "The man of goodwill is one who is unconsciously on the lookout for Christ."

From the older churches, the local church requires encouragement as it grapples with its problems. For a long time the help was prayer, personnel, and material resources. Prayer is the universal communion, which will always be required. It looks as though new methods must be thought of concerning personnel. There is the ever growing antipathy toward foreigners in all regions of the world, the first world as well as the third world, and the progressive antagonism of governments all over the world to religious personnel—all of which leads to difficulties about visas. These are pointers to be interpreted as signs of the times. On the other hand, transcendental truths, like that of the communion of churches, need to be concretized through the presence of members from other churches.

One of the most touchy points of church collaboration is finance. The question can be considered in the context of the world today, and the first point to be raised will be partnership. If one reconsiders the entire question from the point of view of the church, sign and sacrament of God's saving love, incarnate like its Lord, the question will have to be looked at differently. There is no doubt that the benevolence of older churches generally in economically developed countries has affected the life-style of church personnel in the third world. It has made the church "foreign" in the most tragic sense of the word, alienating it, insulating it often from the poverty of the world in which it lives. Sometimes it has undermined the self-reliance of Christians, as aid at government levels has generally done. It is difficult, because it demands a complete metanoia, a heroism, to explain what should be the form of church aid. In any case the local church, including its leaders, should not differ from the economic point of view from its non-Christian brethren. Further, dependency should not be perpetuated. A study is called for concerning the social function and evangelical impact of foreign churches' financial resources on the church in India. Only such an objective study, based on right theological thinking, will enable us to arrive at firm decisions.

This is not to question the good intentions and spirit of sacrifice of the churches elsewhere; neither does it doubt the financial integrity of the local church. This only raises one more point of the missionary dimension of the local church in the present context.

Ecclesiastical study abroad is a good illustration. There is no doubt that a few from each local church should study in other churches. But many scholarships for such studies unintentionally stunt the growth of ecclesiastical educational institutions in the local church, since there is no two-way traffic. They not rarely lead to a betrayal of mission by the student concerned, and later on to problems for both churches. Assistance to build up libraries, or a visiting professor, may do more good.

Mission and Human Life

The mission of the church is to make Christ present to men and women of goodwill. This is the privilege and responsibility of the church: to be Christ's point of contact with the non-Christians as their Savior. The church must be able to speak to the deep yearnings of these people and help them to be submissive to the working of the Spirit in them. The objection is sometimes heard that such a form of missionary activity would aim at "making Hindus better Hindus and Muslims better Muslims" instead of bringing them into the church as Christians. The objection has no validity because we have to take into account the working of the Holy Spirit in these non-Christians, and Christ is the goal and crown of all the religions of humankind.

In the orientation papers of the All India Seminar on the Church in India Today, it was pointed out that the activities of the Brahmo and Arya Samajs, the Ramakrishna missions, the Theosophical Society, and other movements advocating reform in Hinduism are an outgrowth of that Christian ministry that is regarded as the true mission of Christianity in India. Not one of these movements fails to reveal, to the eye that can see, the influence of this wider Christian ministry. These movements may repudiate their indebtedness to the dogmatic Christianity with which alone they are acquainted, but they owe their origin and inspiration to the ministry of Christ.

This form of the mission will not give tangible and immediate results; instead it will be a long and painful process in which the church will concentrate on the integrity of its witness to Christ and leave the results to God. The task ahead is not hopeless; but it calls for a new kind of "presence" of the church in this region. This "presence" is spelled out in *Ad Gentes,* nos. 11–12.

I wish to indicate briefly a few areas of human life in which the gospel influence is needed and will be appreciated by Indian society.

Dignity of the Person (cf. *Gaudium et Spes,* no. 12). In the face of the degradation of millions of human beings on the grounds of caste, it is necessary that Christians by their lives show the respect that is due to every human person. Hindu and Muslim societies have never recognized the personal dignity and rights of women. Non-Christian youth are attracted to this value; one of their strong (though confused) aspirations is for a society that is personalist. Our schools can and must inculcate this value of the dignity of the person regardless of the accidents of caste or social status. The religious Sisters must teach their non-Christian sisters the dignity of womanhood, the rights of women.

Dignity of Mind and Truth (cf. *Gaudium et Spes,* no. 15). The Christian witness can liberate the Hindu mind from its irrational attitude toward ancient traditions, many of which, though outworn and oppressive today, are still blindly accepted. Indian youth are deeply frustrated by the stranglehold of an irrational world-view imposed on them by tradition. Our Christian schools will render great service to their non-Christian pupils by helping them to cultivate critical minds and a respect for objective reality.

Freedom That Is Both Creative and Responsible (cf. *Gaudium et Spes,* no. 17). Due to their "religious philosophy" and the law of Karma, Hindus are strangers to freedom, although modern youth are aspiring to this value. Hinduism has stifled human freedom and reduced the person to a helpless and passive victim of circumstances. Consequently the Hindus have no clear concept of responsible human creativity in history. In their witness, Christians must live this freedom courageously in its response to God; for humankind is God's free and responsible partner in perfecting the creation, in remaking the human self, society, and world according to the plan of God.

The Christian in the World. Christians know that this world is important in God's plan, that their work and sufferings in mastering the world and making it more human have bearing on their salvation. They cannot turn their backs on this world and seek salvation by flight from the human reality. It is Christianity alone that gives a genuine religious value to work, to the world, and to human involvement in the world, while seeking first the kingdom of God. This lesson of the dignity of work and its relevance to salvation is very necessary for the people of this region.

Life as God's Gift. Finally, the Christian witness will teach the acceptance of life in its totality as God's gift, because Christians live with the certain hope that God will never be defeated by evil, and that God's kingdom, for which they work and pray, will surely come, though in ways hidden from them but known to God.

These are some of the human values that the church can try to promote. It must not succumb to the temptation to reduce its mission to development works of a material nature, though it may use the resources available to help the poor to better their condition in life. It will be attentive to their deeper needs and will be the servant who loves them for the sake of God.

In practice how can this be worked out?

Forms of Mission in City and Village

The present forms of mission activity will certainly carry on for a long time simultaneously with any new form that may be thought out. Nobody can know the mind of God fully. Hence no proven method should be discarded as if by a human fiat. The Lord's providence will do that in its own time. So proposing a new vision, a new method, is not equivalent to the condemnation of the old. Possibly one complements the other.

In urban areas the strength of the church is in its institutions. Though started in non-Christian areas, theoretically as pre-evangelization works, they are today largely secular, service-oriented institutions. Through them we have intimate access to thousands of students and to their families, to patients and to their relatives.

The existing educational institutions can be directed to evangelical work by forming the conscience of the pupils through the entire school program. Moral science, which presents morality as obedience to a personal God, which teaches the pupils to pray, is of great value. "Open" religious meetings with prayers, talks, and exchange of views can be conducted in neutral places, preferably not on church premises. These talks will not present Christ at the beginning, but will deal, rather, with the actual deeper needs of the people in their actual situation. This preparatory stage is God-centered and will continue as long as the Holy Spirit wills and as he prepares the people to "open up" to God, who loves them, cares for them, and forgives them.

When the ground is prepared, the Christ-event will be presented as the final revelation of God's love for humankind. The church cannot water down the revelation of Christ crucified, which is both a scandal to the Jews and a folly to the Gentiles, although for people on the road to salvation, it is a revelation of the wisdom and the power of God. There must not be hurried baptism of individuals. There must first be genuine "conversion," which will be evidenced by the change of attitudes and values. Christ will grow in them as an Indian Christ. It is true that the historic Christ was a Jew and lived in a particular cultural milieu; but the Risen Lord is transhistorical and is not to be tied to any particular place or nation or culture. The concern of the mission team will be to preserve the purity of the gospel of God's saving love in Christ, and not to propagate Greek philosophy or Roman law. Since the city is a conglomerate, with many who are influenced by modern ideas, values, and customs, it is not possible at the outset to plan the structured community that will eventually emerge to form the local church in the city. In this apostolate much will depend on the ability to understand non-Christian youth, and to recognize beneath their indifference and aggressiveness, their hunger for values that are human and spiritual. Sensitivity to their yearnings, unexpressed thoughts, and dominant feelings is very necessary here.

The aim is exactly as Pope Paul described in article 17 of *Evangelii Nuntiandi:* to upset, as it were, with Christian values, the existing values of Indian society. The good ones will be nurtured, the others will be purified, till Christ be all in all.

In the villages the situation is somewhat different. Here we have a homogeneous group, wary through centuries of experiencing "clever" teachers, yearning for peace and unity. The church must accept them as its own people.

The missionaries recruited from other local churches not of this region must be prepared to undergo a veritable "cultural kenosis" like Christ in his self-emptying (cf. Phil. 2:6). Missionaries must accept as their own people all those living in this region. They must accept the people in their actual, existential condition, accepting their language, customs, culture. These will be loved and respected. This acceptance will lead to the missionaries' being accepted in turn. Experience shows that non-Christians do not reject the gospel, but the preacher of the gospel, whom they regard as an alien, whereas those who sincerely love and respect the people are accepted, whatever the place of their origin.

Since the Indian village is a close-knit community, the missionary must be open to every sector of the village and not concentrate exclusively on the "weaker section." The evangelists should use the simple village techniques of songs and discourses to respond to the deeper yearning of the village community. The message of God's fatherly love for his children, his concern for them individually and collectively, his plan to liberate them from sin and the consequences of sin, such as selfishness, injustice, fear, especially fear of the occult powers of evil and fear of death, will be the theme of missionary discourses.

Since the popular religion of the villagers is a mixture of devotion, superstitious fear of occult forces, and fatalism with regard to external circumstances, a long-sustained process of purification will be necessary. This may continue for years before villagers are ready for the message of Christ; but the grain of wheat must die if the witness to the gospel is to have its healing influence.

When a sizable section of the village is converted to God, the Christ-event will be presented as the culmination of God's saving love. The catechesis will be adapted to the mentality of the villagers, and will avoid abstruse dogmas. The call should be initially to discipleship with Christ, and not yet to church membership. These disciples of Christ should be encouraged to develop their community life along traditional lines in social and cultural matters, avoiding only what is sinful. The sole concern of the missionary will be to preserve the purity of the gospel in these neophytes. There must be no question of imposing a ready-made pattern of church structures. Yet from discipleship with Christ to membership in the church, the step is a small one, the time element being in God's providence.

Those who desire to be baptized and have faith in Christ should be given deeper catechesis on the sacramental life of the eucharistic community. They should be taught to worship God through Christ in a liturgy that embodies their own proper spirit of worship, but which will no longer be individualistic. In this way they will bring their treasures to Christ. In the words of *Lumen Gentium* (no. 13):

> Since the kingdom of Christ is not of this world, the Church or People of God takes nothing away from the temporal welfare of any people by establishing that kingdom. Rather does she foster and take to herself, in so far as they are good, the ability, resources, and customs of each people. Taking them to herself she purifies, strengthens and ennobles them. The Church in this is mindful that she must harvest with that King to whom the nations were given for an inheritance (cf. Ps. 2:8) and into whose city they bring gifts and presents (cf. Ps. 71 (72):10; Is. 60:4-7; Apoc. 21:24). This characteristic of universality which adorns the People of God is a gift from the Lord Himself.

The stages described above will not be as clearly identified in reality. To begin with, the Holy Spirit moves where he wills, leading some slowly, others more quickly. Then we must not expect all in the village to come to the missionary on the same day. There will be various other extrinsic and internal reasons.

What kind of structured church community will evolve and develop in village India? The answer is that we do not know. It should be patterned on the village community with the minimal apostolic structure given by Christ the Lord. The Vatican Council has given us a deeper understanding of the unity of Christ's church. It is the unity of a living organism with its legitimate human diversity, and not the dead uniformity of a dead organization. Unity is the gift of love given by the Spirit, while uniformity is the product of law enforced by authority. It is not possible at this early stage to anticipate the features of the church that will evolve in village India, but it must preserve the rich spiritual traditions of the people—their spirit of simplicity, contemplation, poverty, asceticism, and devotion. This will be an enrichment for the universal church.

The movement toward inculturation has just begun. It is bound to gather momentum. At present it is limited to a few persons, touches only marginal matters. As the missionary church grows, inculturation will affect the life of the church at every point. While being fully the church of Christ, loyally united in loving communion with churches everywhere, especially with the See of Peter, it will be fully Indian, not only with a world vision consonant with India's past, but in its liturgy, in its laws, in its cultural expression. Serious efforts being made toward inculturation in the seminaries of North India, and in various religious congregations, especially the Jesuits, will bear fruit even though future generations may smile at the faltering steps we are taking today.

What of the Future?

The church in India has very limited options. If it forgets its missionary dimension, it may become a powerful association having at its disposal medical and educational institutions that will be appreciated and used; but it will die, for it will not have been faithful to the fundamental mission of Christ, to be his sign and sacrament. It will have to see, beyond the small number of his followers, the teeming millions of India, and be to them the love of Christ. In the concrete circumstances of India it will mean being the hope that is Christ to the poor, and the voice of Christ to those who exploit them. Such a missionary church will think less of its own rights, more of rights of humanity, and be to all the column of truth. This championing of basic human rights, while being the sign of hope and fraternal love, is a significant aspect of the missionary dimension of the future.

3

ASIA AND INDONESIA

Robert Hardawiryana, S.J.

By becoming flesh the divine Word entered humankind in its solidarity, in order to redeem it from sin and to save it for the kingdom of the Father. Jesus' life on earth was totally taken up by his being sent by the Father, by his mission. Hence, while gathering his disciples, he could not but enjoin them to take part in his own mission by becoming witnesses to him unto the ends of the earth. Thus it is contrary to the Christian vocation to be egotistically concerned with one's own salvation. To the church, drawn from within the solidarity of humanity by divine grace as the universal sign of salvation, the missionary dimension is constitutive. Being sent on behalf of the salvation of all humanity, as a matter of fact, is identical with our catholicity.[1]

The missionary dimension of the universal church reveals the Father's call to the kingdom, concretely actualizes Christ carrying out, now as ever, his salvific mission, whereas the Spirit in our hearts helps to discern in the signs of the times and in events of our personal lives that call to eternal life. Christ's mission is directed to us who already belong to his church, since we remain sinners in need of conversion and renewal in all aspects of our lives: cultural, social, economic, political, religious. This metanoia is continuously to be performed by assuming human values while purifying them according to the gospel. Thus evangelized values become the concrete expression of our faith within daily-life situations.

By the mission of his church Christ addresses himself to those who do not belong to the church as well. Thus this missionary dimension is the Christlike actualization of our solidarity as Christians with the whole of humanity; indeed the sign of Christ's own solidarity is the mystery of his incarnation. It is constitutive for the universal church, and this means constitutive for every particular church.

Christian communities in the past used to be divided into mission-sending churches, (all of ancient Christian tradition) and mission-receiving churches (called "foreign missions"). Both this terminology and its underlying theology, the concept

Robert Hardawiryana, S.J., is presently Rector of the Institute of Philosophy and Theology in Jogjakarta, Indonesia, and professor of Ecclesiology at the same institute. He is also theological adviser of the Indonesian Bishops' Conference.

of a "one-way mission," together with an understanding that all external aspects of church life down to minute particularities were simply to be taken for granted as "the visible church," are now out of date. Churches in Asia, often still referred to as "young churches," are ever more conscious of their being sister churches to the churches of "the West." They have awakened to an ever growing creativity in mission, at a level equal to that of all other churches. In other words, all Christian communities are equally mission-sending and mission-receiving.

I: ASIA

Asian Society as the Milieu of Church Life and the Field of Its Mission

Developments in post-Vatican II ecclesiology rightfully emphasize the importance of particular churches as the concrete presence and realization of the universal church and its salvific mission. The theology of "incarnation of Christian faith" implying participation in the mystery of death and resurrection, and of "inculturation" (which amounts to the same) are being elaborated more than ever as a serious attempt toward counterbalancing the stress in the past, often too heavily laid upon the "universality" or "catholicity" of the church, then often understood in the sense of "uniformity" down to exterior appearances of church life with a rather strong connotation of its being centralized around the highest church authority.

Quite often it has been stressed that the particularity of the local church lies in the very fact that Christian faith has to be lived in community totally immersed in the given conditions of society: cultural, social, economic, political, and religious; and that faith has to grow from within these life situations. This is precisely why we start the first part of this paper by outlining the main features of Asian society.

In our opinion, however, the particularity of the local congregation at times is emphasized in the extent that it is easily overlooked how much people everywhere have in common. And yet exactly in those elements that we all have in common as humans and as being called to salvation in the same Lord, we have as many areas of communication. They will serve as the basis of the universal communion of faith, imbued as they are by the action of the same Spirit vivifying the entire church as the sacrament of union between people and their God, and of the unity of all humankind.

The Main Features of Asian Society

In order better to grasp the missionary dimensions of the churches in Asia, it is imperative to recall some of the main features of this continent of misery and distress, its striking inequalities, oppression, and injustice. It is a continent with countries, like Japan, in which the rising tide of technology, despite its great benefits, threatens to absorb the quality of human life; but also with countries particularly but not only in the "socialist orbit," where human rights and fundamental freedoms are scarcely appreciated. It is the cradle of two of the world's major civilizations, where age-old cultures and traditional religiosity give rise to attitudes and behavior patterns that may obstruct development, while, on the other hand, the continual preoccupation of many with the divine and their quest for religious experience may have much to contribute to the crisis-ridden concepts of liberation and quality of human life. This continent is emerging from dependence on colonial powers and, in fact, is becoming an important and perhaps vital element in the world-power pattern; a reality of people—half the human race—now more conscious than ever of their plight, and determined, especially the 60 percent who are its youth (i.e., one-third of humanity), to struggle for a more just, more human, and more humane world.

Let us realize how much Christians, who are a very small minority, both in number and in resources, are caught up in all the problems of their countries, and how precisely there they are sent as a *pusillus grex* to give testimony to their faith.

Asian Societies and the Family. Technological progress almost nowhere will be paralleled by social development. Confronted with immense technological changes, ever increasing pace, traditional attitudes of mind still remain mostly unchanged, although at the same time one may question: Unchanged for how long?

The process of urbanization is well under way. A United Nations conference in 1980 predicted that if current trends continue there will be fourteen "agglomerations" in Asia with populations of more than 10 million by the end of the century: Bangkok, Tokyo-Yokohama, Osaka-Kobe, Seoul, Shanghai, Peking, Manila, Jakarta, Calcutta, Bombay, Delhi, Madras, Karachi, and Teheran. People from rural areas will leave for the growing cities, which for many are becoming an inimical rather than a friendly environment, without going to new opportunities. Millions have to face the aggravating problem of unemployment.

A number of crises center on the population explosion and the threat of world famine. In many Asian countries the population is being doubled within thirty years (in the Philippines and Thailand in 21 years; Indonesia, 24; Malaysia, 25; Hong Kong and Korea, 28; Singapore, 29; Taiwan, 31).[2] Not only is Asia overpopulated; it is also condemned to suffer more and more from the unequal distribution of the world's resources. The last fifteen years have seen the gap between the rich and the poor countries actually widen instead of narrow.[3] "Development" is either nonexistent or, paradoxically, counterproductive: perpetuating and propagating poverty rather than relieving it.

Amid the process of modernization the older and the younger generation will have ever less values of experience in common. At times the gap between generations seems to be ever widening. Where no continuity of life is felt, many people will sense a vacuum of values, but have no planned way to rediscover values or replace those that have been lost. A process of secularization is going on, different in many ways from that in the West. On the other hand, this is the very opportunity for the church to step in with its mission, and for Christian faith to save cultural patterns and religious values that are being undermined.

Although in many countries medical care is improving relatively slowly, this steady improvement causes life expectancy now to be twenty years longer than that of one generation ago. More and more old people will lose their place in family life. This also will be affected by changing relationships between man and woman. The struggle for life will put a heavy strain on the nuclear family, so that parents cannot implement the role expected from them. The Second East Asian Regional Meeting of the Federation of Asian Bishops' Conferences (FABC) at Suwon, Korea, September 21-25, 1976, stated as a mission of the East Asian Episcopal Conferences the exchange of information about formation in Christian values of marriage and family, and about scientific developments in the field of responsible parenthood.[4] The statement of objectives of the first Australasian Zonal meeting of the International Federation for Family Life Promotion, held in Hong Kong November 8-10, 1976, includes the purpose "to provide leadership, guidance and education in the fields of family life education in general and natural family planning in particular."[5] The Third Assembly of the East Asian Region of FABC, Tokyo, Japan, held March 26-29, 1979, particularly stressed the urgent need of evangelization of the family.[6]

Governments and the Church. It seems that in the 1980s governments will continue to put pressure on the churches. As a matter of fact, the church is considered by many to be "a state within the State," "endangering national unity." The Freedom of Religion Bill passed by the state assembly of Arunachal Pradesh, India (1978), was viewed by Christians as aimed against conversions to the Christian faith. In Bangladesh an ordinance published in December 1978 appears certain to increase government control over the activities of churches and Christian agencies, for example, by registration of all organizations and strict regulations of incoming finance. We shall elaborate on the problems in Indonesia in the second part of this paper. In Pakistan there is a move to introduce separate election groupings for small, minority communities; many feel that the procedure will isolate Christians without any voice in the life of the nation. One's vote will be weighed according to the religion one professes. In Japan Christian groups protested the several attempts to restore various prewar Shinto-related practices and systems; some of these revivals received official sponsorship. In Israel all the Christian bodies expressed their displeasure and anxiety at the antimissionary legislation passed in 1977, attacking also all kinds of social, educational, and charitable activities of the church.[7] It does not seem right to think of these cases in terms of the church being curtailed in its mission. The church should, rather, accept these facts as realities and pose the questions: What, concretely-speaking, is that mission in these very circumstances? Which is the best action the church can take?

Gaudium et Spes (part II, chapter IV, on the life of the political community) as well at *Dignitatis Humanae* (Declaration on Religious Freedom) are mostly written against the background of separation between church or religion and state. The question arises whether or not the guidelines laid down in both documents apply everywhere in the same sense. Among most Asian peoples, the religious aspect seems to permeate the whole of life. Within this context how are relationships between religion and state to be appropriately defined? Here again there is a question mark: For how long will this integration of the religious aspect last? How will secularization develop in Asian countries?

Religions in Asia. While the modernization process is going on, Asia will be the testing ground for religions. To what extent will religions still be able to hold on and resist the adverse forces of modernization? Will they remain free and emerge amid secularizing currents with a renewed vitality? Or will secularism eventually cause their decline?

Among religions are trends of socialism or a deeper commitment to social development. For example, in some cases Buddhists have started to anticipate Marxist criticism toward religion by pressuring Buddhist monasticism from within to renew itself along socialist lines. It is equally significant that since the 1950s Southeast Asia has produced about three different brands of "Buddhist socialism," namely, that of Bandaranaike of Sri Lanka, U Nu of Burma, and the earlier Norodom Shihanouk of Kampuchea. In a meeting that could have particular significance for the pluralistic religious situation of Asia, delegates from nine major world religions discussed the place of human rights within their religious and cultural traditions. The assembly, sponsored by UNESCO, convened for its consultation in Bangkok, December 3–7, 1979, with representatives from Buddhism, Catholicism, Confucianism, Hinduism, Islam, Judaism, Orthodoxy, Protestantism, and Shintoism. The participants offered what may be their most important contribution to present-day interreligious dialogue:

> The delegates to the conference recognized that, although the assumptions on which the Universal Declaration of Human Rights are based may be alien and even unacceptable to some religious traditions, the declaration may provide the most effective starting point for both an internal reform of the self- understanding of each religion, and an external opening to collaborating with the rest of the world to reduce the global stresses afflicting mankind today. The meeting concluded with the recognition that their religions could and should be important contributing factors to a better implementation of human rights in today's world, even if their understanding of religion is different.[8]

It is urgent for Christians at large to be in constant dialogue with people of other living faiths and beliefs. The first Bishops' Institute for Missionary Apostolate (BIMA I) of FABC, Baguio City, Philippines, held July 19–27, 1978, gave an excellent description of dialogue as an important element in the missionary dimensions of the church: "Religious dialogue is not just a substitute for or a mere preliminary to the proclamation of Christ, but should be the ideal form of evangelization, where in humility and mutual support we seek together with our brothers and sisters that fullness of Christ which is God's plan for the whole of creation, in its entirety and its great and wonderful diversity."[9] At the first Bishops' Institute for Interreligious Affairs (BIRA I), sponsored by the FABC Office of Ecumenical and Interreligious Affairs, Sampran, Thailand, October 11–18, 1979, participants coming from Sri Lanka, Thailand, Hong Kong, and the Vatican Secretariat for Non-Christians, listed among the obstacles for dialogue: "Church ties with the colonialism of the past, inadequate inculturation, foreignness attributed to Christianity, mutual ignorance among religionists, the mutual attitudes of religious and cultural superiority, lack of significant contacts and guidelines for religious cooperation, [a] limited number of negative and insufficient motivations for dialogue."[10]

Popular religiosity has an important impact on people. Since throughout the centuries it has developed within the frame of religions, and because it reveals a good deal of their respective spiritual values, it has to be carefully and thoroughly studied in view of inculturation of the Christian faith. Amid increasing humanism and secularization, this religiosity will be put to a severe test. Since it is inextricably intertwined with people's everyday lives, its decline perhaps will bring about a grave crisis in traditional life patterns. Quite in conformity with the mission of Asian churches, the Standing Committee of FABC in 1974 approved a plan "to prepare Asian leaders who will be academically trained to discover the humanistic and spiritual values in the Great Religions of Asia, to interpret these values for the Roman Catholic community and to disseminate the findings of their research."[11]

In the same missionary spirit the Institute of East Asian Christian Spirituality, sponsored by the Chinese Episcopal Conference, affiliated to Fu Yen University, and inaugurated October 30, 1976, offered courses in various spiritualities: Confucian, Taoist, Buddhist, and Christian.[12]

Christianity in Asia. We have touched upon the missionary dimensions of Christianity, in describing Asian societies and family life, the attitudes of governments towards the church, and religions and religious values in Asia. The social question alluded to above—not in a period of idyllic peace, but in a gigantic crisis—affecting this continent in great ferment, will challenge the church to prove its credibility and the relevance of its mission, namely, that Christianity in implementing its mission is indeed truly committed to the poorer masses. Among the contemporary challenges urging Christians to dialogue BIRA I mentioned "the desire for a more just and human society, a better educated and more concerned laity, a willingness to keep cultural identity and to return to cultural roots, a new atmosphere created by Vatican II, a desire for greater incarnation of the Church in its worship, in its theology, in its life-style and structures."[13]

The emergence and further development of genuine Christian communities, deeply inculturated and Asian in thinking, in living and communicating their own Christ-experience, will be decisive. They will have to search for new spiritualities, new faith expressions, new theological articulations, new structural forms, a new dynamism in carrying out their mission of evangelization in their environment. A progressive growth of a plurality of mission theologies is striven after, theologies which are locally and historically bound, truly contextual. The Asian Colloquium held in Hong Kong February 27–March 5, 1977, reflected extensively on the necessity of lay ministries, although as a matter of fact in many Asian churches this is not really a new problem. Questions were raised—as yet not fully answered—on leadership of community life, leadership in the service of the Word, leadership even in the celebration of the Eucharist.[14]

Church Life in Most Asian Countries

Now that we have outlined the main features of Asian society as the milieu of church life and mentioned some of FABC's activities, further reflection is required on the question: What actually is implied in the mission of Asian local churches? How has theological and pastoral thinking on their missionary dimensions developed so far, while being contextualized within life situations in the Asian continent? What are the prospects of evangelization in its comprehensive sense for Asia's future?

Before we recall what particularly the Asian bishops have said during the past decade, let us review a few ideas from Pope Paul VI's Apostolic Exhortation on Evangelization in the Modern World, *Evangelii Nuntiandi.*

The Christian understanding of mission must be integral and truly comprehensive, in order not to distort its meaning or to mutilate its range of action and life. "Any partial and fragmentary definition which attempts to render the reality of evangelization in all its richness, complexity and dynamism does so only at the risk of impoverishing it and even of distorting it" (*Evangelii Nuntiandi,* no. 17).

Evangelii Nuntiandi, nos. 18–21, deal with the elements of evangelization, all of vital importance in the Asian situation as pictured above. The gospel must transform humanity from within to make its values, its interests, its aspirations, and its models of life new. Evangelization reaches into all spheres of human life and culture. The gospel is meant to penetrate them all to their very roots. The church's mission is sharing, witness, solidarity, and service. It is also explicit preaching, formation of the Christian community, its structures and ministries, adherence to the life of the church in its doctrinal and sacramental fullness, apostolic and missionary initiative and labor.

Within the Asian context a central issue in the Bishops' Synod of 1974 and in *Evangelii Nuntiandi* should be mentioned: the relationship among evangelization, salvation, and intra-historical liberation, especially in socioeconomic and political areas. How present this problem is whenever we reflect on the meaning of the gospel in our countries, nowadays, for our peoples!

Pope John Paul II in his address inaugurating the Third Latin American Bishops' Pastoral Council on Evangelization (CELAM) at Puebla, Mexico, January 28, 1979, summarized *Evangelii Nuntiandi's* teaching on the issue of human liberation: if the church makes itself present in the defense or the advancement of humankind, this is in line with its mission. Although this mission is religious and not social or political, it must consider people in the entirety of their being. The Lord outlines in the parable of the Good Samaritan the model of attention to all human needs; in the final analysis he will identify himself with the disinherited, the sick, the imprisoned, the hungry, and the lonely, who have been given a helping hand. The church has learned from the gospel that its evangelizing mission has, as an essential part, action for justice and the tasks of the advancement of humankind. Between evangelization and human progress there are strong links of the orders of anthropology, theology, and love (cf. *Evangelii Nuntiandi,* no. 31). Thus "evangelization would not be complete if it did not take into account the unceasing interplay of the gospel and man's concrete life both personal and social" (*Evangelii Nuntiandi,* no. 29). It is therefore not through opportunism or thirst for novelty that the church, "the expert in humanity," to use Pope Paul VI's description, defends human rights. It is through a true evangelical commitment, which, as happened with Christ, is a commitment to the most needy. In fidelity to this commitment the church wishes to stay free from competing ideological systems, in order to opt only for humanity. Whatever the miseries or sufferings that afflict people, it is not through violence, the interplay of power and political systems, but through the truth concerning human beings, that they journey toward a better future.

People ought to be freed from everything oppressing them, but above all from sin, and to live in the joy of knowing God and of being known by him. It includes reconciliation, forgiveness, the recognition that every human heart can be transformed by God's love. Liberation has definite economic, political, social, and cultural dimensions, but is not reduced to them. Its fuller Christian sense is not to be sacrificed to the demands of any strategy, practice, or short-term solution. Liberation is part of the proclamation and realization of the gospel message.

Asian Bishops on the Mission of the Asian Churches. *The Asian Bishops' Meeting* (Manila, 1970) considered the church's evangelizing mission not in some narrow "ecclesiastical" perspective. This mission is genuinely ecclesial: resolutely facing the people, intimately concerned with its human and societal as well as its more "churchly" aspects. The proclamation of the gospel must involve the concerns of culture, justice, and the aspirations of youth. If it wishes to penetrate the fabric of Asian societies, it must be fully aware of their needs and objectives as inextricably inherent in its agenda. Mission in the future should not be a mere repetition of what the churches performed in the colonial past. It will henceforth be primarily the local church in mission within its own environment. This mission would have something of the breadth of what, in a way, the church in the European Middle Ages considered as its task: to bring the gospel into every sector of human thought and endeavor, into every human heart as well as into every human structure, but facing Asian societies as they are with their own particular histories, cultures, and ways of life.

The recommendations of this assembly dealt with the defense and promotion of human rights; the education and organization of workers and peasants; the equitable distribution and socially responsible use of land and resources; responsible parenthood in response to urgent population problems; trade on an equitable basis; greater openness of markets to the fruits of Asian labor; justice in international commodity prices; the struggle against atheistic communism and imperialism of every kind; cooperation between government and religious and civic bodies in development work; the effective implementation of the 1 percent of GNP of affluent nations as aid to developing countries; and similar matters.

Some more specific "home tasks" were stipulated: the construction of a theology of development with reflection on the meaning of conflict and clarification of the roles of clergy; religious and laity in the concerns of development; a more resolute entering into interreligious dialogue; the development of contextual theology and inculturation of Christian faith and life; greater recognition of the importance of students in the tasks of transforming Asian societies; greater emphasis on education for total human development; more unified practical action in areas of mass media: radio, television, press and film, the establishment of an Asian News Agency, and the like.[15]

The First Plenary Assembly of FABC (Taipei, Republic of China, April 22–27, 1974) had as its theme Evangelization in Modern-day Asia. Its Statement and Recommendations placed the local churches in Asia at the center of focus. The primordial missionary assignment in Asia is the building of the local church, in basic continuity with Vatican II's *Ad Gentes,* with accents more markedly placed on becoming more authentically the local church.

The Final Statement of the assembly says, in part:

> The primary focus of our task of evangelization then, at this time in our history, is the building up of a truly local Church.
>
> For the local Church is the realization and the enfleshment of the Body of Christ in a given people, a given place and time. . . .
>
> The local Church is a Church incarnate in a people, a Church indigenous and inculturated. And this means concretely a Church in continuous, humble and loving dialogue with the living traditions, the cultures, the religions—in brief, with all the life-realities of the people in whose midst it has sunk its roots deeply and whose history and life it gladly makes its own.

The assembly speaks of dialogue with the history, the ways of life, and the cultures of the peoples in Asia. This should be first of all a dialogue of life, especially with the multitudes of the poor, the deprived, the oppressed, in the spirit of the gospel, enabling the task of inculturation, taking ancient and contemporary religions with utter seriousness and reverence; a dialogue too long postponed, too superficially pursued, too peripherally located.[16]

The Asian Colloquium on Ministries in the Church (Hong Kong, February 27–March 5, 1977) was a sustained effort to draw up a preliminary set of rough sketches for adapting the structures, ministries, and methods of evangelization of the Asian churches in order to bring these into gear with their mission as truly meeting the situational challenges indicated above. This sentence from BIMA I of FABC reflects the same realization: "Deeply challenged by these fundamental issues, the participants felt how inadequate our present structures are to realize this our mission in Asia, starting from the central mission organization of the Church right down to the local level. The discussions also revealed the inadequacy of many of our present-day mission methods."[17]

In Hong Kong the theme of the small Christian communities emerged clearly, and with it the new understanding of ministries, particularly lay ministries, that derives from the realization of grassroots ecclesial units. These communities are seen more and more "front and center" on the Asian scene. One effect of Pope Paul VI's *Evangelii Nuntiandi* was the genuine, if guarded, welcome and "right to the city" it gave to small Christian communities, *"communautés de base"* (cf. *Evangelii Nuntiandi,* no. 58).

Synthesizing the results of the brainstorming sessions, BIMA I came to the conclusion, surprising for some, that without intending it, the assembly actually had followed in the footsteps of the Taipei Assembly of 1974, stating clearly the building of the local church as the goal of all missionary activity, a goal to be reached only by a genuine dialogue.[18]

The Second Plenary Assembly of FABC (Calcutta, India, November 19–25, 1978) was an exercise in inculturation and in dialogue with at least some aspects of the religious traditions and prayer ways of other Asian religions. It was, in fact, programmed to be just as much "prayer exercise" (and in this sense a praxis) as reflection and discussion. To quote from the Final Statement and Recommendations of the assembly:

> We renew our commitment too to the tasks which the Gospel and the Spirit speaking in the "signs of the times" have given to us and our communities. These tasks call us to shared responsibility for justice and brotherhood among men and peoples, to solidarity with the men and women of our time, especially when they are poor and voiceless, marginalized and oppressed, deprived of their rights and their human dignity.
>
> It is thus our resolve to "allow Jesus to pray to and live for the Father in our hearts and lives" ever more fully, and in freedom to receive and make ours the gifts of Faith, Hope and Love which the Lord gives to men for their liberation from sin and its consequences in society, for the fulfillment of their earthly tasks, and their pilgrimage to the Kingdom of God.
>
> Our faith "teaches us that liberation from oppressions which weigh upon our peoples will not be wrought, nor the pain and injustice of the world removed from it, except through our sharing, in prayer and self-gift, in the mystery of the Cross."
>
> We believe that finally the power of God's love is the only force which can truly renew the world. This force is the power of the Spirit; it is given to us by the Lord through prayer.[19]

Thus in the Asian churches, even prayer has missionary dimensions constitutive to it. Continuing the theme of the International Mission Congress (Manila, December 2-9, 1979), namely, the Good News of God's Kingdom . . . to the Peoples of Asia, and the theme Your Kingdom Come of a conference in Melbourne under the auspices of the Commission for World Mission and Evangelism of the World Council of Churches, the theme proposed for the Week of Prayer for Christian Unity in 1980 was genuinely missionary as well: Your Kingdom Come.[20]

Thus we see that the centerpiece of the mission of Asian churches is *dialogue:* dialogue in the inner heart with Christ to grasp a little of his meaning for us; dialogue with one another within Christian communities; dialogue in the three wide realms described by FABC I (1974) and confirmed by BIMA I; dialogue with our people in their own concrete historical and cultural situations; dialogue with the religious experience of Asian spirituality and prayer; dialogue in order to create "the poor Church of the Servant" within our own lives.

Some practical imperatives flow from this cluster of interlocking perspectives: the increasing involvement of bishops and other community leaders in this climate and movement of dialogue; the attentive listening to "the signs of the times" in the vast variety of continuously changing situations to be taken account of and boldly ventured into; the creation, activation, and fostering of authentic Christian communities; the growing realization, in ideal and in lifestyle, of "the image of the poor

Church conformed to the pattern of the Suffering Servant of Yahweh"; the opening up and renewal, the intensification of the role of prayer and contemplation, so important in the religious quest of Asia, in our evangelizing effort; the attention to be paid to adequate formation for mission.

The Development of Asian Churches and Their Mission

Now that we have taken a glance at Asian society as the milieu of church life and the field of its mission, we shall consider more closely how Asian churches develop their missionary activities, conscious as they are of their insufficiency if each church were left to itself. How are they responding to their constant need for mutual communication? What are the tensions to be overcome in church life? Along with the development of missionary activities through interchurch sharing, it is necessary for the churches to assess themselves continuously.

The Insufficiency of the Local Church Left to Itself

The life situations of Asian churches are mostly as described in Vatican II's decree *Ad Gentes* (no. 19):

> These Churches, most often located in the poorer parts of the world, are generally suffering from a very serious lack of priests and of material support. Therefore, they desperately require that the continued missionary activity of the whole Church furnish them with those subsidies which principally serve the growth of the local Church and the maturity of Christian life. This mission action should furnish help also to those Churches, founded long since, which are in a certain state of regression or weakness.

A shortage of personnel is often cited as an important reason why local communities in what were once called "mission countries" are thought to be unable to live up to contemporary challenges in Asia. Perhaps thorough reflection on church life is called for, particularly as to who so far have sustained it. Have we relied too much upon priests and religious, many of them coming from other churches, as if they were almost the only ones to keep things going? Does not the Declaration of Concern on Devaluing the Laity, issued by forty-seven priests, nuns, and lay persons at Chicago, December 12, 1977, still apply to many among us? "While many in the Church exhaust their energies arguing internal issues, albeit important ones, . . . the laity who spend most of their time and energy in the professional and occupational world appear to be deserted."[21]

To what extent are the laity in Asian churches conscious of their co-responsibility for the well-being of Christian communities? Are lay people really given ample chance to take part seriously and effectively in church life? If co-responsibility is still lacking, what are the reasons? Perhaps the educational level, in general, is too low. Or is the standard of living so poor that most people are completely taken up by their struggle for life, and have no opportunity and energy left to promote education? Maybe there is as yet no truly felt need for actively belonging to a community of faith. Or there is no sense in it. Possibly certain sociocultural traditional patterns, such as feudalism, are so many obstacles to the growth of common responsibility and participation in the community's mission. Could a traditional image of a "clerical" church play its role? Or could it be also the crisis of missionary spirit and spirituality, so that churches formerly rich with missionaries eventually almost cease to send them?

A second reason for the insufficiency of the local church may be lack of resources, as is frequently the case with third-world churches where, as in Asia, Christianity constitutes a very small minority of the total population. Surely, as long as young churches have not nearly enough resources of their own, these should be provided by the help of churches that are better off. Meanwhile these resources must enable our churches in Asia to mature in such a way that after some time they stand on their own feet as regards funds and forces. Not seldom it has been said that they ought to be helped so that they do not need help any more. Within the young churches possibilities should be explored for raising their own resources. This will have a strong educational impact on the faithful, since by their own contributions, no matter how small, they are helped toward maturity and a fuller awareness of their co-responsibility, so necessary if the local church is to become self-supporting and self-ministering in its mission in society.

Third, in order for faith to become genuinely inculturated, the particular church needs to remain within the universal communion of faith with all churches throughout the world, or—practically speaking—at least with the neighboring churches in the region, and with the entire church tradition starting from the time of the apostles. "Tradition" here is used in the sense given by Vatican II's *Dei Verbum,* no. 8: ". . . everything which contributes to the holiness of life, and the increase in faith of the People of God; and so the Church, in her teaching, life, and worship, perpetuates and hands on to all generations all that she herself is, all that she believes."

Almost nothing is so harmful as isolationism, entailing a rather restricted range of expressions of Christian faith, namely, a definite culture or cultural pattern, resulting in a spiritual inbreeding, an impoverishment of individual as well as communitarian Christian life, and a narrowing of Christian outlook. As *Ad Gentes* says (no. 19): "Stress should be laid on those theological, psychological, and human elements which can contribute to fostering this sense of communion with the universal Church."

Thus dialogue ought continuously to be kept alive among the local churches, so that the overall growth of Christian communities may be incessantly stimulated by inspirational influences from the outside. (From this point of view, no matter how mature a local church is, the presence and valuable contribution of missionaries from other churches—which will be dealt with later—always will be very important, if not necessary.) Thus the depth of the divine mystery of salvation and its richness can be better expressed by endlessly varied ways of Christian life. Hence our next step is to reflect on interchurch sharing in the Asian context.

Interchurch Sharing in Asia

Since a healthy growth of the local church requires communion with the universal church, both "horizontally" by sharing with other contemporary churches and "vertically" by being well acquainted with church tradition and its values for the present as well as for the future, members of the local church are to complete their faith experiences through sharing with those coming from other particular churches. A structure embodying the commonly and currently felt need for interchurch sharing is the episcopal conference. Its foundation, as we all know, is located in *Lumen Gentium,* no. 23. The model used to describe it is the rich notion of the ancient patriarchal churches rather than the more restrictive image of a particular council or a synod. Synods and councils, however, are reaffirmed and the establishment of episcopal conferences encouraged in Vatican II's decree *Christus Dominus,* chapter III, nos. 37–38. Article 38 has been implemented in Pope Paul's apostolic letter *Ecclesiae Sanctae,* chapter I, no. 41 (August 6, 1966), attributing many decisions in particular matters to episcopal conferences, for example, regulations concerning the distribution of the clergy, the care of migrants, and so forth.[22]

The Federation of Asian Bishops' Conferences. Interchurch sharing in Asia is facilitated first of all by the Federation of Asian Bishops' Conferences, which is a voluntary association of episcopal conferences in southern and eastern Asia, established with the approval of the Holy See, to foster among its members solidarity and co-responsibility for the welfare of church and society in Asia. The missionary dimensions of the church in Asia are summed up in FABC's principal functions:

A. To study ways and means of promoting the apostolate, especially in the light of Vatican II and post-conciliar official documents, and according to the needs of Asia;

B. To work for and to intensify the dynamic presence of the Church in the total development of the peoples of Asia;

C. To help in the study of problems of common interest to the Church in Asia, and to investigate possibilities of solutions and coordinated action;

D. To promote inter-communication and cooperation among local churches and bishops of Asia;

E. To render service to episcopal conferences of Asia in order to help them to meet better the needs of the People of God;

F. To foster a more ordered development of organizations and movements in the Church at the international level.[23]

In this respect Asia has been divided into three geographical or sociocultural regions, namely, South Asia (India, Pakistan, Bangladesh, Sri Lanka); Southeast Asia (the Philippines, Thailand, Malaysia, Singapore, Indonesia, Kampuchea, Laos, Burma); and East Asia (Korea, Japan, the Republic of China, Hong Kong, Macau, Vietnam).[24]

The Offices of FABC. In order to initiate and carry out programs and to execute resolutions and instructions of the federation, to establish liaison with other related national and international organs, to conduct studies and to provide documentation and information to member conferences and associate members, five specialized service agencies have been established, as follows:[25]

1. *The Office of Missions:* This office sponsored the First Bishops' Institute for Missionary Apostolate (BIMA I) held in Baguio City, Philippines, July 19-27, 1978, in order to search out ways to animate the missionary activities of the local churches in Asia, and to provide some needed followup on this continent, notably from the last two World Synods of Bishops and Pope Paul VI's exhortation *Evangelii Nuntiandi.*[26]

2. *The Office of Social Communications:* So far we have not been able to avail ourselves of information about particular activities or events at the international level concerning this office.

3. *The Office of Human Development:* This office was instrumental in organizing the Asian Interreligious Forum for Social Action in March 1973, along with the Protestant churches of Asia and SODEPAX.[27] With the Bureau of Asian Affairs (S.J.) and others, the Office of Human Development helped to organize the East Asian Seminar on Population in the Context of Integral Human Development, held in Quezon City, Philippines, June 18-22, 1973,[28] one of a series of regional meetings held to prepare nongovernmental organizations (in this case, the church) to take part in the United Nations Population Conference in Bucharest, Romania, in 1975.

The first Bishops' Institute for Social Action (BISA I) of FABC was held in Manila, March 1-15, 1974, shortly before the Taipei Assembly. Despite the input and the insights, this meeting, with forty-four participants, remained on a rather theoretical level. BISA II (held in Tokyo, April 7-19, 1975) on the Social Dimensions of the Gospel, attended by forty persons, and BISA III, held in Kuala Lumpur, November 2-16, 1975, on the same theme and attended by sixty people, sought "to allow bishops, major religious superiors and directors of social action to come into confrontation with the social, religious, economic and political values of present day Asia; to come to a greater awareness of the task of the Church; and to arrive at concrete programmes which will place the diocese in its role as the basis for the involvement of Christians in the development of their community and country."[29]

BISA IV, held at Antipolo, Manila, March 5-8, 1978, discussed the Collegiality of Bishops for Human Development, and was the first session to be attended by bishops from developed countries as well as those from Asian countries; the former were present as representatives of the member episcopal conferences of the Asian Partnership for Human Development. The thirty participants considered it their primary task "to share with all men the Christian vision of man . . . sharing the noblest aspirations of men and suffering when she [the church] sees them not satisfied, she wishes to help them attain their full flowering, and that is why she offers men what she possesses as her characteristic attribute: a global vision of man and of the human race."[30]

This session took resolutions on episcopal commissions for social action, and for justice and peace or human development; on education, formation, training; on communication and documentation; and on organization.[31]

BISA V, held in Baguio City, Philippines, May 27–June 1, 1979, was different from BISA I–IV in that participants from outside Asia outnumbered those from the Asian countries. The thirty-seven bishops joined the bishops of Latin America in declaring that the church should have a "preferential option for the poor," and expressed an active support for such bodies as the Pontifical Commission for Justice and Peace, the agencies of the United Nations, and Amnesty International. They recommended, among other things, that a future Synod of Bishops in Rome treat the theme Human Rights in the Contemporary World.[32]

4. *The Office of Ecumenism and Interreligious Affairs:* As a followup on the questionnaire sent to every ordinary in the member conferences of FABC, this office organized two institutes on interreligious dialogue (BIRA I and II). Two basic questions were addressed:

a) What should be the *pastoral* position of the Catholic Church in Asia with regard to the predominantly influential religions of Asian countries or regions?

b) What concrete steps should the bishops of Asia take in their pastoral planning during the next five years in order to push forward the interreligious dimension of the Church's apostolate?[33]

BIRA I was held at Sampran, Thailand, October 11–18, 1979. Participants came from Sri Lanka, Thailand, Hong Kong, and the Vatican Secretariat for Non-Christians. People need these pastoral attitudes for dialogue: "a spirit of humility, openness, receptivity, and especially love for Buddhists and for what God wishes to tell Christians through them; a witnessing to the saving grace of Christ, not so much by the proclaimed word, but through love in Christian community, so that its universal validity is seen and felt as such."

BIRA II, held in Kuala Lumpur, Malaysia, November 13–20, 1979, drew delegates from Bangladesh, India, Indonesia, Malaysia, the Philippines, and the Vatican Secretariat for Non-Christians. It appealed for dialogue and for "a change of attitude towards Islam." The dialogue of life was considered the most essential aspect of dialogue, with Christians and Muslims living together in peace. Through the daily practice of brotherhood, helpfulness, openheartedness, and hospitality, everybody should show themselves to be God-fearing neighbors. Several recommendations were made for formal and theological dialogue, the education of Christians for dialogue, and the role of bishops in advancing dialogue. Cooperation with other Christian churches and groups in this dialogue was especially encouraged.[34]

As a direct followup to BIRA I and II a national seminar on interreligious dialogue was held at Fujen University in Taipei, March 10–13, 1980, in which twenty-two representatives from all the dioceses of Taiwan took part.[35]

5. *The Office of Education and Students' Chaplains:* This office held a formation course for university student chaplains at Imus, Philippines, November 6–26, 1978, attended by about seventy people, among them ten bishops. The first week concentrated on an analysis of society and a report of the experiences of the participants

from all parts of Asia. The second part considered the social teachings of the church, which was followed by sessions on management, planning, and the "review of life" methodology. Perhaps the most significant part of this pastoral training was the continued dialogue among the bishops, chaplains and students.[36] A planning session was held in Hong Kong April 23-25, 1979.[37] Twenty-eight participants —bishops, priests, Sisters, and lay chaplains—met at a formation course held at Tansui, Taiwan, from June 10-24, 1979, and came to recognize, among others, these common problems among students in the Far East: "Some aspects of the educational systems, such as competition and exam pressures, do not favor faith growth; there is a lack of concern for the wider society in which they live; there is a lack of Christian Formation Program that integrates faith and action." The participants also called for intensified and new programs for formation of Christian students, including a "social reading of the Bible."[38]

A seminar held in Tagaytay, Philippines (November 23-30, 1979), brought together bishops, student chaplains, and youth to help the development of dialogue and cooperation between Catholic and Muslim youth. After the country reports on the involvement of Christian youth in social issues, the seminar discussed the problems, conflicts, misunderstandings, causes of fear, prejudice, and isolation that have arisen from previous contacts between Catholics and Muslims.[39]

The International Congress on Mission. Two hundred participants from forty-two countries attended the Congress on Missions, jointly sponsored by the Congregation for the Evangelization of Peoples and the Pontifical Mission Aid Societies of the Philippines, which was held in Manila, December 2-7, 1979. Its theme was the Good News of God's Kingdom to the Peoples of Asia. Its purpose was to discuss contemporary orientations in the church's theology of mission, and to clarify and deepen the theological foundations of the work of the Pontifical Mission Societies; to renew the motivation for the church's primary task, evangelization, among those who are involved in this work; to lay down renewed guidelines for policies and planning for the immediate future of the church's missionary effort, and for collaboration with and support for that endeavor.[40]

The participants were divided into several workshops: theology for mission in the Asian context today; local Asian churches and the tasks of mission (inculturation); dialogue with other religious traditions in Asia; the gospel, the kingdom of God, development, and liberation; basic Christian communities and local ministries in Asia; mission, prayer, spirituality, and formation for mission; co-responsible evangelization; mission and education; media and evangelization.

Additional Ways for Interchurch Sharing.

1. A few times religious superiors of Asia have assembled at the international level in order to discuss matters of importance in their service to the churches. A unique gathering of religious women from thirteen Asian countries took place in Bandra, Bombay, November 20-30, 1977; they came together as AMOR IV, an organization of Major Religious Superiors from Asia, started in 1973 in response to the particular needs of Asia. The preliminary report mentioned, among others, these relevant points:

the need to be freed by the poor and the oppressed through sharing their life experiences; the necessity of analyzing and understanding the social and political realities of a country, and of responding as a praying community to injustice; the effectiveness of intercongregational efforts to be present in areas where the needs are greatest, building Christian communities in which programmes are designed and based on concrete needs; the possibilities opened to us when we train people to replace us; the task of re-evaluating and deepening our own formation, for only then can we explore new areas of service; the challenge of dealing with our real fears of Communism while at the same time opening ourselves to possibilities of dialogue; the need to enter into a dialogue with Islam as a political reality in several countries in Asia; . . . a serious study of the Great Religions of Asia in order to discover where we can meet in God; . . . the evaluation of the traditional services of our religious congregations and an assessment of community life styles in the light of the demands of new situations. . . .[41]

The first meeting of representatives of the Conferences of Religious Major Superiors from all parts of Asia was held in Bangalore, India, February 27–March 4, 1978. The participants included forty-five men and women major superiors, representing conferences in India, Pakistan, Sri Lanka, Bangladesh, Indonesia, Singapore, Malaysia, Thailand, Philippines, Hong Kong, Taiwan, South Korea, and Japan. Their attention was primarily directed to the formation of religious and to relationships between the hierarchy and religious. The assembly was convinced that

Asia needs religious deeply committed to contemplative prayer, wanting with their whole being to carry the good news to the poor (to the materially poor and to the spiritually poor), by being with them, . . . daring without fear to fulfil the prophetic mission, . . . to have a vision of the ultimate, . . . to become men and women deeply rooted in faith, capable of using freedom joyously in responsibility, courageously taking risks, open to the Spirit and to the changes required by our times, sensitive to the sufferings of the poor and those who are victims of injustice, ready to lose everything in order to win all for Christ.

2. For the first time theologians from Asian theological institutions gathered at the International Colloquium on Contextual Theology (Manila, June 20–23, 1978). The colloquium tried to limit itself to a situational analysis of the problem as it is experienced in the Asian countries. These were some of the questions posed to authors of working papers: What are the principal characteristics of the sociocultural and political milieu of your country? What challenges and questions do they pose to your theological institutions? How are you meeting those challenges? What new theological and pastoral problems and questions are coming to the fore? What priorities do you propose in order to meet these problems?[42]

3. Representative rectors and deans of Catholic theological seminaries of Asia

met with officials of the Association of Theological Schools in South East Asia (established in 1957), in Manila, June 6–7, 1978. They concluded that "perhaps the most urgent present need is communication among the seminaries themselves. The participants seemed surprised to learn that seminaries in other countries, or even in the same country, are going through similar periods of improvement and difficulty. . . . Among other areas discussed were faculty enrichment, faculty exchange, library improvement, inculturation of preparation for the priesthood, and spiritual formation."[43]

The rectors of all the seminaries of South Asian countries except Burma met in Barrackpore, India, December 1–5, 1978. Using the general theme of inculturation, the participants sought ways to realize what the FABC Plenary Assembly, which had met in the same place just one week before, had held up as an objective of seminary formation: seminarians should be prepared for their ministry so that they become "truly Catholic and truly Asian."[44]

4. Interchurch sharing on behalf of Asian churches also takes place outside Asia. As a result of a fruitful ecumenical dialogue by twenty-two theologians from the third world, held in Dar-es-Salaam, August 5–12, 1976, an ecumenical association of third-world theologians was formed with the aim of continuing development of third-world Christian theologians in order to serve the church's mission in the world and to witness to the new humanity in Christ expressed in the struggle for a just society.[45]

In December 1976 the Missionswissenschaftliches Institut (MISSIO) organized an international meeting of theologians from Africa and Asia, near Frankfurt, in order to exchange views on the life of the churches in both continents, and on what MISSIO could do to assist them in developing themselves, particularly by subsidizing theological publications.

Tensions Resulting from the Development of Particular Churches

The facts on interchurch sharing in Asia just summed up show clearly enough how deeply convinced church leaders in this continent are that the universal faith communion is necessary for their congregations to develop properly. It is at the very least a great advantage that participants of international church meetings, coming from diverse countries, heterogeneous in all aspects of life, can freely exchange their faith experiences and reflections, and are thus enriched by various sources of inspiration and motivation in implementing their mission in their respective societies, in building their communities down to the grassroots.

It is beyond question also that developments of church life in Asia since Vatican II call for a thorough reassessment and renewal of certain traditional structures of church leadership. Here we may recall Pope John XXIII's celebrated opening speech to the Vatican Council on October 11, 1962: "In the present order of things, Divine Providence is leading us to a new order of human relations which, by men's own efforts and even beyond their very expectations, are directed toward the fulfillment of God's superior and inscrutable designs."[46]

The preface of the Decree on the Bishops' Pastoral Office in the Church strikingly refers to the phrase "a new order of things," taken directly from John XXIII's proclamation of Vatican Council II, December 25, 1961, where it says: "This most sacred Synod, therefore, attentive to the developments in human relations which have brought about a new order of things in our time, and wishing to determine more exactly the pastoral office of bishops, issues the following decrees."[47]

The question is: To what extent is institutionalization needed in order to facilitate mutual understanding and reciprocal inspiration among the churches? And when do structures of leadership degenerate so that by overcentralization (just to take one instance) they become counterproductive? Is it not the case at times that by emphasizing uniformity, adverse to the proper meaning of catholicity, or by too strongly insisting on authority, contrary to genuine *diakonia,* initiatives are repressed and even stifled from the outset, and Christian communities are actually prevented from maturing in their own identity precisely by implementing their mission in faithful response to challenges from contemporary society?

By no means do we intend to question the services rendered by central church institutions of government. But the problem, which we probably share with many others and which may be found particularly in young churches or in communities fully conscious of their evangelizing mission in society today, concerns the self-perception of those institutions and their manner of exercising authority: namely, to what extent these are still in keeping with "the new order of things," with "the new order of human relations." We fully acknowledge their often indispensable ministries for the well-being of the universal church. Yet one may question the historical appearance they have adopted in the course of time, which, being contingent upon changing periods of history, ought to be always adaptable, taking into consideration that the universal church is concretely realized in culturally and socially conditioned local congregations at this present stage of history. Is it not true that at times they function in ways alien to contemporary ideals of leadership? Are we aware that by clinging too strictly to structures, practices, and attitudes of a former age we may jeopardize the credibility of those institutions as well as their essential ministry to the churches?

May a critical study be suggested of present patterns of exercising authority in view of adapting them to more relevant modes of functioning in keeping with "the new order of things" brought about by radical changes in human relations? This would seem to involve a study of

the distinction between the essential ministry of the Curial Departments and their incidental historical structures;—the implications of the renewed self-perception of the Church as laid down in the documents of the Second Vatican Council, notably the implications of the Church being primarily the People of God, the implications of lay coresponsibility, of collegiality and of the principle of subsidiarity;—the implications of bishops' Conferences participating in the Magisterium Ecclesiae, which entails that relations should be characterized by trust in their unquestioned sincerity and orthodoxy;—the implications of exercising authority as an office of *diakonia* rather than of power, with a pastoral rather than a juridical attitude, in accord with a prophetic rather than a repressive concept of leadership, and in case of differences of opinion, resorting to dialogue rather than authoritarian commands;—the implications of a modern pluralistic world society and a modern pluralistic Church community; —the implications of modern democratic convictions calling for openness, giving full credit to legitimate requests for information;—the implications of a consistent application of Chapter I of the decree on *the Bishops' Pastoral Office in the Church,* with due attention being paid to "the signs of the times" which are being written with the immanent guidance of the Spirit of God.[48]

An instance that invites us to reflect is a statement issued by the Congregation for the Evangelization of Peoples through its Theological Commission, criticizing the final declaration of the Asian Theological Conference held in Sri Lanka in January 1979. This statement speaks of a theological methodology that "does not come any more from God or from revelation but springs from social conditions and from historical problems"; a theology "lacking in revealed value"; a theology subject to "deep relativism" because rooted solely in an understanding of Asian political and social conditions; and a theology that moves the authentic interpretation of revelation from the bishops to the oppressed poor.

Father Tissa Balasuriya, O.M.I., organizer of the conference, replied that the commission made "many errors of judgment—not to say misrepresentations." To specific criticisms he replied in a letter:

(i) an unbiased reading shows that the declaration often mentions God and Jesus; *(ii)* the declaration said the people are one source for theology, not the only source; *(iii)* the fact that the declaration does not mention bishops does not mean their role is denied; *(iv)* regarding the use of Marxist categories to attack capitalism, the declaration said nothing that Pope John XXIII and Pope Paul VI had not said many times; *(v)* conversion is not forgotten: the declaration itself was an invitation to personal and collective conversion to the values of the Gospel.

He suggests also that the Western background of the members of the Vatican commission was the cause of the misunderstandings, and that the commission's criticism is an example of the failure of theologians to understand the Asian situation.[49]

Another example: in catechetical matters bishops' conferences and local ordinaries apparently enjoy the authority and freedom inherent to their office. The Indonesian Episcopal Conference, however, has wondered why this same authority and freedom are not recognized in liturgical matters. There is no intention of questioning the existence and the service of Congregation for the Sacraments and Divine Worship. Yet it is felt that this congregation is interfering too much in matters that can be fully assessed and arranged only by episcopal conferences or local ordinaries. Also, up to now liturgical books are prescribed for the whole Catholic world; certain texts are even being urged as the only valid ones. Even translations have to be approved. How can the congregation—without any knowledge of foreign vernacular languages—presume to judge whether translations into these languages are correct or not? Such a state of affairs at best can only be called outdated.[50]

The Need for Particular Churches to Assess Themselves

Since Vatican II promulgated its constitutions, decrees, and declarations, all focused on the life of the church and the churches, developments in their lives and their structures have aroused an ever greater awareness of the necessity of reassessing thoroughly traditional patterns of Christian community life and of pastoral care down to the grassroots levels. A regular self-evaluation is requisite not only in view of the growth in depth of Christian faith within the congregation, but also in order to determine accurately in what way and to what extent churches need to cooperate with their sister churches, and to determine what exactly is the role of missionaries and the function of missionary institutions.

Here are some of the factors that continuously stimulate us to reflect: as is evident from discussions in FABC sessions and in conferences sponsored by FABC offices held thus far, Asian churches become ever more conscious of their mission amid society; the rightful autonomy of earthly values as taught by *Gaudium et Spes,* no. 36, is gaining ever wider recognition and enhancing a renewed understanding of salvation; ongoing modernization and technological progress in Asian societies evoke numerous problems of somewhat radical changes in the people's mentality on a large scale, particularly in their religious attitudes; this calls for a healthy process of secularization which, however, does not necessarily mean secularization in "western" shape. Political independence gained since World War II by Asian countries; awareness of their national identity impelling towards a definite stance—even to the point of resentment and resistance—against former colonial powers; the fact that our peoples are determined to rely ever more on their own resources are factors certainly not without impact on church life. We, ourselves, in Asia, as well as "mission-sending" churches elsewhere, have to reckon with these factors while assessing the progressively changing relationships toward missionaries and missionary institutions.

Amid these sociocultural and political transformations, the traditional notion of mission and traditional missionary methods, which in the past were taken for granted, now are being seriously questioned. Without taking any issue on the often heroic self-sacrifice of many foreign missionaries or in any way raising doubts as to their good intentions, while indeed remaining deeply grateful for their genuine efforts of evangelization, our people are posing questions as to what extent missionaries have succeeded in getting the message of salvation across to the hearts of the people, to what extent their preaching of the gospel has been truly relevant in society's life situations, so that Christian faith could take deep root in their daily lives.

Within the general search for new patterns of authentically inculturated evangelization in and by the local church, the problem should be posed anew as to which are the proper roles for the local clergy and local religious right now and henceforth; and insofar as missionaries from abroad are still needed which new roles must be assigned to them, so that their precious contribution will enhance the proper maturing of our Christian communities.

Rethinking the Role of Missionaries and Missionary Institutions

Now that we have considered the life of Asian churches and their mission in society, and have examined their mutual relationships as actualizing the universal communion of Christians in faith in the Asian context, and this specifically as embodied in FABC and its various offices, we shall in this section inquire into the role of missionaries and missionary institutions vis-à-vis Christian communities in progress toward maturity.

What is the bishops' responsibility for mission? Can the fact that churches send forth missionaries be assumed as a sign of maturity? What are some of the symptoms of neocolonialism in young churches? To what extent is financial dependency a help or a hindrance? What are the strains vis-à-vis missionaries from other churches, and how can those tensions be overcome? In other words, how are missionaries to integrate themselves within the new context of their missionary life? How do we describe the role of missionaries in the past, the present, and the future?

The Bishops' Responsibility for Mission

Vatican II explicitly pronounces the *sollicitudo omnium ecclesiarum* of bishops.

> . . . each of [the bishops], as a member of the episcopal college and a legitimate successor of the apostles, is obliged by Christ's decree and command to be solicitous for the whole Church [*Lumen Gentium,* no. 23].

> The bishop . . . together with his own college of priests, must become increasingly animated with the mind of Christ and of the Church, and must think and live in union with the universal Church [*Ad Gentes,* no. 19].

Bishops, therefore, are responsible for their respective churches' mutual sharing —within the context of the one mission of the universal church—of faith experiences first of all, but also of personnel and resources needed for the implementation of that mission. Precisely in chapter III on particular churches the Decree on the Missionary Activity of the Church, referring to Pope John XXIII's encyclical *Princeps Pastorum,* wishes particularly that the young churches preserve an intimate communion with the universal church, and embed their traditions in their own culture, "thereby increasing the life of the Mystical Body by a certain mutual exchange of energies. Hence, stress should be laid on those theological, psychological, and human elements which can contribute to fostering this sense of communion with the universal Church" (*Ad Gentes,* no. 19).

Bishops manifest their responsibility for mission by: (*a*) willingly and wholeheartedly attending to the requests of other churches, particularly those "most often located in the poorer parts of the world," and "generally suffering from a very serious lack of priests and of material support" (*Ad Gentes,* no. 19); (*b*) generously giving their consent when there are among their clergy those who wish to be sent to other churches as missionaries (religious superiors will have to take the same attitude toward members of their congregation opting to dedicate their lives to missionary apostolate abroad); (*c*) seeing to it that during the years of formation, candidates for the priesthood become well acquainted with the life of churches in other parts of the world, with their problems and their chances. For instance, missionaries on leave could be given the opportunity to introduce their field of pastoral activity to students, so that they grow in the sense of being in intimate communion with the whole church, and the missionary spirit be kept ever alive among them. This applies to the clergy as well. They all can join their efforts and render their valuable contribution, even if they never will be sent forth as missionaries.

Sending Forth Missionaries: A Sign of Maturity?

Most people perhaps tend to think first of "consolidating" their own faith before considering the possibilities and their abilities for apostolate. Similarly perhaps most people will be inclined to think that a local church must be mature in itself before sending forth missionaries in order to help out other churches, which then are supposed to be immature by the fact that they still need missionaries from abroad. Or, in other words, the ability to send forth missionaries is still considered by many as a sign of maturity. This thinking, however, more or less along the line of *nemo dat quod non habet,* reflects for us the very traditional concept of a one-way or one-direction mission, of dividing the entire church into mission-sending and mission-receiving churches. Possibly also one of the underlying, unpronounced assumptions is that the salvation of others is secondary to one's own salvation, and thus apostolate is something almost accidental or even supererogatory. It could also mean that the relationship between "living one's own faith" and "giving testimony to that faith" is not rightly understood.

Is it not true that by living our responsibility for the salvation of others in genuine love and unselfishness, we ourselves grow toward ever fuller Christian adulthood? Similarly, for a church to send forth missionaries could mean an enrichment in various aspects. By direct contact with other cultures and by their personal experiences in exploring new ways of expressing Christian faith, missionaries could give new stimuli to the church of their origin, so that this church might renew itself in worship and Christian life, personally as well as in community. By dedicating their lives to an apostolate abroad, missionaries could inspire those at home toward an ever greater generosity in committing themselves to Christian witness, perhaps even to a more direct apostolate.

Of course a certain maturity is required for anyone in order to take some responsibility for others, and to help them develop their personality and their life of faith. For parents the care for their offspring requires that they themselves be mature. Similarly a local church should have reached some degree of adulthood, and be able to take care of itself to some extent, before sending forth missionaries becomes realistically feasible. This *can* be a sign of maturity. But whether or not we could infer that the sending church is mature would still depend on the type of missionaries, their views particularly about church life, and how they translated new ecclesiological insights into practice. The type of missionaries in many respects reflects the type of church life from which they come.

On the other hand, the contact of churches of ancient Christian tradition with other cultures—even in countries materially poor and far less developed, but which may have many spiritual values to offer to technologically advanced societies—may very well be a rich source of inspiration and stimuli to regain their maturity in their highly secularized milieus, and to find new ways of relevantly expressing the richness of the mystery of salvation in Christ. By this universal communion in faith with other churches, and with other cultures as bearers of religious values in which the seeds of God's saving Word are found, the local church grows toward its full maturity in Christ. Here the idea of *sister* churches sharing their faith-experiences should become a reality!

Symptoms of Neo-colonialism in Young Churches

In 1659 the recently established Congregation for the Propagation of the Faith addressing the Vicars Apostolic of China, gave this strong and clear directive to missionaries:

> Do not waste your zeal or your powers of persuasion in getting these people to change their rites, customs, or ways of life, unless these be very obviously opposed to faith and morals. For what could be more ridiculous than to import France, Spain, Italy or any other part of Europe into China? What you carry with you is not a national culture but a Message which does not reject or offend the sound traditions of any country, but rather wants to safeguard and foster them.[51]

The tragic story of the Chinese rites early in the eighteenth century shows how far missionaries were from practicing this directive. Even up to Vatican II a maximum of uniformity was regarded as the ideal, and there was tendency to identify the Western church with the universal church. But have we overcome this tendency today?

And since, according to the synod document *Justice in the World* (1971), participation in the transformation of the world fully appears to be "a constitutive dimension of the preaching of the Gospel, that is, of the mission of the Church for the redemption of the human race,"[52] let us listen to what the Christian Conference of Asia had to say about development:

> We do not accept development as understood, interpreted and imposed upon us by the dominant groups. We do not want it, as it alienates and disintegrates our people. It destroys human values so precious to us. The people of highly industrialized (developed) societies in Asia bear witness to the dehumanizing process of so-called development. . . . We want our way of life, our view of land and family, our languages and cultures to be recognized.[53]

Can the presence of missionaries from abroad be an obstacle to the growth of the church? In what sense and to what extent? Our reflections on the missionary dimensions of the local church and on its need to develop itself within the universal communion of faith have shown how much, even within renewed mutual relationships of sister churches, foreign missionaries can be of service to the local church.

Nonetheless, particularly in young churches in Asian countries that are just now developing or are underdeveloped, the role of those missionaries should be carefully reconsidered. It is not altogether beyond question that here and there missionaries, apparently even in good faith, still impose their ideas and ways of life as well as church structures or institutions they are familiar with in their homeland, so that the local clergy and religious—not to speak of lay people—cannot properly live out and develop their creativity and their initiatives. Thus some missionaries may be an obstacle to inculturation of Christian faith in young churches in Asia by perpetuating some sort of clerical "neocolonialism." It is even possible that this attitude, particularly among newly emerging nations, is met with resentment and resistance not only by the Christians, but by society at large. If government institutions are involved, serious obstacles could arise. A church with a too "Western" or—generally speaking—a too alien appearance is not welcome in Asia, and will be seriously hampered in its mission of evangelization.

Financial Dependency: A Help or a Hindrance?

Churches of Asia cannot but share the situation of most of this continent made up of multitudes of poor, where most people are deprived of access to the material goods and resources that they need to create a truly human life for themselves, where millions are living below the poverty line, and where there is vast hunger, disease, malnutrition, and unemployment.[54]

Particularly where Christianity is a small minority, it is far from feasible to rely upon its own material resources. Christian communities still have a long way to go in order to become mature, and this by wholeheartedly committing themselves to the poor and opting in their favor;[55] by not merely working *for* the poor but, rather, *with* the poor.[56] The areas of church concentration for work with the poor agreed upon by the first three BISAs, namely, people's or communitarian health programs; assistance to workers; massive adult education programs for the poor; efforts to assist the people to design and operate models of development; the use of mass media to provide local, and especially rural, communities with information in order to conscientize them; etc.,[57] are a burden far too heavy for the churches. They are still very much in need of financial support from other, and in this respect, better-off churches, their missionary institutions, and their funding agencies.

And the churches so far have been very generous indeed. For example, according to the Catholic Relief Services (CRS) annual report, from July 1976 to July 1977 this American Catholic agency for aid to developing countries provided $240 million to 12 million people in eighty-five countries. During 1976 the generosity of German Catholics amounted to more than 260 million marks, with MISEREOR contributing 84 million, ADVENIAT 83 million, and MISSIO 77.5 million.[58]

It is to be noted, however, that several forms of financial dependency belong to the factors that may prevent local churches from becoming mature and self-reliant. This may be the case where funds are merely and directly consumed in order to cover running expenses (although there certainly are inevitable expenses, e.g., in vast jungle areas with practically no facilities for transportation except perhaps by motorboat or small airplanes). Instances are known of several projects being "out of proportion" so that they surpass the ability of local Christian communities to sustain them.

The purpose of missionary institutions and funding agencies abroad must be to assist local churches so that these develop into self-supporting, self-ministering, self-reliant communities as soon as possible. Hence local churches in Asia should build up their own resources, not only with regard to personnel, but in material resources as well. Far more necessary and helpful than any other form of support is human investment in its various forms, mainly in education or formation, for example, of local clergy and religious, or of lay leaders.

The general directive laid down in *Ad Gentes,* no. 19, must always be kept in mind: "the continued missionary activity of the whole Church furnish them [i.e., the churches located in the poorer parts of the world] with those subsidies which principally serve the growth of the local Church and the maturity of Christian life." Although it is reasonable that funding agencies are well informed as to how the financial assistance they provide is being disposed, it only stands to reason that they leave the local church to decide substantially the purpose for which funds are to be used, and in what manner they are to be used.

Tensions vis-à-vis Missionaries Coming from Other Churches

During the past few years in several Asian countries that attained freedom from colonialism following World War II, there has been a tendency to resent the presence of missionaries from abroad. Such countries attempt to restrict the presence and the activities of missionaries, to set time limits on their residency, and sometimes to have them expelled. We hear that in some countries, such as Malaysia, India, Sri Lanka, Vietnam, and Burma, missionaries often encounter difficulties in trying to enter or work there.

But even apart from such situations, tensions will arise quite understandably between the local church and those coming from other local churches on account of differences in cultural, social, and religious life. Certain tensions are even inevitable. Let us accept them as a reality, not just as a necessary evil bound to arise whenever missionaries are sent to other local churches, but as an opportunity for dialogue, and hence for deepening of our consciousness of the richness of Christian faith by mutual sharing. Not all tensions can be resolved, especially not by mere discussions, since many cultural discrepancies and many feelings are difficult to express verbally. Perhaps it is a healthy situation for certain tensions to remain in certain areas, so that our minds stay alert and flexible. It is, however, important to foster the right atmosphere for better mutual understanding (which does not necessarily mean agreement or consent) by a continual "dialogue of life" among the local clergy and religious and those coming from other local churches, so that tensions may not harm but, on the contrary, stimulate the dynamism of life in Christian communities.

Integration of Missionaries Coming from Other Churches

Without in any way questioning the readiness and goodwill of missionaries from abroad, the problem of their integration should be considered realistically, while taking the following elements into account:

1. This process of integration, which is reciprocal between the local community and the missionaries, concerns all aspects of human life, external and internal (spiritual/personal), cultural, psychological, and religious. Not only does it concern the field of human awareness. It also affects deeply the realms of our subconscious, and this, at times, causes difficulties in adapting attitudes of mind that are far from easy to tackle.

2. This process also depends very much on how alien the life in the new cultural milieu is to the missionary. Integration will not be achieved with equal ease by all missionaries in all local churches, since not all have the same ability to adjust themselves to new circumstances and conditions of everyday life.

3. Hence it is not reasonable to expect from all missionaries that they will perfectly succeed in suiting themselves to the new ways of life, in becoming Japanese with the Japanese, Burmese with the Burmese, Indian with the Indians. Nevertheless, keeping in mind the example of Christ the Lord, who came to serve and not to be served, and became the son of his contemporary cultural milieu, missionaries are expected to have the mental attitude to learn by living contact with the people in the society to whom they have been sent: how they think and act, individually as well as in community life, how they feel, not just simply to imitate them, but to suit themselves reasonably to this way of life.

4. It is also to the advantage of the local church that missionaries retain some particularities of the culture of their origin, and characteristics of their original world-view, their standpoints, their insights, so that they remain able to take a critical stance toward the local culture and situations in the new field of their activities, and thus help the local church create its own identity.

5. On the part of the faithful an understanding of the aforementioned aspects of the problem is required, so that they wholeheartedly accept the missionaries and stand ready to help them through the often difficult process of inculturation.

II: INDONESIA

Mission is constitutive to the church in Indonesia. Living Christian faith in one's milieu is none other than giving testimony to that faith, bringing the good news to one's fellow humans. Hence we shall consider the church's life and mission as its response in faith to the signs of the times as shown in society, a response to the ideals and aspirations, to the needs and the anxieties of Indonesians, to the unquenchable longing for the Lord of salvation deep down in their hearts.

Religions in Indonesia

Indonesia is not a religious state. Neither is it a merely secular state. Its state philosophy is based on the Five Principles, the *Pancasila,* namely, belief in unitary deity, nationalism, democracy, humanitarianism, and social justice. On this basis (which the Christian groups do not want to be developed into a detailed ideology but left loosely defined so that the various religious groups in Indonesia can give them meaning in terms of their own faith and tradition), the great religions present in Indonesia—Islam, Catholicism, Protestantism, Hinduism, and Buddhism—are recognized by the government and officially given equal status and rights in practicing and propagating their faith (although in practice, predominant Islam is clearly given certain privileges). The Muslims are joined together in the Council of Ulamas; the greater part of Protestant Christians in the Council of Churches in Indonesia; the Hindus in Parisadha Hindu Dharma; the Buddhists in Walubi; and the Catholics in the Indonesian Bishops' Conference (MAWI). Official relations and cooperation between the government and the various religious groups are carried on through these councils. There is a Department of Religion, representing the government in its relations with the religions, always led by a Muslim. Understandably the pressures from this massive Muslim majority are felt strongly by other religions.[59]

There is, besides, the challenge of plurality in Indonesian society: an overwhelming diversity of cultures, from the highest degrees down to the primitive ways of life, even to that of isolated tribes only recently discovered, which have hardly passed the Stone Age.[60]

Our questions are: How is Christian faith to be lived and expressed in order to become deeply incarnate in daily life? How can inculturation of life according to the gospel proceed healthily, without going astray into isolation in self-enclosed and self-centered communities, in continuous dialogue with Indonesian society in whose midst Christians have to carry out their mission of service and evangelization while maintaining communion with other local churches and with the universal church? How are Christians to respect whatever positive values are found in ancient cultural and religious traditions, in the Indonesian *adats,* and to help people become aware of those values heavily challenged today by modernization and technological progress? What contribution can the church render to society, so that the inheritance of cultural and religious values will be preserved, and new values disclosed in all the efforts for development and social welfare?

In order to fulfill this mission of evangelization, which now more than ever should be prophetic, "critical" in the Christian sense, and truly constructive, leading toward the salvation of the whole person and all people, Christians ought to be evangelized themselves, their faith consolidated and deepened, their communities increasingly self-reliant, self-ministering, and self-supporting.

Participation in National Development Programs

Since 1969 the Indonesian government has been focusing all funds and forces on the cultural, social, and economic development of the people through successive five-year development programs, in order to achieve a balance in overall develop-ment as the basis of self-sustaining growth toward the common welfare.[61] Indonesia is presently implementing its third development program (1979-84). The church, deeply aware of its mission to live up to its full responsibility as part of society, plays an active and well-appreciated role in various fields of development (education, health care, other areas of social welfare, and political life). Several times since the first five-year development program was inaugurated in 1969, the participation of the church in Indonesia's efforts for development has been the main theme of study and reflection in annual sessions of the Indonesian Bishops' Conference. In 1970, the conference issued *Action Guidelines for Indonesian Catholics;*[62] in 1974 it re-flected on the church's participation in REPELITA II (the second development pro-gram)[63]; and in 1978 and 1979 papers were presented on the mission of the church in Indonesian society.[64] MAWI's annual assemblies so far have made reflection, deliber-ation, and common policies possible concerning nationwide problems in various aspects of life in society and church, for example, the problems of population and family planning, of education, and of health care. A few times the faithful in all dioceses have been invited to discuss questions proposed by the various bishops' commissions, and thus to contribute to MAWI's deliberations. Particularly in recent years the main theme for conscientization of the faithful by means of Lenten Actions has been the development and promotion of justice.

Catholics in Indonesia presently number only 3.5 million. Yet the role and in-fluence of Catholics are acknowledged and well esteemed by the government. During the 1970's MAWI grew in importance, and by 1980 fully was recognized both by society and by the government. It is frequently consulted about momentous ques-tions by governmental offices and organizations, as well as by private groups.[65]

In order to reinforce the impact of *Pancasila* on the entire Indonesian people, the 1978 session of the People's Consultative Assembly issued a decree entitled *Guide to the Living and Practice of* Pancasila. As its followup the government has held a series of seminars for government officials and leaders in society, including religious leaders. MAWI and diocesan representatives have been invited twice to take part, together with leaders of other religions. Availing themselves of these extraordinary opportunities, MAWI's representatives were able to associate intensively with leaders of Islam, Buddhism, Hinduism, and the Protestant churches.

Problems of Population and Health Care

The population in Indonesia is the fifth largest in the world, after the People's Republic of China, India, the Soviet Union, and the United States of America.[66] Overpopulation due to high birth rate (the increase per annum is 3,108,400 or 2.6 percent) and uneven distribution are two of the gravest problems. The government sponsors a National Family Planning Program heavily supported by international organizations such as the World Health Organization (WHO). By diverse means the government is seeking effective ways to reduce the population growth. A few years ago it issued regulations to the effect that the dependents' subsidy for civil servants and members of the military forces would be limited to the amount needed for the support for the three children, other children becoming the sole responsibility of the parents. Religious leaders, including MAWI, have been officially requested to support this Family Planning Program. We have always tried to secure that rights of free choice and self-determination be respected, and that the parents' sense of responsibility be stressed.

In order to deal with the unauthorized practice of abortion, common in many regions, the Ministry of Health organized a research and preparatory seminar to gather data for legislation on abortion for medical reasons. Representatives of the Catholic position took part in this seminar.[67]

Complying with suggestions of the Association of Voluntary Health Services of Indonesia (PERDHAKI), early in 1978 MAWI issued *Guidelines on Health Services,* stressing the importance of primary health care, self-reliance in health care, coordination and cooperation among health-care units, private health services, and government health services.[68] In collaboration with Cipta Loka Caraka, a Catholic publisher, the Institute for the Welfare of Catholic Families issued two booklets and a book on population education.

According to the new marriage regulations (in force since the mid-1970s), to which MAWI contributed its recommendations, all Indonesian citizens are obliged to register their marriage. There is a tendency to oppose divorce and polygamy, a relevant point in a predominantly Muslim society. Several times MAWI's representatives were requested to submit their suggestions and proposals concerning government regulations to be issued on this matter.

The Churches Participation in Education[69]

Before the 1978 session of the People's Consultative Assembly, government policy in the field of education resulted in negative effects for private education. Some of the points in question were the "integration" of pupils in private schools, the assurance of Muslim religious instruction in schools, the policy of the regional government on the location of schools built by presidential instruction, and the policy on the assignment of teachers in private subsidized schools as government employees. The 1978 session of the People's Consultative Assembly expressed its positive appreciation for private education: "Private education has its role and responsibility in carrying out national education. Hence it is necessary that its growth be fostered in accordance with its potentialities. Private education should remain within the patterns of national education, while at the same time keeping the characteristics of private schools."[70]

Education is most important for the development of cultural life. Nevertheless the MAWI session of 1978 found it necessary to examine carefully the exact reasons why the church's contribution in this field would still be relevant in the future, particularly in regard to school education. In the meantime other ways ought to be explored in order that all levels of society be reached ("adult" or "informal" education), and not just the youth, since in traditional rural societies (roughly 80 percent of the population) the older generation still plays an important role in decision-making, unlike in city areas where the younger generation should be given preference.

On behalf of cultural development, obstacles such as attitudes of "feudalism," "paternalism," etc., which also affect church life, should be surmounted. In this respect, the faithful, as much as all other members of society, need to be conscientized about their ability and responsibility to build up their own future.[71]

At the moment Catholics are in charge of 31 educational institutions at university level (universities, colleges, and academies), 1,060 high schools, and 2,854 elementary schools. Catholic education, generally speaking, is highly esteemed. But the problem of meeting the running costs is a heavy burden. Government financial assistance is far from sufficient, yet it is a token of Indonesian society's appreciation for our contribution. The National Association for Catholic Education (MNPK) helps; the diocesan commissions on Catholic education render their valuable services to our schools, especially where nationwide church policy and relations with government institutions are concerned.

Pastoral Care of the Youth

The fact that youth in the cities are much different from rural youth requires a difference in approach and pastoral care. In the cities many of our young people are actually being severed from parental guidance either by their own choice or due to lack of interest and responsibility on the part of the parents. They are left to search for their future more or less on their own; many are rebelling against widespread abuses such as corruption and injustice, and feel themselves torn by the fact that, while they are determined to foster their idealism, they meet with frustration because they are unable to change life situations. This poses a tremendous challenge to church leaders. The youth in rural areas, although affected by the changes in society, find it almost impossible to break away from traditional views and life patterns that are losing more and more of their relevance to modern life.

Since 1960 the government has established youth centers in many places with the aim of providing physical and mental education for the youth during leisure hours. These centers are also designed to provide training in certain vocational skills for dropouts. Youth centers in the initial stages are usually managed by the private sector, but are later on gradually taken over by government institutions. In 1978 there were 2,042 such youth centers all over the country accommodating around 287,500 persons.[72]

Within the Commission on Lay Apostolate a special section has been established for youth in order to help all youth leaders and organizations in the dioceses. This section is to consult the dioceses on the possibilities of upgrading programs for youth leaders.[73] Interviews at the national level have been held with leaders of the Catholic Students' Organization, the Catholic Youth Organization, and parish youth groups. A guide for the formation of youth and a course on preparing for marriage are to be published.[74]

Church and State Relations

In a society made up of a great variety of ethnic groups and religions, like Indonesia, it is understandable that tensions and controversies arise among the adherents of religions and religious beliefs. The government assiduously promotes and cultivates religious harmony necessary for peace and order in society. This main target of national development in the field of religion is said to cover the development of unity among the adherents of each religion, among adherents of various religious faiths, and between each religious community and the government. For this purpose inter-religious dialogues are arranged concerning social problems, studies are conducted on various social phenomena, cooperation is stimulated among various religious communities, national interreligious seminars are held, etc.[75] The Department of Religious Affairs several times has invited representatives of the five religions to discuss the feasibility of a consultative forum on religious matters.

The publishing of a complete edition of Holy Scripture, which, especially for Indonesian Catholics, would have involved no small outlay of funds, has been granted government subsidies during the past several years. This "Ecumenical Bible" was edited jointly by the Indonesian Bible Association (LBI—Catholic) and the Indonesian Bible Society (LAI—Protestant).

The Department of Religious Affairs, however, not in the least through its Catholic section, which shows a tendency to take over what pertains to the responsibility of the church, so far has proved to be a source of a number of problems, some of them very delicate. Hence the need is felt for studying very carefully what would be the most appropriate relationship between the church and the government in the Indonesian situation. Here are some of the aspects to be considered:

a. Although in principle the freedom of the church (on a par with that of other religions) is officially recognized, some of the guidelines as stated in Vatican II's Declaration on Religious Freedom apparently are not acceptable in practice.

b. The prevailing model of conceiving the relationship between the government and religion seems to be that of the relationship between Islam and the state; thus "religious freedom" and the competence of the state in religious matters are differently understood from what was stipulated by Vatican II. The concept of religious freedom as based on "human dignity" and "fundamental human rights" is even open to suspicion as being "of Christian origin."

c. The idea of separation between religion and state seems to be alien to most (if not all) cultures in Indonesia, where religious values are deeply immersed in cultural traditions and folkways.

d. Within this setting, the tendency seems to be that the government has rather "too much to say" in religious matters and, Islam being predominant, is in a sense rather restrictive to our missionary activities.

A much disputed problem is the question on teaching religion at school. Early in 1978 the government started officially recognizing religion teachers for elementary state as well as private schools. Out of the 16,000 teachers recognized by the government only 475 were teaching Catholic religion. The discussions of MAWI in 1978 centered on the conditions posed by the government, and subsequently on the question whether institutions for the formation of teachers of Catholic religion (PGAK, IAKN) should be established. Apparently situations vary from region to region, so that it seems unrealistic to have one and the same attitude applied everywhere.[76] Also it has been a long-disputed question whether or not non-Catholic pupils in Catholic schools are to be given religious instruction, and in which religion.

Another delicate question is: How is the church implementing its mission by exercising its prophetical-critical function in Indonesian society? For example, the posters and folders on the theme "Promoting Justice" of the 1978 Lenten Action for Development gave rise to evaluations and reactions varying from place to place; in some regions and among several groups they were considered too negative in that they could cause harm to the church; elsewhere they were used by the youth to launch criticisms of the government.[77]

The year before, November 9, 1977, MAWI issued its *Critical Remarks on Developments in Indonesian Society* describing the restlessness and the concerns within society, but also the goodwill and the many efforts to surmount existing deficiencies and weaknesses. The importance of the principles of democracy were underlined, as well as the proper functioning of state institutions; the equality of human rights and opportunities for all groups; the task of judiciary institutions; the need to emphasize in all the dignity of the human person.[78]

Is There Freedom for Missionary Activities?

Here we mention some facts and some decrees of the Department of Religious Affairs that have caused difficulties to Christians, Protestants and Catholics alike:

a. The decree jointly issued by the ministers of Religious Affairs and of the Interior, September 13, 1969, stating restrictive conditions, has for the past ten years hampered Christians in building their churches, and has caused continuous friction between Muslims and Christians.

b. The declaration issued by the Minister of the Interior, May 5, 1975, prohibited Christians from using their homes as places for worship.

c. After a visit to the Vatican upon the invitation of Cardinal Pignedoli without the knowledge of the Episcopal Conference, the Minister of Religious Affairs made the statement that the Vatican already had accepted these proposals of the Indonesian government: Islam is to be taught to non-Catholic pupils in Catholic schools; Catholicism may not be propagated to non-Christians; restriction of foreign aid. The secretary of MAWI then officially declared that the ministerial statement was not in accordance with information received from the Vatican.[79]

d. The decree of the Minister of Religious Affairs, no. 22/1978, seriously obstructed the issuance of visas and residence permits for missionaries. Although there were doubts about the validity of this decree issued when the Cabinet had already resigned, it has in fact been applied by officials of the ministry.[80]

e. The decree issued by the Minister of Religious Affairs, no. 70/1978, banned religious preaching to those who already profess a religion, and decree no. 77/1978 necessitates official approval for any form of foreign assistance (personnel, funds, etc.). The government, however, does not interfere with those who voluntarily change from one religion to another, or of their own will attend sermons, Qur'anic or biblical lectures, and the like, for the sake of just getting acquainted with a religion; nor does the government ban caritative and social activities of religious bodies, for example, in the field of health care and education, since these are the ways adherents of religions participate in national development.[81]

f. The decree jointly issued by the Ministers of the Interior and of Religious Affairs, no. 1/1979, which as a result of the reaction of both MAWI and the Indonesian Council of Churches to decree nos. 70/1978 and 77/1978,[82] modified both decrees into a more acceptable decree stating that (1) religious preaching among adherents of other faiths is forbidden only when strongly persuasive methods are applied; (2) foreign assistance to religious organizations no longer needs to be cleared by the Minister of Religious Affairs, but merely by the national Coordinating Committee for Foreign Technical Cooperation.

The Current Problem of Missionaries from Abroad

For almost thirty-five years, since Indonesia gained its independence after World War II, missionaries from any country at all (except in the past few years those from East European countries) have been free to live and work in Indonesia, although at times they have met with some minor obstacles. This relatively peaceful situation, however, was suddenly disturbed in 1979 when news came that the government would not allow missionaries to stay longer than five years in Indonesia. Church leadership, therefore, should be "Indonesianized" as soon as possible, and evangelization conducted and carried out by the Indonesian clergy and religious. During 1979 thirty-three foreign missionaries were given only a six-month extension of their residency permits and told that no further extension would be granted. If such a policy were carried out consistently, in a short time 926 priests, 284 Brothers, and 891 Sisters would be forced to leave the country. In audiences with several Cabinet ministers and, eventually, with the president of Indonesia, a MAWI delegation declared that the efforts and assistance of missionaries were still needed by the church and that the church had long since engaged in the Indonesianization of its leadership, but that education for the priesthood had to meet high requirements; moreover, on account of the universality of the church, even when there would be sufficient Indonesian personnel, the church always would need the presence of foreign missionaries. In a special parliamentary hearing on November 27, 1979, MAWI's secretary, Archbishop Leo Soekoto of Jakarta, explained that the projected Indonesianization of the clergy would not be completed within five decades, that of the Brothers in not less than thirty years, and that of the Sisters in not less than twenty-five years, an estimate deduced from the current growth rate of the number of Indonesian Catholics. Following MAWI's clarifications, the government decided to withdraw the restriction to six-month residency without further extension for the aforesaid thirty-three missionaries.

The government is allowing foreign missionaries the opportunity to become Indonesian citizens. Six hundred and thirty foreign-born priests, Brothers, and Sisters have already submitted their application. We are awaiting the government's decision as to how long missionaries will be allowed to stay on and work in Indonesia.[83]

MAWI is grateful for being invited by the government to discuss this question on missionaries. Generally speaking, the government so far has been willing to listen to MAWI's proposals and suggestions, and its attitude seems to be moderate compared to that of some neighboring nations like India and Malaysia.

The Mission of the Laity in Indonesia

The just described situation of missionaries from other churches has its positive aspects. Consciousness of the mission and the responsibility of the laity is growing deeper than ever, although ever since Christian faith was introduced among Indonesians early in this century, especially in remote outstations, the faithful have been well acquainted with laity (mostly schoolteachers) playing an active and leading role in Christian communities. Almost everywhere Catholics are ever more aware that the in-depth growth of faith down to the small Christian communities largely lies in their own hands. Everywhere the formation of lay ministers and lay leaders, their in-service training, refresher, or upgrading courses, have become the most urgent of needs.

On this point the Declaration of Concern on Devaluing the Laity, issued by forty-seven priests, nuns, and lay persons in Chicago, U.S.A., had something noteworthy to convey. Lay ministry is now often viewed as "the laity's participation in work traditionally assigned to priests and sisters." Today the impression is often given that one can work for justice and peace only by stepping outside one's ordinary role in the business world, as a mayor, a factory worker, or a government worker. The church now suffers the threat of a new clericalism, for "during the last decade especially many priests have acted as if the primary responsibility in the church for uprooting injustice, ending wars and defending human rights rested with them as ordained ministers. As a result they bypassed the laity to pursue social causes on their own rather than enabling lay Christians to shoulder their own responsibility. These priests and religious have sought to impose their own agendas for the world upon the laity."[84]

The severe shortage of priests is not the only reason why adequate pastoral care cannot be provided to the faithful. A great number of far distant and isolated communities in Indonesia with the widely diverse geographical and demographical conditions in the various regions will not have their own priests in a hundred years. A preliminary survey carried out by the Bishops' Commission on Liturgy showed that the percentage of religious services without Mass varies from 0.5 percent (Jakarta) to 80 percent (Merauke, West Irian). The 1975 plenary assembly of the Indonesian Bishops' Conference arrived at these conclusions:

Opportunities are to be created for the faithful to have religious services on Sundays and days of obligation. This quite often will imply that capable lay persons will conduct the service of the Word. Wherever possible this service should be concluded with H. Communion. The faithful must be well prepared by instructions to accept these conditions. Candidates for lay leadership should be selected among men and women of good reputation in their communities. Leadership of community services is not necessarily connected with traditional (tribal) authority, since teachers and catechists may as well be good leaders. Preferably the leadership of Christian communities is carried out by small teams. It is suggested that lay leaders be installed officially in a liturgical ceremony and that they be assigned for a limited period.[85]

It is of vital importance that the Indonesian bishops be granted full authority to entrust certain ministries to lay persons, not by way of an extraordinary faculty for a limited time, but rather, as part of the ordinary competence of the Episcopal Conference.[86]

Religious Life in Indonesia

The vast majority of church personnel consists of religious (priests, Brothers, Sisters). The fourth Joint Congress of Religious (KONGGAR IV) held in Jakarta, September 6–14, 1978, was attended by fifty-eight religious women, ten Brothers, and thirty-two religious priests, and it issued the statement "KONGGAR on the Inculturation of Religious Life in Indonesia." Since it was felt necessary to consolidate the structure of their federation, a Conference of Religious Congregations in Indonesia (MASRI) was established with the aim of intensifying cooperation and mutual enrichment in life and work, improving the ministry of religious within the church and in society, and fostering good relations with other groups, secular as well as ecclesiastical, especially with the Indonesian Episcopal Conference. Members of MASRI are all religious superiors or provincials, at the national or regional level.[87]

The Indonesian situation of a church anxiously aspiring to its full maturity in Christian life and mission urges all religious communities to set aside the narrow-mindedness of merely attending to their own group interests, as though they were self-enclosed units within the dioceses. The last decade has seen religious coming together regularly in order to arrive at an ever fuller integration in the implementing of the mission of the entire Indonesian church under the guidance of the local bishops. And since ever-expanding missionary activities call for deeper religious spirituality, apparently retreats, conferences, workshops, and seminars for religious are resulting in greater interest on their part.

The Need for "Contextualized" Theology

In view of building a genuinely Indonesian church, that is, of the authentic inculturation of Christian faith throughout all Christian communities, the need is deeply felt for a renewed orientation of pastoral care of the faithful endorsed by a theological reflection that is truly "contextualized" in the Indonesian situation. Of paramount importance are the roles to be played by research institutions (e.g., the Atmajaya University Research Centre, MAWI's Institute for Research and Social Development, or LPPS), pastoral and catechetical centers, the Institute for Consultation on Church Matters, and the like, which, one hopes, will become so many sources for inspiration and animation of lay people, religious, and the hierarchy.

The Bishops' Commission on Seminaries at the 1978 Assembly of MAWI strongly recommended that due attention be paid to the ongoing pastoral formation of the clergy, particularly to the two-month refresher course for priests throughout Indonesia, organized annually by the Pastoral Center of Jogjakarta.

It ought to be stressed how urgently theologians are needed not only to staff major seminaries, but also for other important areas of church life and activities, for example, in the fields of socioeconomics, catechesis, liturgy, and pastoral care in general.

Since 1969 there has been an annual issue of the periodical *Orientasi* ("Orientation") providing articles on philosophy and theology in Indonesian on behalf of seminarians and other interested persons. The need is felt for publications in pastoral theology, not necessarily all at a highly theological level, but at a level that will serve as much as possible the clergy and all others engaged in pastoral ministry.

Notes

1. See *Lumen Gentium,* nos. 13–16.

2. In 1976 there were 738 million children below the age of fifteen in the United Nations ECAFE region (Economic Commission for Asia and the Far East).

3. It has been estimated that 80 percent of the earth's wealth is concentrated in the hands of 20 percent of the people; some believe that by 1990 the figure will be 90 percent belonging to 10 percent of the population.

4. See statement of FABC's second regional meeting, on Catechesis of Young Adults, no. 20.

5. *FABC Newsletter (FABC-N),* no. 16 (November 1976), p. 3.

6. See *Report of the Third Assembly of the East Asian Region of FABC,* "Evangelization of the Family," pp. 3–4.

7. See *FABC-N,* no. 26 (February 1979), p. 3. Also *FABC-N,* no. 27 (April 1979), p. 2; no. 29 (September 1979), p. 3; no. 30 (December 1979), p. 3.

8. Quoted from *The Tablet* by *FABC-N,* no. 31 (February 1980), pp. 1–2.

9. See "The First Bishops' Institute for Missionary Apostolate of FABC," in *FABC Papers,* no. 19 (Hong Kong), p. 15.

10. See *FABC-N,* no. 30 (December 1979), p. 1; the Plenary Assembly in Taipei (1974) recommended that "FABC . . . promote organized efforts, including scholarship arrangements, to explore the deeper relationship between the Christian faith and the Asian religions and beliefs" (*FABC-N,* no. 18, April 1977, p. 3); the University of Santo Tomas opened an institute of Oriental religions and cultures in 1978 (*FABC-N,* no. 23, April 1978, p. 4).

11. See *FABC-N,* no. 18 (April 1977), p. 3.

12. See *FABC-N,* no. 16 (November 1976), p. 2; *FABC-N,* no. 21 (December 1977), p. 2.

13. See *FABC-N,* no. 30 (December 1979), p. 1.

14. See Pedro de Achutegui, S.J., ed., *Asian Colloquium on Ministries in the Church,* held in Hong Kong, February 27–March 5, 1977 (Manila, 1977).

15. See "Message of Asian Bishops," November 29, 1970, Manila; printed in *His Gospel to Our Peoples . . . , Evangelization in Modern-Day Asia, II: Taipei,* published under the sponsorship of the FABC by the Cardinal Bea Institute for Ecumenical Studies (Manila, 1976), pp. 349–55; see also "Resolutions Adopted by Asian Bishops," ibid., pp. 356–59.

16. See *His Gospel to Our Peoples . . . , II: Taipei,* especially "Final Statement of the Assembly," pp. 330–40; "Recommendations of the Plenary Assembly," pp. 341–43; "Briefer Statement of the Assembly," pp. 344–48.

17. *The First Bishops' Institute for Missionary Apostolate of FABC,* II, in *FABC Papers,* no. 19, p. 6.

18. See *FABC Papers,* no. 19, p. 4. On the Hong Kong Colloquium, see *Asian Colloquium on Ministries in the Church.*

19. *Prayer—The Life of the Church of Asia,* part II, "Final Statement and Recommendations," par. 42–45, in *FABC Papers,* no. 13 (Hong Kong, 1979), p. 22.

20. See *FABC-N,* no. 29 (September 1979), p. 5.

21. See *FABC-N,* no. 22 (February 1978), p. 2.

22. See also *Directory on the Pastoral Ministry of Bishops,* part IV, nos. 210-12.

23. *Statutes of the Federation of Asian Bishops' Conferences* (Hong Kong 1975), chap. I, art. 2.

24. On the regional assemblies, see ibid., chap. VII, arts. 26-28.

25. See ibid., chap. VIII, arts. 29-30, and appendix, bylaw II, arts. 1-5.

26. See *FABC-N,* no. 25 (December 1978), p. 2; *The First Bishops' Institute for Missionary Apostolate of FABC, FABC Papers,* no. 19. An excellent description of the missionary dimensions of Asian churches is found on p. 2.

27. The organization that resulted is called the Asian Cultural Forum on Development (ACFOD), with offices in Bangkok.

28. See Cristeta B. Piczon, ed., *The Church and Population in East Asia,* a report (Manila, 1973).

29. See *FABC-N,* no. 13 (March 1975), p. 1. On BISA I-III, see *The Bishops' Institutes for Social Action of FABC, FABC Papers,* no. 6.

30. Quoted among BISA IV's reflections on *Populorum Progressio,* no. 13.

31. Report published by the Office for Human Development of FABC.

32. See *FABC-N,* no. 28 (June 1979), p. 1.

33. Ibid., p. 2.

34. See *FABC-N,* no. 30 (December 1979), pp. 1-2.

35. See *FABC-N,* no. 32 (April 1980), p. 2.

36. See *FABC-N,* no. 25 (December 1978), p. 3.

37. See *FABC-N,* no. 27 (April 1979), p. 1.

38. See *FABC-N,* no. 29 (September 1979), p. 2.

39. See *FABC-N,* no. 30 (December 1979), p. 2.

40. See *FABC-N,* no. 28 (June 1979), p. 4.

41. See *FABC-N,* no. 22 (February 1978), pp. 3-4.

42. The working papers of this colloquium have been published in a special issue of *Philippiniana Sacra,* vol. XIV, no. 40 (January-April 1979), pp. 5-212.

43. See *FABC-N,* no. 24 (June 1978), p. 1; cf. *FABC-N,* no. 23 (April 1978), p. 3.

44. See *FABC-N,* no. 25 (December 1978), p. 4.

45. See *FABC-N,* no. 17 (January 1977), p. 3.

46. See Walter Abbott, ed., *The Documents of Vatican II* (New York: Herder and Herder, Association Press, 1966), pp. 712-13.

47. See John XXIII, Apostolic Constitution *Humanae Salutis,* December 25, 1961, AAS.54 (1962) p. 6; English text, "Pope John Convokes the Council," in *The Documents of Vatican II,* pp. 703-9.

48. See *Report of the Bishops' Conference of Indonesia to the Holy See on the Occasion of Their ad Limina Visit, May 1980,* II, "Some Current Problems Confronting the Catholic Church in Indonesia, 5. Decentralization of Authority," pp. 16-18.

49. See *FABC-N,* no. 31 (February 1980), p. 3.

50. See *Report of the Bishops' Conference of Indonesia to the Holy See . . . ,* II, "Some Current Problems . . . , 2. Liturgy and the Local Cultures," p. 11.

51. Quoted by Parmananda R. Divarkar, S.J., "Reflections on the Problem of Inculturation," in *The Encounter of the Gospel with Culture—A Short Symposium,* in *FABC Papers,* no. 7, p. 12.

52. Quoted in "Summary of Reflections and Conclusions," in *The Bishops' Institutes for Social Action of FABC, FABC Papers,* no. 6, p. 27.

53. Work group report, *Development and Minority Rights,* CCA "Voices," quoted in *FABC-N,* no. 27 (April 1979), p. 4.

54. See, e.g., the analysis of the social reality in Asia in the minutes of BISA III (Kuala Lumpur, November 2-16, 1975), p. 28; cf. *The Bishops' Institutes for Social Action of FABC, FABC Papers,* no. 6, p. 27.

55. See the minutes of BISA III, p. 29.

56. See the minutes of BISA I (Manila, March 1-15, 1974), p. 2.

57. See *The Bishops' Institutes for Social Action of FABC,* pp. 30-32.

58. See *FABC-N,* no. 2 (February 1978), p. 3.

59. For a detailed description of religions in Indonesia, see, e.g., Frank L. Cooley, "The Growing Seed, a Descriptive and Analytical Survey of the Church in Indonesia," *Occasional Bulletin of Missionary Research,* 1, no. 4 (October 1977): 1-33.

60. For a good overall picture of contemporary Indonesia, see *Indonesia 1978: An Official Handbook,* published by Department of Information, Republic of Indonesia.

61. On the five-year development programs (REPELITA), see *Indonesia 1978,* pp. 94-103.

62. See "Pedoman Kerdja Umat Katolik Indonesia," *Spektrum* 1 (1971): 3-47.

63. See "Partisipasi Gereja Indonesia dalam REPELITA II," *Spektrum* 5 (1975): 64–86; synthesis of discussions, pp. 87–97.

64. See, respectively, R. Hardawiryana, S.J., "Panggilan Gereja dalam Masyarakat Indonesia," *Spektrum* 8 (1978): 263–446, and "Meningkatkan partisipasi Gereja dalam hidup kebudayaan, kenegaraan dan kemasyarakatan, *Spektrum* 9 (1979): 145–296.

65. E.g., in 1978 in the questions on *abortus provocatus*.

66. On population census and future growth, birth and mortality rates, and population density, see *Indonesia 1978*, pp. 19–23.

67. *Report of the Plenary Meeting of the Bishops' Conference of Indonesia, November 6–16, 1978*, no. 24, p. 37.

68. See *Summary Report of the Plenary Meeting of the Bishops' Conference of Indonesia, November 7–17, 1977*, II, no. 3, pp. 4–5.

69. On educational and cultural development, see *Indonesia 1978*, pp. 199–202.

70. See *Naskah Garis-Garis Besar Haluan Negara* ("General Outlines of the Indonesian State Policy"), chap. IV.D, "Religion and Socio-Cultural Life," no. 2, "Education," sub e, in *Himpunan Ketetapan-Ketetapan Majelis Permusyawaratan Rakyat Republik Indonesia 1978* ("Decrees of the 1978 Session of the People's Consultative Assembly of 1978") (Jakarta, 1978), p. 212.

71. See *Report of the Plenary Meeting of the Bishops' Conference of Indonesia, November 6–16, 1978*, no. 2.1, p. 7; no. 10, pp. 21–23.

72. See *Indonesia 1978*, p. 192.

73. See *Bishops' Conference of Indonesia—Summary Report, Plenary Meeting, November 8–18, 1976*, B, pp. 5–6.

74. See *Report of the Plenary Meeting of the Bishops' Conference of Indonesia, November 6–16, 1978*, no. 7, p. 19.

75. See *Indonesia 1978*, pp. 210–11.

76. See *Report of the Plenary Meeting of the Bishops' Conference of Indonesia, November 6–16, 1978*, no. 28, p. 39.

77. Ibid., no. 12.1, p. 26.

78. See *Bishops' Conference of Indonesia—Summary Report, Plenary Meeting, November 7–17, 1977*, no. II.1, p. 4.

79. See *Report of the Plenary Meeting . . . 1978*, no. 4.9, p. 16.

80. Ibid., pp. 16–17.

81. Ibid., no. 2.4, pp. 10–11.

82. To this effect a booklet was published entitled *Tinjauan mengenai Keputusan Menteri Agama no. 70 dan 77 tahun 1978*, dalam rangka penyelenggaraan kebebasan beragama dan pemeliharaan kerukunan nasional, diterbitkan oleh Sekretariat Umum Dewan Gereja-Gereja di Indonesia dan Sekretariat Majelis Agung Waligereja Indonesia 1978.

83. See also *FABC-N*, no. 30 (December 1979), p. 3.

84. See *FABC-N*, no. 22 (February 1978), p. 2.

85. See *Bishops' Conference of Indonesia—Summary Report, Plenary Meeting, November 10–20, 1975*, no. V, pp. 8–9.

86. On the leadership of Christian communities in Indonesia, see R. Hardawiryana, *Those Who Minister to the Church*, and *The Layman as Leader of the Christian Community*, Pro Mundi Vita: Dossiers, Asia-Australasia, Dossier 7 (May–June 1978), esp. pp. 19–23, 24–31.

87. See *Report of the Plenary Meeting of the Bishops' Conference of Indonesia, November 6–16, 1978*, no. 21, p. 35.

4

LESOTHO

Alexander Motanyane, O.M.I.

Lesotho is a small, self-governing country in southern Africa, landlocked and bordered on all sides by the Republic of South Africa. It is the enclave of the Basotho people, an ethnically homogeneous group consolidated under the leadership of Moshoeshoe in the early nineteenth century. In response to a request from Moshoeshoe, Lesotho became a British Protectorate in 1868, regaining independence in 1966.

Lesotho covers 11,716 square miles, an area roughly equivalent to the size of Belgium. The western quarter of the country consists of the so-called lowlands, which are high plains at an altitude of 5,000 feet. The lowlands contain seven of the nine (now ten) district headquarters, with one-half of the total population of 1.2 million, which makes them one of the most densely populated areas in rural Africa. They constitute the best agricultural area in Lesotho. In the eastern three-quarters of Lesotho are rugged, almost inaccessible mountains, which rise to heights of 10,000 feet along the Drakensberg range, before dropping steeply into the Republic of South Africa at Lesotho's eastern border. In the mountain region the people live in scattered and isolated villages of thatch-roofed, mud huts with no plumbing or electricity. Many must walk for considerable distances to draw water from unprotected waterholes and streams.

This small kingdom's population grows at the rate of 2.2 percent per year, with 43 percent of the population under the age of fifteen. Lesotho is among the poorest of African nations, plagued by several topographical and social problems. Educational opportunities are fairly good in Lesotho, and the literacy rate is high, by some estimates as high as 50 percent, due largely to the efforts of the missionaries. Eighty percent of the population is Christian. Lesotho is the recipient of considerable amounts of foreign development and relief assistance from private, governmental, and international agencies.

Alexander Motanyane, of the Oblates of Mary Immaculate, is the Secretary General of the Lesotho Catholic Bishops' Conference, and is also the Secretary for Education of the same conference.

The Beginning of Missionary Work

When we speak about the missionaries, we always fear being accused of ingratitude for their good work, while our intention is to examine their efforts and dedication, notwithstanding mistakes that have been made. Lesotho received its first Catholic missionaries from France when the Oblate Missionaries arrived. Similarly the Protestant churches sent their first missionaries from France. This was nineteenth-century France where there were many controversies among the churches. Unfortunately these conflicts were imported into Lesotho by the missionaries, and inherited by the Basotho. Lesotho is one country and its people speak one language, yet there is the big division brought by the churches, in particular by the Catholic church and the Paris Evangelical Missionary Society.

There is no doubt that these missionaries introduced education and development to a greater extent than elsewhere in Africa. Schools were established throughout the country, and the religious congregations played an important part in the educational field. While a priest preached the gospel in the villages, the Sisters taught children in the schools; the teaching of catechism was included in the curriculum.

By 1918 France could no longer send sufficient missionaries to Lesotho. At this stage the Congregation of the Oblates of Mary Immaculate recruited missionaries from French Canada to come and carry on the work of evangelization by the Catholic church.

This group came from a young country that was progressing in big strides, and they imported new ideas. It was at this time that the church encouraged the missionaries to recruit local people for missionary work. These young missionaries had a remarkably strong faith. They established a seminary, and after ten years the first Mosotho priest was ordained. Many young men from southern Africa came to Lesotho to study for the priesthood. Slowly but steadily Basotho young men were ordained priests, and in 1952 the first African bishop in southern Africa was appointed from among them.

Let us remember that we are speaking about South Africa, which is condemned by the whole world for its color discrimination. It was not an easy task for a black man to find himself over a domain that was thought to belong to white people. For this reason we must praise the white missionaries who encouraged young Basotho men to join the seminary and study for the priesthood. We also admire their foresight in the development of the church, by identifying local persons as church leaders. The seminary established in those difficult days has produced eight of the eleven black bishops in southern Africa.

Although it seems that the Catholic church has many local leaders, there are still many parishes run by missionaries from outside. Printing works, training, chaplaincies, and other related works are still undertaken by missionaries. There is still a great need for specialist training of local people. Administrative training of personnel is essential in developing countries, but such training is also important for the church.

The Role of the Missionaries

We have already pointed out that the primary task of the missionaries in Lesotho was to evangelize the Basotho and establish the church. They had to establish the church as they knew it, which means they established the church in accordance with traditions of their places of origin. They built schools, hospitals, prayer houses, and so forth. Through their teachings, several local customs and traditions were dropped because they were labeled as paganism. The missionaries presented their traditions as though they were truths of faith.

It is right that expatriate missionaries acknowledge the fact that their local confreres are equally important in the congregation. They may be younger than the missionaries in many ways, they are younger in age, in religious life, in education, in the knowledge of many things, but their ideas must be respected. When new fraternal workers from Europe and America arrive with special skills, care should be taken that local personnel are trained to take over responsibility for projects as much and as soon as possible. We do not have to repeat that we welcome the interest and generosity of our partner churches in Europe and America. But we must insist that we are responsible for the decision-making in our development programs, the ordering of our priorities, and the setting of our standards. This is a natural corollary of both our political independence and our increasing awareness of our special heritage as an African church. Our insistence on taking final responsibility for our own affairs does not diminish our readiness to hear informed criticism of our plans, nor our willingness to discuss with our partners our problems and opportunities.

Missionaries from the old tradition must be patient and tolerant about the mistakes made by members of the church to which they have come to preach. They must respect the views of the bishops, the priests, and the faithful. They must realize that the logic they use in deciding certain issues may not agree with local traditions.

Lesotho, is surrounded by South Africa, receiving its influences, traditions, and ideas. At times we see that some expatriate missionaries practice color discrimination or have a superiority complex. When a local person is appointed over them, they ask to be transferred to their home country rather than submit themselves to the new superiors. This surprises the local people who, themselves, have given complete and undivided loyalty to white superiors. Of course, we admire some white missionaries who demonstrate true faith. They help our youth acquire skills. Here we think of particularly the white missionaries teaching in our seminaries, doing difficult jobs during these changing times of political, social, and economic developments. As we have pointed out, one of the greatest tasks of the church is to educate the people, preparing and assisting them to answer the political, social, educational, moral, and economic challenges. We cannot achieve this without outside help, since we are still a young church; but we must avoid importing what is alien to our good customs and traditions. Our local people still need more study about evangelization and true faith. Some young priests have already done specialized studies in Scripture, catechetics, theology, canon law, church history, and education.

Lesotho's Turn to Send Missionaries

After one hundred years we must think of what we can do for other people. We have had several requests to send our Basotho missionaries to other areas. We have already sent some to the Republic of South Africa to work in those dioceses with limited missionaries. We have received requests from Botswana, Zaire, and Namibia. At present, we have Sisters who have been sent from Lesotho to do missionary work in Zaire and in the Republic of South Africa. We desperately need our missionaries, but for charity and brotherly love, we must leave our country, parents, and friends to help others.

Lesotho last received missionaries for generalized church work in 1968. After that the missionaries came for specialized jobs, such as teaching in the major seminary. Now whenever the Lesotho government requests specialists, local people are sent for training so that they can replace the specialists at the end of their terms.

Assessment Required in Requesting Missionaries

We need missionaries who can come for short periods to help the local church prepare itself. Very often these missionaries need not learn the language of the people, since they work with local people who speak English. Such missionaries can help by teaching at major or minor seminaries; they can help us prepare for pastoral work, help local religious groups to identify priorities in their work, and conduct retreats.

It might be good if we no longer received outside missionaries so that local vocations could be stimulated. When outside missionaries left Nigeria during the civil war, local vocations sprang up in greater numbers. "Necessity is the mother of invention," and this is still true today.

Self-Sufficiency

It is remarkable to note how the outside missionaries made big sacrifices to raise funds with which they achieved outstanding projects, built churches, schools, and the like. It is worth noting that in Lesotho the policy was for all missionaries to raise all financial resources wherever they could, and when these funds were received they used them to accomplish whatever schemes they wished to achieve. This encouraged the missionaries to embark upon various ways of fund-raising, and as a result, magnificent churches and schools were built all over the country. It should be observed here that there should have been proper planning. Often you see a magnificent church in a remote area in the country, while the church in the town is poorly built. The reason is that every missionary did as he or she wished; a missionary who was more resourceful had more funds available. One would have expected that all the funds received would be collected in one place, either by the bishop or by the provincial superior, who would control the spending of these funds. It should be pointed out that, emerging from this practice, notwithstanding its benevolent achievements, the local people are experiencing great difficulties in the discharge of their work. It is difficult to maintain the magnificent buildings. One observes a beautiful mission in an island of poverty. Sometimes one finds a swimming pool in a mission where the neighboring villages have no drinking water. Would it not have been more suitable if the missionary who built the swimming pool had built a well for the villagers?

Sometimes we observe members of religious congregations who live a more luxurious life than the ordinary people. That is why when we speak of the vow of poverty, people are unable to comprehend, and consequently they do not believe what priests and missionaries tell them. Many missionaries did not educate the Christians to understand that the church belonged to them, and that they had to assist the missionaries. Today when the church is in the hands of the local people, it is difficult to convince the Christians of their responsibilities. This has created problems for the new church, which seems to suggest that the local clergy and local religious are inefficient, while in truth they lack the necessary instruments with which to work. It also suggests that they are incapable of handling money. Surely it will take some time before the local church can provide for itself. No doubt many new churches would like to free themselves from these financial complexities. When we look at the Protestant churches, we discover that they initially educated their Christians to support their pastoral works. Often we notice, too, that their undertakings are not so successful as ours.

Of course, we do not suggest that the church must depend solely on its local resources. For this reason we are very much aware that we shall have to seek aid from church agencies in other countries. In practice, two extremes should be avoided: reducing the level of the apostolate to the dimension of local resources alone, and using excessive resources from outside the country. The first preoccupation should be pastoral and apostolic care. Let it be remembered that interchurch aid is a concrete expression of communion in one and the same Spirit. The local churches are together in the universal mission. There is no point in labeling some churches beggars and others benefactors. If need be, one calls upon outside help for the extension of the church and for launching works. But works are viable only if their maintenance and continuation are assured by local resources. Help coming from outside should aim at gradual self-reliance.

In seeking help from other sources these should be some of the priorities: (1) formation and upkeep of all the apostolic workers, priests, Brothers, Sisters, and lay people; buildings should take second place; (2) present-day apostolic demands over structures inherited from the past (a regular review and adaptation to new demands); (3) evangelical authenticity over traditional forms of financing, which today are liable to be a counterwitness; (4) the apostolic responsibility of Christians; their financial contribution should be seen in this light.

Conscientization and Participation

Whenever Christians participate actively in the administration and control of financial resources, they also are made aware of financial responsibilities. The knowledge of needs, the making public of accounts, and participation in important decisions arouse interest and give rise to a legitimate pride.

Solidarity and Sharing

Preoccupation with self-reliance should not turn into ecclesiastical selfishness. Sharing with the poorest parishes or dioceses is essential to the mission of each local Christian community.

Some Practical Means

In the present situation in Africa, appropriate undertakings of the church give the image of a rich church, which arouses the envy of civilians and of the state, and brings about confiscations. Salaries for priests for pastoral services limit the freedom of the church. The salaries of ecclesiastical personnel, instead of being of use to the Christian community as a whole, are at times liable to create a rich personnel paid for their services, alongside a poor personnel dedicated to pastoral effort. Contributions from the faithful create a true solidarity in the community between pastors and faithful. The idea would seem clearly to be the interdependence of the People of God. In practice interdependence demands mutual consultation: the consultation of parish councils, and so forth, in order to know what concrete forms of ecclesiastical ministry are desired by such-and-such a community, and with what financial support it can respond.

Responsibilities of Local Bishops

In the countries to which the church sent out missionaries there were considerable delays in preparing leaders, namely, bishops to take over. When these countries received political independence, the church, in an attempt to keep pace with political developments, appointed some priests to be bishops.

Administration is one of the most difficult tasks in developing countries. When a local bishop is appointed it seems as though one of the determining ideas is to get a man who will not rock the boat. Therefore local bishops are often people who are afraid to explore new pastoral activities. There are new experiences in some dioceses. Priests who engage in new pastoral activities are not popular with their bishops. Local priests have, in many instances, the same background as their political leaders, and the fact that they are bishops does not necessarily make them good planners.

Another element that militates against young local bishops is the fact that in most parts those holding key positions are missionaries who are more experienced. If their advice is always followed, the complaint will be that such-and-such a priest is running a diocese; the greater criticism will come from the local priests.

Formerly the missionary bishops had the financial backing of their congregations. There were no special contracts with a diocese. Now there are contracts between congregations and dioceses. The local bishops have to support personnel from funds that do not exist. They spend most of their time looking for money instead of planning pastoral activities. In any case, pastoral activities need funds to be realized.

There is no doubt that a bishop as the leader of the church in a given diocese must take responsibility for the development of the church in that section, together with other bishops of the region. The church looks too "foreign" because it has often ignored African traditional values and heritage, as well as the pressing exigencies that a developing country must face. The Declaration of the Bishops of Africa and Madagascar applies here:

> The young churches of Africa and Madagascar must take over more and more responsibility for their own evangelization [i.e., evangelization of the African people] and total development. They must combine creativity with dynamic responsibility. This way of ours must strengthen the bonds of unity within the universal Church and in the first place with the Apostolic See. Missionary co-operation must take on new forms. The missionaries will be available for and participate in the searchings of the young communities under the direction of the local hierarchy.

The words of Pope Paul VI in Kampala, Uganda, in 1969 also apply:

> Today you Africans are your own missionaries. One duty, however, remains to be accomplished: we ought to have in mind those who before you, and even along with you today, have preached the Gospel. It is a story we do not have to forget; it confers on the local church the sign of its authenticity and nobility, the sign that shows it to be "apostolic." It is a story continuing to this very day and which is bound to continue yet longer, even if you, Africans, now take its leadership.

Tensions

The development of the church through the appointment of local bishops and the greater participation of the people have created some difficulties between the missionaries and the local leaders at times. In the first instance, missionaries have been the organizers and planners of the work of the church; now these functions have fallen into the hands of the local people. The missionaries are more experienced than those who have taken over the leadership, and probably have even trained the leaders. They do not realize that they are also priests. Rather than take second place, these missionaries feel that it is better to return to their home country.

In their work with the people some missionaries are inclined to belittle their parishioners and the civil leaders. An independent people are proud that they are no more under colonial rule. It is important that missionaries be careful in what they say, that they show sympathy with the problems of the local leaders. Christians respect missionaries, but missionaries should appreciate that colonial days are over.

Our country of Lesotho was fortunate to receive many missionaries who were able to establish the church throughout the country. They built churches, schools, and clinics. They sought vocations for the religious life and priesthood. They built places for the training of priests and the men and women religious. They trained catechists and teachers. They encouraged many lay activities to assist the work of the Catholic church. One witnesses a living church. Even so we see a number of parishes left without a priest. New towns are growing without any priest. There are more vocations than in the past, but it takes six to seven years before a young man can be ordained. The seminaries themselves need personnel to run them. This type of personnel is so specialized that it will be a long time before a country like Lesotho can be self-sufficient in matters of personnel.

It would be unfair to the missionaries in Lesotho not to say something on their work on development. Lesotho was a backyard of South Africa. It was a place where men were recruited to work in the gold mines of South Africa. There was not much done by colonial powers to improve the quality of life of the people. The missionaries opened hospitals and clinics in the remote points of the country. Nuns served people who could hardly pay for these services. They did not forget the economic development of the people. They established credit unions, because they realized that in working together the people could improve their lives. The missionaries held social courses to teach the people their civil rights, which became a preparation for later political development. There is no doubt that, at the time, the church through the missionaries was helping the people in many ways, but the people did not see these things as their own. Development was too often seen as a consequence of decision-making at the top. The vital need to bring about mass participation was at times sacrificed. Development should not be applied in a paternalistic manner, even with the best of intentions, but should grow out of the realized needs of the society.

Migrant Labor

One has to attend a normal Sunday service in Lesotho, especially in a country church, to understand the problem of migratory labor. This is creating several problems affecting the pastoral work of the church:

1. Adult males are absent for long periods. This has many consequences: (a) much agricultural work must be done by females, old men, or children, which lowers productivity and interrupts the schooling of children; (b) fathers become near strangers to wives and children, which has obvious social consequences, harmful to the family; (c) migrants may acquire a second wife (and sometimes a family), in South Africa, and neglect or abandon their Lesotho family in favor of the town wife; (d) migrants may return with diseases, disabilities, or bad habits (e.g., alcoholism) acquired in the mines, which reduces their ability to support their family.

2. Migrants receive cash wages plus their housing, food, medical attention, and the like, while in South Africa. There are no fringe benefits for families in Lesotho, and the families in Lesotho do not benefit from the employment of migrants in any way except via wages earned.

3. The economic return for the migrant working a shift in the mines tends to be so high relative to the return for a day's work at home that agricultural work is relegated to the status of a secondary, subsidiary activity. For the migrant worker few income-generating possibilities in rural areas of Lesotho appear likely to be sufficiently remunerative, compared to the mines, to make it worth his while to invest time and savings in them. Hence he may choose to spend his time between contracts "resting."

4. The migrant himself probably suffers from various psychological or subjective problems as a result of working in South Africa, and having to leave his family and live in a compound as a "foreign Bantu."

Effects of Migrant Labor on the Nation

Something like half of Lesotho's male labor force is, at any given time, working for enterprises located outside Lesotho. These enterprises cannot be taxed by Lesotho, and they make no contribution to the direct and indirect costs, in terms of the physical and social infrastructure—roads, housing, education, medical services, etc.—of the maintenance of their Basotho workers and their families, other than their direct wage payments.

Earnings of migrant workers are not at present subject to any of Lesotho's taxes on personal incomes, although many migrants now earn enough that, if their incomes were earned in Lesotho, they would be subject to both special tax and income tax. Furthermore, a large proportion of migrant earnings are spent in South Africa, generating incomes there rather than in Lesotho.

The relegation of agricultural activities to a secondary place has serious implications for Lesotho's economy in terms of the productivity of agriculture, agricultural practices, and their consequences for soil erosion. And this is in a country whose primary domestic economic activity remains agriculture.

Exposure to South African patterns of consumption and lifestyles may produce attitudes toward consumer goods and goals of national development inappropriate to a country with Lesotho's resources, declared development aims, and present level of development.

The possibility of migration by skilled and professional workers, together with the wage and salary structure in South Africa, may result in Lesotho's educating workers at national expense who then leave to work in South Africa. Lesotho is then faced with a dilemma: to accept shortages and a "brain drain," or to adjust wages and salaries for skilled workers in ways that would make the income distribution more unequal.

The present situation implies enormous dependence by Lesotho on South Africa! Without the earnings of migrants, Lesotho's consumption standards would fall drastically, perhaps by half. Since the migrants all work in South Africa, and the South African government is sovereign, this situation implies a considerable degree of risk for Lesotho. The chances of a mass return may be small, but the consequences would be so serious that the possibility must be considered. Real costs are incurred in providing some capability to handle contingencies, and the policy choices open to the Lesotho government may be seen as constrained by the fact that some choices, undesirable to South Africa, might increase the risk.

Effects of Migrant Labor in the Family

Migrant labor is a necessary evil. It is an evil because, owing to the husband's absence from home for long periods, the fruits of education, of sanctification, and of social advancement that are expected in a normal family are greatly reduced. This situation explains why the wife comes to assume the control of the house, why she may meet with more dangers to fidelity, and why she may have to work to earn her living when her husband delays sending money. Migratory labor surely contributes to giving a cheap image of the family. When we say it is a necessary evil, we mean that the existing conditions in the country oblige many thousands of men to seek work in the Republic of South Africa.

Conclusion

Once more I would like to say that whatever criticism has been said about the work of the missionaries, this has not been said in any bad spirit. Wherever human beings are engaged in a common enterprise we shall always find certain aspects of that work that can be improved. If there are certain aspects of the missionary work that we have criticized, it is only because we would like improvement.

Catholic missionaries throughout the centuries have done wonderful work. As long as the church exists, there will be missionaries. The way of the missionary may vary, however, during different times.

5

MEXICO

Rodolfo Navarro, M.G.

A Few Words on Terminology

We shall be considering the local church at the national level. That is, the "local church" will be the church of Mexico, in its dynamic development from its origins to our own day—although our examination will be very succinct, with a view to identifying the missionary dynamism of this church and making a projection for the future. We think that the meaning and importance of the local church of Mexico can be transferred and basically applied to nearly all the countries of Latin America.

For our present purposes we make no distinction between "local church" and "particular church." The Vatican Council uses these terms interchangeably.[1]

The Missionary Dimension of the Local Church and the Universal Church

The Catholic church is to the local churches as the soul is to the human body: as the soul is in the whole body, and whole and entire in each part thereof, so also, analogously, the church—its spiritual reality—is present not only throughout the world but also, wholly and entirely, in each and every local church.

The local church is the image of the church universal. "In the particular [local] church, one actually finds the substance and operation of that Church of Christ which is one, holy, catholic, and apostolic" (*Christus Dominus*, no. 11). The ideal of the particular church—or, better, its obligation—is to represent, to re-present, the universal church in as perfect a manner as it can (*Ad Gentes*, no. 20). If the basic community has this obligation (*Lumen Gentium*, no. 26), then surely the local church should have the face and the spirit of the universal church. The bishops, source and foundation of unity in their particular churches, are by that very fact the promoters of this image of the church universal (*Lumen Gentium*, no. 23).

In virtue of these considerations, the dynamism of the church universal, and this

Rodolfo Navarro, Superior General of the Missionaries of Guadalupe, is also the coordinator of the Lay Missioners Group for Mexico. He worked in Korea for eleven years.

same evangelizing dynamism in the local churches, should operate on the same level, stimulating and complementing each other.

If we understand evangelization as the "proclamation of the good news of salvation to all human beings, through word, deed, and life itself,"[2] then the whole missionary dynamism of the church takes its shape in the local churches. They are the conduit of the good news, whatever be the state in which they find themselves at the moment.

From a missiological point of view, the missionary church has made great progress, and this should be continued, in the spirit of the council. The practice of the rich doctrine of collegiality, which has been rather discreet until now, has generated in the bishops of the particular churches a mentality of creative prerogative and imagination, of genuine responsibility for evangelization.

The Sacred Congregation for the Evangelization of Peoples will have as its prime purpose the inspiration and nurturing of this creative impulse in the bishops and their local churches. Of course, an ungainly, centralized organization could, without intending to, actually be a hindrance to the local churches in their missionary duty.

For their own part, the particular churches must understand how urgent it is that missionary organs such as themselves not simply sit around waiting to hear from Propaganda. Initiative on the level of the bishops' conferences is vital in the area of evangelization, especially in the countries we still call mission countries today.

It is a matter of a delicate balance between paternalism and provincialism. "This duty [of evangelization], with which the order of Bishops, presided over by the Successor of Peter, is charged . . . is single, and identical in all places and every situation, even though it not be discharged in one and the same manner, owing to circumstances" (*Ad Gentes*, no. 6).

Reciprocity of the Local Churches

In virtue of the collegiality of which we have spoken, one can also speak of a "subsidiarity" between the particular churches and the universal church. That is, the former accept all their responsibility, and the latter accords them all the needed autonomy, to develop themselves and to cooperate in the process of evangelization.

When we speak of the "reciprocity" of local churches in this context, we mean it in this sense: "There obtain, among the various parts of the Church, certain bonds of intimate communion with respect to spiritual resources, apostolic laborers, and temporal assistance" (*Lumen Gentium*, no. 13).

It is a matter, then, of a cooperation flowing among the particular churches, to enable them to carry out the duty and privilege of the evangelization of all men and women, an evangelization entrusted, in Peter, to each bishop. Doctrinally, the missionary dimension of the local church is clear. The problem will be whether its bishops, and the People of God there, will live it, under the constant inspiration of the church universal and the authority of Peter as supreme shepherd.

Right up to the present day, by reason of the lingering twilight of the era of foreign domination, perhaps unconscious now, by reason of a traditional paternalism, for economic reasons, and—why not come right out and say it?—by reason of a spirit of colonialism still smoldering—for all these reasons, countries like those of Africa, Asia, and Latin America *appear* to be the only ones to have a need of other countries. The underdeveloped countries evidently stand in need of the developed ones. But we think that the factor of influence and power is not going to be the definitive factor. Europe, North America, and other countries also have need of their neighbors in the world—have need of the countries that we call "mission countries" today—in virtue of the integrity and oneness of the one single Mystical Body of Christ, in whom no one of us is more important than anyone else—in whom we all have evangelizing to do.

> From the first centuries of the Church, the bishops, at the head of their particular churches, moved by the communion of fraternal charity and by zeal for the universal mission confided to the apostles, united their strength and their will to promote the common good, as well as the good of the particular churches [*Christus Dominus*, no. 36].

Poor or rich as it might appear to be, there is no church, not a single church, that can say to another, "I have nothing to learn from you," or "I do not need you." The local church that does not know how to receive or share in its wealth or poverty will promptly suffer a spiritual impoverishment. In the words of a missiologist:

> Every particular church must carry out a twofold missionary activity: *one within* its borders, the other, beyond those borders, *"to the ends of the earth,"* as we read in Saint Mark's Gospel. And this latter mission is in virtue of the collegial responsibility of the episcopate, "upon whom devolves the responsibility for proclaiming the gospel throughout the whole earth," a responsibility comporting an active participation in, a "communion" with, the entire work of the Church.[3]

I: The Missionary Dimension of the Local Mexican Church during the Period 1523–72: Birth and Internal Development

The Mexican church of the "primitive period" opens its history very precisely with the arrival of Fra Pedro of Ghent, a Franciscan lay brother (who thrice refused priestly ordination), born in a suburb of Ghent in Belgium in the 1480s. Accompanying this admirable lay brother were Fra Juan de Aora and Fra Juan de Tecto. The year was 1523, and the evangelization of "New Spain," as Mexico was then called, was under way.

In 1524, Ghent and his companions formed the group called the "Twelve," one of whom was Fra Martin of Valencia. Martin died in 1572—the very year in which the second stage of the establishment of the Mexican church began, with the arrival of the Jesuits, who would mark this second period with new methods of evangelization.

In a letter to his confreres, Ghent recounts that by the year 1529, six short years after his arrival, he had already built some 100 churches and chapels, and baptized some 200,000 of the native population—data that betray not only the excellent missioner, but the thrust of the young Mexican church in its very first years.

Characteristics of the Period 1523–72

What are the important characteristics of the period from 1523 to 1572, and how does the missionary dimension of the local church manifest itself? We would say that what was going on at this point was an activity *ad intra*, an activity of the birth and growth of the church in an immense territory, with an inhospitable geography, an extremely varied ethnology, and, in spite of a stubborn hostility on the part of the indigenous population, a profound integration of piety with life—hard proof of the fire and character of the first missionaries and their methods of evangelization.

The First Characteristic. The church of Mexico was founded by religious. It is a "Friars' church." In Mexico in the sixteenth century, in the missions which had been erected by Propaganda Fide, we have

on one side, the bishops, with their not very numerous or effective secular clergy—and on the other, the Friars—completely exempt from the authority of the bishops, even when they were pastors, and, far from being confined to one or another diocese depending on which congregation they belonged to, they were all scattered throughout the entire country. Hence a history of the founding of the Mexican church is essentially reducible to a study of the mission methods of the mendicant orders—Franciscans, Augustinians, Dominicans, and Mercedarians.

The Friars' higher intellectual and spiritual level, along with their considerable numbers, cast the bishops in the shade. The second Archbishop of Mexico City, the Dominican Alonso de Montúfar, would say, "I am not the Archbishop of Mexico, Pedro of Ghent is."[4]

This intense, really excellent work by the Friars does not mean there was no church being founded at this time. No, we have the catalogue of the hierarchy, from the beginning up to 1572:[5]

Mexico City
1528–48: Fra Juan de Zumárraga, Bishop and Archbishop, Franciscan
1554–72: Fra Alonso de Montúfar, Dominican

Michoacán
1538–65: Don Vasco de Quiroga
1567–72: Don Antonio Ruíz Morales

Tlaxcala-Puebla
1526–42: Fra Julián Garcés, Dominican
1546–58: Fra Martín de Hojacastro, Franciscan
1563–70: Don Fernando de Villagómez

Antequera (Oaxaca)
1535–55: Don Juan de Zárate
1559–79: Fra Bernardo de Albuquerque, Dominican

Nueva Galicia (Guadalajara)
1548–52: Don Pedro Gómez Maraver
1559–69: Fra Pedro de Ayala, Franciscan
1571–76: Don Francisco de Mendiola

The Second Characteristic. The sixteenth-century missioners had two different ways of looking upon paganism and pagan civilizations and their values. They used either a *tabula-rasa* approach, or a "providential-preparation" approach. After all was said and done, they opted for a system that was prudently eclectic, for they had absolutely no missionary experience to go by in their time. But one cannot say they were not creative.

The *tabula-rasa* method consisted in an effort to bring the local people to a total and absolute break with their past. The missionary considered corrupt all religious or social institutions, all political modalities, and all interior life of people's minds and souls. You started at point zero and you worked for total renewal. Part of the missionary activity was the destruction of the pagan temples and the eradication of all sacred vestiges of the past. The men of Ghent's missionary training practiced this approach and informed us about it as being something important.

The "providential-preparation" system—that is, the effort to preserve ancient beliefs and customs (whatever in them is "naturally true," whatever is "good"), the method that has seemed obvious to us ever since the middle of the nineteenth century, was not yet clear to missionary giants like Sahagún, nor to ecclesiastics of the stature of Zumárraga or Don Vasco de Quiroga. No, "the evangelizers of Mexico were children of a nation where a horror of everything heterodox is characteristic, and, to boot, their missionary activity coincided with the birth and propagation of the Protestant errors."[6] They lived in fear of a pagan syncretism—although in the course of their arduous labors, through encounters with the bishops and with other members of the evangelizing orders, they managed to arrive at a syncretism of methods.

To be sure, at this juncture we are not going to require of these people that they be specialists in inculturation—although we do have to admit that they founded and consolidated the church not only by administering the sacraments, but by building schools (even agricultural and trade schools), hospitals, and aqueducts as well. One of Fra Pedro of Ghent's daily activities, in which he engaged in the evenings, was keeping contact with his five hundred lay collaborators, especially celebrators of the Liturgy of the Word and catechists, whom he prepared for work in the environs of Mexico City.

In the last analysis, sixteenth-century Mexico knew great missionaries, extraordinary ones. They loved the Indian with a deep passion, and, although they did not make use of all the human wealth of the native culture, paradoxically they always respected the Indians' language, and never tried to "Europeanize" them.

Shortcomings in Sixteenth-Century Evangelization: Paternalism

The missionaries loved the Indians intensely. But they loved them as one loves a child. They protected them excessively, isolating them from their social milieu.

The missionary saw no need of ordaining Indian priests and bishops. All that would have been contrary to the spirit of missionary guardianship. Hence the church of New Spain will have no national character, and its first Indian priest will not be ordained for a long time—Don Nicolás del Puerto, consecrated bishop in 1679 as ordinary of Oaxaca.

The Failure of the Ambitious Project of an Indian Seminary at Tlatelolco

In 1536, on the Feast of the Epiphany, on the outskirts of Santiago Tlatelolco, in the presence of Don Antonio de Mendoza, the first viceroy; Lord Zumárraga, first archbishop of Mexico City; and all the distinguished ladies and gentlemen of the capital, a seminary was founded for the Indians. The number of candidates selected the first year was sixty. They came from the best indigenous families. The faculty was a select one as well, and included Sahagún. The curriculum was contemporary, not omitting Latin and Indian natural medicine. The Indians demonstrated their ability to read and write in three languages: Mexican, Spanish, and Latin. They spoke Latin admirably, and wrote classical Latin better than did the Spaniards themselves. But the project broke down, because of a lack of confidence in the Indian, because of jealousy at the prospect of seeing them ordained priests one day, because of the classism applied in the selection of candidates, and, as always, because of the novelty of such a radical departure in the formation of native Christians.

The so hopeful endeavor of a first seminary failed, and thus evangelization—even in this enlightened and rich period in its evolution—remained incomplete. "What was founded, before and above all, was a Spanish church, organized on the Spanish model, directed by Spaniards, and rendering the native faithful somewhat second-class Christians," even when they received an education, as many of them did.

None of what has been said is to deny the historical fact that this period from 1523 to 1572 was the matrix and basis of the colonial centuries and modern Mexico. The missionary dimension of this local church was, as we have said, *ad intra*, but it was limited only to a territory that is practically subcontinental in its extent, and unmistakably charged with great missionary dynamism from the moment of its birth.

II: The Missionary Dimension of the Local Mexican Church during the Colonial Period, 1572–1821

On December 12, 1981, the Mexican church celebrates the 450th anniversary of the historic apparitions of Our Lady of Guadalupe. A Grand Mission is being prepared to celebrate the event. The preceding year will be the 450th anniversary of the founding of the Diocese of Mexico City.

The apparitions of Our Lady of Guadalupe deserve a chapter apart, but for purposes of our study the following synopsis will suffice: *(a)* Mary's admirable assistance in the hard task of evangelization, an enterprise which she continues to foster; *(b)* her method: when she appears to the Indian, the Blessed Virgin speaks the language of the people, Nahuatl. Should not the missioners of those days have done the same? Should they not do so now? Is it not even more urgent for them than it was for her?

The Blessed Virgin makes use of the theology (the "theogony") of the Mexicans. In explaining that she is the "Mother of God" she uses seven names for God, which were familiar to the Mexicans. The document of the apparitions, *Nican Mopohua,* is written in the Indian mentality, and constitutes a fearless commitment to Indian sensibility and culture.

To Mary's thinking, the actual evangelizer is the Indian—in this case, Juan Diego, the man to whom she appeared. The supposed evangelizer, the bishop, Fra Juan de Zumárraga, was evangelized by the Indian.

Mary's message is one of liberation:

> I earnestly desire that a temple be built for me here, in which I may demonstrate and bestow all my love, understanding, aid, and defense . . . for you and yours who dwell in this land, and for all others who love me, call upon me, and trust me—that I may hear their cries of lamentation, and bear remedy to all their miseries, pains, and sorrows.[7]

Is this not a timely and liberating mission method?

We have already noted the *ad intra* character of the period of evangelization between 1523 and 1572. This arduous task continues to the present day, although events occurred which opened the seventeenth- and eighteenth-century Mission of Mexico to the universal mission of the church.

The University of Mexico and the First Seminaries

Concern for a university had been in the air since 1525, when King Charles V had been asked to found one. The petitioners persevered, and the idea came to fruition on January 25, 1553, Feast of the Conversion of Saint Paul.

The lofty intellectual movement of New Spain in the seventeenth century centered around its Royal and Pontifical University. Theology, Sacred Scripture, canon and civil law, medicine, philosophy, rhetoric, and grammar were all that was needed in those days to form an intellectual class, a governing class, as well as (for this was part of the purpose of the university) priests and ecclesiastics.

Boarding schools had flourished in Franciscan religious houses since 1540. Similar schools of high quality, under the conduct of the Jesuits, arose at the dawn of the seventeenth century. They all fed the university atmosphere, and provided a basis for the Tridentine seminaries that also flourished. It is to the glory of New Spain that, twenty years before Trent, thanks to Don Vasco de Quiroga, we already had the Colegio de San Nicolás de Michoacán, a genuine seminary (and one still in use today) and university—a herald of the mind of the church as expressed in the great reforming Council of Trent.[8]

The Arrival of the Jesuits in Mexico

The arrival of the Jesuits in Mexico, on September 9, 1572, was providential. Saint Ignatius Loyola practically ordered them there: "Let them go to Mexico if they wish to—by invitation if possible, but even without."

The aggressive methods of the new missionaries, who went in search of Indian and Spaniard alike in the streets and squares, were followed up with great involvement and success on the levels of secondary and higher education.

They reached Tarahumara, they reached Chih. They reached Sonora, and Lower California. Great missionaries, of the stature of Father Kino, of Juan María Salvatierra, and Juan de Ugarte, continued to work in our country until the year 1767, when Charles III expelled the Jesuits from New Spain.

The Jesuits provided just the right impulse for an evangelization that could have fallen prey to weariness and routine. They were the right educators for the time, the seventeenth and eighteenth centuries.[9]

Apostolic Schools of the Congregation for the Propagation of the Faith

In 1683 Fra Antonio Linaz founded the Apostolic School of Querétaro, and the Convent of the Cross, the religious house attached to the school. It was a school of holiness and solid spiritual formation, and great numbers of "new human beings" came from there.

In 1707 Fra Antonio Margil de Jesús founded the Colegio Apostólico de Guadalupe Zacatecas, a boarding school exemplary for its religious observance and zeal. October 1773 marked the foundation of the Colegio Apostólico de San Fernando in Mexico City, refuge and inspiration of Fra Junípero Serra.[10]

These were real missionary seminaries, the precursors of our modern missionary institutes. They were the glory of the Franciscans, and the instruments of the evangelization of what is now the southwest of the United States—California and Texas—which were in turn the stepping stones to our only missionary penetration of the Orient, the Philippines.

The great navigators, Fra Andrés de Urdaneta, an Augustinian, and Legaspi, both compatriots of ours, carried out Philip II's order for the conquest of the Philippines. With the famous *Tornaviaje* ("Souvenir of a Journey")—the commemorative coin that was struck for the occasion, bearing the image of Father Urdaneta's ship, *West Wind*—two centuries of commercial and evangelizing interchange got under way between Acapulco and Manila.[11]

One fruit of these contacts was the martyrdom of Felipe de Jesús de las Casas on February 5, 1597, in Nagasaki, Japan, on his return voyage from Manila to Mexico for his priestly ordination, when his ship was driven to Japanese shores by a storm.

Our local Mexican church was born with a clear missionary vocation—just as any particular church is, perhaps, but with very special signs of its own. Its destiny, linked at first with that of Spain, decreed, with the achievement of Mexican independence in 1821, a halt in its progress for nigh on a century—until the early 1900s, which also saw the persecution of 1927-29.

III: The Missionary Dimension of the Local Mexican Church
during the Preconciliar Period

Pontifical Mission Societies

The Society for the Propagation of the Faith—the mission society founded in Lyon, France, by Mother Pauline Jaricot—first came in contact with the Mexican church in 1839 by letters from its Central Council in Lyon to their lordships the bishops of Mexico, inviting them to come to know this society and actually naming particular apostolic endeavors in each diocese which the society would be willing to undertake.

Only three bishops accepted the offer, but from these three dioceses the society spread out to others, in small, decentralized groups.[12] The Nation Council of the Society for the Propagation of the Faith was not established in the Republic of Mexico until 1931.[13] From 1931 to 1952 the work of this organization was, rather, one of laying groundwork, and was of modest dimensions. From 1952 on, the society really began to establish itself in Mexico. It became organized and reached considerable dimensions.

Beginning in 1975 the National Secretariats of the Holy Childhood and of the Union of Missionary Clergy have integrated their organizations with those of the Pontifical Mission Societies of the Propagation of the Faith and of Saint Peter the Apostle in a single National Council.

Progress has been unremitting, and the Propagation of the Faith in Mexico has been very effective in its work for the economic improvement of the Mexican people—who have such a love for the missions—as an intermediary with the more developed countries of the world.

In the works of the spirit the pontifical societies have been even more effective, as will be clear below from their work in organizing mission congresses. But they also carry on other missionary activities in our country, such as the promotion of workshops for priests, religious, and laity, on a high level and with the participation of experts on the missions.

Mission Congresses in Mexico: Missionary Motivation
on a National Level, with Continental Dimensions

The mission congresses have been, and continue to be, an effective source of missionary fervor, ever since they began to be held in our land of Mexico in 1942.

The first of these took place in the city of Guadalajara, from November 11 to 15, 1942. The theme selected was "Go and make disciples of the whole world." One of the initiatives undertaken by this first congress was the founding of a Mexican Foreign Mission Seminary. Thanks to God and the indefatigable zeal of its promoters, this project came to realization seven years later, the fruit of this first congress.

The second congress was held in Puebla de los Angeles, September 25–29, 1947, when the Most Reverend Octaviano Márquez was archbishop. The theme was "Let all the earth adore you." In attendance was the national director of the Pontifical Mission Societies of Spain, Monsignor Angel Sagarmínaga.

The Mexican church was infected by a missionary fervor equal to that of the first congress, and one of the resolutions carried was that there should be an annual "Mission Vocations Day." There has been one ever since.

Once more the Mexican people made a date with itself, this time in Monterrey, for the celebration of the Third Mission Congress, held from the twelfth to the sixteenth of November 1952. Honored at the event were the lord cardinal of Havana, His Eminence Don Manuel Arriaga y Betancourt, and the international president of the Pontifical Mission Societies, from Paris. The general upshot of this congress was the promotion of the mission ideal in the seminaries of the Republic of Mexico. This would be the task of Their Excellencies the bishops and the rectors of their seminaries.

There were also representatives of the Pontifical Mission Societies of Rome in attendance, as well as the world president of the Holy Childhood, from Paris. An event of great interest at this third congress was the presence of actual missioners from Alaska and Africa.

The Mexican Seminary for the Foreign Missions introduced at this third congress the priests it had produced so far—six in all. And the day before the congress adjourned, a seventh was added to their number—Father Alejandro Ríos Zalapa.

The Fourth Mission Congress was held in Mexico City, January 18–25, 1959. One of the most significant activities of this congress was the celebration of a Foreign Missions Day in all the parishes of the archdiocese. It is estimated that more than 600,000 persons filed through the Missions Expo (held as part of each mission congress). At this congress, by special invitation of the Mexican church, His Eminence Don José Cardinal Garibi y Rivera was present as assistant of honor of the Holy Father. One of the fruits of this fourth congress is the deepening of the missionary spirit throughout our nation today, and the overt, palpable penetration of this spirit into our seminaries and houses of religious formation.

Guadalajara, scene of the first congress, became the host once more—for the Fifth Mission Congress in Mexico, November 9–13, 1966. Presiding was His Eminence Don José Cardinal Garibi y Rivera, pontifical delegate to the congress. The business of the congress consisted in a study in depth of the mission decree *Ad Gentes* and its practical application in all sectors of the church. The Holy Father sent a message to the congress for the first time, which further served to stimulate the missionary concern that was already so palpable. The logistics and dynamics of the fifth congress were such that all present—bishops, priests (diocesan and religious), seminarians, religious women, and laity, each in his or her own way—could find appropriate study sessions and discussions and gather their fruits.

The Sixth Mission Congress was held in the city of San Luis Potosí, November 19–21, 1972. Its theme was "Living the faith to spread the faith." The central idea of the Holy Father's message to this congress was: "The Church is missionary in its essence, for it follows the Master's path. And this mission is incumbent upon the whole people of God." In one of the addresses of the sixth congress, Father Esteban Martínez de la Serna, then superior general of the Missionaries of Guadalupe, proposed the foundation of an institute of secular missioners. The project was approved by the bishops and committed to the Missionaries of Guadalupe themselves.

The Mexican episcopate prepared the groundwork for the Seventh Mission Congress by holding regional preconferences, greatly enhancing the congress itself held in Torreón, in Coahuila, November 20–23, 1977. The theme of the congress, as well as of the precongresses, was "The church, universal sacrament of salvation." This seventh congress had the distinction of being not only national but at the same time the "First Latin American Mission Congress." Now the congress was international.

On the national level, it was proposed "To study the pontifical mission societies and consider establishing them in every diocese," and "To found a secular missionary institute." First steps toward such a foundation, fruit of the preceding congress, had already been taken on February 11 of this same year.

On the Latin American level, it was proposed:

—To integrate more fully the Departamento de Misiones of CELAM with the national administration of the pontifical mission societies, with a view to carrying out a joint pastoral mission throughout Latin America.

—To form a Missionary Training Team for all Latin America.

—To found a Latin American Missionary Training Center for national teams.

For its work, the Seventh Mission Congress studied the dogmatic constitution *Lumen Gentium*, the decree *Ad Gentes*, and the apostolic exhortation *Evangelii Nuntiandi*—according the last named great importance and making it the basic document of the congress. The land of Mexico, which had now celebrated six mission congresses and today more than ever felt committed to making the sacramentality of the church something really alive, took as its Proclamation for the Congress: "Salvation for All—Mexico is Committed!"

Today, two years before the next mission congress (the Eighth National and Second Latin American), preparatory steps are already under way. The first planning meeting was held February 11–13, 1980, in the Casa del Sacerdote in Mexico City. Attending at this meeting were the members of the Bishops' Mission Commission, the OMPE national administration team, members of CELAM's Departamento de Misiones, and the bishop of Tlaxcala, the host diocese.

This meeting determined the General Objective of the Congress, to be held in November, 1982:

To provide an impetus for the evangelizing activity of the Church, the universal sacrament of salvation—with Mary, our mother, teacher, and model—in order that the bishops, priests, religious, and laity of Latin America may live their missionary spirit and let it shine forth like a beam of light to the entire world.

Specific objectives were also determined, like the Proclamation:

Latin America—Christ's Missioner!
With Mary—Christ's Missioner!
With Christ and the Pope—One Church!

Some Institutes with a Missionary Orientation

Certain congregations have sprung up in our country, consisting of religious women who wish to respond to their missionary call and charism and so have left us in order to carry the salvation message to other lands. Such, for example, are the Misioneras Clarisas del Santísimo Sacramento, founded in 1948/49, and who at present, besides working in certain parts of Mexico, have spread to Japan, Africa, Indonesia, Ireland, and so on.

Similarly, the Eucharistic Missionaries of the Most Holy Trinity, founded in 1936, sent their first group to China, and later to Japan, Peru, Bolivia, and the Indian territories of Hidalgo State in Mexico.

A fruit of the First Mission Congress of Mexico, as has been pointed out above, was the Mexican Foreign Mission Seminary. On the eve of its establishment Bishop Miguel Darío Miranda stated: "Mexico can and should produce Mexican missioners who will leave their homeland—the apple of their parents' eye, members of deeply Christian families."

On October 7, 1949, His Excellency the Most Reverend Don Guillermo Piani, the apostolic delegate, blessed the new seminary. His Excellency Don Ignacio Márquez read the message from Pope Pius XII:

Mexico's bishops seek to bring down heaven's blessings upon their dioceses by inaugurating this seminary. Here are our first Mexican missionaries—youth filled with dreams, ready to give their very lives for Christ.

A long list of aspirants to the missionary life was begun in 1949 with twelve boys, from various parts of the republic: Zamora, Morelia, León, Aguascalientes, México, San Luis Potosí, Puebla, Querétaro, Tepic, and Veracruz. The bishops' generosity had made this unusual beginning possible.

In charge of the new seminary were the Maryknoll Fathers, to whom Bishop Miranda had applied at the instance of the Mexican bishops. Maryknoll was a missionary congregation, continental in scope, and highly esteemed in the United States. It had been founded in 1911, and its Fathers had developed ardent missionary enterprises in Quintana Roo, Yucatán, and Nayarit in Mexico.

In 1953, on April 28, the Holy See approved the constitutions of the mission seminary, which was erected as the Institute of Our Lady of Guadalupe for the Foreign Missions. Its members were known from then on as the "Guadalupe Missioners," as the First National Mission Congress had desired. Monsignor Alonso M. Escalante, M.M., was designated Superior General of the institute. A native of Mérida, in Yucatán, he had been ordained a priest on February 1, 1931, had been a missionary in Manchuria and China, and in 1943, upon his appointment as bishop and vicar apostolic of Pando, in Bolivia, asked to be consecrated in El Tepeyac, at the feet of our incomparable Missionary Sister of Mexico.

On May 29, 1955, the Feast of Pentecost, Bishop Escalante announced that the institute's first mission would be in Japan. There were three who left for the new mission that year; to date there have been eighty-nine. The second mission, in Korea, was announced by Bishop Escalante on October 3, 1961. Our missionary contingents are growing constantly, and Mexico is becoming increasingly present in mission lands through them.

The third mission was in Kenya, and was announced on October 7, 1965. Today, fifteen years later, work is going on in the regions around Teso, Maragoli, Nairobi, and Kipsiguis.

In 1966 the twenty missionaries who had gone to Korea were entrusted with the Sun-Cheon region. In 1967 Bishop Escalante ended his missionary career, on mission soil—in Hong Kong, where he had begun his work twenty-five years before, in sight of the Chinese coast, and where now he had been struck down by sudden ill-health. In him the Guadalupe Missionaries have received a rich inheritance of virtues and example.

Since 1971 the Guadalupe Missionaries have cooperated in the evangelization of Mezquital, in Hidalgo State. Twenty-five years after the founding of the Mission Seminary, it was announced in the Basilica of Guadalupe that a fourth mission had been entrusted to the Institute: Hong Kong. And most recently, on March 22, 1980, the members were named who would make two new foundations, one in Latin America and the other in Angola.

May the Lord of the harvest grant that our land continue to respond, in numbers and in zeal, to the call of Christ, "Go and teach."

IV: The Missionary Dimension of the Local Mexican Church in Our Own Day

Native Ministry: From Medellín to Puebla

The church of Latin America, from Medellín to the present, fosters a pastoral vector which makes it a special church, a church of the country in which it is living and developing, a church that, in its diversity, has managed to be genuinely Latin American, genuinely Mexican. But this unusual theological phenomenon has not been automatic or mechanical. It had been germinating and growing slowly for a long time, until it reached its flower in Medellín.

Antecedents. Before Vatican Council II, even before the gates of *Ad Gentes* opened wide, a native pastoral ministry in Mexico saw itself as an opportunity for the church to spread out in a vital manner to the Indian communities.

Hand in hand with this desire to bring the church to the Indians went another desire—to share with the Indians the privileges of the immigrant Mexican society. Thus there were initiated, or reinitiated, projects for literacy, elementary school and, especially, health.

The most urgent need of this undertaking was for personnel. And so Archbishop Luigi Raimondi, then apostolic delegate in Mexico, assumed the task of persuading and encouraging almost every congregation of religious women to open one mission house among the Indians. He selected the stations himself, in consultation with the bishops, and indeed managed to install a missionary team of Sisters in nearly every one. At the same time he interested international institutions in financing these experiments.

To coordinate and channel these efforts he founded CENAMI, the National Center for Assistance to the Native Missions, served primarily by laity. As time went on, the Mexican episcopate assumed concern for the evangelization of the natives as its own task and founded the Bishops' Commission for Natives, which in its turn became the Executive Secretariat of CENAMI.

In 1975, after long peregrinations, Vatican Council II promulgated the decree *Ad Gentes*, and the eyes of those who had so long been questioning themselves about the culture, the achievements, and the values of autochthonous elements, and the meaning of these for salvation, beheld a panorama of dimensions hitherto recorded only in the great moments of the history of evangelization.

The mission's horizon was now the autochthonous church. In it the seed of the Word of God was now being sown, deeply planted in the indigenous cultures, and this seed would have to be charged with life and power in order to grow to the maturity of the gospel. This demanded a special preparation on the part of those who would attempt to respond to a missionary vocation. But seminaries and houses of formation were not ready to implement new methods in their programs.

For this reason the Bishops' Commission for Natives sought out qualified persons to advise missionary teams—help them grasp the new world of the indigenous cultures, then go on from there to work out the appropriate pastoral ministry.

Objectives. The best way to discern Medellín's presence and influence in the ministry to the local people is in the objectives that this very Bishops' Commission has set itself in recent years. In 1973 it responded with this objective: "To enable the discovery and implementation of a pastoral ministry of incarnation and liberation in the native cultures with a view to the emergence of native churches."

In 1975 the pastoral ministry to the natives was conceived in a much broader perspective: "To hear, accept, and empower the voice of the native, who is the Church." A special importance attaches to this objective, in view of the fact that it was set after the first national-level evaluation, with the participation of ministers of evangelization from all over the country. It comported a qualitative change in ministry to the natives. This had been a ministry to the natives by non-natives. Now it was ministry to the natives by the natives, with the collaboration of non-natives.

"To hear the native" was understood as allowing his or her voice to come up out of the total concrete situation—historical, social, economic, political, and religious—with all its implications for problems and conflict. "To accept the voice of the native" was to be of service to this voice, to put the resources of the church at the disposition of its projects, and to continue the commitment—maintain it, support it, defend it, bring it to ever higher levels of effectiveness.

In 1976 the pastoral objective was placed in an integral dimension: "To hear, accept, and empower the native as people and as Church." This is a more integral formulation than that of 1975. And as a matter of fact it is not really the same thing to hear a "voice" as to hear a "native." Now the church saw and felt itself to be more credible, reliable, communitarian, and committed.

The beginning of the year 1977 saw an objective more solemn in its formulation but also more profound: "To foster the discovery and practice of an integral evangelization, by which the natives may show forth, in every circumstance, the 'new human being,' as people and as church." In the characterization of evangelization as "integral," one discerns the influence of *Evangelii Nuntiandi*—although this type of evangelization was our concern even before that document appeared.

Early in 1978 a meeting was held of twenty bishops called together by the Bishops' Commission for Natives (CEI), with the objective of reviewing and revising pastoral activities and priorities.

A more concrete, historical thrust in pastoral ministry to the natives in Mexico began in 1970, with a meeting between nineteen natives, and bishops, anthropologists, sociologists, pastoral ministers, and religious who wished to receive from them, and discuss with them, their solution to the problems of native religion, from their own viewpoint.

The continued thrust of this spirit of shared inquiry has enabled native communities to inspire new life in teams, planning, evaluation, and promotional ministries. This dimension of church reality was expressed in Medellín prophetically, then in Puebla with a mightier voice: commitment to the poor and the marginalized. The Puebla event was opened and blessed with the affable presence of our reigning pontiff, John Paul II, during his visit to Mexico of January 26–31, 1979. Puebla synthesizes, for Mexico and for Latin America, the whole birth and growth of a new church, charged with all that is ancient and evangelical.

From the considerations above we can draw the following conclusions.

The local Mexican church has in a way turned to the evangelization of its native population (there are more than 7 million in the country), as it did in the sixteenth century. This concern ought to be ongoing, inasmuch as it is *ad intra*. The Puebla documents demand this. Wonderful! The native continues to be forgotten in Latin America, and it would be tragic if the church made no serious examination of the evangelization of the native, and of its own participation in his and her integral liberation.

But the local Mexican church, like all the churches of Latin America, is the Catholic church, and hence has a missionary duty of universal dimensions. The church of Latin America should not center its concern upon itself to the extent that it forgets to evangelize the world today, in the mission countries as well as on the continents in need of reevangelization.

In view of Latin America's missionary potential for universal evangelization, it seems to us that the Puebla documents devoted very little to the subject. The two specific numbers (368 and 891) that it devotes to mission activity *ad extra* are not to be understood as an exclusive concern with the missionary aspect of the church universal. Proof of this universal concern of the Mexican church is the almost continuous dispatch of Sisters, Brothers, and priests to various mission lands.

Evaluation. Generous, active response:

On the part of the Christian community:

1. Prayer: Days of prayer for the missions.
2. Alms: A generous cooperation with the missions, especially on the part of persons of scant resources—once more, the "widow's mite" of the Gospel. The sacrifice

of the faithful on behalf of the missions is moving.

3. Personnel: Little by little the Christian community is becoming aware of its missionary vocation. Hence the generous response of various lay persons in joining the Mexican Institute of Seculars (IMMIS), or periodically organizing mission campaigns in rural or native areas. Mexican Catholics stand ready to evangelize themselves and to evangelize other lands. The church should send them forth.

On the part of the bishops:

1. By lending their encouragement and support (most of them, at any rate) to:
   (a) missionary endeavors, *(b)* Mexican Foreign Mission Seminary, *(c)* Institute of Secular Missioners.
2. By freeing some of their priests from diocesan tasks so that these may devote full time to mission work in Mexico and abroad.
3. In the mission congresses: *(a)* by their presence, *(b)* by their encouragement, *(c)* through their initiative and support in the actual carrying out of recommended projects, which have always redounded to the benefit of the Mexican church.

On the part of religious communities:

1. Groups of religious women have sprung up whose members desire to take up work in rural, native, or inner-city areas. Their work is proceeding apace.
2. Of the 152 institutes of women religious registered in the CIRM (Confederation of Mexican Religious Institutes), only thirty-five work in mission areas properly so called. Only 4.3 percent of their members work in missions in Mexico. Some ten of these institutes also work in foreign missions.

   Thus also, of the sixty male religious institutes, only twelve are at work in mission areas—5 percent of the total membership of these institutes. Five of these male institutes also have personnel in foreign missions.

Questions and Answers Following Presentation of This Paper

Q: Does this local church speak for the other local churches of Latin America? Are interests, attitudes, and so on, the same?
A: I think so. The problems are the same, and so is the work of evangelization, with incidental differences. And these missionary movements have arisen practically simultaneously in all churches in recent years, following Vatican II, Medellín, and Puebla.

Q: Is Latin America realizing its missionary potential?
A: No. Latin America's missionary potential is constantly more committed and involved, stronger, more conscious and conscientious, and more effective. But there is still a very long way to go before we really carry out the mandate of Christ to "go and teach."

The movement that has brought missionary institutes to Latin America ever since the invitation of Pius XII, and also the formation of institutes of our own today, have generously contributed to the solution of the distressing problem of the scarcity of clergy that is suffered in some localities. But the bishops should not depend on this assistance. This would only perpetuate the lag that has obtained for centuries, and would further retard our evangelization.

In Latin America the local clergy and all the baptized must solve their own problems. Any outside help must be only by way of stimulus and supplement —temporary assistance and a sign of the presence of the church universal. (Every church needs foreign missionaries as a sign of the presence of the church universal.)

What is true for evangelizing personnel is equally true when it comes to the economic means of evangelization. The great evangelizing thrust must come from the countries themselves. They must evangelize themselves and others, from a point of departure in their own poverty, and thus escape both the traditional spiritual underdevelopment of the churches of Latin America and the spiritual neocolonialism of the powerful churches. Grand projects are not needed. The projects needed can largely be financed from within.

We repeat: none of the series of problems we face in Latin America—marginalization, scarcity of clergy, poverty, oppression, in a word, our condition of sin—none of this can exonerate the Latin American church of its decisive role in the evangelization of the world, nor even postpone this duty.

Nor can it be the occasion for the older churches to assume a Big Brother attitude toward Latin America. On the contrary, in the near future they themselves will be able to receive missionaries, from the South—provided we can achieve the necessary conditions for spiritual growth in Latin America, and provided we know how to read the signs of the times.

—Translated by Robert R. Barr

Notes

1. See M. A. Molina, in *Diccionario del Concilio* (B.A.C.), p. 285.
2. *Herder Korrespondenz* (1974), p. 649.
3. Xavier Seumois P. Bl., *Las misiones después del Concilio* (Ediciones Guadalupe), p. 181.
4. García Icazbalceta, *Bibliografía mexicana del seculo XVI* (Mexico City, 1886; F.C.E., 1954).
5. Robert C. Ricard, *La conquista espiritual de México* (Editoriales Jus-Polis), p. 515.
6. Unless otherwise indicated, all citations in this part covering the period 1523-72 are from Ricard, *La conquista*. Ricard's work is particularly admirable for its extensive bibliography. We rely almost entirely on it for this period.
7. CENAMI, *Estudios indígenas*, 7/2:204-6.
8. PLAZA, *Edad segunda*, chap. 14.
9. Mariano Cuevas, *Historia de la Iglesia en México*, 2:495-513.
10. Ibid., 4:170-78.
11. Mariano Cuevas, *Historia de la Nación Mexicana*, pp. 234-36.
12. López Velarde, *Orígines de la Propagación de la Fe en México*, p. 64.
13. López Velarde, *Para la historia de la Obra de la Propagación de la Fe en México*, p. 326.

6

JAPAN

Joseph Hiroshi Sasaki

"The pilgrim Church is *missionary* by her very nature. For it is from the mission of the Son and the mission of the Holy Spirit that she takes her origin, in accordance with the decree of God the Father" (*Ad Gentes,* no. 2). Therefore it can be said that the church is mission or mission is the church. *Missio Dei* is the dialogue of salvation with the totality of creation.

Similarly the church's mission is a continuous dialogue between Jesus-Christ-Gospel and the totality of the situation (context). This dialogue is nothing but an incarnation process of the Word of God into the various cultures of the human race. By this inculturation process is meant "those efforts which the Church makes to present the message and values of the Gospel by embodying them in expressions that are proper to each culture, in such a way that the faith and Christian experience of each local church is embedded, as intimately and deeply as possible, in its own cultural context."[1]

Thus the local church emerges from this inculturation in such a way that it becomes "the realization and enfleshment of the Body of Christ in a given people, in a given place and time."[2] This incarnated and inculturated church is a missionary church which is sent by the Triune God to bring the gospel to its surrounding milieus and also into all the world.[3] Therefore the local church goes beyond the juridical, hierarchical, and territorial frame (i.e., diocese) and refers to an existential situational reality, namely, to the same sociocultural realities.[4]

I: Evangelization of the Japanese Church Itself

"The Church has to be evangelized by constant conversion and renewal, in order to evangelize the world with credibility" (*Evangelii Nuntiandi,* no. 15). The Ja-

Joseph Sasaki, a priest of Sendai Diocese, Japan, is the Director of the Japan Missionary and Pastoral Center, which was set up by the Japanese Bishops' Conference in 1977 in order to coordinate and promote the missionary and pastoral activities at the national level according to the spirit of Vatican Council II.

panese church needs to be liberated from clericalism. That is, a priest-dominated church has to become a genuine and authentic Christian community so that the laity might be promoted at the frontiers of evangelization.

Declericalization—A Church of the People

The Japanese authoritarian and Confucian mentality (the vertical principle) contributes to the conservative character of the Japanese church in which clericalism still lives in the decision-making and even in the financial administration. This clerical church often creates a ghetto that is irrelevant to the common people, especially to the poor people. The teachings of the church are still difficult to understand because of a decidedly Western outlook.[5]

In not going beyond the stage of adaption or imitation of Western Christianity, the Japanese church is often church-centered and introverted, separating itself from society. There is a lack of social awareness or responsibility among the majority of Christians. Consequently the official church has kept a silence regarding social problems and issues of Japanese society such as pollution, the serious distortion of the educational system, corruption in the economic and political systems, and social discrimination.[6]

Therefore the evangelization of the Japanese church requires first of all a declericalization in order to become a church *of* the people.

Building Christian Community

Within and beyond the existing ecclesiastical structures, we have to build up genuine and authentic Christian communities where people can deepen their faith, share with others, and experience fraternal communion by being nourished through prayer, the Word of God, and the Bread of Life.

This community has to be *prophetic* by proclaiming the good news and denouncing whatever is against the kingdom of God. Ongoing Christian formation is necessary for the clergy and religious, as well as for the laity through serious and continuous study and reflection on the Word of God in their lives. Personal and communal prayer are important elements in building up a community that enables the members to experience metanoia daily.

Christian community should become *eucharistic* by celebrating its life-experience in the light of Christ's saving action. The eucharistic celebration has to integrate all activities and events into praise and thanksgiving to God the Father. A group atmosphere will help the members to integrate the various factors of their lives into an existential experience of divine grace. Also through a life that is in harmony with nature, we are able to praise and give thanks to God the Creator.

This community also should become *ministerial* by participating in the ministry of Christ himself. Strengthened spiritually, the community reaches out to serve the poor in particular, and the oppressed within Japanese society as well as outside the country. Expressing Christian love concretely through actions, we need to animate people so that even non-Christians are enabled to participate in Christ's ministry in-and-for society. Doing social welfare work and participating in mutual self-help movements have become very common and accepted in Japan over the past ten years; the Christian community, therefore, has to become an animator of such movements.

Thus this community can also become an animator for building up civil communities in regions and working places. Christians should be a yeast or catalyst in order to build a human community in the civil society.

Christian community, therefore, is a basic reality, a core and nucleus of the Japanese church so that it will become a principal evangelizer of Japanese society, because "it is the *Church,* the visible sacrament of salvation" (*Evangelii Nuntiandi,* no. 23). And this is nothing but the basic ecclesial community in the Japanese context.[7]

Promotion of the Laity—New Lay Ministries

In the Church, there is diversity of ministry but unity of mission. . . . The laity, too, share in the priestly, prophetic, and royal office of Christ and therefore have their own role to play in the mission of the whole People of God in the Church and in the world. They exercise a genuine apostolate by their activity on behalf of bringing the Gospel and holiness to men and women, and on behalf of penetrating and perfecting the temporal sphere of things through the spirit of the Gospel [*Apostolicam Actuositatem,* no. 2].

In the Japanese church we have educated many lay people who are faithful and obedient assistants and helpers of the clergy, but we have not trained enough responsible Christian co-workers. In addition, Christian formation has been based mainly upon intellectual study with a stress on strict moral obligations as presented in Western catechisms. Consequently many Japanese Catholics feel that faith is something added to their daily life, resulting in the separation of faith from their lives. From the pastoral point of view, we are aware of the need of an ongoing Christian formation, especially after baptism, which is often considered by pastors and lay people as a kind of graduation in Christian training.

On the other hand, in the present situation of the church, one of the felt needs among the lay people at the grassroots level is the desire for a genuine and deeper faith experience. Because of this spiritual thirst, many people have been participating in prayer meetings or in groups where there is sharing of the Word of God. Such people have been patiently and seriously studying the Bible through their daily life experiences for many years. Dissatisfied with the formal, fixed prayers and liturgies offered in the parish churches, they feel that the present parish structure cannot meet their spiritual needs.

Many lay people are aware that church activities have to be nourished by a deeper spiritual experience. Some spiritually awakened people have already become involved in social action such as the campaign against pollution and social discrimination, involvement with the poor, the unemployed, and social outcasts such as alcoholics.

"Ministry of the church" is the fundamental "ministeriality" that is the participation in the *diakonia* of Christ shared in various ways by all its members, while "ministries" refers to the various specifications of the church's ministry. Lay ministries are exercised on the foundation of the common priesthood. Therefore they are not a participation in the ordained ministry.[8]

In some dioceses there is an urgent necessity to educate the lay leaders who are going to take care of the parishes where there are no permanent, resident priests. But in the near future we shall also need lay ministries that the laity can exercise in the midst of the world. The creation, formation, and promotion of the lay ministries are crucial issues not only for the future, but also for today.

II: Inculturation Process

"In order to be able to offer all of them the mystery of salvation and life brought by God, the Church must become part of all these groups for the same motive which led Christ to bind Himself, in virtue of His Incarnation, to the definite social and cultural conditions of those human beings whom he dwelt among" (*Ad Gentes,* no. 10). For the Japanese church, therefore, the inculturation process has a fundamental and vital importance if the church is to become a truly local church capable of evangelizing society.

Incarnation Process

The message and value of the gospel, as well as the church itself, have to become incarnate in the Japanese culture and traditions in accordance with the example of the incarnation of God's Son. The church, therefore, should seek to share in whatever truly belongs to the Japanese people: "its meanings and its values, its aspirations, its thoughts and its language, its songs and its artistry. Even its frailties and failings she assumes, so that they too may be healed. For so did God's Son assume the totality of our fallen human condition (save only for sin) so that He might make it truly His own, and redeem it in His Paschal Mystery" (FABC, Taipei, no. 12).

Dialogical Encounter Process

"Dialogue" has to be understood in its deepest meaning, which comes from the salvific movement of the Triune God. "The Advocate, the Holy Spirit, whom the Father will send in my name, will teach you everything and remind you of all that I have said to you" (Jn. 14: 26; cf. Heb. 1: 1-2). Therefore evangelization and inculturation are essentially a dialogical process, which originates ultimately from God's saving dialogue with the totality of creation.[9]

A true inculturation is "far from being a tactic for the propagation of the faith; it belongs to the very core of evangelization, for it is the continuation, in time and space, of the dialogue of salvation initiated by God and brought to a culmination when He uttered His Word in a very concrete historical situation."[10]

Discovery Process

We have to discover the seeds of the Word that lie hidden in the Japanese culture and the living traditions (cf. *Ad Gentes,* no. 11). "Traditions" do not mean something past and dead, but a living reality at the deepest level of the people's lives today. In Japan in spite of the tremendous changes and modernization, some basic factors remain, forming layers and having considerable influence on the cultural background. Therefore we have to study our own culture by going back to its roots and also by tracing its historical processes in order to understand it deeply and develop it fully.

Purifying, Healing, and Transforming Process

As the incarnation of the Son has been fulfilled in the Paschal Mystery, the inculturation process of the church must also experience death and resurrection. This means that the church, as the messenger of the gospel on the one hand, and the Japanese culture and traditions on the other hand, *both* must be purified, healed, and transformed by the saving power of the Gospel-Jesus-Christ.[11]

Some Japanese Cultural Areas for the Inculturation Process

Contemplation of the Absolute in the Phenomenal World. According to Hajime Nakamura, a specialist in Indian and Buddhist philosophy, "the Japanese are willing to accept the phenomenal world as Absolute because of their disposition to lay a greater emphasis upon intuitive, sensible, concrete events, rather than upon universals."[12] In this way, Shinto sees the *kami* (deities, spirits, souls, etc.) in all kinds of things of this world. Buddhism also conceives of the Buddha-nature as inherent in everything.

In these Japanese ways of thinking, we can find the seeds of God's Word: "God saw all he had made, and indeed it was very good" (Gen. 1:31; cf. Wis. 11:24–12:1); "Yes, God loved the world so much that he gave his only Son" (Jn. 3: 16). For the Japanese to *sense* God's love for this world and his commitment to it will not be very difficult, provided that they develop further a clearer and deeper understanding of One-Absolute-Creator-God.

A Sense of Impermanency *(Mujōkan):* The Japanese have a tendency to perceive nature and human life as one and the same in terms of ascribing "unhappiness and misfortune to the transiency and evanescence of nature and things impermanent."[13] This Japanese sense of impermanency (*mujōkan*) seems to have its origins in the Buddhism of the late Heian period (1000–1200), and is still deeply alive in the people's mentality. We therefore have to elevate and cultivate this sense with the biblical understanding of impermanency, which appears especially in the Wisdom Books. But at the same time we need to foster strongly a greater filial confidence in God the Father (cf. Mt. 6: 30–33).

Search for God through Beauty. The Japanese sense of recognizing the absolute significance of this phenomenal world and the Buddhist understanding of the unity of nature and humankind originate from the traditional Japanese love of nature. That is why we seek a momentary consolation for the difficult problems of human relationship by finding refuge in quiet nature.

According to the expression of Takaaki Aikawa, the president of Kanto Gakuin University, "what is natural is beautiful, and what is beautiful is natural."[14] Namely, the Japanese love of nature leads to an aesthetic appreciation of nature. Moreover, he interprets this cultural tendency in a religious sense, saying, "seeking after beauty is in itself *religious,* and 'salvation' can be found in this pure, single-minded devotion to beauty. . . . But in Japan, this search for God in some form of beauty can be traced back even to the Noh [a traditional play] performance of the early fourteenth century."[15]

There is a suitable passage for this Japanese aesthetic inclination in the book of Wisdom (13:3–5):

If, charmed by their beauty, they have taken things for gods, let them know how much the Lord of these excels them, since the very Author of beauty has created them. And if they have been impressed by their power and energy, let them deduce from these how much mightier is he that has formed them, since through the grandeur and beauty of the creatures we may, by analogy, contemplate their Author.

Here, however, we cannot ignore the contemporary and urgent problem of the pollution and the destruction of nature in Japan, due to the awful industrialization and heartless leisure business.[16] There is a serious split between the traditional love of nature and modernization. For the Japanese, therefore, how to integrate our religious love of nature with development is a crucial issue in terms of the evangelization of this world.[17]

III: Ecumenism and Interreligious Dialogue

The first contact of the Catholic church with Japan was made by Saint Francis Xavier, S.J., on August 15, 1549, at the port of Kagoshima. After the flourishing Christian Century (1549–1639), the centuries of Seclusion and Prohibition (1639–1873) began. The restoration of the Catholic church started with the discovery of the Crypto-Christians on March 17, 1865, at Oura church in Nagasaki.[18] The introduction of the Protestant churches was by four American missionary societies between 1859 and 1869.[19] Christianity in Japan has always confronted the other Japanese religions. And since 1859 the Christian churches have faced a divided Christianity.

Ecumenism in Japan Today

In Japan, after Vatican II, a new period of ecumenical movements began. The Prayer for Unity Week is observed every year in many places. Common Christmas services, breakfast prayer meetings, and charismatic prayer meetings have been held at different places. More importantly, the mentality and attitude with regard to the relationship between Catholics and Protestants have changed remarkably.

Nowadays, between individual Protestant pastors and Catholic priests, for instance, there is very friendly contact. In many places they are meeting for prayer as well as for studies. Besides, there are many official ecumenical meetings organized by the official commissions of both churches.

The New Testament of the Common Bible Translation was completed in 1978 and the work on the Old Testament will finish within a few years. The Justice and Peace Commission works together with several Protestant committees tackling concrete social problems within the country as well as outside it.

In the future, also, we can foresee a better relationship among Christians so that we might give joint witness to Christ with credibility.

Interreligious Dialogue

We also have to promote a dialogue with the Japanese religions. Our dialogue should be with persons, by taking into account their religious background and where they are in their relation to Ultimate Reality. "The dialogue in terms of equality and in a common search for God is not to deny the uniqueness of Christ but rather to seek the fullness of Christ—the Cosmic Christ in whom the uniqueness of Jesus of Nazareth is fully and finally manifested."[20]

As the ways of this dialogue, there are the *dialogue of understanding* to promote mutual understanding concerning belief and ideals; the *dialogue of life* to join together in promoting whatever leads to unity, love, and justice; and the *dialogue of prayer and religious experience.*[21]

A dialogue in depth, by giving witness of one's own faith-experience, is sharing. The dialogue transcends human words and can become a listening to God, who comes through the believers of the other religions, for example, conversations between Zen Buddhists and Catholics. Dialogue, however, should not be limited to specialists such as scholars and leaders. It is very important to promote a grassroots dialogue among the ordinary people, who also have a deep insight and practical experience in life.[22]

In Japan especially, we need a deeper understanding of Shinto and Buddhism so that we might discover in them the seeds of the Word of God. And this interreligious dialogue "enables us to find authentic ways of living and expressing our own Christian faith. It will reveal to us also many riches of our own faith which we perhaps would not have perceived" (FABC, Taipei, no. 16).

IV: The Evangelization of Japanese Society

Today Japan has joined the group of developed countries, but the principles of this society do not always coincide with the principles of the gospel. The gigantic economic power has been in control of the whole society where injustice, corruption, and discrimination have been accepted, as it were, as a matter of course. There is excessive competition in every field; a practical materialism; a hopeless situation in the educational system, which is seriously distorted by a materialistic mentality; mass media controlled by commercial interests; and so forth.

"Christ's redemptive work, while of itself directed toward the salvation of men, involved also the renewal of the whole temporal order. Hence the mission of the Church is not only to bring to men the message and grace of Christ, but also to penetrate and perfect the temporal sphere with the spirit of the Gospel" (*Apostolicam Actuositatem,* no. 5).

Evangelization of Mentality (cf. *Evangelii Nuntiandi,* no. 19)

The determining values and lifestyle, which have become quite materialistic, should be changed through an ongoing formation in traditional Japanese spirituality. And this spirituality can be fully cultivated by the power of the gospel. The Japanese people are not only seeking mere material progress and prosperity, but a promotion of their human dignity and brotherly and sisterly communion, which will be fulfilled only through Christ's salvific power. At present the most important factor in changing the people's mentality is *education*. The Catholic schools are challenged to give a strong witness to an education based on the gospel values.

In Christian families the gospel has to be the fundamental source for formation and education. Only by the power of Jesus-Christ-Gospel, can we overcome the worldly mentality. Nowadays many people are inclined to think that they cannot help others as long as they themselves are not affluent. Therefore we have to foster a spirit of sharing with the needy not only from our abundance, but also from the small amount we may have.

Evangelization of the Social Structures

The Japanese *economic system* is becoming more and more centralized, and high standards of living coupled with high industrial output make Japan a consumer society. In the *social system,* factors that affect social standing are money, educational background, type of employment, ancestry, and so forth. In the *political system,* the form of government is democratic but in practice it can be said that politics exists mainly for the benefit of the political party in power and the industrial giants.[23] Therefore the conversion of individuals is not sufficient to bring about a change in Japanese society as such. This is evident from the fact that the setup itself of society contains evil and sinfulness.

Consequently, working for the actualization of justice and participating in the reform of society is an essential and constitutive dimension of evangelization.[24] In the Japanese context, a reform of the society should be started from a conscientization of the grassroots. And in this kind of conscientization, Christians have to become animators and catalysts through a *dialogue of life* with the oppressed and discriminated peoples. This gospel movement has been started in some districts where many outcasts gather.

The Responsibility and Task of Japan in Asia

Japan has been upsetting the equilibrium of people's lives in the developing Asian countries, especially by her overpowering economic aggression and exploitation. Moreover, some large industrial companies have been exporting pollution by constructing their plants in the developing countries.

In this context, the Japanese church, in atonement for the Pacific War, has to take the lead in helping the oppressed and exploited peoples of Asia today through a fraternal sharing of life with them. Fortunately the Justice and Peace movement has been started under the sponsorship of the Japanese Catholic Council for Justice and Peace.

Conclusion

The future-oriented Japanese church has to become a church incarnate and inculturated in the Japanese culture and traditions. In this local church, Christian communities are the core and nucleus, which proclaim the good news to the Japanese people, especially to people who are marginalized, oppressed, and discriminated against in society.

These Christian communities will be animators and catalysts in building up more human communities in the civil society. In order to evangelize the Japanese society, the formation and training of lay leaders are the most important issue in the Japanese church today.

Inculturation is a dynamic process of a continuous dialogue-encounter between the Word of God and the totality of the situation. But this should be done first of all in the Christian communities where the people can share their faith-experiences through a genuine and authentic Japanese spirituality.

Thus declericalized Christian communities will be able to become a living witness to the Risen Lord for the Japanese people as well as for the whole world.

Notes

1. P. Arrupe, S.J., "Letter to the Whole Society on Inculturation," *Studies* (June 1978), p. 11.

2. "Evangelization in Modern Day Asia," *The Final Statement of the Assembly,* FABC, Taipei, 1974, no. 10.

3. Cf. "Message of the Delegates of the International Congress on Mission," Manila, Dec. 7, 1979.

4. Cf. Ernst D. Piryns, C.I.C.M., "The Local Church and Incarnation: A Dialogical Perspective" (mimeographed notes), (Tokyo: Oriens Institute for Religious Research, 1977), p. 2.

5. Cf. Suzuki Noritake and Joseph J. Spae, *Christianity Seen through Japanese Eyes* (in Japanese), (Tokyo, 1968); *The Image of Christianity: A Survey,* ed. James P. Colligan (Tokyo, 1980).

6. Cf. "A National Survey on Missionary Pastoral Problems" conducted by the Japan Missionary and Pastoral Center (Tokyo, 1977).

7. Cf. "Developing Basic Christian Communities," *Asian Colloquium on Ministries in the Church,* Conclusions, part II, section B (Hong Kong, 1977).

8. Cf. Jacques Dupuis, S.J., "Ministry and Ministries in the Church," *Ministries in the Church*

in India, ed. D. S. Amalorpavadass (New Delhi, 1976), pp. 72–87; *Asian Colloquium on Ministries in the Church,* ed. P.S. De Achútegui, S.J. (Manila, 1977).

9. Cf. E. D. Piryns, "Principles of Mission and Missiology: A Dialogical Perspective" (mimeographed notes), (Tokyo, 1979), pp. 23–35; "Contextual Theology: the Japanese Case," *Philippiniana Sacra* 40 (1979): 141–144.

10. BIMA I (The First Bishops' Institute for Missionary Apostolate of FABC), *FABC Papers,* no. 19, p. 15.

11. Cf. *Lumen Gentium,* no. 17; *Evangelii Nuntiandi,* no. 15; FABC, Taipei, nos. 12, 17; P. Arrupe, "Letter," pp. 18–19; P. R. Divarkar, S. J. "Evangelii Nuntiandi and the Problems of Inculturation," *Teaching All Nations* (1978): 230–231.

12. H. Nakamura, *Ways of Thinking of Eastern Peoples* (Honolulu, 1974), p. 57.

13. Hiroshi Minami, *Psychology of the Japanese People* (Tokyo, 1971), p. 57.

14. T. Aikawa and Leavenworth, *The Mind of Japan: A Christian Perspective* (Valley Forge, Pa., 1967), p. 59.

15. Ibid., p. 52; cf. Daisetz T. Suzuki, *Zen and Japanese Culture* (Princeton, 1973), p. 363; Hideo Kishimoto, "Some Japanese Cultural Traits and Religions," *The Japanese Mind,* ed. Charles A. Moore (Tokyo, 1978), pp. 117–20.

16. Cf. Tadashi Fukutake, *Japanese Society Today* (Tokyo, 1973), pp. 115–19.

17. Cf. Edwin O. Reischauer, *The Japanese* (Tokyo, 1978), pp. 422–26.

18. Cf. Joseph Jennes, C.I.C.M., *A History of the Catholic Church in Japan* (Tokyo, 1973).

19. Cf. Stephen Neill, *A History of Christian Missions* (Bucks., 1977), p. 326.

20. BIMA I, *FABC Papers,* no. 19, p. 8.

21. Cf. "Report of the Third Assembly of the East Asian Region of FABC," Tokyo, March 26–29, 1979; E. D. Piryns, "The Church and Interreligious Dialogue: Present and Future," *The Japanese Missionary Bulletin* 33 (1978): 173–79, 246–50.

22. Cf. M. Shirieda, S.D.B., "The Dialogue of the Catholic Church with Non-Christian Religions," Nemi Conference, July 25, 1978.

23. Cf. Edward Gerlock, "Summary-Interpretation of Group Analysis of Japanese Society" (the results of the Social Structural Analysis Workshop, August 1977, Atami).

24. Cf. FABC, *Evangelization of Modern Day Asia,* Taipei, nos. 22–23; "The Future-Oriented Church of Japan: Its Image and Vision," *The Japan Missionary Bulletin* 32 (1978): 129.

Section 2

THE MISSION OF THE LOCAL CHURCH
IN SECULAR SOCIETY

Statement of the Question

There are new questions put to faith because secularization in various forms has emerged as a dominant process in many societies. At times this process is expressed in the negative form of secularism, in which the relativization of cultural value systems, forms of Marxist thought, materialism, or consumerism are major factors. Youth in such societies are conversant with values and symbols that can be unintelligible to persons who grew up in different kinds of societies.

Elements for a Reflection on the Question

- The different types of secular societies
- The fact of religious revival in various forms and its relation to faith-experience as a reaction to secularism
- The church's expression of witness in face of Marxism or other forms of secularism
- The need for cooperation with secular friends
- The need to identify the transcendental values among youth
- The role of small Christian communities in relation to secularism
- The possible collapse of the Western socioeconomic system
- The significant percentage of youth in some places and their role
- The relation of inculturation to secularization
- The role of religious as continual signs of the transcendent and of the radicality of the gospel

Related Questions

- What are the secularizing tendencies in the context of your local church?
- What is being done to promote Christian/Marxist dialogue?
- What are the signs that the gospel is effectively penetrating cultures or societies strongly influenced by materialism?
- What is being done to express the gospel message in language and symbol that is understandable to young people?
- What role do young people play in formulating an effective Christian witness in this society?
- What kind of person is needed for mission in secular society in the future?

7

SECULAR SOCIETY AND THE KINGDOM OF GOD

Tissa Balasuriya, O.M.I.

We can understand secular society as the whole human community in a given area. It is looked at from the point of view of being secular, that is, not strictly as belonging to a religious group or under a religious authority. It may or may not be open to motivation by spiritual and transcendental values according to one's understanding of the term "secular." Strictly speaking the whole of society is secular. Even the church communities are only part of such a secular reality. The churches are not outside secular society.

We may approach the question of the mission of the church to secular society by viewing *secular society as the locus of the coming into being of the kingdom of God.* It is the whole of society (i.e., secular society) that has to be transformed into the kingdom of God. The values of the kingdom of truth, love, justice, sharing, and peace must pervade and prevail in the whole human society. Secular society is therefore the area of the church's mission. For a local church, its secular locality is its primary and closest area of mission.

However each local church has also to consider its mission in terms of the relationships of different geographical areas or sociological groupings to which its own locality is linked. Thus the local church in Sri Lanka must also consider its mission to the British who were, and are, some of the main beneficiaries of the economic activity and exploitation that goes on in our villages, plantations, factories, and urban areas. Correspondingly the local church in Britain has to consider its moral responsibility to all the exploited peoples of the world from whom the British empire built up its capital. British churches should also consider the relationship to the lands that Britain has occupied and colonized, and that are still open to the British for settlement.

The secular society is not only a term or object of the church's mission. It is also a *subject of mission.* It can bear a message from God to all others, including the

Tissa Balasuriya, Oblate of Mary Immaculate, is presently Director of the Centre for Society and Religion in Colombo. He is the author of *The Eucharist and Human Liberation.*

Christians and organized churches. God is present and active among all human beings. His grace includes an enlightenment to know God's will in a given situation. It is a continuing revelation from God to humanity. In this sense revelation is not limited to the apostolic times, to the church's magisterium, or to the Christians. God still speaks in many and multifarious ways.

We must therefore be open to listen to what God tells us through the voice of secular reality. This can include the advances of learning in scientific knowledge, as well as the growth in consciousness of good and evil, of right and wrong in our evolving world. Thus the churches have to learn from the movements for colonial liberation that they were deeply and wrongfully involved in the exploitation of the two-thirds world by the Western Europeans and North Americans. In this the light of God's revelation came to Christian churches long after these exploited peoples had made their own moral judgments concerning colonialism.

The same may be said of almost every major event of modern (secular) history. It is the secular society that taught the churches as institutions many positive values, which in fact the churches should have been the first to foster. This can be seen from the history of modern science, of democracy, of socialism, of the human right to liberty, of the women's movements, of the emancipation of the workers. In the sphere of personal and interpersonal morality, too, the churches have learned much from secular society.

Secular society has much to teach the churches through the challenges that the youth culture offers to the traditional values of societies, especially in interpersonal relations. The youth and the older generations have to learn from each other.

If we accept that secular society is also a subject of mission, then a grave responsibility is cast on the local church to listen to the groanings of the Spirit of God within its locality and in relation to it. The churches then would not have a monopoly of being missionary to others. The churches must also be open to conversion. This requires an attitude of readiness to listen, of not being dogmatic and cocksure of one's positions, of being prepared to make amends where we have been wrong.

Many of the mistakes and misfortunes of the churches in the past were due to their being unwilling to listen to God speaking through the secular society. Naturally such a voice may not always come in a pleasant form or without any error or impurity. Thus in the nineteenth century, European churches did not hear the groanings of their cruelly exploited working classes. The churches were scandalized by Marxism, but would hardly imagine that God may have been giving them a message through Marx and Engels and the socialist movements in the context of a sinful but advancing capitalism.

Mission therefore demands of Christians a very great sensitivity to others. The churches too have their share of sinners. Sin or ignorance may dominate any church for long periods of time. Unfortunately we, at the receiving end of both colonialism and Christian mission, have experienced this for centuries. How blind were Christian churches to the heinous barbarism of colonial exploitation during more than four centuries!

In the present phase of human history it is fairly clear that in the foreseeable future the Christian churches will be only one of the many faiths of humanity. In fact the churches are a minority, and are often at conflict among and within themselves. Ultimately the churches themselves will disappear in the final realization of the kingdom. Then there will be no faith, but only love. The churches are based on faith, whereas the kingdom is where genuine love prevails, with or without explicit faith.

Since God is active among all human beings taking human history to its term and building a genuine community among all humankind, the mission of the churches must be guided by a careful discernment of the demand of the kingdom of God at a given time and in any particular conjuncture of events. The mission of the churches and our personal sanctification depend on them and our option in those circumstances.

From the universal trends in human history we can discern the elements for the *universal mission of the church.* In that sense the universal direction of mission would not be the prerogative of one single church or body of persons. No one can claim such an absolutely clear awareness of God's will for humanity. It is from the interplay of the human forces all over the world, and the interrelations of humanity, nature, and the universe that all the churches can try to find out the goals, the priorities of their mission in a given time. Thus today's global crisis, the environmental perils, and the threats of nuclear destruction indicate some general imperative for all human beings, including Christians. Similarly the emergence of youth, women, the oppressed, and the poor as conscious determinants of history give further guidelines for mission. Within such universal orientations of a global nature we can try to understand the mission of local churches.

Mission and Local Churches

Christian mission includes the witness to Christ and listening to him in a given locality. Therefore it is important that the local church have an initiative and a freedom to be docile to the Spirit manifesting itself in different times, places, and groups. Inculturation is one aspect of this process.

If we accept that God can and does speak to human beings and different peoples according to their situations (as he did to Israelites in bondage in Egypt), then the local church must be free and disposed to respond to such a call from God. Thus the call to the oppressed people of South Africa or of Brazil may be to overthrow the burden of exploitation. For women it may be to struggle for their right to be full human beings, equal in rights and dignity with the long-dominant males. This message of God often comes to a local church through secular society. Then the local church must respond to it and be converted to the justice, love, and true reconciliation required by the situation.

The problem arises as to whether the universal church, or the central authority in the church, will hear or understand this message. For this it is necessary that the local churches articulate their message, which in the case of the poor countries has to be the voice of the voiceless. For the local church to do so, it must listen to its own poor and marginalized. What Saint Paul says about mission is true here also. How can the universal church (authority) know unless it hears from the local church? How can the local church speak authentically unless it listens to its base? Being the church of the poor demands that the world's poor have an opportunity to speak to and decide on behalf of the church. Then the poor in the church will be a most challenging voice interpreting the demands of the gospel to all believers.

Unfortunately the local churches of Asia, Africa, and Latin America have been more recipients from the central church authorities in Europe and North America than communicating to them what the poor of these exploited two-thirds-world countries would want to express to their exploiters in the central "mother" churches. Thus the content of the catechesis in the local churches was often a repetition of what was being said in the North American churches. This may be acceptable in the fundamentals of the content of belief concerning the revelation of God in Jesus Christ, but it can be very inadequate concerning the application of Christian moral demands to a given situation. It is not surprising that European and North American churches did not deal in their preaching, catechesis, and overall theology with the grave evils of exploitation of the colonial peoples. It is sad that the episcopates, pastors, and seminaries of Asia did not relate with a Christian judgment to these issues for several centuries. It is an indication of something seriously lacking at least in the local churches.

Local churches cannot fulfill their mission by being merely *dependent churches*. The temptation for them and the "universal mother churches" is to reproduce the relationships of center and periphery that exist in international economic and political life. The local churches of the two-thirds world, or the "mission" countries as they are called, then become *domesticated churches*. Their message to their people is one of echoing the voice of their "mother" churches, which often happen to be in close alliance with their political dominators and economic exploiters. These churches at the periphery then do not have an authentic existence of their own. If they do try to speak of, or on behalf of and for, their poor peoples, they tend to be suspected of orthodoxy by the central authorities of the "mother" churches. The "mother" churches tend to equate their own thinking with the universal and unerring message of the gospel and of God.

The relationship can be further complicated when the "mother" churches send missionaries, as in the past; or send financial assistance as at present. In either case the "mother" churches need a great deal of sensitivity, openness, and humility not to impose their views on the ones to whom they present the gospel or give financial aid. It is easy for the patterns of domination in the outside world to be reproduced in intra-ecclesial relations. This is contrary to the teaching of Jesus, concerning both power and the use of money.

For the local churches to be able to respond to the demands of secular society, it is necessary that the local churches be organized or organically linked in relation to the levels at which the issues or problems arise. They must be small enough to deal with some specific issues, such as those of workers in a factory or industry, or of youth in a region. On the other hand, they must be big enough or have linkages to be able to understand and respond to large issues such as the transnational corporations, the arms race, human rights in Southeast Asia, refugees, and tourism.

It is not enough that each local church communicate only vertically with its "mother" church in Europe or North America. The local churches need to be in ecumenical relationship with their closest neighbors, or those with whom they serve in the same area. Thus the churches in Colombo must first get together to deal with their own problems of slums, or foreign and local exploitation and liberation. It is only then that they can speak clearly and unitedly as believers in Christ from a given area. Thereafter they can convey their views to their different centers in Rome, Geneva, Canterbury, Moscow, or New York. Similarly the different religious congregations in a given locality should try to meet together to understand and fulfill their mission there. Unfortunately the local churches have been divided even within themselves by the genetic roots of their communions, be they lay movements or religious. On the other hand, the secular reality often impinges as a totality in a given locality. The church responses are widely divided due to the nature of the historical roots of church groups.

This is true also at the wider level of an entire region or continent. The churches of South Asia, Southeast Asia, and the Far East do not meet often. They do not meet ecumenically. Yet some major problems are common to the areas concerned, for example, the poverty of the masses of the people, the impact of modernization, their worsening terms of trade, and so forth. This is another direction in which the concept and reality of the local church has to be evolved. The historical divisions of churches into denominations is less relevant for these peoples than the very exacting demands of witness to the gospel.

The Asian women religious have been meeting regularly since 1972 in AMOR I–V. It would be useful if the religious congregations of men in Asia could also meet to articulate their thinking and, where possible, program common action.

It is, however, understandable that the universal "mother" churches insist on the need of international togetherness within each church, religious congregation, or lay movement. In this context we must insist that the same global approach should be taken by those who exercise international authority over the churches. They should get together in the name of humanity to respond to the demands of secular reality that challenges all churches. It is irrelevant to insist on vertical relationships and loyalties if, at the same time, there are not corresponding horizontal linkages and partnership in mission, and struggle for human liberation. The mission of the local churches can be better understood in relation to secular society, where the universal authorities of the churches grapple together with their common mission to the overall global secular reality.

A characteristic of many local churches in the world is the predominance of anti-kingdom values such as oppression, injustice, exploitation, marginalization, and alienation of persons, groups, and cultures. On the other hand, the mission of any church is to build the values of the kingdom of God for the full realization of human persons, communities, and cultures. Therefore the local churches have to be energetically engaged in combat against such counterkingdom values for the promotion of justice, truth, peace, sharing, and love. However, this requires of the local churches a clear vision and analysis of the local and related global reality, and action against the evil forces that are generally enthroned in power.

Unfortunately an earlier concept of mission, which gave an almost exclusive priority to the building up of local communities in a somewhat "ghettoish," self-centered manner, did not train Christians to be active for the building of strong secular communities founded on the kingdom values of justice. The domestication of Christians was related to the tight control in thought, action, and finance that the central church authorities exercised over the local Christian groupings. These latter had hardly a personality of their own. They were almost everywhere in the world reproductions of a prototype of Christian groupings around a church, a school, an institution of social service, a priest, a religious, and some pious sodalities or imported lay apostolate associations. The movement of life of the local secular communities hardly pulsated within the Christian communities.

This anemic condition of comparative irrelevance was maintained partly by the manner of choosing the leaders of the local communities. Thus the bishops were generally nominated in the Catholic "mission" churches on the advice of apostolic nuncios who stayed only a few years in a country, and who were often unrelated to, if not unsympathetic to, the people's struggles for personhood, identity, dignity, and nationhood. The type of bishop chosen was very often a docile communicator of the decisions and wishes of the central church authority that was thought of as having direct, immediate, and universal jurisdiction over all persons and places in the entire globe. The formation of many bishops in the guarded sanctuaries of small seminaries, major seminaries, and the pontifical institutes in Rome or elsewhere did not help them to be aware of the secular reality of the struggle for existence of the vast majority of their people. They had hardly any experience of people's movements. Their spirituality was largely one of withdrawal from the world *(fuga mundi),* which was considered a source of contamination. They ruled over their spiritual children in a paternal manner, but did not often understand their people's problems in personal, family, or societal life. Until recent decades the leaders of the local churches almost everywhere in the two-thirds world were like this—with, of course, an exceptional person or so breaking through due to rare abilities or sensitivities.

Since the diocese was considered the main locus of ecclesiastical jurisdiction, it was to such bishops that the main orientation of the local churches was entrusted. They in turn tended to bring up their clergy, religious, and laity on the lines of a similar spirituality that was largely uninvolved in building the kingdom values in secular society except in the sphere of education, health, and social services.

Seminary formation continued from generation to generation within more or less the same mold. The theology taught was that which had been thought out mainly in western Europe during the previous half-century. A good many seminary professors, too, had been brought up in the closed tradition of the central churches. They handed down from generation to generation the thought patterns of the past, which were alien not only to the cultures of the people of the colonies, but much more to their human struggles. The content of seminary education was to form the type of pastor suitable for maintaining and expanding the Christian group. The task of the clergy was conceived more as being the dispensers of the sacraments and animators of the faithful than as being builders of the wider human community. Thus their formation involved little contact with the outside "world." Even in more recent years the greater flexibility of seminary training does not often include participation by these young men of eighteen to twenty-six years in the main struggles of the youth and the masses of the people of our country. They find it difficult to get so involved, since the clergy already in the field to which they are sent are themselves seldom concerned seriously with such issues. Where some clergy are so engaged, it is a rare bishop who would consider them suitable for training their seminarians in action in secular society. The dependence of seminary finances on gifts from the central churches helps to reinforce the theological and pedagogical dependence of the diocesan, national, and regional seminaries of the local churches.

The formation of men and women *religious* is similar to that of the diocesan clergy. One or other religious congregations may be more open or more closed to the secular society than the diocesan directions. But this is generally a matter of degree than a radical difference of orientation. Otherwise there would be major conflicts within the churches in the country. Some of the women religious in some countries such as the Philippines have been particularly sensitive to the exploitation and struggle for liberation of their people. But by and large the young nuns are even more secluded and sheltered from the societal problems of their wider secular environment. The nun is seldom expected to be active outside her traditional roles of educator, social worker, and parish assistant. Today development action is included as part of her role; but this does not often include a participation in the people's struggles. The result is that many nuns who begin to think of the deeper and wider issues grow frustrated by their inability to contribute meaningfully to their people's full human development. Some of them live traumatic lives, torn between their enlightened and sensitive consciences, and the often less relevant orientations and exigencies of their religious communities. They do not know what to do. If they question too much, they are considered bad religious. If they keep quiet, they are internally tormented by their sense of futility. If they leave the congregation, they are often lost to the cause. They may not even be able to earn a living, or find an acceptable place in a society where religious traditionalism is strong. Sometimes they get little understanding from their international headquarters or "mother" houses. The difficulty of changing the formation of younger clergy and religious is also due to differences in understanding spirituality itself.

The best approach to such issues is that the entire Christian community should grow together in consciousness and commitment to the promotion of values of the kingdom of God in the local churches. This is likely to have the best impact on both the secular and the Christian community as such.

8

THE EXPERIENCE OF THE LOCAL CHURCH OF CHIMBOTE, PERU

Héctor Humberto Herrara Herrara, O.P.

We cannot speak about the church of the Prelature of Chimbote, in Peru, without considering it in the broader context of what is occurring in the Latin American church as a whole. It is well known that the latter has begun to be subjected to intense questioning, based on the experience of Medellín, where it made a clear option for the poor. Its gospel witness, lived by innumerable laity as well as by various priests and bishops, is rejected by the groups in power. These feel themselves to be questioned in their system and interests, and they are beginning to persecute Christians who seek to build the Beatitudes and the values of the kingdom of God, for these values are in opposition to those upon which what they call "Western and Christian society" is built.

The post-Medellín Latin American church is living the experience of the primitive church. Its witness is written in the blood of so many martyrs—workers, peasants, priests, even bishops who discover the liberating presence of Jesus Christ in walking with their people—for, as Father Rutilio Grande, a Salvadoran priest assassinated in 1977, was to put it:

> What is at stake is being faithful to the mission of Jesus or not being faithful to it, in the midst of this concrete world which it has fallen to our lot to be living in. . . . Practically speaking, it is illegal to be a Christian in our country, for necessarily, in the eyes of the world which surrounds us, founded as it is on the established disorder, the mere proclamation of the gospel is subversive.[1]

The hour of the cross, of hope for the liberation announced by Christ, has a dynamism of its own, and no amount of murder and violence perpetrated by the

Héctor Humberto Herrara Herrara, a Dominican priest from Peru, was ordained in 1976. Since that time he has been involved in youth work and communications in Chimbote.

powerful against the poor can stop it. And the voice being heard is the prophetic voice of a church taking up the defense of the rights of the poor, and becoming the voice of those who have no voice even if it costs the church its life. Such was the understanding of Salvadoran Archbishop Oscar A. Romero, faithful witness to Jesus and defender of the rights of the poor. He was killed for defending the lives of his people, and their right to live as human beings.

The Latin American church assumes its role as evangelizer and liberator of the continent's poor in a context plagued by regimes founded on the doctrine of National Security, propagated by powerful interests both within and without our countries. Archbishop Romero made a fair assessment of reality throughout the continent: "Political power is in the hands of an unscrupulous military, who only know how to oppress the poor and further the interests of the oligarchy."[2]

We may say that the Latin American church is undergoing a process of conversion to God and the poor. At least that is what our Christian communities, together with their pastors, are experiencing. This, then, is the context in which I propose to speak about the mission of the church and of the Prelature of Chimbote in Peru.

I: The Situation of the Local Church: The Chimbote Prelature

Vital Data

The Prelature of Chimbote has its seat in the city of that name, 420 kilometers north of Lima. It was created February 10, 1963, for the provinces of Santa (Chimbote) and Casma, with a population of some 750,000—farmers, laborers, fisher folk, artisans, teachers, and so on. It has 18 parishes, 33 priests, 5 Christian Brothers, 16 seminarians, 4 Dominican postulants, and 36 religious Sisters.

Before the erection of the prelature, this area, then part of the Diocese of Huaraz, was served by the Oblate Fathers of Saint Joseph, and by Father Bertino Otárola, a diocesan priest. Upon the erection of the prelature, it was entrusted to Monsignor Carlos S. Burke, O.P., as bishop, and it was he who directed the church in Chimbote from his installation on April 14, 1965, until July 10, 1978.

Bishop Burke exercised his pastoral charge side by side with other ministers, both religious and laity. His farewell Mass of July 10, 1978, was marked by the presence of various Christian communities who wished to give testimony to his characteristic of making the cry of an exploited and believing people his own. As he himself put it in his prophetic Easter Letter of 1978, "The Church in Chimbote has moved from a pastoral ministry, which turned the poor person into a beggar, to a ministry of liberating evangelization." This was the time of Medellín and the Peruvian bishops' documents. Since then the concern of the church in Chimbote has always been the defense of the weak and the poor, since preaching the gospel to an exploited people means restoring them to the dignity of human personhood, to the dignity of children of God. Pastoral ministry in Chimbote always keeps in mind that the purpose of mission is not to palliate the situation, but to transform it. The poor, whom we meet every day, are cast out into the streets. They languish in the public squares, or shuffle from place to place in search of work. Their whole unhappy lot is reflected in the faces of their hundreds of children deprived of childhood. It is not a question of isolated instances. This is a whole people, victims of the scourge of hunger and injustice produced by an economic and political system that does not consider the poor to be persons.

Our own words on the occasion of Bishop Burke's farewell included the following: "His prophetic denunciations have been the mark and brand of the pastoral ministry of this bishop who is our brother. To be the voice of the voiceless, of the lowly people of the new ghettos, of the fisher people, of the teachers, of the iron workers—this was the mission he has fulfilled."

In token of our gratitude for his work we compiled a collection, *In the Path of Pain and Hope: Pastoral Letters 1963–78, Orientations for Evangelization, Testimonials of* Comunidades de Base *and Pastoral Ministers*—a whole doctrinal compendium of Burke's presence, a bishop who walked with his people at their every step, and a bishop who defended his priests. "Never," he said at his farewell, "shall I forget the toil, the hours of gladness, hope, and pain which I have shared with you—together with my brother priests."

Chimbote is a fishing port—ironically known as the "First Fishing Port of the World." In 1967 Bishop Burke denounced the atrocity of the concentration of the wealth of the fishing industry in the hands of foreign and domestic capitalists to the detriment of a people who lacked the necessities of life—water, bread, housing—with the ensuing moral degradation. Finally the concentration of wealth in the hands of a few, the abuse of power by the exploitation of the poor, a whole new traffic in real estate, the rise of public immorality, and so forth, put an end to fishing. Below we shall examine Burke's denunciation of the concrete, hidden injustices in our society, when we come to 1977 and the contribution of our Christian communities. For it is in examining the present situation that we shall best be able to understand the experience of the church in Chimbote.

The Pastoral Presence of the Church

The church in Chimbote underwent a process of conversion, undertaking an ongoing evaluation of its pastoral ministry. That ministry began as one of pastoral assistance: it built buildings, it gave to the poor. But it did not attempt to advance the cause of the poor themselves. It felt unsure of itself, and called itself to account. The changes that were taking place, the exigencies of love, and the testimony of a people that were poor, had reached their mark. It analyzed its own role and nature in the midst of all these problems. And it opted for a frank evangelization of liberation. Thus, for example, we see that all the documents from 1967 to 1978 question the adequacy of ministry's presence with and commitment to the poor. The most salient examples are "The Easter Pastoral" (1972), "Letter Denouncing the Assault on Fishing Rights," "Pastoral Guidelines" (1974), "Diocesan Labor Day" (1977), "Letter of the Christian Communities on the Occasion of the Feast of Saint Peter," "Pastoral Guidelines: The Puebla Contribution," "Pastoral Letter on the Situation of the Iron Workers," and "Pronouncement of the Christian Communities on the Occasion of a Change of Bishops."

On July 25, 1978, the direction of the Prelature of Chimbote was assumed by Bishop Luis Bambarén, S.J.

Pastoral View of the Situation in the Chimbote Prelature

For purposes of the present treatment, we shall take the elements of the work of reflection carried out by our Christian communities in the prelature in their study of the Puebla document, and set them in relationship with the set of problems in which our country lives. As Puebla says:

> Taking inspiration from the great mission of yesteryear, we want to draw closer to the reality of today's Latin Americans with a pastoral eye and a Christian heart, in order to understand and interpret it. Starting off from that reality, we want to procede to analyze our pastoral mission [no. 14].

This is the only way to convey the feelings of our people—by approaching this real situation.

The first question we formulated in our study of the Puebla document, then, was: How do we see the description and analysis of society in the Puebla document reflected in the situation in Chimbote? Our answers fall into six categories:

1. Economic.

a. The gap between rich and poor: the Peruvian economy is currently oriented toward exportation, thereby favoring the Association of Exporters through CERTEX (free exportation), which is waging a struggle with the other large companies of the industrial society, themselves oriented toward an internal market, for a greater share of the bread of the poor.

b. The absence of any regulation of commerce.

c. Low salaries: the economic crisis through which the country is passing invariably affects the disadvantaged classes.

d. Galloping inflation, in function of world inflation. Thus the dollar, according to the Banco Central de Reserva,[3] will be quoted in July 1980 at 290.52 soles, and for December 1980 it will be at 323.28 soles—which means a devaluation of 29.6 percent as compared with 1979.

e. In Chimbote the capitalists have turned to CERTEX as part of their plan to reach the maximal point of the "fishing boom." As they have practically exterminated anchovies, they have concentrated on taking other species for the manufacture of fish meal. In 1973 the proportion of the taking of other species was 24 percent. In 1977–78 it rose to 57–60 percent. Fish meal is made from fish fit for human consumption. "As long as they are used to feed chickens, hogs, and cattle, people can't even buy a yellow jack," according to the *Newsletter* of the Prelature's Commission on Justice. Pickle factories are appearing everywhere. In 1973 the country consumed 63 percent of its take. In 1979 it consumed only 31 percent, or 214,000 metric tons, or 12.5 kilograms per inhabitant—enough protein to satisfy the minimum daily requirement for forty days. There is no meat or milk available. In a country that is rich in natural resources, people are dying of malnutrition—Peru, a fishing country where 40 percent of the people are tubercular and 70 percent of the children are undernourished.

f. Unemployment: the situation in Chimbote is particularly serious, but I shall refer to the national situation. Of a work force of 6.2 million, only 2.5 million are employed.

g. Population: of 300,000 inhabitants, 117,600 are children under sixteen years of age.

2. Cultural.

a. Culture shock, from the mountains to the coast.

b. Foreign culture permeating the communications media.

c. The acquisitive society, and the felt need to "get ahead."

d. The failure of the Education Reform.

e. Dehumanization of the person.

f. Abandoned families.

g. Machismo.

3. Juridical.

a. Laws that oppress the poor for the benefit of the rich: for example, the labor decrees on "stability of employ"; state contracts with oil and mining corporations; return of files to former owners as these return to power. All this occurs on a national level.

b. Corruption of the legal system, locally as well as nationally.

c. Repression and torture of workers and the leaders of their labor organizations.

d. Arbitrary detention.

e. Absence of respect for human rights: unarmed workers are shot down in the streets, as happens when there is a municipal strike.

4. Political.

a. Popular participation prohibited.

b. Repression of popular organizations.

c. Moral corruption of the authorities.

d. Abuse of power: Absence of any concern for the problems of the people.

5. Religious.

a. Proliferation of the sects, which attempt to foist an ahistorical, fundamentalist message on the people.

6. Social.

a. Class Differences—too obvious for anyone to miss.

We offer an interpretation of the causes of this situation just outlined. The system in control in Peru cannot but engender injustices—that is, the violation of the rights of the poor. The system is supported by institutionalized violence. Repression. The inequitable distribution of national wealth. The economy's politics favors the large capitalists by concentrating on exports. (According to the president of the Banco Central de Reserva, the economic crisis will cost the country 500,000 children.) Combined with the drought, the result is a 4.7 percent decrease in the agrarian sector, even in the hands of agribusiness. Comestibles are down (and are not available to the people)—for instance, carrots by 31 percent, and meat by 11 percent (which the common people have not seen for some time). High school matriculation is down 40 percent.

The most striking consequence of the economic crisis is that in Peru 169 children out of every 1,000 are dying before they reach the age of three. (Evidently they have no right to live.) And here in Chimbote, we see it and feel it—without statistics, but without exaggeration. It is the tumultuous outcry of a whole suffering people —hunger, malnutrition, unemployment. There is fishing, but it is not available to the people because of the depredation of the species carried out by the fishing industry. The short-term profit goes to the capitalists, and the people are exploited.

The second question formulated in our study of the Puebla document was: According to Puebla, what are the most urgent roles that the church should assume in the face of this concrete poverty, injustice, and violation of human rights?

Among the church's roles and activities noted were:

a. A more powerful thrust in the direction of evangelization; a true grassroots evangelization.

b. Preaching based on actual reality.

c. Courage to denounce injustices in the light of the gospel. Conversion at a personal level, and the proclamation of the gospel.

d. Knowledge in depth: of the Word of God (the Bible), and of the reality of our situation.

e. Better organization and unity, for evangelizing in the context of the actual reality in which we are living.

f. Formation and consciousness-raising of leaders and pastoral ministers.

g. Restraint of the tendency to paternalize—promotion of the people as the active vessels of their own history.

h. Promotion of dialogue—community consciousness.

i. Dissemination of Puebla doctrine, documents.

What advances and what shortcomings did we note in our own church with respect to these roles? The advances included: *(a)* evangelization and catechesis; *(b)* identification with the poor; *(c)* concern for youth; *(d)* pluralism; *(e)* use of the communications media; *(f)* participation of the laity; *(g)* family involvement; and *(h)* prayer groups.

Among the shortcomings listed were: *(a)* once-a-year Christians; *(b)* indifference; *(c)* lack of commitment; *(d)* abuse of religion for economic or political purposes; *(e)* fear of denunciation; *(f)* scarcity of priests and pastoral ministers; *(g)* failure to study the concrete situation in depth; *(h)* church silence; *(i)* the division into two currents, conservative and liberating (with the people); and *(j)* lack of a spirit of search and inquiry.

The work group assigned to study the theme "The Truth about the Church," in the Puebla document of the same name, made the following response:

What qualities of the church of Christ are present in our local church of Chimbote?

It is the people of God in history.

It is an evangelizing church, exercising the function of service to the Father and its neighbor in which Christ constituted it.

It has deeper roots in the poor. It is a people's church, incarnate in the history of those sectors of the population that make an ever firmer option for the poor.

We have the increased participation of the laity, as well as of youth, in the roles and ministries of the church.

There is a family spirit, a spirit of brothers and sisters, in our church. However, there are tensions and divisions as well.

The Church of the People is born of the people's faith, and identifies with the struggle for justice and dignity for all the children of God.

There are certain problems and shortcomings to be noted in the church of Chimbote:

A lack of missionary commitment, and of commitment in general, on the part of the laity.

Certain priests lack confidence in the laity.

There are aspects of popular spirituality that are not well received by church structures.

There are two currents: the "spiritual," and the committed ("suspect of politics").

It is within this actual reality that our church experiences its faith. Thus in his 1979 Christmas message our bishop, Monsignor Luis Bambarén, summarized the drama of Jesus as it is lived by our children:

In Chimbote, in 70 percent of our children under five, Jesus is growing up with some degree of malnutrition. Sometimes Jesus gets tea, bread, and noodle soup every day; sometimes he only gets *nicovita*. And he often risks his life on the docks or trucks, in the skinny little children looking for fish to take the edge off their hunger. Sometimes Jesus grows up, goes to school, and plays. But sometimes he has no medical supplies or doctors. . . . Sometimes he has no water, and plays in the garbage dump because there are no playgrounds or recreation facilities.

We seek to proclaim a gospel that restores to a human being the hope of being recognized and accepted as a child of God, of being able to build that kingdom of God that is present in Jesus, the Poor One of Nazareth, who took upon himself the condition of poverty.

II: The Mission of the Church in the Popular Movement: Christian Openness

As far as the question of the Christian-Marxist dialogue is concerned, I think the problem is not with the nonbelievers. This is not the experience on our continent.

That is, we pose the question from another point of view. Latin America today numbers 320 million people, and by the year 2000 the population will double, to some 600 million. What concerns us is that our youth constitute more than 70 percent of the population: young adult Indians, peasants, miners, fishers, laborers, and even children, who are obliged by their poverty to work as adults. This year, according to data from the Economic Commission for Latin America (United Nations), there are 35.5 million children among the poor, and by the end of the century the number will not be less than 51 million. Of the total number of poor people, 160 million live in urban areas, 85 million in rural areas, without minimal human conditions. And the politico-economic and social system that determines our lot is not responding to the needs of the poor. The wealthy classes rely on the multinational corporations—on the capitalist system—and this generates an explosive situation of institutionalized violence, as our bishops stated in Medellín. The Christians of our grassroots ecclesial communities have arrived at a clear consciousness of this fact, and their option for the poor leads them to a critical attitude, to an openness to the human sciences, which help them give better definition to their commitment to live their faith by taking into account the history in which God is speaking to us.

The participation of Christians in the popular and revolutionary movements goes without saying. Our faith requires us to make a commitment in the very midst of our people. And if the Latin American church seeks to opt for the rights of the poor, in order to bring about a real and effective change, it cannot ignore the existence or the contribution of

> philosophical materialism as a method of coming to know, and transforming, reality, or ignore the fact that such acceptance is no obstacle to a believer's exercise of his or her faith, in the recognition that, in the progress of history and its popular struggles, they are fighting for revolutionary transformations that liberate human beings.[4]

The presence of Christians who are taking responsibility for their faith, and for their loyalty to the gospel of Jesus Christ, is a presence that involves a particular understanding of the will of God. Our committed Christians understand that the will of God is precisely to build the community of brothers and sisters announced by Christ. And they understand that this cannot be some kind of theoretical building of that community with mere abstract ideas. The love of Christ for women and men translates into deeds, in the concrete history of brothers and sisters who live their lives deprived of that community. There can be no community of brothers and sisters where injustice reigns. "If a man who was rich enough in this world's goods saw that one of his brothers was in need, but closed his heart to him, how could the love of God be living in him?" (1 Jn. 3:17). The words of John, like the whole biblical message, are charged with a profound truth: we cannot love God without loving our sister and our brother. And this truth, this reality, can only be understood if we clothe it in flesh, if we incarnate it. This comports a radical change, a change of structures plagued by sin, to allow the poor person to actualize himself or herself precisely as a person.

Building the new human being in Latin America today means taking one's point of departure in a radical option for Christ. It means an actual, concrete deed of love and solidarity, the kind performed by Christians who have committed their lives to brothers and sisters who are not understood. This is why the contribution of the human sciences impels us to seek the path of involvement, of search, and of bold challenges. Hence, in the experience that the Peruvian church is living, the local Christian community involves itself in a concrete history, which aids it in redefining its faith as a faith that accepts God as Father and men and women as brothers and sisters, children of that same Father, whose love has been revealed to us in Jesus Christ. Surely in Christ we have learned the truth that makes us free. In him we have discovered the transforming road that recreates the world and makes all things new. But men and women in Latin America are living outside this community of sisters and brothers, and this liberty, proclaimed by Christ. We Christians, then, are beginning to understand that receiving the gift and grace of God consists precisely in breaking with this sinful situation, which sets itself up in opposition to friendship with God and human beings. This is why "the faith does not eschew historical means and methods, or socio-political analyses of real situations."[5]

The presence of Christians in our people's struggles consists in a defense of the rights of the poor, like the right to work and the right to job security. Christian presence means accompanying a whole people in its search and demand for justice. Christian presence in struggles like these is a sign of the presence of a church seeking to build the kingdom of God and to condemn sin.

Through this attitude of openness, a good many Christians are living their faith in a mature way, and are making an effort to understand and accept the gift of the Spirit of Truth.

There are those, however, who conceive a certain fear when they study the document. They are afraid of "Marxist infiltration." These persons do not wish to see. They are unwilling to accept reality. They are not willing to be questioned because it makes them feel insecure. I should like to point out that this fear exists in Latin America—in certain sectors—where a dominant ideology plays an important role. In these circles there is no bold quest. Concern is limited to the area of "intra-church conflicts." Here Christians who commit themselves to justice and the kingdom of God are accused of seeking only people's political or social liberation. This shows that these persons have not assimilated the liberating aspect of the faith, a faith whose hallmark is precisely the following of the poor Jesus of Nazareth, and accepting the lot that was his because he had the courage to love the poor. "The Good News is proclaimed to the poor" (Mt. 11:5) was Jesus' answer to John's disciples. The poor know how to grasp the wisdom of God. They are the living gospel that keeps us aware of the living presence of God as it works itself out in everyday history. How many lessons of faith and wisdom issue forth from the simple! They look to the church for a more meaningful response to their problems, and the church must be constantly in an attitude of search if it wishes to be faithful to God and to his poor. It is true that we are laden with our limitations, and that we shall encounter suffering and difficulties. But this search must be authentic, full of respect for human beings, for our people, for believers. We must not be concerned to impose our own criteria on them. It is not true that this common search of ours is limited to social concerns.

Christianity's contribution goes much further than that. Rather, through the intermediary of history, we seek the light of Jesus Christ, in whom the hope of the poor finds its pinnacle and crown (cf. Lk. 4:18-21).

III: Signs of God that Penetrate a Culture Influenced by Materialism

There are clear, living signs of the presence of God among our people. There is a deep sense of religion, which demonstrates its attachment and love for God and all men and women. There is a search for a community of sisters and brothers, a thirst for justice, a hope for the day of liberation. Our people cherish profound values of hospitality and common enterprise, the fellow feeling of compatriots, a sense of family, and a respect for others, as it pointed out in our document applying Puebla to the situation in our local church.

The most atrocious form of materialism among Latin American people, and the one that besets our own in Peru and Chimbote, is that of the *idols of power,* with their instruments of murder (the arms race) for the oppression and stifling of the people. The money idol fills the coffers of the great ones of the earth, by encouraging the spoliation of our land in order to hand it over to the large multinational corporations, and by furthering a political economics of exportation, which results in hunger among the people. The mass media are manipulated by the powerful in order to create a competitive, disunifying, demobilizing mentality that will ensure the viability of their system—a system that goes so far as to rob the people of their religious sentiments through the "officialization" of religious feasts by the state. (We shall consider this below, when we examine popular religion.) The principle of National Security creates a vested state, by terrorizing, imprisoning, and persecuting the people. In Peru it is subversive to demand the right to be human. This is the most dehumanizing of materialisms—even when it calls itself "Christian humanism."

Our people have a rich faith. They discover, in their history of oppression, that God's will calls them to engage in a concrete search for this community of which we have been speaking, this community of brothers and sisters. Our people are discovering that all their actions can be an expression of this wisdom of God, of which Jesus spoke when he said it was revealed only to the little ones (cf. Mt. 11:25). Our people are discovering the signs of God in history, for they have their theological task: "Authentic theology springs forth from the spirituality of the people, is nourished with the people's living experience, and creates a system—to which the professional theologians then make their contribution. Authentic theology is an ecclesial reflection, born of the warmth of communion among the people of God."[6]

The Role of the Christian Communities

In the hands of their pastoral ministers, the Christian communities have been maturing. They have been reflecting on their faith in Jesus Christ, via their incorporation into the parish communities. Laborers, youth, farmers, fisher folk, domestic servants, couples, catechists, teachers, the unemployed—all are joined together in these new, vital communities, which meet in small groups to reflect on their faith, taking their point of departure in the historical situations in which they are presently living. They attempt to render the Word of God incarnate, by means of their vital concern for the world of the marginalized. It is these communities that take part in the popular organizations—precisely because their faith makes them feel in solidarity with others. Every parish is the expression of the community within it, which unites all these various sectors in a mutually enriching search that they all engage in together.

The presence of the church in different areas of endeavor motivates the faithful to assume their own responsibility, to make their own contribution to the task of evangelization.

In the Family. The family is "the first teacher of the faith," and as such is the principal promoter of the faith of children and youth. Hence our emphasis on sharing responsibility with parents when it comes to the reception of the sacraments. We are currently in the stage of initial experimentation with "family catechesis" in three parishes, seeking to involve parents with each other in preparing their children for the sacraments.

Working People. The presence of the church among the working classes is important for helping people to recognize that they are children of God, with all the implications this has for a continual restatement of ways to live one's faith with justice in the world of working people. The same applies to ministries with fishers, iron workers, the unemployed, and so on.

Domestic Servants. The young mother or single person who works as a maid in someone else's home is appropriately styled a "servant." Rarely does she receive a living wage. At times she is paid, but less than enough to live on, and at times she is simply handed an alms and some used clothing. Recently, however, some of these young mothers and single persons have discovered, in the light of their faith, that theirs is the dignity of human beings, and this has motivated them to organize to defend their rights. Their progress, their participation in the Christian assemblies, and the rich contribution they make as they speak out in simplicity are a matter of admiration and astonishment.

Teachers. Teachers meet to carry out a reflection on their role in the field of education.

Rural People. Here there is the slow, interesting task of forming leaders to assume a role in communities where there is no priest.

Youth. Half of our population consists of children and young people. Their faith life is making a mark on our church, and this is a very interesting experience for us. As I have been involved in youth work, I shall attempt to synthesize the three criteria proposed by Puebla and their development by our youth with the help of our pastoral ministry.

The Puebla Criteria and Pastoral Ministry to Youth

The Truth about Jesus Christ. We open a youth meeting with a question like, "In what actual way do you think of Jesus as your friend and liberator?" And we help our young people to respond:

"Because he shares our sufferings and our hopes, and guides us by his Spirit into the path of liberation."

"Because he frees us from our selfishness. He gave his life for us, and to teach us to give our lives for our friends."

"He opens our eyes to see things around us."

"He is our friend. We find support and encouragement in him. He helps us become free, and not just individually, but by liberating our neighbors as well. He teaches us the truth, love, and justice we should have among ourselves."

The deep aspirations of youth for freedom and true love find in Christ a path they can follow. Christ gave the example of genuine friendship, and of the radical commitment to people required in order to build a new society (cf. Puebla, no. 1183).

Youth may not have a deep knowledge of Christ. But they have intuitions, and these enable them to find in him an answer to their search for genuine values like solidarity, love, and generous commitment.

Youth in the Church. "Young people should feel that they are the church, experiencing it as a place of communion and participation." For they are a people that is new, poor, contemplative, and ready to listen (Puebla, no. 1184).

What do young people do to build the church of Christ? Hear what they have to say:

"We reflect on the upbuilding of our faith in Christ and our commitment to the poor."

"We deepen our faith in our communion with God and people."

"We try to feel that we are church, by action."

"We encourage people, by means of the faith in Christ we share in common with them, to play a part in their own liberation."

The church must respond to youth's uneasiness. It must give them a clear presentation of the gospel. The church in Chimbote has been making its own the goals and aspirations formulated in Medellín: "The Church must discover, in youth, a sign of itself, of the need it has to be ever engaged in a process of renewal, for the Church is 'the true youth of the world' " (*Decree on Youth,* December 8, 1965).

The Truth about Human Beings. In the poor Christ, young people find a human being who rejected a society devoid of all respect for the dignity of human beings, a society that prevented people from bringing about the community of brothers and sisters that God gives us all as his gift. In Jesus they meet the person who came to liberate men and women so that they could build a society of sisters and brothers and decide their own destiny. He is youth's friend, and young people will discover this if they mediate his message and his presence in history through the men and women who demanded solidarity with and commitment to the poor and the exploited.

The young person who seeks to assume, in his or her life, the same attitudes as Christ assumed, necessarily seeks to proclaim this ideal—and not to someone far away, but to someone who is part of his or her life. The young person seeks to communicate a liberating experience, one which unites and builds. And the young person realizes that the concrete reality in which human beings live, the facts of human life, stand in need of being transformed by the light of Jesus Christ.

Concrete Actions for Youth Ministry. (*a*) a deepening of knowledge of Jesus and his gospel; (*b*) a critical vision of reality, a vision enlightened by faith in Christ; (*c*) a deep knowledge of human rights, of the right to be children of one Father and brothers and sisters in Jesus Christ; (*d*) education in the gospel values of love and solidarity, of deep respect for the human being, and of commitment to the task of a transforming liberation from "consumerism" (cf. Puebla, no. 56).

Furthermore, in the face of the "deterioration of family values" (Puebla, no. 58), youth should be offered family security and education toward the formation of genuine families, whose members foster justice and the liberation of the continent. In the face of the crisis of moral values (Puebla, no. 69), we should strive to form the "new person," who will take up the task of building the kingdom of God.

The pastoral ministry of the church must allow itself to be marked by the impressions and attitudes of our youth—by their legitimate aspirations arising from a true and living faith within a context of conflict, where they are discovering what it means to be faithful to the Lord and to his poor.

Puebla asks us to encourage youth movements such as the JEC, the young JOCist workers, and rural people who are meeting and carrying out their mission of evangelization. It is there, in the young Christian communities, that vocations will be found, and these should be fostered in a new way, so that future pastors will be truly evangelized people—"so that, evangelized, they may evangelize."

The Grassroots Ecclesial Community and the Encounter with Christ

The faith-experience of our Christian communities is precisely a product of their view of Christ and of the church. Hence it is also the result of a reflection.

How do we meet Christ? What is the face of Christ that we meet, live, and proclaim? We meet Christ in those who suffer and live in profound poverty; in the depth of faith of a simple, suffering people, impelled by this faith to go in search of their liberation; in children who are abandoned, or struck down spiritually by an unjust and oppressive society; in children who die from disease for lack of economic resources and medical aid; in victims of injustice who are imprisoned; in our people, who wear the face of Christ, bloodied and abused.

The positive aspects of our encounter with the face of Christ are to be found in the concern of the church to help resolve the problems of the people; in persons who share their hope with those who suffer; in those who denounce injustice, and persevere in their acts of solidarity.

How do we live Christ? At times we attempt to live a Christ who asks no commitment of us, for fear of losing our security. But by living the faith, respecting others, and practicing what he teaches us, we live the real Christ.

What is the true notion of Christ, and how are we to proclaim it? A Christ we make for ourselves, who asks no commitment to the poor, or a Christ who punishes, a Christ who is strict in his laws and rules, is a negative proclamation. In positive terms, through our life and witness, we can proclaim a Christ who is: (*a*) in solidarity with those who lack the necessities of life; (*b*) committed to a people in their actual history—an integral liberator, who frees us both through faith and through justice;

(c) the brother of the people who share the Father's love; (d) the hope of the poor; a sensitive Christ, faced with problems and difficulties, burning to live in a more simple and committed fashion.

The vision held by the church translates into activity, and these activities can be expressed as tasks: (a) The church should be more incarnate in the people, making denunciations and proclamations on their behalf, and evangelizing by preference the poor and the suffering. (b) In view of the suffering of the people, the church should carry out a frank evangelization of liberation, in defense of human rights. (c) The church should promote the grassroots Christian communities, the *comunidades eclesiales de base*. (d) Preparation for the sacraments, and participation in the liturgy, should be encouraged more by the church. (e) Fundamental to all these activities is true conversion to Christ so that all who make up the church will be closer to their brothers and sisters.

There is in our people a profound sense of confidence in God, and of solidarity in the struggle for a just world. They know how to pray. The reason is that the living experience of their faith is expressed through the promotion of justice. Here a good deal of credit is due the Commission for Justice of the Prelature of Chimbote, with its different fields of endeavor: women's rights, prisoners' rights, and the rights of the poor. The commission's *Bulletin* is a valuable contribution, both by reason of its serious study of the series of problems we have to face, and because of its involvement with the people. Thus the Center for Social Intercommunication (CINCOS), another organ, represents the church in the communications media: radio—cultural and religious programs for local stations, and broadcast of the Sunday Eucharist; the press—by the publication *Pido la Palabra* ("May I Have the Floor?"), an effort by the grassroots communities in the form of a periodical for reflective essays; audiovisuals and books—various undertakings.

We have named these organizations here because their work is linked to Christian communication. Their efforts are directed toward small groups as much as possible, to help youth, and older people as well, learn a new method of evangelization, via minor popular communications media such as modest publications, audiovisuals, theater, and music. These are expressions of a church that must ever be engaged in searching.

Our Christian communities are waxing, inspired by their faith in Jesus and by their desire to search out solutions. And since the great majority of these communities consists of young people, I should like to pass on to you the sentiment of our youth:

> Because we understand that Christ liberates human beings within concrete history, we young people must carry out the liberation process motivated by faith in Christ and in the poor as the sole agents of our people's liberation. We seek to review our lives, in the light of the gospel—to review the meaning of our actions and our problems, in order to be more effective. The gospel demands our conversion to God and neighbor: hence we must deepen our faith, by sharing our reading of the Bible, and by celebrating the Eucharist in such a manner that it may be the expression both of our people's sufferings and of their hopes for liberation.

IV: God's Message in the Language and Symbols of the People: Evangelization and Popular Religion

The Origins of Popular Piety in Chimbote

During the eighteenth century, a number of families moved to the Cove of Chimbote from Huanchaco. With them they brought "Saint Pete," San Pedrito, the patron of the fisher folk. Then during the years between 1940 and 1970, there was a heavy migration from the Libertad range and from Ancasho. So rural people and mountain people met and mingled, sharing their beliefs, devotions, and religious celebrations. From the very beginning it was a piety of the poor and the oppressed, and such it has remained to this day. It is a piety of tension between two poles: resistance and identification, resistance to and identification with the incorporation of the mountain people, and of all the youth, into a difficult and strange world. Its principal context is the search for a concrete, material salvation in communitarian and collective fashion.

Evolution

There is a process of change under way in this piety. The changes are the result of pastoral activity as well as a whole context of the impoverishment of the majority of the people together with the dream they cherish of bettering their life. The following aspects stand out.

The Privatization of religion. This consists in an evolution of popular piety from a concentration on God's salvation of all his people (as expressed in a devotion to the saints) into more individualistic devotions. People become victims of the modern myth that each one makes his or her own life. "My saint, my devotion, helps me."

The Utilization and Manipulation of the Religion of the Poor. The religious festival of the fisher people has been absorbed, partially, by "Chimbote Civic Week," established by governmental decree in Belaúnde in 1967 (by Public Law No. 16597). More recently, the iron works makes use of San Eloy as the occasion of a "circus for the people, with floats and queens" instead of a Christian celebration. In this way the civil authorities and company management not only gain prestige, but actually inject themselves into the religious life of the poor.

The Fundamentalist Boom. The evangelical sects attack the people's own faith tradition, firing their enthusiasm with their "miracles" and their fundamentalist conception of the faith.

Backlash

A reawakening is taking place in the area of religion and popular piety. Many Christians are coming to a greater sense of social commitment, a more generous and profound faith. A ministry of liberation is developing, allowing the masses to express their faith in the Lord from a point of departure in their situation of oppression and their anxiety to be freed from it. This ministry is described and fostered in various ecclesiastical documents. In his Easter Message for 1972 Bishop Burke pointed out that the people have "a profound religious piety, demonstrating their love for God and all men and women."

In 1977, on the occasion of the Feast of "San Pedrito," the Christian communities wrote a letter. "While the people are expressing their faith," they said, "there are others who move in to deceive them and grow rich at their expense." Puebla made a special contribution here in 1979 by emphasizing the evangelization potential of simple people through their life of prayer. Pointing the way of the faith of the simple who trust in the Lord, poor people engage in a justifiable protest action, expressing their faith in the attainment of a life according to the will of a God who seeks justice, their confidence in the possibility of crushing evil on this earth by concrete action (cf. Puebla, nos. 1153–65).

The pastoral team of Señor de los Milagros Parish has made an effort to strengthen the faith of the oppressed in that "Lord of miracles." This is one of the parishes in which, as mentioned above, the parents nourish the faith of their children by means of catechetical programs.

Recovery and Reaffirmation of Popular Piety

The piety of the people is looked down upon because it is judged by the standards of the Westernized culture of the middle, urban class. Instead, Medellín extends an invitation to view it with the eyes of the poor: "Popular religiosity can be the occasion, or point of departure, for a proclamation of the faith" (*Catechesis,* no. 2).

The Theological Value of Popular Piety. Medellín places the emphasis on the religious values of the oppressed poor, and on a reevangelization in view of the "seedlings of a call from God" expressed in those values. This piety contains the "light of the Word" (*Popular Pastoral Ministry,* nos. 2, 4–5). Even before Puebla there was a theological respect throughout the continent for the religion of the people, as expressed, for instance, in the statements of the Peruvian Bishops' Conference. Thus a break was made with modern, rationalistic, middle-class criticism of the religion of the poor, which considered them ignorant and superstitious.

The magisterium of recent popes contains pronouncements along these same lines: Paul VI, in *Evangelii Nuntiandi,* no. 48, laments occasional contempt for popular piety, which he defines as "a thirst for God known only to the poor and the simple." John Paul II, in Mexico, complains that it is judged as a "lower form of religious expression."

For my presentation of the foregoing material I have used the notes of Diego Irarrázaval, a researcher who has developed an investigation in depth on this theme. It would take too long to retrace the whole, but I should like to point out that Puebla blazes trails for the recognition of our peoples' religious values with the observation that these peoples are permeated with the Christian faith and the condition of an unjust poverty (Puebla, no. 436). These unjust structures, the document goes on, arise from the dominant ideologies, and are incompatible with the particular faith of our popular culture (no. 437). Then the document warns us against the "ideological, economic, social, and political types of manipulation" of popular religion (no. 456).

As I have said, there is a power of liberation within our people. *Their* hope is born of "their deeply religious sense" (Puebla, no. 73), and this is why they "ask for the bread of God's Word and demand justice" (no. 93). And because the people, out of their own sense of faith, recognize the sacred value of personal dignity and the solidarity of sisters and brothers, religious piety often becomes a cry for a genuine liberation (Puebla, no. 452).

The piety of our people contains, as Puebla points out, a potential for evangelizing, for it is based on the Word of God. It is constantly purifying itself, it belongs to the church, and it makes a commitment. Puebla sketches practical directions for grasping interiorly the rich paradox of a God who is transcendent and yet close by (nos. 413, 913): attachment to Christ in one's life and ministry (nos. 171–72, 454), as well as to Mary (nos. 285, 459, 913); membership in the church (nos. 232, 454); a deep sense of prayer (nos. 454, 898, 905, 913); and values like friendship, personal dignity, human solidarity, family unity, and a capacity for suffering and heroism (nos. 454, 913).

We are being challenged to take up an evangelizing task among our people. We are called to liberate them from totalitarian ideologies, which seek to make use of religion to oppress. But our people have a lively consciousness of a Christ who is Liberator, who is close to their problems, and who takes a position against the idolatrous cult that divorces religion from the process of the integral liberation of the human being.

The Christian Commitment in Society

Our people are coming to understand the gospel message. The building of the brotherhood and sisterhood proclaimed by Christ is a task demanding personal and social conversion. And this conversion cannot take place on the margin of politically and socially conditioned history. On the other hand, we realize, the system is a product of people's selfishness and blindness, hence is constantly reinforcing its methods of breaking people with its repression. It makes use of, it utilizes, religion. It proclaims itself to be "humanistic and Christian." These attitudes must be protested, and opposed, by the power of the gospel. Christians, and especially the poor with whom we work, are coming to realize this. It is a matter of taking upon ourselves the Beatitudes, of accepting the condition of sons and daughters of God, of accepting Jesus Christ. It is becoming a deep question within the hearts of the poor why the vast majority of them cannot live a life worthy of a human being. Thus, with the pain of the cross and the hope of full liberation in Christ Jesus, our poor are evangelizing *us*—for what is new in our Latin American churches is "the deepening of the faith in the popular communities."[7] This implies great theological ferment, whose point of departure is not in abstract questions, but in a situation of oppression and a thirst for justice. Numberless written and oral messages, stamped with suffering, prison, torture, or death, are leaving their mark on our churches. They demand a disquieting search, questioning, and encouragement.

Our Christian communities look upon these extreme situations of injustice as incompatible with the Christian message. This is why, in 1979, we circulated a document on the part of the Christian communities of Peru, a declaration by various priests and religious working in our country. No notice was taken of the document in the official press, for it was entitled, "Give Us This Day Our Daily Bread," and described how much nearer death our children were every day. How is it possible to proclaim the Lord of Life, we asked, in a country where thousands of children are sentenced to death, or to irreversible physical and mental retardation, for lack of food and medicine?

Our youth are frustrated by their deficient educational system, while their parents struggle desperately for a wage of next to nothing. The indigenous peoples are robbed of their land. Unemployment is rising. We are beset by administrative corruption, a lack of morality, the brutal repression of any struggle for human dignity, the violation of human rights, an arms race, and the dishonest acquisition of wealth by a special few. We speak in the name of this people (and we go on to say we wish to make the gospel a political and social reality). We speak in the name of those who seek bread, and who ask their shepherds for a liberation and that liberation does not come. The poor seek justice and bread and they receive repression and death. These are the challenges. These are the hard realities of their life, and these hard realities are maturing us, evangelizing us for the proclamation of the Lord with all our strength. The day of reckoning is at hand, for the system, and for the elements within the church itself that refuse to understand.

VI: Viewpoints and Avenues of Action for the Mission of the Church

We are being taught the lines of action to take by the communities themselves. Here is what we have to do:

1. Deepen our reflection on the Bible, by means of a critical reading from the point of view of the poor and their situation of oppression.

2. Deepen our creative search for a liturgy that may express Christ's gift of liberation.

3. Study the human sciences, and learn from them a better understanding of actual social and political situations, and thus be aided in our continual search.

4. Form lay leaders.

5. Promote a sharper consciousness, among pastoral ministers and people alike, of the Christian view of the human being.

6. Deepen our work of evangelization and catechesis of children, youth, and parents.

7. Maintain a vigilant and critical attitude toward those in power when the rights of the poor are at stake.

8. Promote the social doctrine of the church in our high schools and youth centers. Foster a greater presence of the church in popular organizations.

This is what the Peruvian bishops urge us to do in their "Declaration of the Permanent Council of the Peruvian Bishops' Conference on the Occasion of the National Elections." The document begins by asserting that there are changes to make today that can no longer be postponed. Then it continues:

The painful situation of the great majority of our people ought to be a source of concern on the part of all. It ought to be subjected to the painstaking analysis of everyone in our country at this time of the national elections. . . . And its urgency is such that it ought to be the first consideration of the government to assume power after the elections. The problems of hunger, health, housing, employment, and education are of a magnitude calculated to engage the responsibility of every citizen, and demand a great joint effort to overcome them [R.S., no. 6L, March 8–14, 1980].

I think the church will discharge its role very well if it is careful to be sensitive to its people and to accompany them on their journey.

The contribution, and the conversion, of the missioners who have come to our church from other places is very important. Some of them have had the courage to recognize reality and preach a liberating evangelization. Others have suffered culture shock and adopted the "cultural values" of the status quo, thus producing a division in the church from the viewpoint of pastoral ministry.

The future of the local church is in its vocations, which are rising up in abundance out of the Christian youth communities. But this work demands a common effort of critique and adaptation in the area of training, so that our new ministers may be able to respond to the questions of men and women of today.

How can we discover a deep sense of God in our history? How can we accept Jesus as our people's Liberator? How can we put a stop to the rise in violence, hate, and lack of respect for life and for every human right? We human beings must turn our eyes toward Jesus Christ Risen. He is making himself present in a new way in the Latin American church, and it is in him that we encounter the full meaning of life and respect for the human being.

Our brothers and sisters of the churches of the first world must help us in our struggle to keep those who are in power in the underdeveloped nations from continuing the arms race, which serves to support regimes of terror and oppression. We demand the right to live in a human community. That means the right to bread, to work, to education, to housing, to clothing. Only thus can we recognize ourselves, and be recognized by others, as children of God and beloved of Jesus Christ. For it is Jesus who has shown us that a human being can be neither human being, nor brother or sister to others, as long as he or she lives in terror, unrecognized as a person.

VII: Personnel Working in the Ministry of Our Local Church

3 Oblates of Saint Joseph (2 Italians, 1 Peruvian)
8 Dominicans (6 North Americans, 2 Peruvians [1 by nationality])
5 Holy Cross Fathers
8 Fathers of Saint James the Apostle
6 Spanish Missionary Institute
5 Diocesan Clergy (Majorcans: 1. And two other diocesan priests as missioners)

NOTE: Of the diocesan priests, one is Director of the Regional Seminary in Trujillo, another is assigned to the Archdiocese of Piura, and a third resides in Lima for studies.

Religious Brothers

4 Brothers of the Christian Schools

Religious Women

12 Mercedarians
7 Dominicans (from two congregations)
4 Carmelites
4 Missionaries of Mother Teresa of Calcutta
3 Missioners of Charity of the Child Mary
3 Mothers of Saint Joseph of Corondolet
4 Canonesses of the Cross

There is also a lay institute of Peruvian missioners, and three young people working in the field.

—Translated by Robert R. Barr

Notes

This presentation is based on the experiences of the Christian communities of Chimbote, and on the various reports of our pastoral workshop on Puebla. The author is particularly indebted to the contribution of the Diocesan Commission for Justice, under the direction of Father Lino Dolan.

1. *Lo Mataron por defender la causa de los pobres* [Killed for the Cause of the Poor], brochure of the Centro de Publicaciones (CEP) (Lima: CEP, 1980).
2. Ibid.
3. Cf. *RS Lima,* April 26–May 2, 1980 (3rd year, no. 68), p. 9.
4. Alfredo Pastor, *¿Liberación del pueblo o proclamacion del evangelio?* Centro de Informacion, Estudios y Documentacion (CIED) (Lima: CIED, 1980), p. 81.
5. Gustavo Gutiérrez, *Signos de liberación: testimonios de la Iglesia latinoamericana* (Lima: CEP, 1973), introduction.
6. Maximiliano Salinas and Diego Irarrazabal, *Hacia una teología de los pobres* (Lima: CEP, 1980).
7. Ibid.

9

THE MISSION OF THE CHURCH AND NIGERIAN REALITIES

Mercy Amba Oduyoye

Let me begin by sharing with you four preliminary considerations. The Christian religion lays claim to the Johannine affirmation that the Word of God has made a home in the world. It is also true that there are many who have not received this Word, while others have in varying degrees and from differing standpoints. This universal observation has its particular manifestations, for although one can say that Christ has found a home in Nigeria, Christianity has not become a fully accepted part of the Nigerian heritage. It continues to present itself as a foster child, and several see it as such. The traditional religions of Nigeria, all would say, are the pre-Christian, pre-Islamic "ancestral cults." It is, however, never said of Islam that it is a colonial religion, whereas in fact it is, for it too came to Nigeria as a conquering religion from the north.

Second, Christianity by nature is an evangelizing religion. Christians are like hungry people who, when they have found food, because of the nature of their finding are compelled to go round telling other hungry people where the food is. Christians are on a perpetual mission or they cease to be Christian. The church, the overt carrier of Christianity, has accepted it as a duty from Christ to carry the good news that this world is the sphere of activity of God, who is King. The good news of the sovereignty of God, not only over human affairs and history but also over the whole cosmos, is the burden of the church's mission. It is this Christian affirmation that prompts the question: How is the church to go about the work of making Christianity at home in Nigeria, and Nigerians at home with Christianity?

Third, in Africa as a whole, the words "mission" and "missionary" are associated in our minds with foreigners, mostly people of another color and mostly Euro-Americans. The reason is simply this: setting aside the ancient churches of Ethiopia

Mercy Amba Oduyoye, originally from Ghana, is Lecturer in Early Church History and Christian Theology in the Department of Religious Studies at the University of Ibadan. She has been youth education secretary for the World Council of Churches, and youth secretary for the All Africa Conference of Churches.

and Egypt, the ill-fated ones of North Africa and Nubia (Sudan), and the "Aladura churches,"* all others belong to the World Confessional Families (WCFs) and are in Africa as a result of Euro-American missionary activities, which began in the middle of the nineteenth century. The earlier attempt, that is, the Latin or pre-Reformation effort, had very little effect beyond the Portuguese trading posts on the coast of Africa; neither did the Spanish involvement in this effort yield much fruit. At any rate missionary societies were always *foreign* societies based outside Africa and sending people to Africa "to do them good." This was the sum total of mission as described by Robert Brookling, a Wesleyan missionary to the Gold Coast of the 1840s. As a result the definition of a missionary can be simply put as a white man or woman who has come "to do us good" or "to disrupt and to disturb our traditional life," depending on who is speaking. Consequently, to speak of a Nigerian as a missionary sounds grotesque, and the local (Nigerian) church as a missionary body is simply incomprehensible. The church and Christians in Nigeria are recipients of missions.

One last comment: although I speak of Nigeria, I wish to say that I live in Oyo State, in the west, and that I have only very limited knowledge of other areas of this country, which has a population close to 80 million, and a land area of 923,769 square kilometers, the largest single geographic unit along the west coast of Africa. Also, though born a Methodist, I have had too much ecumenical exposure to consider myself a parochial Methodist. I am therefore taking the general perspective of "the mission of the Nigerian Christian community" as a whole. This is the "local church" as used in this essay. It is to the context of this local church that I now turn.

The Nigerian Scene

As I was considering how best to present a collage of Nigeria today, two things happened. Dr. Tekena Tamuno, a professor of history and former vice-chancellor of the University of Ibadan, presented a paper at a seminar at the Institute of African Studies of that university, entitled "Crime, Security, and Military Rule in Nigeria." Second, Dr. Tam David-West, professor and consultant, virologist of the University of Ibadan and the University Teaching Hospital, had a book, *Philosophical Essays,* published in Ibadan, and launched by the Oyo State governor, Bola Ige, a lawyer and a well-known figure in ecumenical circles both in Nigeria and on the world scene. The two professors provide me with takeoff points: the history and the philosophy of Nigeria. I also went through back copies of three newspapers that in my judgment together give a fair coverage of Nigerian events. I had already chosen 1960 as the terminus a quo, when Nigeria became independent. I had also been looking at the writings of social commentators like Wole Solarin, the educator, and Tola Adeniyi,

*I use "Aladura" to cover all the churches begun by Africans in Africa that are characterized by an emphasis on the work of the Holy Spirit and by fervent prayers. In this I do not include those that came into being as a result of a direct break between whites and blacks in a World Confessional Family. The WCF is a term being used to cover a number of major denominations, such as Roman Catholics, the Eastern Orthodox family of churches, Methodists, Lutherans, Reformed, etc. It is not a very happy term, but a convenient one all the same.

the journalist. To attempt to summarize and analyze all this would be a major work. *How to Be a Nigerian* by Peter Enahoro, himself Nigerian and a well-known journalist, has a perspective on the value of Nigerian society that is well worth reading if one wants to understand human relations in this country.

This presentation, then, is a kaleidoscope of events and attitudes that, for me, characterize Nigerian society. The hues and tones are entirely as I see them.

Nigeria is a multiethnic, multilinguistic, and multireligious community. The traditional social structures, as well as the superimposed Western and oriental ones, produce such a mosaic effect that to call it a pluralistic society sounds like an understatement. As far as Nigerian history goes, one can see five periods, which may be described as follows:

1. a complicated, partially recorded precolonial history that is yet to be unraveled;

2. a colonial period, which had until recently been recorded and interpreted only from the perspective of European history;

3. the first civilian regime or first republic, which Tam David-West describes as characterized by personal cults and tribal unions;

4. the thirteen-year military interlude, begun by Aguiyi Ironsi and ended with Olusegun Obasanjo. The military had hoped, in the words of Yakubu Gowon, to hand over to a civilian government a united Nigeria devoid of "sectarian politicking." He postponed his 1976 target date because an atmosphere of sufficient stability had not been generated. He was ousted and the 201 Day national hero, Murtala Muhammad, sworn in. He was head of state from July 29, 1975, to February 13, 1976, when he was assassinated;

5. the fifth and current stage, the second civilian rule and second republic, which was inaugurated on October 1, 1979, amid doubts as to the legitimacy of the interpretation of two-thirds of nineteen states. Happily one should say this unease has been dissipated, and the nineteen states have settled down to fulfill their electioneering promises, of which there were many and toward which there was a lot of justifiable cynicism.

Nigeria as a modern entity came into being in 1914, but its modern missionary history predates this by some seven decades, having begun in 1842. Although it is the whole time span from the precolonial period to the second republic that has shaped the entity called Nigeria and the people called Nigerians, for the purpose of the future mission I am concentrating on the period during which Nigeria has been a sovereign state, namely, from 1960 to 1980, or from Balewa to Shagari.

Looking at the economic structures of Nigeria, one could describe the country as a mixed economy verging on capitalism rather than socialism. The constitution declares it to be a mixed economy, but the debate goes on as to which predominates or should predominate in reality. To some Nigerians socialism is a panacea for all our social ills. Nigeria does have a lot of theoretical Marxists and socialists but, as Professor Tam David-West observes, their style of life is nowhere near that of the suffering masses. Socialism, however, does provide a utopian ideal to work toward, and thus Nigerian socialists, both religious and the few atheistic ones, hold on to it, and properly so, for "where there is no vision the people perish." Like the professor, I "can hardly see the strict relevance of the traditional or classical rhetoric between capitalism and socialism to our contemporary Nigerian society." The debate itself is irrelevant. Nigeria's economy is mixed, and social structures, both traditionally and in terms of the modern state, are imbued with the principles and practices of a welfare state. Private and state enterprises are found side by side, and attempts are made to provide some free social services.

The economy itself was agrarian and peripheral to Western Europe until the oil boom, which some insist is the "oil doom." It has brought in its wake the civil war, thirteen years of military rule, and a local inflation quite apart from the worldwide trends. Most significant is the fact that is has successfully pushed agriculture down to the extent that the groundnut pyramids of northern Nigeria are now only facts in history books. Government after government, realizing the gravity of the situation, has come out with "bold plans": Operation Feed the Nation, land reform, green revolution, integrated rural development, and so forth are part of Nigeria's political vocabulary. Worse still, Nigeria has of late witnessed what it means to have "living waters" polluted with oil spillage and farmlands laid waste with mining. The first oil export was in 1958; by 1969 oil formed 88 percent of Nigeria's export earnings, tenth in the world and third in Africa, according to the *Nigeria Year Book.* In all this it is the 80 percent or so rural population that bears the brunt of the mismanagement of our resources, and the unequal distribution of the economic benefits accruing therefrom. The quiescence and fatalism of our rural people has been broken more than once. Take the 1969 Agbekoya farmers' agitation and the current protests of farmers on oil lands in several parts of the country. The rural has become a periphery of the urban, and so the law of the migration of labor is operating, leaving those areas to decay in the hands of "the old folks at home." The economic question here is not a matter of class, but one of distribution.

From this one sees the political wisdom in the decision to create more than three states in the federation. There are now twenty capitals for young people to flock to, and if the several petitions for the creation of more states succeed, more capitals will bloom and the "urbanization" of the rural areas will take place. The ordinary social problems created by rapid worldwide urbanization is compounded by the accompanying apparent loss of cultural roots that migrants suffer when they leave a relatively simple and homogeneous village community for the complex anonymity of city life.

Thus the socioeconomic realities of Nigeria have bred all sorts of evils. The "tribalness" of traditional rural life has become "tribalism" on the national scene and grown to be one of the sources of political unrest, nepotism, and favoritism in employment; it has successfully clothed our national unity with a superficiality that makes it utterly vulnerable. Even the country's new constitution recognizes this, and tries to combat it by decreeing against mono-tribal political parties.

Tribalism is also an element in the universal corruption that seems to be endemic in the society and taken as acceptable in the business world. With people who are after the higher social status that comes with wealth, and who want to climb at all costs, there is no limit to the use of the tool, bribery. This has created situation after situation calling for probes, commissions, bureaus of corrupt-practices investigation, and so on—all to no avail. Some have thrown in the towel, declaring bribery to be advanced payment for services to be rendered in the future. Nothing is solved, nothing changes.

The urban-rural axis is but one way of looking at Nigeria. As a community of people we do have a social setup that can be aptly described as a pyramid of human beings with a very wide base, consisting of the majority of the people, who are poor, and tapering very sharply to a rich tip. This situation too is endemic, but not easy to highlight because few could be said to be overtly starving; and there is the traditional "sharing," which ensures that only the down-and-out are truly destitute. So, it is not easy to whip up genuine concern for the Marxist's suffering masses, although their presence is a fact. Moreover, there is an articulate fringe of people with sociopolitical and economic power who make it their business to advocate social justice geared to improving the lot of those at the base of the pyramid. Their aim is to secure "the greatest happiness for the greatest number of people," not as the surplus from the tables of the affluent, but as a right.

By and large the country seems to have reached an equilibrium that makes it difficult to undermine the status quo. The poor have either accepted their lot, or they have been "conned" into thinking that "their time will come." Traditional culture often advocates recognizing and maintaining one's ascribed position in life. Only in extreme hardship is it suggested that one had made a pre-mundane choice of hard luck. The treatment for such is by religious ritual, not by clamoring for social justice.

Onto this picture of the Nigerian society transpose an economy that produces a per capita income of under U.S. $300 per year, and superimpose upon it all the far-reaching arm of religion.

Religion in the Society

Basically Nigerians (like other Africans) are said to be religious. What this means is that at the roots of their way of life are assumptions that are basically religious. Religion is one of the reference points in their lives. I do not join easily in the chorus of scholars and others who have declared the African, and therefore the Nigerian, as being incurably religious. There are people, Nigerians, who have declared that the feeling of dependence and of creatureliness that inspires worship has either left them or they never had any such feelings. I would like to respect their declarations about themselves, as I expect them to respect mine. There are others who claim to have cured themselves of religion or at least of its organized manifestations. Such people in Nigeria are a small fringe, but is by no means an insignificant one, for it consists of vocal, articulate persons who therefore wield influence out of all proportion to their numbers.

These people are not simply religious, they are social crusaders and are themselves people of admirable principles. I am referring to people like Tai Solarin, the educator, columnist, crusader for social justice, and a declared atheist. There is Fela Anikulapo-Kuti, son and grandson of Anglican priests, popular musician and social commentator, who has a song showing up all religious leaders as charlatans and religion itself as a confidence game. Then there is A. O. Awojobi, a professor of mathematics, social commentator, and crusader for probity and integrity, who is simply angry at how Nigeria runs its affairs. He spends himself making sure that "truth" is not thwarted. These have a large following of people, mostly young, who are not necessarily atheists, but who understandably admire their stand on life.

The rest of Nigerians, however, are described by Tai Solarin as "Fair-weather creatures, casual, illogical, outrageously sentimental, *ludicrously blinkered by obfuscating religion.*" Hard words from a member of the sector of Nigeria that would prefer secularism as the doctrine for running Nigeria's affairs. They aim at excellence in public conduct; integrity and service are their watchwords, and they propagate a form of atheistic humanism. Most of these, usually very well educated (by Euro-American standards), have come to this stand because of the obvious domestication associated with Christianity and Islam, the paternalistic policies of Christian missions, and the dubious styles of some Christian leaders. These atheistic elite cannot be overlooked, for they constitute a strong and penetrating voice. As far as their political allegiance is concerned, some have associated themselves with parties that have socialistic tendencies and in which, together with Christians and Muslims, they try to direct the affairs of some of the nineteen states of the federation. Others of them would have preferred parties that were more overtly socialistic.

There is no state religion in Nigeria; the constitution subscribes to religious freedom, but operates in a way that shows a sensitivity to the integral nature of religion in the life of this nation. An interesting example of the modus vivendi of religious institutions and the state is the overt assistance to religious pilgrims, now mostly Muslim, but becoming increasingly Christian too. This is validated by a constitutional clause which says that the government should make adequate facilities for leisure and for social, religious, and cultural life. There is also the teaching of religion in the educational system, its propagation via public media, radio and TV, based on the argument that religion is an integral part of culture. In exchange the state requires prayers and cooperation of religious bodies to foster state policies and for state occasions. Fine, as long as the visions of the two for society are not in conflict.

On the personal level, most Nigerians would fill out legal documents declaring themselves to be either Christian or Muslim, but there is a substantial, and I suspect a growing, number who would declare for the traditional religion (i.e., the pre-Islamic and pre-Christian ancestral cults). Again there are no official statistics; my hunch is that at present there are as many Christians as there are Muslims. The official policies of the government reflect the average Nigerian's prayer for the peaceful coexistence of these two world religions and others. Most Nigerians are at pains to see to it that the latent conflict demonstrated in the Federal *Shari'a* Courts' debates that went on during the formulation of the current constitution should not become real. The inherent contradiction of having a vast population of Muslims administered outside the *shari'a,* and the practicability and justice of having two legal systems in one nation, became very clear.

For the moment there prevails what I consider to be a precarious truce, but it is becoming apparent that wherever there is a church, a bigger mosque is springing up. Several Muslim youth organizations are becoming more and more visible as they buy buses and throw squash parties. Several Euro-American usages are appearing in Islam; white wedding complete with rings and wedding cakes; car stickers with Islamic religious quotations have joined Christian ones in competition for our car parks.

In the face of this new dynamism of Muslims in Nigeria, various Christian communities that would not join together in the Christian Council of Nigeria have now deemed it fit to come together in the Christian Association of Nigeria (CAN), not to confront Islam but to be able to present a united front to government and society at large. The Roman Catholic church in Nigeria is a member of CAN. In fact, the meeting of August 27, 1976, which led to the formation of CAN, was held in the Roman Catholic Secretariat in Lagos. Some church leaders of various denominations had met to submit a memorandum to the federal government. They became convinced that a united force of Christians in Nigeria would achieve much for God through Christ. There are other forces at work in Nigeria striving to make Christianity a real option. There has been, for instance, "Operation Good News" in the past two years, launched by the National Congress on Evangelism in 1978. This program aims at giving every Nigerian the opportunity to become Christian within a few years. Its motto is "Good News for Everyone." An Anglican bishop, the Right Reverend J. A. I. Falope, Diocese of Ilesha, in his presidential address to the Second Synod (May 30, 1980), commenting on the necessity for the operation, said: "Every Christian of our time knows that, more than ever, the world is nearing its end." A bishop of the Methodist church in Nigeria comments on the religious scene as follows: "If we achieve a 'healthy competition' for the good of the country it will be a blessing from God. We would have learned *love* and *obedience*."

Both Christianity and Islam, but more particularly Islam and the "Aladura" churches, have more occasions for making open denunciations of ancestral cults of Nigeria. Nevertheless, on the wings of cultural revival and especially with the Festival of Arts and Culture staged in Nigeria in 1977 (Festac 77), the traditional religion has been given a boost. Drama on television and on stage seems to be consciously structured to show the impotence of Christianity and Islam and the efficacy of the rites of the ancestral cults. In this context Christianity is often the target for ridicule. There is an even more subtle promotion of these cults. This comes with the difficulty of adjusting to urban life. When we are at our wits' end we always seem to say that the rural and the traditional hold the answer. For instance, with the difficulty of dealing with crime, there is a harking back to the past. The suggestion is that in rural Nigeria, with its smaller units of virtually mono-ethnic groups, life was more tolerable and crime minimal. In these communities characterized by fear, superstition, respect for elders, age grades, secret societies, guilds of diviners, priests, and ancestral cults, religion was an ingredient in the complex system of social defense. These communities, it is argued, are marked more by obedience than by the infringement of laws.

One cannot say that all this was pre-1914; this society runs side by side with the superimposed modernization, and it is not only rural, but also urban. The difference between them is only a matter of degree. In the streets of Ibadan, persons have been lynched for theft or for alleged witchcraft even in very recent months. In 1978–79 witchcraft-purging tribunals were still being held in some parts of the federation; in this same period there was a spate of mysterious disappearances of people in the Ijaiye quarter of Abeokuta, some of whose badly mutilated bodies were discovered later. These are not economic crimes, at least not directly; they can only be attributed to the operation of traditional rites and "medicines," some of which are geared toward the well-being of others. There is no gainsaying the fact that the ancestral cults, although not organized as "public corporations," are very much alive as the personal religion of many.

The insistence that Nigerians, whether Christian or Muslim, still continue to practice aspects of the ancestral cults and at crisis points in life, sometimes unavoidably so, is no empty boast. It has to be taken seriously as the traditional religious festivals gain more and more prominence, and traditional rulers reassert themselves as the reference points of Nigerian culture. Since it is often nearly impossible to isolate the religious aspect of traditional culture, any plea or attempt on behalf of the culture (e.g., the use of herbal medicine) is seen as a desire to revive the religion in all its ramifications. This, of course, has given rise to a lot of misunderstandings. The same can be said about Christianity, for those who want to hit at Christianity often do so by hitting at Western culture, which carried it. Even more serious is the fact that there are Africans who do not want to see any attempt at separating the two. We do have in our midst conservative unbelievers as well as conservative believers, and both species are a danger to the church's mission.

This is the context of the Christian mission in Nigeria. The divisions within Christianity are most glaring and constitute a handicap to the mission of the church. Not only are the major World Confessional Families represented; we have churches of our own creation, which are growing daily. One is dealing with a situation of general revival in all three sectors.

Of the three religions, Christianity seems to carry a lot more negative heritage than the others. The vestiges of Constantinianism in the British administration of its colonies tied Christianity and colonial exploitation together in the minds of the nationals. The observance of Sunday rather than Friday or any other traditional "holy" day, though taken for granted by Christians and the British administrators, did not go unnoticed by others. At independence the national holidays doubled as Muslims produced one for every existing one that the Christians had. The ancestral cults have not done so well, but feast days are considered holidays for those involved, and the periodic cultural festivals and the mammoth Festac 77 have more than compensated for the lack of nationwide "holy days."

It is also a fact that while no eyebrows are raised at the predominance of Islamic/Arabic culture, religion, and laws in the country, negative comment is always passed on "Westernized," "hybrid" Nigerian Christians. The spirit of *Uthman dan Fodio* is the determination to plant the flag of Islam beyond Ilorin. This spirit is just as disruptive to traditional religion as the spirit of the white man with Bible in hand. The church's mission, then, is not to bring about a religious revival. The country is already experiencing that phenomenon. The church's mission is not in the building of church schools to compete with the state system. The three religions are already being taught in that system. The question is whether or not the nurturing that leads to commitment can happen in the context of an exam-oriented system. The hospitals that used to be a symbol of Christian concern for the health and wholeness of the human person are now, mostly by the request of the workers in the institutions, state hospitals. The question is: How is the church going to demonstrate this concern? Much has been secularized, but the secularization of Nigerian society is without secularism. There is no overt antireligion stance by government and people of this country. At the same time, I do not consider the Christian Pentecostalism, the electronic churches, and other varieties of nonethical approaches to Christianity that are fast inundating Nigeria a service, either to the mission of the church or to the health of the country. This type of Christianity serenades rather than awakens peoples' consciousness to the world and to God.

Is Christianity at Home in Nigeria?

The mission of the church in Nigeria depends on whether or not the religion it propagates is at home in Nigeria. This central issue cannot be analyzed without going back to the colonial/missionary period, namely, pre-1960. This propagation of Christianity in Nigeria was tainted with the ethnocentrism of the white man, which even as early as 1888 the indigenous people were protesting against. The mission had also been in the nature of an attempted overthrow of the indigenous culture and could not be said to have been entirely devoid of racism while lip service was paid to the declared intention of developing self-supporting, self-propagating, and self-governing churches.

The missionary enterprise was also characteristically a denigration of the culture and ancestral cults of the peoples, and sought to replace these with alien norms and mores. In our missionary heritage we also have to recognize the intense competition of the missions: the Roman Catholic Mission versus the Church Missionary Society (CMS); the CMS versus the Wesleyans; the arrival of fresh missions where others had been laboring; and so on. This, of course, has not gone without notice and comment, and has not disappeared with the movement from mission to church. Acting together as Christians has not been easy. We are finding it difficult to live down our history. Even adopting one syllabus for the teaching of Christianity in schools is a problem for us. If we cannot agree to use the same textbooks in the state system, who will dare talk of one common catechism and other Christian-education materials, let alone of a common effort at evangelization, especially in the narrow sense of efforts toward church growth?

Even if one can sustain the sweeping claim that Nigerians are a religious people, one should still ask: Is Christianity at home in Nigeria and are Nigerians at home with Christianity? More than a third of the population, if not half, would claim to be Christian. In a society that is fast developing a consumer mentality, which imports all the technical gadgets of the industrial world and parades an exaggerated sense of dependence on material wealth, how does one preach the simplicity of the "life that is life indeed?"

This materialism has not been copied from the West; it is part of the traditional culture. It is endemic in the cults that operate an almost "deuteronomic" quid pro quo of righteousness and prosperity, and attributes the penury and the suffering of the righteous to witches and the "evil eye." Any catalogue of the ills of Nigeria may be traced to the search for material things, wealth, and status. The heights to which this search has reached is only the result of the availability of more things for which to reach. It is the natural outcome of the interaction between the traditional culture and the impinging technological culture, so that basically the original question remains: How is the good news of the kingdom understood in such a context?

Let me add here a word on the "youth." When Yakubu Gowon became head of state he was unmarried and thirty-one years old. One can cite many "young people" in responsible positions in Nigeria. If one is to talk of those under thirty, or even of the teenagers, there is very little that one could add to the general character of the Nigerian society sketched above. The youth are found at all levels and in all categories. They simply reflect the values of the society. The demonstration effect of the adult world is too strong. The values and demands of society on them are too strong to allow them to develop a counterculture; they also preclude radical action and radical thinking. Several of the demonstrations of "student power" that I have witnessed have had to do with their own well-being as students: scholarships, accommodation, structure of courses and exams, number of units to be taken and passed, type of certification agitations for or against removals of school authorities, a national service they did not want to do. Only once did they protest in relation to a strictly national event, namely, the assassination of the head of state, Murtala Muhammad. They are just as busy collecting gadgets. In fact most undergraduates are looking forward to driving a Peugeot 504 as a first car.

There is evidence of the beginnings of drug abuse among the younger elements, but this is not limited to the "affluent" youth. There are allegations that most young people involved in crime are also involved in drug abuse, and that it is found in the army, too. These are simply allegations; I have no statistics. But if they are true they do emphasize the fact that our young people have nothing special to offer this society, and that to isolate young people as a special object of mission may prove a failure if based on some starry-eyed idea that they are different. It is true, however, that both Christian missions and Muslim institutions are busy doing this. In numerical growth they may be succeeding, but if one is looking for radical change of their style of life, then I dare say all this effort is a colossal failure. To be effective in this area one will need to change the whole ethos of the society.

It is also a fact that it is not only the urban that is touched by Westernization, and its inherent materialism and the unavoidable cultural components. Tai Solarin, in his usual penetrating way, selected for comment Dr. K. C. Anyanwu's indictment that most of us (referring to the Western-educated elite) are "rooted not here, but there in Europe and America and Tierra del Fuego." The rural Roman Catholics may not connect *feijoun* with Brazil, but they do take it as being Roman Catholic. Christians are to be found in all states, cities, and hamlets.

No culture is static. What is jealously guarded as Nigerian traditional culture today cannot be said to be "pure." What is traditional Hausa culture and what has taken on Arabic/Islamic accretions? Even internally there cannot be a purely Igbo culture that has not subtly added or subtracted either Western elements or those of neighboring ethnic groups. The emergent Nigerian culture is bound to be a "new creation." Whenever people speak of "our culture," one ought to listen carefully in order to locate the culture and discover its content. There are naturally common elements that cut across the diversity, and even more important, a richness that needs to be fed into human culture. Through all these, whether consciously or not, some Christian elements have entered.

What Sort of Mission Does Nigerian Society Call For?

In such a complex religious and social context, the mission of the church cannot be effective if it is only a potted plant. Neither can a blueprint, even one devised by nationals, stand much chance if it remains inflexible. It goes without saying that, given Nigeria's history, the missionaries who stand a chance of being acceptable to the government are not those who are foreign nationals; and even if the Christian community itself is open to other nationalities, they naturally are not going to take racist elements or ethnocentric preaching. It is also clear that there is more to be done by the church in Nigeria than preaching and increasing membership. These are important, but we have now entered a period when proclamation has to be not only by word of mouth and symbolic acts but by effective action. To highlight but one possible action: the prophetic voice of the church has to be heard against all that dehumanizes and on behalf of all that brings fullness of life. But there is also the prophetic act as well as acts of mercy. A holistic approach is the only viable and effective method of preaching Christ and the kingdom that he came to announce and to bring.

The new sociopolitical forces at work in Nigeria and their resultant stress on human life and human relations are glaring. I have tried to present a kaleidoscope of the atmosphere and the religious response to it. People are simply bewildered. Nigerian prophets, like Obadare, can draw crowds of distressed people for months on end. People seeking life, children, wealth, promotion; people afraid of witches, of the machinations of evil people; people who fear that they themselves may be witches, and these are not all in material penury. An Obadare crowd is typical of the Book-of-Common-Prayer description of "all sorts and conditions of men." The motivation to preach Christ is to announce the Christian Victor. We do not preach Christ in competition with Islam or with the ancestral cults; we preach Christ because, in our evaluation of the situation, he is the answer. He is not being preached as the Aladdin's lamp to provide all our material needs, nor as the source of a spirituality that is a tranquilizer to keep us from experiencing reality. Rather, we preach Christ because in our estimation there is nothing so revolutionary as his total dependence on God, which manages also not to be fatalistic. The new situation in Nigeria, that is the heightening of the struggle to get material comforts, as well as to feel like people whose past is rooted in Africa and in God, demands a gospel of the lordship of God over the whole cosmos and the whole of history. This is the mission of the church: to announce and denounce, to break down and to build up, to encourage and to dissuade. It is the work of the church universal. But the "local" church stands a better chance of getting to the heart of the matter and the hearts of the people.

The mission is universal, but I submit that after two thousand years one ought to be able to say that in whatever nation Christianity exists, the responsibility for mission in that locality should be primarily that of the local church in that place. This does not preclude the utilization of distinctive insights and skills from other places; but the latter should not be the predominant element. Although, in general, one can say that the state is open to the universal church, one has to take into account indigenization laws that seek to regulate the participation of non-nationals in the workforce of the nation. Preaching is definitely not seen as an area needing foreign technical assistance. In practice, therefore, "unskilled foreign missionaries" will find it difficult to justify their presence in Nigeria. In fact, even church leaders tend to seek non-nationals who have "secular skills" needed in the work of the church, and there are many. A missionary wishing to serve in Nigeria ought to train in some secular service that is in short supply in Nigeria.

This problem is not specific to Nigeria. Wherever African governments have felt the heavy hands of colonialism, imperialism, and neocolonial exploitation, and have associated their ills and woes with the white man, the church has gone into the basket as a companion to these systems. Therefore, for the health of the local mission and of the universal church, multiracial, multicultural ecumenical teams of missionaries would be the ideal face of Christianity to present—and to me, the most authentic face of the religion.

Naturally this will mean that in Nigeria, too, Christians must be oriented to see themselves as "sending churches." Nigeria is a "wealthy" country, not so much in terms of oil wealth as in its culture. Nigeria has skilled people and ardent Christians who, even without formal theological and pastoral education, will enrich many Euro-American churches, not to mention other African countries, or Asia and Latin America. Nigeria does have a mature Christian community and ought to be seen to be contributing to the universal church.

Some Specific Areas for Mission

The work of the church in teaching and health care, in social welfare and personal counseling has become traditional. What a Nigerian-church-in-mission needs to rethink is the specific forms of this ministry, which will serve the needs of Nigeria. Take the teaching ministry. Education has been interpreted to mean schooling, and so, with increased government participation in this aspect of education, the church has been thrown into consternation. What shall we do now that we do not have any specifically "mission schools"? Even in this regard, the thinking has centered around the teaching of religion in these schools. In principle our three major religions—Christianity, Islam, and ancestral cults—are permissible throughout the formal educational system, and the government entrusts to them what shall be taught to the adherents of the religion, at least at the junior levels. At the moment a spate of syllabi development and textbook writing is going on in this area. The project brings into the limelight several delicate and complicated questions, and much in-depth work is still needed and will be needed even after the projects themselves shall have been completed. The difference in theology and ecclesiastical authority alone is enough to thwart the project. To mention another question, should a Christian teach Islam?

This structured teaching of religion in the educational system consumes so much

attention that the church has done little to improve catecheses and Christian education among its members. This does not, of course, apply to all families of the Christian community; some do put a high premium on this duty and execute it honorably.
This most vital aspect of the church's mission should have a high priority in the
church's planning. Now that all forms of media are becoming increasingly utilized by
all who have something to tell the nation, the church will need to make more effective
use of these means of communication. The variety in the form of presenting a message is inexhaustible; all the church needs is a little more creativity.

While the church in Nigeria tarries, countermessages are being fed to the nation;
"more" has become the aim of all advertisement. Tracts are flowing in from the
United States while the "electronic" media are being utilized to denigrate Christianity or to promote certain versions of it whose sponsors can pay for the time. Meanwhile the Roman Catholic church and other World Confessional Families sit smugly
in their pews splitting hairs as to who can legitimately distribute the "Holy Elements."

Take another aspect of mission, the healing ministry. Health care in Nigeria is
principally in the hands of the government, but not nearly enough is being done, and
so private participation has not been banned. Moreover, not nearly enough attention
is paid to preventive medicine, including environmental sanitation. Thus this area
of service is also wide open. Any Christian community that can help to train water
and sewage engineers, garbage-disposal specialists, food-preservation specialists,
drought- tsetse- and mosquito-control personnel, and make sure that there are facilities to enable them to function efficiently, will be doing "God's work." All these
should be the churches' concern, not necessarily to develop structures to deal with
them directly, but train and orient and equip Nigerians to want to do these things.

Welfare services can be as varied as the needs of people are varied and complicated. The care of the physically handicapped, and their involvement in the mission
of the church, is an old area needing new thinking. The care of the aged and the
motherless and other disadvantaged people are traditional in Christianity, but they
are not obviously so in Nigeria. The nurture of young people into adult life and the
inculcating of professional ethics into all is a service the church can render as part of
its mission. The whirlwind pace of life in Nigeria is such that many people feel lost,
while others are swindlers to various degrees. The church's mission is to both categories: How does one cope with such a life? Educational, vocational, marriage, family,
and other types of counseling services have to replace impotent lamentations against
abortions legal and otherwise. The Christian vocation to lay all emphasis on the
sacredness of the human being is rendered unconvincing by our attitudes toward
other forms of dehumanization.

For me to speak of social welfare is to be reminded of the needs of the individual
person. Other philosophies and ideologies may operate on the concept of the
"masses." Not so the church. Caring for individual needs and recognizing people as
persons is not individualism; neither is it against the "communal ideology" of traditional culture. Therefore, in any missionary enterprise the church to be true to itself
should build into its plans the needs of *persons*. Small prayer groups, work teams of
threes and fours, group counseling and therapy are necessary antidotes to the ano-

nymity of Lagos, Ibadan and Port Harcourt, and Kano. But the traditional "confessional ministry" remains a model still valid for individual counseling and serves a good purpose if we can broaden the scope of "confession."

An individual congregation like Saint Christopher's, near where I live, when it becomes the focus of mission may find it necessary to hold group discussions for petrol-station attendants, "wayside mechanics," farmers, domestic workers—most of whom will also be attending their town's union meetings. Congregational worship alone is not sufficient. Christian education events ought to be designed to fit into evenings, weekends, school vacations, and the many public holidays. This latter may be profitably utilized for evangelistic events of the revival type. In this way we shall see both souls and bodies of people fed, and we shall be preaching the whole gospel to the whole human being—and worldwide to the whole human race.

Work and Worship

For me it would be an anomaly if the church should undertake the humanizing work suggested above without reflecting that work in its worship. The controversies as to how the eucharistic liturgy could be adapted should not be allowed to stifle other developments in relevant worship. The Eucharist may be left medieval and said in Latin, if people wish to keep its mystifying effect (I personally do not believe it should be so); but that should not preclude other acts of worship that focus on the realities of miners in mining areas, and of traders in commercial centers. The whole of life should come before God for renewal. In the ancestral cults of Nigeria, tutelary gods play significant roles. Worshipers of Sanno, the god of thunder, have broadened their base from traditional blacksmiths to all who use iron implements, especially drivers and mechanics; and all of them take part in the traditional festival geared toward securing success in the coming year. Whatever acts of worship the mission enjoins cannot afford to be unrelated to the experience of the worshipers. Worship should reflect life, not only as it should be lived but as it is lived, for even what is contrary to the design of God must be brought to God so that God may purify and utilize it in the service of the kingdom.

In the year of King Uzziah's death I saw the Lord Yahweh seated on a high throne; his train filled the sanctuary; above him stood seraphs, each one with six wings: two to cover its face, two to cover its feet and two for flying.

And they cried out one to another in this way,
"Holy, holy, holy is Yahweh Sabaoth.
His glory fills the whole earth."

The foundations of the threshold shook with the voice of the one who cried out, and the Temple was filled with smoke. I said:

"What a wretched state I am in! I am lost,
for I am a man of unclean lips
and I live among a people of unclean lips . . ." [Isa. 6:1-5].

Only as we confess our lack of effective work of the past and are cleansed by burning coals from the altar, can all of us Christians in Nigeria and those of the universal church effectively say, "Here I am, send me." Until then, all and any human plans to go on God's errands are doomed to failure.

10

A REFLECTION FROM THE CONTEXT OF THE LATIN AMERICAN CHURCH

Juan Marcos Rivera and Moisés Rosa Ramos

For today's Christians, "the world is broad and strange," to borrow the title of a novel by Ciro Alegría. The twentieth century has gradually dissociated itself from traditional Christian values and assimilated the values imposed upon it by material interests and technocracy. This secular historical development has not been linear, however. Society has passed through, and is still passing through, a series of contradictions. Christianity, confronted with this process, and yet holding fast to a utopia of the kingdom of God·as the finality of history, has been unable to work out a material basis upon which to erect its powerful moral standards and demands, its search for and order of justice and love. Of course, this deficiency has not prevented it from responding aggressively to any attempt to deify the secular order. Nevertheless, Christianity has continued to lose ground to the process of secularization, powerful in its own right, which is inflicting itself upon our world.

One of the great handicaps of Christianity in our milieu has been the "privatization" of faith, the reduction of faith to the purview of the individual. "Christianity is a value of universal spirit, having its roots in the most intimate recesses of human individuality."[1] This is how Miguel de Unamuno begins his book, *The Agony of Christianity.* Spanish and Latin American Christianity is one of the loci of this privatization of the faith, of piety, and of pastoral practice, and the result is a docility, on the part of the individual as well as on that of the Christian community that is the church, in the face of the advance of the secularizing process. In the face of the challenges of Latin American history—the wars of independence, industrialization, imperialism, and militarism, all facets of this same secularizing process—the church's advances and retreats have resulted in a loss of historical time, of physical

Juan Marcos Rivera, from Puerto Rico, is presently in charge of the Pastoral of Comfort and Solidarity in the Latin American Council of Churches. For the past eight years he has worked in ecumenical activities leading to the formation of the Council. Moisés Rosa Ramos assisted him in the writing of this paper.

and moral space, and of the precious lives of many Christians and non-Christians concerned about the dehumanizing direction taken by the history of the Latin American peoples.

Another point to be made concerning the situation of the Latin American church has to do with the power of Christians who are sensitive to our condition of poverty and exploitation. Latin American people are dramatically poor. It all began with the history of colonization—Latin America's incorporation into the European world. Our later incorporation into the economic empire of the United States, while occasioning the collapse of exploitative structures of a feudal ilk, also impoverished the vast majority of the people. In response to this situation a poor church has arisen, a church of poor people and those who opt for them, in contrast with and opposed to those sectors of society that profit by this impoverishment. It is also opposed to the traditional church, which clings to the individualization of the faith and its alliances with the dominant classes.

What has been the church's response to the concrete process of secularization being suffered by the peoples of Latin America? We shall attempt an answer to this question by taking into account three aspects of our history and our reality: Latin American Christianity's deep roots; the course of the secularization process and of the church's responses; possibilities for a response to the present situation of exploitation and militarist secularization that the continent is suffering.

Once this question has been considered in these three aspects, we shall be in a position to answer the unavoidable challenge that the process of secularization presents to the Latin American church.

First, however, it is necessary to establish a basic presupposition. We are making a serious attempt to work out a theology whose point of departure will be our option for the poor. This option obliges us to look at Jesus in his poverty, as the Gospels show him.

Jesus as a Poor Person

Jesus was born into a poor community. Mary brought forth her son, wrapped him in swaddling clothes, and laid him in a manger, because there was no room for him in the inn. His first visitors were some shepherds, who evidently were poor, for they were engaged in keeping watch by night over their flock in the vicinity of Bethlehem. On the occasion of the presentation of the child in the temple, Mary offered the sacrifice prescribed in the law for a mother who was poor—which, according to the book of Leviticus, was two turtledoves or two young stock doves. According to the law, faced with a lack of means to offer a lamb, poor mothers offered these instead: "If she cannot afford a lamb, she is to take two turtledoves or two young pigeons . . ." (Lev. 12:8).

According to the Gospel of Luke, this was Mary's offering, which shows her lack of means and her poverty: "And when the day came for them to be purified as laid down by the Law of Moses, they took him up to Jerusalem to present him to the Lord . . . and also to offer in sacrifice, in accordance with what is said in the Law of the Lord, *a pair of turtledoves or two young pigeons"* (Lk. 2:22,24).

A second datum that bears on our examination of the Gospels is Jesus' preference for the poor. This is shown in the choice of his disciples, who were selected from among poor and laboring people. When he took up a relationship with persons such as Matthew or Zacchaeus, he demanded a change of attitude toward wealth. He did not depreciate the rich, but he did demand that they join the chorus of those who were seeking justice, by an act of renunciation of what they had unjustly acquired. In the case of the rich young man the demand is radical: "Jesus said, 'If you wish to be perfect, go and sell what you own and give the money to the poor, and you will have treasure in heaven; then come, follow me'" (Mt. 19:21).

Jesus' concern for the poor is demonstrated by his special attention to the outcasts of Israel: the sick, women, children, and poor people in general. The Beatitudes, in Matthew as well as in Luke, express his most intimate sentiments toward those in need. In Luke's Gospel, in enunciating his program Jesus cites a text of Isaiah in which this predilection becomes altogether explicit:

> *The spirit of the Lord has been given to me,*
> *for he has anointed me.*
> *He has sent me to bring the good news to the poor. . .*
> [Lk. 4:18; cf. Isa. 61:1–2].

One last datum is recorded in Jesus' death. He died between two robbers, by the side of the royal highway, facing the garbage dump of the city. The gospel kerygma makes a special point of this.

> In your minds you must be the same as
> Christ Jesus:
>
> His state was divine
> yet he did not cling
> to his equality with God
> but emptied himself
> to assume the condition of a slave,
> and became as men are;
> and being as all men are,
> he was humbler yet,
> even to accepting death,
> death on a cross [Phil. 2:5–8].

In this sense Jesus is the heir of God's solicitude for the poor, which is so salient in the law and the prophets. Albert Gelin has written:

A few texts will suffice to summarize the whole struggle on behalf of the poor, whose portrait we have attempted to sketch. It is said that our age has discovered new traits of poverty. Nevertheless, the circumstances of poverty in which the people of God found themselves in the Old Testament were substantially the same, and the disinherited form an immense procession, which cries out to Yahweh over its state of dehumanization, its utter lack of security and any possibility of fashioning a future for itself, and its oppression and hopelessness. And the prophets are like the echoes of these lamentations.[2]

Our investigation of poverty must be brief, and cannot take into account all variations on the biblical theme. The aspect cited represents the main course of biblical thought in this area. It also represents God's option in the Old Testament and Jesus' option in the New. And there is no doubt that, for its part, the primitive Christian community made that same option: "they sold their goods and possessions and shared out the proceeds among themselves according to what each one needed" (Acts 2:45).

The ideal of evangelical poverty still endures. It is embodied in the medieval orders, as a protest against the boundless concern for wealth in some circles of the church. In Latin America today the church is going in search of the gospel poor. The attainment of this state and attitude has been a long historical process, in which the church has been recovering its own identity and dissociating itself from the false conceptions imposed upon it by the domination, both cultural and economic, to which we are heir.

Below we shall describe the process and the difficulties that we have had to go through in order to achieve our present understanding of the church's mission, in the face of the thrust of secular conceptions of life and history.

The Epic of Latin America: A Secularizing Process

Latin American thought is pervaded by a Christian conception of the world. The Spanish Christianity arriving with the *Conquista* not only spread over vast geographical expanses; it took deep cultural root as well. We have the clearest example in the effort to re-create the image of Christ in our thought. The epic of the South American Christ traced by Juan A. Mackay[3] still persists, and is reappearing in the thought of José Miguez Bonino, Leonardo Boff, and Jon Sobrino, to name the Christologists most read in our milieus.

The basic finding of this research was a surprise to no one: Christ's image in our milieus conforms to the vision of him held by the dominating power. One facet presents him in his agony, utterly defeated. The other—in order to justify the domination—presents a Christ victorious, distant, and terrible.

Because Latin American thought has been permeated by the Christian perception of the world, the three stages of our peoples' struggle have occurred on two fronts. One is that of the recovery of the image of Christ as the agent of liberation. The other is the struggle with the process of secularization. The wars of Latin independence, the populism that survived until the middle of this century, and the search for a Latin American way of development (harassed by imperialism and its instrument of domination, militarism) are, in their inmost essence, various efforts to erase the image of a Latin America riveted to the static condition of traditional Catholicism.

It is not our intention to establish our thesis by overwhelming the reader with all the evidence. We shall content ourselves with a summary description of the structure of production characterizing the three eras mentioned and the church's response to each.

The Wars of Independence

It is no wonder that the process by which our peoples won their independence was guided by elements that were functionally non-Christian. It was the liberals, the positivists, the Masons, and the most anticlerical elements of our society that struck alliance against traditional, Catholic Spain. The anticlerical ideals of the French Revolution influenced the liberators as well. This process of secularization was not only a break with the church, but a break that launched a search for something else—the search for a place in the world, and the incorporation of Latin America into the modern world.

Painful as was the struggle for independence, the search for a place in the world was and is even more painful. From the point of view of the structure of production of goods and wealth within our countries, there still persists the battle between the production sector of the economy and the commercial sector of the exporters. Political independence did not necessarily mean economic independence. As Javier Iguiniz has pointed out, "Latin America's independence was mainly a military event. It brought about the breaking of economic bonds with the mother country, but it did not mean an independence from the colonial past."[4]

The colonial relationship was supplanted by a new form of outside interference, which came from the United States and which has a history of its own. This new intervention resulted in the creation of the colonial, semicolonial, and dependent capitalist models that obtain at the present moment in Latin America's history.

The response of the church, and especially the European church, was of a missionary character, directed to the preservation of the colonial relationship through the employment structure and patronage.[5]

The End of the Liberal Era and the Rise of Populism

Beginning with the decade of the 1930s, Latin America had to respond to the economic collapse of the capitalist world. That decade was truly a terrible one. The deep suffering of our peoples was greatly intensified. But at the same time it was an era of increased hope, for now the poor were involving themselves in the political struggles. This is the age of populism, blooming in the hot day of the *caudillos,* the new heads of state. The church's slow response was to begin to incorporate itself within the social processes and to ask itself the great questions pervading our theological atmosphere today. From now on, secularization, the religious hoax, and the almighty social structure will be challenged by the new popular classes on the upsurge.

This second era was the product of a grave crisis. Freed from the markets of the United States and Europe, Latin America turned inward. It joined the great industrial advance. Large sectors of the population were incorporated into the new social changes. The core population of peasants, which had been so docile to efforts at evangelization, turned toward heavy industry, and traditional Christianity underwent a sclerosis and a loss of momentum in favor of a religious expression that was more political and civil in character, as well as more rootless.[6]

The church continued to involve itself with the social processes, now for progress, now serving as a mechanism for the retardation of these processes. The ecumenical movement in the Catholic church, the result of imminent threats to that church, had its echoes in Latin American Protestantism, provoking new attitudes there as well. At the same time the *comunidades de base,* the grassroots ecclesial communities, arose within the Catholic church, and a great number of Christians there were concerned with all these rapid social changes.

All this flowed together in the second Latin American Bishops' Conference, at Medellín in 1968. There the church redefined its task. It made a clear option for the poor, and reinforced the whole theological development that Vatican II had initiated in the Christian world.

From that moment on, the mission of the church was an immense methodological and practical problem, resulting in Latin America's contribution to the world of theology: the theology of liberation. One of the driving forces of this new reflection is the theme of the poor. This approach consists in the identification of the poor in Latin America with the poor of the Gospels. Little by little the poor who organized the grassroots ecclesial communities formed a new church, the people's church, the church of the vast majority.

The church that opted for the poor at Medellín now walked in the company with them. As a result the more conservative elements of the church were compelled, by the option for the poor and the dynamics of the new church, to make an adequate response to the situation. This is the era in which the mission of the church redefined itself in terms of liberation.

The era was a short one. Populism was supplanted by militarism, and the decade of the 1960s came upon Latin America with its tragic ledger of pain and death.

The Present Stage: From Populism to the Military Dictatorships

The third era that we wish to sketch is also the result of a crisis, a new one: the crisis of the capitalist system, which took a turn for the worse during the latter part of the 1960s and climaxed in 1974-75. There is a great deal of general documentation on this whole crisis, to which one may refer for its causes and its consequences in the global purview. What we should like to do here is discuss it a bit from the viewpoint of Latin America. The social scientists have worked out a construct for the crisis in our particular context, which they call the "theory of dependence." Then they make use of this theory to rationalize our situation of poverty and underdevelopment.

A general characteristic of these estimations of our situation is their profound contempt for world history in general and that of our lands in particular. This is the only possible explanation for the reappearance of the so-called "non-economic factors." And indeed, a disdain for history, or its caricaturing as a movement of the stock-market index, is perfectly understandable in the imperialist thinker. No one enjoying power likes to be reminded that he is flesh and bone, that he was born, and that he will have an end.[7]

Beginning with Raúl Prebisch's discovery in 1949 of the root cause of our dependency,[8] thinkers like André Gunder Frank, Ruy Mauro Marini, Fernando Cardoso, Enzo Faletto, Theotonio dos Santos, and Agustín Cueva worked out the theory of dependency methodologically. We have discovered that its causes are structural in nature, and neither racial nor owing to some inability to carry forward our own projects of development and of actualization as a people.

While the theoreticians were busy searching out the causes of underdevelopment in Latin America, the people, in their search for an escape from poverty, were taking initiatives that finally threatened the stability of the domination. Beginning in 1965, when the military assumed command in Brazil, the specter of militarism arose all over the continent. Argentina, Chile, Bolivia, Paraguay, Uruguay, Ecuador, Peru, Panama—all combined the classic old dictatorships with the new, totalitarian, fascist-style militarism. It is not just a matter of the rebirth of the old personal and despotic dictatorship. We are in the presence of a new phenomenon: militarism. Prebisch writes:

> The personalism of the *caudillo* is replaced by a bureaucracy. The military is no longer confined to the role of arbiter in disputes arising between various factions of the middle class, without ever eliminating anyone, and the assignment of defending the national territory against the threat, or the actuality, of aggression from without. The armed forces have taken control of the entire apparatus of state, which they now strive to mold to their own image. The military has come to power. Military values are substituted for civil principles in the organization of society. The new parameters presiding over this enterprise of restructuring have been codified in a doctrine—the doctrine of National Security. It is a war doctrine, whose first effect is to identify the friendly camp and the enemy camp and to work out appropriate strategic manners of approaching each.[9]

While it is not a monopoly of this region of the globe, militarism does have its peculiarities in Latin America. One of its most significant contributions is its secularizing nature, in spite of its appeal to the defense of Western Christian civilization. In the limits it imposes on the activity of almost all liberal sectors of society, civil as well as ecclesiastical, it betrays its deeply anti-Christian character. We are witnessing a ferocious attack launched by a sector of society represented by the military, with the purpose of bringing our peoples to terms, in the global context of a world in crisis, and of maintaining global equilibrium in the midst of the crisis of capitalism, at the cost of even the most fundamental human rights.

The terrible thing about this new situation is that it is erected upon a traditional Christian vision, while its actual working out constitutes in every respect a secularizing process that permits the introduction of a foreign system of values—the massive sterilization of women, the devaluation of the person, and the technologizing of the state to its most brutal extreme in the use of torture.

The response of the church in such a situation has not been long in coming. A document concerned with Chile asserts: "The church has had to make a radical choice between loyalty to the people, and thereby to itself, and submission to the military junta," and then adds: "The Chilean church has recovered its role as political critic."[10]

In general this has been the response of a Latin American church confronted with a new brand of secularization, which attempts to use the church's symbols to justify total war on the people. The response of the church at the present moment deserves a particular description and study of its own. But it would be impossible to cover the whole extent of the conflicts our church is going through in the space of this article, so we shall only touch upon a few aspects of the various situations in which we must function within the national churches, and say something about the general responses of the third general Latin American Bishops' Conference (CELAM) in Puebla, Mexico, and the Latin American Council of Churches, which met in Oaxtepec, Mexico, in 1972.

The Latin American Church in the Face of the Secularization Process

The process of secularization is the product of a more scientific view of the world. Viewed as such, the process itself can have a positive moral evaluation. Its essential nature can be the object of inquiry. But its actuality, its evident advance in all areas of human affairs is undeniable.

There is no doubt that the first two stages can be evaluated as positive, inasmuch as they supplied liberty and alternatives for a self-realization to be attained by our peoples. The independence of the Latin American nations, and the populist response, activated the masses and incorporated them into history as agents. At bottom what we discern here is the thread that runs through the very history of humanity on the planet—the search for new orders of justice and peace. This thread of continuity has seen its interruptions, its steps backward, at the hands of social groups, then dictators, and more recently the militarism of North American inspiration. It is evident that the present situation, with its dehumanizing character, has the qualities inherent in the process of the de-Christianization of the world. The latter movement, proclaimed by the new prophets, arises in obedience to the demands of the search for more rational forms of the distribution of goods and wealth, and the concerted efforts of human beings to snatch away nature's secrets. This should not be interpreted as God's withdrawal as if he were no longer interested in us. It does not even destroy our traditional conception of the faith. What is happening is that Christ is being crucified in the living flesh of the poor. This is a new instance of what the Gospel of John (1:14) defines as incarnation:

> The Word was made flesh,
> he lived among us, . . .
> full of grace and truth.

The Christian faith survives the vacillations of reason and human intelligence. This is why, every passing day, the church, which is identifying with the cry of the poor, is finding ever new meaning in the cross—and is recovering the hope of resurrection.

Various national churches bear witness to this new theological position—El Salvador, Chile, Nicaragua, Brazil. The church has answered the challenge of military repression in each of these countries by committing itself to solidarity with the oppressed.

The Church in El Salvador. The church in El Salvador has recently been crucified in the person of its archbishop, Oscar Arnulfo Romero. On March 24, 1980, a sharpshooter entered the chapel where he was celebrating Mass and dispatched him with a single bullet to the heart. This bloody deed is but one more added to the list by the military government and the fourteen families who govern the most densely populated country of Central America. Catholic priests have been threatened, abused, exiled, and assassinated in the effort to silence the voice of the church. "One of the ways in which the Salvadoran episcopate has demonstrated its ideological fortitude and total fidelity to the gospel is by not succumbing to the temptation of a false 'Christian love' which fails to demand justice right to the very end."[11]

The Church in Nicaragua. The following statement, made by Ernesto Cardenal in 1977, exemplifies the response of Nicaraguan Christians to the criminal offensive launched against the people by the tyrannical Anastasio Somoza.

ERNESTO CARDENAL: "I AM A MEMBER OF THE SANDINISTA FRONT,
OUT OF LOYALTY TO THE GOSPEL"

I consider my sentencing to prison as a matter of much honor. I am accused of illicit association with the FSLN. I take the occasion publicly to declare that I actually am a member of the FSLN—another matter of much honor.

The FSLN is a clandestine organization, and obviously while I was in Nicaragua I could not make this declaration, but in the present circumstances I can make it, and the high command of the Frente Sandinista de Liberación Nacional has judged it opportune that I do so.

I have considered it my duty, as poet and priest, to belong to this movement. In Latin American countries struggling for liberation, the poet cannot remain aloof from the struggles of his people. Much less a priest.

I belong to the FSLN first and foremost out of loyalty to the gospel. I seek a radical, a profound change, a new, just society of brothers and sisters, as the gospel teaches. And I consider this a "sacerdotal" struggle as well, just as Camilo Torres did.

The FSLN is a movement of the most valiant and precious of Nicaraguan youth. By their struggle they have made it a proud thing to be a Nicaraguan. As the poet José Coronel Urtecho said, they are the best youth of Nicaragua and of all America, and many of them are genuine saints.[12]

The Chilean Church. The response of the Chilean church to the military coup that overthrew the constitutional government of Salvador Allende in 1973 reveals the enormous difficulty faced by the whole Latin American church in its struggle to serve the people. Bishop Sergio Méndez Arceo, of Cuernavaca, Mexico, gives the following description:

> The most excellent and hopeful characteristic of the local Chilean churches, separately and together, has turned out to be the encounter of socialism and Christianity in the revolutionary praxis. This vital confrontation is not an academic one, although reason and science were indeed shattered by the growing threats of violence against the regime of Salvador Allende, already weakened by concerted opposition as well as by the errors of the parties of the Unidad Popular.
>
> When the coup occurred, the Chilean hierarchy was not abreast of things, because it had not dissociated itself from the capitalist system—which Paul VI had condemned indeed, but without either serious political analysis or clear theology.[13]

This is perhaps the most typical response of the Latin American church, which cannot be faithless to the people, and yet has found no clear path leading to the full actualization of our peoples.

Brazil. This emporium of wealth and forest has for fifteen years been the scene of a military exercise, the establishment of a dependent capitalism as a form of domination, and the castration of the popular struggle. Its model and symbol, the Brazilian militia, has unleashed a specter of torture, war, and death—and not only against men of war, but against many Christians committed to the poor.

The exemplary loyalty of the church of Brazil had been organizing since before the military coup of 1965, in the grassroots ecclesial communities inspired by Vatican Council II. Brazil played an important role at Medellín, and the strong voices of a handful of bishops from this huge country made themselves heard in Latin America and the world as an expression of evangelical commitment. The resounding voice of Dom Helder Cámara, the apostle of nonviolence, stands out among all the rest. This is the bishop from whom we hear words like these:

> Permit me the humble boldness to take a position:
>
> I respect those whose conscience obliges them to opt for violence—not the violence of the armchair guerrillas, but that of those who have given proof of their sincerity by the sacrifice of their life. It seems to me that the memory of Camilo Torres and Che Guevara deserve as much respect as that of the Reverend Dr. Martin Luther King.
>
> I denounce the wounders of justice and preventers of peace, both on the right and on the left, as the real fomenters of violence.
>
> My personal vocation, however, is that of a pilgrim of peace, following the example of Paul VI. Personally I had rather be killed a thousand times than kill.
>
> This personal position is based on the gospel. A whole lifetime of effort to

understand and to live the gospel leads me to the deep conviction that although the gospel can and should be called revolutionary, it is revolutionary in the sense that it demands of every one of us a conversion. We have no right to close ourselves up in selfishness: we must open ourselves to the love of God and also to the love of human beings. And we need only look at the Beatitudes—the quintessence of the gospel message—in order to see that for Christians the choice rings loud and clear: we Christians are on the side of nonviolence. But this is by no means a matter of choosing weakness and passivity. To be nonviolent is to believe more in the power of truth, justice, and love than in the power of war, murder, and hate.[14]

The Church in Cuba. Perhaps the most difficult situation through which the church in Latin America has passed has occurred in Cuba. This country of 10 million inhabitants, located in the eye of the Caribbean hurricane, has lived a socialist type of revolution for twenty years now. The Cuban secularizing process was and is comprehensive. The whole society is directed toward national reconstruction on scientific principles. The transition from a situation of exploitation and social marginalization to the intense involvement of all sectors of the Cuban population in its political life went far beyond the social doctrine of the church, and the church entrenched itself in its counterrevolutionary positions. This damaged it not only in the eyes of the government, but in those of the whole Cuban people, although this people continues to be Christian.

The earmarks of social redemption—a campaign against illiteracy; a fight for the right to work, for personal and national dignity, and for solidarity with the peoples of the world; a primary interest in infants and children; a public-health program; the disappearance of straw-hut housing; and the struggle against all the consequences of underdevelopment and poverty—all this meant little to the church as compared with the loss of certain individual liberties, the collectivization of life, and the loss of its own prestige in Cuban society.

It should be pointed out that Catholic and Protestant churches alike had been closely linked with the prerevolutionary regime and glorified and legitimized exploitation and poverty, drinking at the table of the tyrants.

Although the traditional sectors of the church still have not found their place within a socialist society, the popular church has been making its contributions to the revolutionary process. "Church" here includes Pentecostals, Presbyterians, the Union Seminary, the MEC, and other ecumenical movements, which have seen today's Cuban society as the vehicle of a secular and humanizing process with a clear potential for convergence with the gospel.

The Church in Puerto Rico. Seen from the outside, the Puerto Rican church centers around two great nuclei, the Apostolic and Roman Catholic church, and the Protestants. The latter are divided in turn into the Episcopal church, the Lutheran and other mainline Protestant churches, the Pentecostals, and the lesser sects. The history of Puerto Rican Christianity has two aspects that must be examined before that history can be adequately understood in the twentieth century. They are (1) the profound link between culture and religion, and (2) the long battle between traditional Catholicism's tenacious resistance in the peasant culture, and the aggressive, transcultural Protestantism accompanying the colonial domination of the United States over Puerto Rico.

On the other hand, the Puerto Rican form of religious piety has been the result of a long process of internalization, appropriation, and adaptation of the content of the faith to the content of native culture. This is revealed by the high degree of cultural resistance on the part of Puerto Ricans themselves to the heavy-handed process of "rebirth" and transculturation hammered away at by the imported church.

During the long period of the colonial struggles of the twentieth century, once the peasant culture was destroyed the Protestants began to win the battle. The conversion of the Puerto Ricans to the "gospel" has to be seen as massive if one takes into consideration that the process of secularization advances in step with it, and that it must do its recruiting from traditional Catholicism.

All this has ultimately resulted in a highly motivated, militant church, no longer centered on a conflict with Protestantism, which is creating church expressions in response to the basic conflict under which the Puerto Rican people struggle: their colonial situation. Here the Catholic church has generated the pastoral approach of the *comunidades de base,* which, along with the projects, efforts, and organizations of the Protestants, has come forth as a decolonializing and liberating response. On the other hand, the Protestant church has managed a consensus and regimentation based on coercion, very similar to that generated by the authority of the Catholic church, and making the most of the current political situation, or assiduously glorifying Puerto Rico's colonial status as a territory of the United States.

The church, supported by the middle class, gives that class the system that is most to its advantage, and so the church holds a preferred status in the political structure—supporting (and softening) the unfair advantage of that preferred status with a certain effort at raising the consciousness of Puerto Ricans, in a tentative manner, with regard to their situation of exploitation.

As a result of all this, there is an impasse in the church. The church has not been able openly to take a position against the cultural and political assimilation. Its voice within Puerto Rican society has been silenced. Its influence and identity in the Latin American world has been very poor, except in the case of the precious exception of those Christians who are involved in the liberation process, and who have managed to achieve something through the Latin American ecumenical movement.

From Medellín to Puebla: The Option for the Poor

The thinking of the Latin American church made a great qualitative leap forward in the second Latin American Bishops' Conference in 1968 in Medellín, Colombia. Medellín denounces the situation of external dependency and internal injustice that shapes the Latin American panorama, and denounces it as sinful. Thereupon it exhorts all Christians, and all men and women of goodwill, actively to commit themselves to the building of a true peace. Then the document continues:

Human beings can fulfill themselves as human beings where their dignity is respected, their aspirations satisfied, their access to truth assured, and their personal liberty guaranteed—in an order in which human beings are the agents of their own history. Where, then, discriminatory injustices exist among human beings and nations, a criminal act is being committed against peace.[15]

The third Bishops' Conference, in Puebla, Mexico, in 1979, in spite of the multiple pressures exerted on the church, reaffirms the option taken at Medellín, that is, its preferential concern for the poor. The Latin American church reaffirms its preferential concern for the poor, the marginalized, and the oppressed.[16] Thus the view of the church is that peace cannot be established in Latin America without the antecedent achievement of justice. And the church and its peoples extend this challenge to all the peoples of the globe who colonized us once upon a time and are therefore in our debt. We look to them for understanding and solidarity.

On the Protestant side, the churches of Latin America met in 1978 in Oaxtepec, Mexico, not only to found the Latin American Council of Churches, but also to make a response to the situation of injustice in which the poor of our continent are living. After a certain amount of preliminary wavering, they did manage a profound grasp of our real situation, and responded with a denunciation, and a declaration of solidarity in the search for justice and in the challenge that had been proposed. The transparent and unambiguous response of the ecumenical movement had already been pronounced, for, since the foundation of ISAL (Iglesia y Sociedad en América Latina), the ecumenical movement had already started down the road to liberation with ASEL, MEC, ULAJE, and more recently with COPEC.

Now we have seen how the secularizing challenge, in its liberating aspect, has been the churches' companion on their search for justice and peace. Colonialism and the personalist and military dictatorships have been unable to stifle the voice of Christians. Now there is a new challenge, that of a new secularism, in which technology allies with oppression in order to deny people the enjoyment of life. The church has no answers of its own to this new situation. Its response will be conditioned on its base—the poor among our peoples. There, where it recognizes that there is hope, where it sees the possibility of rooting out hunger, disease, political arrests, helplessness, torture, prison, and genocide—there, with the people—the church has taken its stand.

Conclusion

Whoever takes the long road to our peoples' liberation is going to have the church for a companion on the way. Whatever the nature of the dilemmas that may present themselves, the church is now part and parcel of the social processes on our continent and will have to respond to them and take part in their solution. This will be the criterion of its nature and of its right to exist. The threats that pursue this church of the people so relentlessly resound like a drum roll, challenging both the institutional church and the One Church. Thanks to the people and their hierarchy, history is now moving ahead toward peace and justice. This is a general affirmation, and does not deny the confusion that seems to block the vision of the most influential echelons of the institutional church. But neither can we deny the plain fact that even this institutional church is charged with a tension arising from its providential dilemma: it lives amid an ever worsening poverty among its people, and yet it is placed squarely in the path of Christian elements advancing toward the future with eyes of hope.

True, the secularizing process stifles our aspirations for a victory of the peoples, disclaims the deepest expression of faith, and challenges the practice of all who live the gospel in the option of a commitment to the poor. But at the same time we have to admit that in Latin America this same process has been a positive factor in the rise of the people and their struggle for liberation, even if on occasion it has dealt a blow to the Christian conception of the world.

All that we have observed inclines us to believe that no process is repressive enough to hold back the people. Though they be crucified, and a thousand times, they only reappear as a sign of the kingdom. Thus the secular process, when it accompanies a struggle for liberation, only lends them more strength; and men and women of goodwill join it, for it does not contradict their search for a more just and humane order within the framework of the divine will.

—Translated by Robert R. Barr

Notes

1. Miguel de Unamuno, *La Agonía del Cristianismo* (Buenos Aires: Losada, 1938), p. 13. Eng. trans.: *The Agony of Christianity,* trans. Kurt F. Reinhardt (New York: Frederick Ungar).

2. Albert Gelin, *Los Pobres de Yavé* (Barcelona: Tierra Nueva, 1965), p. 19. Eng. trans.: *The Poor of Yahweh,* trans. Mother Kathryn Sullivan, R.S.C.J. (Collegeville, Minn.: The Liturgical Press, 1964).

3. Juan A. Mackay, *El otro Cristo español* (Mexico City: Casa Unida, 1952).

4. Javier Iguiniz, *Teoría de la Dependencia* (Peru: Tarea, 1978), p. 2.

5. Cf. Justo L. González, *Historia de las misiones,* Biblioteca de Estudios Teológicos (Buenos Aires: Aurora, 1970), p. 437.

6. Cf. Juan Luis Segundo, *Acción pastoral latinoamericana: Sus motivos ocultos* (Buenos Aires: Búsqueda, 1972), pp. 28–30. Eng. trans.: *The Hidden Motives of Pastoral Action,* trans. by John Drury (Maryknoll, N.Y.: Orbis Books, 1978).

7. Iguinez, *Dependencia,* p. 4.

8. Raúl Prebisch, *Problemas, teorías y prácticas para el crecimiento económico* (United Nations, 1952).

9. A. Mattelart, *Comunicaciones e Ideologías de la Seguridad Nacional* (Barcelona: Cuadernos Anagrama, 1978), p. 44.

10. DOCET/CELADEC, *Documento Iglesia: Chile* no. 2.

11. DOCET/CELADEC, *Situación de la Iglesia de El Savador,* Iglesia, series A, no. 6, p. 50.

12. *Cuadernos del Tercer Mundo,* no. 17, November 1977.

13. DOCET/CELADEC, *Nicaragua: Dignidad o muerte,* series B, no. 5 (1978), p. 22.

14. *Informaciones Católicas Internacionales,* Spanish version (Ixtapalapa, Mexico, 1968), p. 7.

15. Medellín, document no. 14.

16. Puebla, nos. 1134ff.

Section 3

CHRISTIAN MISSION
AND ECUMENICAL RELATIONS
IN THE CONTEXT OF THE LOCAL CHURCH

Statement of the Question

Divisions among Christians and between various Christian communions continue to erect stumbling blocks in the proclamation of the gospel, especially in areas that are co-inhabited by people of other world faiths or secular ideologies. This scandal increases in local situations where Christians of different confessions make little attempt to overcome whatever indifference, isolation, and/or rivalry have marked their relationships to each other. This behavior has distorted the witness of Christians even to that unity, although still partial, with which God has already blessed them.

Elements for a Reflection on the Question

- The role of the Holy Spirit in Christian mission
- Often the reasons for these divisions are not strictly theological, but historical, social, and political; and they have been exported from one place to another
- The fidelity of the church to the gospel message and the related credibility of the church in the eyes of those who accept religious pluralism, for example, Hindus
- New proliferations of indigenous, independent churches and Christian groups
- Types of proselytic behavior that induce adherence to a church through false means and motivations
- The different Christian confessions and the relation of this plurality to the diverse ways in which these confessions are incarnating the Christian faith in various parts of the world
- The obstacle posed by internal divisions in the Roman Catholic church as well as in other Christian churches
- The relation of multiracial, multicultural, ecumenical teams of Christians to a common Christian witness

Related Questions

- To what degree are Christians cooperating in theological reflection and social concerns in your local church: for example, defense of human rights, promotion of religious freedom, eradication of economic, social, and racial injustices; campaigns against illiteracy, hunger, alcoholism, prostitution, drug traffic . . . ?

- To what degree is there collaboration for the production, publication, and distribution of Scripture translations, of catechetical materials, and for joint use of mass media?
- What is the extent of common prayer and acts of worship for each other and the world?
- To what extent is it feasible to have joint surveys and planning for proclamation of the gospel in areas as yet unreached? What is the feasibility of joint action through ecumenical teams?
- In what ways will the present relations among Christians in your local church determine their way of acting together in the future?

11

THE PACIFIC

Leslie Boseto

Introduction

The topic that I have been asked to share is a challenging one—challenging because it is not so much a question of more research, but simply a question of living out and sharing in practice God's love. It is a question of obedience to the imperative of our Lord's new commandment to love one another. It is a question of stepping further out and yet nearer to the deep reality of the pain and joy of witnessing to the living and active love of accepting and serving one another for Christ's service.

Before I proceed to the principal subject matter of this paper, I must emphasize two things. First, there is the question of the *owner* or source of Christian mission. Second, there is the question of the *urgency* to accomplish its purpose here and now. These two interrelated vertical and horizontal dimensions of Christian mission cannot be merely studied. While it is important that we consider the future of mission, we can never own or preserve it neutrally. Nor can we make a timetable for it. Its forceful source is always from outside our natural existence, and its urgently and sensitively right response to situational challenges and to local expectation and need can never be delayed or rescinded without accomplishing its purpose.

Because of these two dimensions, the "local church" can never be organizationally defined or controlled when the presence of the living Christ is both felt and experienced by people in their own contextual situation. Hence ecumenical relations in practical terms cannot be merely worked out conceptually and doctrinally but must be deeply experienced and openly shared. Any human-made structures and historical traditions must be responsibly responsive to the realities of the living situations.

Leslie Boseto is a member of the Central Committee of the World Council of Churches, and an executive member of both the Melanesian Council of Churches and the Council for World Missions. He completed his term as moderator of the United Church in Papua New Guinea and the Solomon Islands in 1980.

Why Christian Mission and Ecumenical Relations
in the Context of the Local Church?

"Ecumenical relations" is a foreign idea to those who have not yet become familiar with the terminology that is continually on the lips of people in Geneva and in the Vatican. Yet in reality a society that feels and experiences God's whole concern for his whole society appears to know more about ecumenical fellowship than those who have written a lot about ecumenical relations.

Again, a similar question can be raised in relation to "Christian mission." What is Christian mission on this planet Earth where only about one-quarter of its total population claim to be Christian? What is the aim and goal of Christian mission while it is continually confined and isolated within its historical and political organizations?

While we want to speak about ecumenical relations and Christian mission in the context of the local church, it must be remembered that Christian mission is Christ's mission. It is he who sends. It is he who gives power. It is he who through his perfect sacrifice is the Yes of God in order that lordship of Christ may be directly confessed by individual believers within the fellowship of the local church in every place.

Today, in our discussions and studies it has become clear and challenging to us that we can no longer define the "local church" according to each church's tradition. Ecumenical relations are forced to see their local context in terms of national context. National context must be the context of their local church. Therefore I can say that the whole country of Papua New Guinea or the whole nation of the Solomon Islands must be seen in a local-church context. We can no longer speak of the local church without taking seriously into consideration and planning the whole People of God in mission in their own national context. Even our own definitions of "local church" according to our traditional orders and structures is as much a mission field as "national context." Hence Papua New Guinea presents a local church within its national context.

Since here I am dealing with not just Christian mission and ecumenical relations but ecumenical relations for Christian mission, I must stress that by "local church" I mean God's people in their national context—God's people who have direct relationship with their creator and hence experience his presence and discover his revelation and the exercising of his gift of authority.

Hindrances and Barriers to Leadership of the Holy Spirit

The Holy Spirit became very clear in the Gospels and the Acts of the Apostles as the revealer, leader, and guide. The Holy Spirit worked outside the religious center and made it possible for us to see that God was made incarnate through an ordinary woman. The Holy Spirit led Jesus to challenge the world's strategies for mission and development, as presented to him by the ruler of this world in Matthew 4:1–11. The Holy Spirit revealed to the disciples and those who believed in Jesus Christ the truth about God. The Holy Spirit touched the hearts of people with love beyond written dogma or creed and made every believer a living educator and instructor of one another. Hence every believer was a missioner of Christ. The gospel then was spread by scattered individual missioners after the promised blessing on the day of Pentecost was freely given and freely received.

Four major hindrances to leadership of the Holy Spirit are:

1. Tradition. The letter of Paul to the Galatians teaches us that the Jews' religious tradition must recognize the universal and unconditional love of God on which the formulation of their national constitution, namely, the Ten Commandments, was based—because it was he, the Lord, who brought them out of Egypt, where they were slaves, and gave them the Ten Commandments.

The relationship that the Holy Spirit brought to the Gentiles was a direct gift of the gospel of love, which had to be accepted by faith wherever they were and as they were. Tradition, then, is not a reality of the promise. When the promised reality is received and experienced, tradition is no longer taking an essential place, because it is simply a pointer and is powerless to do anything.

Saint Paul says that now that the time of faith is here, the law is no longer in charge of us (cf. Gal. 3:23–29). Christian mission, if it is God's mission by the leadership of the Holy Spirit, must bring believers to a deeper level of relationship not because of what the law (tradition) says but through faith that they are God's children in union with Christ Jesus. It is not merely "ecumenical relations," but union with Christ and with one another. This act of uniting one's life to Christ is a voluntary act of individual believers. Hence an individual believer has equal right of accepting the age of faith in Christ in whom there is no Jew or Gentile, male or female, slave or free, archbishop or ordinary communicant member, because all are one in Christ Jesus. It is this oneness that took place when the promised blessing of the Holy Spirit on the day of Pentecost was experienced by all who were present. This means that God's promise to everyone of his children must be experienced as a reality, not just as a written statement of belief.

2. Organization. An organizational structure is necessary as long as it is responsive and subject to life in a given situation and locality. A denomination can never organizationally and doctrinally own people. I cannot accept it when we say, for example, "70 million Anglicans, 40 million Methodists, 80 million Lutherans. . . ." Each individual person is free to respond voluntarily to God and be responsibly responsive to his or her neighbor. The first and the second commandments (Mark 12:29–31) demand from an individual person that he or she live beyond and above organizational orders and rules and doctrines. They are direct demands to individual persons and the individual person's voluntary response to God and to neighbor. It is an individual reply to the commandment, with the assurance that one is not far from the kingdom of God.

Only when we hold a concept of organizing our people to an extreme of calling them our own possessions does the question of proselytism come in. If all Christians in a given locality show their faith by relating to one another in love and fellowship, the Christian community in that locality witnesses the leadership of the Holy Spirit.

3. Sin in us. The greatest hindrance to the leadership of the Holy Spirit is our sinful nature. However much we might have done in terms of teaching and preserving *pure* doctrine, in keeping the *right* discipline and traditional practices and interpretations within our church organization, our sinful nature usually tempts us to believe, and indeed assures us, that what we have done and are doing is for mission. Hence we can never be open to the leading of the Holy Spirit in the way that he led Peter to meet Cornelius, in the way that he led Jesus of Nazareth to form a redeemed and restored community outside the religious center of his days! God fought for reconciliation and unity because of sin, not only in individual persons but in organized and institutionalized and constitutionalized groups of individual human beings. And when human beings are operating under a cover or a mask of a structure, the outside is painted bright and attractive but inside is full of corruption. In Luke 11:37–52 Jesus said some very strong words to the teachers of the laws, but they themselves, because of their sins, were far from practicing what *they* demanded and expected others to follow! Saint Paul revealed this after his conversion. In Romans 7 and 8, and also in Philippians 3:1–11, we learn that Paul's old life under the organized structure, where good laws were taught, did not change. It was only after he was changed from within that we was able to relate to the Gentiles.

Jesus, who was born into the demands of his religious, tribal, and constitutional laws, confessed in public this hidden sin in human community. Jesus' openness toward God and toward people was made possible through the cross. It was at the cross that Jesus of Nazareth confessed the power of sin and the power of the love of God. God's "amen" on Jesus was not announced because of Jesus' obedience to the law, but because of his openness to accept and commit himself to the demands of God's *unconditional* love. The question of the Holy Spirit's leadership cannot be considered only outside the human being's sinfulness. Division in the church is simply the result of sin in our human community. The question that we as Christians must ask is: How far does the gospel of Christ reach out to our people? If our people see the gospel as something that each church leader and theologian formally treats as a secret and confidential parcel that only certain specialized and appointed leaders can open and handle, then there is no life in the church. This is because members of the church cannot only *think* of their right and direct access to the presence of Christ himself. Each one must *feel* the presence of the Lord Jesus Christ whenever the person is in a situation permitting him or her to be open to other persons in that situation. So Christian mission is not something to be organized by missionaries or church leaders before it can take place. It takes place where individual persons share the living presence of Christ in that exact situation where their immediate needs are felt. This brings us down to earth, for ecumenical relations are not just something to do with documental statements, confessional creeds before Christian mission. Christian mission must help sinners who feel the presence of Christ to be open and to accept one another as neighbors.

4. Ecclesiastical Structure. If the church is to witness to the world as a structure that shows Jesus of Nazareth, then the ecclesiastical structure, because of its formal and oppressive operation, is a great barrier to the leadership of the Holy Spirit and the showing forth of Christ. Jesus came to be "among" and "to serve" the human community. He did not come to be served.

The World Council of Churches' Conference on World Mission and Evangelism

(Melbourne, 1980) dealt, in part, with the question "The Crucified Christ Challenges Human Power." One of the "powers" was the institutional church, which continues to reflect the structure of our worldly society. The church has become more and more powerless and hopeless to challenge the societal structures of the world. A part of that conference's final report (no. 17, "Repentance and Restructuring in Mission") is relevant to my vision of the Christian mission and ecumenical relations:

> Churches are tempted to be self-centered and self-preserving, but are called to be serving and sharing. Churches are tempted to be self-perpetuating, but are called to be totally committed to the promises and demands of the Kingdom of God. Churches which are tempted to continue as clerical and male-dominated are called to be living communities in which all members can exercise their gifts and share the responsibilities. Churches which tend to be decaying or morbid from stifling structures are called to be living communities in which all members can exercise their gifts and share the responsibilities. Churches are tempted to be exclusivist and privileged but are called to be servants of a Lord who is the crucified Christ who claimed no privilege for himself but suffered for all. Churches tend to reflect and reinforce the dominating exploiting structures of society but are called to be bodies which are critical of the status quo. Churches are tempted to a partial obedience but are called to a total commitment to the Christ who, before he was raised, had first to be crucified.

Let me say that the churches are not only tempted but have been caught into the world system of educational, economic, and political privileges. If we are to break the barrier that isolates the so-called ecclesiastical structure in order to experience "living communities," the term "churches" does not give meaningful and helpful encouragement to those of us who have our deeper security in our own cultural and racial and even national identities.

"Churches" are thought of as something belonging to priests, bishops, archbishops, moderators, and the like. They belong to the employees within organized and institutionalized churches, especially the "ordained priests." The gospel today requires new structures, responsive to the urgency of communicating the gospel. We need the kind of structure that encourages trust relationships with responsible leaders at every level and in all their diverse situations. This is where the "local church" must be seen as a reality of each geographical and social locality, not as an organizational structure, the property of a religious order.

Ecumenical Relations Responsive to the Living Presence of Christ for Mission

In Melanesia we have been encouraged by the openness of churches to come closer and closer together. The challenging context is Melanesian—and also the whole Pacific—not just a few members of different churches here and there under a priest or a bishop.

The movement of the Holy Spirit has brought us to where people *are* the love of

Christ. The Holy Spirit is no longer seen as channeled only through a priest or bishop or through a certain accepted traditional channel. Many sensitive and experienced Christians in Melanesia today, mostly laymen and women, have begun to ask serious questions on the irrelevance of many aspects of traditional structures and attitudes and teachings of our institutional churches. We see that charismatic renewal has begun to create awareness of many living and active architects of structural unity. This is a challenge to the dominating, controlling, self-perpetuating institutional churches. Many members of the church of Jesus Christ see their diverse gifts not just from the ecclesiastical church identity but as individual Christians. Therefore the question of ecumenical relations must not merely repeat what has been said for more than fifty years. It must not deal only with written statements but with church leaders, too. Church leaders are simply human beings, exactly the same as the other church members. They can claim the grace of God only as others beneath them can. Therefore they must be with and among the people, not isolate themselves within a formal system in which, albeit, they often feel comfortable and secure. Responsive ecumenical relations must take seriously the question of decentralization of power, and trust relationship with all the people of God. It must challenge the church structures with the living presence of Christ.

Christ is always at the side of the least, the ignorant, the poor, and the weak. When God moves in his mighty Spirit he can work and move with and through his people whether within the church structure or outside it. He works with and through the so-called laymen and laywomen. He works wherever men and women, boys and girls are. This is where members of the Christian community in each given locality must experience the power of the presence of the resurrected Christ in relation to his leadership and authority. Today many people, during their study of the Bible and praying directly to the Lord wherever they are and as they are, have come to experience the power to preach, to heal, and to share this living experience of Christ. They have come to see what Saint John said: "But if we live our lives in the light, as he is in the light, we are in union with one another, and the blood of Jesus, his Son, purifies us from all sin" (1 Jn. 1:7). This particular verse talks about ecumenical relations between Christian leaders and members, not between organizational churches.

Another passage that has become more alive and reassuring to individual Christians in this age of charismatic renewal is Philippians 3:10–11, where Paul says: "All I want is to know Christ and the power of his resurrection and to share his sufferings by reproducing the pattern of his death. That is the way I can hope to take my place in the resurrection of the dead." These verses show how Saint Paul experienced the reality of Christ. His relationship to the Gentiles came about because of his experience of the power of Christ's resurrection and his continued fellowship with Christ the crucified. It is not the relationship between his confessional statements or dogmatic statements. In 1 Corinthians, chapters 1–3 Paul defines the role of church leaders. They are given a task to do: the work of a servant, working in a garden. Some of them are to sow the seed, some are to water the plant, but God who gives the plant life makes it grow. These leaders, who argue from their traditional leaders' points of view, must learn that their faith in Christ does not rest on human wisdom but on God's power.

When we today want to pursue ecumenical relations, simply repeating ourselves again and again in confessional statements or theological interpretations of each denominational organization does not bring us closer together. It is a waste of time and money, and hence we are not good stewards of our given resources. God's Holy Spirit works outside and beyond any human statement, however wise. The Spirit works with people for people in each locality. I cannot forget what one church leader said during a discussion on confessing Christ and the unity of the church: "The Holy Spirit of God is busy bringing his people together for his mission while church leaders and theologians are busy drafting and redrafting statements!" And what he said about people is what I see taking place everywhere in charismatic renewal.

The following statement for the ecumenical movement is from the report of the Consultation on the Significance of the Charismatic Renewal for the Churches, which took place in Bossey, Switzerland, in March 1980:

A new sense of community binds together people of multiple denominations, transcending historic divisions and demonstrating the urgency of the quest for the unity of the church. The charismatic renewal has added new and significant ecumenical experience to the people of God, and that must be taken very, very seriously. It also puts pressure on Church leaders to move more forcefully on unity concerns.

Responsive ecumenical relations must be sensitive and responsive to Christ at work at each given locality and each given national context as the local church's context. It is true that all charismatic manifestations should be tested and validated, as Saint Paul requests us to do (cf. 1 Thess. 5:10–22). But our testing and validating rods or criteria must not be the traditional status quo, which tends to control and formalize without life.

The ecumenical experience in the Pacific is not going to be much concerned with artificial statements. Apart from encouraging the churches to close cooperation for partnership in development and service, more and more will be coming from within the Pacific's growing identity and the challenges to the so-called mother churches in the West to be prepared to be responsive theologically, doctrinally, and organizationally to the living situations in the Pacific. Are you prepared and are you sensitive enough to the leadership of the Holy Spirit?

Ecumenical Witness in Melanesia

Within the last five years, the ecumenical cooperation to witness the lordship of Christ has been very encouraging not only within Melanesia but within the whole region of the South Pacific.

In 1976 for the first time the member churches of the Evangelical Alliance of the South Pacific and the Melanesian Council of Churches came together in Lae to discuss evangelism. The Roman Catholic church fully participated as a member church of the Melanesian Council of Churches. Most questions raised by this Evangelism Seminar will be followed up.

In 1977 the churches and Christian organizations in the Pacific were represented at Pacifique '77, held in Honiara, Solomon Islands. There were a number of recommendations covering different areas of development. The following recommendations need the attention of the overseas churches in the West, and their agencies:

> Pacifique '77 has taken note of the need for overseas partners, sensitive to the needs and aspirations of Pacific people, especially the spirit of this meeting, and further notes that if they are to be true partners they should be active in raising awareness in their own countries, and that in raising funds they should attempt to present a truthful and dignified picture of countries overseas.

> Knowing that not all overseas agencies, even those that call themselves "Christian" are true partners in this spirit, [Pacifique '77] recommends to the churches and ecumenical groups in the Pacific that they do not accept money blindly, and consult where possible the partners they already know first if approached by new agencies.

The first paragraph above was later expanded thus:

> Pacifique '77 believes that it is important for agencies overseas to be involved in awareness-raising in their own countries. We recognize that this means less of their resources will be available directly for development projects in the Pacific, but we believe that it is in the long term for the whole world more important for them to direct a substantial proportion of their incomes to this work in their own countries.

What we in the Pacific want our overseas partner churches and their agencies in the West to do is to listen more to us, to be very sensitive to our priorities and our aspirations rather than maintaining what they see as priority and our needs. The donor agencies are strongly requested to undertake and communicate a program of awareness-raising of what the Pacific people are saying to them. Those who already know what is best for us are deaf to any other ideas. Therefore, they are unable to educate their people to be a true voice of the Pacific people.

In 1978 there was another seminar in Lae, with the theme "Religion and Development." This seminar was attended by representatives of churches and Christian organizations, and our national politicians, planners, and university lecturers. From 1979 to May 1980, the member churches of the Melanesian Council of Churches and those of the Evangelical Alliance promoted the theme "Partnership in Mission and Development under the Reign of God." This particular program was undertaken in order to prepare our delegates for the Melborne Conference and also to further an understanding, from one another's experience and visions, of the kingdom of God and its challenging and demanding message of repentance from our sins to commitment to its higher expectation within our human community in Melanesia.

Resolutions Presented by the January 1979 and 1980 Workshops

1. Common Worship
    a). We believe prayer for one another aids unity. We encourage congregations to
    pray for one another.
    b). Where there are towns or areas where more than one denomination holds
    services, we encourage congregations to come together for services at appro-
    priate times. For these services, we encourage congregations to draw up a
    form of worship that is acceptable to them for use.
    c). We ask MCC [Melanesian Council of Churches] to consider a common hymn
    book for Papua New Guinea.
    d). We are convinced that a way in which a deeper understanding of ecumenism
    will grow will be through the establishment of cross-denominational Bible
    Study and Prayer groups. We encourage all the churches to promote these.

2. Sharing of Resources
    a). We see that partnership can be strengthened if churches share their manpower
    and material resources: e.g., exchange of pulpits; exchange of teachers,
    nurses, students and other workers; sharing of vehicles, buildings, finances
    and land and contributing to the running of activities.
    b). Congregations should be informed of establishments that are of an ecumeni-
    cal nature and we encourage congregations to support these through prayer
    and financial help: e.g., Kristen Redio, Kristen Kaset, Bible Society, Wantok
    Publications, the Melanesian Institute, etc.
    c). We ask the MCC to produce a directory that will inform congregations of
    ecumenical institutions and other projects and establishments of the member
    churches.

3. Partnership with Overseas Churches
    a). We encourage overseas church agencies to share with us in prayer for the
    promotion and development of the unity of all God's people in our countries
    of Melanesia.
    b). We are grateful for the considerable assistance that overseas churches and their
    missionary agencies have given us in setting up our churches. We believe now
    the churches in Papua New Guinea and Solomon Islands should be self-
    supporting as much as possible. A mature church requires that we not only
    receive, but that we are willing to share our resources with our partner
    churches. However, overseas financial help is still needed and we remind
    churches of their responsibility to be good stewards of these financial re-
    sources. We see that a way of exercising a good stewardship in order to reach
    our goal for self-supporting and self-reliance is to utilize these resources ecu-
    menically. We strongly recommend to overseas churches and their funding
    agencies to support schemes that we determine as priorities in our ecumenical
    ventures.
    c). We see there is still a need for overseas workers as an expression of the universal

nature of the Gospel and the Church of our Lord Jesus Christ. Their role must be to discover with us the active presence of Christ in our own contextual situation. We recognize the importance of overseas workers' expertise, which we may need from time to time. However, our need is for men and women who are willing to participate in the power shown in the resurrection of Christ, the crucified Messiah. We ask our partner churches in their training of candidates for overseas service to be sensitive to God's leading in our struggles to bring about the Kingdom of God in our unique situations. This can necessitate setting aside pre-conceived knowledge and becoming co-discoverers of the challenges which face God's Kingdom in Melanesia.

4. Melanesian Reflection

a). To develop our thinking and to share our experiences of God first hand, we see the importance of having conferences and study groups. We thus encourage our theologians, church leaders and educators to be fully involved in such conferences and study-reflection groups.

b). Further series of articles, papers and booklets which will help in the formation of our own theology should be developed on an ecumenical basis.

c). We should study in depth the areas of our faith and practice where we are both like-minded and differ. Where there are differences these should be openly discussed and studied. Hence we recommend to MCC/EA and SICA (Solomon Islands Christian Association) the possibility of the formation of a Faith and Witness Commission for Papua New Guinea and the Solomon Islands.

5. Theological Colleges

a). At this stage of development and partnership we see it is important that there is an interchange of staff and students within our theological colleges and recommend to the Melanesian Association of Theological Schools (MATS) that this receive immediate consideration.

b). We believe serious thought should be given to uniting our theological colleges so as to minimise our expense and use of resources.

c). We stress the importance of including sociology and anthropology in college programmes. We bring this to the notice of MATS.

d). We are further concerned that the programmes of our theological colleges have followed too much the traditions of our overseas churches and we see them becoming steadily more academically oriented. We would like to see far more integrated courses of study which would include knowledge of agriculture, bookkeeping, mechanics, carpentry, typing, health care, politics. We believe practical and theoretical training should receive equal emphasis. To carry out such a programme will entail the appointment of both lay and theological trained Melanesian staff to institutions.

The May 1980 Conference, Port Moresby, Papua New Guinea

The Conference in May 1980 held in Port Moresby immediately before the Melbourne Conference on the theme "Your Kingdom Come" presented the statements and questions in our Bible Study, summarized below, and also the resolutions printed below.

BIBLE STUDY'S GOSPEL MESSAGES
(SUMMARY OF STATEMENTS AND QUESTIONS)

The church shall deliver the message for the totality of life in all its dimensions. It is a message for the whole person, including what we are doing with our mind and bodies. We are doers of the words—doing truth, doing justice, and doing peace. The church is compelled to go and tell the deeds of God to all nations. The message is ecumenical in the broadest sense and we are placed on the alert to reach the world with the good news.

We in Melanesia, who have been one of the most evangelized people, should look to contributing to the churches abroad by sending church workers and missionaries. We have certain gifts, which we should share. Example: Our attitude to communal living and the spirit of ecumenism that is apparent in this country are two areas where we can help others in their struggles.

The spirit of shared discipleship is something that churches must learn and communicate to the grassroots. We must make disciples of Jesus Christ. "Making disciples" means following someone and continuing in his or her work. Here the church must avoid doing things for its own glory. It is for Christ's glory: we must remember that we are not bringing people to denominations but into God's church where Christ is the King. People are not coming to institutions but to a person, Jesus Christ.

RESOLUTIONS

1. We believe church leaders at all levels need to be familiar with the national constitution so that there may be constant interplay between government and church to maintain and implement the true aims of both the constitution and the eight point plan.
2. A sub-commission be set up under MCC to look at the fundamentals of faith and their interpretation to Melanesians.
3. A conference be organized for only Melanesians to attend in order to discover our common basis for witness. This will allow freedom to discuss imported thought forms and theological interpretations which are foreign. Later, expatriates are to be invited to attend.
4. Individual churches be encouraged to do more in presenting the gospel in the local cultural forms. This is preparation of hymns, litany, etc.
5. The Churches of Melanesia have a responsibility for the public scene in areas of both spiritual and social concern both at home and abroad. National Christians need to face their responsibility of accepting and carrying the cross and suffering alongside their expatriate co-workers. The "we" attitude rather than the "they" attitude must emerge.
6. This conference requests our churches to consider communicating to their overseas counterparts that one of the challenging mission fields in Papua New Guinea is in the government and private sectors. We invite qualified overseas lay Christians to be involved in these areas.

7. Mutual communication be established at the local level between pastors, ministers and church workers wherever there are MCC/EA member churches. (This is to be initiated at first by delegates from the Conference.)

8. We encourage churches to work together at the local level to study problems and to come up with an agreed joint programme.

9. Areas of co-operating on a partnership basis should be discovered and implemented at the local level.

10. MCC/EA should work together in identifying areas of need and when clarified this should be brought to the notice of WCC.

11. MCC/EA should look into the possibility of promoting adult education.

12. Churches in order to help in nurturing their members and adherents should aim at improving the quality of ministerial training through upgrading courses and through running regular refresher courses for ministers.

13. We recommend that Dr. John Strelan's Bible Study notes be printed for distribution to participants and others so as to encourage further study on the theme "Your Kingdom Come."

The Ongoing Search

The full significance of this 1980 conference can only be felt if all those who attended the conference returned to their own situation to take up the challenges raised at the conference. At both workshops, at Lae and at Sirinumu near Port Moresby, the groups saw that the Port Moresby conference was not going to be the culmination of this endeavor but, rather, a continuing process. It was seen very much as a further and an important mark in the ecumenical outreach of the churches in Papua New Guinea.

At the conference, although one session was spent studying the affirmations, it became immediately obvious that the conference was not the right time to relook at the affirmations. It is now the responsibility of small groups gathering together in both denominational and ecumenical groups to relook at the affirmations and to submit their thoughts to the Port Moresby planning committee. The Port Moresby planning group will continue to have the overall responsibility for assisting and aiding smaller groups with their discussions. If the feeling is strong, and the committee feels it is needed, it may arrange for further specialized workshops to look into aspects raised.

Let us all remember that Christ has challenged us. How can we be faithful witnesses to the lordship of Christ in the same way that Jesus showed to the people, the leaders, and the authorities of his time? Does this require a radical change of heart and a change in the structures?

Areas of Commitment

Besides our desires and longings for future directions summarized above, there have been areas where we have brought member churches of our Melanesian Council of Churches and Evangelical Alliance to commit themselves. These are the areas of communications and of Christian education.

In the area of communications, through the Churches' Council for Media Co-ordination, the churches have been working closely with our National Broadcasting Commission on matters of religious programs; they have also given encouragement by helping with communications programs of the member churches and with their communications organizations. Wantok Publications is one area of ecumenical commitment for Christian mission.

In the field of education, apart from the churches' close cooperation with the government in formal education and health training and services, we have an ecumenical institute, namely, the Melanesian Institute, which has stated: "The objective of the Institute shall be to offer pastoral and socio-economic service to the People of Melanesia." In order to achieve this objective, the institute lists the following program of work:

a. Organize regular orientation courses for church workers;
b. Conduct inservice courses for church workers either alone or in co-operation with other bodies;
c. Conduct specialist courses and seminars either alone or in co-operation with other bodies;
d. Undertake research relevant to the pastoral and socio-economic field;
e. Publish material in the pastoral and socio-economic fields relevant for Melanesia.

The institute is run by its Governing Council, which is appointed by its Association. The council's functions, in draft form, are as follows:

a. To present the Institute with pastoral and socio-economic needs as communicated by the bodies represented in the Association;
b. i. To evaluate past programmes of the Institute;
    ii. To evaluate projected programmes as formulated by the Institute;
    iii. To make major policy decisions based on recommendations from, or in consultation with, the Institute;
c. To present the programmes and aim of the Institute to the bodies represented in the Association;
d. To appoint committees as required;
e. To appoint permanent members of the Institute;
f. To terminate the membership of permanent members of the Institute;
g. To accept the resignations of permanent members of the Institute;
h. To appoint the officers of the Institute;
i. To accept other churches or organizations as members of the Association and to accept the withdrawal of present members;
j. To be responsible for all assets, from wherever derived, used by the Institute;
k. To appoint a treasurer for the Association whose duties are as in by-law no. 2.
l. To receive, evaluate and approve audited annual financial reports of the Institute;

m. To appoint auditors who will hold office at its pleasure;

n. To receive a proposed budget for the Institute's operations, as prepared by the Institute;

o. To adopt a budget for the Institute;

p. To ensure that the provisions of the constitution are being upheld;

q. To submit proposed changes to the constitution to members of the Association;

r. To enact or amend by-laws appropriate for the implementation of the constitution.

Local Community for Christian Mission

A local community within a given locality or nation is both a mission field and an evangelizing community, for it is the people of a particular locality, or nation, who are called to carry out the total concern of the whole gospel of Christ. Therefore Christian mission in a local church means Christian mission within the whole context of Melanesian society. "Local church" to me means the People of God in a given nation or province. It is not a question of each denomination's definition according to its theological interpretation and organizational structure. And those who have to determine priorities and lead the responsive planning must be the members of that national community. This is where my strong vision for the new conciliar community, or fellowship, comes in.

I want to challenge all missiologists and theologians and church leaders of the so-called mother churches to be very sensitive to which direction the wind of the Holy Spirit is blowing for Christ's mission. It is no longer always from Rome or Geneva or England or New York or Pittsburgh, or even from the West. I see that the strong wind of God's Spirit has been and will continue to blow within Melanesia and from within to outsiders, even to those for whom there has been only a one-way traffic in communication previously.

What are your sensitive and responsive answers regarding this challenge? What can you do in terms of preparation of all candidates for mission and your releasing of financial help in order to be both open and strongly supportive of a confessing and witnessing of Christian community in a given national context? This is a question that we in Melanesia and the Pacific region as a whole will address to you more and more urgently, because of the Holy Spirit's leading for his whole Pacific community today.

Conclusion

The urgency of mission is at our homes, doorsteps, and nations. What is our responsive commitment? We can no longer organizationally and constitutionally control and own the People of God. Trust them in their own diverse and itinerant situations to redeem the time by communicating the deeper touch of the gospel. The power of the gospel is people who experience the deeper touch of Christ's love, not an institutional and organizational power. All of our societal powers and their pressing demands will at last come to an end. The power of Christ and his gospel will remain forever. This power of the gospel, which is directly experienced by our people, needs new wineskins, not the old skins of an organizational status quo. The movement of the leadership of the Holy Spirit, who is the leading missionary and missiologist to bring about Christ's nature in each given locality, can never be permanently housed or even tented within our temporary and earthen vessels. We can only share our experiences of him whom the Holy Spirit brings into our lives under his lordship.

12

EAST AFRICA

John Mutiso-Mbinda

The search for unity among Christians is one of the priorities in the Catholic church today. This is because Christian unity, born out of ecumenical relations, is at the very center of Christian mission. As Pope John Paul II wrote in his first encyclical, *Redemptor Hominis*: "It is also certain that in the present historical situation of Christianity and the world, the only possibility we see of fulfilling the Church's universal mission, with regard to ecumenical questions, is that of seeking sincerely, perseveringly, humbly, and also courageously the ways of drawing closer and of union" (no. 6). In his message to the delegates of National Ecumenical Commissions, on November 23, 1980, the Holy Father put this priority in a way that no previous pope had ever put it so emphatically: "Let no one delude himself that work for perfect unity in faith is somehow secondary, optional, peripheral, something that can be indefinitely postponed."[1]

The concern for ecumenical relations in the African context is as old as Christianity in Africa. Thomas Merton once observed: "Among the martyrs of Uganda, all one in the witness of their death and of their blood, were several who were not Roman Catholics. Who is to say these were not canonized along with the others? A great sign is seen in Africa."[2] Despite this great sign, in Africa divisions among Christians and between various Christian communions continue to erect stumbling blocks in the proclamation of the gospel, especially in areas which are co-inhabited by people of other world faiths or secular ideologies. This scandal increases in local situations where Christians of different confessions make little attempt to overcome whatever indifference, isolation, and/or rivalry have marked their relationships to each other. This behavior has distorted the witness of Christians even to that unity, although still partial, with which God has already blessed them. The de facto situation in Africa, as elsewhere in the world, is that we are very divided. This is not a new realization. At the World Missionary Conference in Edinburgh (1910), the fact of the multiplicity of churches in the missionary territories was already a major con-

John Mutiso-Mbinda, priest from Kenya, is the Vice Director of the AMECEA Pastoral Institute and Director of the AMECEA Research Department. He is also a consultant to the Vatican Secretariat for Promoting Christian Unity.

cern. The conference had to admit sadly that the proliferation of churches was a major scandal and caused a lot of confusion not only to the new African converts, but to potential ones as well.

Divisions and rivalries among the various Christian churches are believed to have weakened and confused Christian life in Africa more than anything else.[3] People have witnessed, historically, old traditions of bitterness, mistrust, and missionary attitudes of hostility being passed on to new generations of Christians. What was particularly perplexing to the Africans was that each overseas nationality preached a different brand of Christianity. Thus the Africans could not help associating the English with the Anglican church, Scotsmen with the Presbyterian church, Italians and Frenchmen with the Roman Catholic church. This unfortunate, yet true, association may have given rise to the birth of the independent churches mushrooming in Africa today. "If the English have their church, the Americans their church, the Italians their church why can't we have our own Church too?" the Africans would argue. This is only one explanation, among many, for independence in Africa today.

The effects of division are far more reaching than we realize. We have every reason to be scared of the scandal it causes among the people being evangelized. Hence Pope John Paul II points out: "Disunity is a scandal, a hindrance to the spread of the gospel; it is our duty to strive by God's grace to overcome it as soon as we can."[4] The urgency of this task was expressed clearly by the pope in Nairobi. This call by Pope John Paul II is even more urgent here in our African context where Christianity is the direct result of a divided mission. Brian Hearne writes:

> With this division in mission went competition and rivalry between the various missionary groups: sometimes, indeed there was open hostility, especially between the so-called "Evangelicals" and Catholics. For this reason the wound of division is in some ways harder to heal in Africa than elsewhere even though it is of more recent years, and even though there is no centuries-long history of conflict, as in the West.[5]

This sin of division in Africa, as elsewhere, is both the indicative and the imperative for the church's urgent call to conversion and deliberate work for Christian unity in its mission.

The Christian "mission" or the "mission" of the church must be understood before we can speak of it in the precise context of the local church. We refer here to a specific mission, which is by its nature Christian, based on the person of Christ himself. Hence there is no other mission apart from that of Christ himself. Pope John Paul II centers his first encyclical, *Redemptor Hominis,* on the mysterious truth affirmed by Vatican II: "By his incarnation, he, the son of God, in a certain way united himself with each human person . . . " (no.13). This leads the pope to look at the church's mission to all people from the aspect of God's universal saving plan in his creation, finding its visible expression and meaning in Christ and in the church's activity in the world. Brian Hearne clarifies this point as follows:

> The Church exists not for itself but for Christ, and for the world. All its activity and methods must be constantly referred to the unchanging standard of the

life of Jesus, to the way he did things, and to his purpose in life. The New Testament makes plain that this purpose was "the Kingdom of God."[6]

The Christian mission is the same as the mission of Christ. In his proclamation of this mission, Christ makes it clear that his mission is one of creating communion rather than divisions. Jesus inaugurates a new world order. His presence and deliberate day-to-day activity transform the world and all people; diseases are cured (Mt. 8:16–17), struggle is transformed into joy (Lk. 7:11–17; also Mt. 5:41–43), the elements obey him (Mt. 8:27), death is transformed into mere sleep (Mk. 5:39), sins are forgiven (Mk. 2:5), and the Lord's year of favor has begun (Lk. 14:19).

This mission begins to take shape when the present sorrow is gradually turned into joy and hope, *gaudium et spes*. It includes a process whereby the marginalized come to the center, the oppressed are set free, the powerless are in control of their own lives and destiny, the voiceless speak, the uprooted are rooted in their own culture, the absent ones are present, and the noninvited feast at the heavenly banquet. Only by looking at the mission of the church in this way can we see that the church "is in nature of sacrament—a sign and instrument, that is, of communion with God and of unity among all men" (*Lumen Gentium,* no. 1).

By "local church" throughout this paper I do not mean just an administrative unit of the organization called the Roman Catholic church, but I mean the Catholic church in a particular place. In the strict sense and in the official documents of the church, the local church is to be found in the diocese (cf. Constitution on the Sacred Liturgy, no. 41). However, for the purpose of this paper, I would like to restrict the usage of this term "local church" to a much higher level, usually referred to as "particular" or "regional" churches (cf. *Ad Gentes,* chap. III). I am restricting the scope to one geographical or regional group called AMECEA (Association of the Member Episcopal Conferences of Eastern Africa), which includes Ethiopia, Sudan, Uganda, Kenya, Tanzania, Malawi, and Zambia. However, the data collected and used here exclude both Ethiopia and Sudan. Fortunately I happen to be working at this same regional level on a four-year research project on "Attitudes and Initiatives Toward Christian Unity in Eastern Africa." However, in such a short paper it is impossible to cover in detail all the aspects of the topic in question. A brief analysis of some of the major elements and events in AMECEA countries will suffice.

Major Aspects and Events

The Local Context

Historically Christianity came to Kenya, Malawi, Tanzania, Uganda, and Zambia very divided. Missionary routes were opened by early explorers. However, the arrival of Roman Catholic and other missionary personnel were interspersed. In Malawi, for example, David Livingstone arrived on the shores of Lake Malawi in 1859, and two years later the Universities Mission to Central Africa (UMCA) was founded and sent missionaries to Magomero and later to Zanzibar. By the time the Roman Catholics arrived in Malawi (1889), the people were already being evangelized by

UMCA and the Church of Scotland. Jealousies regarding early feelings of territoriality seem to have increased in recent years. The flag may have also been the cause for hostilities. As Hastings points out:

Inevitably much depended on the religious sympathies of the colonizing power. In Belgian Africa Protestants developed very justifiably a deep sense of grievance, while in British Africa Catholics could generally feel that they were carefully kept out of inner circles of political power, though not so directly discriminated against in an easily provable way; wherever the Union Jack flew Anglican Missionaries managed to carry with them the status of a quasi-Establishment.[7]

Politics mixed with religious issues, along with socioeconomic ones, to form major obstacles to early evangelization, as Alan Moorehead points out: "There was another obstacle before the Christians in Africa, and it was more fundamental. Unlike the Muslims, they were divided among themselves . . . ." What Moorehead says was true of the Uganda situation from the very beginning, with mounting hostilities between Protestant Alexander Mackay and Roman Catholic Simon Lourdel. In the same book Moorehead points out: "Mackay and Lourdel continued to weaken themselves by acting independently. Each one built up his mission as rapidly as he could. Each encouraged his followers to look upon the rival Christian faith as heretical and vile."[8]

One Ugandan seminarian, reflecting on the current situation in Uganda, made the following observation:

There was little social communication between Catholics and Protestants. Even minor things became very important as "identification marks": Catholics called Jesus "Yezu" and Mary "Maria,"while Protestants used the names "Yesu" and "Mariamu." Culture was mixed with theology, and even different political parties for Catholics and Protestants resulted from this—the UPC (Protestant) and DP (Catholics).[9]

In the 1980s, with the present political crisis in Uganda, we are back to the same situation of political divisions along religious lines. The UPC (Uganda Peoples Congress) is still nicknamed "United Protestants of Canterbury" and the DP is referred to as *Dini ya Papa* (Swahili for "the pope's religion")!

In Kenya the profusion of missionary churches and their national character is still seen by critics as a continuous cause of division. The Kenyan author Ngugi wa Thiong'o, in his controversial Kikuyu drama *Ngahika Ndeenda* (literally "I will marry when I decide"), which landed him in detention during the Kenyatta era, points at the multiplicity of "national" churches imported to the African soil. He is critically puzzled by the way Christ is so divided and wonders how such a divided house as Christianity could be a carrier of truth and salvation. In a word, Ngugi is saying with Marx that the religion taught by these churches is an opiate of the people.

The situation was the same in both Zambia and Tanzania. One Zambian of the United Church of Zambia (Anglican) pointed out recently at a meeting:

> Most Christian churches in Zambia were founded by missionaries from overseas countries like England, Europe and America. These set out to the task of founding new Christian communities. This was done on individual denominational bases, according to geographical areas, and in extreme cases according to tribal areas. Among other things, this was the beginning of separateness: opposition between churches transplanted from overseas to our situation.[10]

The Reverend Mr. Lumbama just quoted, points out the presence of defensiveness, based on self-righteousness and fear of "spiritual pollution" from other mainline churches. Very much like the situation in Malawi, Roman Catholic missionaries began active work long after other mainline churches, in 1860 from Reunion Island. Again due to the multiplicity of Christian churches and the claiming of particular territories for evangelization, quarrels continued to exist among the missionaries for many years. Catholics were not allowed to attend weddings of Protestant relatives or friends.

All these attitudes of hostility and bitterness, as pointed out before, are based on missionary history. It is very unfortunate that psychological and religious wars were transported from Europe and America to the African context. The background to missionary expansion into Africa is marked by strained ecumenical relations between Catholics and Protestants, especially in Europe. The political flag was another obstacle to ecumenical relations. In this regard Townsend writes that the missionaries of all nationalities were eager

> to make native people German, British, Italian, Belgian, as the case may be; and expansionists of all countries let no opportunity slip to employ missionaries, dead or alive, to advance the "Kingdom," not only of God, but of nationalism and the economic power overseas. The Church Missionary Society supplied money to the British East African Company to enable it to remain in Uganda.[11]

By the end of the nineteenth century the Protestants had a larger share than the Catholics in the "planting" of Christianity in Africa south of the Sahara. The Church Missionary Society (CMS; Anglican) arrived in Kenya in 1844 (Krapf) and 1846 (Rebmann), both of whom were not Anglicans but Lutherans. Alexander Mackay, a Presbyterian, also came under the CMS umbrella, arriving in Uganda in 1877. The Roman Catholics arrived on the scene much later in both Kenya (1890) and Uganda (1879). The pattern of arrival is the same for Malawi, Tanzania, and Zambia.[12]

Another phenomenon that must be taken into consideration in the context of this subject is the presence of Islam in Eastern Africa. In many ecumenical efforts, the local church tends to ignore this factor, and yet it is the oldest influence in Eastern Africa, as old as Islam itself. Parrinder writes:

A Muslim expedition besieged Dongola in Nubia in 652, but made a treaty of non-aggression and mutual trade, in the name of God, the prophet Muhammad, the Messiah and the Apostles. . . . The kingdom of Dongola fell about 1320, and though many people were still Christian the Arab tribes now flooded the country towards the richer lands to the South which Nubia had blocked.[13]

Islam had already spread widely on the east coast of Kenya, Tanzania, and Malawi by A.D. 1290. Christian contact with Islam in Eastern Africa began only after Vasco da Gama's visit in 1498 and especially after the Portuguese entered and controlled the coast from 1530 to 1698. During this period bitter religious and political wars were waged on the east coast. Arabs gained control again in 1698. By 1844 Arabs arrived in Buganda, making converts to Islam gradually. When King Mwanga killed the Christians in Uganda in 1884, the Muslims supported him. Because of the slave trade a severe hatred for Arabs and Islam developed among the Christian African chiefs, encouraged by the colonial rulers and missionaries. However, Muslim influence has remained in these countries ever since. To quote Parrinder again:

In Kenya Muslim influence was limited chiefly to the coastline. In Uganda there is a strong Muslim minority, principally to the north of Lake Victoria. In Tanzania there is Islamic dominance on the coast and areas of strong influence inland, especially since the influx of Muslims from Mozambique. The north of Mozambique up to Lake Nyasa is predominantly Muslim, along the old trade route and in Malawi, particularly among the Yao people who have taken to Islam more than other people in these parts.[14]

Despite this presence of Islam in Eastern Africa (a majority in the coastal but a minority in the inland or up-country areas), there is very little, if any, ecumenical relationship between Christians and Muslims. No credible and genuine mission can remain indifferent to this phenomenon.

Religious Pluralism

Related to the context of the local church within the AMECEA countries is the question of religious pluralism, which cannot be ignored. The local church finds itself in the midst of this pluralism, which should not in any way be seen as mere diversity, but diversity in unity. The many elements are brought together to form a unity, each element being enriched thereby. Africa's three religions, namely, Christianity, traditional religions, and Islam should ideally form such a diversity in unity. No one religion should take it for granted that they are right and the rest are wrong. However, as we have already seen, this is not the case. Religious pluralism is increasingly becoming a stumbling block to ecumenical relations. Within Christianity internal divisions are increasing daily. In 1970 one observer wrote:

Careful study has finally been given to the phenomenon of the "African Independent Churches." Within the past fifty years, two-fifths of the sub-Sahara tribes have seen the spontaneous generation of over 5000 schisms from the historic "mother" Churches, and from each other. Most of these communities are small, but together they number over seven and a half million members.[15]

The problem of African independent churches has to be taken into consideration in the African ecumenical movement, since this seems to be a phenomenon peculiar to Africa. This concern was raised by the African delegates at the meeting of Delegates of National Ecumenical Commissions in Rome in 1979. African independent churches were considered as an issue of common pastoral concern "which cannot be ignored in working for Christian Unity." Since many studies on this phenomenon have been made, producing several theories (e.g., Barrett, Sundkler, Daneel, Turner, Welbourne and Ogot, Perrin-Jassy), it would be a good starting point to have this phenomenon as a basis for ecumenical dialogue. According to Dr. Barrett, by the year 2000 these independent churches may have increased to eight thousand! There is another hidden giant, called African traditional religion, with which there is an urgent need for dialogue at the local level. Christians and Muslims cannot take for granted that they are the only true worshipers of God. The question of pluralism raises a number of issues that cannot be adequately dealt with here.

Ecumenical Relations and Proselytism

Proselytism has been said to include any improper attitudes and behavior in the practice of Christian witness; whatever violates the rights of the human person, Christian or non-Christian, to be free from external coercion in religious matters; whatever, in the proclamation of the gospel, does not conform to the ways God draws free people to himself in response to his calls to serve in Spirit and in truth. The history of evangelization in the area of study is marked by bitter complaints of both Protestants and Catholics of "proselytizing" attitudes or "sheep-stealing," usually behind each other's backs.

The joint working group of the Roman Catholic church and the World Council of Churches at its meeting of May 1970 summed up the issue of proselytism as follows:

> Christian witness, to those who have not yet received or responded to the announcement of the Gospel or to those who are already Christians, should have certain qualities, in order to avoid being corrupted in the exercise and thus becoming proselytising. Furthermore, the ecumenical movement itself had made Christians more sensitive to the conditions proper to witness borne among themselves. This means that we should be completely
> - conformed to the spirit of the Gospel, especially by respecting the other's right to religious freedom, and
> - concerned to do nothing which could compromise the progress of ecumenical dialogue and action.

In some countries, for example, Kenya, where the freedom of worship is so plentiful, proselytism is worrying many parents and teachers in secondary schools where numbers of free-floating preachers seize the opportunity of religious education periods or break periods to preach at length to the students. At least one religious education supervisor feels that it is about time the Christian churches united in dealing with the problem of proselytism in secondary schools.

Nontheological Reasons for Christian Divisiveness

The reasons for division among Christians in the region under study range from beer to political-party affiliation. One observer points out that "in many African countries, beer and cigarettes are more pressing problems than are any doctrines of faith; and the political complications in a country like Uganda loom far larger in the minds of Catholics and Protestants than questions like infallibility or the interpretation of the Bible."[16]

Socioeconomic reasons usually run very deep. So much so that to hold a fund-raising meeting for one particular church automatically means strengthening the membership of that church. But perhaps all these nontheological reasons for division could be traced to basically one reason, namely, prejudice, which is very present in every one of us no matter who we are.[17] This prejudice is built on very deep-seated psychological attitudes toward the other, which lead us to excessive exaggerations and bigotry. One African bishop, Ndingi Mwana a' Nzeki, made the observation from experience that Africans are very cooperative before conversion, but once they become Christians they begin to oppose each other.

Ecumenical Initiatives as Indicators of Future Orientation

Since the publication of *Unitatis Redintegratio* (Decree on Ecumenism) in 1964, many initiatives have taken place in Eastern Africa, at both regional and grassroots levels. Recent ecumenical initiatives have included theological colloquia, joint integral development work, Bible translations, joint religious education syllabi, joint production and delivery of mass media, common prayer, and joint planning for evangelization.

Theological Reflection

A Kikuyu proverb tells us *Kwaria ni Kwendana*, which means "To talk is to love one another." This may seem to be a rather simple expression but it points at the very purpose and object of dialogue at all levels, namely, the creation of a loving relationship. This is the ideal that is achieved in informal reflection but rarely in formal theological reflection. However, formal theological reflection prepares the way for better mutual understanding and gradually leads to genuine dialogue. That is why in our African context we never rush our meetings or reflections. "We talk till we agree," Julius Nyerere once said.

From experience, missionaries in Africa realized that divisions were defeating the purpose of evangelization. Shortly before and after the World Missionary Conference (Edinburgh) in 1910, there were several attempts by the Protestant churches in Kenya: Masseno Conference (1908), Kijabe Conference (1909), and Kikuyu Conference (1913). The main churches represented were the Church Missionary Society (CMS), the Church of Scotland Mission (CSM), Africa Inland Mission (AIM), the Seventh-Day Adventists (SDA), the United Methodist Mission (UMM), and the Lutherans. Among the aims of these conferences were three major concerns: (a) to stress what was common among the churches and to enhance it; (b) to create a self-governing, self-supporting, and self-propagating native church; (c) to agree upon the proposed constitution of the Federation of Missions, which was done at the Kikuyu Conference. Among other things, it was agreed that each church have an area of evangelization; one set of rules of discipline; the same form of words for baptism and Eucharist; and the acceptance of the Bible as the only source of revelation. The divinity of Christ and his atoning death were also stressed.

For the Catholics there was little if any initiative for theological reflection aimed at working toward ecclesial unity until after the Decree on Ecumenism was published in 1964. The decree is very clear with regard to what has to be done:

> The term "ecumenical movement" indicates the initiatives and activities encouraged and organized, according to the various needs of the Church and as opportunities offer, to promote Christian unity. These are: first, every effort to avoid expressions, judgments and actions which do not represent the condition of our separated brethren with truth and fairness and so make mutual relations with them more difficult. Then, "dialogue" between competent experts from different Churches and communities; in their meetings, which are organized in a religious spirit, each explains the teaching of his communion in greater depth and brings out clearly its distinctive features. Through such dialogue everyone gains a truer knowledge and more just appreciation of the teaching and religious life of both communions. . . . Finally, all are led to examine their own faithfulness to Christ's will for the Church and, wherever necessary, undertake with vigor the task of renewal and reform (*Unitatis Redintegratio,* no. 4).

It was in view of the directives above that the bishops of AMECEA in consultation with AACC (All Africa Conference of Churches) decided to carry out research on "Attitudes and Initiatives Towards Christian Unity in Eastern Africa" (cf. letter to Canon Burgess Carr, July 30, 1975, and Burgess Carr's response of Sept. 8, 1975). This consultation led to a joint planning meeting, which was held at Trinity College, Nairobi, October 5–7, 1976. At this meeting both AACC and AMECEA were officially represented by Right Reverend Raphael Ndingi Mwana a' Nzeki (the vice chairman of AMECEA), and Mr. George K. Mambo (director of research, AACC, Nairobi). It was at this meeting that the delegates, representing National Christian Councils, episcopal conferences, university departments of religious studies, seminaries, theological colleges, Bible societies, joint religious education syllabi, and ecumenical foundations, agreed upon the aims and objectives of the joint research project, outlining the methods and areas of investigation. One of the methods of the project would be theological colloquia at which theologians and teachers of theology would exchange views on ecumenism in order to help propose some practical steps to be taken toward Christian unity. The research project is funded jointly by the World Council of Churches and the Vatican.

Since 1977 there have been five theological colloquia in Eastern Africa (Zambia— Nov. 1-2, 1977; Kenya—Nov. 4-5, 1977; Malawi—Nov. 28-29, 1977; Tanzania —June 13-15, 1978; and Uganda—Oct. 30-31, 1979).

During the three years of theological reflection, thirty-one papers were presented at ecumenical colloquia. These papers were mainly aimed at stimulating thinking and discussion. They raised a number of issues: theological, historical, biblical, cultural, spiritual, and general questions having to do with everyday life. The experience of being together, working together, eating together, and praying together was in itself a very important process of education for ecumenical awareness. As one participant put it at the end of one theological reflection, "I have discovered that it is not so much the theological issues that divide us but the nontheological issues." At the end of each theological colloquium a national ecumenical follow-up committee was formed to implement some of the recommendations that emerged from the various discussions. It seems a pity that in all these discussions, ecumenical relations with Islam were never dealt with.

Human Rights and Integral Development

Pope John Paul II, in his speech in Washington, D.C., in 1979 spoke of "joint witness in the defence of the rights of the human person, in the pursuit of goals of social justice and peace, and in questions of public morality."[18] The church in Africa as a whole must be actively involved in this joint witness if it is going to be credible to the African person. The issue of human rights and social justice was the main theme of the pope's speech to the Diplomatic Corps in Nairobi on May 6, 1980. The churches in Eastern Africa are increasingly aware that the end of alien rule is not identical with the attainment of full human rights by all of our people. The Khartoum Human Rights Consultation organized by the World Council of Churches and the All Africa Conference of Churches, February 16-22, 1975, was aimed at deepening this awareness. The Roman Catholic church was represented. Although none of the countries studied has an established justice and peace commission, at the AMECEA Plenary of August 1979, the issue of setting up a regional commission was raised. The AMECEA board members, meeting in Eldoret, Kenya, on September 23, 1977, issued a strong statement in protest about social injustice in Eastern Africa.[19]

In the area of integral human development, the churches in Eastern Africa are becoming aware too that development in the fullest sense is essentially part of their mission. In the five countries studied for this research there have been various levels of cooperation between church councils and Catholic secretariats. In two countries (Kenya and Malawi) there is a Joint Medical Board. In Tanzania, Zambia, and Kenya there have been joint refugee services, although in the Kenya situation the Joint Refugee Services of Kenya (JRSK) did once run into problems arising from two National Christian Councils of Kenya (KCCK). Perhaps the best example of cooperation in integral human development would be the Christian Service Committee (CSC) in Malawi. The projects carried out by the Christian Service Committee include relief operations, for example, in flood and famine disasters; and welfare, for example, school feeding, water projects, self-help schemes, credit schemes, preventive health-care programs. A good summary of what is happening in the rest of Africa in general is contained in Father Kibirige's booklet "Our Needy Brother."

Joint Religious Education Syllabi

In most of the countries of Eastern Africa, major steps have been taken in joint religious education syllabi in both primary and secondary schools. Vatican Council II noted the importance of common witness in religious education in stating: "Church renewal therefore has notable ecumenical importance. Already this renewal is taking place in various spheres of the Church's life: the biblical and liturgical movements, the preaching of the Word of God and catechetics . . ." (Unitatis Redintegratio, no. 5).

The question of having joint religious education syllabi was already being discussed in 1970 at the AMECEA Seminar on Ecumenism. The participants in this seminar made the following findings:

1. It was agreed that a common syllabus for religious education in secondary schools is not only desirable but necessary.
2. A common syllabus will require a teacher's handbook which will have special inserts for the points where there is a difference in the teaching. These would be prepared by competent people for their respective denominations.
3. The texts for the religious education of students in secondary schools should be common to all denominations, since according to present methodology they provide matter for discussion taken from life experience and are not a doctrinal presentation.[20]

At an AMECEA Consultation on Primary School Religious Education held June 2-11, 1980, in Eldoret, Kenya, a detailed evaluation of the historical background leading to primary school joint syllabi was done. Commenting on the government's role in joint religious education syllabi in primary schools, a government representative said:

One of the most outstanding examples is the degree of practical support by the majority of Governments and Ministries of Education in Eastern Africa. After the nationalization of the schools there was concern that children of mixed denominations and different religious backgrounds should be helped to grow and develop as religious persons. The governments and Ministries were anxious that religion should not be a source of division in the schools and so recommended a joint Christian syllabus and an accompanying set of books. The Churches were encouraged to produce these. Not only were the rights of the Churches respected but their responsibilities were stressed. As a result there has been considerable ecumenical cooperation at the national level in many countries.[21]

The same government representative in addressing the participants of the consultation had the following to say on joint Christian syllabi for primary school religious education:

> Many groups of people—professional and Church—have been consulted and involved in drawing up Joint Syllabuses—in writing of lessons and the ongoing evaluation of materials. Kenya and Zambia have been particularly fortunate in this regard. In each country where the Joint Programmes exist, the Episcopal Conference and Joint Church Panels have given their approval before material has been submitted to the ministry of Education.[22]

It is important to note here too that teachers being prepared for teaching these joint religious education syllabi in primary schools in both Kenya and Zambia use joint churches' syllabi. At the end of the consultation the participants gave seven recommendations. The first three are as follows:

1. We recommend that each AMECEA country continue developing its own Primary R.E. Syllabuses and programmes, but that further reflection can be done about the feasibility of international ecumenical Primary R.E. programmes for Eastern Africa.
2. We recommend that Catechesis (family/community/parish) and Religious Education in schools be seen as separate entities. It should be clearly known in each of our countries who is responsible for each:
   a. Which department?
   b. Which Bishop?
   c. Which Secretary?
3. We request that further AMECEA Consultation on Primary R.E. be held in 1981 and 1982, with observers from other Christian communities.[23]

At this consultation, a country-by-country report on the present situation of primary school religious education was presented. This was both very encouraging as well as being an eye-opener for most participants.

As far back as 1968 Catholic teachers of religious education in secondary schools requested a program of religious education that would be both ecumenical and relevant for the youth of Eastern Africa. Their request was referred to the AMECEA Pastoral Institute, which in turn sought the collaboration of other Christian churches in the five countries. A Working Team for Secondary School Religious Education was established, with headquarters at the AMECEA Pastoral Institute. The team consisted of Father Mike Pierce, Sister Gemma McKenna, Brother Richard Kiley, and Sister Josephine Lucker. By 1975 the collaboration among the churches of Eastern Africa through the coordination of a core team had resulted in the production of syllabi and textbooks on the themes "Developing in Christ" and

"Christian Living Today." In Kenya and Uganda the official reference for the "Christian Living Today" syllabus is "Syllabus 223" (Examination Council number) in order to distinguish it from another joint religious education alternative, "Syllabus 224." Both are officially recognized by the Ministries of Education. Both are used for "O" Level examinations in Kenya and Uganda.[24]

The demand for "Developing in Christ" and "Christian Living Today," however, has increased and gone beyond Kenya and Uganda to all eastern as well as western and southern African countries. A detailed analysis and evaluation of this joint initiative has been outlined in a case study done especially for the Joint Working Group on Common Witness, at the world level. This study "Common Christian Witness in Religious Education in Eastern Africa," made in 1977 by Okullu, Kiley, and Lucker, is, as its title implies, specifically on the Eastern Africa situation. The international dimension of this joint initiative is mentioned by one of the coordinators and co-authors of "Developing in Christ" and "Christian Living Today":

> The new courses are already being used in many countries outside the AMECEA regions and in some, countries have been helpful to the local committees preparing their own syllabuses and books, such as Papua New Guinea, Hong Kong, Sierra Leone, Ghana, Liberia, and parts of Rhodesia (Zimbabwe) and South Africa.[25]

In June 1979 a Consultation for Religious Education in Southern Africa (CRESA) was held. This consultation was triggered by the Joint Initiative in Religious Education in Secondary Schools in Eastern Africa, as confirmed by the initial statement from the report of the consultation:

> Over the past ten years, Churches in Eastern Africa have collaborated with Ministries of Education in the production of agreed-on teaching materials for Christian Religious Education in secondary schools. During 1978 invitations were sent from most countries in the Southern African region for representatives from East Africa, to share their experiences. The Eastern Africa team conducted initial training sessions in Botswana, Lesotho, South Africa, Swaziland and Zimbabwe—Rhodesia, following which many places introduced experimental use of the Eastern Africa materials in their schools.[26]

Obviously a lot is being done on common witness in this area of joint religious education syllabi in both primary and secondary schools as well as in teacher-training colleges. At "A" level, a joint syllabus was produced in 1975 on an experimental basis.[27] The formation of the Association of Theological Institutions of Eastern Africa has also made a valuable contribution in the promotion of joint religious education syllabi at higher levels of learning.

Conclusion

Owing to limitations of space, this paper has covered the situation of ecumenism in Eastern Africa rather sketchily. The context of the local church, where ecumenical relations happen, has been emphasized. More space would be needed to show clearly the pastoral implications of the main hypothesis presented. It is hoped that the outline presented will serve as a starting point for further consideration leading to practical recommendations for pastoral action. A number of areas for which there is collaboration at regional and local levels have not been sufficiently covered. These include common prayer, mass media, biblical apostolate, and joint planning for evangelization.

The Holy Spirit is working gradually in the hearts of people, enabling them to see the need for genuine ecumenical relations at different levels. The signs of the present moment are hopeful in Eastern Africa. The prayer that follows shows that "we are on our way":

> Lord, your Churches quarrel,
> Bishops feel superior,
> Behave as if they were our Lord himself,
> From Europe they import traditions
> And book-learning.
> We don't want their division.
> We want one Church.
> Lord, has your Son not prayed for this one Church?
> Lord, we ask you for one Church in Ghana,
> One Church in Africa. We are on our Way.
> Give us so much love in our heart
> That the separation may be drowned in it. Amen.[28]

Notes

1. *L'Osservatore Romano,* Dec. 3, 1979.

2. Thomas Merton, *Conjectures of a Guilty Bystander* (New York: Doubleday Image Books, 1968), p. 30.

3. Cf. A. Hastings, *Church and Mission in Modern Africa* (London: Burns and Oates, 1967), p. 238.

4. *L'Osservatore Romano,* Dec. 3, 1979.

5. Brian Hearne, *Seeds of Unity* (Eldoret, Kenya: Gaba Publications, 1976), p. 4.

6. Brian Hearne, ed., *Spearhead No. 60,* vol. 5 (Eldoret, Kenya: Gaba Publications, 1979), p. 3.

7. Hastings, *Church and Mission,* p. 240.

8. Alan Moorehead, *The White Nile* (Harmondsworth, England: Penguin Books, 1963), pp. 292-95.

9. B. Muhumuuza, "Pastoral Problems in the Area of Christian Unity" (manuscript, 1975).

10. E. K. Lumbama, "Ecumenism, Attitudes and Initiative" (manuscript, 1977).

11. M. E. Townsend, *European Colonial Expansion since 1871* (1941), p. 57.

12. Cf. B. Pachai, G. W. Smith, and R. K. Tangri, eds., *Malawi, Past and Present* (Blantyre, 1971); Roland Oliver, *The Missionary Factor in East Africa* (London: Longman, 1952); P. Bolink, *Toward Church Union in Zambia* (Netherlands, 1967).

13. G. Parrinder, *Africa's Three Religions* (Sheldon Press, 1969), p. 191.

14. Ibid., p. 197.

15. Thomas Stransky, "Ecumenical Action for the Christian Mission in Africa," *Seminar on Ecumenism* (Nairobi: AMECEA, 1970), p. 13.

16. Hearne, *Seeds of Unity,* p. 20.

17. Ibid., pp. 25-35.

18. *L'Osservatore Romano,* Nov. 5, 1979.

19. AMECEA Documentation Service, no. 9/77/128; cf. also ADS, no. 9/77/127, in which the Catholic church in Kenya supported Sister Janice when she was imprisoned in Rhodesia.

20. *Seminar on Ecumenism* (Nairobi: AMECEA, 1970), p. 79.

21. J. Malesu, in "Report of the AMECEA Consultation on Primary School Religious Education" (June 1980, Eldoret, Kenya), p. 3.

22. Ibid., p. 4.

23. Richard Kiley, in "Report of the AMECEA Consultation," p. 9.

24. Cf. East African Examination Council, *Regulations and Syllabuses 1980–1981* (Nairobi, 1980); and AMECEA Documentation Service, no. 8/77/126.

25. AMECEA Documentation Service, no. 5/77/1 (119), p. 6.

26. CRESA, "Report" (1979), p. 1.

27. Jomo Kenyatta Foundation, *Christian Religious Education,* "A" level teachers' guide (Nairobi, 1975).

28. A. Shorter, *Prayer in the Religious Tradition of Africa* (Oxford University Press, 1975), p. 128.

13

AUSTRALIA

John Reilly, S.J.

The Australian Context

Australia is still very much a land of the future. In fact, only recently have the majority of Australians begun to show an interest in their past. In 1988 the second centenary of the white settlement here will be celebrated, for it was in 1788 that the first fleet bringing convicts and their guards from the overflowing jails of the British Isles landed in Sydney Cove on the eastern coast of Australia. They discovered that a black-skinned people were already sparsely scattered throughout the forests, plains, mountains, and deserts of this great land, a primitive people who built no cities or towns or even villages but lived simply from their hunting and food gathering, moving from place to place, yet rooted to the land by an intimate and sacred relationship which is only now beginning to be understood by modern Australians.

Though it has been estimated that there must have been 300,000 of these black aboriginal Australians at the time of the first white settlement, there remains today out of a total population of 14 million Australians just a little over 100,000 persons in Australia who claim to be aboriginal. In an increasingly pluralistic society, especially since World War II and the great influx of immigrants from European countries and, in recent years, from Asian countries also, the aboriginal Australians have on the whole been unable to integrate themselves into what is now becoming a multicultural country. Some have suggested that the simplicity and sharing of aboriginal Australians and their close relation to the land in which they live is a message that many Australians need but have so far failed to hear. Yet, as many a visitor to Australia asks, where are the aboriginal Australians? And all Australians might wonder, will the aboriginal Australians always be here to continue to speak the message that consumer-conscious Australians need to hear?

The Australian way of life, like the cultural heritage of any country, is a complex thing to which many different factors contribute. The vastness of this southern con-

John Reilly, S.J., is presently engaged in the direction of retreats mainly for priests and religious and lecturing in theology to various groups throughout Australia. He worked for several years in North India and taught theology at the East Asian Pastoral Institute, Manila.

tinent, the fierceness of its burning sun and the great solitude of its silent deserts, personified already for long centuries in the nomadic life of the aboriginal Australians, have certainly been fundamental elements in determining the Australian character. The aloof confidence of the English, the rebellious enthusiasm of the Irish, and the dour determination of the Scots, together with the other native endowments of these races, have interacted and blended within the historical events and challenges of their new home in its geographical isolation from the rest of the world to produce what has come to be known for several decades now as the Australian way of life.

At the risk of a gross simplification, which could lead perhaps to a caricature of the ordinary Australian if wrongly understood, it is possible to describe Australians as a people who by and large like to *do* things rather than talk or think about them, to do them *together* rather than on one's own, and to do things that will succeed and be useful for the *future* and not simply perpetuate what has always been done in the past. The Australian way of life has, therefore, these three main cutting-edges; it is practical, democratic, and future-oriented.

If this is the way of life that has become largely separated from religion, then the Christian churches in Australia face the challenge and the task of bringing Christianity into the Australian way of life at these three cutting-edges in particular. Without such a genuine insertion into the Australian way of life, the Christian religion ceases to be the life-centered gospel that Christ clearly intended it to be. Perhaps the failure of the Christian gospel to reach the hearts of the great mass of Australians in the past was the failure of the churches to bring the gospel in word and deed to bear effectively on these and other key features of the burgeoning Australian way of living.

Christian life in Australia was introduced by the white settlers and former convicts. These came mainly from England, Ireland, and Scotland. It is the descendants of these people who have continued to control the development of Christian life in this country until the 1970s. From the beginning, Anglicans from England, Catholics from Ireland, Presbyterians from Scotland, and Methodists from Wales formed the main Christian churches. They brought to Australia from their homelands their own customs, ways of worship, and prejudices, so that from the beginning the Australian experience of Christianity has been one of denominational rivalry and sectarian bitterness. In recent years the growth of the Orthodox church among the more recent immigrants from Greece and other Eastern European countries has introduced another vital and influential element into Australian Christianity.

Perhaps because of these sharp divisions among the Christian churches and possibly also because of the harshness of life and the struggles to exist that the new land imposed on the nineteenth-century settlers who came here, the majority of Australians, when they did not leave their religion completely to one side, soon learned to separate it from their public and professional lives. This "privatization" of religion, as it might be termed, has become characteristic of the average Australian and has become a cultural pattern that many recent immigrants find unnatural and strange. Religion is sacred and life is secular, and most Australians would consider that both function best when kept separate. Once they were separated, however, it soon became necessary, especially as the quality of life in Australia rapidly developed to the highest levels, to choose one's priorities. For Australians at the present time, the option appears to have been already made, probably not consciously, for life rather than for religion. The result has been that while most Australians remain nominal Christians, Christianity has ceased to be an effective force in their lives. For the practicing minority, who would still worship in one of the churches in any kind of regular way, religion has become in many cases a strictly compartmentalized affair with little apparent influence on their lives as a whole.

The Mission and Unity of the Church

Mission

The mission of the church is first and most simply to be what Christ wished it to be in the world. The true nature of the church as Christ willed it to be from the beginning has been beautifully and profoundly presented to the world in our times by Vatican Council II in the Dogmatic Constitution on the Church *(Lumen Gentium)*, universally acknowledged as the key document to come from that council. In the first three chapters of that constitution a balanced understanding of the church is presented in three broad dimensions.

The church is, first, the mystery made visible. It is the hidden entry of the Triune God into human history to bring to humankind the salvation willed by God from the beginning and now made present by his incarnate Word and his Holy Spirit. The church, then, is a kind of fundamental sacrament, that is a sign and instrument, which by reason of its relation to Christ makes visible and effective in the world humankind's union with God and the unity of all people (cf. *Lumen Gentium,* no. 1, and generally chap. 1).

Second, the church is a pilgrim community of faith. It is the new People of God struggling in faith to recognize God and serve him in holiness. Born to faith from the seed of God's living Word in Christ, it already lives by the foretaste of what it moves forward to receive in its fullness, not in a merely natural way but in the sacramental water and the Holy Spirit (cf. *Lumen Gentium,* no. 9, and generally chap. 2).

Third, the church is called by Christ to be a visible institution in the world. Its institutional reality, which the church itself must constantly struggle to perfect, is already given in broad outlines by Christ our Lord when he established, in the church that he founded, leaders with authority directly from him, for the good and for the service of the whole body (cf. *Lumen Gentium,* no. 18, and generally chap. 3).

This rich teaching of Vatican II on the nature of the church has been drawn together into a higher perspective by the Synod of Bishops, which met in Rome in 1974, and by the Apostolic Exhortation of Paul VI *(Evangelii Nuntiandi)* in 1975, in which the pope summarized and personally synthesized the mind of the synod fathers. The grace and vocation that is proper to the church and reveals its deepest identity is evangelization, its task to bring the gospel into the world (*Evangelii Nuntiandi,* no. 14). The kernel of this gospel is salvation, which means liberation from all that oppresses humans (no. 9). It is a salvation whose foundation, center, and summit is a clear proclamation of Jesus Christ in his life, death, and resurrection (no. 27).

Ecumenism

Ecumenism, which began in its modern form at the World Missionary Conference in Edinburgh in 1910, has its origin at the very heart of Christian tradition in the clearly expressed desire of Christ himself that his disciples would be one in their missionary thrust into the world (Jn. 17:23). He wished them to be one not only interiorly in a spiritual sense, but externally also as one flock under the one Shepherd (Jn. 10:16). They would thus visibly reflect the mysterious union with the Father and the Holy Spirit, which Christ revealed to his disciples and shared with them through their faith in him (Jn. 17:21–22). Ecumenism, therefore, is as essential to the church as mission is.

It was Vatican Council II that gave to Catholics throughout the world the first authoritative guidelines toward modern ecumenism. These are clearly expressed in the Decree on Ecumenism *(Unitatis Redintegratio)* especially, which is generally regarded as one of the most progressive documents of that council. It is also one of the documents whose essential message has failed to reach the grassroots level of the Catholic church in Australia.

It was, moreover, one of the chief concerns of Vatican Council II, which explicitly stated that it saw the divisions among Christians as a flagrant contradiction of the will of Christ, a scandal to the world, and an injury to the preaching of the Gospel (*Unitatis Redintegratio,* no. 1). The Vatican Council also explicitly recognized modern ecumenism, which originated from the initiatives of non-Catholic Christians, as a movement that had been fostered by the grace of the Holy Spirit for the restoration of unity among all Christians (no. 1).

What is probably the most significant ecumenical truth of Vatican II, which has failed to reach the great mass of Australian Catholics, is the important distinction, though not a complete separation, made between the church of Jesus Christ and the Catholic church over which presides the successor of Peter, the bishop of Rome. Though the council teaches that the church of Jesus Christ subsists, or has its full, concrete, and visible reality, in the Roman Catholic church, it cannot be identified exclusively with this church, since there are genuine elements of the church of Jesus Christ, real Christian truth and holiness, present in other Christian bodies to the degree in which they have remained faithful to all God did in Christ his Word and have remained obedient to the movement of Christ's Spirit within them. The Catholic church, therefore, while maintaining its claim to be the true church founded by Jesus Christ cannot hold itself aloof from other Christian bodies as the exclusive possessor of Christian truth and holiness, into which all others must transform themselves. On the contrary, the Catholic church must be a church that is prepared to enter into a sincere dialogue with other Christian bodies. This means not only a readiness to share its own riches but to learn from these other Christian bodies more clearly and more concretely what is the will of Christ for his church, given by Christ from its foundation but not always consciously accepted and welcomed by its members.

In a general view of Australian ecumenical relations, it might be said that four main kinds of motivation for church unity operate in the members of the various churches in Australia. Each of these motivations is characterized by its principal focus on Christ, on mission, on church, or on the world. For some, their ecumenical interests and activity are motivated by fidelity to Christ, who wanted his disciples to be one. Looked at negatively, this fidelity may manifest itself as a kind of guilty conscience on the lack of unity among Christians. Second, others focus on the mission of the church. These are motivated in their ecumenical concern by a longing for a more effective missionary activity among nonbelievers, which church disunity prevents. Third, others find their ecumenical motivation chiefly in the need they feel for the survival of their church in the world as an institutional structure. Finally, others are motivated in their ecumenism by a concern for the social issues around them, which they believe can be met effectively by the churches only if they are united as one.

Catholic Principles of Ecumenism

Unitatis Redintegratio declared three basic principles for ecumenical activity by Catholics today, but these principles still do not seem to be known by the majority of Catholics in Australia and do not appear to affect significantly their attitudes toward non-Catholics. These three basic principles are:

Action of the Holy Spirit. It is the Holy Spirit that is the principle of church unity. Dwelling in all those who believe in Christ and pervading the entire church, it is the Spirit who brings about true communion among them. By his action he brings about the faithful preaching of the gospel, the proper administration of the sacraments, and the right governing of the church as Christ desired from the beginning. The Spirit leads the church toward the common witness of one faith, the common celebration of one worship, and the fraternal harmony of one family of God serving one world (cf. *Unitatis Redintegratio,* no. 2).

Real though Imperfect Communion. Persons who believe in Christ and have been properly baptized are already in a real though imperfect communion with the Catholic church. This unity, based on a real incorporation into Christ through a personal justification by faith in baptism, persists and needs to be recognized by Catholics within the variety of differences of doctrine, discipline, and structure that exists between the Catholic church and the other Christian churches or communities. Liturgical actions, reverence for the Word of God in the Bible, a manifest life of grace, lives that are lived in faith, hope, and charity, signs of the interior gifts of the Holy Spirit, as well as many other visible elements, bear witness to this already existing partial communion. These and other visible means of salvation and signs of the Spirit of Christ, evident in other churches or communities, must be acknowledged by Catholics and understood by them to derive their efficacy from the same fullness of grace and truth that has been entrusted to the Catholic church by Christ, even though on account of the imperfection and sinfulness of its members this fullness has been frequently obscured and not clearly and faithfully manifested to the world (cf. *Unitatis Redintegratio,* no. 3).

Tasks for Catholics. Catholics are exhorted to recognize in the present efforts among non-Catholics toward unity the influence and grace of the Holy Spirit, and signs of the times, to which they are called to respond, become involved, and profit by contacts and meetings with their separated brethren. Either in such meetings or among themselves Catholics should try always to maintain truth and fairness when representing the position of their separated brethren. Dialogue undertaken by competent experts from the different churches is a special help toward this just appreciation of the truth and goodness in each church. Such shared studies by experts can lead further to shared service of humankind, shared prayer and fresh incentives toward renewal and reform within their own churches. Little by little differences will be overcome until all Christians can one day be gathered by a common celebration of the one Eucharist into the unity of the one church of Jesus Christ.

This desired unity of the one church of Christ, as we have seen, and which Catholics believe already subsists, that is, already has a concrete and visible expression in the world, in the Roman Catholic church, is something which has never been and, by the will of Christ, never can be lost or absent from the world, in spite of all the imperfection and sinfulness of its members, but which must go on increasing until the end of time. By this assertion, however, Catholics are not in any way excused from bettering themselves personally as Christians or from playing their role in the continuing renewal and reform of their church. In this ongoing renewal, Catholics are urged toward a proper freedom in spirituality, discipline, liturgy, and theology, which, done in charity, will bring a richer expression to the authentic catholicity and apostolicity of the church of Jesus Christ (cf. *Unitatis Redintegratio,* no. 4).

Cutting-Edges of the Australian Way of Life

Genuine Sense of Democracy

The average Australian has from the beginning had a strong sense of the basic equality of all people and has been quick to react against any person or group that tried to impose authority or leadership from above in a manner unacceptable to the majority, or in the face of the majority's opposition. Leadership was to be tolerated only when it was clearly acceptable to the majority of the people concerned, and it was always preferable that wherever possible this authority or leadership should come from below, from among the ordinary people, and not be arbitrarily imposed from above.

In Australia, Anglicanism especially, and to a lesser extent Catholicism, have tended to project an image of churches where leadership is imposed from above. However, this has been offset somewhat by the severe separation of life and religion in Australia from the earliest days of the white settlement, so that the full impact of this basic egalitarianism in the Australian way of life has yet to be felt in these two major churches of Australia.

Importance of the Ordinary

Closely linked with this rejection of authority imposed from above is the Australian's prejudice in favor of a truth or a person proved from below. Australians' sensitivity to what is popularly called "bulldust," and their instinctive and total rejection of this, determines their attitude both to persons claiming authority or some kind of superiority and to truth claiming their acceptance and allegiance. Anyone or anything that has not been proved to have evident links with the ordinary and necessary processes of life merits this somewhat vulgar label of "bulldust." Such a characteristic attitude of Australians is not so much a form of anti-intellectualism as a deeply rooted belief that the real truth will always prevail in the demanding testing-ground of the ordinary activities of life, and that the really superior person will be known only in fair competition with his or her peers.

Broad Tolerance

A corollary of the genuine regard that the average Australian feels for what has proved itself by fair competition within the ordinary affairs of life, which all know and experience, is an innate sense of tolerance, especially toward the struggling underdog. Though often blind to one's own prejudices, the Australian will usually maintain the broadest tolerance as his or her ideal and will generously admit any latent intolerance when this is pointed out to him. A sense of fair play is one of the Australian's absolutes. "Fair go, mate!" is a phrase constantly heard in Australia, and this sums up what is meant here by the broad tolerance of the average Australian. It means that the other fellow should give the speaker or some other third party a chance to prove his or her mettle. No underhand or unfair means are to be used which might prevent the best person coming to the top or stop that person from winning.

Primacy of the Practical

Like the three previously mentioned characteristics, this fourth one is another aspect of the focus on the grassroots level of life, which is the perspective always operating throughout the so-called Australian way of life. In particular this primacy of the practical is manifested within the various churches today by concerns that are directed toward difficulties and problems arising from pastoral needs and from growing requests for a deeper spiritual formation. It has never been seriously questioned by the majority of Australian Christians that theology and church administration should directly serve and should be consciously subordinated to the pastoral needs and spiritual formation of church members.

Challenges for the Churches

Keeping in mind these cutting-edges of the Australian way of life, or the salient features of the Australian character that will largely determine the manner in which Australians will progress into the 1980s and 1990s, let us now look at some of the main challenges that all the churches in Australia will face in these decades before us. These challenges in different ways call the churches to a common effort and a united response, not only because that was and always remains the express wish of Christ for his disciples in their mission to the world (Jn. 17:21), but also because that is clearly necessary if Christian witness in the present situation is to be effective.

Decline of Sectarianism

Christianity in Australia has been colored by antagonism and strife among the different church denominations from the first coming of the Christian churches with the first white settlers. The chief form of sectarianism has been in the form of an anti-Catholicism on the part of the Protestant churches and, on the Catholic side, an aggressive form of defense against their attackers. Happily, however, anti-Catholic sectarianism has steadily diminished in recent years. It still exists, but among what appears to be a small and decreasing minority of Protestants. This sectarian prejudice is only partly religious, since it appears to be inspired also by fear and jealousy of the Catholic church, which is strong, well organized, and still steadily increasing in numbers. The roots of sectarianism are to be found in the historical situations of England, Ireland, and Scotland, from where the forefathers of about three-quarters of the present Australian population originated. Prejudices, bitterness, fears, and hatreds developed in those countries were transported to Australia and formed the hard core of sectarian attitudes manifested in Australia. It is understandable, therefore, why sectarian bitterness appears to be diminishing as links with the British Isles are more and more reduced. It seems reasonable to foresee a time in the near future when it will cease altogether to be an effective factor in interchurch relations. This will mean a greater freedom for ecumenical activity, especially for more positive contributions and deeper involvement by the Catholic church in Australia. In this regard it is also interesting to note that some surveys indicate that anti-Catholic feeling may now be found more among secularists who profess no particular religious affiliation rather than among churchgoers.

Development of Ecumenism

In the nineteenth century ecumenism in Australia consisted of mergers between groups of similar denominations, especially among the Methodists, but also among the Presbyterians and the Congregationalists. In the twentieth century the focus has changed to unions between the different denominations. This activity in the first half of the century has consisted mainly of attempts to bring about union among themselves by the Methodist, Presbyterian, and Congregational churches, with the Anglican church involved as an interested observer favoring and actively fostering such a union. The Catholic church did not participate. This first half of the century, however, witnessed only failure to bring about union among the denominations. Various reasons have been suggested for this lack of success, the chief ones being institutional resistance to change, fear among the clergy of the inevitable disturbances of their vested interest and power, and a laity too exclusively concerned with their own local enterprises. But the second half of the century has already witnessed some remarkable developments. In 1977 the Uniting Church of Australia was inaugurated as a union of the Methodist, Presbyterian, and Congregational churches of Australia with a nominal membership of about 15 percent of all Australians. It therefore became, after the Anglican and Catholic churches, the third largest body of Christians in the country, although some of the Presbyterians chose to continue as a separate Presbyterian church. From the time of Vatican Council II the interest of the Catholic church, both at the level of leadership and among the laity, has grown dramatically. Survey polls conducted in the mid-1960s revealed Catholics as the most union-minded of all the denominations. However, it may not become a practical activity for some time, since most Catholics do not yet seem to consider ecumenism to be of the same vital concern for the identity of the church as its sacramental or missionary activity. For most Australian Catholics ecumenism is still a side-issue.

Secularization in Australia

The phenomenon of secularization has a unique quality, which distinguishes the situation in which the Christian churches find themselves in Australia from the situation of the churches in the developed countries of Europe and North America. Europe has centuries of Christianity at the base of its secularizing processes, and North America had strongly motivated Christians among its chief founders. Australia, on the other hand, was secular from the beginnings of the white settlement and, when secularity was written into the laws of the nation, Australia had never really experienced any other situation. If the aboriginal Australians had been able to exercise any real influence on the development of modern Australia, things might have been very different, for they were a people with a simple but deep religious sense of the sacred and its place in life. The causes of secularization in Australia are complex, but the divisions among the churches and their failure from the beginning to speak with one voice greatly diminished their influence upon the development of the country in its ordinary life. The separation of the sacred from the ordinary functions of social life was enhanced further by the Protestant doctrine of individual justification by faith, thus bypassing institution and works, which led naturally to the autonomy of the individual and secularization as a logical consequence. Likewise the Catholic attitude of separation from the state and defending itself from the Protestant majority by a well-organized institutional church tended to keep Catholics apart from the mainstream of life in the nation, and separated their life as Christians from their life as Australians. The separation of the sacred from life has led to a laxity and indifferentism toward religion among Australians, which are especially evident today among the young. This and the constant challenge of the secular condition of Australian social life for the churches to find new ways of bringing the sacred into ordinary life again demand a common effort on their part. How is the sacred to be made a visible and public reality in a way that speaks to the hearts of secularized Australians, especially the great numbers alienated from the churches? How can the Australian in his highly secularized way of life be effectively offered a spiritual formation that will enable him to experience deeply the sacred?

Cultural Pluralism

In this century, in fact since the end of World War II, Australia has passed from cultural uniformity, through a stage of cultural assimilation of new elements from outside, to its present chosen position of cultural pluralism. The experience of cultural pluralism, which has only begun to have a real impact on the majority of Australians over the last few years, poses a new opportunity for the churches. The rejection of Christian faith by so many Australians, possibly now the majority, if not in theory then at least as a serious factor in their daily living, is being confirmed for them by their experience of cultural pluralism. For their rejection, signified in their increasing alienation from the churches, does not appear to be based chiefly on any intellectual or reasoned arguments. Though these may be used to support their rejection, this is based primarily on what they consider to be their practical experience of Christian faith as something of no real consequence for their lives.

By such a practical rejection of faith, Australians are saying to the churches that in the worship, holiness, doctrine, and social concern which they offer to their members they are offering nothing of real substance that cannot be found elsewhere within the vibrant and rapidly increasing cultural pluralism of the nation. The social relativism that is coming to predominate in modern Australia has produced a widespread skepticism toward churches that claim to offer an absolute truth and goodness to people and yet cannot agree among themselves on the meaning and practice of what they offer. Such a situation clearly calls for some form of united action on the part of all the churches. Only then can they remain faithful to their common belief that the gospel must always be in some way an essential element in the final solution to any human problem. As Pope John Paul II has stressed emphatically, it is only in the gospel revealed in Christ that humankind attains the full truth about humankind.

Returning Foreign Missionaries

Another striking phenomenon on the Australian scene today, and one that affects all the main churches and so offers again a challenge that can best be met by a united effort, is the return of many foreign missionaries to their native Australia. Men and women, clergy, members of religious orders and missionary societies, and many lay people have returned to Australia because their term of service has finished or because of the restrictions of foreign governments on the protracted residence of outsiders, sometimes especially Christian missionaries, in their countries. Many of these men and women are in their prime, and most have years of useful service ahead of them. The presence within all the main churches of Australia today of such men and women offers a tremendous source for a renewed creative and energetic missionary thrust within Australia itself.

Such returned missionaries are usually dedicated and highly motivated. Their transcultural experience ideally equips them to face the new situations within Australia today. It helps them to make any necessary adaptations in the way of expounding Christian doctrine, structuring Christian worship and community at the local level, or organizing Christian pastoral service according to the needs of the people. Thus they can readily become spearheads for the churches as they move into new areas of Australian life. Their presence also brings a new flexibility to their churches, helping to overcome the inertia of settled habits built up over the years, which are possibly no longer relevant. At least missionary awareness, the core of the church's identity, will be reawakened by the presence of these returned missionaries. Many of these missionaries, moreover, have had creative and mutually enriching ecumenical experiences during their missionary service in foreign countries. Their presence, therefore, within the Australian churches brings a new dynamic element into Australian ecumenical relations. Church leaders already sensitized to the importance of ecumenism in the life of the churches in Australia have in them a new and creative source of collaboration.

Nuclear Families

One important factor in the Australian situation today to which many of the returning missionaries are particularly sensitive, especially those coming from the so-called underdeveloped countries, is the shrinking of the extended family generally, and in big cities especially, the absence of such extended families. The extended family, where three generations live under the same roof and where aunts, uncles, and cousins live in close proximity if not under the same roof also, is very difficult to maintain in Australia today for many reasons. The nuclear family, consisting of parents and children, is also becoming smaller, usually two or three children. The breakup of these small families is frequent. Nearly half of all marriages contracted in Australia are now ending in divorce or separation of some kind. In addition, the phenomenon of one-parent families, where one parent, usually the mother, tries to bring up a child or children on her own, is common.

Family life in Australia is finding difficulty in surviving, or at least in enjoying much of the richness and vitality of the family life typical of previous generations. There are many and complex reasons for this, but one thing seems clear. The nuclear family, and much more the one-parent families, are in need of a support and assistance that possibly only the churches can effectively provide. In fact, according to the recent teaching of the Catholic church since Vatican Council II, the family is a church, "the domestic church," and so it is basic identity of the church in its simplest form. In supporting this basic unit, therefore, the churches can find themselves again in a manner that can both unify and call for common efforts from all the churches to provide assistance.

Mobility of Australians

Linked with the problems of the increasing isolation of Australians is the increased mobility of people in Australia over recent years. Australia is a huge land mass with a small population and is still in the early stages of the full development of its immense natural resources. This, combined with the ready availability of modern means of transport to all levels of the population, has made modern Australians a highly mobile people. Tourism within and outside Australia is a big business today. Change of one's place of residence is frequent. In one year, 1978–79, a survey showed that one out of every six Australians changed residence. This was especially characteristic of the young in their early twenties and of the unemployed. Such a situation offers a big challenge to the churches for united efforts to meet a problem that obviously has to be tackled on a national level. When a population is so mobile, local churches and the individual denominations have to work with one another if they are to be effective in their mission to communicate the gospel of Christ. Church resources need to be pooled in order to reach a moving population of church members. The media, such as television, radio, and newspapers, are one of the few constants in such a moving population and need to be properly utilized by the churches in their mission. Yet the use of such means usually requires more resources than the local church can provide and also even more than the individual denominations are able to call upon.

Public Morality

Private morality is the concern of the churches, for Christian faith brings moral imperatives into the life of each individual Christian. Public morality, however, challenges the churches with a special urgency of its more universal consequences for Christian living by church members. There are urgent challenges given to all the churches in Australia by the contemporary decline in public standards of morality. This decline is particularly noticeable among the young where it is manifested in the increasing frequency of drug addiction, violent crimes, overindulgence in intoxicating drinks, infidelity in marriage, a lack of integrity and pride in one's work, and a lack of respect for old age and for authority in general. The consumer mentality, which leads to the stimulation and the full satisfaction of every possible human feeling and inclination without a real concern for the overall direction of one's life, is also particularly evident among the younger generation.

It appears in many cases that the young have yet to experience seriously that there is any alternative way of living in a modern society. The consumer mentality challenges the core of the gospel carried by the churches, for it denies the simplicity and dependence that Christ taught as a condition to enter into the life of the kingdom. Closely associated with the problem of consumerism is the right use of leisure, which the new technology and increased standards of living are putting into the hands of so many Australians in a constantly increasing measure. These are challenges that the churches can best meet by united efforts to offer that essential assistance toward the solution of these human problems which only the gospel of Christ can offer.

Oppression and Injustice

An area of public morality to which the Christian conscience may need a more vigorous awakening in Australia, if the churches are not to fail by neglect, is the world of big business and financial investment. Individual Christians and the churches as communities may contribute to, or even be primarily responsible for, situations of injustice and oppression against those who have no voice. This can happen through their lack of a Christian consciousness in the way money is invested and business transactions are conducted. Situations need to be revealed with the assistance of the churches where injustice is caused or aggravated by indiscriminate investments of large amounts of capital in powerful enterprises and international institutions where financial profit is the overriding motive. The churches can stimulate one another to a greater awareness in this whole area. By their united efforts they can bring more effective pressure on individuals and companies to take into consideration factors other than sheer profit and loss, or at times they can use their influence to bring direct pressure on the profits of such individuals or companies in the language they best understand. By such concerted action the churches will not only be more effective in producing concrete results in the struggle against injustice, but will also be drawn closer to one another by their mutual cooperation.

Urgent Social Issues

In Australia at the present time there are a number of social issues that are of special importance because of the frequency with which they are being brought to the attention of the nation by the media and because of the inherent human need and suffering on a widespread scale that they represent. The churches by their common title of discipleship toward Christ are challenged by these social needs. Fidelity to the gospel demands of all the churches that they seek the most effective means to bring relief to suffering and disadvantaged people.

In most cases the churches in Australia are faced with the same social issues. These call for the most effective solution possible and therefore one involving the gospel, if not directly based on its principles. Such a solution based on the gospel is best offered when it is done by a united church response. In situations where the government at the national or state levels has been providing some measure of relief, plans and programs already exist. Such is the case in Australia today in social relief for insecure families, especially one-parent families, for the large body of unemployed, for migrants newly arrived in the country, for the aged and the handicapped, for the numerous alcoholics, and for the aboriginal Australians. The plans and programs of the government call for cooperation and assistance from the churches with their integrated and comprehensive vision of humankind derived from the gospel and their ready access to dedicated and deeply motivated persons within their communities. An increasing involvement in such government social programs rather than an exclusive concern for initiating separate responses from their own denominational churches could greatly further the cause of church union.

Catholic Schools

The widespread organization of Catholic primary and secondary schools, spread throughout the country, educates more than 20 percent of all children in Australia. The history of the Catholic schools in Australia is one of the great factors in the development of the strong, vital, and unified Australian Catholic church that exists today. Extraordinary sacrifices were made by Catholics from the second half of the nineteenth century to provide the finance and personnel for these schools. Only quite recently has the government accepted the principle of state aid to the nonstate schools. Yet the situation today is changing. Tertiary education in Australia has always been secular and state-controlled.

Though the issue is highly sensitive, emotionally charged, and extremely complex, many Catholics in Australia appear to question the need of a separate Catholic school system at the secondary level as an effective means of either secular or religious education in Australia at the present time. The dramatic decrease over recent years in the numbers of religious Brothers and Sisters committed to the educational apostolate, who have until recently carried the main burden of the teaching in Australian Catholic schools, constitutes an obvious and immediate reason to reconsider the future of a distinctively Catholic school system in Australia. The need for Catholic primary schools and their effectiveness does not seem to be questioned seriously. In fact, there are reasons indicating a need to expand Catholic primary education in Australia. Several basic factors, however, suggest the need for serious consideration of the possible phasing out of Catholic secondary education. These are, for example, the tendency of Catholic education to foster a state within a state, the development of schools for the elite who can afford them, instead of schools that are genuinely catholic, or universal, and the separation of Catholic children from Protestant children during the critically formative years of adolescence and early adulthood. Moreover, the situation in Australia during the nineteenth century, when fear and hatred of Rome led secularists and Protestants to combine their efforts and secularize education, has for the most part ceased to exist.

Certainly if all the Catholic boys and girls now in Catholic secondary schools were to mix freely with their compatriots of the same age in the one Australian school system, the challenges to the churches and the opportunity for united efforts to continue the formation of these young men and women in gospel understanding and gospel living could have a dramatic effect on the whole ecumenical effort in Australia. Would the Catholic church, both in its leadership and in its members, be prepared for such a sacrifice toward both national unity and the union of the churches? Could the Catholic church in fidelity to Christ make such a move? Would the government consider it feasible?

Conclusion

From what has been written I think it is evident how much I believe the future missionary activity of the churches in Australia is inseparably bound to the slowly accelerating activity of these churches toward a union in the one church of Jesus Christ in Australia. The churches may have in their mission within Australia a call from Christ just as challenging as the traditional foreign missions of recent times and one demanding the same readiness to cross cultural barriers and the same flexibility to make the adaptations that will be asked of the churches. Ecumenical activity is not an added extra to the mission and life of the churches in general, but an essential element in the missionary calls Christ gives to them through the signs of the times in the Australian situation of today. Ecumenical union of the churches will be more likely to occur when a common and united effort is made by all the churches together to be faithful to Christ and his gospel in and through the needs and service of their fellow Australians.

Two factors especially seem to suggest that all of this may be much more than theory and wishful thinking. These factors are two movements taking place in all the churches in Australia today. The first movement is from *outside* to *inside,* when foreign missionaries are returning to Australia and finding that the missionary situations they have experienced overseas are to be found more and more within Australia itself. The second movement is from *above* to *below,* when ecumenism which for many years has been the concern and interest of many of the leaders in the various Australian churches is now beginning to be felt with the same urgency and longing, but possibly with less patience, at the grassroots level in the ordinary, good but unsophisticated members of the Australian churches. Both these factors, more felt than planned, may indicate that the finger of God is already here.

14

CATHOLIC, EVANGELICAL, AND REFORMED: AN ECUMENICAL STRATEGY FOR TOTAL EVANGELIZATION

Harry E. Winter, O.M.I.

During the 1960s the insight appeared and was systematized within American Protestantism that Christianity is catholic, evangelized, and reformed. This insight is vital and essential for both ecumenism and evangelization. First, we shall look at each of these characteristics, and then see how witness is carried out by those churches and groups that typify one or the other of the three tendencies. We shall propose some strategies for ecumenical evangelization, and close with some areas for further study.

Several important analyses of evangelization in the United States (Southern Baptist, Texas, 1975–77; Roman Catholic, 1976–78) have demonstrated that if the local community is not renewed, evangelization is worthless. Developing the consciousness that each parish includes people of catholic, evangelical, and reformed temperament has proved valuable in renewing parishes for mission.

The Meaning of "Catholic," "Evangelical," and "Reformed"

Catholic Christianity

The best simple and biblical explanation of these three characteristics of the church is found in the Consultation on Church Union's *In Quest of a Church of Christ Uniting.*[1] Of course, the Reformation churches such as the Lutheran, Presbyterian, and Reformed churches have always vindicated catholicity as one of their characteristics, in contrast to the churches that came out of eighteenth-century pietism (with some heritage from the Anabaptists). The catholic Christian is usually

Harry E. Winter, Oblate of Mary Immaculate, is the Pastor of Holy Family Catholic Church in Pearisburg, Virginia. He is also the Secretary-Treasurer of the Giles County Ministerial Association and Editor of the newsletter, *Mission/Unity.*

a cradle Christian, baptized at infancy and steeped in the sacraments. This type of Christian, in the Roman Catholic church, was caught off-guard and ill-prepared for Vatican II, and still is skeptical, if not of the changes mandated by the council, at least of the interpretations proposed by many devotees of the Council. They note that when Pope John XXIII opened the windows to let in fresh air, many bugs entered too.

Catholic Christians quite naturally and often unconsciously consider the church to be simply and unqualifiedly the body of Christ, and sense that, in the Pauline metaphor (1 Cor. 12:4–11), the hand is somehow more important than the fingers. Catholic Christians thus give a great dignity and importance to the hierarchy, sometimes waiting until ordered to do something, before action takes place.

The universality of the church comes to mind first for the catholic Christian, and perhaps only much later does the local church enter into importance. Theoretically at least, cultural and ethnic diversity are easily admitted and pursued, especially if they stay at a safe distance.

The catholic Christian tends to emphasize structure, order, and the institution. Structures do not prevent decay and laxity. But as James Hastings Nichols, Princeton Seminary's church historian, has noted, once such decay has been detected, structures permit quicker renewal than in churches that have downplayed or almost eliminated them. This has important missiological consequences.

Evangelical Christianity

The Consultation on Church Union (COCU) tells us that evangelicals emphasize the authority of the Scriptures and the *experience* of the gospel, with a strong missionary role for the entire church. It should immediately be recognized that much of the Protestant missionary movement, at least in its English-speaking form (and probably also in the French *reveil* and the German *Erweckung*) depends on the pietist strand, and not on the fundamentalist strand. Thus today's evangelical Protestant missionaries are much more moderate than the American sects, cults, and fundamentalist Bible-thumpers. Billy Graham (the preacher), Oral Roberts (the healer), and Francis Schaeffer (the philosopher) all represent a kind of evangelical Protestantism increasingly willing to make common cause with Roman Catholics, especially charismatics, and even mainline (often viewed as "liberal") Protestants.

Glenn Igleheart, director of the Department of Interfaith Witness in the Home Mission Board of the Southern Baptist Convention, U.S.A., summarized this moderate stance in "Evangelism and Ecumenism in the Eighties." He wrote:

> For all their affinities, it is unfortunate that evangelism-oriented people and ecumenism-oriented people do not talk or work more with one another. What usually occurs is in-house talk about other-house people and their shortcomings. One challenge of the 1980's is for evangelists and ecumenists to meet on a deeper level, to acknowledge and applaud one another's gifts, and to challenge one another on the basis of both biblical exegesis and contemporary needs.[2]

Granted, not all evangelical Protestants are so ironically disposed, especially in Latin America. But even there a growing number of evangelical Protestants, especially after the Lausanne Covenant (1974) and the emergence of the charismatic movement and basic communities within Roman Catholicism, are interested in evangelizing together.

Protestant historians admit that there has always been, to use James Hastings Nichols' felicitous expression, an "evangelical undertow" in Roman Catholicism. (The question arises: Can Roman Catholics admit that there has always been a "catholic undertow" within Protestantism?) Saint Francis of Assisi and what Louis Hertling, S.J., called "monastic waves" are generally cited by most historians as examples of reform and renewal in Mother Rome. (Hertling made it clear that the word "monastic" was misleading; generally the renewal of the religious orders was but the tip of the iceberg of renewal in the entire church.)

A most important renewal, as far as this author is concerned, is the charismatic renewal, dated in the Roman Catholic church, U.S.A., from Duquesne University, Pittsburgh, Pennsylvania, 1967, and shortly before that in the mainline Protestant American churches. That it has important contacts with classical Pentecostalism is admitted by all. Cardinal Suenens[3] and Father Kilian McDonnell, O.S.B.,[4] have each demonstrated that elements of both evangelization and ecumenism exist in the charismatic movement. What interests us here is the closeness between the baptism in the Spirit of the charismatics and the "born-again" experience of the evangelicals (Jn. 3:3). The majority of participants in most Roman Catholic, or even interdenominational, prayer groups probably do not speak in tongues, but the majority would have had the usually shattering, emotional experience of the Lord's love, which they call "baptism in the Spirit," and which evangelicals call being born again in the Lord. *And this experience is both mission-oriented to witness and unity-oriented to ecumenism.*

When Latin American Pentecostals Luis Paulu and Manoel de Mello work with Roman Catholic charismatics, they offer us a priceless example of how evangelization, ecumenism, and spirituality can come together, overcoming the hatreds and hurts of the past. Charismatics, evangelicals, and Roman Catholics represent overlapping categories. Especially in black Africa, with the emergence of many populist, grassroots movements in Christianity, it should be asked if these represent a universal tendency within structured churches: evangelical groups do not necessarily have to be revolutionary, but may simply be the age-old impulse of the Spirit. The Roman Catholic charismatic movement demonstrated its appeal to the third world by the inclusion of third-world representatives in the group that met with Pope John Paul II on December 11, 1979. Thus we have an important indication that contact between classical Protestant evangelical and Pentecostal groups, and the renewed Roman Catholicism represented by the charismatic movement offers great possibilities for both evangelization and ecumenism.

Scripturally, evangelicals tend to the image of the church as the People of God (1 Pet. 2:9-10; Rev. 5:8-14), and to use the ecclesiology of this image to develop basic communities with strong lay leadership. As Cardinal Willebrands stated so forcefully in the presence of Cardinal Krol, when the former addressed the 1970 National

Workshop on Christian Unity, in Philadelphia, Pennysylvania, democratization of the church's structures does not mean that we teach that the church is a democracy. Participation in decision-making by the people whose lives are touched by those decisions does not mean a renunciation of authority by those in charge, but only a wise use of that authority. And it is an old monastic principle!

Reformed Christianity

COCU hints that the reformed strand of Christianity is more a corrective to the other two than a full-fledged strand.[5] In a church that is constantly renewing itself (and some portions of Roman Catholicism still prefer the term "renewal" to "reform"), nothing is final. Reformed Roman Catholics instinctively grasp that the key distinction used by John XXIII when he opened Vatican Council II ("the substance of the ancient doctrine of the deposit of faith is one thing, and the way in which it is presented is another"[6]) is subject to simplistic interpretations, for one never has nude substances walking around. No form is final; everything is subject to continual growth and reform.

It can be argued that Karl Rahner, S.J., and Yves Congar, O.P., the two lights who did the most to prepare the Roman Catholic church for Vatican II, are much closer to Karl Barth, the Niebuhrs, and Paul Tillich (the classical exponents of neo-orthodoxy, or "Reformation theology"), than they are to the more traditional proponents of Roman Catholic Scholastic theology. Both, especially Congar, work out of historical theology, profoundly aware of the vast fluctuations in doctrine and discipline during our history. Yet when we view all history as relative, we are not falling into relativism. Within the constant flow of time, customs, and circumstances, there are anchors, tether-hooks, and benchmarks. But the appearance and outer clothing of these change.

The missiological impact of reformed Christianity is considerable, especially in the area of inculturating Christianity. All cultures and civilizations both affect Christianity and are affected by it. Christianity can never renounce its claim to judge all cultures; in this, reformed Christianity is adamant. The reality of sin, evil, and the demonic are reinforced by reformed Christianity's existential philosophical base, and an optimistic existentialist seems a contradiction in terms.

Yet the critical stand of reformed theologians means honest dialogue with the world. The reformed strand is thus the closest to coalition-building and emphasizes the servant role of the church. In its Protestant expression, reformed Christianity has always been in close touch with the world of science and modern civilization. Major portions of the Pastoral Constitution on the Church in the Modern World (*Gaudium et Spes*) could probably be laid at the door of reformed Catholic Christianity.

H. Richard Niebuhr caricatured liberal Christianity as "a God without wrath, leading men without sin, into a kingdom without judgment, through the ministry of Christ without a cross."[7] Reformed Christians thus instinctively use the model of tensions, rather than syllogistic reasoning from major through minor to conclusion. God is both wrathful and lamblike; humankind is deeply wounded, yet capable of enormous good; the church is both a kind mother and a stern judge; and the cost of discipleship is great. Hand in glove with these tensions goes the scriptural image of the church as a pilgrim (Heb. 11:29, 37–12:2; 13:12–14). The community of Christians is never at home in this world; and in order to travel light, it is continually stripping off (and being stripped of) its excess baggage. Thus the reformed strand tends to be very eschatological, yearning and looking forward to the city that is being built every day. (Yet a pilgrim is not a wanderer; the route may be vague, but the destination the pilgrim searches for is somehow known.)

One of the surprises of Paul VI's *Evangelii Nuntiandi* was the insistence that the church not only evangelize, but first and continuously must *be* evangelized itself (no. 15). "Constant conversion and renewal" sounds refreshingly like reform.

Having seen each of these strands, and recognizing that the Roman Catholic church, even as it embodies the community Christ founded *(Lumen Gentium,* no. 8), needs to embody each of them more fully, let us see how each does its missionary work.

Evangelization by the Three Tendencies

Catholic Christian Evangelization

The great advantage of catholic Christians in evangelization is the attention they pay to structure and past history; the great disadvantage is their lack of awareness of the role adult, individual conversion plays in building up the local community. The work of Matteo Ricci, S.J., in China can be cited as catholic Christianity at its best. And the inability to make common cause with evangelicals, to appreciate the psychological and spiritual dynamism of the "born-again experience" can be cited as their greatest problem and failure.

Traditionally, catholic Christians have tended to delegate the responsibility for evangelization to the clergy and the Legion of Mary. Yet a distinctive mission consciousness is growing within catholic Christian groups.

The catholic Christian will instinctively tend toward stability and order, and almost naturally emphasize the sacraments over against Scripture in this age-old tension within all worship. Those passages of the New Testament that find Paul at his most "pastoral," establishing structure and acting with authority, are instinctively favorite passages of catholic Christians. The following passage from a highly respected sacramental handbook of American Protestants illustrates that this passion for order and stability is not peculiarly Roman Catholic:

The Order should not be tampered with. The minister should not introduce experiments into the service. He should let the Sacrament speak. . . .

The closing rubric of the first order should be carefully followed. "After the celebration reverent disposition of the Elements which remain shall be made by the ministers and elders." Too often regarding this there is a carelessness and irreverence, which is frequently noticed by the people and especially by the young.[8]

The same author, though, illustrates a tendency in catholic Christians to be uneasy with powerful biblical preaching. Due in part to abuses by evangelicals, the catholic Christian stresses the objectivity of sacrament, over against the preacher's feelings.[9] The great emphasis in English-speaking Catholicism during the late 1950s on kerygmatic preaching seems to have been neglected, and needs to be resurrected, needs to be seen as a vital part of the cornerstone of Vatican II, *Dei Verbum* (Constitution on Divine Revelation), and made a part of the catholic tradition, if that tradition is to recover and deepen its evangelization possibilities. Again, Paul VI showed a new (for most of us) emphasis when he underlined the place of preaching and the liturgy of the Word in evangelization *(Evangelii Nuntiandi,* nos. 42–43).

Two other aspects of worship are vitally concerned with missionary work, and will probably best be developed within the catholic tendency. One is the use of the lectionary. The United States Bishops Committee on Liturgy has written:

> The revised lectionary has been adopted and enthusiastically used by those Churches which for centuries shared with the Roman Church the one-year cycle; the excellence of its inherent rationale has also caused it to be widely used in other Churches, unaccustomed to a fixed lectionary. Thus this lectionary, supported by the serious, positive criticism of biblical scholars, has been of inestimable value in the promotion of Christian faith and witness.[10]

If the lectionary is followed, the evangelizer must balance hellfire and brimstone with God's love. The lectionary, if used as a guide, will ensure that evangelization will be complete, and not just the favorite texts of the missionaries. The local community will be nourished on all of God's Word and will hear more than the pet peeves of the group mainly responsible for evangelization.

If worship is a three-legged stool, and the sacramental system needs the other two legs of personal prayer, and family church year devotional prayer to support it, then what Paul VI called "popular religiosity," and termed "at the same time so rich and so vulnerable" *(Evangelii Nuntiandi,* no. 48) needs real attention. In the United States, at least, the Hispanic culture, especially in the Southwest, shows definite signs of using its popular piety well, while the Anglo culture is in real danger of having an anemic, weak devotional life, especially outside of charismatic groups.

Another approach of catholic Christianity to evangelization, which should be lauded and developed, is that of the "soft sell." English-speaking Roman Catholicism fears proselytism, partly in reaction to fundamentalism, and partly due to temperament. When Paul VI spoke of "innumerable events in life and human situations which offer the opportunity for a discreet but incisive statement of what the Lord has to say in this or that particular circumstance" *(Evangelii Nuntiandi,* no. 43), he struck a cord that catholic Christians everywhere recognize.

With the great veneration that catholic Christians have for the medieval synthesis, as illustrated in nostalgic titles such as *The Thirteenth: Greatest of Centuries,* the use of the arts and culture to bring out the best of humankind's potential is another direction that catholic Christians can be expected to take in evangelization. Yet as Paul Tillich's companion, Richard Kroner, pointed out, the attempt of the papacy to baptize the Renaissance ended in corrupting the papacy. The fear that the reformed strand has of getting too close to culture and the arts needs to be remembered here; Vatican II's balance between optimism and fear of the demonic has not always been kept since Vatican Council II (cf. *Lumen Gentium,* no. 16; *Ad Gentes,* nos. 9, 11).

When Paul VI finally defined evangelization, he refused to eliminate the society side: "the Church evangelizes when she seeks to convert, solely through the divine power of the Message she proclaims, both the personal and collective consciences of people, the activities in which they engage, and the lives and concrete milieux which are theirs" (*Evangelii Nuntiandi,* no. 18).

The problem is that the catholic tendency has always given the pride of place to the societal collective, and little to the personal. Even the parish mission seemed to remain outside the structure of the parish, and was never fully incorporated into Roman Catholicism. The difficulty that United States bishops are having in fully accepting and structuring the Ad Hoc Committee on Evangelization also illustrates the relative newness in contemporary Catholicism of viewing the church as ongoing mission.

The catholic tendency offers rich possibilities for evangelization, especially as worship emphasizes its quality of commissioning and strengthening for mission and witness. Yet much must be done to incorporate the born-again, adult commitment within the catholic tendency.

Evangelical Christian Evangelization

Evangelism is one beggar telling another beggar where to find bread, wrote D. T. Niles in a celebrated definition. It is no coincidence that this description of evangelism suits Christians who play down the societal side of life and prefer to work one-on-one. It is also no coincidence that evangelicals still fear incarnational theology, with its real possibility of suffocation in ritualism. The Puritan element within evangelical Christianity surfaces in many ways.

Evangelical Christianity places a great deal of importance on lay people witnessing, even in a foreign missionary situation. The exaggeration of celibacy in a situation where the only missionaries are priests, or perhaps nuns, is thus avoided, and married life assumes its rightful role as the normal vocation of most Christians. Yet the fear of celibacy also does not allow this gospel calling to develop as quickly as it should, and even as the catholic tendency exaggerates celibacy, so the evangelical tendency exaggerates marriage. The sending out by groups such as Maryknoll of both priests and nuns on the one hand, and married couples on the other, offers real hope that this last of the Reformation-Tridentine exaggerations is being corrected. So too the charismatic side of evangelicalism, within the Roman Catholic church, offers real hope that celibates and married couples, witnessing out of the same basic community (even though probably not living under the same roof), can overcome the dichotomy between the two kinds of gospel witness.

The charismatic groups are developing a worship that is witness-oriented and complementary to the sacraments. It is no coincidence that the Pentecostal and summer ecumenical charismatic conferences in the United States feature worship that is vibrant, missionary, and nonsacramental.

The evangelical strand does tend to fall into the hard-sell, hitting people over the head with the Bible. It needs to be more nuanced and subtle. Its great strength—adult commitment with a natural desire to witness—has done work of inestimable value in building sound family life, overcoming alcoholism, reinforcing work habits, and evangelizing prisons. Yet this can be Band-Aid social work unless evangelicals also commit themselves to the long-range problems of rebuilding, or at least reforming, an unjust economic and social structure. Richard Quebedeaux's *Young Evangelicals,*[11] *Sojourners* magazine, the Lausanne Covenant, and the "Chicago Call"[12] are all signs that just such a maturing of evangelical-charismatic thought is occurring. These developments urgently need to be studied in mission institutes and programs for the updating of missionaries.

Reformed Christian Evangelization

Because reformed Christians are totally convinced of the reality of sin and the demonic, and the need for explicit evangelization, such liberal themes as "A moratorium on missionaries," or "The world sets the agenda for the Church," cause them to gag. Since reformed Christians generally come from a background of strong historical consciousness, they recognize the concern that these two slogans represent. But such concern only increases the need that reformed Christians see for witness and mission.

With the ties that reformed Christians have to both liberals and evangelicals, they are the ideal ones to deepen the dialogue about secularism and secularization (cf. *Gaudium et Spes,* no. 36; *Redemptor Hominis,* nos. 8, 15–16). Harvey Cox's *Secular City*[13] is a seminal book to which Christians must return, and as Claude Welch pointed out in *Secular City Debate,* philosophical questions (perhaps not systems) must continue to be recognized as playing a vital role in modern thought.[14] Reformed Christians generally have a deep respect for philosophical matters and so play a vital role in developing missionary strategies, particularly in the difficult question of separating harmful elements from positive elements in each culture, especially the modern secular culture.

Reinhold Neibuhr's *Moral Man and Immoral Society* (1933) has had enormous influence on modern Protestant thought. Reformed Christians have been in the vanguard of the effort to bring Christian values to an increasingly unjust national and international economic structure. Bishop Francisco Claver's statement that "economic power, painstakingly gained by cooperative effort among the farming and working classes, could not long be sustained and held on to without corresponding political clout" points out the danger of those who would separate the church's teaching on social justice from politics.[15] If the church is to witness in all the areas mentioned by Paul VI, then the contribution of reformed Christians, both Protestant and Roman Catholic, is crucial.

A Methodology for Strategy in Evangelization

It would seem that those churches, denominations, and ecclesial communities that profess belief in the three characteristics sketched in this paper, and the desirability that each parish should consciously incorporate all three, are ripe for a renewed effort at witness. It should also be evident that, in those places where bishops and major superiors are faced with hard choices in withdrawing full-time personnel because of the drop in the numbers of priests, this methodology furnishes a tool for reinforcement of parishes and/or missions, or for curtailment if that seems advisable.

The Lund Principle has not always been grasped as an evangelization principle, but if, in the words of Robert McAfee Brown, we "should act together in all matters except those in which deep differences of conviction compel us to act separately," then our witness would seem to be a prime area for cooperation.[16]

One wonders why the hesitation. Certainly the conciliar and papal teaching is clear on this point: evangelization needs Christian unity. The Decree on Missionary Activity blazed the way (*Ad Gentes*, nos. 6, 15-16); Paul VI minced no words (*Evangelii Nuntiandi*, no. 77), and was even clearer when he opened the Holy Year of 1975: "We wish, lastly, to proclaim that reconciliation among Christians is one of the central purposes of the Holy Year. The reconciliation of all men with God, our Father, depends, in fact, on the reestablishment of communion among those who have already recognized and received in faith Jesus Christ."[17]

John Paul II's *Redemptor Hominis* is equally clear on the need for ecumenism if evangelization is to be effective (cf. nos. 6, 11-12); when he met with the patriarch of Constantinople, he several times insisted on "the necessity of realizing full unity in order to bear a more effective witness for our time." Asking the Lord to make us "impatient for unity," he hoped that the coming millennium would find Roman and Orthodox "standing side by side, in full communion, to bear witness together to salvation before the world, the evangelization of which is waiting for this sign of unity."

The statement "Common Witness and Proselytism," issued by the Vatican and the World Council of Churches in May 1970, and the Lausanne Covenant of the evangelical churches (1974) demonstrate beyond a shadow of a doubt that joint planning is desirable. "Common Witness" put it this way:

> The missionary effort of one Church in an area or milieu where another Church is already at work depends on an honest answer to the question: what is the quality of the Christian message proclaimed by the Church already at work, and in what spirit is it being proclaimed and lived? Here frank discussion between the Churches concerned would be highly desirable . . . with the hope that it would help to determine the possibilities of fraternal assistance, or of complete withdrawal.[18]

Yet when such suggestions have been made by this author, both to missionaries and to bishops, in the context of only the Orthodox and Anglicans, consternation resulted. Certainly when Walbert Bühlmann looked at the need for more effective evangelization of places like São Paulo, Brazil, he did not hesitate to affirm: "Here again it is evident that such tasks can only be undertaken in ecumenical cooperation."[19] Nor did Bühlmann gag at working with evangelicals: although there is still "fierce anti-Catholicism, . . . contacts are being multiplied and a certain degree of co-operation is developing."[20]

This author views with sadness and discouragement the closing of flourishing parishes in the state of Texas simply because of a lack of priests. No thought was given to an ecumenical analysis of those parishes that were near Orthodox or Anglican parishes. The possibility of ecumenical cooperation in opening those few new parishes that are being opened seems never to have been raised.

This does not mean that the ecumenical criterion is the only one, or even the most important. One bishop, not known for being especially innovative, appointed two nuns as co-pastors of a parish where for years his priests had either resigned because of ill-health, or withdrawn from the priesthood. Certainly lay leadership is one criterion that needs to be considered. And this author has met permanent deacons who are the only "clerical" presence in entire counties in the United States. But one is concerned that in the instruction given to permanent deacons and emerging lay leaders, the dimension of evangelization and mission is sadly absent. The people are eager and anxious for the theology and spirituality of ecumenical mission, but our leadership seems petrified by the problems of oversight that do result.

One remembers the efforts of the Hudson's Bay Company to persuade Oblate and Anglican missionaries to evangelize in separate areas of the Arctic and sub-Arctic, so that the Eskimo and Indian would not be competing over different religions, and thus avoid duplication of efforts by two of the more similar churches. Perhaps the children of this world are wiser than the children of light (cf. Lk. 16:8). While it may be naive to expect any "gentleman's agreement" ever to have come about between Anglican and Roman Catholic missionaries in the late 1800s and early 1900s, it is strange today to find no trace of any ecumenical strategy in missionary planning.

Promising efforts to renew the Hispanic community in the United States are just now beginning to work ecumenically. Bishop Raymond Peña, of El Paso, Texas, prepared a significant study, "Special Report on Evangelization and Hispano Community" (November 16, 1978), which looked at the Protestant efforts rather ironically, and probably influenced the American bishops finally to structure a Hispanic into the regrettably "Ad Hoc" Bishops Committee on Evangelization.[21]

More directly important was the October 24-28, 1978, meeting of Protestant and Catholic Hispanics at the Mexican American Cultural Center in San Antonio, Texas, with its "Message to the Hispanic Community of the United States and Puerto Rico and the Christian People of North America."[22] For the first time in the United States, Hispanic Protestants and Catholics talked about the hurts of the past, and what it means to be Hispanic Christians in countries predominately viewed as Anglo-American. This statement too seems to have been met with thunderous silence.

Even individual Southern Baptist pastors are telling their Roman Catholic fellow pastors that it makes no sense to try to evangelize Catholics who are actively practicing their faith. Such an attitude seems to be the first step toward acknowledging that every parish needs to confess that it fails to embody the three strands of catholic, evangelical, and reformed, and needs to work in mission with other denominations and churches. Such cooperative work should lead to the question of duplication of efforts, and a better use of already scarce personnel.

While the economic motive is not to be disregarded (stewardship can be biblically based), one does wonder if covenanted churches and shared buildings are entered into for the purpose of more effective witness or simply to save money. It is a shame with such a model at hand (parishes that aim to be catholic, evangelical, and reformed for the sake of mission and unity), that there is not more dynamism, joy, and vibrancy in the expectation of what the Lord can do.

It is growing more and more evident that in the increasingly critical area of social justice, no one church can decisively influence legislation and reform. As John A. Coleman, S.J., points out, all that the combined efforts of interested groups can do is to *tilt* legislation away from bad effects, and toward good efforts. All that the combined efforts of all American religious groups, labor unions, and professional educators were able to obtain in the critical issue of the Panama Canal treaties was a legislative margin of one vote (two-thirds of the United States Senate). If any one component of that coalition had been missing, the morally sensitive issue of the treaties would have been defeated.

Given the enormous problems of social justice between Latin America on the one hand, and North America/Europe on the other, the failure of the Puebla pronouncements to take an ecumenical approach could be crippling, as Harvey Cox has observed.[23] The recent conflicts and tragedies in Nicaragua and El Salvador make ecumenical and interfaith pressure on unjust structures all the more urgent. To the names of João Bosco Burnier and Rutilio Grande, S.J., daily are being added many other modern martyrs. It makes chilling reading to see the name of Archbishop Oscar Romero in William O'Malley's *Voice of Blood: Five Christian Martyrs of Our Time,*[24] when he recounts Father Grande's assassination, and to know that now the archbishop has given his life too. Unless we answer the call of John Paul II for "Christians," and "all men, especially those belonging to the social groups that are dedicating themselves actively to development and progress today," to be "more open to others, especially the neediest and the weakest" (*Redemptor Hominis,* no. 15), then our evangelization will be but a noisy gong or a clanging cymbal, words and no action. Coalition-building with all people of goodwill, for social justice, is essential for evangelization.

John Paul's indictment of "the rich, highly developed societies" (*Redemptor Hominis,* no. 16) will not sit easy in North America and Europe, nor will Tissa Balasuriya's *Eucharist and Human Liberation.*[25] Yet if the latter is read as a commentary on the former, it may be more digestible. Those Christians who are introduced to the methodology of striving to integrate the three strands of catholic, evangelical, and reformed into their personal lives and into their religious community will be more likely to strive also for social justice in the face of the overwhelming odds of vested interests.

Further Exploration

The exciting article by Bishop Claver, referred to earlier, should not be read too simplistically, especially its division of Roman Catholicism into the two ecclesiologies of the church as institution and as people.[26] Yet the elements cited by the bishop are very close to the "catholic" and "evangelical" terminology used in this paper. However, in at least one church, the United Presbyterian Church, U.S.A., there have been three distinct "catholic" ecclesiologies in the past thirty years.[27]

The most thorough work done recently in ecclesiologies is Avery Dulles's *Models of the Church.* Of his six models, the first two, the institutional and the sacramental, correspond to "catholic" as used here; the mystical communion corresponds to "evangelical"; and the herald, servant, and eschatological models correspond to "reformed." As Dulles himself observes, the Anglican church has tried with the greatest explicitness to maintain within itself models that, on the surface at least, conflict with each other.[28] And from a historical viewpoint, Anglicans such as Evelyn Underhill, with her pioneer work *Worship* (1936), blazed the way in showing that each church and denomination is sadly impoverished if it maintains only one of the traditional forms of worship.[29]

Catholic efforts at "born-again" experience have not been seriously examined; Jay Dolan's work on the parish mission, *Catholic Revivalism,*[30] shows that the evangelical undertow was present in the form of the parish mission in the late 1800s and early 1900s. Today the evangelical-charismatic movement needs to be seriously examined, especially for the theological issue: What is the relationship between basic ecclesial communities and the born-again experience? Are basic ecclesial communities doomed to fail unless a core has experienced the shattering, memorable event of being born again in the Spirit?

Such tools as the *New Oxford Review,*[31] with its avowed purpose of furthering the dialogue between evangelicals and catholics, need to be seriously examined. The fact that many parishes that belong to evangelical denominations such as the Southern Baptist count over a thousand families in a parish should give us pause as we examine the basic ecclesial community phenomenon. How do such "institutions" combat the inevitable problem of numbers and bureaucracy?

When one looks at works such as Johannes Hofinger's *Evangelization and Catechesis*[32] and John R. W. Stott's *Christian Mission in the Modern World,*[33] and realizes how close they are in spirit and content, it is surely time to use all deliberate speed to further the dialogue on evangelization between catholic and evangelical, for the sake of mission.

Notes

1. Princeton, N.J., 1976.

2. Glenn Igleheart, "Evangelism and Ecumenism in the Eighties," *Ecumenical Trends,* May 1980, p. 78.

3. Cardinal Suenens, *Ecumenism and Charismatic Renewal* (London, 1978).

4. Kilian McDonnell, *Charismatic Renewal and Ecumenism* (New York: Paulist Press, 1978).

5. COCU, *Principles of Church Union* (Cincinnati: Forward Movement Publications, 1966), p. 62.

6. Walter Abbott, ed., *The Documents of Vatican II* (New York: Association Press, 1974), p. 715.

7. H. Richard Niebuhr, *The Kingdom of God in America* (Chicago: University of Chicago Press, 1937), p. 185.

8. Hugh Thomson Kerr, *Christian Sacraments* (Philadelphia: Westminster Press, 1944), pp. 96–97.

9. Ibid., pp. 27–29.

10. *Newsletter,* December 1978, p. 142.

11. New York: Harper & Row, 1973.

12. Cf. *Ecumenical Trends,* September 1977, pp. 119–20.

13. Harvey Cox, *The Secular City,* rev. ed. (New York: Macmillan, 1966).

14. Claude Welch, *Secular City Debate* (New York: Macmillan, 1966), p. 163.

15. Francisco Claver, "Prophecy or Accommodation, the Dilemma of a Discerning Church," *America,* April 26, 1980, p. 354.

16. Robert McAfee Brown, *Ecumenical Revolution,* rev. ed. 1969, p. 41.

17. *L'Osservatore Romano,* April 24, 1975, p. 11.

18. *Ecumenical Review* 23 (January 1971), p. 18.

19. Walbert Bühlmann, *The Coming of the Third Church* (Maryknoll, N.Y.: Orbis Books, 1978), p. 360.

20. Ibid., p. 218.

21. See Cecilio Morales, Jr., "Hispanic Home Religion," *America,* April 19, 1980, pp. 344–45, for an account of Bishop Pēna's work.

22. A copy of the "Message" is available from the National Council of Churches, Room 1268, 475 Riverside Drive, New York, N.Y. 10115, U.S.A.

23. Harvey Cox, "A Puebla Diary," *Commonweal,* March 16, 1979, p. 145.

24. Maryknoll, N.Y.: Orbis Books, 1980.

25. Maryknoll, N.Y.: Orbis Books, 1979.

26. Francisco Claver, "Prophecy or Accommodation," pp. 356–59.

27. See Harry E. Winter, "Catholic, Evangelical and Reformed: The Lord's Supper in the United Presbyterian Church, U.S.A., 1945–70" (Ann Arbor, Mich.: Xerox University Microfilms), esp. p. 5.

28. Avery Dulles, *Models of the Church* (Garden City, N.Y.: Doubleday Image Books, 1978), p. 16.

29. Evelyn Underhill, *Worship* (New York: Harper & Row, 1957); first published in 1936.

30. Jay Dolan, *Catholic Revivalism* (Notre Dame, Ind.: University of Notre Dame Press, 1978).

31. Available from Dept. KK, 6013 Lawton Ave., Oakland, Calif. 94618, U.S.A.

32. New York: Paulist Press, 1976.

33. Downers Grove, Ill.: Inter Varsity Press, 1975.

Section 4

THE MISSION OF THE LOCAL CHURCH AND THE MISSIONARY INSTITUTES

Statement of the Question

The recognition of the local church's responsibility for mission and the recognition of the laity's role in carrying out that responsibility pose questions for missionary institutes about their orientations and methodologies at a fundamental level. Underlying these questions is the basic relation of mission to the local and official, universal structures of the church in the post-Vatican II world.

Elements for a Reflection on the Question

- The need to identify and study whatever emerges in recognizing each level of the church responsible for mission
- The theological relation of the local to the universal church
- The call to mission as a gospel imperative
- The situation of Christians who are out of touch with the church
- The recognition that the universality of the church, if imposed from one direction only, creates a situation where mission is no longer creative and active on the receiving side
- The possibilities for coordinating placement of personnel
- The question of reverse mission
- The structures needed for six-continent mission formation
- The role of the church in relation to nationalism
- The relation between ecclesiastical structures and the structures of missionary institutes in the sending of missionaries
- The risk that bishops see missionaries as replacement for missing local clergy

Related Questions

- When does a local church become *truly* a local church?
- When should a missionary institute leave a local church?
- What forms of ministry by missionary institutes are needed in different local cultures, contexts?

- What concrete planning is being done to integrate the laity into the mission of the church?
- What is the relation of the small Christian community to this whole question?
- In terms of the evolution taking place in the local church, what will be the criteria for missionary institutes to determine their commitments in the future?

15

THE UNITED STATES OF AMERICA

John T. Boberg, S.V.D.

The issues and problems confronting missionary institutes today are deeper and more far-reaching than structures, though structures are definitely part of the problem. The conditions, the presuppositions, the motivations, even the concepts on which most missionary institutes were founded during the heyday of missionary activity in the nineteenth and early twentieth centuries have since that time totally changed. It will be sufficient to name just a few of these elements: the Western attitude of cultural superiority; the political, imperialistic expansion of Europe; the necessity of baptism to be saved from hellfire; mission-sending and -receiving countries. All of these elements have not only changed but have been reversed—at least in principle. The residue of structure and of attitudes that remain from this period, however, are a major part of the problem for missionary institutes as a new era of mission begins.

What are the characteristics of this new era of mission? Limiting ourselves just to the reversals of the elements listed above, we have strong affirmation of the plurality of cultures; a new international order with a diffusion of global power; the belief in the availability of God's saving grace to all peoples even before the gospel is preached; the reality of six-continent mission. None of these new elements is inimical to mission as such; indeed, all of them, in one way or another, are more favorable to authentic witness to the gospel.

The problem lies in making the transition: in shifting the attitudes and changing the structures to correspond to the new situation. As the Statement of the Question for this paper puts it: missionary institutes are being questioned "about their orientations and methodologies at a fundamental level."

The response, in this view from the United States, has three aspects: mission as universal call; the relationship of mission and church (mission—church—mission); tensions between the universal and the particular (or local).

John Boberg, Divine Word Missionary, is the Director of the World Mission Program and Professor of Mission Theology at the Catholic Theological Union in Chicago, Illinois.

Mission as Universal Call

No attempt will be made here to provide an exhaustive theological basis for mission, but simply to sketch the outline of an understanding of mission that will meet needs of the present, changed situation in the world and in the Church.

Mission Is God's Call to Unity

The vocation of all peoples is one: to be united in love with God and with one another. This unity of humankind is not just to be realized beyond death; the increasing globalization of our planet is bringing everyone closer together and making them more interrelated. The challenge is to oppose the exploitive and destructive aspects of this planetary process and to foster human solidarity on the basis of mutual trust, respect, and love. Meeting this challenge is the explicit concern and purpose of mission. The affirmation of pluralism and the ability to deal with the complexity of global issues are basic requirements in carrying out such a mission.

Mission Is Witness to Jesus Christ

To make sense today mission has to be much more than the response to a mission mandate as recorded in the Scriptures (cf. Mt. 28:19). The meaning of mission has to be seen much more directly in the meaning of Christ himself: in the intrinsic reality of who he was in relation to all humankind, and in the actual reality of how he carried out his mission.

Christ's Relation to All Humankind. Vatican II saw in the confession of faith in Jesus as God, Lord, redeemer, and sole mediator the specific character of all Christian churches (*Unitatis Redintegratio,* nos. 1, 20). It gave this doctrine, however, a certain relevance to more contemporary problems by emphasizing Christ's relationship to humankind as the answer to the question of human existence (*Gaudium et Spes,* nos. 10, 22), as the head of a renewed humanity and the fulfillment of human aspirations (*Ad Gentes,* nos. 3, 8; *Gaudium et Spes,* no. 38), and as the culmination of human history (*Ad Gentes,* no. 3; *Gaudium et Spes,* no. 45).

This relationship to humankind, stated by Vatican II, finds a more explicit, theoretical basis in "transcendental" theology, that is, a theology that understands the human person as being concretely and existentially oriented to God's self-communication in such a way that humankind finds its fulfillment only in union with God, in living the divine life. "This divinization (which does not mean a pantheistic identification with God), in an absolute final culmination of the history of nature, spirit and freedom, is the self-transcendence of the world; in it God himself (through his free act) is not merely the cause but the actual reality of the world's perfect fulfillment."[1] In God's plan it is in Christ that his promise and total gift of himself in judgment and mercy is effected definitively, supremely, and irrevocably. In Christ human self-transcendence achieves its total goal, makes its breakthrough to fulfillment and union with God in such an absolute and definitive way that Christian faith professes this event as "God's final promise in Jesus and as 'incarnation' or 'hypostatic union.' "[2]

This "transcendental" understanding of Christ's relationship to humankind provides several basic orientations for missionary activity: one with regard to God's saving presence preceding the missionary, the other with regard to the unity that exists between promoting human authenticity in a world of peace, justice, and love and the upbuilding of the kingdom of God.

The first important orientation that "transcendental" theology gives to mission is its identification of the saving reality of Jesus Christ as the culmination of human self-transcendence, as the total achievement of the process inherent in the structure of human existence. Participation in the saving event which is Jesus can be seen then as participation in the same process of self-transcendence. Wherever and whenever persons find within themselves the freedom to renounce their self-centeredness and give way to selfless concern for others may be described as a process of self-transcendence, as a dying to themselves and a rising to new life—as a participation in Christ's paschal mystery. This would seem to be what Vatican II is stating in *Gaudium et Spes,* no. 22: "The Holy Spirit in a manner known only to God offers to every [person] the possibility of being associated with this paschal mystery." The achievement of self-transcendence, however, the victory over self-centeredness, is not experienced as a personal triumph. It is experienced as a gift, a gift that transcends the persons themselves, that they want to share with others, and for which they expect no credit or reward.

In this "transcendental" perspective mission cannot mean bringing God's saving presence to people, but can only mean discovering how that gift is already present and operative in the culture and lives of people. Mission is witness to Christ in the sense of helping to make the reality of the paschal mystery explicit and of helping people to integrate this explicit reality with the rest of their lives. Such an approach to mission is not the basis for a new kind of triumphalism that claims all the "good" people for our side, since they are already implicit ("anonymous") Christians; rather, it is the basis for deep humility and respect on the part of missionaries in approaching people whose cultural and religious expression of God's gift is often so radically different from their own that missionaries need to spend a long time listening, learning, discovering, in order to recognize it for what it is.

What we perhaps need to emphasize more is the attitude expressed by Saint Paul in his "woe to *me* if I do not preach the Gospel"; he was more concerned about his own responsibility to his faith in Christ than about the needs of nonbelievers. All too easily our motivation for mission expressed as concern, or sometimes even pity, for those who do not share our faith and life in Christ is only a cover for our own need to feel superior, to feel secure that our efforts are meaningful.

The second important orientation that "transcendental" theology gives to mission is a solid basis for the unity between humanization and Christianization, between witnessing to Christ and promoting human authenticity in and through a world of peace, justice, and love. I have always found Bernard Lonergan's approach most helpful here. In his analysis and description of the act of human knowing as a process of self-transcendence guided by the innate dynamism of the questioning human spirit, he shows how persons are spontaneously led from awareness through questions of meaning (What is it? What does it mean?) to understanding, and from understanding through questions of truth (Is it so? Is it true?) to judgment about the true and the real. This self-transcendence on the level of knowing is then led further by the same dynamism of the human spirit through questions of values (Is it good? Is it worthwhile?) to deliberation and decision and choice. When human decisions and choices are made on the basis of this self-transcending process, when they are made on the basis of objective values and not of self-interest or comfort, then real or moral self-transcendence—authentic human existence—is achieved. The dynamism of the human spirit, based on questioning, is an unrestricted capacity for knowing and loving, for self-transcendence. This capacity finds its fulfillment not through its own achievement but in the gift of God's love. The gift of God's love does not deny or abrogate human authenticity, the process of self-transcendence; it raises it to a new level, places it within a new horizon in which the love of God transvalues our values and the eyes of that love, faith, transforms our knowing. Such transformed knowing and loving is the life of religious faith and love. Human authenticity and human progress, therefore, are inseparably linked to religious faith and love, rooted as they both are in cognitional and moral self-transcendence. This is condensing and leaping to the conclusion of a much more nuanced and reasoned argument in Lonergan's chapter on "Religion" in *Method in Theology,* but I think enough has been given to bear out the conclusion that faith is linked to human progress and that to promote one is to promote the other indirectly; there is, therefore, a basic unity between humanization and Christianization. It may be helpful, though, to quote—even somewhat at length—Lonergan's description of the way the two interact:

> Faith places human efforts in a friendly universe; it reveals an ultimate significance in human achievement; it strengthens new undertakings with confidence. Inversely, progress realizes the potentialities of man and nature; it reveals that man exists to bring about an ever fuller achievement in this world; and that achievement because it is man's good also is God's glory. Most of all, faith has the power of undoing decline. Decline disrupts a culture with conflicting ideologies. It inflicts on individuals the social, economic and psychological pressures that for human frailty amount to determinism. It multiplies and heaps up the abuses and absurdities that breed resentment, hatred, anger, violence. It is not propaganda and it is not argument but religious faith that will liberate human reasonableness from its ideological prisons. It is not the promises of men but religious hope that can enable men to resist the vast pressures of social decay. If passions are to quiet down, if wrongs are to be not exacerbated, not ignored, not merely palliated, but acknowledged and removed, then human possessiveness and human pride have to be replaced by religious charity, by the charity of the suffering servant, by self-sacrificing love.[3]

How Jesus Carried Out His Mission. The importance of the life and mission of the preresurrection Jesus has gained new importance among theologians recently. They were always important to the average Christian and missionary, even though there was often the tendency to spiritualize the mission of Jesus: the conversion he urged and the kingdom he proclaimed. Salvation was too often seen as something pertaining to the next life only; it was not concerned with the transformation of the concrete world in which we live.

Since Vatican II, however, and especially due to the awareness aroused by "liberation theologians," the concreteness and this-worldly dimension of Jesus' mission can no longer be ignored. In describing his mission, Jesus used the words of the prophet Isaiah:

> The spirit of the Lord has been given to me,
> for he has anointed me.
> He has sent me to bring the good news to the poor,
> to proclaim liberty to captives
> and to the blind new sight,
> to set the downtrodden free . . . [Lk. 4:18].

If nothing else, this passage emphasizes the privileged place in Jesus' concern for the poor and the outcast, the marginal people of society. What is clear from the gospel's portrayal of Jesus and his mission is the centrality of his concern for people: people with all their individual concerns and weaknesses—the hungry, the sick, the blind, the crippled; but also people caught up in oppressive structures, even the oppressive structures of religion. In Mark's Gospel at least, the key confrontation with the Pharisees and Herodians that persons are more important than rules and regulations ("Is it against the law on the sabbath day to do good, or to do evil; to save life, or to kill?" Mk. 3: 4) was the beginning of their determination to seek his death (Mk. 3: 6).

From the Gospels it is clear that for Jesus his mission was just that, a mission, a movement, that was aimed at the transformation of this world, including the social structures in which the sinfulness and oppression of people were embedded. He plunged into this world to penetrate and alter it in concrete ways, which his followers of every generation must determine anew (cf. *Gaudium et Spes,* no. 38).

This renewed understanding of Jesus' mission as concerned with the transformation of people in the concreteness of their life in the world is frequently discussed in terms of two conflicting views of mission and church: church as ark of salvation; church as light of the world. These conflicting views will be looked at more closely in the next section.

The Relationship of Mission and Church: Mission—Church—Mission

For the last forty years there has been much disagreement about the meaning of mission. At one end of the spectrum of opinion are those who would limit mission to a very specific activity of primary evangelization (the initial preaching to those who have never heard the gospel message); these authors make a clear and sharp distinction between missionary activity and pastoral action. At the other end of the spectrum are those who would seem to identify mission with any pastoral action of the church.

In the first view the task of missionary institutes is clearly related to just that initial stage of primary evangelization. Their members should turn over the continuing "pastoral" development of the church as quickly as possible to local people and not get suffocated into becoming foreign pastors rather than missionaries. In this view missionary activity would be restricted to those areas traditionally known as missions.

The second view sees missionary activity in a much broader way as the effort to bring about the explicit presence, life, and meaning of Christ into any situation or group of people where his message is not operative and effective. In this view missions definitely are not conceived as "foreign" and the distinction between sending and receiving countries loses all meaning, except to recognize that all countries must be *both* sending and receiving countries. In this view the line between missionary activity and pastoral action begins to fade. Mission becomes more identified with church and the chief challenge is to establish priorities in the one mission rather than to draw distinctions between missionary and pastoral activities.

There are, of course, many variations on the spectrum between these two poles. My own understanding, for example, which I shall describe below, is a significant variation that aims to combine the advantages and eliminate the disadvantages of the two extremities. Given the ambiguity surrounding the term "mission," one has to be careful in judging the meaning of other writers who might differ from one's own understanding. The temptation is to set up "paper tigers" of extreme positions and shoot these down—without adding much clarity to the real issues involved. Before describing my own position, however, it does seem safe to say that most missionary institutes were founded, and carried out their work for years, theoretically at least, on the basis of the first view of missionary activity as primary evangelization. It also seems safe to say that their present structures and basic orientations, fund-raising for instance, are generally *still* operating from this perspective. On the other hand, it also seems safe to say that the actual involvement of most members of the institutes reflect the second view. Added to this actual situation is the growing support for the ideas that also reflect the second view: every Christian is a missionary, mutuality of mission, six-continent mission. The tensions that have developed in this schizophrenic situation are inevitable.

Vatican II made major contributions to the basic issues in question here, but it by no means resolved all the ambiguities; indeed, it probably added to the schizophrenia. Clearly and emphatically the Vatican Council said that the whole church is missionary and that this mission "is carried out by means of that activity through which . . . the Church makes itself fully present to all peoples" (*Ad Gentes,* no. 5). The Mission Decree then goes on to say (no. 6) that this mission, which is "one and the same everywhere and in all situations" differs according to the variety of circumstances in which the mission is exercised. Thus the document distinguishes between missionary activity, pastoral work, and ecumenical undertakings.

Rather evidently the council fathers were concerned about maintaining specific missionary activity, or "missions," as a distinct and important undertaking. Their distinction may have succeeded in achieving the exact opposite. The problem, it seems to me, is not with the distinction itself but with the impression it gives. It seems to say that the three activities of the one mission of the church are parallel activities

—some people do this activity, others do that one. Such an impression almost necessarily contributes to the attitude already so prevalent: missionary activity is what some "others" do in far-off places; it is not a concrete concern of the average Christian who is really only involved in pastoral situations. In this context, being essentially missionary is not something that touches the immediate lives of every Christian; it means supporting the "missionary" effort of *others* through prayers and money, until the day the "missions" reach maturity and can take care of themselves through pastoral work. In this context, not only does missionary activity remain "foreign" to the average Christian, but pastoral work also becomes truncated and closed-in on itself. It is all too easily seen as a self-servicing undertaking for an in-group; its purpose is to meet primarily, if not only, the spiritual needs of its own members.

A solution to these distorted views, which result from seeing missionary activity and pastoral work as parallel functions, does not lie in the direction of identifying the two. For one thing, the distinction seems to be a real one; at least it has been with the church for a long time. As Ferdinand Hahn points out in *Mission in the New Testament,* already in the later writings of the New Testament itself (1 and 2 Timothy; 1 Peter; 2 Thessalonians) "the work of the mission, which was directed outward, and the work of developing, consolidating and caring for the churches, became distinct; one may perhaps even say to some degree separated."[4] Both the political situation with its incipient persecutions as well as the danger to the churches through false doctrine induced efforts toward a stronger consolidation of the churches. Hence much more weight is laid on preaching with the church.[5] In this process the mission's task is not lost, is not in dispute, but becomes a thing by itself, needing its own style of preaching and particular activity.

Without denying or trying to eliminate the distinction between the missionary and pastoral functions of the church, however, it is possible to *relate* them in a way that could prove very fruitful. Rather than seeing them as parallel activities, they could be united in a continuous chain of cause and effect. This reality becomes clearer if we change the names of the two functions and speak of *sending* (the outward thrust, the movement beyond its own boundaries, *missionary activity*) and *gathering* (the inward thrust, the consolidation and care of those within, *pastoral action)*. For a healthy life in the church the two functions—sending/gathering—work in mutual relationship: sent in order to gather, gathered in order to be sent. The function of gathering, of building up the inner life, through worship, service, and teaching is distinct, but its purpose is to prepare for sending, for mission. Mission has its own special qualities and needs, but its purpose is to gather, to build up the people of God as sign and instrument of God's kingdom.

Another way of speaking of this same relationship is to use the terms "mission" and "church." For a long time now "church" has been considered both the primary and the ultimate reality with regard to mission. The church has a mission in order to establish the church. Just the opposite is true: mission establishes a church in order to continue the mission. The proper order then should always be "mission—church— mission." This may seem a subtle difference, but it is more in line with the theological reality, and the effect on attitude is profound. (Both *Lumen*

Gentium and *Ad Gentes* describe mission as beginning from God. He sends his Son and the Spirit to the world. Church is first of all a result of mission, and then a participant in mission. It is the continuation and instrument of God's mission.) When church is seen as the prior reality, mission can be (and is) considered just one of its functions. Depending on one's priorities it is a function of greater or lesser importance, and all too easily is removed to the fringes of the church. When mission establishes a church for mission, then mission is of the essence; it is not just one of several parallel functions. Everyone is involved in it; everyone in the church is essentially missionary.

The acceptance of the intimate, causal relationship between sending—gathering—sending, between mission—church—mission does not resolve all the ambiguity surrounding mission, but it is a step in the right direction. It needs to be correlated with the renewed understanding of Jesus and his mission, indicated above in the section "How Jesus Carried Out His Mission," that is, a movement directed to the transformation of the world. At the same time it helps us to choose between the two radically opposed views of mission and church alluded to there: church as ark of salvation; church as light of the world. We need to examine these two views more closely.

Church as ark of salvation. In this view church is more or less identified with the kingdom of God on earth. Its purpose is to gather as many people as possible within its ranks and lead them to eternal life. Its main task is maintenance-oriented: to care for the people who already are members; its mission is to convert people who are not yet members.

Church as light of the world. In this view church is clearly distinguished from the kingdom of God on earth. The kingdom of God is larger than the church; it exists wherever people are living together in peace, justice, and love. The church is the sign and instrument of the kingdom; its task is to be a witness to every human community, proclaiming by its own life how people can be liberated and live together in unity and peace, justice and love. In this view church is directed primarily outside itself; it is mission-oriented, not maintenance-oriented. This does not mean that membership in the church is unimportant. Church is not just a task force for spreading the kingdom; it is the body of Christ. But like Christ, its head, it does not exist for itself alone. He poured himself out completely for the sake of the kingdom. The church must do likewise. In order to proclaim and serve the kingdom effectively, church must have a vibrant life of its own: it must gather in prayer, in celebration, in solitude, not in a simplistic way of recharging batteries in order to get back to the business of mission, but in order to be transformed by God into an effective witness of his love for the world.

Clearly, the second view of the church as the light of the world is more acceptable today. It maintains both the distinction and the unity between missionary activity and pastoral action. At the same time it includes a broadening of the concept of mission/sending. Mission/sending is not directed to extending the limits of the church in order to *save* as many people as possible; it is witness to the kingdom, it is the effort to bring about the explicit presence, life, and meaning of Christ into any group of people or situations where his message is not explicitly operative. Such witness has nothing, as such, to do with geography, with near or far. But if we are truly compelled by God's love to share his love in Christ, then we can never rest content with meeting the challenge of the near and not the far; neither can we play leapfrog by being concerned with far-off problems, while ignoring those on our doorsteps: the racial discrimination, the flight to suburbs, the urban blight, the sale of arms, the unequal trade agreements, the alienation of the young, the amoral secularism of business and science laboratories. Bringing the message and love of Christ to bear on these situations is as much mission as evangelizing the Masai or dialoguing with Buddhists. There has recently been some recognition of the correctness of this approach, even though the efforts along this line by members of missionary institutes have been given the misnomer "reverse mission." In this perspective these efforts really belong to the mainstream of missionary activity.

Understanding mission in this way does not make everything the church does "mission." Mission retains its specific nature; it is outreach, it is going beyond boundaries into "areas" untouched by Christ's presence. It is not "gathering," but gives new meaning and dynamism to all the pastoral efforts, preventing them from becoming simply self-centered and self-serving activities.

The most important consequences of such an understanding of mission is that it brings mission into the immediate concern of every Christian; it gives relevance to the truth that every Christian is essentially missionary. Though at first glance this might represent a crisis situation for missionary institutes, whose members have been the "specialists," it is surely evident that such an enriching and broadly engaging understanding of mission offers much more opportunity than it does danger. It is up to the institutes to make the most of the opportunity.

Perhaps as a way of recapitulating, as well as of being more specific, it might be helpful to suggest some of the implications for missionary institutes of this understanding of missionary activity.

1. Promotion of the reality that every Christian is a missionary; that is, that the missionary task is concerned with the deed-and-word outreach of all Christians into all areas of life not influenced by Christ's message, not just with "foreign" peoples and places. Mission includes in its mainstream the sort of activities that have recently been called "reverse mission."

2. The laity's participation in all phases of missionary activity needs to be helped, but not usurped. Attitudinal change in line with the conviction that "the whole Church is missionary, and the work of evangelization the fundamental task of the people of God" (*Ad Gentes,* no. 35) is most important as a first step. The evolution of new ministerial roles needs to be supported. Missionary institutes need to be ready and able to share in providing the supportive structures that are necessary as the whole church becomes involved in mission. Appropriate missionary education, shared community, opportunities for reflection, religious experiences that build on the particular style, and needs of the laity are some of the support structures that immediately come to mind. Appreciation of the unique contribution that laity can make probably means that collaboration with independent lay organizations is more significant than "opening our doors" to lay members.

3. With the expanded view of mission, the challenge to missionary institutes is, on

the one hand, to let go of any exclusivism that keeps missionary activity "foreign" to the average Christian and to promote personal involvement in outreach into areas where the gospel message is not present and yet touch people's daily lives. If I may elaborate on a well-known slogan, mission means the whole church (nonspecialist and specialist) bringing the whole gospel (deed and word) to the whole world (near and far). On the other hand, though mission has nothing to do with geography, with "near" or "far," the old cliché that "charity begins at home" has to be constantly challenged that it does not end there. "Some two-thirds of the world's four and half billion people have had no proper opportunity to receive Christ," according to the Thailand Statement of the meeting at Pattaya sponsored by the Lausanne Committee for World Evangelization. Establishing priorities in mission has to keep these "unreached" people high on the list. As Waldron Scott, the general secretary of the World Evangelization Fellowship pointed out in his address to the 1980 meeting of the American Society of Missiology: "The reformation and renewal of Christian communities must not be carried out at the expense of those [hundreds of millions of people] who have every right to hear what God has done in Christ." New symbols have to evolve that capture the outward, nonimperialistic, nontriumphalistic thrust of mission beyond the boundaries of church. New ways of understanding and expressing the significance of sharing explicit faith in Christ need to permeate the Christian community. Some work in this direction is being done. One thinks of Schillebeeckx's books on Christology, of Kung's *On Being a Christian,* of David Tracy's *Blessed Rage for Order.* Missionary institutes with their traditional commitment to cross-cultural mission need to highlight and continue to develop this kind of theological research and motivation for mission.

Tensions between the Universal and the Particular

One of the most exciting contributions of Vatican Council II was the affirmation given to the particular (local) church. Since the council, there has been much development both in clarifying the basic theology of the particular church and in spelling out its practical implications. There is, of course, still a long way to go, especially in the area of concrete application.

Aided by the social sciences, however, it has become clear that one of the basic meanings of the church as universal is, paradoxically perhaps, that the church is local in many different places. The universality of the church is only realized through multiple particularities. Unity of the church cannot mean uniformity. Unity demands variety and diversity. Universality cannot be realized by spreading a single particularity that imposes one particular cultural expression on all peoples.

There is a healthy tension, therefore, between the church as one and universal, and the church as multiple and local. And this tension must remain. The particular church, because it is an expression of universal church, can never be an isolated, self-enclosed world of meaning; precisely insofar as it remains open and in dialogue with other particular churches any one particular church remains a legitimate expression of the universal Spirit who unites the churches.

Granted this healthy tension between universal church and particular church, it nevertheless seems to me to be inaccurate and misleading to speak of the relationship between "local" and "official, universal structures" of the church as is done in the Statement of the Question for this paper. The "official, universal structures" should probably more accurately be described as the central administrative offices and institutions in the church, whether these be the Vatican with its congregations and secretariats, or the general headquarters of missionary institutes. At any rate, the issues that seem to me crucial in this relationship are pluralism and coordination of efforts.

Pluralism

The issue of pluralism is one of the thorniest problems in our *world* today, not only in the church. How to achieve unity in diversity? How to promote peace and harmony and not strangle cultural identity? We state these as our goals easily enough; they are difficult to put into practice.

In our rapidly contracting world the reality of cultural pluralism has become increasingly significant. One would think that as we are exposed more and more through the media and actual travel to the great diversity of peoples and cultures, we would become more adept at dealing with pluralism. Eugene Nida in an address to the American Society of Missiology in June 1979 argued just the opposite:

> When people become insecure and uncertain under the impact of pluralism, they normally retreat to a conservative position and demand greater and greater conformity. . . . Intolerance of cultural differences is on the increase in the secular world, and a similar phenomenon is present in Christendom, despite all that is written and said about "dialogue" and "ecumenicity."

Earlier in his address Nida had suggested that this intolerance for diversity especially affects us with regard to people who are *closer* to us:

> The cultural differences of an out-group are much easier for people to recognize, understand, and accept than the pluralism within an actual or potential in-group. We expect other people to be different, but we find it difficult to accept the fact that people within our own Christian group or those of other Christian groups can or should be different from us. . . . People argue that after all, truth must be unitary, not multiple; and though multiple hypotheses may be all right for scientific inquiry, they cannot be accepted as a basis for religious instruction or thought. . . . Relatively few Christians in the Western World are able to or willing to accept fully the differences in other Christian groups, especially those nearby.

In this context the reflections of Father Arrupe in his letter on inculturation to the Society of Jesus seem especially appropriate. After describing the need for a "new and continuous inculturation of the faith everywhere" as well as providing an excellent list of the attitudes required for effecting this inculturation, he comes to what he calls "the personal interior inculturation," which must be a basis for the external task of inculturation.

> Although we admit in theory the necessity of inculturation, when it comes to practice and touches us personally, demanding of us profound changes in our attitudes and scale of values, often there is insensibility and resistance. . . .
>
> If we want to let ourselves be caught up in the process of inculturation, theory and study are not enough. We need the "shock" of a deep personal experience. For those called to live in another culture, it will mean being integrated in a new country, a new language, a whole new life. For those who remain in their own country it will mean experiencing the new styles of our changing, contemporary world—not the mere theoretical knowledge of the new mentalities, but the experiential assimilation of the way of life of the groups with which we must work, the outcasts, Chicanos, slum dwellers, intellectuals, students, artists, etc.

What Father Arrupe is stressing, and what I agree with most heartily, is the need for personal interior conversion for the acceptance of pluralism. Such a conversion is a simple matter, but it is *not easy.* It is as simple as a shift from one particle to another: from "the" to "a." It is the shift from thinking of my culture as "the" culture, to thinking of it as "a" culture. A conversion that accepts and gladly affirms that my way of thinking, of doing things, of evaluating is *not* "the" way, but "a" way.

Such a simple shift is not easy. Since it touches attitudes, it cannot be effected merely by study and new knowledge. It needs an experiential component. The whole person needs to be touched. Normally the kind of experience that will effect such a conversion will be achieved in a situation in which persons feel their powerlessness, their own inadequacy to deal with some present reality, their dependence upon, and the need to learn from, other people: experiences, for instance, that I have heard veteran missionaries describe as so significant for them, like learning from local villagers to fish among the coral reefs off the shore of Papua New Guinea or, more simply, learning from an Aymara Indian how to wash the mud from one's feet after a reed-boat ride on Lake Titicaca. It needs to be an experience in which one gets "shocked" out of one's feeling of superiority and self-sufficiency. My own experience in trying to prepare people for cross-cultural mission and ministry is that a combination of theory and practice is essential, and that the practice—the experiential field component—is most effective when trainees have to deal with the most marginalized people of society. The challenge and demands of taking the really poor seriously, of being vulnerable with them, is much more significant for transforming attitudes than simply living and working with another cultural group.

Coordination of Efforts

When Walbert Bühlmann says that "the central authority of the Church needs to be a universal collective genius to give a just appraisal to all developments and not strangle them at birth,"[6] it seems that he is looking for some such conversion, some such "personal interior inculturation" in these authorities. Internationalization of these central organizations will not do it alone; the ability to "experience the other side," in Martin Buber's words, is essential.

As absolutely essential as this attitude is for whatever structure the organization of the church has, it alone is not enough either. Structure, the type of structure, is also important. As indicated above, to think of Rome as the "universal" contrasted to "local" structure is wrong and misleading. The why and how of "centralized authority" is the real issue, as Bühlmann rightly points out.[7] I do not think there is any question about the need for a central authority. The world today has become a single world and its unity is increasing. This means that the whole church as such has duties in respect of the shaping and further development of this unity; the church as a whole must be in a position to act in regard to the world as a unity, and it needs new and appropriate ways to meet the responsibility.

In addition to being able to deal with such responsibilities, central authority is demanded for good organizational structure. Organizational structure with clear job descriptions and lines of accountability is essential to getting any job done. Who's responsible for what, to whom do they report, whom must they keep informed. And yet such structural questions seem to be the most neglected aspect of the church today. I would also venture to say that there is as much resistance to appropriate organizational structure from the people at the bottom as from those at the top. Maybe even more. The average missionary or pastor, it seems to me, is as reluctant to be accountable as any official. They should be allowed "to do their thing"! Institutional planning with its demands of goals clarification, job descriptions, areas of responsibility, lines of accountability, evaluation and feedback are no panacea, as some religious groups have discovered, but they are basic to any organized effort to get a job done. It seems to me to be an area that has been neglected for too long at most levels within the church.

Concluding this paper with the spotlight on method (planning) and structure may seem a cop-out. Where are the answers to all the issues and problems raised in Elements for a Reflection on the Question and Related Questions? Yet no other conclusion is possible. In an age in which scientific inquiry and the social sciences have made elaborately clear that truth and objectivity cannot be encapsulated in neat formulas deduced from general, universal principles but are part of an ongoing, open-ended process, then surely the important thing is not finding any specific answer but developing a method that guarantees the correctness of the process.

Bernard Lonergan set out to do this for theology in *Method in Theology*. Discerning a method in the very processes of the human mind, which moves from attentiveness to data, through understanding and judgment to responsible action, he formulated the Transcendental Imperatives: Be Attentive, Be Intelligent, Be Reasonable, Be Responsible. Faithfulness to these imperatives constitutes a process of self-transcendence and leads—more often through correction of error and repentance of sin than through unidirectional progress—to a threefold conversion: intellectual, moral, religious. These conversions, partial as their achievement will ever be in any one person, are the foundations of authentic subjectivity, which in turn is the only basis for genuine objectivity. Authentic subjectivity with persistent application of transcendental method to specific areas is the way to truth and progress.

In his final chapter on "Communications," Lonergan points out how following these principles and method in communicating the Christian message involves the church in a process of self-constitution that is structured, outgoing, and redemptive, and how this process will become fully conscious "only when theology unites itself with all other relevant branches of human studies."[8] The aim of integrating theology with scholarly and scientific human studies is "to generate well-informed and continuously revised policies and plans for promoting good and undoing evil both in the church and in human society generally."[9] What he then says about the implementation and goals of these integrated studies seems worth quoting in full:

> Needless to say, such integrated studies will have to occur on many levels, local, regional, national, international. The principles of subsidiarity will require that at the local level problems will be defined and, in so far as possible, solutions worked out. Higher levels will provide exchange centers, where information on successful and unsuccessful solutions is accumulated to be made available to inquiry and so prevent the useless duplication of investigations. They will also work on the larger and more intricate problems that have no solution at the lower levels, and they will organize the lower levels to collaborate in the application of the solutions to which they conclude. Finally, there is a general task of coordination, or working out in detail what kinds of problems are prevalent, at what level they are best studied, how all concerned on any given type of issue are to be organized for a collaborative effort.[10]

As difficult and perhaps overwhelming as the implementation of this challenge might seem, our contemporary world with its ever increasing change due to an ever increasing expansion of knowledge demands no less. "To operate on the level of our day is to apply the best available knowledge and the most efficient techniques to coordinated group action"; but such an approach will not only meet the demands of our present day; it "will also set the church on a course of continual renewal."[11]

This is a large vision; it is a challenging vision. We have, I hope, the courage to begin at least to work toward its implementation.

Notes

1. Karl Rahner, "Jesus Christ," *Sacramentum Mundi III* (New York: Herder and Herder, 1969), p. 203.
2. Ibid., p. 197.
3. Bernard Lonergan, *Method in Theology* (New York: Herder and Herder, 1972), p. 117.
4. Ferdinand Hahn, *Mission in the New Testament* (London: SCM Press, 1965), p. 137.
5. Ibid., p. 139.
6. Walbert Bühlmann, *The Coming of the Third Church* (Maryknoll, N.Y.: Orbis Books, 1978), p. 179.
7. Ibid., p. 180.
8. Lonergan, *Method in Theology*, p. 364.
9. Ibid., p. 366.
10. Ibid.
11. Ibid., p. 367.

16

AUSTRALIA

Cyril T. Hally, S.S.C.

Prolegomenon

A certain clarification of terminology might be useful as a preliminary. *Ad Gentes* treats of the mission of the church, and hence one may use the expression "mission" also of the local church. The decree states that it is from the mission of the Son and the mission of the Holy Spirit that the church takes its origin and so is missionary by nature. Hence mission is prior to the church, which will be judged by its fidelity to the mission of God. In *Ad Gentes,* no. 6, we read: "the differences which must be recognized in this activity of the Church, do not flow from the inner nature of the mission itself, but from the circumstances in which it is exercised." Missionary activity is defined in footnote 19 as that which is carried on in favor of peoples or nations that do not believe in Christ and whose culture has not been transformed and elevated by the gospel. My understanding, then, of mission is that each local church (assembly of Christians), under the guidance of a dynamic Holy Spirit, has to translate the one mission into provisional objectives or priorities at each stage in the history of the "people" to whom the assembly belongs. This it does by interacting with the total culture of that people. The research seminar therefore concerns "reading the signs of the times" so that each local group, in communion with other Christian groups, may respond in faith to the promptings of the Holy Spirit in the construction of the kingdom.

The second term to require some comment is "missionary institute." In point of fact the vast majority of the members of SEDOS are not missionary institutes but, rather, religious congregations. A few religious congregations are also exclusively or predominantly missionary, and usually, but not always, subject to the Sacred Congregation for the Evangelization of Peoples (SCEP). A few (18) societies of men, living in common without vows, are exclusively missionary institutes. They are, however, predominantly clerical. Lay missionary groups are in the wilderness. The

Cyril Hally, Columban priest, is the Director of the Pacific Mission Institute. In the past he was in charge of the Asian desk for Pro Mundi Vita and also secretary of the National Missionary Council, Australia.

Code of Canon Law did not make provision for exclusively missionary institutes as such, that is, for a distinctive institutional form of the missionary charism. In the practical order the SEDOS seminar is important, for it is superior generals and provincials, and not SCEP, who are responsible for the selection, formation, appointment, and withdrawal of the vast majority of missionaries. Hence it might be useful to reflect that such superiors send missionaries where the people are already Catholic and the cultures strongly influenced by Catholicism. For example, according to calculations I made in 1969 there were 18,000 expatriate priests in Latin America, 1,868 in the Philippines, 12,000 in Africa, 5,749 in the rest of Asia, and 690 in Oceania; 51 percent were in Latin America and the Philippines (basically because of the shortage of priests?). The law appears to be: the higher the percentage of non-Christians in a region, the lower the percentage of missionaries appointed to that region. These decisions were made predominantly by religious superiors, many of whom have no mission experience or training. It is also probably true that the majority of religious appointed to missionary activity have received no prior missionary formation. Fortunately the main missionary agent is the Holy Spirit.

The modern mission era, which began in 1492, witnessed the development not merely of the term "missionary" (European religious going out to non-European non-Christians) but of a special department of the Curia (Propaganda Fide) and of mission-sending agencies. The mission era came to an end in 1949, with the coming to power of the communists in China and the total expulsion of missionaries. A new age in human history commenced.

Perhaps the most significant characteristic of the new period is the interdependence of all peoples politically, economically, and culturally. Just when humankind enters this stage in its history, Christian communities have come into existence within practically every people and culture. A genuine *communion* of churches breaking through the barriers of race, language, culture, and ideologies would be a sign to the whole of humankind of the possibility of genuine worldwide human union. Each local church is called to contribute positively, according to its charisms, to the fostering of such communion by stimulating and correcting other churches and being in turn stimulated and corrected.

Another universal characteristic of our age is the rate of multiple change to which every people and culture are subjected—hence once again the significance of the contemporary existence of a Christian community within each people and culture. Each such Christian community is called to go out into that newly emerging culture and evangelize it. The human missionary agent today is the local Christian community responding to the unique and constant prompting of the Holy Spirit for the building of the kingdom, the *new* creation. Hence the Christian community within a people is to be a salvific sign to those people by its witness and willingness to attribute to its donor the gift of consciously sharing in the life of Christ, and of being open through dialogue to where the Spirit is already active outside itself. Hence the missionary role of each community has a local and a universal dimension.

The primary missionary agent is the local community, in the concrete, particular "churches," built up not only of people but also of "aspirations, of riches and limitations, of ways of praying, of loving, of looking at life and the world, which distinguish this or that human *gathering*," assembly, or ecclesia (*Evangelii Nuntiandi*, no. 63). Such gatherings are prior to historically determined structures of parish, diocese, or national/regional episcopal conference. Even more so are they prior to clerical ministry, let alone "missionary institutes."

Each such community has a threefold function, in the terminology of Father Arevalo: to *discern* where God is at work in its environment, to adopt a *prophetic* stance by denouncing evil, and to become a *saving* community through cooperating wherever grace is at work.

Another characteristic of our age is the massive movement of persons across national frontiers, whether as tourists, diplomats, business people, conventioneers, migrants, or refugees. Allied to this geographical movement is the corresponding social mobility characteristic of most societies today. There is an absolutely unprecedented crossing of cultural and religious frontiers today by goods, ideas, and persons.

In the modern mission era the missionary was at least as significant as the diplomat, soldier, or merchant who, sharing the same religious affiliation, more or less willingly granted to the missionary a certain precedence. Among those moving today, the missionary has not the same significance, but surely has just as much pastoral responsibility to help those crossing national frontiers to be aware of their missionary responsibility. Is there not a striking similarity to the situation in the Roman empire during the initial period of Christianity? All one may do here is mention the impact of modern transnational political, economic, and social structures on the consciousness of humankind. In particular the aspirations for participation, equity, and humanization are so significant a set of characteristics of our age that each church's contribution to the fostering of peace and justice has become almost the criterion of credibility. Of course, the Catholic church as an institution is the transnational corporation par excellence. It was precisely the missionary/ religious institutes that built up the transnational structures of the contemporary institutional church.

The Australian Local Church

Only in March 1976 did the Australian church cease to be technically in the category of "missions," subject to the Congregation for Evangelization. However the arrangement with the Pontifical Mission Aid Societies, whereby one-third of the funds collected remain in Australia, was not abolished. Much of that money is utilized for the Aboriginal apostolate and some to finance the National Missionary Council. The change in juridical status had absolutely no symbolic meaning for Australian Catholics. A brief glance backward into the origin of the Australian church is necessary in order to understand the present situation.

European settlement in Australia began with soldiers and convicts. One-fourth of all convicts were Irish, the majority "political." Only in 1820, thirty years after the commencement of the settlement, were Catholic chaplains allowed into the country. Under such circumstances there was no possibility of a mission to the Aborigines.

In the 1850s gold drew very large numbers to Australia, of whom again one-quarter were Catholic, mostly Irish (in British colonies). The pastoral care of the settlers in a land occupied by Stone Age nomads diverted attention from the Aborigines. The pastoral care was undertaken by Irish bishops, priests, Sisters, and later Brothers. The physical environment was hostile, the social environment characterized by secularization, industrialization, and urbanization.

In the 1870s the question of universal education presented the young church with a challenge of kairos proportions. A decision was taken to supplement the basic parish structure with a network of Catholic schools staffed by religious, managed mostly by the parish priests and paid for by the laity. In effect the mission of the church, in terms of priority use of material and personnel resources, was the preservation of the Catholic faith with particular stress on its transmission to the rising generation.

By the 1930s the young church may be said to have come of age. By then over 90 percent of the Catholics were Australian-born, the first Australian-born and educated bishops were beginning to be appointed, and the leadership of religious congregations was passing into Australian hands. In the 1920s the Irish enthusiasm for missions was brought to Australia by one of the new foundations, the Columban Fathers. They began a nationwide mission animation campaign. By the 1930s the Pontifical Mission Aid Societies were organized on a national basis also.

The only Aboriginal mission of the nineteenth century to survive was that undertaken in Western Australia by Spanish Benedictines. At the turn of the century, the French Sacred Heart Fathers and the German Pallottine Fathers opened missions in the northwest. None of these had much impact on Australian Catholic consciousness until the 1960s. World War II, apart from stopping all expansion of the material plant of the church, had one consequence of significance. Australians became conscious of their neighbors, particularly of Papua New Guinea (an Australian colony—mandated territory) and of Asia. However, defense considerations initially were dominant. The result was the beginning of a massive migration program that has drastically changed the composition of the Australian Catholic population, still one-quarter of the total population.

Though relatively isolated from the rest of the world, the Catholic population is now 44 percent ethnic (24 percent overseas-born and 20 percent Australian-born of overseas-born parents). The languages spoken in Catholic Sydney homes in order of frequency are English, Italian, Arabic, and Spanish, together with some ninety additional languages or dialects. Despite state aid to the extent of 70 percent of costs beginning in the 1960s, only 57 percent of Catholic children are in Catholic schools. In Sydney and Melbourne over 50 percent of these have at least one parent born overseas. Beginning in the 1960s a sudden decline in the number of religious (13 percent of Sisters between 1966 and 1976 alone) has changed the situation also, for in Australia there have traditionally been three Sisters to every priest.

It is against this background that Australian "missionary" involvement should be situated. A survey conducted in 1972 revealed that sixty-two of the Australian religious congregations had some personnel engaged in missionary activity (eight congregations being exclusively missionary, mostly of recent arrival in Australia). Some 10 percent of priests, 9 percent of Brothers, and 5 percent of Sisters were missionaries. By region they were distributed as follows: 48 percent in Papua New Guinea,

24 percent in Aboriginal missions, 7 percent in the Pacific Islands, 19 percent in Asia, and only 1 percent each in Africa and Latin America. Two-thirds of the congregations began missionary activity only in the 1960s, together with three lay missionary organizations. Lay missionaries accounted for 22 percent of the entire missionary personnel (probably the highest proportion in the world).

Since 1972 there has been a considerable decline in the number of missionaries. One may note that Australian missionaries have been heavily concentrated in Papua New Guinea (recently an Australian colony), among Aborigines (internal colony), and the South Pacific (much of it economically dominated by Australia). In the nineteenth century Sydney, because of its geographical location, functioned as headquarters for mostly French congregations, among them Marist and Sacred Heart Fathers, engaged in the evangelization of Oceania. Hence there is no long tradition of mission-sending among Australian Catholics, let alone of missiological reflection. (For the number and location of Australian missionaries in September 1978, see tables 16.1 and 16.2).

Table 16.1

Number and Location of Australian Missionaries, September 1978

Pacific Region		Asia		Latin America		Africa		Middle East	
Papua New Guinea	576	Philippines	59	Chile	12	South Africa	8	Israel	2
Fiji	56	India	54	Peru	9	Ghana	6	Egypt	1
Solomons	48	Japan	48	Brazil	3	Kenya	2		—
Gilbert Islands	16	Singapore/		Venezuela	3	Algeria	2		3
Samoa	14	Malaysia	29	Paraguay	2	Ethiopia	1		
New Caledonia	11	Korea	29	Mexico	2	Nigeria	1	Australia	
Maori, New Zealand	10	Indonesia	15	Equador	1	Lesotho	1		
Tahiti	7	Bangladesh	7	Guatemala	1	Uganda	1	Aborigines	398
Nauru	3	Sri Lanka	4	Colombia	1	Zambia	1		
New Hebrides	2	Pakistan	4	Uruguay	1				
		Thailand	3						
		Hong Kong	3						
Total	743		255		35		23		

Table 16.2

Number and Location of Australian Missionaries, September 1978

| | Priests | | | Brothers | | Sisters | Lay | |
	Religious	Diocesan	Total	Clerical	Non-Cler.		Miss.	Total
Papua New Guinea	115	8	123	29	72	291	58	573
Asia	169	–	169	20	7	57	2	255
Aboriginal Missions	61	11	72	38	14	223	51	398
Pacific Islands	22	1	23	7	9	129	2	170
Africa	1	–	1	–	3	17	1	22
Latin America	15	10	25	2	–	6	–	33
Middle East	–	–	–	–	–	3	–	3
Total	383	30	413	96	105	726	114	1454

The comments that now follow this background presentation of the missionary effort of the Australian church are my own views from my stance as the first secretary of the National Missionary Council (NMC) and as the present director of the Pacific Mission Institute (for missionary formation) and the NMC Resource Centre.

Statement of the Question

The recognition of (*a*) the local church's responsibility for mission and (*b*) the laity's role in carrying out that responsibility questions missionary institutes about their orientations and methodologies at a fundamental level. Underlying this question is the basic relation of the local and official universal structures of the church in the post-Vatican II world to mission. Notice that I have rephrased the last sentence because I believe that the church, the local church or the communion of churches, is judged by its fidelity to the mission of God revealed in Christ and now guided by the Holy Spirit.

The theological paradigmatic switch to the model of the People of God for the church sanctioned by Vatican II does not mesh well with the structures of either local church or communion of churches, both of which reflect a hierarchical model that has been sacralized by centuries of experience. The Federation of Asian Bishops' Colloquium on Ministries in the Church (Hong Kong 1979) stated (nos. 30-31) that

> the Christian mission is incumbent on the entire Christian community of each local Church in its own situation and human environment. Just as the whole Church is missionary, so is it ministerial in its entirety, for all her members

participate in the common mission, though in various ways. All Christians are called to serve as Christ did. The Church is a communion of service in which, even though there are a variety of functions, services and ministries, all persons are equal, co-responsible, and interdependent. It is within this context and against this background that the various distinctive ministries of the Church find their raison d'être and their specific character. Charisms are enduring gifts of the Holy Spirit given to the Church members to be put to use in services and ministries. Endowed with them, different members render different services, thereby contributing, each in his or her own manner, to the Christian mission.

In practice this is what occurs according to the fidelity of the Australian church, thus signifying to some extent the presence to fellow citizens of Christ's saving action. Unfortunately the activity of Catholics is not conceived of by them as such, nor is it reflected as yet in local church structures. It is doubtful that even the majority of the clergy conceive of the Australian church as a local church drawing upon Australian culture, and criticizing and perfecting it in communion with, even, neighboring local churches.

Historians of the local church disagree as to whether the Australian church reflects predominantly Irish or Roman influences. (My own interpretation favors the latter.) Irish bishops sent to Australia belonged to the Cullen faction related to the Irish College in Rome. Practically all the Australian-born bishops appointed before the war had studied as seminarians in Propaganda College, and nearly all clerics with ecclesiastical higher degrees acquired them in Rome.

Just as the Australian culture itself is predominantly derivative, a factor reinforced by the use of the English language, so also the bishops and clergy have shown little pastoral initiative, but have carried out instructions from the Roman Curia provided not too much incongruity was involved. The Episcopal Conference lacks an adequate secretariat to help it to undertake a thorough examination of the options open to the Australian church. Access to the conference by lay people is almost impossible. The religious congregations only recently have established a national secretariat, largely in response to the felt needs of the congregations of women religious. A national Pastoral Institute has come into existence but in practice it is substantially a catechetical center of higher studies.

With the advent of state aid for Catholic schools and the substantial subsidizing of Catholic medical and social welfare institutions, Catholic organizations of professional competence, largely staffed by the laity, have come into existence in the 1970s. Of particular significance are the various Catholic education offices and the Catholic teacher-training colleges. The Catholic education system never extended into the tertiary level. Hence these new structures plus the staffing of the Catholic schools predominantly by the laity may have some impact on the laity's recognition of its responsibility for mission.

The rather extensive undertaking of missionary activity in the neighborhood of Australia by religious in the 1960s was the result of prompting by the contemporary apostolic delegate. The only local initiatives in the specifically missionary sphere came from lay missionary "movements" and diocesan priests who volunteered for overseas service in Papua New Guinea and Latin America. Neither initiative was integrated into the structures of the church.

While these comments might seem unduly critical, the lack of initiative must be understood against the background of a doubling of the Catholic population between 1947 and 1971 (119 percent). The diocesan clergy were confronted with the daunting task of practically doubling the physical plant of the church. The pastoral care of the non-English-speaking migrants was handed over to migrant chaplains, mostly religious, imported for the purpose. The religious, on the other hand, had the even more daunting task of trying (for an increasingly multicultural cohort of students) to double the Catholic educational system, particularly at secondary level, without any state aid until late in the 1960s. Even less than in the civil area do migrants have access to decision-making positions in the Australian church to date. Nevertheless the ethnic variety within the church will undoubtedly be an asset in the days ahead. For example, in 1979 more migrants from Asia than from the United Kingdom were admitted to Australia.

Given the factors described above, any questioning by religious/missionary institutes in Australia of their orientations or methodologies was prompted by involvement in Asian or Latin American churches rather than by developments in the Australian church.

Elements for a Reflection on the Question

The Need to Identify and Study Whatever Emerges in Recognizing Each Level of the Church Responsible for Mission. As mentioned above, the Australian Catholic church, as a minority in what was perceived to be a hostile environment, Protestant or secular, developed no structures to reach out to the Aborigines until after 1900, or to practical non-Christians. Mission was understood to refer to foreign missions. They were taken care of by the Pontifical Mission Aid Societies. The structure consisted of a national director and a small staff, plus diocesan clerical directors, usually part-time. Mission Sunday in October was the major occasion for the laity to contribute to the missions throughout the entire church. The bulk of church finance in Australia is collected from the people attending Mass. The annual collection has built up to over Australian $2 million, which on comparative standards is very good. Lacking a regular magazine the societies can do little to promote a post-Vatican II concept of mission among adults.

The exclusively missionary institutes, Divine Word and Columban Fathers, have national mission animation programs. Some other clerical religious, such as the Sacred Heart, Marist, and Jesuit Fathers, have full-time mission procurators. The religious sisters are severely handicapped through lack of access to pulpits, the only way of reaching the mass of Australian Catholics. The same applies even more to the fledgling lay-missionary organizations. Mission still remains the responsibility of specialists.

In 1964 the hierarchy set up Australian Catholic Relief (ACR), separating the relief work from the control of the Federal Catholic Immigration Committee. ACR started Project Compassion as the Australian Lenten Bishops Fund for socio-economic development. The inspiration came from overseas. Staffed predominantly by lay persons, ACR soon adopted a progressive approach to aid based on reciprocity between local churches, symbolized perhaps best by block grants, together with those of several other Western churches, to the Asia Fund for Human Development; these contributions are allocated by the receiving churches themselves. In its animation programs, ACR moved from publicizing the symptoms of inequality and poverty to identifying their causes. This later approach has provoked something of the backlash treated by Lissner in *The Politics of Altruism*.

In 1968 the hierarchy set up the Catholic Commission for Justice and Peace (CCJP), financed by ACR. This organization is also lay-staffed. It has been given the responsibility of publishing annual Social Justice statements, as well as attending to matters of justice both within and outside Australia. The commission does not speak in the name of the hierarchy, but is often considered to do so. Hence not a few bishops are rather sensitive about its choice of issues, which by definition must be ones with considerable political and emotional implications. The CCJP so far has failed to win the cooperation of the majority of parish priests and hence access to all the laity through the parish structure. Structures that have been sacralized are particularly resistant to innovations. Consequently the clerically operated traditional Pontifical Mission Aid Societies and the lay-staffed ACR and CCJP ran along parallel lines for several years with no cooperation and with considerable latent hostility. This did little in the post-Vatican II era to promote an understanding among Australian Catholics of the interrelatedness of mission, justice, and development (let alone liberation). Some religious teachers have been influenced, partly at least, by the animation efforts of ACR and CCJP to experiment with justice education programs, which in turn have led some congregations and conferences of religious superiors, of Sisters and Brothers, to release religious to undertake full-time work in the justice area.

A further innovation has been the establishment of an ecumenical organization called Action for World Development (AWD). Once again this is a lay-staffed organization predominantly of a grassroots nature, in marked contrast to the other organizations, which all operate exclusively at the national or state levels. The numbers involved, unfortunately, are very small.

In my personal opinion none of the above (nor all together) has the influence still exerted by the National Civil Council (NCC), a lay organization started during World War II to prevent a communist takeover of industrial unions, which exert a very powerful influence on the Labour party. Expelled from the Labour party in 1954 and declared by the hierarchy not to be an ecclesial organization, the NCC gave rise to the Democratic Labour party. The Movement, as it is often known, sponsors a weekly periodical of conservative political comment and its founder has a weekly column in a national newspaper and a weekly TV program. The NCC influences some of the older bishops, many of the older religious and clergy, and probably most of the older missionaries.

On the other hand, ACR, CCJP and AWD have certainly taken the initiative away from the Pontifical Mission Aid Societies (PMAS) among the younger clergy and religious and probably from the missionary institutes. For example, there is a widespread assumption that the most important contribution younger Australian Catholics can make to the third world is in their homeland and not abroad, that feeding the hungry has priority over preaching the gospel, and that the causes of injustice are mostly in the first world.

Finally, in response to a Roman recommendation, the hierarchy established the Episcopal Committee for Missions in 1970 and the National Missionary Council the following year. There was no felt need for either at any level of the Australian church. The National Missionary Council did, however, provide the missionary and religious institutes with an opportunity to cooperate among themselves, with the Pontifical Mission Aid Societies, and with the hierarchy. The secretariat has been staffed by the missionary institutes.

A resource center has been established as both an information and a research facility for those interested in missiological development and news and information concerning missionary activity and other local churches. Likewise a missiology program was started to provide formation for those with a first missionary appointment, missionaries on furlough, and those working with Aborigines and migrants within Australia. Both services have been utilized predominantly by the women's religious institutes.

An effort was made to start Mission-in-Focus programs at a parish level. The idea, copied from Canada, was an attempt to build into parish councils a mission dimension marrying local and universal concern. The program gave some indication of being useful in rural dioceses but failed in the large cities. The basic reason is the hostility of the metropolitan environment to all forms of adult formation based on the parish.

Greater success was achieved in attempting to bring about some coordination between the educational work of the Pontifical Mission Aid Societies, ACR, and CCJP. This has resulted in the appointment of a common education officer to promote the mission/justice/development curriculum in the teacher-training colleges of Sydney. A further initiative has been the hiring of a few educational experts to provide teaching materials for both primary and secondary Catholic schools for integrated formation in mission/justice/development. It is hoped that the demonstration effect of the three agencies working together through one of the major institutions of the church will bear fruit in time.

A certain amount of systematic input now flows into the formation programs set up by the major superiors for different cohorts of religious. The mission institutes have both initiated and cooperated with ACR in exposure programs for religious in third world countries. It should be noted that very few adult laity are directly influenced by any of the initiatives above.

The Theological Relation of the Local to the Universal Church. This question troubles me. What, theologically, is the *universal* church? Surely it is not the pope and the Roman Curia; yet, for example, in the recent Dutch Synod the curia claimed to be exactly that. Theologically the universal church is the communion of local churches sharing a common faith and sacraments, in apostolic union with churches of the past and present, and bearing one another's burdens.

The *local* church poses problems also. In the widest sense I consider that it refers to any grouping of Christians who feel united by some nonecclesial bond, such as neighborhood, locality, nationality, or culture. Hence I would include regional churches, such as that of Latin America, with a certain common culture and history, national churches such as that of Japan, dioceses, parishes, and what are now known as basic ecclesial communities. The present rigid territorial divisions have become inadequate. Personal groupings do exist, such as Eastern Rite churches, national "parishes." It is doubtful if at present there is a right of free assembly within the so-called universal church. Sooner or later non-Western forms of grouping will have to be recognized as legitimate and pastorally functional. The missionary institutes have a serious responsibility at this stage in Christian history to promote both the concept and the reality of the communion of local churches. This calls for much greater horizontal sharing and reciprocity in place of the former exclusive spokes-of-the-wheel model, each local church at the receiving end from the curia in Rome, and to a minor extent from centralized missionary institutes.

The Call to Mission as a Gospel Imperative. The Holy Spirit retains the initiative in directing the churches toward the building of the kingdom. This he does by means of *charisms*. These are granted to individuals, or to groups and institutes. Charisms are given for the building up of the body so that it can be faithful to the mission of God. More often than not they respond to that need, but not necessarily so. It is the responsibility of each community to discern what genuine charisms are being granted to its members individually or collectively and for the legitimate authority in a church to authenticate the charism.

The missionary institutes themselves should be particularly sensitive to the possible existence of charisms of a strictly missionary character. In this context the phenomenon of the massive movement of people across national and cultural boundaries takes on a particular significance. It could also be that in the future the missionary institutes may function primarily as a support group for innumerable persons with temporary charisms scattered throughout the various churches.

The Situation of Christians Who Are Out of Touch with the Church. Once again I do not like the use of the concept "church" in this context. In reflecting upon this reality I believe three phenomena should be considered. The first is those local churches that find themselves living under Marxist regimes, particularly when the Christian community is a small minority. All present ecclesial structures have developed within capitalist societies and hence are capital- rather than labor-intensive. There is the historical example of the Japanese church ministries during centuries of repression, which was very similar to that exerted by Marxist regimes. I cannot think of a single church in danger of being overrun by Marxists in which structures possibly appropriate to the future situation have been even imagined. This could be a challenge to "professional" missionaries.

The second area is that of local churches, particularly where the Christians are recent, as in African churches, in which access to the Eucharist is extremely limited, for example, a few times a year. Nonsacramental Christians by definition are out of touch with the "church." This points up the importance of the third area, the basic ecclesial community new-ministry approach. Missionary institutes have a significant role to play in fostering the necessary attitudinal and structural changes. Too many "missionary" pastors are tied to the parish and too many religious to some institution.

The Recognition That the Universality of the Church, if Imposed from One Direction Only, Creates a Situation Where Mission Is No Longer Creative and Active on the Receiving Side. Once again I do not like the wording of the concept. The universality of the church cannot be imposed, for ecclesial universality is communion, which calls for reciprocal, free exchange between equals. What is imposed are external patterns of relationships, which frequently are of a dominant/dominated character and hence not creative even on the dominant side.

The missionary institutes, as mentioned above, are transnational corporations. Hence each individual missionary has the power of his or her institute's organizational, material, and personnel resources behind him or her, not withstanding their individual intentions or lifestyles. One of the ways of lessening the power impact is by breaking the missionary personnel into small and relatively scattered groups. The vow of obedience is concerned with the *right use of power*. This calls for constant discernment. The lines of communication established by missionary institutes between churches can be useful in denouncing cases, for example, where human rights are violated, and so bringing legitimate moral pressure to bear on oppressors.

Another aspect of missionary institute behavior is related to the vow of poverty, *the right use of material goods and services*. Once again we are confronted with the phenomenon of collective wealth and capital-intensive pastoral and missionary structures.

The Possibilities of Coordinating Placement of Personnel. I have a feeling that, in the not too distant future, the normal pattern for placement of personnel will be much the same as that operating with regard to financial aid. Increasingly the latter is granted in response to a request. If we look closely at the latter, we might be able to learn some lessons. The CIDSE effort at more or less international coordination broke down, I understand, because some local churches, for example, in West Germany and the United States, were too powerful. Hence the size of a church open to requests has to be taken into account. The two churches mentioned are too big and powerful in terms of financial resources for genuine equality to be established with any receiving church. Hence the right level at which cooperation should be fostered will have to be found by means of experimentation.

Whatever happens it is important that Cor Unum does not get control of the allocation of funds. The Pontifical Mission Aid Societies pride themselves on supporting the "universal" mission of the church in a fair and equitable manner. Witness the bringing of national directors to Rome every year to foster a democratic procedure. While there are doubtless sincere efforts to help local indigent churches to be relatively self-supporting, the analysis of the causes of the indigence is either nonexistent or woefully inadequate. No one in Rome or Paris is likely to give up control of a $50 million enterprise.

The parallel with the coordination of personnel is not exact. As mentioned above, the placement at present is predominantly in the hands of either superiors general or provincials. Theoretically the NMC or a regional missionary council could be the receiving agency for requests to a particular local church from other local churches. I cannot see much possibility of this happening in Australia in the near future. The Major Religious Superiors Conference, especially of women, is beginning to be approached and responds through its members in an ad-hoc manner.

Protestant missionary bodies many years ago attempted to separate the financing of the exchange of personnel between local churches from the actual exchange of personnel. This resulted in the exchange of personnel among third world churches, with first world churches footing the bill.

In this context the missionary institutes, for the time being, could perform an essential task in providing formation and backup for temporary personnel responding to a request in another local church. To some extent this is what the Pacific Mission Institute (PMI) tries to do in Australia. The PMI has grown out of the missiology program established by the NMC. Likewise the missionary institutes could, and sometimes do, act as reception personnel for such temporary missionaries in the receiving institutes, and the like, in cooperation with the local church.

A lot of this is utopian at present. Most bishops and superiors at both ends are concerned primarily with the staffing of institutions rather than the identification and testing of charisms.

The Question of Reverse Mission. As pointed out, the majority of missionaries from Australia who have returned belong to religious provinces with minimal mission involvement. Some provinces had a policy of rather rapid circulation of members to their remote mission post so that the religious would not be away long enough to have trouble fitting in on their return. Not a few returned missionaries suffer culture shock in reverse or feel frustrated in not being able to utilize their experience and insights. The Mission-in-Focus program was designed to offer them an opportunity to share their experiences at the parish level.

The lay-missionary experience is even worse. A few years ago we were able to get the hierarchy to set up a Lay Missionary Gratuity Fund, to provide the minimum financial help to lay missionaries returning with no savings while they looked for a job, and so forth. The Mission-in-Focus program was designed to help them also. We felt that lay participants should receive some remuneration while participating full-time in a team, but this made the operation rather expensive.

It was hoped that the Pacific Mission Institute would be able to provide reentry programs for returning missionaries that might help them to reflect on their experience and discover ways and means of making use of it. Only members of missionary institutes have availed themselves of the program.

A proposal was made that returned religious or lay missionaries be employed full-time by the diocesan directors of the Pontifical Mission Aid Societies for mission animation, given that the directors are part-time clerics. Only one or two such experiments have taken place so far.

Hence mission in reverse is undertaken and reflected upon only by members of missionary institutes. One institute takes young people on exposure tours of its missions with a view to their contribution to the church of origin. Another institute has appointed members to justice and peace work and to mission animation, in addition to the normal or traditional promotion work (finance, vocations, and prayer). It was found that the same missionaries could not combine all three or even two of the activities. Since the roles are new the appointees have to pioneer. The most difficult part is winning reasonably widespread understanding or expectations from the clergy or laity. Their work at present tends to be supportive of those already converted or interested.

Finally both the missionary institutes and the ACR invite representatives of other local churches to engage in conscientization programs in the Australian church. While generally reinforcing the convictions of the already converted, some of these importees are utilized by the radio and TV national networks.

Two comments are in order on this matter. Many of the returned missionaries are suitable for and capable of only the traditional promotion work. Those who have been heavily committed to basic ecclesial community, justice, or development programs suffer severely from culture shock in reverse, sometimes from extreme alienation in their church of origin. This is in addition to the lack of structures through which to work on their return. Hence the importance of reentry programs. Since most of such missionaries use some form of structural analysis they are likely to be accused of Marxist leanings, and so dismissed as incompetent or as fanatics. The other matter is that not a few middle-aged missionaries, realizing that they should hand over to younger local priests, would be willing to return for reverse mission work if they were sure such work would be available. They do not feel capable of a pioneering role, however.

The Structures Needed for Six-Continent Mission Formation. After several years of experience in trying to provide this type of formation I have reached certain conclusions. A process must be employed that facilitates the communication of vision and commitment. Such attitudinal or value change requires cognitive, affective, and directive dimensions. At the first level two skills must be acquired: analytical and evaluative. Some introduction to economics, political science, and social anthropology seem to be essential at the cognitive level. Often persons who have studied philosophy, Scripture, and theology experience some sort of blockage with regard to the social sciences. The consequence is that the first step in reading the signs of the times at either the local or the global level tends to be uncongenial.

In themselves none of these disciplines (or all together) necessarily communicates a vision. In my experience this is either caught from people consumed by a vision or results from an exposure experience that shocks the participant into a questioning of internalized myths or ideology.

The most difficult challenge is to include in the formation what might be called a missionary spirituality adequate to living on an exposed frontier, engaged in genuinely open dialogue at the deepest level, and committed to a project that is never absolutized. Of course, such a spirituality develops only in the situation outlined above.

The Role of the Church in Relation to Nationalism. Undoubtedly, nationalism is the strongest "natural" force in the contemporary world. Allied to state symbols and organization, it is capable of mobilizing very large numbers of people and of rendering them uncritical of national goals, for example, warfare. In one sense it is the modern form of idolatry calling for absolute sacrifice. In another it turns patriotism into extreme ethnocentrism.

It seems to me that the centralized structures of the institutional church have failed significantly in the area of peacemaking. In this context the development of a genuine communion of churches has an enormous contribution to make, particularly in the protection of basic human rights. It is minorities, utilizing national/state machinery, who today violate the human rights of their own citizens, for example, atheistic propaganda and restriction of religious freedom or the exploitation of religious symbols and institutions for ideological reasons.

As the FABC "Conclusion" (no. 113) states, "A deep renewal of the episcopal ministry is called for, if the bishop is to be an effective sign of unity in the ecclesial community and the guiding spirit of the Christian mission in the world." The text sees bishops as members of the Episcopal College, as the rallying point between local churches, as visible signs of the communion of churches—a communion presided over by the successor of Saint Peter. Their specific charism is that of unity and spiritual leadership. Hence their ministry is eminently pastoral rather than administrative. Among their main tasks is discerning the voice of the Spirit speaking through their people and those of other local churches. To some extent this is beginning to happen in regional conferences of bishops and even in the Roman synods.

In this context it seems to me that missionary institutes, particularly if their membership is international, have an extremely important contribution to make at present. In some such congregations the internationality of the membership is suppressed as much as possible. In others, in which the tension is faced up to, an example is given of overcoming false national loyalties and ethnocentrism. Such congregations then have a moral authority to speak directly to hierarchies in situations where basic human rights are being violated. In many ways they can contribute toward reconciliation among peoples.

In our contemporary world there would seem to be a special missionary function to work, at the same time, for the protection and development of minorities within states and for the suppression of excessive nationalism in favor of the universal common good of humankind. If this were lived out there would be a deepening of the theological understanding of the communion of churches.

The Relation between Ecclesiastical Structures and the Structures of Missionary Institutes in the Sending of Missionaries. As mentioned above, in discussing coordination of personnel, it is, substantially, religious superiors who decide who will work where and at what task. Hence in a sense the question is tautological. In Australia the hierarchy has absolutely nothing to do with the appointment of members of religious/missionary institutes. The bishops do release a few *fidei donum* priests and Sisters from congregations of diocesan rite. The Melbourne Archdiocese has two overseas "missions," one in Venezuela and the other in Papua New Guinea. The former seems to have come into existence through a friendship between the archbishop of Melbourne and a bishop in Venezuela. Now that the former has moved from the diocese the mission is to be closed.

In the "mission" situation, now that the *jus commissionis* has come to an end, in theory missionary institutes enter into a contract with the local bishop, often the first indigenous bishop of a diocese. Such a contract frequently determines who will "place" the expatriate missionaries. Ideally a healthy tension develops between a bishop, pastorally oriented in the sense outlined above, and the members of the local missionary group, who discern on the basis of their missionary charism. It seems to be utopian to expect that the local Christian community will have effective say in the arrangements. Perhaps the very notion of a contract places administrative before pastoral considerations, and institution before community.

Risk that Bishops See Missionaries as Replacement for Missing Local Clergy. This is not a risk but a reality. Given the present ecclesial structures, insisted upon by canon law for every diocese in the world no matter what its stage of evolution or type of culture, and expected by the vast majority of clergy and even people, the bishop has little choice but to maximize, from whatever source, the number of clergy. Taking clergy in the wider sense of ministers, this phenomenon covers religious Sisters and Brothers also. It is simply a consequence of the consistent priority given to institution over community/charism. The bishop as the head of the institution is caught more than anyone else. A radical change of attitudes and symbols is required. To the bringing about of such changes, missionary institutes can contribute much, on condition that they remain faithful to their missionary charism. They are also likely to see their role as building a diocese or running parishes rather than helping communities to form that are outward-looking and missionary.

Related Questions

When Does a Local Church Become *Truly* a Local Church? A few years ago in *Mondo e Missione* the following were listed as characteristic of a mature local church:

—localization, namely, the consciousness of a local community that is a church with its own specific responsibility to continue the mission of God, in building the kingdom among its own people and beyond its own people;
—relative autonomy in ministries and services appropriate to its contribution to the mission of God, in financing such ministries, and in self- evangelization plus responding to the missionary charism of going out to other people, a necessary stage in the maturing of a church;
—inculturation, namely, the purification and perfection of the local culture plus the contribution of original insights into the knowledge of the person of Christ shared with other contemporary churches;
—positive building of communion of churches in solidarity with other churches and in union with the pope as supreme pastor.

These criteria break down the division between old and young churches, now that a Christian community exists nearly everywhere. The real division is between mature and immature churches, the latter including many old churches.

When Could a Missionary Institute Leave a Local Church? No universally valid answer can be given to such a question. One of the most difficult actions for any ecclesial institution is to stop doing something it has started. Ideally the missionary institute engages in a process of discernment with the local Christian community. Factors involved would be promotion of the maturity of the local church by withdrawal of specifically missionary, as distinct from pastoral, expatriate help; fidelity by the missionary institute to its missionary charism to avoid the danger of undertaking properly pastoral tasks in the local church; the need elsewhere for scarce missionary resources of personnel; ideally the understanding of the community of the church or churches of origin.

What Forms of Ministry by Missionary Institutes Are Needed in Different Local Cultures, Contexts? Once again such a question cannot be answered outside a concrete culture and context. Further, it depends upon the initiative of the Holy Spirit in the granting of charisms. It is difficult to overemphasize that all churches have entered into a new missionary era. The future is pregnant with unimagined possibilities. As the FABC Colloquium on Ministries in 1977 insisted, prior to any form of ministry is the development of genuine local community. The community as it forms discerns the charism that the Holy Spirit provides it with so that the body of Christ may be built up in order to further the mission of the Father. We are dealing with a new creation. While there is continuity with the past, there is also radical innovation.

The formation of such ministries, in a sense, is prior to the development of ministries by missionary institutes. In not a few regional churches, the bishops' conferences have given broad guidelines, which some missionary institutes have used to make more specific their own priorities for this period and the relevant region. They in turn provide criteria for initiating or giving up various ministries.

For example, one such specification of the missionary role of crossing boundaries of language, culture, and faith to assist local churches in bringing the knowledge of Christ to the unevangelized resulted in the following priorities: facilitating dialogue between Christians and non-Christians; preferential option for the poor and oppressed; helping in the task of inculturation of gospel values in cultures not one's own; promoting communion between churches through the exchange of ideas, programs, and personnel.

What Concrete Planning Is Being Done to Integrate the Laity into the Mission of the Church? I do not like the framing of the question. It situates the church over against the laity. I come back to the point I have made so often in this paper. It is not the function of the clerical members of the Christian community to define the pastoral/missionary priorities of the community. Rather, their first responsibility is to identify the charisms given members of that community for building it up to carry out the mission of God.

In this perspective the role of "mission animator" as distinguished from that of "institute promoter" is to help increasing numbers of the laity (and of the clergy) to realize that they constitute a local church which by nature is missionary and that each person has a role to play corresponding to complementary charisms. These manifest themselves usually in aspirations. It is the task of missionary institutes in particular to be sensitive to where the Spirit may be granting specifically missionary charisms, to help the community to recognize them, and to provide moral and perhaps institutional support.

One concrete example of such experimentation is the offer of temporary membership in missionary institutes to laity aspiring to undertake some form of missionary activity in one's church of origin or in other local churches. Probably the majority of the members of clerical missionary institutes are not convinced of the usefulness or practicality of such gestures. The basic obstacle is centuries of differential status between clergy and laity. Perhaps the "vocation" crisis is the only way left for the Holy Spirit to bring about a radical alteration in relationships between persons in the Christian community, at present defined entirely on the basis of a hierarchy of functions.

What Is the Relation of the Small Christian Community to This Whole Question? As indicated earlier, it is in the family (the domestic church) and in "primary" or *gemeinschaft* groups that the "faith" is transmitted, developed, shared, supported, and related to nearly all other aspects of life. From a sociological point of view, while the traditional parish functions as if made up of a mass of individuals, in fact each individual normally belongs to a parish as a functioning member of a primary group. Unfortunately the parish ignores the "natural" group as a group, including increasingly even the family. These natural groups are prior to any formal institutional aspect of the church.

In third world countries in particular, such basic ecclesial communities have been developed in rural areas and in urban slums. In both of these situations persons need primary group membership in order to survive. Urban middle-class persons are accustomed to a multiplicity of secondary (impersonal) relationships and often lack membership of a *gemeinschaft* group, which most certainly an urban parish in Australia is not. Since an increasing proportion of people are entering the urban middle class, a most serious pastoral imperative is the development of primary groups for such people. This is an aspect of modern culture that has yet to be evangelized, and hence calls for missionary strategies.

I believe strongly that in these primary Christian groups the activity of the Holy Spirit is most likely to be recognized—where all fundamental evangelical activity begins. Hence the contemporary missionary requires skill in identifying different types of human groups in diverse cultural settings and in helping them to become evangelizing agents for their members and those they come to contact.

In Terms of the Evolution Taking Place in the Local Church, What Will Be the Criteria for Missionary Institutes to Determine Their Commitments in the Future? As mentioned in the prolegomenon, there are very few exclusively "missionary" institutes, and they all belong to the modern mission period, mostly to the last decades thereof. That period has come to an end. Hence the possibility must be allowed for that missionary institutes may have to die in order that structures more appropriate to the contemporary age may develop. The same, of course, applies to the Congregation for the Evangelization of Peoples to which the missionary institutes are subject more or less. For example, the missionary institutes could merge into some kind of national or regional missionary council at the service of a local church in building the communion of churches.

In the meantime the institutes could pay much more attention to the aspirations of the young who join them, even if in decreasing numbers. This is a frustrating task at present, partly due to lack of formation processes that take seriously the implications *for the institute* of the aspirations of the young members. Discernment, of course, is needed. Some are very "conservative" and experience difficulty interiorizing the basic insights of Vatican II. Others are charismatic with a tendency to ignore the environment in which mission takes place today. Still others are excessively socially active. Some are genuine prophets.

In the early 1980s most of these institutes have an aging membership as a consequence of the severe hemorrhage of younger or experimental members in the last decade or so. Many of the survivors have been able to cope only with the utmost difficulty with the missionary implications of Vatican II and the multiplicity of radical changes that have taken place, and still are, in third world countries. It is precisely such members who are called upon to read the signs of the times and to carry out future commitments. Hence an extreme sensitivity to the prophets in their midst is essential at the present time.

These prophets seem mostly to be disciples of the ecclesial prophets in the third world churches. We will put aside the increasing frequency with which missionaries from the West are denied entry into third world countries or expelled therefrom, except to remark that the analysis and evaluation of this trend constitutes an important dimension of the discernment process concerning future commitments of missionary institutes, and calls for contingency planning for the placement of relatively large numbers of middle-aged or elderly missionaries following upon a sudden expulsion from a mission region. Not a few of the third world prophets are calling the first world churches to conversion.

It could be that in the near future missionary institutes will be heavily engaged in helping to build communion between local churches from the base of their churches of origin, which is perhaps another name for mission in reverse.

17

INTEGRATING THE MISSION SOCIETIES INTO THE LOCAL CHURCH

Bernard-Antoine Joinet

The presence of mission societies in the local church, in the North as well as in the South,[1] seems to pose certain problems for these societies.[2] I have neither the ability nor the desire to carry out a theoretical theological or sociological investigation of this subject. The only thing I can do is share with my missionary brothers and sisters the fruits of my prolonged practical reflection, based on events of daily life, on the presence not just of individuals but of *structured missionary groups in the local church,* both in the North and in the South.

Free Associations

As a White Father, I am not only an individual at the service of the Tanzanian Bishops' Conference, as indeed I have been these past fifteen years; I am also a member of one missionary society among many others.

Indeed, since before Saint Benedict, but especially since the fifth century, a curious phenomenon has occurred in the universal community that is the Catholic church.

One fine day a man or a woman has a spiritual experience, whether at Manresa, Subiaco, or Avila. Or he or she discovers the people's distress, as Monsieur Vincent, or women's need of liberation, as Mlle Pelletier. Whereupon groups of companions form around the person, sharing his or her lifestyle and specific mode of service. Gradually the new group adopts a specific aim and a rule. After numerous difficulties, the purpose and the rule of this group are recognized and approved by the hierarchical church as being in conformity with the gospel and the universal mission of the church. A religious society, or congregation, or order is born.

Bernard-Antoine Joinet, White Father, has been in Tanzania since 1966. He is economic adviser to the Episcopal Conference, and also Chaplain to the Faculty of Medicine, Dar-es-Salaam University. He is likewise Honorary Lecturer in psychology and psychopathology.

In sociological terms, we would call these groups of men and women, these societies, "free associations." They freely choose their end and aim, and they may even change their ends, as the needs of the contemporary world change. Their members meet regularly in chapter to elect their superiors and revise their constitutions. They choose their candidates, and form them in their own fashion, within the framework of the general directives handed down by the institutional church.

These associations are not "free" in the sense that their members do what they please. They are bound by both the general mission of the church and the original act of institution of their founder. Sociologists call them "free" because their members enter them freely, freely adopt a common goal and a common strategy, are freely admitted into the society, and in certain circumstances can detach themselves from it by mutual consent.

The existence of such groups of men and women, priests and laity, who adopt a goal and a strategy for attaining it, as well as a certain form of common life, is recognized and approved by the church, and forms part of the life and dynamism of the church. This is a matter of historical fact. Popes and councils alike, and more recently the Roman Curia, recognize the existence of these groups as something of great value for the church. For historical reasons, these free religious associations began and developed especially in the churches of the North. Do the churches of the South wish to receive—or better, do they wish to allow to be born within themselves—such free religious associations? Only they can give the answer. Are the bishops of the churches of the South willing to allow to spring up in their dioceses free associations of apostolic men and women over which they will have but partial control? It is a question that can be asked. The bishops' actions will give the answer.

Sometimes, too, these free societies lose sight of their purpose, which is the service of the church and humanity. They concentrate on their own interests, occasionally even exploiting peasants who live on "their land," or placing themselves at the service of the dominant class. They become parasites. This is also a fact. It is striking to observe that in France, some of the most de-Christianized regions of all are to be found in the vicinity of great old Benedictine abbeys like Cluny. The history of the Benedictines, from Saint Benedict, through Saint Bernard and the Abbot of Rance, to Bernard Besret, can be viewed as the history of continual deviations and reforms.

Religious societies, congregations, and orders have a gift, a special charism—that of being free associations. But this freedom, which is their particular gift, is a two-edged sword. It can be employed for better or for worse. The proof is in history.

Schools of Risk-taking and Creativity

The members of religious societies, because they have chosen one another and form relatively united groups, enjoy evident advantages. But these precious gifts are also ambiguous.

As a member of a free association, I enjoy great material security. If I am seriously ill or injured, I know that the "Flying Doctor" will come by plane to evacuate me to the best hospital in East Africa or Europe, so that I may be treated by the best specialists. I need have no anxiety about my later years: I know that I will receive a state pension, and that my society has several houses for aged Fathers and Brothers. If I so desire I can grow old peacefully in the suburbs of Paris, surrounded by my friends of this same society, and even enjoy a weekly cultural outing on the Left Bank, twenty minutes away by public transportation.

If I have need of an automobile in my ministry, and lack the wherewithal to have one, I need only apply to the mutual assistance fund maintained by my confreres, and I receive a part of the necessary assistance. Or if I belong to a society that has the vow of poverty, that society will simply furnish me the vehicle of which I have need.

I also enjoy great spiritual security, if there is such a thing. When I feel that the Spirit calls me and moves within me, I am mistrustful. Is it actually the Spirit working within me, or my unconscious wishes? Or is the Spirit making use of these desires to tell me something else? I do not know. I must apply the "discernment of spirits." Here I have many things I can do. I can consult my friends, for months and years. The Spirit always works slowly. There is no hurry. When things become clear, I broach the matter with my superiors—and the dialogue continues. Or sometimes the Spirit calls me by means of something proposed to me by my superiors. Often I balk. But eventually the light becomes so clear that I can no longer fail to see it. The moment has come to make a decision with my superiors.

I have had a deep experience of freedom during a retreat given by a blind Jesuit Father, locked up in his blindness but with a very keen ear for the Spirit. He told me quite simply, "Father, the superior's role is not to give orders, nor to see that they are carried out—but to help the 'inferior' discern the will of the Spirit in his regard." Ever since that retreat, I like to talk to superiors. Naturally I do not consult only the members of my society, I also consult my Tanzanian superiors of the Bishops' Conference, and my friends, priests or laity, Catholics or Protestants. But in the last analysis the practical decision is taken in common with the superiors of the society which I have freely chosen and which has admitted me. Even when I feel I am drowning in a sea of doubts, I know that all around me, within arm's reach, there are several lifebuoys. This certainty makes me relatively comfortable even in my anxiety.

Likewise I enjoy a great intellectual security. When after six years of parish work, or teaching, I have the feeling of going around in circles, of making no theological progress, I manifest myself to superiors. I consult them. We make a diagnosis together. They give me the green light, and advise me to do a year of special studies, garnished with a thirty-day retreat. After the year is over I am ready to set out for a new assignment in a new diocese.

The physical, intellectual, and spiritual security that a group gives its members is one of the gifts, one of the specific charisms, of these free associations. It is a gift that can be apostolic. It permits creativity and initiative. In other words it permits risk-taking. If a religious tries to introduce liturgical reforms that go "too far too fast" for a particular diocese, his or her superiors can send that liturgist off to another diocese, one that is more open—and precisely in need of a liturgist. If the person manages to be expelled from South Africa for fighting apartheid, he or she can work in Tanzania or Mozambique. If a Father or a Brother has a talent for youth ministry but cannot bear the regular life of a teacher in a minor seminary, he can try his gift among the youth bands, the "parking boys," of Nairobi or Abidjan. In successive tasks—by "groping"—a member of a free association can discover his or her gifts and the manner in which the Spirit wishes them to be used. For it is the Spirit who is the source of these gifts, as well as the guide of the church and its religious societies in their use (cf. *Lumen Gentium,* nos. 4, 7–9, 12). One can even discover that one does not actually possess the gifts one thought one possessed. In all cases, the certainty of being able to find a new assignment, of finding a new opportunity in case of failure, the certainty of being able to carry out successive tasks that permit one to discover one's gifts, afford the security necessary for taking the initiative, for making bold options—and accepting the risk that these entail.

This security that the group offers its members, and the range of tasks it gives them for the exercise of their talents seem to me to be one of the specific gifts of religious societies. They permit risk-taking, initiative, mobility, and flexibility. This is not to say that these societies hold a monopoly of these gifts. Nor is it to say that their members are willing to use their gifts. On the contrary, there are societies that seem to be suffering from sclerosis.

But this security offered by the group, whose experience often includes the secular, is ambivalent. It can block both vision and action. For if, as the church asks of me, I should take sides with the poor—if, as the 1977 Synod affirms, "action in favor of justice, and the transformation of the world, seems to us to be one of the constitutive dimensions of the proclamation of the gospel," then what about the fact that my security prevents me from sharing and living the insecurity of the oppressed and the poor? I can choose to live the life of African peasants, and live every day on balls of meal or maize, sleep in a hut, a classroom, or the co-op shop as I go around to the villages for most of the months of the year. But when it is time for vacation in Europe, there is my plane ticket—which costs the equivalent of the joint annual income of twenty-eight of my peasant friends—right on my table, poverty or no, and I pack my bags and say, "Be seeing you!"

In fact it seems to me that, in certain dioceses, this security is one of the principal sources of friction between members of missionary societies and the diocesan clergy, who do not enjoy the same system of security. In the 1960s the security of the diocesan clergy was one of the main themes of discussion in several national associations of diocesan priests.

Like liberty, security is one of the gifts or charisms of the free religious associations.[3] And like liberty, it is a two-edged gift. It can be a source of initiative, flexibility, and risk-taking in the service of the church and humanity, or it can cut the religious off from the poor and the oppressed and encourage them to lead a life of beatific comfort, concerning whose source they dare not ask too many questions. Like liberty, security can be used for the best or for the worst.

Multinational Corporations in the Church

I hesitated for a long time to have recourse to the analogy of the multinational corporations for a better grasp of the nature of religious societies in general and the missionary congregations in particular. The multinational corporations have a bad press, and are theoretically excluded from certain countries. But I think the comparison casts sufficient light on the present situation of the mission societies to make it worth the risk of being misunderstood.

In technical terms, a multinational corporation is an enterprise largely composed of subsidiaries in countries other than that of the parent company. These subsidiaries are altogether rooted in the country in which they are located. The labor force, most of the management, the raw material, and a part of the capital come from the host country, which purchases a part of the product of these local affiliates. Opinion is divided on the good or bad effects of the multinational corporations on world economy, and I do not intend to take up this question. My purpose is to study the *power* of these corporations.

The central fact, upon which everyone agrees, is that the subsidiaries of the multinational corporations can make only short-term decisions, and then only to resolve local problems. Major decisions concerning the subsidiaries are made by the parent company. For example, a multinational corporation can decide to close a textile factory in France in order to open one in the Ivory Coast where labor is cheaper.

Since the development of the multinationals, national governments have less and less control over their own economy. As powerful and nationalistic a political personality as General Charles de Gaulle, who was able to withdraw French armed forces from NATO, was unable to prevent American companies from winning a monopoly of raw materials in France. Whatever the multinationals' economic effect may be, their political effect is sure: they gradually limit a state in its power to make decisions on its own economy. World economy is gradually slipping from the hands of small businesses and governments and beginning to depend on a few hundred technocrats and bankers whose avowed aim is to turn a profit. Thus there is a latent conflict of interest and power between local governments, who wish to direct their own economy, and the multinationals, who actually direct it from the outside. A frequent solution is collusion between the local elite and the multinationals, at the expense of the peasants and laborers. The rise in unemployment in the industrialized countries of the North is one of the most tangible signs of this.

Thus there are two sources of power, and two sources of decision: the local government, and the parent company abroad. A government can choose to raise the minimum wage, and the multinational corporation can decide to close its subsidiaries in that country and move to Hong Kong.

Certain religious orders and most mission societies are rather strongly centralized. They have their local superiors in the mission fields, but they also have their provincials in Europe and North America and a superior general in Rome. A large teaching order can decide to withdraw little by little from its middle-class schools in order to devote itself more to the apostolate of the working class, without either the parents or the bishops having a word to say in the matter. A provincial or general of a mission society can very well decide not to send any more money or personnel into a diocese in Asia in order to reroute both toward West Africa, or vice versa. Naturally this will be done gently, with a velvet glove, but in the last analysis, with or without any cooperation and consultation, the free religious associations make their own decision. They have the last word. In a certain sense they function in the manner of the multinational corporations, whose decision centers are beyond the borders of the country concerned.

However, there is a telling difference. The goal of the industrial multinationals is the financial gain of the parent company. The goal, at least in the ideal, of the mission societies is the proclamation of the gospel, the service of the church and humanity on a continental or world scale, which is the same service that the local church is called to render.

The free associations in the church, multinational for the most part, and the diocesan churches, pursue the same mission, but in parallel fashion, and are guided by different decision centers even if consensus and collaboration provide a basis for coordinated action.

A Continual Source of Conflict and Friction

Thus there is a source of conflict within the church owing to its very structure. On the one side, the whole earth is divided into geographical units, the Latin dioceses, under the direction of a bishop with his presbyterium around him. On the other side are the free religious associations, who select their own goals, their rules, and their style of life, with the approval of the hierarchical church. As long as this structure remains intact it will be a source of conflict. It is not of divine institution. There is no evidence that Christ wished to divide up the whole world into dioceses of the Latin Rite. This most useful division was copied from the organization of the Roman empire after the conversion of Emperor Constantine. And of course, it is not a rigid division. Nowadays in Palestine or in Canada there can be, in the same city, one Catholic community under a Ukrainian bishop, another under a Latin bishop, and a third under the Melkite bishop, all three of them being bishops of the Catholic church and all three being bishops of the same city. But the diocese, begun sixteen centuries ago, is certainly not about to disappear.

On the other hand, the decisions of the popes and the councils and the decrees of the Roman Curia make it very clear that free religious associations are considered a source of dynamism in the church. Certain popes did attempt to prevent, by decree, the formation of new religious societies. But the Holy Spirit raised up more founders, and these popes' successors recognized and approved the foundation of new religious societies. The source of possible conflict inherent in the two parallel centers for decision-making is part and parcel of the present structure of the church, and doubtless will continue to be in future centuries.

Of course, conflict is not necessarily negative. Some conflicts are, surely. But generally they are a source of dynamism and progress. When a group, religious or diocesan, is always of one mind, it must be caught up in a routine and going around in circles. It is in a rut. It runs the serious risk of remaining static in a world of change. On the other hand, not everyone can do everything. One and the same individual cannot be administrator, confidant of persons in difficulty, youth minister, assiduous visitor of the sick and aged, and analyst of the economic and cultural changes in the world all at the same time. A division of labor and a training suited to each task are necessary. The existence of religious societies corresponds to this need for specialization and division of tasks. Nowadays, however, they have no monopoly. It is easy to find diocesan priests, religious, and parents collaborating in teams, for high school catechesis, in the struggle for social justice, or a missionary endeavor.

In days gone by, bishops, isolated in their dioceses, did not easily see the problems posed by the church's mission on a world scale. But now they are set up in bishops' conferences, national, transnational, and even continental. Their representatives meet regularly in world synods. Consequently the global vision of the church on a world scale enjoyed by the "multinational religious corporations" is more and more complete, animated by post-conciliar bishops who by virtue of the synods and Vatican Council II have become "bishops of the entire world." This gradual upbuilding of a world awareness both among the bishops and within religious societies greatly facilitates cooperation, planning, and common decision-making, for it affords a common planetary vision of the needs of the world and the church. There is still the tension—but confrontation and planning make it fruitful.

The Traditional Situation in the North

The churches of the North, and their several hundred religious associations, are accustomed to this situation of conflict. They look upon it as a fact of the life of the church, one that can move and stimulate. Indeed, curiously, numerous free religious associations have been founded by bishops, such as the Mill Hill Fathers by Cardinal Vaughan, the White Fathers by Cardinal Lavigerie, and the Oblates of Mary Immaculate by Bishop de Manezod, among many others. In other words, certain bishops felt the need of having, alongside a diocesan clergy and an organized laity, free religious associations with a specific task, like witnessing to the Christian faith among the Muslims, or the evangelization of the more de-Christianized parts of France.

That the founding bishop recognized a society's usefulness, however, did not eliminate conflict. Perhaps the most typical instance is that of the first superior general of the White Fathers—who had been elected by his confreres, then resigned and left the society following a clash with Cardinal Lavigerie, the founder, over a few acres of vineyard. Actually those wretched Carthaginian grapes were only a surrogate bone of contention. The real conflict was between a person who had founded a free association and then refused to recognize it as such, and a superior general elected by his confreres and responsible to them for the direction of their society.

The churches of the North, then, and their hundreds of religious orders are accustomed to these tensions. The Dominicans, founded for the ministry of the Word, originally had no regular parish or diocesan assignments. Originally they simply preached the Word, in dioceses governed by bishops, without even wishing to participate in the government of these dioceses or the parishes through which they passed. Originally these orders lived a life of tension, as they cooperated in the mission of the church. The history of the church is in part a history of the conflicts between the diocesan clergy and the religious orders, especially the mendicant orders, who traversed the countryside preaching and begging alms and by no means pleasing the parish clergy who were reduced to the bare necessities of life. In the churches of the North the diocesan clergy and religious are accustomed to cooperate in an atmosphere of tension, and the cooperation goes ahead. As we have already remarked, this cooperation has become much easier since Vatican II, which enabled bishops and religious to share a broader common vision of a world in change, thanks to the bishops' conferences and the synods.

A New Situation in the South

We missionaries may be members of free religious associations, but we are not yet accustomed to behaving as such. When we arrived in Africa, Oceania, or America, we were not put to work in accordance with our particular goal in territories governed and served by local bishops and priests, as the Dominicans or Jesuits were when they were first founded. We were the bishops and priests. The bishops were chosen from among us on nomination of our superior general. In case of a minor conflict, provincial or regional superiors straightened everything out. Everything was in the family.

We were free associations in the service of the evangelization of the peoples. We left home to proclaim the good news abroad. When we arrived there, we built parishes and set up diocesan administrative structures. Within a few years we were functioning as diocesan clergy, bound to a territory. We found ourselves speaking of "my" parish and "my" diocese. The belfry spirit developed very quickly, and many is the man who has never climbed to the top of the belfry to look beyond the limits of his parish or diocese, to lift his eyes to the horizons of all Africa, for example—for whose evangelization, after all, and not just parochialization, he has asked to be admitted to a free society such as the White Fathers or the African Mission Society.

Doubtless this stage had to be gone through. Doubtless we had not only to proclaim the gospel, but also to found and form the local church—which seemed to mean setting up parish and diocesan structures that the local clergy could simply slip into just as their homologues in the churches of the North had been slipping into them ever since the conversion of Constantine.

Yes, the step was a useful and necessary one. And partially successful. But during the course of it we simply forgot what we were: free religious associations, groups that constantly call into question not only their strategy, but sometimes even their original aim, in a changing world.

And so we are uneasy. Most of us are foreign-born diocesan clergy—yet we wish to be treated as religious, participating in decisions, engaging in dialogue in order to discover the will of the Spirit regarding a transfer from parish A to parish B. Doubtless I am talking in a vacuum. Numerous missioners are so accustomed to being pastor or assistant in a parish that it is impossible for them to behave otherwise. I know missionaries working in the city who would like to throw themselves into the "youth apostolate." Well, nothing is stopping them. They work in urban parishes and they can dispose of their daytime hours as they see fit, since the adults are at work. They would have plenty of time to get in contact with the bands of youth in town, high school graduates and dropouts looking for work that cannot be found. But they spend their time in the parish structures, with its registers and its office hours for meeting with candidates for the sacraments. They are extremely busy, yet they complain. Of what? Of not having time to do work that seems to them to be more in keeping with their missionary vocation. Actually, materially, they have the time. But *psychologically* they cannot take the time, for they would be "neglecting" traditional parish tasks that they have been accustomed to perform for two or three decades now, and which have become part of their life.

The Bishop, Minister of Unity or of Monopoly?

For their part, the bishops of the churches of the South with which I am familiar, mainly those of Africa, especially East Africa, are the true successors of the missionary bishops. They are not yet accustomed to seeing groups of men or women, recognized and approved by the church, arriving in their diocese for a precise project along the lines of their founder's original concept, with their own methods, houses, and finances, with the permission or at least the tolerance of the local ordinary, as has been done in the North for more than fifteen centuries.

Like their missionary predecessors, they have a tendency, with a few exceptions, to think that these religious have the mission and vocation of planning everything, supervising everything, running everything. They are also inclined to utilize the free associations of men and women for their own projects instead of giving them the opportunity of using their talents to follow their own dynamism, as the expression of the dynamism of the church. To be sure, there are changes being made, as is demonstrated by the new foundations of contemplative groups, or Mother Teresa's Sisters of Charity. But missionaries are still frequently considered to belong to the diocese, to be there mainly for parochial assignments.

The Crucial Point: A Double Reciprocal Conversion

This means that both the missionaries and the local clergy, including the bishop, ought to find out what missionary congregations are in the church—free associations with their own goals and their own methods; approved by the hierarchical church; not bound to a territory; making use of their freedom, security, and flexibility in order to respond constantly and rapidly to new needs that arise in a world changing with dizzying speed. For example, the rural population of Africa is moving more and more to the cities, like Kinshasa, Nairobi, and Dar-es-Salaam, each of which is growing at an annual rate of 100,000 or more. Who can respond to the call of an uprooted population determined at all costs to avoid returning to their villages? Perhaps the arrival of African members of religious societies who are oriented toward the urban apostolate would be a partial answer, along with the solution attempted by Cardinal Malula with the laity in Kinshasa. In a word, the missionary societies must rediscover their identity as free associations, rediscover their flexibility and mobility. But as I have already pointed out, most of their members are incapable of making this change. They can only be asked not to block the efforts of those who are.

This means too that the missioners must discover that a local bishop does not necessarily consult the religious working in his diocese in making his decisions. They must discover and accept what a southern bishop is: more often than not a bishop who appears very authoritarian to missionaries who come from the North. All the studies on the exercise of authority agree on one point: adults unconsciously exercise their authority in the same manner in which their father or mother exercised it. If a bishop was born into a family where the father gave his children orders without discussing them, the bishop will act in his episcopal function as his father acted in his childhood, and not discuss his decisions with anyone. "Dialogue," to him, will simply mean *explaining* to his priests why he makes such-and-such a decision; it will not mean asking them what would be best to do and making a decision together with them. But this is exactly what is expected of him by missionaries brought up by parents who consulted them constantly as children, asking them, "Well, what shall we do this weekend?" and the like. Very simply, it is a matter of accepting the local bishop and his culture, along with his personal problem of how to be faithful to his culture while following the example of Christ washing the feet of his disciples. It is also a matter of accepting the diocesan clergy for what it is, that is, a group of men who have chosen to be bound to the land, to diocesan boundaries, to the service of the people living within its limits. Finally, it is a matter of accepting the free associations, that is, groups of men, in this case, bound together for a common apostolic goal that they have freely chosen.

Of course, I know that the tradition of the free associations in the church was born in the North. If the churches of the South wish to have no part of this tradition because it is foreign to them, that is their right. In this case it would be most desirable if they would be plain about this with the missionaries—discreetly and indirectly as is their wont, but clearly. They would thereby spare those who are accustomed to it a great deal of moral suffering.

But the missionaries themselves, the multinational corporations in the church, must come to realize what enormous pressure they exert (without realizing it now, probably) upon the local clergy and their bishop—a pressure, *mutatis mutandis,* similar to that exercised by the industrial multinationals on the civil states. When a bishop with four or five diocesan priests finds himself face to face with a mission society of several thousand members, with their own superiors, their own governments, their own meetings, how can he fail to be afraid of no longer being master in his own house?

So here are all the mutual fears that we must recognize and exorcise. It will be long and hard. Only to the extent that the religious and bishops who work in the same country discover the needs of Christians and non-Christians on a national and even continental scale will they be able to make common use of the flexibility and mobility that is or could be the gift of the mission societies.

It will take time. The local bishop is a prudent man. When a religious society moves in with its personnel, its knowledge, its experience, and its finances, the bishop does not know how it is going to use all these power sources. He wants to get acquainted with them first, strike a personal relationship with them. He wants to be sure he can trust them. But trust is a delicate flower that takes root only very, very slowly. Will he feel he must be absolutely familiar with them in order to understand them sufficiently? For a bishop, being absolutely familiar takes time—a great deal of time. And a great deal of time is incompatible with the flexibility and mobility that is the gift and charism of the free religious associations. The paradoxical task of building deep human relationships while remaining flexible and mobile is one of the problems that the members of the mission societies have to solve.

In the last analysis everything boils down to a fundamental problem of contradictions in constant need of resolution: between clergy bound to a territory and religious bound to one another by a common purpose; between stability and mobility. These contradictions give the church its dynamism. Without them, everything would either stagnate or move too fast.

But perhaps all these considerations are useless. Perhaps there will be no more missionaries in the year 2000.[4]

The Future of the Missionaries and the Missionaries of the Future

A great number of mission societies are passing through, or have already passed through, an identity crisis. General chapters have asked questions like: What is our proper charism? What is our specific purpose? Are we still useful? Before asking these questions it would perhaps be in order to take certain facts into consideration—even though it may be difficult to accept them, and still more difficult to draw practical conclusions from them.

Aging Societies

The first fact that strikes us is that we missionaries constitute groups of persons whose average age is constantly rising. In the greater number of mission societies the mean age is in the vicinity of fifty years. I know perfectly well that John XXIII and Cardinal Bea bore their fruit in their eighties, but these are the exceptions that prove the rule. Zealous missionaries who have performed a sacramental ministry in farm parishes for thirty years cannot be expected suddenly to come to town and busy themselves with juvenile delinquency. The desire to set oneself new objectives, to start a new, pioneering apostolate, seems to me to be a security-inspiring possibility and attitude, but one that is altogether futile on the practical level. Starting a new apostolate generally comes down to doing the same thing somewhere else.

A Childless North

Meanwhile the phenomenon of aging continues apace. The simple reason for the scarcity of vocations in Europe and America is that there are no more children in these countries. Today the "normal" family means one or two children. Three children make a large family. But traditionally missionary vocations spring up in large families—families averaging 6.1 children for the French White Fathers in 1950. I know missionaries who are only children; leaving one's family and risking letting one's parents grow old all alone demands an exceptional vocation. And indeed many parents exert pressure on their only children not to "abandon" them—for that is how their departure is seen.

We have to accept the fact that only a few young people, among fewer and fewer young people, will answer the call of the Spirit. The religious congregations will not grow any younger. On the other hand, the presence of these young people even in reduced numbers should lead the societies that admit them to ask themselves certain questions, whether or not the young persons ask them themselves.

I have met these young Fathers and Brothers, secure in their vocation and without any questions about their future. Most had already served in Africa for several years, and knew what sort of life awaited them.

Then I saw these same young missionaries, one after another, arrive in their parishes and set ardently to work in the Christian communities and seminaries. Within a few years they had become diocesan priests, by reason of their attachment to their new diocese and their assimilation of a new language and culture. Now they supplement a local clergy that still has too few indigenous priests at its disposal. They are happy. They have also lost their openness to the world at large, their concern for the universal church, and their mobility and flexibility.

A Church Turned Inward

Missionary vocations depend on the openness of a country or a local church to the world. It is difficult to wish to proclaim the good news in China or in Tristan da Cunha if one does not know they exist. The great missionary countries have been either colonial nations, like France, Belgium, and the Netherlands, or countries from which there is a great deal of emigration, like Ireland. Surely the Spirit works where he will. But even if Canada, with its long border and deep cultural affinity with the United States, has supplied a large number of missionary vocations, it is equally true that Catholic lands like Austria, Hungary, and Croatia or Slovenia have seen few mission vocations.

At present the countries of the North are in the process of closing themselves off more and more from the South. They are turning inward. They are taken up with internal problems, such as the energy crisis or unemployment. Only a few groups of "third-worlders," of a few dozen persons each, in the cities, retain an active interest in North-South relations. This turning inward cannot but present an obstacle to missionary vocations.

For these two major reasons—a turning back upon themselves and the absence of children—I think that within a few years the mission societies will be made up of a majority of men and women in their sixties. Yet at the same time, year in and year out, they will be receiving a few excellent candidates. What will be the effect of these extremely committed young people, along with the few senior members capable of a change of orientation, on the others? What will be the reaction of the aging majority, altogether adapted to and quite content in their parish work, a work recognized as worthwhile, and particularly in demand in the South? It seems to me that these are the two basic questions the mission societies should ask themselves. If they think they can have a renewal by adopting new aims that the majority of their members cannot pursue, they are deceiving themselves.

New Vocations from the South

There is a relatively new phenomenon in the church, in the form of the massive influx of young people of the churches of the South into the mission societies. The majority of the young professed and of those in formation in several mission societies, such as the Society of the Divine Word and the Medical Mission Sisters of Philadelphia, are already from the churches of the South. The same thing is happening to a lesser degree in many other congregations, like the Scheutists, the Holy Ghost Fathers, and very recently, the White Fathers. It could be just a passing phenomenon, but nothing points in that direction when one considers the rising rate of diocesan and religious vocations in the majority of the churches of the South.[5]

Mission Societies of the Year 2000

If we take these facts as our basis we can sketch a profile of the majority of the mission societies of the year 2000. We are altogether aware of the hypothetical and problematical character of this profile: (1) The vast majority of the members coming from churches of the North will be living out their old age in retirement homes (in serenity, we hope) or still engaged in useful parish work. (2) A small group of somewhat less elderly members, of northern origin, deeply rooted in the churches that have received them and enjoying the confidence of their hosts, will be capable of change, creative initiative, mobility, and flexibility according to the movement of the Spirit and the new requirements of an evolving world. (3) A few young new members from the North will regularly be added, each year—some capable of flexibility, mobility, and adaptation to new tasks, and others not. (4) A growing proportion, soon to be in the majority, of young members will come from the churches of the South.

This profile suggests that the free missionary associations will no longer be homogeneous groups. They will consist of several age groups, doubtless united by a common spirit, but endowed with different abilities and gifts. This in turn means that they will no longer be able to set themselves single goals. They will have to have differentiated aims, reflecting the abilities and gifts of their members. Of course, these aims will be the concrete expression of a single goal, the one common to all Christians—the proclamation of the good news and the evangelization of every human activity.

May I propose three aims here, as a basis for dialogue both within the mission societies and between these societies and the local churches of North and South alike.

1. **Fidelity to Our Traditional Purpose in Its Traditional Framework.** One of the differentiated purposes of the mission society of the future may well be the evangelization of the world and of every human activity within the framework of the parish, under the direction of the bishop and in collaboration with the diocesan clergy. In other words, most missionaries will continue to serve the church as diocesan clergy,

since that is what they have become in the course of the evolution of their mission. It is a necessary service, and by no means inferior to any other. If I may take Tanzania as an example, several dioceses there are less than 6 percent Christian. In the parish in which I have just finished a three-year term as associate pastor, the northeastern region, with a population of over 100,000, had barely 1,000 Christians, and there was a seminomad group that had never heard the Word at all. There is still room for primary evangelization in the churches of the South. This evangelization is the responsibility of the bishops, but we can help them to fulfill it. They ask us to help—why should we refuse?

It is not enough to baptize people. The entire life of a Christian must be penetrated by the gospel, professional life as well as family life. And so there must be a family apostolate, a preparation for marriage, a special ministry to teachers, health professionals, agricultural technicians, Christians who are active in political life, and so on and on. So many tasks, as traditional as they are exciting! But how difficult they are. How should we go about helping people to live the gospel in their destructured urban environment? In any case it will be the task of a parish apostolate. The field is vast. But all this demands a certain set of parish priorities, for example, preference given to urban parishes, or to dioceses where only a small part of the population has been evangelized. Since the available personnel decreases year after year, this will entail the abandonment of certain parishes, which is always a painful and difficult choice.

2. **The Rediscovery of Our Charism as a Free Association.** We function as diocesan clergy. This is a fact, and many bishops of the churches of the South ask us to do so. It is a service we render, the only service that most of us can render. And this is well. Let us thank God. But we must also rediscover the fact that we were founded as free associations, that is, groups of persons who have freely gathered together and provide one another with the security necessary for facing the constantly new needs of a world in change. New tasks arise that are difficult to carry out in the context of parish service to a Christian population demanding the satisfaction of their thirst for the sacraments.

In the thirteenth century, the northern countries saw the birth of a moneyed middle class concentrating on profit. In that century the church raised up Saint Francis, scion of that same urban and commercial society, to remind it of the demands of evangelical poverty lived as service. In Africa today we are witnessing the birth of a new elite, which is gradually being structured into a moneyed or political middle class, and this in the socialist and the capitalist countries alike. One need only listen to the statements of President Julius Nyerere or Bishop Sarpong of Kumasi to have an idea of the ravages of corruption in Africa, as on the other continents. Africa has need of a new Saint Francis, or at least of children of Saint Francis, who will not be just zealous pastors, but will challenge this elite by their radical poverty. The youth of the churches of the South are leaving their villages in search of work in the cities, and they do not always find it. The number of bands of young people without resources is becoming a social problem, which is disturbing the authorities. The churches of the South have need of a new Don Bosco, or of disciples of Don Bosco, who will not be too burdened by the keeping of the parish records or by meetings of the mothers who teach religion to be at the total service of these bands. Since their inception, the White Fathers have had a special connection with Islam. Vatican II calls Christians to a dialogue with the other religions. This requires specialists who will help Christians in the parishes better understand their Muslim brothers and sisters. As a university chaplain, I am in constant contact with Muslim professors and students. Fortunately a Tanzanian priest who is a specialist in the dialogue with Islam teaches in a nearby seminary. He can advise me, help me better to understand Islam. This demonstrates that specialization is not the prerequisite of the free religious associations. But they are more adapted for it.

Thus I think that the free missionary associations ought to study very carefully the new needs of the churches of the North and of the South, and, in concert with the bishops, prepare the right members for these new tasks.

It will not be easy. There are bishops who are very sensitive to the necessity of these new tasks. But there are others who are less so, and scarcely understand why missionaries, be they from the North or from the South, would want to devote themselves to a dialogue with the Muslims when they themselves are obliged to close parishes for lack of personnel.

The solution would seem to be for some members of the free missionary associations to work in the churches of both North and South as the old religious orders—Dominicans, Jesuits, Franciscans—have done in the North for centuries. This fidelity to one's proper gift as the member of a free religious association will not be without difficulties and friction. It has never been easy. It demands a continual dialogue between the local church and the free associations, a dialogue whose first objective is the identification of the needs of the world of today.

These new tasks are not the "specialty" of the free religious associations in any exclusive sense. But they are so difficult that they require the support of a community. It would seem that the free religious associations are in a good position to give this support. When I hear the statements of President Nyerere and other African statesmen I realize that Africa has need of a new type of witness: the laborer, the office worker, the professional, who will demonstrate by his or her daily conduct that a position of employment, a "job," is not just a source of income but a service as well. The African members of the mission societies could be these witnesses, as some diocesan religious women already are—as schoolteachers, nurses, accountants, in government employ.

3. **A Special Ministry: In the Service of the Universality of the Church.** The gifts thus far cited, and the tasks proposed, are those of any and every free religious association. The Jesuits, the Dominicans, and the Franciscans have been bearing this witness for a long time. But, it seems to me, certain members of the mission societies have a special gift: they belong to two cultures, that of their country of origin and that of their adoptive country. Naturally they do not have a monopoly of this gift. Certain Fidei Donum priests, certain priests of the churches of the South who are invited to serve for several years in the churches of the North, as some of my Tanzanian friends have been, share this gift as well. And some members of mission societies lack it. But it is within the mission societies that one encounters it most often. For example, it is true that certain missionaries who came to the South when they were young are being gradually cut off from their native church and no longer feel

comfortable there when on vacation leave, if indeed they take such a leave. On the other hand, one meets persons in these missionary associations who are well rooted in their own culture, have kept up contact with their friends in the North, follow "home" affairs by radio and newspaper, and after a few days' vacation feel entirely at ease with their families without having constantly to repeat their stories of Africa or Asia. And yet they know the language, the economy, and the political situation of their adoptive church as well as they know their own. They truly belong to two cultures.

Vatican II never tired of repeating that the difference in cultures is a source of mutual enrichment for local churches. This is true theoretically. But if two cultural eras or two churches have no bonds, no exchange is possible. Thus the church has need of a new kind of minister, who will be at the service of communication between cultures and between churches, a witness to diversity in unity. We need a new ministry: that of communication between churches and cultures. The church needs bridges, which will link the churches of the North with those of the South in both directions.

Until recent years, communication generally went in one direction only—north to south. Finances and personnel only flowed south. It must flow both ways. Otherwise it is only the religious counterpart of the economic neocolonialism now raging in the South.

Let us look at a specific example. We hear much about the exploitation of the South by the North and of the need of an international new economic order. A great number of Christians of the North are completely unconscious of this. But as a missionary I have been in actual contact with this ongoing impoverishment of the South, living as I have in Tanzania. This country has to export 45 percent of its currency (shortly the percentage will have reached 50) in order to purchase an inadequate supply of gasoline. The reason is simple: the countries of the North are willing to purchase gasoline at any price on the open market. Now, as someone from the North myself, I also understand the difficulties my compatriots are in. I appreciate their fear of inflation and unemployment. Thus I am in an ideal position to explain to them the influence their lifestyle has on the economy of the Tanzanian villages in which I have lived. They are surprised, and begin to think about this.

We hear much about justice in the church. The gift, the charism of many missionaries, could be pressed into service precisely to help the North become conscious of the deepening chasm separating North and South. The missionary can likewise bear witness to the dynamism of the churches of the South—the activities of their parish councils, the formation of base ecclesial communities, the catechumenate maintained by Ivory Coast youth in the high schools. The South has all this wealth to share with the North. Television and newspapers help, but direct testimony is essential—even if it is via television. This testimony is one that can be given by certain missionaries, who thereby become genuine bridges between the two churches.

The church has need of men and women rooted in two cultures, as much at ease in the one as in the other, who can put each in communication with the other. This seems to me to be the charism of many missionaries, precisely because they are missionaries. The church needs only a few hundred of these ministers, these witnesses of diversity in unity, but it will need them till the end of the world.

The North needs men and women from the South to strike roots in the North and participate in this ministry of communication. But to strike roots they need a North-South communications network. The missionary associations have them. They have built these communications networks, among cultures, among churches, patiently, over long decades. These aging missionary associations have the right, and it seems to me the duty, of placing their experience and their intercultural communications networks at the service of the burgeoning youth of the churches of the South.

This is only a personal opinion—but perhaps the influx of young people of the South into the free missionary associations is a sign of the Spirit. African missioners to Europe, working with Europeans . . . European missioners to Africa . . . all in the service of diversity in unity! This vision is already a reality, albeit a tenuous and fragile one. Its future? Strangulation by criticism, or development by an openness on the part of all. The answer will depend in large part on the attitude of us missionaries, the members of the aging multinational corporations of the church. It also depends on the ability of the bishops of North and South to transcend the boundaries of their little dioceses, and become in deed what they are in theological theory: bishops of the whole world, who are not afraid to delegate their powers and missions to free associations animated by the same vision as themselves.

—Translated by Robert R. Barr

Notes

1. The Euro-Americans are generally distinguished as follows: the Western bloc, or first world; the Eastern bloc, or second world; the rest of the world, or third world.

A distinction is also made between developed nations and developing nations. African political theorists and economists make a distinction between the industrialized nations, whether in the East or in the West, and the nonindustrialized nations, since the former are situated in the northern hemisphere and the nonindustrialized nations are situated in the southern hemisphere. They also distinguish North from South, speaking of a "North-South dialogue" or the "impoverishment of the South by the North." It is this view of the world and its division into North and South that I have used in this paper.

2. It likewise poses problems for the local churches, but it is up to them to express them. I cannot pretend to be their spokesperson.

3. We need not consider a gift or charism as coming down directly from heaven. It is the fruit of second causes. Intelligence, too, is a gift, but its degree depends in large part on a child's family environment. Thus the free religious associations have structures favorable to freedom and security, and these structures are their gift.

On the other hand, a religious society cannot assert a priori that it has the gift of youth education or the dialogue with Islam. It is only through the daily work of education or dialogue that it will discover whether it has this gift or not. The endeavor of some general chapters to define their "proper charism" in a meeting hall would seem to me to be an exercise in futility.

4. I hope that certain readers will not be annoyed by my speaking only of priests, bishops, and missionaries, and seldom of the laity. This would seem to constitute an outrageous piece of clericalism. But I have done it for a very simple reason. I know very well that the laity make up the majority of the People of God, and that the missionaries and other religious are first and foremost at the service of this people. But look: as a missionary, desirous of serving the People of God, I have need

of a government visa. And the procurement of this visa, except for the relatively rare case of the missionary who holds a government position, for instance in public instruction, depends on the bishop, not on the People of God.

The possibility of relating to the People of God depends on the missionary's relationship with the bishop, who approves or disapproves requests for a residential visa.

5. Perhaps SEDOS could provide statistics on this apparent phenomenon in churches of the South.

18

THE PHILIPPINES

Julio X. Labayen, O.C.D.

Perhaps the best way to begin is to give several examples of a local church dealing with missionary institutes of various types. This should help us to be concrete. After the examples, some theological reflection based on the examples will be offered. In the examples I limit myself to my own Prelature of Infanta in the Philippines, since it is the one I know best and the one I can talk of most freely. "Local church" in this paper will be equivalent to diocese or prelature.

Carmelite Contemplatives

In April 1980 three Carmelite Sisters began their work in Infanta. Their coming was written up in the Asian Catholic press as follows:

> Three Carmelite Sisters have arrived in this coastal town east of Manila to begin a radical experiment in contemplative living.
> The Sisters, all Filipinas in their 30s, will lead a contemplative life of prayer, but the farmers and their families and social action people will be invited to visit the Sisters to discuss their problems and to take part in the liturgies.
> Before the Sisters arrived, the priests and people of Infanta were asked by their bishop if they wanted the Sisters to come, and also what they wanted the Sisters to do if they did come. The Carmelites and their superiors responded with ideas of their own. Infanta Bishop Julio Labayen described the process as a model for how missionary groups should deal with a local church.
> Some things have been agreed upon already: the people and the Sisters will build the monastery together and it will have no walls. "They're our Sisters, so we will protect them," one man told Bishop Labayen. "Sisters shouldn't stay by themselves behind walls," said one priest. "Especially not in the Philippines where the people are so warm and person-oriented. This way they'll really be one with all of us, not in their own world."

Julio X. Labayen is the Bishop of Infanta, Quezon, in the Philippines.

282

The Sisters will farm to support themselves as much as possible. The people will provide anything else that is needed.

"The Sisters will challenge our prayer lives," said 54-year-old Bishop Labayen, former head of the Office for Human Development, a branch of the Federation of Asian Bishops' Conferences. "They will be the prayer-heart of the diocese. They will know the hopes and problems of the people and the things social action workers are struggling for, and bring them to God. They won't join our mass actions but they'll pray for their success.

"It's a dream I've shared with some Carmelite Sisters for many years," said Bishop Labayen, himself a Carmelite. "When I told Mother Mary of Christ, a Sister who is now 81, that we are finally going to do it, she shouted with joy.

"Are we ready for the Sisters? For a deeper praying community? I can't say. I do know the people are excited. The Sisters' coming has answered some deep need in their hearts. Two young girls are already interested in joining the Sisters."

The three Sisters will return to Manila after four months and report to their superiors before settling down permanently in Infanta.

The main reason for citing this example is the discussions we had with the people and priests about what they wanted the Sisters to do. These were extensive and there were disagreements. Also important I think was the openness of the Carmelite superiors: they didn't have a rigid program that they felt they had to impose on the people. Rather, they were open to the suggestions and needs of the local church.

The Calama Group

Another group that has come to work in our prelature is the Calama Group. This is a group of priests, religious, and lay people that began in Chile and has worked in other parts of Latin America and Europe. In ways it is similar to the worker-priest movement, for example, in its desire to live and work (manually) as closely as possible with the ordinary people. The Calama Group in the Philippines is predominantly Dutch.

The appearance of Calama went unnoticed for a few years, but then different church leaders attacked it for allegedly being communist and intent on destroying the church as we know it today. There has been quite a hue and cry, and as usual nothing has been settled. Calama works now in our prelature in one of the poorest areas. The group members share the life of the people, quietly witnessing to Christian values. Socially they are quite progressive and liberal.

Again before accepting Calama in our area we had long talks with the priests and the people. Calama was invited for several dialogues. The priests sketched their pastoral plan and Calama determined how it could fit in. We discussed their theology and politics. It was only when all practical and theoretical questions were resolved that we welcomed them and suggested a place where they could work. But now that they are accepted, they are our people and we defend them against criticism just as we would defend one another.

The Carmelite Fathers

The American Carmelite Fathers began the work in Infanta. The first bishop was an American Carmelite. We are benefiting today from their hard work and wisdom. Until 1970 there were only a handful of diocesan priests so the prelature was still mostly staffed by American Carmelites. Then two trends coincided. Several of the Carmelites left the country for one reason or another; others were getting old. At the same time we had a good number of young diocesan Filipino priests, some local vocations and some from Manila.

We discussed at length the implications of this and finally decided that we would split our forces. The Filipino clergy would cover the southern half of the prelature (it is 300 kilometers long), which is slightly more developed and accessible to Manila, and the Americans would take the northern half.

Why did we do this? One reason was that our Filipino priests, being young, were full of enthusiasm and ideas about the work; for example, using priest teams instead of pastors in individual towns. We thought they could develop more freely and make less-harmful mistakes if they were by themselves. The future of the local church is tied up with the Filipino clergy, so I kept them around Infanta town in the southern half of the prelature where I would be close to them.

I look upon the Carmelite Fathers who shifted to the north as true missionaries. They subordinated their interests to that of the local church. They were part of the discernment involved in the decision, so they went north knowing it was the best thing for the local church. They see themselves responding to the changing needs of the prelature. If we have enough Filipino diocesan priests in the future, the time will come when we shall have to ask the Carmelites to give up the parishes in the north as well. There will always be a role for these American missionaries as far as I can see, but it will always be an *ad hoc* and supplementary one.

Criteria for Mission Groups

We have other individuals and groups working in the prelature; for example: the Rural Missionaries, an intercongregational association of Sisters who do social action in the barrios, paramedic health workers, community organizers, and so forth. To all of them we apply the same criteria: Will they complement the ongoing work of the prelature? Will they help to execute the present pastoral program? Will they work in harmony with the other church workers? These questions are answered in prayerful dialogue between the local priests and people and the "missionary" group. Ultimately it is the local people-priests and laymen and women who make the final decision about what groups will work in our area and what the nature of that work will be. On the part of the "missionary" group there must be a willingness to operate as the local people want, on the people's terms.

It is easier for us to do this in Infanta than in a big diocese because we are few in number, which makes dialogue and sharing easily possible. Also not many groups volunteer to work in our rather remote area.

In the July 1, 1979, *SEDOS Bulletin* Father Frank Ponsi sketched five concepts or models of mission. The concept that closely relates to what I have been saying is the third, namely, "Mission as Mutual Assistance of Local Churches," epitomized in the verse from Acts, "Come across to Macedonia and help us" (16:9). Developing this concept, Father Ponsi writes:

> It is undeniably true that the church in mission territories has already been planted. In some sense, there are no longer mission churches. There are only churches faced with varied and ever-changing pastoral needs in different geographical situations. This fact, together with the post-Vatican II heightened awareness of the predominant role of local church leadership in setting up pastoral policies, is the major premise for this view.

Some strategies for implementing this concept are, according to Father Ponsi,

1. Personnel exchange between younger and older churches according to the skills needed to meet specific pastoral needs.
2. The initiative for personnel re-allocation should therefore belong to the receiving church, rather than continue to reside with any of the mother churches or with Rome, or with mission boards, since there is a limit to the amount of personnel and capital a local church can realistically absorb.
3. From this perspective, there is room for temporary limited assignments and exchange of personnel.
4. Lay people can play a major role in providing the needed skills for the required time.
5. International ecumenical teams of specialists can be formed and deployed according to demand.

Subscribing to this concept of mission vis-à-vis outside missionary groups does not mean that this is our total concept of mission. The local church must have a deeper and richer notion of mission, which must be grounded in the incarnation, in the life of Jesus, God, and humankind, struggling to become aware of His destiny and announcing with even greater clarity the coming of the kingdom of God.

An interview with Father Raymond Hill, former superior general of Maryknoll (in *Info for Human Development*, FABC), also clarifies the role of the missionary in the local church. Says Father Hill:

> I saw very little real missionary work in Maryknoll when I was Superior General. I think the same is true of other missionary groups. Most of our men were overseas pastors, taking good care of practicing Catholics, but not reaching out to non-Christians, to the non-evangelized.
>
> There's still a real need of missionaries. Our approach in Maryknoll now is to have small groups of men and women, including lay people, work with non-believers. We try to find some specific work through which we can make a contribution and only stay for a limited time, say three years or so. These

teams should have a good community life based on prayer. We should develop local people and move on somewhere else.

If I understand Father Hill, he is saying that missionaries today should perform the tasks that are outside the normal pastoral work of the local church, that is, outside the concern for baptized Christians. Later on in the interview he says that we should get away from the clerical model in mission work and look more to Brothers and lay people.

In a completely Christian area like Infanta we have to say that missionaries should do what the local church can't do, whether it be with Christians or non-Christians. I think this is what has happened in Infanta. The Carmelite Sisters clearly provide a charism that is necessary in a diocese and yet outside the abilities of the local church workers. Calama too is a special witnessing to justice and gospel values that we can't expect of local priests or religious. The move of the Carmelite Fathers to the north is in its own way a role that the local priests cannot play at present.

Like Father Ponsi, Father Hill stressed that mission work may be temporary and that lay missionaries are of special importance because with them, and not with missionary priests, there is a chance that they can serve the local church in novel ways, for example, as agricultural consultants or researchers.

The key in all this is for the local church to set the priorities and choose the outsiders that it wants, for as long as it wants them to do the work that it wants done. This approach is in line with the traditional philosophy of social action that the people of an area must make the decisions that affect their lives and that development decisions made from outside without genuine consultation and participation of the people will ultimately fail.

Some Problems

Such a position presupposes that the people of an area are engaged in discussing the life and future of their church and that the bishop and priests are responsive. But what if they are not? Can outsiders do anything if the local church remains static?

And what if the local church asks for assistance—personnel and financial—from outside that seems to go against any sensible pastoral plan. Suppose, for example, that a local church asks for foreign missionaries because these will ensure a big influx of money for schools, churches, and social projects. How should the outsiders react?

Or suppose that a group of missionaries initiates a well-thought-out withdrawal from an area to make way for the growth of the local clergy, only to find that the bishop is rushing in more missionaries from other congregations to replace them. What should one do?

Obviously these are difficult problems without easy answers. I don't think we should argue, "The local church right or wrong." We don't want to make the principle of local-church autonomy an absolute. Yet how wise is it in the long run to move and take decisions without the support of the local clergy and the people?

The Mission of the Local Church

What we have said so far is intramural, since we have talked of relations between groups active within the church. The impression may be given that in discussing the local church vis-à-vis missionary groups we are mainly interested in establishing good relations between the two or, as they say, forming one big happy family. That is not the prime concern.

All of us have a prior task—to preach the kingdom of God as Jesus did, and we must be totally identified with this task, as was Jesus. In the concrete, to preach the kingdom today is to work for total human development as sketched in the writings of Pope Paul VI and Pope John Paul II. If we—local church and missionary groups—cooperate, it is solely for the purpose of making our preaching of the kingdom more compelling.

We are interested not so much in the development of the church as in the development of the people and *their* involvement in the kingdom. The local church and the missionary groups must focus on this. "Ecclesia pro sua vita aut pro mundi vita?" Cardinal Kim of Korea asked at the 1974 Roman Synod. Our ecumenism is at the service of the people. The same concern for the service of God's people must determine how a local church and a missionary group cooperate. Both are "pro mundi vita."

19

THE BIRTH OF A "NEW PEOPLE": THE MISSION OF THE DISCIPLES OF JESUS CHRIST IN TODAY'S BLACK AFRICA

Philippe Nkiere Kena, C.I.C.M.

One of my tasks in our congregation (Immaculate Heart of Mary Mission Society) is to pay regular visits to certain countries of black Africa: Zambia, Zaire, Cameroon, Nigeria, and Senegal. These countries are all different, to be sure. Their peoples are different, and so are their mentalities. And yet, basically, we are confronted with the same black African reality in all of them, and the same questions arise concerning the current evangelization of these countries. Their local churches have known more or less the same history of evangelization: they have been evangelized originally by missionaries from the West or from North America, who for the most part have been members of the missionary institutes born in the latter half of the nineteenth century. That evangelization was mostly carried out at the same time as their colonization.[1] Today these countries are all independent.

Tormented by a thirst to live their own identities, these countries are at the same time confronted by the economic, social, political, and cultural problems of the world of today. The members of their local churches are seeking a solution to the problem of how to be faithful to Jesus Christ without at the same time denying their proper identity, and faithful to their culture without denying Jesus Christ. For their part, the members of the missionary institutes who have assisted at the birth and blossoming of these local churches feel somewhat out of their element, "strangers in the house of the Father"! And so they are wondering how to be missionaries in a situation of this kind without paternalism, and yet without simply stopping work.

Both the churches and their missionaries, then, are seeking a way to live and proclaim the gospel at the heart of a new society, one torn between modernity and the ancestral tradition. The protagonists of each accuse the other of failing to take

Philippe Nkiere Kena, originally from Zaire, has been an Assistant to the General Superior of Missionhurst for the region of Africa since the General Chapter of 1974.

account of reality, of imposing preconceived notions. The context is one of quest, hence inevitably of tensions as well. It is in this context that the gospel will have to shape a new world, an "other" world, in the reality of the present. It is this new situation in which the gospel finds itself—in the midst of the reality of black Africa—that will define the mission of the local church and of the missionary institutes as well. It is the same mission, in distinct modes of action, for it is one and the same Spirit who accords the distinction of gifts in view of the good of all.

The Function of the Novelty of the Gospel in Black Africa Today

Black Africa, like the other parts of the world, is undergoing the radical change and mutation that is shaking our whole contemporary society. It is the logic of efficiency and of production which prevails in that society. The ideal striven for seems to be to acquire the means of dominating the world of things and to become the masters of the "others" even at the ideological level. The value of human persons and their societies is often set in function of their situation in terms of economics and technology. One even hears of "human capital." But modern society is also a society sorely thirsting for world communion—a communion ceaselessly torn apart in actuality by wars and fratricidal divisions, and forever at the mercy of the great political and economic powers. Modern society, then, is one smitten with a love of technological and economic progress, yet parched with thirst for the unity of human-kind—both facets of modern progress being often disfigured by the domination of some human beings by others. This same hesitation and polarity exists in Africa; in fact it is all the more violent there, owing to the determination with which black African society today means to live its values and its own proper tradition.

In the African conception, the human being is defined essentially as a complexus of vital relationships linking him or her to God, to his or her neighbor, and to the universe.[2] The fundamental value, in black Africa, is community, communion.[3] But how can we live in community and communion where money takes the ascendancy over the human person, where ethnic group or race causes divisions among human beings, where politics crushes creative individuality? In the human dough of black Africa the gospel should be a leaven, the transforming force of a new world united in a new and everlasting alliance. But the gospel is Someone. It is Jesus Christ, living today by his Spirit, who guides and unifies the entire universe through men and women who wish to live by him and for him. In him they form a new humanity, born "not out of human stock or urge of the flesh or will of man but of God himself" (Jn. 1:13). Thus the novelty of the gospel touches all the root relationships of human life: that of the human being with the things of this world, of the human being with his or her neighbor, and of the human being with God.

In the relationship linking the human being with the things of this world, the gospel opposes every attitude or ideology that would reduce that human being to his or her needs and their satisfaction. The human being is more than bread. He or she is a partner in a dialogue with God, whose word is life: "Man does not live on bread alone but on every word that comes from the mouth of God" (Mt. 4:4). On the other hand, a human being is not lord of his or her existence. Life is not the property of human beings. They have received it, and the moment is approaching when, perhaps unexpectedly, they shall have to divest themselves of it (cf. Lk. 12:16-21). Neither slaves nor masters of the things of this world, human beings are called to share what they have freely received. God, who cares for the things of this world, cares for men and women as well (cf. Mt. 6:25-32). In like fashion, men and women should feel responsible for their brothers and sisters, and so be recognizable as children of the Father in his act of creation. Thus they are to transform the world of things into a place where God, and the communion of brothers and sisters, each receives full recognition and acceptance. A new economic order must be brought into being, to transform a world where slavery to things is on the increase, and where flagrant social injustices rage.

In the relationship linking men and women with their fellow human beings, a new, reciprocal dignity bursts into bloom for all. Every human being, and especially the little one, is the place and abode of God. Men and women are above law. The relationship of human being to human being is now the sacramental locus where the relationship of the human being with God is manifested. Any refusal of the gift of oneself to another is a refusal of God as well. Every welcome of another, every act of self-giving is a welcome and a gift of self to God as well (cf. Mt. 25:40-45). One's neighbor is not just one's brother or sister of the same race, religion, or social condition. One's neighbor is every human being encountered along the human road, especially the one in need (cf. Lk. 10:29-36). A new world is dawning, a world where all men and women, in him who is "the firstborn of numerous brothers and sisters," are children of the same Father, and each other's sisters and brothers—a world where the only reciprocal duty is that of brotherly and sisterly love expressed in service, in the gift of self to others. A new social order is being born at the heart of a society torn between a thirst for a world community and the reality of the wars and conflicts that divide humanity.

At the level of the relationship linking human beings to God, the arrival of Jesus Christ places humanity in a new context. No longer can anything sunder the love that unites God to his favorite creature, the human being. Indeed, Jesus is God's total Yes to humanity, as well as humanity's total Yes to God. God is a father for the human being, and the human being is a child for him. Henceforth it is the kingdom of God, his coming among men and women, that is the central event for the entire universe. It is also the event that is radically to transform human life by orienting the human being totally toward God. One must abandon everything for the kingdom of God. On the other hand, God forces no one: we are free to accept him or refuse him. In this new world God is neither a tyrant nor a solitary being far removed from the preoccupations of human beings. He is a Father, who loves all his children and scorns none of them. It is the New Order for a political and religious world where habitually the great have crushed and despised the little in the name of law and order and religious orthodoxy!

Thus, at the heart of a society in search of its own identity, torn between modernity and the tradition of the ancestors, the gospel reveals a new world, an "other" one. It is not simply a model society that is presented. Nor again is it a paradisiac ideal impossible of realization.[4] The gospel establishes a new link among human beings, new relationships among persons and human groups. The gospel is a "movement," to be fostered today in the concrete economic, social, political, and religious situation of the society in which the various local churches of black Africa live. In the power of the Spirit, these Christian communities will be able to read and interpret reality, and finally to act in fidelity to the gospel and to the signs of the times.

Now become children of the same Father in Jesus Christ, and brothers and sisters of one another, Christians are called to insert this twofold reality into the heart of the various relationships of their life. This is the common mission of all Christians, the members of the local churches as well as the members of the missionary institutes. Today more than ever, in my opinion, the novelty of the gospel ought to burst forth here. Let us hear the call of a world athirst for a true communion of sisters and brothers, yet at the same time torn apart by social injustices, tribalism, and authoritarianism. This is a mission that requires the genuine conversion of everyone, a mission with its own characteristics, and yet a mission according to the charism of each person within it. In this perspective, then, let us first examine the mission of the local churches, and then that of the missionary institutes, in black Africa today.

The Mission of the Local Churches

Amid the contradictions that divide various countries, internally as well as externally, a new future is about to be born: a new people, no longer divided but gathered. As People of God, the members of the local churches have the mission of living and proclaiming a new oneness among themselves and with those on the outside, in several different areas: the economic, the social, the political, and the religious.

New Economic Relationships

In various countries of black Africa, the contrast between the wealth of a few and the poverty of the great majority of the population is compensated somewhat by internal bonds of blood relationship. But not only is this system proving to be less and less efficacious in today's world; it also leaves those who are without highly placed relatives and acquaintances in a hopeless situation. Furthermore it favors a certain parasitism, which is itself one of the causes of the disparity. On the other hand, in a value system that places all the emphasis on money and efficiency, money becomes more and more an absolute value determining interpersonal relationships, even within the Christian community. As in the episode of Ananias and Sapphira (Acts 5:1-11),

[the] fascinating power of money blinds its possessors to the true content of social relationships, first and foremost within the church itself. Never neutral in this situation, money has a tendency to substitute itself incognito for the person in his or her relationships with others, and thereby produces an alienat-

ing structure, inasmuch as the threat weighs upon the whole body. The corporeal death of the minor personages of the account expresses the necessity of the death of the mercantile relationship within a social body that wishes to live.[5]

It is impossible to live a single alliance of brothers and sisters in the name of Jesus Christ when one has closed one's eyes to the needs of one's brothers and sisters, when one makes of money one's god. This is why, in the local churches, we must seek concrete means of assisting our members to enter into a real solidarity with our less-favored brothers and sisters—and to share with them, to make material goods a locus of communication and encounter among children of the same Father, within the community as well as with other communities. Each person, according to his or her own opportunities and personal vocation within the community, should live this communion of brothers and sisters by really making a gift of what he or she is and of what he or she possesses. This is the way in which they can live the very generosity of God: "Give, and there will be gifts for you: a full measure, pressed down, shaken together, and running over, will be poured into your lap" (Lk. 6:38).

All people are called to free themselves from all servitude with respect to the goods of this world. As God feeds the birds of the air and clothes the grass of the fields, so also—and how much more!—is he concerned with the life of human beings (cf. Mt. 6:25–32). Thus a human being can never have a reason for feeling uneasy about tomorrow, for God watches over each person (cf. Mt. 6:34). Confidence in God is henceforward part and parcel of the relationship uniting a human being with the things of this world, and this confidence proclaims the presence of God in the life of every creature, and God's attachment to that creature: "Can you not buy two sparrows for a penny? And yet not one falls to the ground without your Father knowing. Why, every hair on your head has been counted" (Mt. 10:29–30).

As the locus of solidarity and of sharing, economic relationships become the locus of filial gratitude to God as well. For it is God who liberates men and women from all turning in upon themselves, who frees them from all servile fear. Only a reconciled and liberated man or woman can allow the rest of the world a life of reconciliation and freedom. Thus, thanks to the practical recognition of the other, economic relationships become genuinely human and liberating. It is the task of the members of each local church to be sufficiently creative to make this reality possible at the heart of their society, and thus usher in a new economic order.

New Social Relationships

Originally divided into many ethnic groups, several of the tribes of black Africa were forced by colonial authorities to form larger unities. Such unity was ever precarious—and is still difficult to maintain. To boot, a new rift has opened and continues to widen—that between those who have had the cultural openness to assimilate the technology and knowledge of the West, and those who have not. Told to live as a nation, the various groups still feel torn between the external fact of national unity and their mistrust of the "stranger," who is anyone of a different race, group, or social condition. Here again the local churches of black Africa have the mission of living and proclaiming the new bond that unites human beings among themselves beyond the boundaries of race or group, sex, and social condition (cf. Gal. 3:28). A real Christian "conversion" is required. In order to see persons united, it will not suffice to gather them together. It is a matter of fleshing out God's own project in the quality of the relationship demanded by the gospel. But according to the gospel the interhuman relationship should be endowed with two qualities: gratuity and universality. Human relationships should be gratuitous because the call to life is gratuitous. Life is something received, like one's race, one's sex, one's country. The call to enter into brotherhood and sisterhood with Jesus Christ is gratuitous as well: "You did not choose me, no, I chose you; and I commissioned you to go out and to bear fruit, fruit that will last" (Jn. 15:16). Hence the disciples of Jesus Christ cannot boast that they are the initiators of the interhuman relationships by which they live. They can love only because they are loved themselves. They themselves have received the love to which they wish to be witnesses. This is the reason why, being reconciled with God by his pure goodness and mercy, they ought to live reconciliation in their turn, and proclaim it at the heart of black African society—a society in which race, group, and social class are all too strongly felt.

Interhuman relationships should be universal. The interhuman relationships propounded by the gospel are no longer based on blood or social condition, and hence should be available to all, without any conditions or limits. They exclude no one. On the contrary, the disciples of Jesus Christ ought to give priority to relationships with the marginalized, with all those who have no one, with all those who are left to their own devices. Every human being, especially the human being in need, is our neighbor—is the brother or sister whom we are to love and help. We are to love even those who do us harm—our enemies. In this manner we break the vicious circle of vengeance, we break free from the sense of having to turn back in upon ourselves. Finally, the love we bear the "other" should enable that other, in his or her own turn, to "go and do likewise": no one may be permitted to break the chain of love that is meant to extend to all humanity. Each and every person is to be a link to all the others in the bond of charity.

It will devolve upon members of the local churches to seek the concrete expressions by which a reciprocal, gratuitous, and universal love may be lived and borne witness to, within the Christian community as well as between the Christian community and other communities.

New Political Relationships

A lamentable phenomenon, which truly strikes one in the countries mentioned above and doubtless in many of the other countries of today's black Africa as well, is the abuse of power—civil, military, and religious. Society frequently finds itself divided into a dominant class, that of the leaders or rulers, and a dominated class. Against this background the words of Christ are cutting, and challenge Christians to a real conversion: "You know that among the pagans their so-called rulers lord it over them, and their great men make their authority felt. This is not to happen among you. No; anyone who wants to become great among you must be your servant, and anyone who wants to be first among you must be slave to all" (Mk. 10:42-44).

Within the local churches themselves, members have the task and calling of refusing to adulterate their faith in Jesus Christ with considerations of persons by scorning the poor and honoring the rich (cf. Jas. 2:1-4). God's choice is not based on appearances. On the contrary, it is those whom the world deems poor that God has chosen to confound and confuse the prideful (cf. 1 Cor. 1:26-29). And thus it is with the manner in which we should treat others. One cannot look simply to titles and honors, but must consider the value and dignity of each human person, especially those "without dignity."[6] A love that stops at mere appearances is unworthy of the name, and it transforms the Christian community into a breeding ground of rivalries and fratricidal jealousy. The Christian community will cease to be a place of communion and encounter. Finally, those who exercise authority in the Christian community are challenged to exercise it first and foremost as a service, and not as the imposition of their person. The mission of authority is first and foremost a ministry of unity, and of the common good of the members of the community.

The members of the local churches are called to seek ways of implementing this new political order within society itself, within the milieu in which they live. Let no one be scorned or harassed with regard to his or her fundamental human rights. Let authority not set itself up as an arbitrary power that represses the creativity of individuals. A genuine attitude of nonconformity is called for in those societies of ours where the relationship linking those in power with the rest of the people is stiff and rigid, a locus of servitude. The gospel challenges us to renounce the sacralization of power, and strive for a community of brothers and sisters.

New Religious Relationships

In the area of religion, the populations in these countries, as also in the rest of Africa, are essentially "believing." Belief in God is a common element in the various religions or sects. Christian religious rivalries have been introduced by evangelizers from Europe and North America. The dialogue among Christians is generally a positive factor in the relations among the different confessions. The dialogue with Islam is still a difficult one, and is becoming more and more so. Conversions to Christianity are frequent. Here the local churches must become increasingly the forum of true dialogue among human beings, agencies of a transformation of rivalries into a confrontation among searchers, by means of new bonds. For God is no one's private property. He wishes to be the God of all, and God for all. Special consideration will have to be given any persons who feel themselves to be "strangers" to all dimensions of religious life.

In their response to the call to live by, and bear witness to, the gospel today, the members of the local churches of black Africa will have to insert the "gospel of human relationships" into the very fabric that unites humanity in the various areas of its life, that all may become brothers and sisters through a real, effective solidarity with one another in God's covenant with his people. This is how the New Order of the world will be created, and men and women will discover themselves to be children of the same Father and brothers and sisters of one another.

The Task of the Missionary Institutes

Just as was true of the primitive church, there are still men and women today who are "reserved," set aside, for the work and task to which the Spirit will send them (cf. Acts 13:2). Thus they receive, in the bosom of the entire Christian community, a specific gift, or charism, for rendering explicit through their person the mission of the church to the world. They set out to live and proclaim the love of the Father, who wishes to reach every man and woman—and the whole man and woman—in this world, "to the ends of the earth" (Acts 1:8).

Born for the most part in the nineteenth century, the missionary institutes ought to be considered first and foremost in the perspective of charism. They are made up of men and women who have responded to a call of the Spirit to open up the church to the dimensions of the entire world, beyond the boundaries of their culture, their country, or their social milieu. Throughout the course of the human history of the colonization of Black Africa, and often enough in anticonformist fashion, the missionary institutes have made an effort to proclaim the gospel to the black African peoples according to the methods and means of their era. Local churches were born that today are growing by leaps and bounds, and are taken up with a search for their own identity. But this does not mean that the task of the members of the missionary institutes has been accomplished. Today that task will be found in the context of the "evangelization of human relationships" of which we have been speaking. Today that task will be found in the radical character of the universal dimension of Christian love in human relationships, and we propose to describe this task in various areas of economic, social, political, and religious life.

The Economic Sector

Economic relationships have not always proved to be the medium of human beings' practical recognition of one another. This is the case both within a given nation and among different nations. Economically powerful persons and nations often continue to close their eyes and their heart to the reality of their economically poor brothers and sisters. Here is where one of the prophetic tasks of the members of the missionary institutes will have to be carried out. Every human being, and especially the least advantaged one, ought to have a fair share in all economic relationships. No one may be neglected for any reason, neither within the local church nor in civil society. The members of the missionary institutes ought to be a critical conscience, insisting upon sharing all things with those who are left out of account simply because they have no one to turn to.

The members of missionary institutes should become the brothers and sisters in action of those who enjoy no economic recognition or acceptance. The same principle is valid where economically favored nations neglect or exploit weak ones. The members of the missionary institutes may not sit back in complacent silence while some of their brothers and sisters die of hunger and others of overeating! And it will not be enough to protest. A prophet is someone who fights for a better tomorrow, and the fight begins in one's own flesh. Becoming the sister or brother of one who is economically weak means being willing to renounce the methods of might when it comes to oneself or one's work. A so-called "development" that employs means beyond a people's capabilities is only digging a ditch between the local population and the members of the missionary institutes. Where there is no actual solidarity in a life relationship, there is no really human (and Christian) "development" either. Anyone wishing to become the sister or brother of someone economically deprived must be willing to share the latter's insecurity as well. There has to be an actual sharing, both of what one has and of what one is.

Sharing what one is involves putting one's abilities and talents at the disposition of one's less privileged brothers and sisters in order to seek, together with them, ways to live a more human life. But the willingness to live with others as sisters and brothers is essential, too, and it is with great justice that the apostle Paul says, "If I give away all that I possess, piece by piece, and if I even let them take my body to burn it, but am without love, it will do me no good whatever" (1 Cor. 13:3). The struggle for a better tomorrow, in company with one's less privileged sisters and brothers, presupposes a genuine commitment on the part of the latter to their own welfare and that of others. (But respect for one's brother's pace, one's sister's pace, out of love for that person, is more important than a task well done!)

When the members of missionary institutes answer the call to give practical and concrete recognition to the underprivileged in the area of economics, they are living a sign of God's concern for human beings, especially for the little ones: "I tell you solemnly, in so far as you did this to one of the least of these brothers of mine, you did it to me" (Mt. 25:40). The desire to inscribe on the fleshy tablets of the heart of human society a respect, a brotherly or sisterly regard, for whoever lacks the goods of this world is not the simple product of considerations of philanthropy, but flows from a faith in the resurrection. For

> the affirmation of one's faith in the Resurrected One together with a multitude of brethren is a call to light up the world with all one's goods. And it is a call to foster, through those goods, the expansion of an effective brotherhood and sisterhood among human beings which stipulates, as a necessary prerequisite, an open economic system. It does not permit one to block one's vision by piling up those goods in front of oneself. Life "in communion" is animated by this violent form of eagerness to find the means and procedures that the Lord himself loves to use when it is "the human being in distress who is at stake."[7]

Living in a culture, a country, or a social milieu different from their own, the members of the missionary institutes wish to be witnesses in the name of Jesus Christ to a new solidarity of sisters and brothers which extends the community of goods to all, and in particular to the brother or sister most in need of them. This efficacious concern for the one in need is a quality of love. It should be present everywhere.

Here too, mission is a mission on six continents: the transformation of economic relationships into an economy of grace!

The Social Sector

Humankind's division on the basis of differences in racial, ethnic, or social origin is a fact of life. Here, as well, both within the local church and out on its frontiers, the members of missionary institutes have a specific task. In black Africa today it is a real challenge. More and more men and women find themselves uprooted, alone, strangers in a world where everyone is turned in upon himself or herself, or is content with relationships that become more and more purely functional. At the same time a thirst for encounter and communion gives rise to new associations, and not merely religious ones, but social and secular as well. New associations easily become ghettos.

The members of the missionary institutes are at the heart of the local churches as a critical conscience with regard to all ghettoization based on race, group, or social status within these churches. By their word and by their life, they prevent the Christian community from being a group that "loves only the ones who love us," and whose directors and guides are always the same people, who know one another and set themselves up in a private club! "For if you love [only] those who love you, what right have you to claim any credit?" (Mt. 5:46). The uprooted, strangers, the lonely can be integrated into the human community only through brothers and sisters who will accept them and help them to open themselves to others. It is the prophetic task of the members of missionary congregations to give Christian agape its universality.

The Christian community should be the place where those who have no one can find brothers and sisters. By their presence at the heart of a culture, a country, or a social milieu different from their own, the members of the missionary institutes hope to be, in their own person, the sign of a new community without borders. In opening themselves by preference to strangers, to those alone, to the abandoned, they testify to the reality of a new people, where all are one in Jesus Christ (cf. Gal. 3:28). Thus the differences and the human limits due to sex, race, and social condition are no longer a barrier, but become a locus of communion. By their presence at the heart of a culture, a country, or a milieu different from their own, the members of the missionary institutes write a question mark on society's heart, inserting there a movement toward communication with the other, with the one who is different from oneself. For the problem is not to reach everyone, but to give rise, by the commitment of one's own "flesh," to a transformation of mentality, of persons, in the area of one's encounter with others.

One cannot live the communion of sisters and brothers inaugurated by Jesus Christ if one closes one's heart to the brother or sister who is a stranger, alone, or abandoned. One cannot pretend to be a disciple of Jesus Christ if one does not encourage a brother or sister to open out to others. But only God can break the narcissistic circle enclosing human beings and groups of human beings. Thus this task of the members of the missionary congregations is a humble one, devoid of human pretension or the might of ideology. It is the task of a midwife, assisting at the difficult birth of a humanity of brothers and sisters beyond the contradictions that divide and isolate them, the birth of a humanity in which the precious worth of the other is affirmed and recognized regardless of who he or she may be, in a continuous departure for "an unknown land" after the manner of the departure of Abraham (cf. Gen. 12:1). Here too, as for Abraham, the only thing that counts is a promise made by the Other: "I will make you a great nation. . . . All the tribes of the earth shall bless themselves by you" (Gen. 12:2–3).

This departure, in order to reach every human being along the road and recognize each one as brother or sister to Him who is "the eldest of many brothers" (Rom. 8:29), is symbolized in the "leave-taking" of members of the missionary institutes. Its only justification is one's real love for every brother and sister, whom one must love as oneself after the example of the Samaritan in the parable (cf. Lk. 10:25–37). It is a radical form of love, of which certain of the disciples of Jesus Christ, today and everywhere, are to be the privileged witnesses. The missionaries must be the focus of reconciliation among the men and women of different races, groups, and social classes.

The Political Sector

In countries just emerging from the colonial era and living in a certain political instability, authoritarianism is far from being a thing of the past! Human relationships are all marked by the tag "superior" or "inferior." Here the members of the missionary institutes have a different task. The first part of their task is within the local churches themselves and concerns the members of the church communities as well as the members of the missionary congregations. There are members of church communities who are undervalued or even looked down upon within the community itself. Members of the missionary institutes must fight for their proper recognition. They must rise up against every form of oppression by which their rivals and dominators are attempting to crush these little ones. In a Christian community, authority is service! By their words and their acts they will be present in the midst of those whom society calls "public sinners"—for Jesus says, "It is not the healthy who need the doctor, but the sick"! He is not exaggerating for effect: this is hard reality, and it ought to be writ large in the life and activity of those sent to others in Jesus' name. It is a matter of opening out the Christian community to the world of all these brothers and sisters, that the community may live its vocation of mercy. Without mercy there is no true Christian love.

As regards themselves, the members of the missionary institutes are sent in the name of Jesus Christ, and not in the name of a civilization or a culture to be imposed upon others. Their mission, then, is in the spirit of the love a servant has for a master: the washing of the feet (cf. Jn. 13:1–15). Within the local church they are on the alert to hear the poor and the oppressed, in order that the voice of these latter be heard and answered by all. Only in humility will they be able to fulfill this mission. In these local churches in search of their own identity, hearing and humility alike must be all the more acute in view of the need to discover new paths in a new world. This will be impossible without communication with the "Master of the harvest," without prayer. Here prayer acquires its maximal self-effacement of sharp attention to the fact that God alone is humanity's rock and salvation (cf. Ps. 62).

Outside the Christian community, the members of the missionary institutes will have to live this same humility in the context of nations in search of their proper visage and identity. This humility will take the form of love, for it will be expressed in the renunciation of all condemning and belittling comparison. It calls for a respect for the concrete reality of each nation, its errors, its hesitations, and its particular pace and stride. Thanks to the bond fashioned by humility, the members of the missionary institutes will be the link between the great (the authorities) and the small, with neither fear nor diplomacy. The cause they should espouse and defend is that of the oppressed. And they should espouse and defend it not in a spirit of temporal messianism, but as the expression of a new world established by Christ: new and special relationships with the poor, with captives, and with the oppressed (Lk. 4:18), relationships whose origin is the Spirit, relationships that inaugurate a new era in the history of humanity. It is a continuation of the mission of Christ: the advent of the kingdom of God among human beings—a kingdom where all are sisters and brothers before they are anything else, both those who have the authority and those who must obey it.

In a world that easily crushes those who have no power, in many different fashions and in many different areas, the members of the missionary congregations are called to live and to proclaim that all members of a society have the right to human dignity—not because of any doctrine or culture but because of God and Jesus Christ, who not only is no respecter of persons, but manifests himself especially to the little ones, thereby undoing diametrically any and every network of determined privilege in the area of human interrelationships. The members of the missionary institutes are called upon to implement, as members of Jesus Christ, his genuine revolution in the political logic of a world where human relationships are often dominated by the important or unimportant place one holds in society.

The Religious Sector

The members of the religious institutes are, and should be, the critical conscience of the local churches with respect to the bonds that unite the latter to the other Christian confessions, religions, or sects. The local churches may not be allowed to close in upon themselves, pretending to be the unique and privileged locus of the manifestation of God. No one can claim to possess God wholly. The members of the missionary institutes will encourage the local churches to open themselves to a dialogue with the other religions, and thus strike a blow against all claims of religious absolutism. The only way they will be able to do this is by becoming "men and women of dialogue" themselves, without hint of paternalism or propaganda. It is the Lord who saves, not we. And he wills to save every human being. Ecumenism is not a matter to be left to each one's goodwill; it is a real missionary task. The same is to be said of respect for religious freedom. In a world becoming more and more pluralistic in the area of religion, it pertains to the human relationship to open the way to genuine encounter, even with those who live no religion, even with those who are against Christianity. A free and universal love is the only true response of the disciples of Jesus Christ. To love without ulterior motives, to love for the sake of persons as they are in themselves—this is the sign of a new religious world.

Thus it is possible to describe the mission of the members of the missionary institutes in terms of the reality of human relationships. This aspect of life seems to me to be most urgent in black Africa today. It is here, I think, that evangelization ought to take flesh for the sake of a human race of brothers and sisters. And this is valid not only for black Africa but for all men and women on earth. Whatever the various forms of economic, social, and political life that are pulling it in different directions, black Africa will be able to be itself, to find its true identity, only in living out its profound aspiration for "communion."

In today's world this communion among human beings is at once ardently desired and fiercely opposed—and it is precisely at the heart of this contradiction that the gospel must become the good news. But the reality is that in the local churches, which we have considered above, this is not the central preoccupation. Instead they are more often concerned with the safeguarding and promotion of a set of structures and a framework. Organization takes precedence over human relationships; forming a competent staff takes precedence over the formation of a genuine community of sisters and brothers; finance and statistics take precedence over the task of becoming acquainted with one's fellow human beings. And these same standards often enough become the criteria for judging the vitality and viability of the young local churches!

In a world of such radical change, in a world parched with thirst for communion, the church's response cannot be a response on the doctrinal, functional, and administrative levels. It must be directly and immediately concerned with the birth of a true community of brothers and sisters. Ideas divide. Structures disappoint. Only a deep communion of the human being with the earth, with his and her human brother and sister, and with God, liberates, creates something new. It is here that the churches of black Africa must do something new. It is here that the members of the missionary institutes are called to a qualitative change in their lives and those of others: by living and proclaiming the universal dimension of a communion of brothers and sisters, one that reaches beyond the familiar, narrow circle of their habitual human relationships. They are called to foster a community of brothers and sisters whose limits are the confines of the universe, and to foster it in and by their Christian communities, linking them to one another by bonds of a new covenant— where the disadvantaged, strangers, and the oppressed have a place. The basic ecclesial communities could become genuine focuses of this universal communion. They gather men and women together in viable human communities. Through them, human relationships will become the locus and point of departure of the new and everlasting covenant begun in Jesus Christ.

The evangelization of black Africa and of the world can take place genuinely only within the communion of human being with human being and human group with human group. This is not to say that the problem of the task of the missionary institutes and of the local churches is thereby resolved. When the mission will have been taken over by the various local churches, how does one justify the continued existence of the missionary institutes?

Challenges of the Future

In this context of *mondialisation*—the thirst for universal communion—and of a preoccupation with human rights, the task of the missionary institutes is to go forth from a kind of ghetto they live in—with respect to themselves, with respect to the local churches, and with respect to the church universal.

With Respect to Themselves

Missionary institutes today are passing through a time of crisis, like the rest of society. They are moving from one cultural world into another, into a world in search of a new economic, social, political, and religious order, transcending the bounds of efficiency, ideology, and narrow nationalism. And at the same time we are witnessing a resurgence precisely of ideological, nationalist, and religious movements! Reality can be paradoxical. In this case the paradox touches the very heart of the missionary institutes. They are drawn back to their initial "charism," their original purpose. But how? In any case not by closing up within themselves. The Spirit is not bound by our structures and our institutions. These are but human means and media through which the mission of a new People of God to the world becomes incarnate.

The question, then, is not the life or death of the missionary institutes. The question goes deeper than that. In which human situations today is the unity of humanity threatened? These will be the situations in which that unity has special need of being lived and proclaimed according to the covenant in Jesus Christ. Men and women who permit themselves to be summoned by various situations will interpret the meaning of their summons in collegiality, and seek a way to answer it "in the flesh," concretely. No one can be excluded a priori, neither priests nor laity nor religious, neither black nor white, neither men nor women. God calls whom he will, as he will, when he will. Hasty attempts to resolve the problem of the missionary institutes according to our human categories run the risk of renewing the exterior without really touching the inside.

On the other hand, solutions inspired by fear and human prudence will fail to give today's church the women and men it needs as the living environment of the Spirit's movement "toward the nations." But

> . . . the movement of the Spirit, his outward thrust, can actually take place only where relationships among "believers" have managed to take shape in an organic structure. The twin coordinates of this structure are described for us: constant newness, as life itself is constantly new; and constant risk, with an orientation toward ever new risks. This operation can never be reduced to any ritual or juridical apparatus. On the contrary, its nature is constantly to create conflict, within the community of "believers" as well as between the "be-

lievers" and the "others." Indeed its success will consist precisely in its ability to bring forth, from a pluralism ever generative of conflict, some relationship that, for a given time, will be the concrete expression of "communion." This communion, then, is inseparable from the resurrection, for the resurrection is acquired for all men and women in Jesus. Thus what this movement and operation has at stake is the global destiny of the human race, the global destiny of "all nations."[8]

With Respect to the Local Churches

The missionary institutes cannot allow themselves to take shape in so heavy a body that they leave their stamp on the local church. The local church is the "place of communion" for all. A form of exchange among the members of the various missionary institutes ought not to be merely possible, it is actually desirable. Since the missionary enterprise is no longer a one-way street, it is clear that each local church ought to be willing not only to send out missioners, but also to receive them from the other churches. Here too, then, the members of the missionary institutes ought to be willing to enter this "interpersonal" exchange among churches. Within the local churches themselves, in the various sectors and aspects of life, they will call upon various men and women, each having the charism to live and proclaim a different aspect of that interchange, to do so in the name of the local church. Thus there will be a division of sacred labor, so to speak; for the accumulation of tasks of diverse quality in the same persons invites superficiality, and forms the seedbed of a certain counterfeit totalitarianism in the Christian community.

Finally, the missionary institutes are also the focus, within the local churches, of a concrete sharing of adapted forms of Christian life and ministry, with a view to manifesting, through these adapted forms, a "communion of brothers and sisters."

With Respect to the Church Universal

In their prophetic refusal to turn in upon themselves, the missionary institutes will exercise the same prophetic function with respect to the universal church. The church may never be allowed to become installed, to become bureaucratic heavy machinery. It should be out on the road, the road of humanity and human life. Within the church, the members of the missionary institutes will be a critical conscience, on the alert for any settling down by the wayside. An itinerant group composed of various members of several missionary institutes might be formed, to be the focus of sharing and renewal of mission life for all the members of all the institutes for the world of today. Similarly, wherever there are meetings and encounters on a world scale, certain members of the missionary institutes should be there, responding to their call to foster the universal communion of humankind in all its evangelical intensity. "The little ones of this world," they must cry out, "and especially they, are also your sisters and brothers!"

—*Translated by Robert R. Barr*

Notes

1. J.M. Ela, "Ambiguïtés de la mission," *Lumière et Vie* 137 (1978): 22–27.

2. E. Mveng, "Liturgie cosmique et langage religieux," *Bulletin de Theólogie Africaine* 1, no. 1 (January–June 1979): 101.

3. Mveng, "Essai d'anthropologie négro-africaine," *Bulletin de Théologie Africaine* 1, no. 2 (July–December 1979): 235.

4. Cf. E. Haulotte, *Actes des Apôtres: Un guide de lecture* (Supplement to *Vie Chrétienne,* no. 212), p. 62.

5. Ibid., p. 66.

6. Borrowed from the title of *Concilium,* vol. 150 (1979).

7. Haulotte, *Actes,* p. 64.

8. Ibid., p. 55.

20

WHAT IS THE ROLE OF THE MISSIONARY INSTITUTES?

Raymond C. Rossignol, M.E.P.

It is not easy to give a clear-cut definition of a missionary institute. The Decree of Vatican II on the Church's Missionary Activity does not attempt to do so. But we find in that document what we can call a descriptive definition:

> So the Holy Spirit . . . implants in the hearts of individuals a missionary vocation and at the same time raises up institutes in the Church who take on the duty of evangelization, which pertains to the whole Church, and make it as it were their own special task.
>
> Those people who are endowed with the proper natural temperament, have the necessary qualities and outlook, and are ready to undertake missionary work, have a special vocation, whether they are natives of the place or foreigners, priests, religious or lay people [*Ad Gentes*, no. 23].

A footnote spells out further: "By 'institutes' are meant the orders, congregations, institutions and associations which work in the missions."

This descriptive definition is fairly satisfactory. It is clear enough that the expression "missionary institute" is used to designate groups of people who, because of a special vocation, are committed to missionary work. They may be men or women. They may be priests, religious, or lay persons. But they all have in common a special calling and a special commitment to missionary work.

Missionary Institutes Today

Missionary institutes used to be very much in the minds of the popes when they were writing encyclicals on the missions. In fact, such documents used to contain

Raymond C. Rossignol is the Vicar General of the Paris Foreign Mission Society. He worked in India from 1954 to 1980. While there he was rector of St. Peter's Pontifical Seminary in Bangalore from 1960 to 1973 and secretary of theological publications in India from 1969 to 1980.

large sections where the successor of Peter was giving instructions and exhortations to the personnel engaged in missionary work, and these were mainly members of missionary institutes.[1]

The missionary institutes are still mentioned several times in *Ad Gentes* and *Ecclesiae Sanctae*; but somehow, the Apostolic Exhortation *Evangelii Nuntiandi* never mentions them. Granting that this exhortation deals with evangelization in general and not simply with the mission *ad exteros*, it is nonetheless surprising that missionary institutes should be left out. One full chapter of *Evangelii Nuntiandi* deals with the workers of evangelization. It speaks of the "perspective" of the universal church and of the individual church, of the role of bishops and priests, of religious, of the laity, of the family, the youth, and so forth, but nothing is said about missionary institutes as such.

It matters little whether the omission was deliberate or not. It may be an oversight. But then it is perhaps all the more significant. The fact that today one may list the workers of evangelization without thinking of the missionary institutes shows that their place in the planning of missionary work is no longer what it used to be.

Several reasons can be given to explain this change:

Missionary activity belongs to the very nature of the church's life. The ecclesiology of Vatican II makes it clear that the church is missionary by its very nature (cf. *Ad Gentes*, no. 2; *Lumen Gentium*, no. 1). The missionary activity of the church can no longer be located on its periphery. One obvious implication is that Christians cannot simply pass on the responsibility of undertaking missionary work to a few "professionals." Any member of the church is duty-bound to do his or her share. "Since the whole church is missionary, and the work of evangelization the fundamental task of the people of God, this sacred synod invites all to undertake a profound interior renewal so that being vitally conscious of their responsibility for the spread of the Gospel, they might play their part in missionary work among the nations" (*Ad Gentes*, no. 35).

Pope Paul VI pursues the same idea in *Evangelii Nuntiandi*. He stresses the personal duty of every Christian to be an evangelizer. In that perspective one can understand the omission of any reference to "specialists" of missionary work such as missionary institutes.

Missionary institutes no longer give a clear priority to the mission *ad exteros*. There seems to be another reason that explains why today one can propose a program for missionary work—as is done in *Evangelii Nuntiandi*—without thinking of the missionary institutes. It is the present position of missionary institutes with respect to missionary work. This position is the outcome of an evolution in their role. In the past members of missionary institutes were sent to non-Christian areas. They were entrusted with the task of planting the church. Insofar as they succeeded, they were invited to hand over the responsibility of the new Christian community to the local personnel and to move on to new areas. Subsequently, as the local churches in mission countries were increasing in number, a new policy was adopted: the members of the missionary institutes were invited to stay on in the "newly planted" churches and to help the young Christian community.[2]

When giving such directives the church never meant that the mission *ad exteros* should be suspended. It meant that the new Christian community itself should take over this responsibility with the help of the missionary institutes—which had perhaps a special charism to that effect.

Unfortunately, at least in some countries, things did not work that way. Members of the missionary institutes did stay on. They contributed their share to the life of the new churches. But for various reasons the new churches devoted the best of their energies and resources to the formation of Christians or to the socioeconomic development of the Christian community—sometimes with the help of mighty institutions that gave some prestige to the Christian community—but did little to foster its missionary dynamism.

All too often the missionary institutes fell in line with the program of the new churches. They may not have given up their missionary ambition, but—rightly or wrongly, consciously or unconsciously—they opted for a further evangelization of the existing Christian communities, with the hope that the new Christian communities would later on reach out to non-Christians. Gradually missionary institutes gave up pioneering work.

It may be an oversimplification to say that missionary institutes have lost their missionary specificity; but it would be hard to deny that today, by and large, the members of the missionary institutes are engaged in activities oriented toward the service of the existing Christian communities and their institutions.[3]

Even if there are many exceptions to confirm the rule, we should probably acknowledge that today missionary institutes can hardly be identified with the task force for the evangelization of non-Christians. No wonder Pope Paul VI failed to single them out as a particular group of evangelizers!

Are Missionary Institutes Still Necessary?

Starting from the ecclesiology of Vatican II one might build a case showing that missionary institutes can be conveniently phased out. Indeed, if the church is missionary by its very nature, it follows—and *Ad Gentes* as well as *Evangelii Nuntiandi* stress these points repeatedly—that every local church is to be a missionary church. Every bishop, every priest, every Christian is to be a missionary. Every Christian community, be it a community of religious or of lay people, is to be a missionary community. If so, is there still any raison d'être for missionary institutes? By keeping up missionary institutes are we not relieving the majority of Christians of their missionary obligations, and placing such obligations on the shoulders of a few? Are we not pushing missions out to the periphery of the church's activities?

By asserting so emphatically that the church is missionary by its very nature, Vatican II makes it imperative to take a new look not only at the theology of missions, but also at the concrete organization of missionary work. On this new ecclesiological background is there any place for missionary institutes?

The structures of the church should reflect its missionary nature. From the organizational point of view, apart from the missionary institutes there is little in the church structures that reflect its missionary nature. It is not difficult to show how the present church structures were devised in Christian countries to cater to the pastoral needs of a Christian population. Territorial units like dioceses and parishes and the corresponding territorial jurisdiction were obviously conceived to distribute pastoral responsibilities and organize pastoral work in territories inhabited by a majority of Christians. Now we find exactly the same type of organization in mission countries. Some territorial units may still go under the name of Vicariate Apostolic or Mission Center; but this is supposedly a temporary situation. As soon as possible the Vicariate Apostolic will become a diocese, the Mission Center will become a parish. Thus from the organizational point of view we have a somewhat uniform pattern all over the world. There is hardly any difference between the church structures in Ireland and those in Japan. Unfortunately, it so happens that these structures are much more suitable to take care of the Catholics in Dublin than to reach out to non-Christians in Tokyo.

If the church is truly missionary by its very nature, this should be written concretely in its structures. It can be done in many ways. Episcopal commissions for evangelization, diocesan animators, evangelization teams, and the like may help the church to function as a missionary church. But eventually, if the church is to function as a missionary entity, there may be no substitute for groups of people who opt mainly, or even exclusively, for missionary work. That is the purpose and the raison d'être of missionary institutes. In their absence the church would still be missionary by its very nature, but practically it might not function as a missionary entity.

Many local churches need outside help in order to assume their missionary responsibilities effectively. There is first of all a problem of numbers. However numerous the candidates to priesthood and religious life, in mission countries usually the young churches are short of personnel. One may deplore the acute vocation crisis in the so-called Christian countries. But one should not forget that there are still more priests in the tiny country of France than in the two continents of Asia and Africa put together.[4] The total population of France is hardly more than 50 million, while the population of Asia and Africa exceeds 2,700 million.[5] When a small Christian community is lost among a vast majority of non-Christians according to a ratio of 1 to 50,000, it is clearly in need of outside help to reach out to the surrounding masses of non-Christians.[6] Missionary institutes may come to their rescue.

Apart from numbers, there is also a problem of the relationship between the small Christian minority and the overwhelming majority of non-Christians living in the same area. The Christian community may not always be a good starting point to reach out to non-Christians.

In many Asian countries Christian communities do not seem to belong to the mainstream of the society. In a country like Taiwan, for instance, Christians are either tribal people or Chinese who came from the mainland. There is hardly any Taiwanese among the Christians. In Malaysia Christians are of either Chinese or Indian origin. In India there are many dioceses, especially in the south, where Christians do belong to the bulk of the society. But there are also many dioceses, particularly in the north, where Christians do not belong to the mainstream of the society. Some are coming from the south; others, however wrong the reasons, may find themselves outside the pale of the "recognized society" because they happen to be Harijans or tribespeople.

Thus the local church may be constituted by people who for some reason are considered outsiders. They belong to minorities, and not simply because of their religious affiliation; there may be some ethnic, linguistic, or sociological distinction.

Several explanations can be given to account for this situation; some could be found in the gospel itself. In the gospel some kind of priority is given to the poor, the downtrodden. No wonder the church has gone to them; no wonder that the poor, the oppressed, the refugees are the first to accept the good news. Some other explanations are less evangelical. One could speak, for example, of the ghetto mentality obtaining in some Christian communities.

Whatever the explanation, it is a fact that often enough Christians are considered as outsiders, nay as intruders, and are looked down upon by the bulk of the society. In that case, are such Christian communities a suitable starting point for the evangelization of non-Christians? Of course, one should not underrate the power of the Word of God; one should be mindful of the reversal of values proclaimed by the gospel. Still it is a fact that the social position of the Christians may constitute, for the non-Christians, a psychological blockage. It is extremely difficult for them to envisage that liberation and salvation might come from those whom they consider as inferior to themselves. To this must be added the consideration that these Christian communities do not always project the image of the ideal Christian community.

Consequently, one wonders whether or not the local church is always the best possible starting point for the evangelization of non-Christians. It goes without saying that evangelization cannot be undertaken without reference to the existing Christian community. But from the organizational point of view it may not be realistic to rely mainly on these local churches to evangelize non-Christians living in the same area. Here again the missionary institutes may have a role to fulfill. It is probably with reference to such situations that the Vatican II document on missions says:

> If it happens that in certain regions there is a group of men which is impeded from accepting the Catholic faith because they cannot adapt themselves to the particular guise in which the Church presents itself in that place, then it is desirable that this situation should be specially provided for, until all Christians can gather together in one community. If the Holy See is able to provide missionaries, then bishops should invite them to their dioceses; they should welcome them and actively assist them in their undertakings (*Ad Gentes*, no. 20).

The Specific Role of Missionary Institutes in the Local Church

This amounts to a problem of identity. Even if the vast majority of its members are fairly satisfied with the type of work they do, and suffer no personal identity crisis, there may still be a problem of identity for the institute as such, insofar as its specificity may no longer be clearly perceived. This problem is already basically solved if one accepts the missionary institutes as a task force available for work among non-Christians (a role suggested earlier in this paper). The place of missionary institutes in the local church and their relationship to the local bishops should be further spelled out, however.

First, negatively, missionary institutes are not meant to serve Christian communities. No one can deny that by serving a Christian community one may indirectly serve the missions *ad exteros,* all the more so if one helps a Christian community to become a missionary community. Nevertheless, this cannot be considered the specific task of a missionary institute. An institute whose members would be exclusively at the service of Christians and Christian institutions might render a precious service to the church, but it could hardly claim the title of "missionary institute." This applies especially to priests assuming pastoral responsibilities. They may do so with commendable missionary zeal. Still, insofar as they do not try to reach out to non-Christians, they do no more than what *Evangelii Nuntiandi* expects from every priest the world over (cf. no. 68).

Second, positively, missionary institutes should be committed to missionary work in the local church. It is certainly legitimate to try to reach out to non-Christians through Christian communities and Christian institutions—and at times this may be the only practical way. However, this does not imply that all the members of missionary institutes should work exclusively among non-Christians. One may be a member of a missionary institute without having the necessary aptitudes to work always and exclusively among non-Christians. But missionary institutes should set right their priorities. If missionary work is to be the specificity of the institute, its members should normally opt for work among non-Christians. They cannot make it a rule to be available for any kind of work in the diocese, even if the diocese happens to be located in a mission country. They cannot become mere helpers of the diocesan clergy. If their professed aim is the evangelization of non-Christians, they should be at the service of non-Christians.

It is, obviously, possible to serve non-Christians from within a community and through it. But one should be mindful of the risk inherent to the position of missionaries who assume pastoral responsibilities. They are likely to devote most of their time and energy to the service of the Christian community. The Christian community will normally welcome their presence and claim their services; on the other hand, non-Christians may prove indifferent if not hostile. In a way, the missionary is in the position of a salesperson whose goods are appreciated and readily purchased in one place, whereas in another place nobody cares for the goods. Is it surprising if the person stays where there is a good market?

Although I do not belittle the role of Christian communities as a starting point for missionary work, it would be hard to deny that a Christian community may also hold back the missionary. Hence it is important that some members of the missionary institutes put themselves in a position where they cannot run away from missionary work. As long as their function leaves them an alternative, the odds are that they will give preference to their work among Christians to the detriment of the evangelization of non-Christians.

To be faithful to their charism the members of a missionary institute may have to get away from the Christian communities and put some distance between themselves and the existing church structures. Because missionaries are at the service of non-Christians, it is only normal that they should work at times outside structures for the service of Christians.

Nevertheless a missionary should never forget that evangelization is an ecclesial act. "No Evangelizer," says *Evangelii Nuntiandi* (no. 60), "is the absolute Master of his evangelizing action, with discretionary power to carry it out in accordance with individualistic criteria and perspectives; he acts in common with the Church and her Pastors." Evangelizers may be pioneers, breaking new ground in new milieus. It is nonetheless necessary that they should be "in communion with the Church and her Pastors." Concretely they should not only be in communion of mind and heart, but also make sure that the local bishop is well aware of what they do, and approves of it.

Evangelizers committed to missionary work may be justified in saying that they are not at the service of the local Church. (If they were, they might find themselves at the service of the local bishop in some Christian community.) Evangelizers are at the service of the mission in the local church. To carry on its missionary activities, they may need a certain amount of autonomy. Nevertheless, if they were to deny the local church the right to assess their work, their evangelizing activities would no longer be an ecclesial act.

The Place of Foreign Personnel in a Local Church

Missionary institutes used to recruit their members in "Christian countries" and send them to "non-Christian countries." It was taken for granted that a missionary was usually a foreigner. In the minds of many the word "missionary" still carries a connotation of "foreign."

But there has been an evolution. Foreign missionaries have been expelled from many countries, and many local churches have had to manage without the help of outsiders; in consequence, more and more attention has been paid to the theology of the local church and to its corollary principles of inculturation and "incarnation." As a result there is a tendency to consider foreign missionaries as poor assets or even as liabilities.[7] Granting that their presence may still be a necessity here and there, foreign missionaries should be considered as a temporary solution to the shortage of personnel until such time as the local church can manage without their help.

This prompts the question: Is there now normally any place for foreigners in a local church?

Before answering that question, we should review the principles basic to twentieth- century missionary activity:

1. Although it may not be easy to spell out clearly all the practical implications of inculturation in a given country, the principle itself cannot be called into question. Inculturation is not optional for the church. It is an integral part of evangelization.
2. It is normal for the direction of the local church to be in the hands of the local people.
3. Any local church should aim at self-sufficiency in the sense that it should not be

unnecessarily dependent on outside help to carry on and develop its activities.

4. Nevertheless no local church can achieve such a degree of self-sufficiency as to be totally independent of outside help. This applies to churches in the West as well as in the East, in the North as well as in the South. All churches have much to learn and must be at the receiving end at times.

5. Missionary help can no longer be considered a one-way activity from those who have and know to those who have not and do not know. *All* churches are in a position both to give and to receive.

We can now answer the question just raised: The presence of foreign personnel in a local church—any local church—can be a blessing. Several considerations underlie this answer:

1. The theology of the local church, rooted in the mystery of the incarnation, should not cause us to forget the otherness, the transcendence of God. "For my thoughts are not your thoughts/my ways not your ways—it is Yahweh who speaks. Yes, the heavens are high above earth/as my ways are above your ways/my thoughts above your thoughts" (Isa. 55:8–9). Jesus himself remains other: "You are from below/I am from above/You are of this world/I am not of this world" (Jn. 8:23).[8]

God comes to us from elsewhere. God is different. *God is a foreigner.* But God who comes from elsewhere has much to bring us. Likewise, in a very limited way a foreigner may be in a position to bring us something that we do not have, just because he is a foreigner, rooted in a different culture, brought up in a different milieu, living his Christian faith in a different way.

By rejecting the cooperation of others on the ground that they are different, that they do not belong to the place, that they cannot understand, we are depriving ourselves of a precious source of enrichment. In a positive way, by welcoming foreigners we open ourselves to the plenitude of God's gifts, distributed in manifold ways in a plurality of races and cultures.

2. Scripture as well as the history of the church show that God uses foreigners as his messengers willingly. There is no reason to assume that he will not use them in the future. At any rate, experience still shows that people are not always and everywhere indifferent to foreigners living in their midst. On the contrary, many welcome the foreigner with an open heart and an open mind. They like to get acquainted with a foreigner. They are interested in the different way of life, in the person's motivations.

Of course, precautions should be taken (especially in countries that have experienced the yoke of colonialism until recently) not to give the impression that foreigners are trying to export their own culture, their own way of life. Nevertheless, in today's context (barring some local exceptions) there is no evidence to show that people automatically build up a defense system against the ideas and convictions of foreigners, just because they are foreign. True, some Muslims, some Hindus, some Buddhists may build up a defense system against the Christian missionary; but they will do so whether the missionary is a foreigner or not.

3. Evidence is not lacking to show that the Holy Spirit pushes some people to leave their own country in order to carry the good news to the ends of the earth. In the Old Testament story, for instance, Jonah was sent to Nineveh. In the New Testament we read of the evangelizers being sent out almost systematically. Jesus himself feels the need to push on toward other places: "Let us go elsewhere, to the neighbouring country towns, so that I can preach there too, because that is why I came" (Mk. 1:38). In his turn Jesus urges the apostles repeatedly to go out to the whole world (cf. Mk. 16:5; Mt. 28:18–20; Lk. 24:47; Acts 1:8).

The history of the early church and the history of missions is the history of evangelizers on the move. Persons today hear a call to leave their own country and to go elsewhere. Some discernment is needed to make sure that it is not simply a desire to evade something or an urge to see the world; but this discernment is possible, and in many cases it is clear that the Holy Spirit is at work in the hearts of those who volunteer to proclaim the good news in foreign lands. Obviously it would be an aberration on the part of the local church to close the door to such laborers on the ground that the personnel available locally can manage.

Thus it seems clear that there is a place for foreigners in any local church. It follows that, barring exceptional circumstances, no local church should deliberately and systematically close the door to foreign personnel. It follows also that foreign missionaries should not leave a country simply because, in their own estimation, the local church does not need them any more. They may have valid reasons to move on to other places, for instance, a matter of priorities with regard to evangelization; but the sole consideration that a local church has become self-sufficient in personnel does not justify the departure of foreign missionaries.

Conditions for Fruitful Missionary Work

If missionary institutes are to fulfill their role in today's context, their members must assimilate the teachings of Vatican II and *Evangelii Nuntiandi*. They must take into account what Vatican II has to say about inculturation, religious freedom, dialogue and the other major religions of the world. They must be well acquainted with the teachings of the Pastoral Constitution on the Church in the Modern World, on the relationship between the church and secular society. They must reflect on the dimensions of evangelization as described by *Evangelii Nuntiandi* and, in a special way, the relation between the mission of the church and the struggle for justice and liberation. No evangelizer can ignore these and other orientations formulated by the church during and after Vatican Council II. But members of the missionary institutes should also pay special attention to the following points.

Witnessing to Prayer

In some Muslim countries Christians are known as those who do not pray. No wonder. Even though many Christians may have a real prayer life, the Christian communities as such do not project the image of praying communities. Unlike Muslims, Christians do not kneel down in public several times a day. In a country like India, the church is known and appreciated for its services in the fields of education, medical care, and social work; but few non-Christians see in the church an organization entrusted with a spiritual mission. When priests and religious reflect on their position in the society, they have to acknowledge that, barring the case of Christians who solicit sacraments, most people look up to them often for material help, but rarely for spiritual guidance.

The church projects the image of a welfare organization. This may be indeed an integral part of its mission, especially in a country where hundreds of millions live below the poverty level. As has been written in *Indian Theological Studies*: "But the Church cannot renounce her identity and be simply the agent of social and economic needs along with other forces working in the same realm. Her Mission is determined by the Mission of Jesus Christ to proclaim God's kingdom and to call for a renewal of heart. . . . Whenever economic, cultural or political goals are connected with the missionary activity, the real aim of the Mission of the Church must be kept in mind: the conversion of hearts without which no real progress can be achieved."[9]

Obviously the church should not give up its efforts to relieve poverty and suffering; but it should also project the image of a community of believers who attach the greatest importance to spiritual values. This seems particularly important in the context of India's spiritual traditions; a similar need is felt in several other countries of Asia. The flourishing Hindu ashrams and Buddhist monasteries are a clear sign that the church should have its own ashrams and monasteries. Of course, any Christian community should be a praying community, any evangelizer should be a man or woman of prayer. There is a clear need for people who witness to prayer in the midst of non-Christians, and in such a manner that non-Christians may see in them possible spiritual guides. Some members of the missionary institutes could adopt such a program.

Creative Imagination

The chapter on the methods of evangelization in *Evangelii Nuntiandi* begins with a clear appeal for a creative imagination. The Apostolic Exhortation does not in any way rule out traditional methods of missionary work, such as schools, medical care, and social work. On the contrary, it is clear that such activities may perfectly fit in with the all-embracing concept of evangelization as described earlier in the same document. But while insisting on a "complete fidelity to the content of Evangelization," *Evangelii Nuntiandi* speaks of the "responsibility of reshaping with boldness and wisdom the means that are most suitable and effective for communicating the Gospel message to the men and women of our time. . . . This question of 'how to evangelize' is permanently relevant," the same document says, "because the methods of evangelizing vary according to the different circumstances of time, place and culture, and because they thereby present a certain challenge to our capacity for discovery and adaptation" (no. 40).

It might be difficult to find a precedent in a papal document for such an unmistakable appeal to creative imagination. By their very nature papal documents are meant to give instructions and clear guidelines. Obviously Pope Paul VI, who had in hand the reports of the Synod of Bishops, was impressed by the diversity of the new situations obtaining all over the world. Suitable methods of evangelization to face these new situations cannot be found in Rome. It is for the evangelizer on the spot to look for new ways and means of reaching out to the world. This calls for common, prayerful reflection. It calls also for courage and boldness.

Because of their commitment to Christian communities, diocesan priests who assume pastoral responsibilities, and also religious who are running institutions, may not feel free to launch new ventures. But missionary institutes should be in a position to try out new methods of evangelization. If it is agreed that missionary institutes are at the service of non-Christians, there is no reason why they should not feel free to look for new ways of approaching the people.

Teamwork

Pioneering work may carry a connotation of individualism. Indeed, often pioneers were setting out alone. In the case of missionary work one might point to pioneers who did an excellent work single-handedly. This may have been the only way to reach out to non-Christians at a time when missionaries were very few, when Christian communities were practically nonexistent, and when communications were extremely difficult. But circumstances have changed. It is today much easier for missionaries to avail themselves of the services and cooperation of others. Teamwork is not only possible; it is a necessity.

It is not simply a matter of mutual help and mutual encouragement. There is also a need for complementarity to face the complex task of evangelization. Because of the rapid development of education and means of communication, people are much better informed of world news, of political problems, and the like. Evangelizers cannot dissociate their action from this widespread knowledge. Missionary activity is probably more complex today than ever in the past. This complex task demands cooperation and teamwork.

There is also a problem of effective witnessing. One should not minimize the value of individual witnessing. It is enough to look at the popularity of some gurus in India to realize how easily people can be influenced by the personality, spirituality, and lifestyle of an individual. Gurus are normally surrounded by disciples; they do not stand alone. Indeed, in most Asian countries, a lonely witness carries little credibility and is easily labeled "eccentric." Group witnessing is more effective.[10]

It will be all the more effective if the composition of the group reflects some kind of catholicity. It would be a drawback to have a team constituted exclusively of foreigners. But the presence of some foreigners on the team may prove a real asset. Apart from the advantages of mutual enrichment for the evangelizers, there is also the fact that the universal dimension of the Christian mission is an integral part of the Christian message. An international and interracial team will witness to the universal brotherhood willed by God and desired, consciously or unconsciously, by all human beings.

Hence, whenever necessary, let missionary institutes reconsider their criteria for membership. Clerical missionary societies had good reason in the past not to recruit, in mission countries, candidates for their own societies. By accepting such candidates they would have defeated their own purpose, which was the promotion of the local clergy. Such reasons are no longer valid. In most countries there is a local clergy and the time has come for this local clergy to set apart people from among themselves for missionary work. It is imperative that all these volunteers for missions work together.

In case of religious institutes who never had any restrictions in their constitutions regarding admission of candidates from mission countries, there may be a tendency to keep everyone in his or her country. This attitude of "We can manage," "Let them manage," may be detrimental to missionary work. One should start from the assumption that no local church—whether it is in a Christian country or in a mission country—no religious province is really self-sufficient. This notion of self-sufficiency should be reconsidered in the light of the enormous advantages that may accrue to the local church from mutual enrichment and the experience of an interracial community.

Humble Service

The fact that today missionary institutes have lost something of their preponderance may be providential. The fact that missionary societies are short of vocations may be a blessing in disguise. Because they experience poverty, missionary institutes may learn to serve from a position of weakness.

In the days when missionary institutes were entrusted with the responsibility of planting the church, they were often in a position to claim some credit for their achievements. In the days when the successor of Peter was dependent almost entirely on missionary institutes to break new ground in non-Christian countries, such institutes were rightly conscious of their importance. Today the responsibility of evangelizing people in any given area is incumbent on the local church. The work of the missionary institutes will be less visible. So much the better! Let the local church grow and let the missionary institutes be satisfied with a humble service.

Evangelization can be viewed as both a centripetal activity and a centrifugal activity. The growth of the local church will reflect the centripetal aspect of evangelization: "Day by day the Lord added to their community those destined to be saved" (Acts 2:47). As for the missionary institutes, let them concentrate their efforts on the centrifugal aspect of evangelization. By their presence and their discreet action among non-Christians, let them diffuse the gospel values in non-Christian milieus. Let them sow the seed that will grow in its own time. To that effect, let them rely mostly on the power of the Word (cf. Rom. 1:16). Let them not be afraid to go to non-Christians empty-handed, relying, like Saint Paul, not on any human stratagem but on the power of Christ crucified. "For Christ did not send me to baptise, but to preach the Good News, and not to preach that in the terms of philosophy in which the crucifixion of Christ cannot be expressed" (1 Cor. 1:17; cf. 1 Cor. 2:3–5; 2 Cor. 9:12).

Notes

1. E.g., *Maximum Illud* (1919); *Rerum Ecclesiae* (1926); *Princeps Pastorum* (1959).
2. This actually describes the evolution of the role of clerical missionary societies without vows; but *mutatis mutandis*, one can verify a similar evolution in the role of religious missionary societies.

3. True, many of them have manifold contacts with non-Christians. But usually these contacts take place through Christian institutions, in which case it can be said that non-Christians come to the missionary; but it can hardly be said that the missionary goes to non-Christians, and that makes a difference.

4. *The Statistical Yearbook of the Church* (Vatican City, 1976), pp. 94ff.

5. Ibid., p. 44.

6. One should use with caution the expression "self-sufficiency in personnel." This is an ambiguous expression and its indiscriminate use may lead to practical aberrations. When saying that a diocese is self-sufficient in personnel, one means usually that "the Bishop has enough priests to provide all parishes with a parish-priest, that he can run efficiently all the institutions in the diocese and perhaps that he can even spare some people either for some inter-diocesan programme or for higher studies or for some specialization. In other words, a diocese is said to be self-sufficient when enough personnel is available to fill up all the posts of a well established community. But, behind this conception of self-sufficiency it is not difficult to detect a rather static conception of the Church" (*Indian Theological Studies,* St. Peter's Seminary, Bangalore, September 1979, p. 173).

7. Foreign missionaries may be considered as a liability for several reasons. First, when foreign missionaries are relatively numerous and play a preponderant role in the Christian community, the local church may unduly project the image of an imported religion without adequate local roots. Second, the presence of foreign missionaries may at times actually retard the process of a necessary inculturation.

8. On these points, see *Echos de la rue du Bac* (Séminaire des Missions Etrangères, 128, rue du Bac, Paris): "Aux sources de l'étrangeté," by M. Navant (January–May 1979) and "Allons ailleurs," by L. Legrand (April 1980).

9. *Indian Theological Studies,* March 1980, p. 28.

10. Group witnessing does not necessarily demand that all members of the team should live under the same roof; but it implies that there be a common planning and a coordinated teamwork in complementarity.

21

WAYFARERS IN A NEW AGE

John N. M. Wijngaards, M. H. M., and Peter Dirven, M. H. M.

In 1975 two young missionary priests, Michael Cypher and Ivan Betancourt, wrote the following open letter from Honduras:

> We believe that the world can be changed. It can be changed through persons who follow Christ. People need priests to guide them on this road. If you were to decide to respond to this vocation, don't promise yourself a comfortable life. You will be laughed at, ridiculed, declared daft. You will walk with us to distant mountain villages where the poor are waiting to hear the good news. There you will sow love, justice, and truth in their hearts.
>
> Some who profit from lies and oppression may be displeased at your work. They will attack you, may even try to murder you, as happened to Jesus Christ.
>
> If you are prepared to undertake such a life, join us. We need you as a partner.[1]

Shortly afterward they took part in a demonstration of agricultural workers. They were arrested and killed.

We begin our reflection with this incident because it touches the heart of what mission is all about. Mission happens where Christ's disciples bring the good news, where they witness to his truth and his love, where new communities of faith are formed. Mission is a work of the Spirit. Mission arises from being sent as Christ himself was sent. Mission reaches out to people, is concerned with human life, is always a becoming flesh in living men and women. Mission means enthusiasm for Christ and the service of newly discovered brothers and sisters. Mission is first and foremost a spiritual reality, a matter of conviction, a power of the heart.

John N. M. Wijngaards is the Vicar General and Councilor for Home Regions of the Mill Hill Missionaries. He worked in India from 1964 to 1976 where he was professor of Sacred Scripture at St. John's Regional Seminary, Hyderabad, and a member of several national planning committees for the church in India. He is the author of a number of books and articles on Sacred Scripture. Peter Dirven, a priest of the Mill Hill Society, assisted him in the writing of this paper.

We remind ourselves of this, right at the beginning. As most of this paper will be concerned with practical considerations, with organization and structure, we might lose sight of its spiritual nature. The perfection of structures, as C. N. Parkinson tells us in one of his inimitable essays, is a symptom of decay. Saint Peter's at Rome and the monumental Vatican palaces were completed only after the era of the papacy's real temporal power. The Colonial Office at London had five times more staff in 1954, when the colonial era was virtually at an end, than in 1935 when the British empire flourished. The vitality of an institution is inversely proportionate to the perfection of its planning![2]

Yet, plan we must and even such a spiritual reality as mission needs structures. The question is: What structures does it need? And, more specifically: Do *missionary institutes*, societies exclusively dedicated to missionary work, still have a task in the future? In the past two centuries these institutes have proved themselves effective instruments in channeling men and women to distant posts. Have these instruments now outlived their usefulness? Are new tools required for the church of tomorrow? To borrow from Buddha: Are our missionary institutes rafts we should be prepared to abandon because we have reached the other side of the river?

Fundamental Questions

The history of the last few decades records many factual changes in the third world, that is, in the countries that were considered par excellence the scene of mission. Between 1946 and 1980, seventy-seven of these countries gained independence. In 1945 the United Nations counted sixty-six member states; the present number is over 150. In the church, too, developments in these countries have been spectacular. In 1929 only one in every 150 mission ordinaries was indigenous; now indigenous bishops form 80 percent of the total.

On February 24, 1969, the Congregation for the Evangelization of Peoples recognized the new situation officially. In an instruction of that date it laid down new norms concerning the relations between local bishops and missionary institutes. The congregation abrogated the previous arrangement by which certain territories, by the *ius commissionis*, had been entrusted to religious orders or missionary institutes. From now on it was the local bishops' conferences and the individual bishop of each diocese who were to hold the key position in the organization of personnel. It is the local bishop who draws up an official contract with the missionary institute, which, under the patronage of the Roman Congregation, is then acknowledged as a "mandatum"; before, however, the mandatum is given, the local bishop has to submit to the Holy See in writing the opinion of the episcopal conference about the contract. The local bishop can also admit other institutes without a mandatum and without the obligation of prior consultation with an institute that already possesses a mandatum.[3]

Able Managers, Poor Mandataries?

From a missionary point of view, the new arrangement was the right one. It was the logical consequence toward which mission had worked from its beginning. It gave concrete expression to a general realization that the time was ripe in many countries for the local church to take over full responsibility for its own management and future. By acknowledging the central position of the local bishop, the new arrangement both crowned the work of previous missionary effort and laid the foundation of enduring new growth.

However, it cannot be denied that the new situation also presented societies with new problems. First of all, many missionaries were not really prepared for the new servant role expected of them. Cardinal Malula of Kinshasa, Zaire, described the new situation in no uncertain terms:

> Missionaries should understand and humbly accept that it is the Africans themselves who in the first place Africanize Christianity. . . . Specifically this means: in the past it was the foreign missionaries who designed, conceived and executed the plans for the pastoral apostolate; now it will be the Africans who design, conceive and execute those pastoral plans. The roles have been reversed.[4]

The reversal of roles took many missionaries by surprise. In their day they might have been good managers; they certainly felt uneasy as "mandataries."

In a number of conflicts between local bishops and individual missionaries, matters were more complicated. In some of these instances the missionaries were the wronged party. Superiors of the institutes concerned often were at a loss whether it was their duty to support the prophetic role played by their own members or the official position of the bishop. What should one do if a particular bishop forbids concelebration, or denies his personnel the chance to take part in updating courses? Such differences of opinion, we know, should be resolved by open dialogue between "partners." The real problem, however, lies deeper. To what extent can a missionary institute insist on demanding a certain church policy or specific mission strategies? If it lays these down as conditions, does it not de facto claim the position of the "stronger partner"? The much-acclaimed withdrawal of the White Fathers from Mozambique, however legitimate in itself, raises questions about the kind of partnership we are in. Is staging a "walkout" the ultimate weapon?[5]

Another result of the new arrangement, which was not so obvious at the beginning but which becomes clearer day by day, is a disruption in the overall organizing process. In the past the mission areas of the world were roughly divided by Propaganda Fide and apportioned to societies and orders. Whatever the defects of the system, from an organizational point of view it worked extremely well in ensuring that personnel and resources were proportionately spread to all parts of the world. For the societies and orders involved it meant a clear definition of responsibilities; each community could expend its energies and available resources on a well-defined number of territories. The new arrangement has totally upset this overall structure. By making the local churches centers of organization in their own right, a process of decentralization has been begun of which the consequences cannot be gauged.

Acknowledging the central role of the local church was certainly a step forward. But it also created a climate of insecurity. As someone put it facetiously: missionary institutes that once monopolized particular markets and thus could export their goods (read "personnel") without restriction, now have to sell their ware to critical customers. And what if it turns out that nobody wants the merchandise?

"Go Home, Missionary"

The position of insecurity was strengthened by the repeated call for a moratorium on Western missionaries. For the average missionary who was so sure of being needed and of doing a worthwhile job, nothing could have been more unsettling. But the reasons for making this drastic suggestion were serious enough.

Ivan Illich was one of the first to call for such a moratorium when in a critical article in the magazine *America* (1967) he expressed misgivings regarding the new missionary concentration on South America. As Illich pointed out, instead of helping the local churches, this influx of European and North American personnel consolidated dependence and stifled real growth. In that same year 220 foreign priests working in Chile wrote an open letter to their bishops in which they expressed the following doubts:

Is our priestly presence in Chile an effective solution or does it delay the solution? Are we solving the problems, or is our presence the reason that the search for and the discovery of the real problems are postponed? What are we really achieving? Suppose that we were to leave the country today, would we not thereby promote the imagination and creative spirit of the national church so that it would look for more authentic and indigenous solutions?[6]

In 1971 the Reverend John G. Gatu of Kenya, chairman of the General Committee of the All Africa Conference of Churches, made an appeal that received wide publicity: "The problems of Third World churches can only be solved if all missionaries can be withdrawn in order to allow a period of not less than five years for each side to rethink and formulate what is going to be their future relationship."[7] In the next year the World Council of Churches Joint Committee on Ecumenical Sharing of Personnel, meeting at Choully, listed four components of the concept of moratorium:

1. withdrawal of present and discontinuation of future personnel sent into the service of receiving churches by foreign church agencies;
2. discontinuation of money given to support churches and their institutions by the same sources;
3. provision of a reasonable length of time to allow for review, reflection and reassessment regarding the revenues of money and personnel in response to the mission of God in our day and the searching for the selfhood of the church in mission;
4. seeing anew the living Lord incarnated in the local situation and expressing that lordship without foreign domination.[8]

At the World Council of Churches Assembly in Bangkok in January 1973 and again at the Assembly of the All Africa Conference of Churches at Lusaka in May

1974, the desirability of a "moratorium on missionaries" was once more publicly defended. Working Group 3 at Lusaka stated in their report: "Thus, as a matter of policy, and as the most viable means of giving the African Church the power to perform its mission in the African context, as well as lead our governments and peoples in finding solutions to economic and social dependency, our option has to be a MORATORIUM on the receiving of money and personnel."[9]

The Case for Pulling Out

The cat was out of the bag, the floodgates were open. By this time within Catholic circles, too, public discussion flared up. Those familiar with conditions prevailing in many missions recognized from the start that the moratorium idea has its merits. In particular the following facts were noted:

1. Many missionaries continue to extend Western cultural chauvinism. The process of indigenization and inculturation is greatly hampered by them.

2. By a kind of theological and ethical imperialism many Western missionaries impede the contextualization of theology in the local churches.

3. By clinging to traditions of authority Western missionaries often impede the growth of genuine local leadership.

4. Foreign missionaries generally receive more aid than their indigenous colleagues. Missionaries build up economic systems that contradict the lifestyle of the country and that cannot be continued in the future without dependence on outside help.

5. The presence of foreign personnel often slows down the recruitment of local leaders. The expulsion of missionaries has at times led to an unprecedented increase in local vocations.

Some advocates of the moratorium went much further by stating that the whole present missionary structure needs to be abolished. They attacked not only the mistaken attitude of individual missionaries, but the system as such. Fabien Eboussi, a Jesuit from the Cameroons, suggested that the missionary effort of the West may at present even function as an escape from its own religious crisis. He said that the present organization of mission is culturally a form of colonialism and therefore a system of violence that can only be terminated by a violent act. "The answer can be short: Europe and America should first convert themselves and the orderly departure of missionaries from Africa should be taken in hand."[10]

Even though a vast majority of bishops reaffirmed the need of missionary personnel "for many years to come," the legitimate questions raised by the discussion left many missionaries wondering.[11] And for many others, next to the rational arguments, a new sense of unease, an emotional insecurity was born. Are we really wanted? Is our work as necessary and useful as we pretend it to be? Or are we fooling ourselves? Healthy criticism was often mixed with self-pity, common sense with the childish desire to give up everything. Why be legionaries in a distant land if your services are not appreciated? And also, how long can the battle be fought without reinforcements?

Signs of Impending Death?

In its Decree on the Renewal of Religious Life, Vatican II envisaged the possibility, yes even the duty, of terminating religious orders or societies that are judged "not to offer any reasonable hope of further development" (*Perfectae Caritatis,* no. 21). In a later instruction of Pope Paul VI in 1966 it was made clear that the principal norm for deciding whether a religious institute has hope of further development should lie in its ability to attract new members:

> In attempting to reach a decision concerning the suppression of an institute or monastery, the following are the criteria which, taken together, one should retain, after one has taken all the circumstances into consideration: the number of members remains small, even though the institute or monastery has been in existence for many years, candidates have not been forthcoming for a long time past and most members are advanced in years (*Ecclesiae Sanctae II,* no. 41).

The decline of vocations in the West has seriously affected missionary societies. As a result some societies seem to present precisely the picture outlined in the norms suggested above. They hardly receive any new candidates and the vast majority of their members belong to the higher age brackets. Holland, for example, had 5,570 missionaries out in the field as of January 1, 1979 (compared to 8,806 in 1963). Their relative ages were: 7 percent under forty; 38 percent aged forty-one to fifty-four; 32 percent aged fifty-five to sixty-four; 19 percent aged sixty-five to seventy-four; 4 percent over seventy-five. During the 1970s the United States saw a decrease in missionaries abroad of 30 percent, West Germany of 15 percent. The number of Irish missionary personnel for 1979 was 5,613, compared to 7,085 in 1965. Some countries and some societies are doing better than others, but the decline has been felt everywhere.

The shortage of recruits has become another important factor in the critical self-examination that has begun. From a theological point of view J. B. Metz's book *Zeit der Orden?* helped to focus attention on the positive value of dissolving religious orders and societies at the right time:

> Our religious orders should cultivate something like an *ars moriendi*. They should do this not to express resignation, but to witness to the Spirit himself who teaches the art of "letting go" as an element of the topsy-turvy world of evangelical counsels and as a condition of being able to put them into practice. What is at stake here is the "art" of being able to stop and die, not only individually, but also together, as a religious foundation.[12]

Practical considerations often press for an immediate answer. Is it justified to keep many people involved in recruitment and formation work when the results are so meager? Should one continue to attract personnel for work abroad when the home church itself is in desperate need of vocations? Is it wise to accept new candidates, knowing that they will be greatly outnumbered by older members in an aging society? Father G. Linssen, Dutch provincial of the Scheut Fathers, put it this way:

> If we continue to try and bring young people into our ranks, we cause frustration both in the older members who do not understand the younger ones, and in the young members who can hardly come into their own because the older section of our societies has become too massive. The young people present now have enough problems as it is. In most cases they are not representative and go their own way, more or less apart from or only marginally concerned with, the activities of the society as a whole.[13]

"Hodie Mihi, Cras Tibi"?

Missionary societies of our day have to face the fundamental question about their future. Should they be encouraged to continue or should they be helped to die a graceful death? Are not the latest developments—resistance in the local churches and the lack of vocations at home—signs of the Spirit calling for a radical handing over?

It cannot be denied that missionary societies from the West should be prepared to face this question honestly. Preparing the way for others, self-effacement, yielding to successors are essential elements of the missionary task. Even the founders of missionary societies must have realized that the organizations they created had a specific and time-bound purpose. Cardinal Vaughan, the founder of Mill Hill Society, may be taken to speak for them all when he wrote in 1866:

> It must ever be borne in mind that a foreign missionary college is, by its very nature, only provisional and introductory; the end to be kept in view being to provide everywhere a good native clergy. . . . It may be said, therefore, that the duty of a foreign missionary college is to work towards its own extinction, by rendering its own existence superfluous through the formation of a sufficient native clergy.[14]

Although many of the problems discussed had their roots in earlier decades, it was mainly in the period 1970–80 that the future of missionary societies came to be questioned. It is true that the bulk of missionaries resisted any such idea and probably continues to resist it even today. But minority groups everywhere have started to raise doubts. On the missions it took the form of pushing for a planned phasing-out. At provincial and even general chapters, voices spoke of "bringing the sinking ship to harbor" and "winding up gracefully." In some countries recruitment is apologetically called "promotion." Many militant missionaries on home leave were saddened and angered by this *malaise,* this "sagging of missionary zeal," this "betrayal of Christ and the gospel." Prospective candidates for membership were put off by the disagreements and uncertainties, and joined other professions. For missionary societies the era of 1970–80 may truly be characterized as one of confusion, search, malaise, reproach, and self-examination.

Church history reckons in centuries, not in years. It is rare that such a flourishing movement as the missionary institutes should be so radically questioned in so short a time. Most societies are hardly a hundred years old. Their peak of world membership was reached only in 1965. Small wonder that for many the question seems too sudden, too drastic.

In this situation a clear answer is called for. If missionary institutes are to be discontinued, they owe it to the church and to their members willingly to go to the slaughterhouse. For what is the use of a band of Templars when the era of crusades has passed? But if, on the other hand, their work is to be continued, they should be able to do so with joy and conviction. For without motivation and enthusiasm mission work is doomed.

The missionary movement derived its strength from the conviction that mission work was what Christ wanted. The missionary knew he or she was doing a good job and this realization made him or her tenacious and adaptable. Till almost the day they were sent out, most men and women did not know whether they were going to be sent to Arctic regions there to live in igloos and learn Eskimo, or face the sweltering heat and unknown hazards of the African jungle. Some worked with their hands and built up hospitals, schools, churches. Others learned sophisticated skills and became experts in languages and cultures no outsider had ever known before. This sustained and monumental effort of hundreds of thousands of people was made possible by the underlying conviction that it was worth doing, that whatever the final outcome the task deserved sacrifice.

If missionary institutes will no longer serve a purpose in tomorrow's church, they should be laid to rest with honor. If, however, their usefulness remains, they need to be strengthened and encouraged.

Sociological Analysis

A missionary institute is a subgroup in a large social system. To understand the changes affecting such an institute, we need to analyze its position within the total system, that is, within the world church. That the church functions as a macro social-system can be deduced both from factual observation and from its theological definitions. Pius XI stated: "Three necessary societies exist, which are distinct from one another. . . . Two of these, the family and the civil state, are of the natural order. But the third, namely the Church, is a supernatural society . . . in which persons, through the rite of baptism, enter the life of divine grace."[15] Leo XIII wrote: "The Church is a perfect society, complete in nature and rites, not less than the civil state."[16] In the words of Vatican II: "This family [the Church] has been constituted and organized as a society in the present world by Christ and provided with means adapted to its visible and social union. Thus the Church, at once a visible organization and a spiritual community, travels the same journey as all mankind and shares the same earthly lot with the world" (*Gaudium et Spes*, no. 40). The church is also *seen* to be a social system because it unifies individuals and subgroups toward a common aim through the mechanisms known from other social systems.

The church is certainly a mystery. The sacramental presence of Christ, the action of the Holy Spirit, and internal grace are realities that cannot be observed. In this respect the church is a social system that cannot be fully covered by sociological analysis. On the other hand, because the church is by definition truly incarnate in human realities, it follows that the church is *at the same time* a social system that will exhibit all the idiosyncrasies of human organizations. Just as a psychiatrist may have valid insights regarding a religious vocation even though some aspects of it may transcend scientific observation, so sociologists can offer reliable insights regarding social changes in the church.

The sociological approach is all the more justified in the particular study we are engaged in now. Because what we are considering is not the nature of the church as a whole but the specific position of missionary institutes within it. The existence of such institutes can in no way be said to be essentially linked to the nature of the church. They are human inventions created at a particular moment in history to respond to a specific challenge. They are not indispensable. They clearly belong to that part of the church's organization that is human, external, and time-bound. They can rightly be subjected to the scrutiny of the "human" science of sociology.

Approaching the discussion from a sociological point of view will, we hope, also contribute to making it less emotional and subjective. We need to find objective norms for establishing whether missionary institutes will also in the future respond to a real need. The study of comparative social processes can be very helpful indeed. When the coal pits in Holland were closed and people switched to natural gas and electricity for heating, some professions went out of business altogether, such as the mining engineers and the chimney sweeps. Other professions adapted their role to the new situation: shops that used to furnish fireplaces now specialize in gas furnaces and electric hearths. Why does one group survive when the other does not?

In this section we shall try to work with generally accepted sociological terms.[17] As there is some latitude in the way some of these terms are handled by different authors, we shall briefly explain under each heading our particular understanding of the terms used.

Social Changes

Social systems are held together by values commonly adhered to, by regulative norms of expected behavior and roles attributed to individuals or subgroups. When the inner structure of a society changes, the effects will be seen in all these elements. What we witness in the church today is precisely such a process of social change.

The subgroup we are discussing has relationships with many other subgroups among which the principal ones are the home churches, the churches in the third world, religious orders, and the Roman congregations. These groups could be divided again into more specific subdivisions. The home church, for instance, can be broken up as comprising the hierarchy, circles of benefactors, national missionary offices, aid agencies, the local Catholic press, and so forth. With all these subgroups and further subdivisions of these subgroups a missionary institute has an intricate network of relations. It is this network of mutual relationships that is held together by values, roles, and norms.

When we examine *the values* prevailing in the church today, we may first identify a large block that have remained unchanged from former times. Such lasting values, which were accepted in previous centuries and are still considered valid today, are, for instance, belief in Jesus Christ, the sacramental system, organizational unity, catholicity in brotherhood, and so on. Certain values, on the other hand, have been considerably modified in the past few years. To mention just a few that are relevant to the mission task, we observe that instead of emphasis on apologetic defense of one's own orthodoxy there is now more appreciation for what is good in Protestant churches or in non-Christian religions. The new values involved are generally referred to as "ecumenism" and "dialogue with other religions." In the past there was a tendency to look on mission as planting the church, as establishing it as an institution. Nowadays concern will focus more on the faithful as living Christian communities, on their everyday life in a concrete human situation. The former concept of a Christian Europe giving aid to pagan and primitive races is rapidly giving way to the discovery that all six continents have equal standing and are equally in need of mission.

We observe similar changes when we study *the role* and *the status* accorded to missionaries. The social role of a subgroup consists of its cluster of obligations toward the other groups. Its status is the cluster of corresponding rights, the obligations that other subgroups have in return. Whereas missionaries in the past were in charge of the mission, were expected to take the initiative and to have full responsibility, now this role is defined, rather, in terms of assisting the local bishop and of serving the young church. This has resulted in a considerable loss of status. The missionary of today has become much more vulnerable. His superiority is no longer taken for granted. As Cardinal Malula said: "A real reversal of roles has taken place."

Regulative norms within a social system are specific patterns of expected behavior. They describe the limits of permissible action, what some category of persons must do, may do, or must not do. Norms too have altered appreciably in the missionary world. In previous decades missionaries had a rather free hand; they could make their own decisions. Today, whether they are parish priest or matron of a maternity ward, principal of the school or development director, they are expected to act only after consultation. More than in the past, missionaries now need to show respect for the local culture and customs of the country they are working in. Other norms have remained unchanged. As in the past, missionaries are expected to be available to anybody at any time, to treat people justly and impartially, never to shame someone in public. But the requirement of language has become stricter; people will be more critical if missionaries do not speak the native tongue or if their mastery of the language is grossly defective.

It is in no way our intention to be exhaustive in describing such changes. Obviously there are vast differences between countries and their Christian communities. For our purpose it suffices to show that the position of missionaries and missionary institutes is being subjected to new social pressures. The organizational change from the *ius commissionis* to the mandatum and the call for a moratorium on Western missionaries reflect these social pressures in tangible form. But does this transmutation of values, roles, and norms overturn or reduce the *function* of missionary institutes?

What Does "Function" Mean?

The notion of "function" plays a key role in analyzing social processes. It is important to understand it properly. The term originated in biology where it came to express how a particular organ was useful to an entire organism. So one could ask: "What is the function of the taste buds on the human tongue"? In an analogous fashion the term is now applied to the services and usefulness of a part for the whole social system to which it belongs. "Any partial structure—a type of subgroup, a role, a social norm or a cultural value—is said to have a *function* if it contributes to the fulfilment of one or more of the social needs of a social system or subsystem; any partial structure is said to have a *dysfunction* if it hinders the fulfilment of one or more of these needs."[18]

Function needs to be distinguished from purpose. On the death of a chieftain, members of the clan may gather from far and wide with the purpose of paying him the last respects and assisting at his funeral. Within the social system of the tribe, however, the funeral celebrations may well have functions different from the purpose, such as affording the opportunity of communication and of keeping the clan together. Some functions that are clearly perceived are known as "manifest functions." Other functions, which are not normally adverted to, yet significant for the survival or welfare of the social system, are referred to as "latent functions." The custom, widespread in Asia, of marrying with preference a daughter of a maternal uncle, has a latent economic function, namely, it keeps agricultural property within the family and so favors economic stability. Latent functions are unrecognized and unintended.

Not all functions are "primary." Some are called "secondary" because they are of less significance, or benefit only part of the total social system. Support to the social system as such can be given by helping it retain its structures (pattern maintenance), by making it respond successfully to new demands (adaptation), by securing some of its desired objectives (goal attainment), and by harmonizing relationships between groups (integration). The primary function of the army in a particular country may be that it guarantees the national security and stability of law and order. Another primary but latent function may be that it solves part of the unemployment problem. The army may also have secondary functions such as absorbing aggressive elements of society by giving them a useful purpose and stimulating basic research, which also benefits commercial industry. All these functions are distinct from the army's "roles," which may change from time to time. The army may, for instance, be called upon to guard prisoners, to exercise police functions during a time of social unrest, or to man the fire stations when the firemen are on strike.

Recognizing something as a function or dysfunction does not imply an ethical judgment. In primitive society polygamy had a very useful selective function: it ensured procreation through the most competent male leaders. The caste system in India helped to maintain an almost immutable structure of roles and statuses. It is clear that polygamy and the caste system also have dysfunctions for the society in which they are practiced so that these societies might well be better off without them. The ethical judgment on the intrinsic merit, on its being conducive to the common good or not, can be made only after an objective assessment of the social functions involved.

The question that now lies before us is: What were and what are the functions of missionaries as a subgroup within the overall system of the church? What does this group actually *do*? How does it fulfill the needs of the church or of subsystems of the church? Can we distinguish primary and secondary functions? What consequences have the recent social changes for these functions?

The Functions of Missionaries

Within the overall church the missionaries as a subgroup have fulfilled and are fulfilling fourteen functions. We shall list them here with a short description and justification for each. Most of the facts we relate will be known to those familiar with the missionary scene so that we feel excused from substantiating them at length. Although the order in which the functions are listed is not altogether at random, we do not by it want to imply any form of priority rating. At this stage our only intention is to distinguish the various functions of the missionary subgroup as factually as possible.

What then are the functions of the missionary subgroup?

1. *It provides witnesses to Christ and the Gospel:* If we take seriously Christ's words "You will be my witnesses . . . to the ends of the earth" (Acts 1:8), it should be recognized that precisely this kind of testimony has been given and is being given by numerous missionaries in countries and cultures where the gospel has not yet been widely accepted. Vatican II reaffirmed the need of such a witness in our own time: "In that case [when direct preaching is not possible] missionaries, patiently, prudently, and with great faith, can and ought at least to bear witness to the love and kindness of Christ and thus prepare a way for the Lord, and in some way make him present" (*Ad Gentes*, no. 6). In many countries missionaries have fulfilled and are fulfilling this function on behalf of the church.

2. *It starts new communities of faith:* In many countries where no community of believers existed, through the action of missionaries such living cells of faith have begun to flourish. To mention but one example: Zaire now has 12 million Catholics (50 percent of the population) divided over fifty-one dioceses. "Missionaries, the fellow workers of God, should raise up communities of the faithful, so that walking worthy of the calling to which they have been called they might carry out the priestly, prophetic and royal offices entrusted to them by God. In this way the Christian community will become a sign of God's presence in the world" (*Ad Gentes*, no. 15).

3. *It expands the church throughout the world:* "The special end of this missionary activity is the evangelization and the implanting of the Church among peo-

ples or groups in which it has not yet taken root. . . . With their own hierarchy and faithful, . . . they should contribute to the good of the whole Church" (*Ad Gentes,* no. 7). We are here highlighting the aspect of establishing the international structure of a hierarchically linked church. At present practically the whole world is covered by a network of dioceses that are united in ecclesiastical territories under archbishops. The ecclesiastical territories of one or more independent countries are coordinated by bishops' conferences. In the territories under Propagation of the Faith alone there are sixty-six such episcopal conferences.

4. *It educates an indigenous clergy:* Much has been achieved in this field. In Africa, for instance, there are fifty-six major seminaries with a total of 4,836 students of philosophy and theology. In 1979, 293 priests were ordained, bringing the total of indigenous African clergy to well over 5,000.[19]

5. *It stimulates evangelical ventures:* Studying the history of missions in the past century we observe that small groups of missionaries often experimented with new approaches and thus initiated important developments. Dialogue with ancient religions, indigenization of the liturgy, and the use of the mass media in the apostolate, for instance, had been advocated by missionary groups before they were commonly accepted as values. Even though the bulk of missionaries may not have been directly involved, by providing creative minds and prophetic spokespersons the missionaries as a subgroup made a significant contribution to the church's need for constant adaptation. Consider the example of Muslims in India, who now number well over 70 million. "Up to the time of Vatican II," writes Charles Troll, "Father Victor Courtois, S.J., has been the only Catholic in India to propagate consistently the need for an apostolate among Muslims and, as part of an over-all vision, to evolve a concept of the methods to be used, the attitudes to be fostered."[20]

6. *It promotes mission awareness:* In the traditionally Christian countries the activities of missionaries have greatly helped to make Catholics aware of their responsibility toward the missions. For purposes of recruitment and fund-raising, missionaries preach in churches and address children in the schools. The 285 Catholic mission magazines in the West reach a vast proportion of Catholic homes. In third world countries, too, the presence of missionaries helps to keep the purpose of evangelization alive.

7. *It strengthens human and religious values:* In many ways all over the world the missionary presence has had a great influence in safeguarding human and religious values. The abolition of slavery is an achievement mainly of Protestant missionaries, although Catholics too had their pioneers in this field, such as Bartholomew de las Casas. Or, to take another example, the emancipation of women in India was furthered most by the Christian mission. V. A. Smith writes:

> The targets of disapproval, though not all brought forward at the same time, were suttee [suicide of a widow at her husband's death], infanticide, child marriage, the plight of Hindu widows, purdah [seclusion of women from public society], polygamy and temple prostitution. The first two of these were regarded as general moral evils, and as such were attacked by the government itself, the first by legislative enactment and the second by a mixture of pressure

and prosecution. The rest came within the scope of local custom and as such escaped official action. It was the missionaries who supplied the positive foil to negative government action not only by criticism, but also by setting forth a conception of womanhood new to the India of the day and by providing living examples of its nature.[21]

8. *It builds up new service structures:* In many parts of the world missionaries have been and are the pioneers in building up service structures that are of great use to the people. Under this heading may be comprised educational institutions (from the classical system to present-day adult literacy programs), health care, youth movements, and development projects. Many states now reap the fruits of the research, the experience, and the organizational skills that have gone into establishing such social services. To cite just one testimony: "This world has seen many wonderful teachers, but among the most wonderful are surely the missionaries. . . . The Society of Jesus was one of the most powerful educational forces the world has ever felt; it could educate a French nobleman, an Indian chief, a Chinese mandarin's son and a Polish squire with the same tact and charm, towards approximately the same ends."[22] It is interesting to note that in the present discussion on educational systems, Jesuits take a leading role in proposing radical reforms.[23]

9. *It aids the process of international integration:* For a large social system such as the church it is a great advantage if constituent parts are linked not only from the top through subordination to leadership, but also directly by immediate contact at all levels. This has been achieved to a great extent. Missionaries injected useful ideas from their countries of origin and, vice versa, their experience in young churches sparked off new initiatives at home. The archbishop of Seoul writes: "Missionaries bring to the Korean Church aspects of the universal church, be it French, German, Dutch, or whatever, which keep the local church aware of its international nature."[24] In a penetrating article S. H. Sekimoto of Japan points out the theological and practical advantages of having foreigners involved in the local church.[25] An example of inverted mission may be the influence of liberation theology and the basic community approach, which has come to Europe and the United States from South America.

10. *It supports church structures in third world countries:* In many countries of the third world a large proportion of missionary personnel is engaged in pastoral care for already baptized Christians. Running parishes, schools, and hospitals, they support—some would say "prop up"—the ordinary pastoral structures found in dioceses all over the world. The reason given for this situation is the lack of indigenous personnel. A look at Kenya may show what we mean. The twelve dioceses of that country number a total of 2,140,000 Catholics. There are only 102 indigenous priests, so that the pastoral responsibility for them falls mainly on the shoulders of the 649 missionary clergy. Also the majority of the 209 religious Brothers and 1,607 religious Sisters are foreign.[26]

11. *It impedes the growth of the local church:* The demand for a moratorium on foreign missionaries discussed earlier in this paper illustrates vividly that in many of the young churches the continuing presence of foreign missionaries is felt to be

counterproductive. It would seem that at least in a number of instances the misgivings are supported by facts. Dependence on foreign missionaries hinders the development of self-reliance, slows down recruitment, and obstructs inculturation. One clear incident may exemplify the implications. The Muslim government of Malaysia expelled, between 1970 and 1973, thirty out of the forty missionary priests in the Diocese of Sabah. The diocese had then only nine local priests, four of whom were Chinese from mainland China. The initial shock was traumatic. Eight parishes had to be closed; many of the 234 outstations could be visited only with great difficulty. But the population rallied in an unexpected way by a much greater lay involvement and a wave of new vocations. Now, ten years later, there are twenty-three local priests and the church is flourishing.

12. *It enhances the status of the West:* Missionaries went out with the best of intentions, but also with prejudices about the country and the people they were going to serve. "Men and women of their age, they too considered that the infinite superiority, from every point of view, of Western society over the heathen world was beyond question," writes McKeown.[27] In modern times the missionary's personal attitude may have improved, but the psychology underlying much aid-giving has not. The chief motivation is still pity, rather than respect and love. Missionaries tend to hold out the church of their home countries as examples of Christian faith and practice, while stressing the helplessness and backwardness of third world peoples when back in their countries of origin. It all shows that mission work, however good in itself, was and is fulfilling a psychological need of the West, namely, to prove to itself and to others its own superiority.

13. *It fulfills the heroic self-image of Western missionaries:* We don't want to call into doubt the sincere religious commitment that motivated missionaries. Yet it should be recognized that the missionary movement coincided with a century of discovery and adventure for the West. In the missionary ideal Western youth found a cause worthy to live for, a program that would fulfill deep-seated desires to open new avenues and conquer the world. It is significant that the biggest explosions of missionaries came from Catholic communities that were struggling to free themselves from oppression, such as the Irish and the Dutch. One of the most successful magazines in attracting vocations was called *Heroes of the Mission Fields*.

14. *It serves as an escape from problems in the West:* Fabien Eboussi maintains that the recent efforts to reanimate the flow of missionaries from the West is a defense mechanism that seeks to divert attention from the serious religious crisis in the West to problems in the third world.[28] Although it is difficult to substantiate this hypothesis, he may be right to some extent. In any case, it can be argued that some individual missionaries prefer to work in third world countries either because they cannot cope with the religious changes in their home churches, or simply because they find a better response abroad.

Brief Sociological Assessment

As far as we can judge, the fourteen functions and dysfunctions enumerated above are factual. Three are obviously dysfunctions, namely, the impeding of the growth of the local church (no. 11), enhancing the status of the West (no. 12), and serving as an escape (no. 14). Some may partly be dysfunctions. The three obvious dysfunctions are all latent in the sense that they are unintended and usually not adverted to. Also latent are fulfilling the heroic self-image (no. 13), aiding international integration (no. 9), and, perhaps, stimulating evangelical ventures (no. 5). The directly evangelical functions (nos. 1–7) are clearly primary; the others would seem to be derived, and hence secondary.

The questions we shall have to answer now are the following: *(a)* Are the dysfunctions intrinsic to the missionary movement? If not, how can they be counteracted? *(b)* Have any of the functions outrun their usefulness? Have they been completed? *(c)* Are there functions that would need to be preserved in the future for the good of the whole social system, the church? *(d)* Are missionary institutes a good way of preserving those necessary functions?

We shall answer these questions in the next section. Our reply will rest on a wider basis than purely sociological considerations. Yet the parallel with ordinary social systems is close. John LeCarré describes in his novel *The Spy Who Came in from the Cold* how a spy organization tries to prolong its existence after the war. When the country needed its services, the organization had been highly successful; but now it hardly serves any function. By a kind of natural impetus the organization starts to produce reasons to justify itself, with fateful consequences for a misguided agent who is sent on a futile and self-destructive mission. Could missionary institutes be validly compared to this?

Or are missionary institutes, rather, in the same situation as the renowned research institute for poliomyelitis in the United States? This institute, with a staff of more than one thousand members, was totally geared to research on that particular disease. When the appropriate vaccine had been discovered, the institute seemed to have become redundant overnight. However, an analysis of its functions revealed that, although its immediate function of research into poliomyelitis no longer had a justification, its latent primary function of serving medicine in general was as valid as ever. What had been set up for poliomyelitis research became the Salk Institute for Biological Studies. Over a number of years the personnel were retrained, the laboratories transformed, and the library extended to adapt fully to this new objective. The institute flourishes as never before.[29]

Future Needs

A study of the functions described in the previous section leads to the conclusion that, while some may have become redundant, others have not. In our view it would be a mistake to disband the missionary institutes that are *ex professo* fulfilling such functions in the church. For the sake of clarity we shall marshal our thoughts as a chain argument, to show that the task of evangelization still needs to be done, that full-time missionaries will be required in the carrying out of this task, and that missionary institutes continue to be useful mechanisms for bundling the contribution of such full-time missionaries. However, missionary institutes will need to be adapted in line with the functions they will have to exercise in the future.

Springcleaning

Our sociological analysis brought to light that the mission endeavor of the last few centuries contained a hidden element of religious colonialism. Western countries held the third world in a stranglehold grip. Willy-nilly, missionaries too were caught up by the social structures of the day. Unknowingly, by their very zeal they became one more mechanism by which the West furthered its superiority. The ambitious aid given to millions of the "poor and needy natives" of newly conquered countries greatly enhanced the status of the West (function no. 12). Without realizing it, intrepid missionaries confirmed their own self-image of Western enterprise and heroism (function no. 13). Their very efficiency, not less than their complacent clinging to Western cultural and religious values, hindered the growth of the local church (function no. 11). In some cases frenzied activity in countries where they felt lord and master may have disguised the inability to cope with the religious problems at home (function no. 14). Both mission and missionaries have become tainted with a streak of colonialism.

This was far from the intention and explicit motivation nurtured by the missionaries. Missionaries, in fact, were one powerful factor that speeded up the end of the colonial era; they fought for human values (function no. 7) and built up service structures that educated people to self-reliance (function no. 8). But neither the avowed intentions nor these valuable services could prevent that the whole *system* of missionizing indirectly perpetuated forms of dependence. It is obvious that a good springcleaning was and is necessary in this field. A whole new situation has arisen that requires a fresh approach. When a mother wants her teenage daughter to become independent and mature, she may have to rethink the way she runs the house. To become an adult partner the daughter too will have a say in how things should be organized. The new developments in the church demand a similar transformation: a removal of "paternalism" and a reshuffling of relationships.

The church has already acted by handing the responsibility for the ecclesiastical territories to the local hierarchy. Much more needs to be done. Western feelings of superiority need to be unmasked where they are hidden. Our structures as well as our thinking need to reflect the realization that there is need for evangelization in the whole world. Mission work is not a prerogative of the West; from now on missionaries should be recruited in all countries where Christian communities grow strong. We shall have more to say about these matters under the heading "Transformations."

Withdrawal

There is a saying in Holland: "As long as the master keeps an eye on the horse, it will grow fat." The proverb derives from a time when the Dutch farmer was more concerned about his horse than about its groom. The unnerving effect of the farmer's watchful presence on the farmhands was not even adverted to. This is characteristic of paternalism. Leaders imagine that they know best and so take personal responsibility for all details. They carry out tasks that others should do, in the belief that they themselves can do them better. They guide others in all things firmly convinced that they are helping in this way. In actual fact they often are an obstacle, hindering true progress by their interfering presence.

In such cases the only cure is withdrawal. Words cover up, good intentions avail nothing. Only the deed counts. Parents withdraw by allowing their adolescent child to take up a separate residence. The retiring manager withdraws by vacating his office for his successor. The commanding officer withdraws by leaving it to his platoon leaders to choose their own route to a target area. After a state of emergency the government withdraws from the press by no longer interfering in what it publishes. Withdrawal can take different forms, but withdrawal there has to be. The call for a moratorium was right in affirming its necessity.

In many countries—not only of the third world—missionaries support church structures by fulfilling pastoral ministries (function no. 10). As we shall point out later, one great disadvantage of this state of affairs is that it ties down men and women who should be mobile and employed in front-line evangelization. But another drawback, the one we are discussing now, concerns the psychological health of the emerging communities of faith. The continued presence of missionaries can indeed stifle local growth and stand in the way of true indigenization. The priority need of the local church should be honestly examined and withdrawal should be effected as soon as it is possible. It has been pointed out that a local bishop may sometimes not be a safe guide in judging the indispensability or dispensability of foreign personnel. A number of bishops may have vested interests. Foreign missionaries may be easier to control than indigenous personnel. They also guarantee the uninterrupted flow of financial aid. By keeping the traditional sacramental ministry well staffed the bishops may unconsciously want to delay necessary reforms.[30] In quite a few cases missionaries may well render the greatest service by a determined policy of withdrawal.

A word of caution may not be out of place here. We should not forget that many of the churches we are speaking about are relatively young and have had no time to build up the economic, social, and psychological resources needed to be truly self-reliant. Zaire may illustrate the point I want to make. Of its population of 25 million exactly half is Catholic. If we restrict ourselves to a consideration of the available clergy, we find that the fifty-one dioceses are served by a total of 2,506 priests. No more than one-third are indigenous. Even as things stand now there is one priest for every 5,000 faithful. Compare this to, let us say, England which, with a Catholic population of 4,220,750 and 7,315 priests, shows an average of 576 Catholics per priest. Even now the average priest in Zaire has to look after nine times more Catholics than his colleague in England, in a country fourteen times the size of England! If the foreign clergy were to be withdrawn, the task for the remaining African clergy would be made three times more demanding. It would be damaging and unfair to this young church, which counted 400,000 in 1923 and underwent a thirtyfold growth in fifty years to reach its present size of 12.5 million.

The same needs to be said regarding the building up of service functions (function no. 8) and the education of indigenous clergy (function no. 4). Minor and major seminary formation, Catholic education, health and welfare schemes, development projects, charitable works, and other organizations fall squarely under the competence and responsibility of the local bishop. Where help is genuinely needed, missionaries should remain involved. It is, after all, a "rounding off" of the overall missionary task. Yet here, too, there is need of withdrawal as soon as the local church can take over. The withdrawal should be gradual and deliberate. Even if a total disengagement cannot be effected, responsibilities and positions should be relinquished in stages.

But what about the moratorium itself, the total withdrawal? Can the missionary task not be left in principle to the local churches?

Mission Completed?

It is not uncommon these days to hear people glibly speak of "the end of the missionary era." What these will say can be summarized in a few lines: "The purpose of the missions was to plant the church all over the world. This has now been done. The gospel has been announced in all countries. Local churches have been set up everywhere. From now on there will only be the need of an exchange of help between sister churches." To anyone who knows what church is about and is aware of the real situation in the world, the absurdity of the statement is apparent. It is like saying that we have solved juvenile delinquency in Europe because Interpol has been established; or that economic progress in the third world is now ensured because the World Bank has branches in all countries. To many people, however, the statement seems to be plausible enough. So, with apologies to readers who may feel we are flogging a dead horse, we shall set about demolishing the fallacy. Nothing is as pernicious as a plausible untruth.

Have local churches been established everywhere? If by "local church" one means "having a bishop from the same country," then the answer can be Yes. Most countries now have been divided into dioceses, and the care for these dioceses has in most cases been entrusted to a bishop from the same country. A new hierarchical network spans the world. If this is what planting the church was supposed to do (see function no. 3), then the church has been planted almost everywhere, and this particular function of missionaries has been concluded to a large extent.

But surely this would be too restricted an understanding of local church. In fact it would seem to portray an entirely inadequate view of what "church" is all about. In the words of Avery Dulles, it would amount to an acceptance of the institutional model at the expense of the church as communion, as sign, as herald, and as servant.[31] We cannot speak of a "church" unless there is a community of faith capable of being a sacrament of salvation, a herald of the good news, and actively involved in bringing about the kingdom of God. To be a "local" church it should be rooted through membership and ministers in the people of a particular place.

What happens if we apply these notions to the world as we know it? Let us consider the case of a diocese in northern India: Satna in the state of Madya Pradesh. In a population of 4.5 million there are 825 Catholics distributed over ten mission stations. A large proportion of these do not belong to the local Hindi population, but are Anglo-Indians or businessmen who have emigrated from the south. All the missionary personnel, with possibly one or two exceptions, come from the state of Kerala: the bishop, his twenty-eight priests and sixty-seven religious. Let us realize what these facts mean. Out of the 4,000 towns and villages in the diocese only ten have small Catholic congregations. Moreover, even in these congregations Hindi-speaking society is hardly represented either in leadership or in composition. May this be called a "local church"?

It is not an isolated example. In 1976 the total population of the Hindi states of Uttar Pradesh, Madha Pradesh, and Bihar was estimated to be 194 million. If we don't include the half-million Catholics in the ethnic areas of Ranchi and Raighar, Catholics in this vast area number only 350,000.[32] The overall picture is much the same as that found for the Diocese of Satna. A large proportion of the faithful and the bulk of church personnel hail from non-Hindi ethnic groups. Even if in a number of localities a new beginning has been made and real indigenous communities of faith are emerging, these are only a few drops in the ocean of the Hindi world, a bare 2 per 1,000, a sprinkling of 12,000 small groups[33] in a total of more than 170,000 townlets and villages in that part of India. If in an average village of 850 inhabitants forty families are Catholic, does that make them the "local church" for that village, *and* for 1,000 totally Hindu villages surrounding it? Would it not seem rather preposterous to pretend that the local church has been established in such areas? Should we not, rather, speak of "some local churches springing up in isolated places"?

These observations would seem to hold, by and large, for the whole of Asia. Most of its 49 million Catholics are made up of the pockets of the Philippine Islands (30 million), Kerala (4 million), and Flores (1 million). The remaining 14 million form less than 7 per 1,000 of all people in Asia and, let us not forget, we are dealing here with some of the largest countries in the world: China, India, Indonesia, Japan, Pakistan, Bangladesh, and so forth, many of which are composed of populous and important national subgroups. When they will have grown out to 60 percent of humanity in the year 2000, reaching the 3 billion mark, the Christian proportion will be even smaller than it is today. The framework of 363 ecclesiastical divisions that now link these churches in diaspora, however much an achievement in itself, cannot be taken as a sign that mission has been completed.

The Great Commission

In the previous paragraphs we were somewhat preoccupied with geographical considerations when discussing the question: Has mission been completed? We saw that even from a territorial point of view, large areas of the world have not yet been evangelized. We should now like to extend the discussion to other, undoubtedly more important, dimensions of evangelization. Again we ask the question: Has mission been completed, has our world been evangelized?

We live in a world where unemployment, destitution, and starvation ruin the lives of millions of people. The gap between rich and poor countries increases as time goes on. National and international systems of oppression are sustained by violence or by unjust economic means. The average citizen of the rich countries uses up thirty times more of the world's resources than his or her counterpart in underprivileged countries. A worker in these latter countries may have to work, without social security, a ten-hour day to earn the same amount of food that can be earned by a worker in an affluent society in well under ten minutes.

It is not our intention here to repeat such well-known statistics. But we need to remind ourselves constantly of their reality. And we need to face these realities as they are experienced by thousands of millions in their daily lives. It is individual people who suffer. Follereau writes:

> When you want to eat, don't say, "I am hungry!" but think of the 400 million young men and women who will have nothing to eat today. . . . One day when I was traveling in Asia I was called to a dying leprosy patient. She was young, twenty-two years. I saw her breathe out her pitiful life in brief spasms. When she had died, I felt a bizarre urge to weigh her. I took her emaciated body, still warm, onto my arms and carried her to a scale. This young woman of twenty-two years weighed 25 kilograms [3.5 stones or 49 pounds]. Now you know what she died of.[34]

Untold misery and an unforgivable violation of human life lie hidden in every such case.

In terms of our functions it means that today as never before there is a need for defending human and religious values (function no. 7). The urgency of this need was recognized by Vatican II and has been repeatedly stressed by the last four popes. The world needs to be evangelized by an aggressive program for justice on all levels. If anywhere, it is here that we find one of the frontiers between church and world, a border area where mission will need to continue.

Another reality of our world is the fact that humankind is divided by a number of ideologies. The principal systems of thought outside Christianity are communism, secular humanism, Islam, and the ancient religions of Asia. Each of these four groups poses a major challenge to the task of evangelization.

In this task the only effective tool available to Christians is witness. Political force or economic pressure, even if they could be brought to bear on the issues, would prove utterly useless. Education, the mass media, and other social mechanisms can only provide additional help. The basic approach will have to be one of Christian witness. In the past, missionaries were engaged in witness by their voluntary presence among peoples of totally different cultures and religions, by their concern for the poor and the needy, and by their way of life (function no. 1). Yet the aspect of witness was often overshadowed by the urgency of other commitments. Most energy and time were poured into evangelizing those who could readily be converted, in constructing buildings, and in external organization. In many places the missionary was admired more for indefatigable devotion to work than for resemblance to Christ in lifestyle and prophetic detachment.

Witness is the essence of ecumenism and dialogue. To achieve results in this field nothing short of a metamorphosis will do. The many initiatives that have already been begun need to be supported and intensified. A new generation of Christians needs to be raised who will give a new meaning to Christ's words: "You will be my witnesses . . . to the ends of the earth." The question is: Should there be professional missionaries among them?

Front-line Troops?

So far we have encountered three functions of the missionary subgroup that would need to be continued in the future: (1) starting new communities of faith (function no. 2); (2) promoting human and religious values (function no. 7); (3) witnessing to Christ and his gospel (function no. 1). It is obvious from a little reflection—and from reading the documents of Vatican II—that these forms of evangelization are the responsibility of the whole church. Bishops, priests, religious, and the laity all have their part to play. But if this is the case, is there still a specific role for full-time missionaries?

There is no contradiction between a general obligation involving the whole church and a specific full-time task entrusted to a few. On the contrary, this is the way social systems work. If a country needs to defend itself, it creates an army of professional soldiers to bear the brunt. Similarly, to maintain law and order it trains police; to impart education, teachers; to staff its hospitals, doctors and nurses; and so on. In much the same way the overall obligations of the church have given rise to various ministries and religious professions. Deacons were set aside to minister to the poor, priests to preside over communities as assistants to the bishops. The call for repentance produced anchorites and monastic orders. When the duty to pray and worship was in danger of being neglected, contemplatives came forward to endorse the point. When the life of priests became encumbered by wealth and landed property, the church called forth its mendicants. Small wonder that a church anxious to evangelize encourages full-time missionaries.

However, there is a realistic danger too in creating such professional bodies. The services rendered by the welfare state, for instance, have lowered people's care and love for one another. Why bother about your neighbors if every kind of eventuality —sickness, fire, juvenile delinquency, unemployment, and old age—are dealt with by state-appointed specialists? In an analogous way the existence of "specialist" missionaries could easily lead to a lessening of interest and involvement among the rest of the faithful. The exact role of the full-time missionary needs to be defined.

The missionary is a living expression of Christ "on the move": We read in the Gospels that Christ refused to "get stuck" in any limited locality. When people in Capernaum wanted to cling to him, he replied that he was called to proclaim the good news in other places too: "Let us go elsewhere . . ." (Mk. 1:38). In spite of his success in Sychar, he stayed there for only two days (cf. Jn. 4:40–41). Christ's ministry was seen as a journey and the Great Commission as an extension of that journey "to the ends of the earth." Many of Christ's instructions given to his disciples concerned their apostolic travels (cf. Lk. 9:3–6; 10:1–16).

In the early church it was soon recognized that the Christian communities needed a resident group of leaders and ministers. Their presence, too, was an expression of Christ's love. Each bishop was a steward appointed by God (cf. Tit. 1:7), a householder entrusted with the care of God's family (cf. 1 Tim. 3:4–5). But apostles were called to embody Christ's concern to move on: they crossed borders and opened up new communities. The difference can be clearly seen in the presbyters installed by Paul at Lystra (cf. Acts 13:23) and Timothy whom Paul recruited from Lystra one year later. "Paul . . . wanted to have him as a travelling companion" (Acts 16:3).

Although the imagery of physical displacement spoken of in traveling and moving on may not always apply literally, the reality described through it is actual enough. Today the gospel needs to move into large areas of the world that have hardly been touched so far: communism, secular humanism, Islam, and the ancient religions of Asia. To cross such boundaries is as challenging a task for the church of the future as it was for Saint Paul to enter the cities of Macedonia or for nineteenth-century missionaries to penetrate the jungles of Brazil.

To carry out this task of "Christ on the move" then as now, the services of specially called ministers will be required. This is, we are convinced, the specific missionary vocation spoken of in the Vatican Decree on the Church's Missionary Activity:

Although the obligation of spreading the faith falls individually on every disciple of Christ, still the Lord Christ has always called a number of his disciples, those whom he has chosen that they might be with him so that he might send them to preach to the nations (cf. Mk. 3:13 ff.). So the Holy Spirit who shares his gifts as he wills for the common good (cf. 1 Cor. 12:11), implants in the hearts of individuals a missionary vocation and at the same time raises up institutes in the Church who take on the duty of evangelization, which pertains to the whole Church, and make it as it were their own special task [*Ad Gentes,* no. 23].

The missionary is "set apart" for new apostolic ventures: All Christians have to leaven the world through their secular involvements. All Christians are supposed to be witnesses to Christ through the way they live. All Christians should preach Christ when the occasion arises. In this sense a dentist, a mechanic, a nurse, and a housewife can and should be apostles of Christ. But there are things that dentists, nurses— all those in secular professions—cannot do because they do not have the time and the charisms that are required. The first community at Antioch—which was very apostolic in the general sense—realized this. The Holy Spirit told them: "I want Barnabas and Saul set apart for the work to which I have called them" (Acts 13:2). This was the beginning of Paul's missionary journeys. Barnabas and Paul were designated to take up the apostolic ventures that were beyond the scope of the ordinary Christians.

In Saint Paul's time the charisms needed were no doubt the ability to travel, familiarity with Greek and Roman culture, a working knowledge of *koine* and other languages, a flair for striking up new acquaintances, the gift of rhetoric. But this was not all. Apostles had to be unencumbered and free. Had not Christ himself demanded such freedom by insisting that those who were to preach the kingdom should give up the three social securities of property, job, and family? Peter and Andrew, James and John, had to leave their nets to become fishers of men (cf. Mt. 4:19).

Candidate disciples were told they should not expect to possess even a stone to lay their heads on; they should leave the care of their families to other relatives: "Leave the dead to bury their dead" (Lk. 9:60). They should give up their home and their property, father and mother, brothers and sisters, wife and children (cf. Mt. 19:29). Barnabas and Paul were set apart for the missionary task because they not only had the abilities, but could also forego the social securities that tied down the other Christians at Antioch.

The demands of discipleship quoted here are rightly applied also to religious in general. Christ's words have a seminal character. His radical vision called forth, in the course of time, such later institutions as the three vows and a wide range of active and contemplative orders. But it should be noted that in New Testament terms *the missionary charism* is more fundamentally and directly linked to discipleship than any of these later forms of organization. To put it crudely: in the New Testament perspective the church could well do without Jesuits or the Daughters of Saint Paul; it could never be without full-time missionaries. Or in a different way: many Jesuits and Daughters of Saint Paul are full-time missionaries; this is more basic to their discipleship than belonging to either of these organizations. When Christ commissioned his disciples to preach the gospel to all nations, he could not but imply that among these disciples there would be, until his command be fulfilled, full-time missionaries who express in their lives a "going out," a "crossing of borders"; and who have the inner freedom and external detachment to do this effectively.

In our sociological analysis we observed that missionaries have stimulated evangelical ventures (function no. 5). This was made possible through a combination of a pioneering spirit and the freedom of the gospel described above. In future years such a creativeness and the willingness to risk all for Christ will be very much in demand. When Paul VI spoke of missionaries in *Evangelii Nuntiandi* (1975) it was those characteristics that he singled out for special mention:

> Other religious, in great numbers, give themselves directly to the proclamation of Christ. Their missionary activity depends clearly on the hierarchy and must be coordinated with the pastoral plan which the latter adopts. But who does not see the immense contribution that these religious have brought and continue to bring to evangelization? Thanks to their consecration they are evidently willing and free to leave everything and to go and proclaim the Gospel even to the ends of the earth. They are enterprising and their apostolate is often marked by an originality, by a genius that demands admiration. They are generous: often they are found at the outposts of the missions and they take the greatest of risks for their health and their very lives. Truly the Church owes them much [no. 69].[35]

The missionary should act as the church's conscience in the matter of its apostolic duty: We have already noted that missionaries promote mission awareness (function no. 6). Formerly this consisted mainly in recruitment and fund-rasing for mission in third world countries. Now this function will have to be given a new orientation. Wherever they are, missionaries should by their very existence, by their example, by the initiatives they undertake, and by proclamation remind the church of its obligation to evangelize. Do contemplatives not have a similar function? Surely their special dedication to prayer is not seen by others as a reason that would absolve them from their own obligation to pray; rather, it prompts them not to forget this dimension in their own lives. The presence of full-time missionaries should jog people's memories and consciences in much the same way.

And people's consciences need to be prodded. It is surprising how soon the established church settles into a situation of nonevangelization. In some European countries, for example, church directories will only indicate the number of Catholics in a diocese, not the number of *inhabitants*. Parish priests rarely step outside the circle of their Catholic parishioners; in fact, they may not even know *how many* other people belong to their area. This is indicative of a widespread apostolic lethargy, which sees the status quo as the attainable goal. The time has come for missionaries to raise their voices about this and to bring about a revolution.

Also in third world countries, in the traditional mission fields, much less evangelization is done than is generally realized.[36] Diocesan priests, religious, and laity alike are absorbed by the wants of their own Christian communities. Especially when evangelization seems unrewarding, the temptation to become inward-looking is amazingly strong. Here too the prophetic voice of missionaries should be heard, not to accuse the church but to keep alive its missionary charism.

These three then are the specific functions full-time missionaries will continue to have within the overall apostolic task of the church: to represent "Christ on the move," to undertake creative apostolic ventures, and to act as the church's missionary conscience. These functions are not opposed to the missionary obligation of others in the church: they underline it and are integrated with it.

The Bishops' Synod of 1974 provided an opportunity for high-level discussion on the merits and demerits of the moratorium idea. Although the need for withdrawal of various kinds was pointed out, it also resulted in a reaffirmation of the charism of professional missionaries. This is clear from the passage in *Evangelii Nuntiandi* (1975) quoted above. Pope Paul VI repeated his stand in his message for World Mission Sunday of 1977. We cite his words, not so much to lend magisterial authority to conclusions we have arrived at independently as to show that international thinking in the church endorses full-time missionaries. In fact, the call for future missionaries arises from the same international awareness and coordinating authority that clarified the apostolic obligation of the local churches. Accepting the latter does not exclude the former:

There is need, therefore, for apostles trained especially for the mission *ad gentes*, in accordance with the criteria laid down in the Council Decree of that name. If they are trained for this special task, with a developed sense of universalism, based on a true feeling for human and ecclesial values, then we shall have new apostles who will turn even difficulties into so many opportunities for evangelization. Only a thorough training which leads to a generous dedication of oneself will create the conditions for a new and flourishing missionary era. And this is a goal that cannot be improvised but must be pursued courageously in prayer, study, reflection, dialogue, commitment. And it is a goal that we would point out not only to future missionaries, but to all priests, religious, seminarians and laity.[37]

And What about Missionary Institutes?

The organization of full-time missionary work can be done in five different ways: (1) by free-lance initiatives; (2) through structures set up by the receiving church; (3) through structures set up by the sending church; (4) through religious orders; (5) through missionary institutes. All five approaches are being followed and all have proved their validity. In line with the purpose of this paper we shall focus special attention on missionary institutes. Our quarrel is with those who contend that these institutes should be disbanded because they "arose in a time of Western colonialism that has passed and in a missionary era that has been completed." Our reasoning will flow from a brief comparison of the five possibilities offered.

Free-lance missionaries are individuals or groups who take upon themselves evangelization without belonging to any recognized organization. A Christian doctor and his wife might decide to emigrate to Yemen to set up a medical practice there. The express purpose of this unusual step might be missionary as well as humanitarian. The notion of such "non-professional missionaries" was elaborated by Roland Allen in 1929. Allen pleaded for men and women of secular professions to go out to mission countries and live their Christian witness there. He wanted them to go independently from missionary societies and to see their main task in fulfilling their secular job in a truly Christian fashion. This witness would be more valuable than that of "professional" missionaries, Allen stated, because the latter are considered to belong to a special class and thus to be different from ordinary people.[38]

It is to be hoped that many convinced Christians will in the future take up such an apostolate.[39] However, this approach will never be the universal answer to mission. First of all, the witness through a Christian life needs to be complemented by the kerygma of spiritual ministers, as Allen himself conceded. Second, the missionary challenge is too wide and complicated for it to be tackled by such a haphazard approach. Third, since World War II many Christian lay men and women have been involved in missionary endeavors. Experience has shown that they require the guidance and support of an organization. Quite a number of lay missionary institutes have been formed, thus demonstrating that the free-lance approach may not be practical. Fourth, if missionary efforts were to be left to free-lancers only, little would in fact be done. To achieve the kind of "mass movement" that could have an impact on evangelization in the future would itself require a continuous and intensive campaign within the church. This in turn cannot be done without organization —bringing us back to square one. Mission cannot be left to free-lance initiatives.

In some parts of the world, *structures set up by the receiving church* try to attract full-time missionaries. An example of this is a seminary or novitiate in a missionary diocese recruiting candidates for its own needs from other dioceses or other countries. This works well when there is a natural relationship between the area that provides vocations and the area that needs them. In this way Ireland provided many priests and religious for English dioceses, Kerala and Goa for dioceses in the north of India. But the arrangement has its shortcomings too. It usually ends up in tying down the imported personnel in pastoral ministry. Above all, recruitment and the initial stages of formation have to be done in the candidates' place of origin. The organization required to recruit, train, and support personnel from a diversity of countries is well beyond the means of most missionary dioceses. What a number of such dioceses might then have to do, of course, is to entrust such recruitment, formation, and support to an intermediate organization. This might then develop into a missionary institute, as happened in the case of some of the new Indian missionary societies.

The organization of mission work could also be entrusted to *structures set up by the sending church*. Initiatives in this direction have been the Fidei Donum priests for Africa, the twinning of dioceses, and so forth. Its appeal lies in the persuasion that the whole home church, and not just a particular group within it, should carry the missionary burden. Here too the dreams of the 1960s and 1970s have given way to sober reflections. To sustain a many-sided and long-term missionary program, the appointment of some Fidei Donum priests will not do. Each sending church would need to establish a structure of experienced and capable persons to guide the planning, recruitment, formation, and support activities indispensable for such an intricate operation. Since mission requires the learning of new languages and cultures, short-term volunteers have only a limited usefulness; life members need to be enrolled. The structure that emerges would, for all practical purposes, become a parallel to the existing missionary institutes, most of which are already organized on national lines. Why should the church in France create a new institute when it has the Missions Etrangères de Paris? Or the church in Switzerland when it has the Bethlehem Missionaries? Rather than building up extra structures, the correct response would seem to lie in a better integration of the existing missionary institutes with the home churches from which they spring.

Religious orders have channeled more full-time missionaries to mission areas and apostolic tasks than all the other mechanisms taken together. The total commitment enshrined in religious life can easily be actualized in full-time missionary work. Many orders and congregations see evangelization as one of their explicit aims. Does this, however, mean that missionary institutes are redundant because religious orders could do the job equally well? In our opinion the answer is clearly No. Why should a person who wants to be a missionary have to embrace the life of a religious? Is the call to religious life not a special vocation, a vocation that is not necessarily linked to the missionary task? Franciscans, for example, have been among the most numerous and successful missionaries of the past centuries. But surely the ideal of Saint Francis—his simplicity, his love of nature, his radiant joy—and the specific Franciscan rule may not necessarily appeal to the spiritual and practical vision of a would-be missionary. In fact, it could be argued that an order such as the Franciscans was founded in the Middle Ages to respond to a particular need and that missionary institutes with their more flexible rules and modern spirituality are better suited to the missionary requirements of our times. The spiritual sons and daughters of the religious founders of the past will certainly fulfill their own ideals also in their missionary involvements. But why should this rule out the validity of exclusively missionary institutes, which put their discipleship totally at the service of evangelization in forms of organization suitable to our times?

It is obvious from what we have said so far that we strongly believe that *missionary institutes* still have a rightful place next to the other approaches and structures mentioned. If any particular institute fails to attract a sufficient number of vocations or if it cannot adapt to the changing demands that will be made on it ("Transformations," below), it should be terminated, as should any religious order in the same situation. But the contention that missionary institutes as such have had their time and should therefore be wound up has—to put it plainly—no leg to stand on. Missionary institutes will be needed simply because full-time missionaries need the fellowship and support that they can give them, because mission work cannot be done in a haphazard way, because any endeavor to organize the missionary input effectively will almost spontaneously give rise to missionary institutes. The present missionary institutes may have their bends and scars, as one would expect from veterans in a draw-out battle. Many of them will have the inner strength to respond to the new demand.[40] Other institutes will be founded to coordinate the missionary energy of the young churches or to meet the demands of new forms of apostolate. Missionary institutes are here to stay.

Transformations

It is remarkable that the university system, founded in the Middle Ages, has remained intact till our own days.[41] The reason for this is that its basic functions—educating graduates and furthering research—are as valid now as they were then. Yet when we compare Salamanca of the fifteenth century and Harvard of the twentieth, we notice that some changes—we call them "transformations"—have taken place. Many of the *concepts and values* adhered to by the professors and students are different now. Inductive science, standards of recording, approaches to education itself, and so on, have changed almost beyond recognition. *Structures* too have been adapted to modern requirements; the appointment of staff, examination procedures, and forms of consultation belong to our century. There has also been a notable shift in *the models* that unconsciously influence the behavior of lecturers and students alike. No longer will anyone today emulate Thomas Aquinas; they might worship Isaac Newton or Albert Einstein. We find a social institution still exercising its basic functions, but with a transformation of concepts, structures, and models.

This is what will happen to missionary institutes. They will remain because their functions still serve a purpose. Yet they ought to be transformed if they are to meet the needs of the church in the altered circumstances of tomorrow. A missionary institute that fails to keep up the pace will soon be as much an anachronism as a university in Oklahoma that would copy the early rules of the Sorbonne.

Concepts and Values

It is beyond the scope of this paper to attempt a listing of all the concepts that are currently being reassessed and transformed. We shall be satisfied if we shall have somehow indicated the extent of the transformation required in this area. Many new ideas are floating around. They will need to be tested and refined. Many of the recent insights have remained in the notional sphere. They have not yet been given flesh and blood in tangible projects. There is still an enormous gap between the traditional values believed in by the rank-and-file missionary and the ideals proposed by the avant-garde. We are witnessing the chaos before creation!

What does "kerygma" mean? How does it relate to "primary evangelization," "cross-cultural evangelization," "missionary outreach"? It now seems quite generally accepted that elements such as secular involvement and liberation cannot be separated from kerygma. The emphasis in the future will hardly be on obtaining as many converts as possible; rather, it will be on witness and dialogue. This dialogue in turn will need to be initiated not only with the great religious traditions, but with the whole existential world of the people one approaches. Its purpose will be that Christ may be discovered from the inside and then explicated. Numerical results in terms of converts may be meager or even nonexistent for a long time, but it is hoped that an incarnated Christianity will be the eventual outcome. What is initially the kingdom of God could gradually become the church of Christ.[42]

Talking about church raises many questions regarding the kind of church that is wanted. The aspect of church that receives most attention is *koinonia*. The local church should be seen as a true community of God's People in Christ rather than a juridical-hierarchical structure. There is also a search for church at grassroots level: the basic Christian communities. As communities where Christian love can be celebrated at its most intense and personal level, they have been called "a hope for the universal Church" (Paul VI); "the primary cells of the whole ecclesial edifice, centres of evangelization and an important factor for human development" (Cardinal Pironio); "the most local incarnations of the one, holy, catholic and apostolic Church" (East African bishops); or simply "the future of the Church" (Paul VI).[43]

The mutual assistance of sister churches, the *diakonia*, is also being scrutinized. In this area the task of the laity is receiving increasing attention. The role of the foreign missionary vis-à-vis the local bishop (servant and/or prophet) is closely linked with one's view on the interdependence of charisms. How can the service extended by aid agencies by interpreted in ecclesial terms? Should new ministries be called into existence and give concrete expression to forms of diakonia relevant to our world?

The implications of *missio* have been studied by groups and individual authors. In 1963 the CWME/WCC meeting in Mexico City coined the term "mission-in-six-continents," thereby seeking to replace the notion that "the missions" lie in third world countries. Apart from this geographical extension ("The church is in a missionary situation everywhere"), the concept is widened in ambience ("Mission is the crossing of all frontiers, whether geographical, cultural, social, ethnic, or spiritual"). Such a sweeping change in the definition of mission signals the advent of important new values. One problem is that the notion may become more of an adjective than a noun (or would it be wrong to say that China is more mission than Ireland?). Moreover, by a tendency to call everything mission its contents are eroded. It is like saying that everyone, somehow, is a Christian; or a pagan, for that matter.

This sketch of present-day discussion of concepts and values may suffice to show that much is at stake. One thing is certain: the old concepts are inadequate and should be corrected. The successful updating of missionary institutes will depend to a great extent on their ability to accept and integrate the motivating concepts that will rule the future.

Structures

Under the heading "Springcleaning" above, we have pleaded for adjustments that will of necessity demand structural changes. We have seen that the West dominated missionary organization. This led to such dysfunctions as Western missionaries impeding the process of acculturation, enhancing the status of the West, and fulfilling their own heroic self-image (functions 11, 12, 13). This state of affairs cannot be put straight by good intentions or soothing words. It has to be rectified radically and through *structural reforms*. One is already taking place: new missionary institutes are being formed in the young churches which will take their place next to the older, Western ones. Another structural adjustment might consist in internationalizing the membership of the older institutes. Further, it may be prudent to keep the number of foreign missionaries working in a local church to within a percentage that does not produce resistance.[44]

A great deal of missionary and pastoral work going on in Third World countries is financially supported by aid agencies and foundations in the West. According to the prevailing form of organization, the decisions on projects are taken in the West: by executives, consultative boards, or traveling agents of Western offices. This makes the young church dependent on policies formulated, or at least sanctioned, abroad. The efforts at working out "partnership agreements" between bishops' conferences and aid agencies signal a new development that should be vigorously pursued.

Some authors foresee that the apostolate of the future will be "less centralized and less rigidly directed."[45] This may well be so and to no harm. Rigorous control is rarely a sign of good management. Yet some new ways of coordinating mission work are badly needed if waste of personnel is to be kept to a minimum. Before 1969 the whole organization hinged on a geographical division of responsibilities; with the *ius commissionis* withdrawn, all 2,500 dioceses of the world are potential partners of any religious order or missionary institute. Unless some *efficient intermediate planning bodies* are established, new contacts will be made either in a haphazard way or by everyone having to search the whole market on their own. Can we expect every bishop to know the potential of all male and female religious orders and societies? Or can the latter have the information required to make priority judgments on requests coming from every part of the world? A particular ecclesiastical province has been shopping around for years to find a liturgy professor; an excellent candidate for this post was available but the need became known only accidentally. One congregation of Sisters pulls out of a diocese because it feels the task has been completed; another foreign congregation takes its place. A highly qualified architect offers his services to the missions; the offer is turned down because he cannot be placed; later it appears he would have been very welcome and useful in a big diocese.

The ingredients of a better coordination of structures could be the following: *(a) Overall priorities and strategies* could be worked out by consultation between the

Congregation for the Evangelization of Peoples, the missionizing orders and societies, and bishops' conferences. These priorities might concern geographical areas (e.g., Asia), ideologies (e.g., secular humanism, Islam), or world problems (e.g., urbanization). *(b)* The priorities and strategies could be given concrete form in *long-term global projects*, which could be sponsored by a number of bishops' conferences, religious orders, and missionary institutes (e.g., twenty-year plan for dialogue with Islam). *(c)* An efficient and fast *network of communication* could be established between the secretariats of bishops' conferences and the headquarters of religious orders and missionary institutes. Its immediate function could be the regular transmission of personnel offers and vacancies.

The new structures that might arise from an attempt to realize the three objectives we have spelled out should avoid certain pitfalls. They should not introduce an unwanted, pyramidal, top-heavy organization; rather, they should be based on the principles of "systemic" management.[46] They should leave full scope for the personal priorities, idiosyncrasies, and charisms of all partners. Its planning should not be exclusively or mainly based on the advice of "experts"; the visions and gut feelings of the men and women in the field as well as the aspirations of the communities of believers are to be fully drawn in. Overall plans should not lead to a monopolizing of areas or apostolic tasks. And finally, initiatives have to be encouraged even if they deviate from the accepted approach or from a common plan. "For strong, healthy grass to grow, all that is needed is a crack in the pavement."

Models

When we speak of "models" here we refer to persons who express the ideals of a social group. In the early Middle Ages King Arthur, Charlemagne, Sir Galahad, and Saint George were models for the ubiquitous knights. Knights were an influential group in a society that was torn by endless conflicts between neighboring fiefs, by revolutions, civil wars, and systematic robberies. Within this turmoil the knight arose as a stabilizing factor. Through the models that society accepted and hallowed, knights were constantly reminded of the expectations people had, of the attitudes that should be cultivated. The models taught the virtues that we still associate with "chivalry" today: trust in God, loyalty to one's overlord, valor and courage, honesty and fair play in all circumstances, protection of the weak, and courtesy to women.

Many authors today write about the new role expected of missionaries. They mention the element of servanthood,[47] identification with local culture,[48] competence in interpersonal communication,[49] acceptance of oneself as "a foreigner,"[50] and other requirements.[51] All agree that it is fundamentally a question of attitudes that cannot be imposed by legislation or taught by logic. What we are really looking for is fresh models that enshrine the attitudes and ideals demanded in our own times.

The models that motivated missionaries so far were of particular types, for example, Saint Francis Xavier for pioneers, and Saint Thérèse of Lisieux for religious Sisters in supporting roles. It is time we recognize the limitations of these models.

Anyone who has studied the life and letters of Saint Francis Xavier is bound to acquire a great admiration for him as a missionary; we can learn much from him.

But at the same time we become quite aware that Saint Francis, as a "model," incorporates some attitudes that would need correction—attitudes that were the result of the theological, spiritual, and colonial climate of his time. It would take too much space to enumerate these attitudes. Most of them, in fact, are to be found in the missionaries of that age, but they are more striking when perceived in a man of Saint Francis's caliber. A few examples may be given by way of illustration.

Francis was so absolutely convinced that baptism by water was essential for salvation that he baptized thousands with hardly any preceding instruction; that he, though very sadly, felt compelled to tell his Japanese listeners that their ancestors were consigned to the eternity of hell; that he urged his colleagues in India to baptize as many children as possible because their (almost providential) high mortality rate would secure heaven for them.

Moreover, he had a low opinion of his Indian converts (the Catholic community would be unable to produce Indian Jesuits; Europe would have to provide them; he had a very negative attitude toward the Malabar priests). He despised the Hindu religion. He urged the children to tear down the temples and idols and took a great delight in their destructive zeal. He did not even attempt to understand the ancient religions but condemned them and their leaders a priori in the most forceful and negative terms: "The Brahmins are liars and cheaters to the very backbone. . . . They exploit most cunningly the simplicity and ignorance of the people." Obviously then, in spite of his saintly, all-consuming heroism and his undaunted pioneering spirit, he can no longer be accepted as a "model" of what a missionary should be like today.

In our search for models we might think of people such as Charles de Foucauld, Martin de Porres, perhaps even Camillo Torres and Archbishop Romero of San Salvador. The ability to conduct dialogue should feature prominently in any future model. A stimulating article on this topic by J. T. Boberg describes what a person of dialogue is like. We adapt it here as an indication of the kind of model we need:

A person of dialogue experiences the other side, listens to others, learns from them.

A person of dialogue enters completely into the real life situations of people, suffers their lived reality with them.

A person of dialogue gives up "power," does not yield to the temptation of imposing ideas, discovers *with* people—not *for* them—what their needs and programs are.

A person of dialogue meets people on their own terms, in their own time, realizing that waiting may well be a more powerful force than acting.

A person of dialogue accepts the fact of not *possessing* the truth or the only right way of doing things, is disposed to the message of others, and continuously open to further conversion as a result of dialogue with them.

A person of dialogue develops deep personal relationships, realizing that in listening to others, taking them seriously, identifying with their world, he or she is saying Yes to them, affirming them in a way that is tremendously creative, mysteriously salvific.

A person of dialogue is so immersed in the world of others, like Jesus in our world, that he or she can begin to ask questions which endorse and which challenge basic human values, and in that context—from within—can announce the good news and denounce sinful structures.[52]

Conclusion and Proposing a New Term

Saint Paul's assessment of his missionary vocation in 1 Corinthians 9:15-27 may well provide some guiding principles for missionaries and missionary institutes of the future. The task remains. "I should be punished if I did preach it [the Gospel]!" (vs. 16). It is the missionary who needs to adapt to people and not vice versa. "I made myself all things to all men in order to save some at any cost" (vs. 22). The future will not be easy. It will require conversion, application, self-discipline. "All the runners at the stadium are trying to win, but only one of them gets the prize. You must run in the same way, meaning to win" (vs. 24). The metaphor suits our time. Ancient and modern systems of thought compete in a struggle that will make or break the lives of millions. People are waiting for athletes who will enter the race with them and who will take them to the finish: God. Missionaries will be athletes for God.

1 Corinthians 9 reveals that Paul understood his missionary role through a multiplicity of metaphors and images. Apart from seeing himself as an athlete, he compares his work with serving in an army, planting a vineyard, tending a flock, harvesting a crop (vss. 7-11). He draws a parallel with priests ministering in the temple (vs. 13) and with servants trying to please their masters (vss. 19-22). He knows himself sent ("Am I not an apostle?" vs. 1) and alludes to his profession as tentmaker ("Are you not my handiwork?" vs. 2). Paul anticipates the many self-definitions and titles applied to his successors in the missionary task throughout the ages.

This brings us to a last and weighty consideration. Might it not be harmful to the task itself that its image is at present determined by only one term, that of "missionary"? This is all the more serious because the term has accumulated in itself a number of connotations that are less fortunate. In third world countries missionaries are often seen as relics of a colonial period. They have the image of being builders, organizers, pushers. Their involvement has been so forceful that many of the attitudes of former generations are being associated with the notion of "the missionary" itself.

We realize that the term "missionary" also has its positive content. Yet, in the light of the thorough transformations we have called for in this last section, *we believe the time may have come for deliberately coining a new term* to fit the realities of the future. Words are influential tools in liberating from unwanted associations and in giving a new direction.

One term that could be used for the "missionary new style" is *wayfarer.*[53] Obviously there is an arbitrary element in any term, and its adoption will only result from a policy decision. But there are a number of reasons that would make adopting this term an attractive option. First of all, the term is a *tabula rasa,* fresh, devoid of connotations so far. Second, it has its roots in Scripture. Christ's disciples were known as "followers of the Way" (Acts 9:2). Apostles instructed catechumens "in the Way of the Lord"; they gave "instruction about the Way" (Acts 18:25-26). Discipleship is portrayed as wayfaring with Christ (cf. Lk. 24:15, 32). In fact, Christ himself is "the Way" (Jn. 14:6; see also 2 Pet. 2:2; 1 Cor. 4:17). Third, wayfaring expresses admirably the characteristic feature of the missionary as "Christ on the move," discussed earlier. Finally, the term is not aggressive. It will lend itself to a self-definition in the context of dialogue. All religions start from the belief that a person is a wayfarer traveling to God.

Genuine wayfarers will be welcome anywhere. The world needs wayfarers who proclaim Christ, who travel with him. They will be the missionaries of the future, the wayfarers in a new age.

Notes

1. Translated from the German: *Beispieltexte* C/26/40 (Aachen: MISSIO, 1979).
2. C. N. Parkinson, "Plans and Plants," in *Parkinson's Law* (Harmondsworth, England: Penguin Books, 1965), pp. 76-85.
3. The full text was published in *Omnis Terra* 20 (1969): 230-34.
4. From a conference of Nov. 26, 1973; CIM (Brussels) 30 (1974): 23.
5. J. M. Hogema, "To Stay or to Leave?" *African Ecclesiastical Review* 14 (1972): 126-29.
6. *Information Catholique International* 297 (Oct. 1, 1967): 28.
7. Gerald H. Anderson, "A Moratorium on Missionaries," *Christian Century* (Jan. 16, 1974): 43-45.
8. C. P. Wagner, "Colour the Moratorium Grey," *International Review of Mission* 114 (1975): 165-76; quotation from p. 166.
9. *Ecumenical Press Service* (June 20, 1974), p. 11.
10. Fabien Éboussi, "La Démission," *Spiritus* 15 (1974): 276-87.
11. *Outlook* 13 (1972): 103ff.
12. J. B. Metz, *Zeit der Orden?* (Freiburg: Herder, 1977), pp. 19-20 (freely translated).
13. *Bijeen* 11, no. 5 (1978): 4-7; *Millhilliana* 30 (1978): 41-46.
14. Herbert Vaughan, *Missionary College Chiefly for Pagan Natives* (London: Knowles, 1866), pp. 15-16. In those days Vaughan still spoke of a missionary "college." The same principles were later applied to "society."
15. Pius XI, *Divini Illius Magistri,* Dec. 31, 1929; *Acta Apostolicae Sedis* 22 (1930): 49ff.; Denz. 2203.
16. Leo XIII, *Immortale Dei,* Nov. 1, 1885; *Acta Sanctae Sedis* 18 (1885): 166ff.; Denz. 1869.
17. Our main sources are: R. K. Merton, *Social Theory and Social Structure* (New York: Free Press, 1949, 1965); H. M. Johnson, *Sociology: A Systematic Introduction* (London: Routledge and Kegan Paul, 1961); J. A. A. Van Doorn and C. J. Lammers, *Moderne Sociologie, Systematiek en Analyse* (Utrecht: Spectrum, 1962); W. E. Moore, *Social Change* (Englewood Cliffs, N.J.: Prentice-Hall, 1963); H. DeJager and A. L. Mok, *Grondbeginselen der Sociologie* (Leiden: Stenfert Kroese, 1971); J. M. G. Thurlings, *De Wetenschap der Samenleving* (Alphen aan den Rijn: Samson, 1977).
18. H. M. Johnson, *Sociology,* p. 63; the full classical descriptions are found in R. K. Merton, *Social Theory,* pp. 19-82; H. M. Johnson, *Sociology,* pp. 48-79.
19. *Annuario S. Congr. per L'Evangelizzazione dei Popoli* (Rome: Urbana University Press, 1980), p. 440.
20. Ch. W. Troll, "Christian-Muslim Relations in India," *Islamochristiana* 5 (1979): 119-45; quotation from p. 126.
21. V. A. Smith, *The Oxford History of India* (London: Oxford University Press, 1958), p. 725.
22. Gilbert Highet, *The Migration of Ideas,* pp. 43, 47; quoted in D. M. Stone, "Changing Patterns of Missionary Service in Today's World," *Practical Anthropology* 17 (1970): 107-18; quotation from p. 107.
23. Cf. I. D. Illich, *Deschooling Society* (New York: Harper & Row, 1971); also, Penguin Books, 1973.
24. "The Need for Missionaries," *Outlook* 13 (1972/73): p. 105.

25. S. H. Sekimoto, "La fonction propre du missionaire étranger," *Église Vivante* 15 (1963): 457-65.

26. *Guida delle Missioni Cattoliche* (Rome: Propaganda Fide, 1975), p. 417.

27. F. McKeown, "Rethinking the Missions," *Heythrop Journal* 7 (1966): p. 316.

28. Fabien Éboussi, "La Démission," esp. pp. 285-87.

29. Our attention was drawn to this example by Mrs. P. Serrarens, Drs. Soc.

30. H. Maurier, "Le Missionaire: Serviteur?" *Spiritus* 14 (1973): 174-89, esp. pp. 178-80.

31. Avery Dulles, *Models of the Church* (Garden City, N.Y.: Doubleday, 1974; London: Macmillan, 1976).

32. *The Catholic Directory of India* (New Delhi: Catholic Bishops' Conference of India, 1977).

33. This is counting all parishes and substations.

34. R. Follereau, *Appell an die glückliche Jugend der Welt* (Munich: Zielfelder, 1975), p. 146.

35. Catholic Truth Society translation (London, 1976), pp. 93-94.

36. In 1965 Fr. Quéguiner, superior general of the Paris Foreign Missions, wrote: "The vast majority of the priests exercising their ministry in mission countries, foreigners or natives, are absorbed by the pastoral care of baptized people. . . . A reliable review recently estimated at 1,000 the number of priests occupied mainly, if not exclusively, in this task. . . ." (Preface to J. Dournes, *Le Père m'a envoyé* (Paris: Cerf, 1965). The observation is valid, but the number 1,000 rests on shaky foundations. The "reliable review" referred to is obviously *Christ to the World,* in which Fr. F. X. Legrand had argued to the figure in the following manner: "S. C. de Propaganda Fide desired [in 1895] that there be at least two of them [missionaries exclusively or mainly devoted to the apostolate among non-Christians] in each vicariate apostolic. At this rate, as there are 505 vicariates or dioceses under the jurisdiction of this S. Congregation, there would be 1,010 priests in the world—out of 392,000—mainly or exclusively dedicated by the church to the evangelization of the immense mass (1,900 millions) of non-Christians" (*Christ to the World* 6 [1961]: 28). We would like to ask Fr. Legrand how, with so few priests involved, 100 million people were converted in the past fifty years. But Legrand keeps quoting this figure in later issues (e.g., vol. 19 [1974]: 484).

37. *Osservatore Romano,* English ed. June 30, 1977, p. 3.

38. Roland Allen, "Non-professional Missionaries" (1929), in *The Ministry of the Spirit,* ed. D. M. Paton (London: World Dominion Press, 1965), pp. 63-86.

39. The great value of such apostolate of witness is indisputable. See also *Ad Gentes,* nos. 21, 41; *Lumen Gentium,* nos. 32-36; *Apostolicam Actuositatem,* nos. 5-6; *Evangelii Nuntiandi,* nos. 21-22, 26-27, 41-42.

40. The General Chapters of most missionary institutes express both the willingness to change and the determination to preserve their original missionary charism; cf. S. Stracca on the Milan Fathers (PIME), *Avvenire* 25 (January 1972); F. Rauscher on the White Fathers, *Theologisch-praktische Quartalschrift* 124 (1976): 143-59.

41. R. Nisbet, *The Social Bond* (New York: Alfred A. Knopf, 1970), p. 305.

42. Interesting in this discussion is the role played by third world theologians. See "Final Statement, Ecumenical Dialogue of Third World Theologians, Dar es Salaam, Tanzania, August 5-12, 1976," in Sergio Torres and Virginia Fabella, M.M., eds., *The Emergent Gospel* (Maryknoll, N.Y.: Orbis Books, 1978), pp. 259-71.

43. Paul VI, *Evangelii Nuntiandi,* no. 58; Pironio, *Pro Mundi Vita* 62 (September 1976): 6; AMECEA, *Spearhead* 60 (1979): 17; Paul VI, *Pro Mundi Vita* 62 (1976): 4.

44. H. Maurier points out the sociological fact that large foreign groups naturally provoke irritation ("Le Missionaire," p. 180).

45. N. Hanrahan, "Missionary Today—A New Vision," *Catholic Gazette* 65, no. 1 (1974): 317.

46. P. F. Rudge, *Ministry and Management* (London: Tavistock, 1968), esp. pp. 43-46; J. N. M. Wijngaards, *What We Can Learn from Secular Efficiency* (New Delhi, 1969), pp. 123-37.

47. J. C. Shenk, "Missionary Identity and Servanthood," *Missiology* 1 (1973): 505-15.

48. W. F. Muldrow, "Identification and the Role of the Missionary," *Practical Anthropology* 18 (1971): 208-21.

49. J. A. Loewen and A. Loewen, "Role, Self-Image and Missionary Communication," *Practical Anthropology* 14 (1967): 145-60; "The 'Missionary' Role," ibid., 14 (1967): 193-208.

50. B. Joinet, "Je suis étranger dans la maison de mon Père," *Spiritus* 13 (1972): 191-202; Ivan Illich, "The Missionary as the Foreigner," *Outlook* 15 (1976): 15-16.

51. Eugene A. Nida, "The Ugly Missioner," *Practical Anthropology* 7 (1960): 74-78. F. X. Clark, "The Role of the Overseas Missioner in the Local Churches Today," *Teaching All Nations* 10 (1973): 38-50. D. J. Hesselgrave, "The Missionary of Tomorrow—Identity Crisis Extraordinary," *Missiology* 3 (1975): 225-38.

52. J. T. Boberg, "The Missionary as Anti-Hero," *Missiology* 7 (1979): 410–21; material quoted adapted from pp. 418–19.

53. The term resulted from a name-seeking competition at St. Joseph's College, Mill Hill. It was suggested by M. Faulkner.

Section 5

MISSION IN THE LOCAL CHURCH IN RELATION TO OTHER RELIGIOUS TRADITIONS

Statement of the Question

The concrete expression of the church's mission is basically at the level of a Christian community where persons interact with other persons, often of other religious faiths. Christians' dialogue with persons of other faiths must be related, on the one hand, to respect for what the Spirit is doing in these religious traditions, and on the other hand, to the duty of witnessing to the Christian faith. Missionaries coming from other cultures could help in crossing cultural and historical obstacles between people of different religious traditions, and assist in the creation of new styles of living together.

Elements for Reflection on the Question

- The need for greater understanding, on the part of Christians, of persons who adhere to other religious traditions
- The fact that dialogue has its own integrity in a religiously plural society
- The question of syncretism
- The need for openness to receive from another religious tradition before witnessing in its presence to the Christian faith
- The extent to which resurgence in some of the major religions is a reaction to secularism, to nationalism, to political/economic factors
- The extent to which this resurgence is a help/hindrance to the future progress of the world

Related Questions

- To what extent can Christians assume a supportive role toward another religious group when the Christians are in a minority?
- To what extent are Christians, when in a majority, obliged to defend minority groups of other religious traditions? What are some concrete possibilities?
- At the level of human community, how can Christians build on another religious tradition with Christian revelation?
- How is dialogue related to evangelization?

353

- What is the significance for mission of the mutual influence of the different religious traditions, including Christianity, upon one another in relation to the growth in dialogue?
- What is the experience of dialogue to date leading us to understand about the relation of church and mission to the kingdom of God?

22

ZAIRE

Boka di Mpasi Londi, S.J.

I am limiting my reflections on the mission of the local church in relation to non-Christian religions to the context of the Diocese of Kisantu, 31,000 square kilometers in area, 300 kilometers in latitude, in the southern part of Kinshasa, in Zaire, with some half-million inhabitants, of whom more than half, or 60 percent, are Catholic. The region is considered 90 to 95 percent Christian,[1] and its population is mostly rural and agrarian.

In its present configuration, as bounded by the Archdiocese of Kinshasa and the Diocese of Kenge on the north, Angola and the Inkisi River on the south, the Diocese of Matadi (the railroad) on the west, and the Diocese of Popokabaka (Kwango River) on the east, the territory of Kisantu makes up part of the old kingdom of the Congo. It received its first evangelization in the sixteenth century, and its second (which we shall be considering here) by the ministry of the Jesuits since 1893.[2] Until 1931, when the vicariate was established, Kisantu was the cornerstone of the Kwango Mission and from it were successively detached the dioceses of Idiofa, Kenge, Kikwit, and Popokabaka. The Diocese of Kisantu is currently in the hands of the diocesan clergy, assisted by a few small Jesuit communities, the Consolatine Fathers (recently arrived), and the Sisters of Notre Dame and of the Sacred Heart.[3]

It is in this framework that we shall be making our reflection. We shall center our attention on three aspects: (1) the mission of yesterday and today in the face of tomorrow, (2) the impact of the Christian communities on the basic clan community, and (3) a liberating mediation. (For lack of space and time, this third aspect is not treated in these pages.)

The Mission from Yesterday to Tomorrow

Yesterday: Uprooting

Yesterday the mission consisted in planting the church. To a number of well-instructed persons whose consciousness has been raised by demands of authenticity,

Boka di Mpasi Londi, S.J., is the Editor of the review *Telema*, a journal for Christian reflection and creativity, in Africa. He is also Visiting Professor at Lumen Vitae, Brussels.

the concept of "planting a mission" readily evokes that of the importation of a value from the outside. And indeed the agents of the "planting of the mission" were, as it happens, Jesuit missioners, hence religious, sent[4] from Belgium.[5] Being thus "set apart" (Acts. 13:2), they were strangers thrice over: geographical, cultural, and sociological. They were governed by a religious rule that reflected their culture and their original milieu; and they formed a kind of elite corps, rather uniform and homogeneous, by their manner of life. These factors condition a mission. (Mission teams have been compared to certain expeditionary forces.) In any case their methods were not unlike a conquest, as witness the rivalries between Catholics and Protestants for mastery of the territory from Kinshasa to the Kwango and the Kwilu.[6]

Furthermore, the planting of a mission aimed at conversion has its immediate result. In the concrete, the converted people adopted the culture of the missionary occupation.[7] It took on its religious traditions, and by this very fact saw itself as somewhat removed from its own culture.

Finally, the missionary enterprise was crowned by the establishment of a local clergy.[8] It reached its culmination in the inauguration of a hierarchy, that is, the establishment of the means of survival of the church that had been planted—the guarantee of the "imported" ecclesial structures and institutions! In sum, from the point of view of the people converted, the planting of yesterday's mission consists schematically of territorial occupation and cultural annexation.

Any number of examples could illustrate the point. Let us limit ourselves to that of the liturgy.[9] When Africans entered the church they brought with them nothing of their own culture, with the possible exception of their language. The melodies and rhythms of their chants, like their musical instruments, remained outside. The festive, ebullient spirit of their village was shut out. The dialogue character of their manner of speech could not enrich the homily and make it a living thing. The spirit of participation in a common activity, so firmly anchored in their social customs of meeting and celebration, were not allowed inside. The spontaneity and sense of community that mark their clan gatherings yielded to a system equally marked by individualism. In such conditions, to dream of liturgical dance, for instance, would have been dreaming indeed—although dance, from the African's childhood on, is an expression of soul that is not only characteristic, but indispensable.[10] The fixed, foreign aspect of church buildings also affected their prayer and its themes: people grew afraid to depart from stereotypes and formulas and acquired a kind of repugnance for prayer arising spontaneously from life. This was most inhibiting for a Christian such as the Mukongo,[11] who had been reared in a prayer of spontaneous, concrete expression, and in an atmosphere of familiarity with the world of spirits and departed ancestors. The ancestors, of course, could not even be invoked, although they are the saints of the clan.[12] In a word, the Christian was uprooted.

Today: Recognition of a Community's Values

Today the mission is no longer a sort of elite undertaking or professional speciality. It is an attitude, a Christian dimension of life at the heart of a community. The agent of mission is no longer an elite corps, come in from elsewhere. The foreign missionary is no longer "sent," but "called," or "invited."[13] It is the believing community itself, in its entirety, with its various functions, which is missionary, radiating its faith life and sharing it with others around it.

Little by little, yesterday's rivalry among the various Christian denominations[14] is today becoming a stimulating emulation among sisters and brothers inspired by a single ideal, bearing one and the same life, charged with the same mission. Thanks to the efforts of ecumenism, a common Christian consciousness in the face of the surrounding life values is beginning to develop—especially spiritual and religious values, unrecognized yesterday, and even looked down upon, but today intimately felt as an integral part of the patrimony of the universal faith.[15] To sacrifice them would be to mutilate what is essentially African for the Mukongo.

Since well before the official inauguration of the campaign for authenticity in 1971, there has been suddenly an irresistible need to return to the inalienable values of Kongo society, especially the relationship with one's ancestors, intimacy with the spirits, a vital communion with the beings around oneself, the primacy of the spiritual in the human being and the communitarian nature of everything that exists, and the concrete, vital referral to the Supreme Being of everything that happens. Music and rhythmic chanting, dance and symbolic gestures impregnate the liturgical atmosphere. Works of art enter the churches, right to the foot of the altar. Musical instruments—the tom-tom, the drum, the rattle, and the *ngonge* (a special metal percussion instrument)—appear in eucharistic celebrations. The disembodied, dryly individualistic style in the liturgy is being replaced with one characterized by the communion of body and spirit, hence by the harmony of the individual with his or her community, and the concrete integration of the past and the present. Yesterday's rigidity is giving way to movement. Bodily expression is finding its language again, is rediscovering the symbolic character of the gesture. The eloquence of posture, of cries of sacred exaltation is restored to its rightful place. Thus attuned to its real, human milieu, and reflecting the intensity of faith that dwells within a person and his or her community, liturgy is becoming life. In this stage, the Mukongo reinterprets, reintegrates, and rehabilitates his or her own community values, snatching them back from a contempt for everything labeled "pagan."

The reappearance of the Christian sects, the return to certain ancestral practices —such as the oracles of the *Nganga,* or prophets, healing by means of incantations, formerly considered as superstitious, and the use of the *nsikilu-nitu,* or "body-stay"[16]—do attest, entirely apart from any judgment of value, to the need to regain direct contact with one's cultural milieu—the need to live one's faith in one's own person, to reinsert one's traditions into a new, modern context. The imported religious traditions come into inevitable confrontation with ancestral values —yesterday rejected and today recovered—within the believer. Both have to meet the challenge of modernity in order to survive, and this is the principle that determines the imperatives of the mission of tomorrow.

Tomorrow: Rooting through Kenosis

Tomorrow the mission of the local church, or Christian community, evolving from an uprooting toward a cultural rooting, will bear the mark of the *kenosis* (cf. Phil.

7), the "self-emptying," the despoiling of oneself in order to become available for exchange, for sharing, for creativity, for communion.[17]

Having served in its first stage as the vehicle obliged to introduce Western traditions identified with Christianity, the mission has permitted the Kongo people to step back from themselves, as it were—to acquire the beneficial, strategic distance from their ancestral culture that they need in order to discern and extract its permanent values, values that can be handed on because they will be viable in modern times. In its second stage, which is taking shape for tomorrow, the mission must encourage believers to make the necessary break with the Western, so-called Christian, traditions in which they have received a faith that does not identify with these traditions but transcends them (cf. *Evangelii Nuntiandi*, no. 20).

This break with Western traditions does not mean a desire to create a vacuum for the sake of a vacuum, but the hope and wish of restoring to one's own local traditions their values, renewing them, enriching them, strengthening them for the inevitable shock of modernity. For example, Western culture is characterized by a profit-orientation—a resolve that nothing should be for nothing. The invasion of this value ought to be countered with the mentality of a local tradition forged within a gift-civilization—everything for nothing—in order to develop and transform the latter into a spirit of gratitude and generosity. The spirit of sharing, that keystone of the clan's solidarity, should animate the Christian communities *de base*, the grassroots ecclesial communities, now so timidly arising and so full of promise.[18]

In the past a global, integral society, organized on a principle of "all in everything, and nothing outside of anything else," fashioned values that were fundamentally spiritual. Today that society has come face to face with a differentiating type of society, one in which each element is outside every other, so to speak: the sacred outside the profane, the religious separate from the political, the economic from the spiritual, and so on.

It is by a creativity capable of breaking away, one generously laced with *kenosis*, that the Christian community will manage to maintain its balance between its past and its future, between its faith and the weight of what might be called a modern civilization of a commercial kind (nothing for nothing).

It must be remarked that the *kenosis* here recommended is not optional. It is necessary and urgent. Indeed, each of the traditions here present, the local one and the imported one as well, must accept its part of the effort to break away, and thereby seize the opportunity for renewal.

In the gospel, as well as in the history of the church, the practice of *kenosis* is synonymous with conversion. Both terms, like their reality, comport both a detachment, or break with one value, and a thrust toward renewal and creativity. There is a continuous evolution involved, inspired by the Spirit of Christ.

Individual *Kenosis*. Jesus, the model and founder of mission, strikes us by his example of *kenosis*. Born at the heart of Judaism, in a history and culture that were thoroughly Jewish, he grew to adulthood in the traditions of that culture. And yet, in his teaching as in his behavior, he ceaselessly and unequivocally broke with certain received values. Witness his continual confrontation with the Pharisees, who were the bulwarks of tradition.[19]

And in what John the Evangelist calls the Jews' incredulity, must we not see a lack of courage to free themselves from certain traditional burdens? Their inability to thrust toward new horizons, to hear new emphases, to respond to unaccustomed calls, to start down new roads—all this betrayed a lack of the courage and faith to break free from their moorings and head for the open sea, to cut the umbilical cord and to risk, in hope, a leap into the unknown. You cannot be born and leave the umbilical cord intact.

Cultural *Kenosis*. The Lord's disciples assimilated his lesson of *kenosis* very well. It had its repercussions in the life of the newborn church. The apostles presented a moving spectacle of *kenosis*. A single example will suffice to underscore the raising of their consciousness in this respect, in the footsteps of the Master. At the time of their meeting in Jerusalem (cf. Acts 15:1–35), the apostles were forced to choose between a Christianity that would be nothing but a prolongation of an Old Testament, Jewish culture, and a mission founded on the break with the Jewish civilization that was needed with a view to creating a new community. In other words, was believing in Jesus Christ purely and simply equivalent to entering the religious traditions of the Jews, or did it transcend that—and transcend it to the point of renouncing traditions that would contradict the universal gift of the Spirit?

After the example of their Master, the disciples submitted to a basic cultural *kenosis* with respect to Jewish traditions. It is upon this model of a cultural *kenosis* that the local Christian community will henceforth have to base its search for ways to break with tradition with a view to pastoral creativity. And so we see that the personal *kenosis* of Jesus, as well as the cultural *kenosis* of the apostles, already contained the truth so resplendently proclaimed by *Evangelii Nuntiandi*:

> The gospel, hence also evangelization, is by no means identifiable with culture. Both are independent of all cultures. . . . While independent of cultures, the gospel and evangelization are not necessarily incompatible with them, but can impregnate them all without submitting to any. The gospel's break with culture is doubtless the drama of our age, as it was also that of other ages. Hence every effort must be bent toward a generous evangelization of culture, or, more precisely, of cultures. They must be regenerated as a result of the impact of the Good News [no. 20].

Mental *Kenosis*: From Imitation to Creativity. For tomorrow the kenotic stage will entail a break with the traditions in which the gospel message has been transmitted, and a rooting—or, better, incarnation—in traditions that will have to be newly created. New traditions will have to be formed by combining selected elements of the imported values with those of the local patrimony, both in the light of the faith and in accordance with the exigencies of modernity.

The kenotic obligation of Christian communities, and hence of the particular local church, is ultimately reducible to that of the incarnation of the faith in concrete life. This incarnation presupposes discernment, the courage to break with inappropriate tradition, and the daring to be really creative. Thus from the beginning, through today, and into the future, the *kenosis* implicit in every authentic conversion, the *kenosis* implicit in the process of deepening the spirit of the gospel marks the axis of an evolution worthy of the Spirit of Christ.

It is in deep and vital awareness of the evangelical *kenosis*, then, that our reflection must now proceed, as we examine the impact of the Christian communities upon the community of the clans.

The Impact of the Christian Communities on the Community of the Clans

The basic notion in Kongo thought and Kongo society is life. Accordingly the soul of that thought and of that society is the bond with the ancestors, who are the intermediaries of life.[20] It does me little good for God to be the creator, the source of life, if I do not receive that life from my parents. And the thread goes back through them to my ancestors. But the life-mediating function ascribed to the ancestors is not limited to the biological aspect of life. It invests every area of life. Here the "all in everything" principle is at play, for we are dealing with one of the "global," societies. The concept of "intermediary" implies two extremes. The ancestors, then, are the intermediaries of life between God and us. And since the all-good God is never responsible for evil, evidently the ancestors must in some way be God's allies against evil.

This traditional thought-framework is an ideal preparation for Christ's special place as mediator of revelation and redemption. In this respect the deep roots of the Christian spirit among the Bankongo of the Diocese of Kisantu are indicative of these people's genuine culture, without the shadow of caricature.

It will suffice simply to lay out the functional diversification of the clan community in order to demonstrate the necessity of a range at least as broad, if not broader, of the ministerial roles that must respond to the concrete needs of the believer in other communities. Attention to people's needs is, of course, one of the first criteria in the discernment of means to be employed for the satisfaction of the deeper aspirations of the soul. Authentic mission, in the sense in which mission is coextensive with pastoral praxis, will be found in this effort to seek out ways to respond to the legitimate aspirations of the concrete human being.

Traditional Kongo Society in the Service of the Human Being

The concept of Kongo society at the service of the human being is that of an alliance with Almighty God as the source of life and goodness.[21] Leaguing oneself with God against the powers of evil is practically a definition of the role of the good person, or of the mission of the believer. The determination to take sides with God in order to deal with earthly evil translates into a series of very specialized social roles. The titles of the various service people, which we are about to cite, all carry the connotation of "specialist" or "expert."

The Ancestors: Mediators. Between God and the generations of humankind there intervenes a mediation of biological and moral life. Not only is life transmitted, but those virtues as well which express the vital bond with God. The agents of this mediation are the *bakulu*, or ancestors. The first thing that must be said about them is that they are not simply the deceased. They constitute the line of forebears who have walked in the way of goodness, justice, and the will of God. In other words they are the saints of the clan.[22]

The *bakulu* represent the incarnation of God's beneficent activities. Sculpture scarcely attempts to individualize them. Unlike the saints of the Catholic church, whose quite particular traits Western sculpture attempts to represent, situating them in time and space, statues of the Bakulu are stylized, symbolical, since they underscore a transhistorical community reality, while Christian sculpture is readily historicizing.

Ultimately the *bakulu* are equivalent to the ideals that at a much lesser distance from us, our parents actualize. But parents alone would not be equal to so diversified a task as maintaining all these virtues in vital harmony. Other specialized roles intervene. Let us mention some of them.

The Diagnostician, or Detector. The diagnostician (*nganga ngombo*, "expert in the occult," or "professional in the area of the diagnosis of the hidden") is at the center of Kongo social relationships. Convinced as they are that the basis of life is the spirit, the Mukongo do not believe that anything having its roots in the spirit can be without its effects. The detector of occult causes, of spiritual causes, is precisely a seer deemed able to scrutinize the depths of one's being, to detect the hidden influences that are invisible to the naked eye. He is a person endowed with an eye like a microscope. He is the central focus of all truth, and his word is sacred and peremptory. In case of illness, for example, the people rarely accept the organic etiology proposed by white physicians or paraprofessionals without having heard the verdict of the *nganga ngombo*. Westerners notoriously ascribe a physical ill to a physical, material cause. For the Mukongo, any cause producing its effect in a *person* must be a spiritual cause. It goes without saying that in the majority of cases any care administered to the sick in a hospital is preceded, accompanied, or followed by consultation and other procedures with the diagnosticians,[23] and by their reassuring "oracles." He alone will be the key to society's progress or retardation, for he is the object of a genuine cult of blind confidence.

The Chief "Priest." The *nganga-bakulu*, or person in charge of ancestor worship, is often also the head of the group. As the one who offers sacrifice, and as the guardian of the ancestral blessings, it is he who performs the public, official act of cultic contact with the spiritual world dominated by the *bakulu*. He is the clan's priest, its intercessor and advocate, and even its scapegoat. He is sought in every misfortune and, when all his attempts are unsuccessful, he can be accused of complicity with the malefactor, the *ndoki*, and hence of *kindoki*, or sorcery."[24]

The Antisorcerer, or "Exorcist." Evil is real, evident, nagging, persistent. One must protect oneself. There is a professional for this purpose—the *nganga nkisi,* or antisorcerer. It is he who confronts the presumptive cause of the misfortune, the sorcerer, or *ndoki,* the ally of the malign invisible powers. The antisorcerer can simply be a healer—a *nganga-buka,* or connoisseur of medicinal herbs and healing therapies. Or he can be a detector of occult causes, like the diagnostician. But unlike the latter the antisorcerer cannot rest content with the localization or diagnosis of the malady. He must propose the means by which it can be cured. The antisorcerer is not a stereotype. His social role varies with its application in society.

The Orator. Speech is an essential of every human society. We need to make ourselves understood—transmit our ideas, knowledge, and opinions. Hence the importance of the *nzonzi,* the orator. Man of science and rhetoric at once, the orator is sage, savant, and historian. He is the clan's walking library. For the living, he is judge and referee, the defender of the communitarian values. In case of dispute, he is the one everyone counts on.

Artists. Among the several kinds of artists, the musician and sculptor predominate. There are various uses for the statuettes carved by the latter.

Frequently, in the eyes of foreigners, all these services are eclipsed by the flamboyant, spectacular figure of the "fetish sorcerer," the *nganga-nkisi.* He is a kind of magician, with his paraphernalia of "fetishes," statuettes, and magic rings. But in Kikongo the term *nganga-nkisi* is used to denote the beneficent antisorcerer as well as the malign sorcerer.

Until recently Western ethnologists and anthropologists considered him to be a unique and "globalistic" type.[25] The attention paid to the "fetish sorcerer," especially with all its errors, resulted in a contempt for him that warped all perception of the social roles fulfilled by the various specialists we have noted here.

Taking its cue from these roles and structures in the community of the clan, which retains a great deal of influence,[26] the mission can create a series of ministries appropriate to the cultural imperatives of this particular social milieu, so attached to its traditional specialists or experts.

Some Cases That Provoke Reflection

After a century of evangelization, one cannot escape the impression that as far as specific traces of Christianity in the actual life of the population is concerned, in the Diocese of Kisantu as a whole the second mission has been as unsuccessful as the first, in spite of what historians may say about the latter's alleged residue.

The same impression of failure is obtained elsewhere, for instance in the neighboring dioceses of Kenge, Kikwit, and Idiofa.[27] The explanation is that faith in Jesus Christ, even when genuinely accepted and lived, finds adequate cultural expression only very slowly. Consequently its chances of survival are diminished. The lack of proportion between an isolated religion, detached from the culture that surrounds it, and the complex of traditions and practices that call to the believer from that culture, results in a parallelism that depresses, destructures, and disconcerts.[28] The accompanying internal disorientation reinserts the Christian into the traditional system of securities that the clan has established. Hence an unbridled recourse to the "exorcists," those who rout the evil spirits or the "sorcerers," to good luck charms, and to every sort of advice-seeking for reassurance against the terror of evil persons and evil spirits.[29]

Case No. 1. Nearly every family attempts to reconstitute, on the advice of the diagnostician mentioned above, the elements of its ancestral security. A good example is the "recovery," or *tombula,* of the *bankita,* who are the tutelary spirits responsible for the protection, good fortune, happiness, prosperity, fertility, and longevity of the members of a given family now alive. The *bankita* consist of a set of three pebbles, taken from nearby waters, and symbolize the succoring presence of one's ancestors.[30] Family members walk in procession to the riverbank, and there search for the three stones. The one who finds them will automatically become the priest, the person in charge of the new cult. The procession returns to the village, and now the stones, lying in their sacred casket, which is sometimes kept in a corner of the dwelling, become the object of cultic attention. Cola nuts are offered them, sprinkled with fresh palm wine, and certain set prayers are said.

The reappearance of such a practice after more than a generation[31] poses problems even to indigenous evangelizers.[32]

Case No. 2. Another practice that has reappeared is the *vwela,* a kind of periodic cure. The *vwela* is both a cure and a retreat.[33] For a minimum of three days and a maximum of nine, the patient is kept in seclusion and fed by the "priest-healer,"[34] who is not content to treat a material body but endeavors to cure the whole person, who is after all also a member of a clan, someone who has ties with the ancestors and with God.

In every illness, the "priest-healer" seeks out the spiritual, moral, and social causes that are disorganizing a person's vital harmony on both the individual and the community level. Thus, far from being considered as a purely somatic phenomenon, illness is viewed and treated as a dissonance, an imbalance of the whole being, which is conceived essentially as a bundle of relationships, a "being with," a locus of communion. By reinstating this being within his or her network of communion, one repairs the patient's disintegrated unity at the same time as restoring the person's health. It is the whole person, then, that is restored to vital dimensions.[35]

Case No. 3. Another striking example of the "global" and vital view of society is the case of the matrimonial dowry. Nowhere up until now has anyone really been able to suppress the practice of the dowry for the validation of a marriage. In this matter the Christian community, including the leaders and catechists, has been as helpless as anyone else. And yet the institution of marriage is so important for the transmission of Christian values to the child, through the first catechetical school, which is the family, that the local church cannot afford simply to fold its arms and stare at this stumbling block. This is a test of the authentic rooting of the faith in the life of the cultural milieu.

One of the reasons for the persistence of the dowry is its basis in the notion of social responsibility. Another is its sacred character as bequeathed by the ancestors, hence its nature as a vehicle of their blessing and solidarity. Administrative prohibitions, being extraneous to conviction, produce only intimidation, which begets clandestinity. Hence instead of continuing to attack or despise this institution, which has carried the day for decades over every attempt to suppress it, and seen every legislative prohibition to its grave as a dead letter, we should endeavor to "convert" it, encourage it to evolve, through a conscious and deliberate *kenosis* in its own regard. It should be evangelized. In its pastoral stage,[36] the mission will have the task of transforming the custom—not by simply adopting it, to be sure, but through a creative evolution, a kenotic renewal.

Case No. 4. A fourth example, along the same general lines as the above, will suffice to convince us of the need to redirect our mission in the direction of *kenosis*. In no region of Zaire is polygamy in any danger. The reason it is surprising to find it in the Diocese of Kisantu is that Kisantu is a very fine example of the viability of the Christian life in Zaire, as well as an important test of that viability, for Kisantu is in a sense the senior diocese of the country.[37] But we have to say that a genuine pastoral praxis with a view to the eradication of polygamy has not yet been found, and there is no evidence that we are on the verge of finding it.

It is generally assumed that polygamy is essentially a response to a sexual need. This is very probably in error. Most polygamic situations, and the motivation behind them, cannot be explained in terms of sexual drives. We are going to have to accept the social and spiritual reasons of clan morality as much more compelling. In the first place, the generation of progeny is not only an individual need, it is also the clan's need to prolong itself. This is a duty, and a sacred one. Second, when you give a child the name of its ancestors, you honor its ancestors. Hence the desire to have as many children as there are ancestral names to transmit. Here again is a moral obligation, and one incumbent on many persons. Finally, of course, children stand in the place of any social security. They are the parent's insurance for old age, sickness, and burial. For the moment, children are the real savings accounts and health and disability insurance.

It is unthinkable that normal persons, for reason of personal considerations, could dispense themselves from such obligations. Unless and until the system evolves and everyone changes at once, on the deepest level of consciousness and conscience, it will be deemed appropriate to take a second wife if, for instance, the first is infertile. And indeed it is sterility that impels relatively many men to bigamy. On the other hand, there are not many cases of sterility in the region. The main reasons for polygamy are social, reducible to the necessity of providing a second wife to help with the homemaking (hence, a kind of social work) when the first wife is passing through a critical time (pregnancy, childbirth, nursing, or the leisure imposed by custom), or to spare one wife the duties of the marriage bed (prohibited by custom during lactation), to be of service to her during the time immediately following childbirth, and so on.

Kill the custom? But it is extremely deeply rooted, and would surely be replaced by other solutions, possibly worse and, what is more, irresponsible.[38] No, the custom must undergo an evolution, under the thrust of a *kenosis*—a break with tradition, with creativity stepping into the breach. For example, the Christian community could make an effort to create a form of social welfare that would assist women at childbirth. Thus the Christian community would largely resolve the polygamy problem, thereby also encourage the continued cooperation of the members of the community at large who favor monogamy.

The solidarity of the clan when it came to "social work" was still a possibility yesterday, when teenage girls readily assisted their aunts, cousins, and older sisters in childbirth, thereby themselves undergoing an initiation into the duties of the homemaker. This is no longer customary, since teenagers go to school. From time to time a family will still withdraw a girl from school to help with immediate home needs, but they dislike doing so and reproach themselves afterward. Until recently the employment of teenage girls in homemaking tasks took the place of courses in home economics. Today the "modern school" is too attractive to the girl herself for this custom to be kept up. Instead, another formula must be invented, in order to obviate the need for polygamy by providing social services for women in childbirth. Here the Christian community might well create a social endeavor in support of its morality of monogamy. Otherwise what will develop in place of institutional polygamy will be the pirate form of polygamy called in Zaire *bureau*[39]—a veritable matrimonial banditry, where the woman pays the price.

Our review of these few cases is sufficient illustration of the cultural *kenosis* that must be promoted by tomorrow's mission as its basic principle of evolution. It will be essentially a matter of discernment, as exercised both in regard to the Western religious traditions that have served as the vehicle of the gospel message, and in regard to those of the local culture, which should be reevaluated and updated. In this way the gospel and the faith it arouses will be the locus of purification for every culture.

In sum, the mission of the local church tomorrow will be identical with a *kenosis,* in order to bring about a deepening of faith and thereby

to evangelize—not in the fashion of adventitious decoration, but in a vital manner, in depth, all the way to their roots—the culture and the cultures of humanity. . . always taking our point of departure in the human person, and ever returning to the relationships among those persons and with God [*Evangelii Nuntiandi,* no. 20].

Thus mission will be tantamount to "inculturation," in the sense in which that word implies both conversion and *kenosis,* both the break with the old and the creation of the new—creativity in fidelity. In a word mission will consist in an ongoing and continuous *renewal* of cultural values, and the gospel will realize its potential as the "leaven in the dough," the "salt of the earth" and of the earth's cultures, and the "light of the world," with all the world's cultures and traditions.

When all is said and done, why should Christ's title of Liberator not become full and concrete reality?

—*Translated by Robert R. Barr*

Notes

1. Many parents, however, for reasons ranging from indifference to a thirst for freedom, tend less and less to have their children baptized in infancy.

For the peculiar African sense of "religion" and its proper structure, see "A propos des religions populaires d'Afrique," *Telema,* no. 2 (1979): 19–50, esp. 20–36.

2. E. Laveille, *L'évangile au centre de l'Afrique (Le P. van Hencxthoven, fondateur de la mission du Kwango)* (Louvain, 1926); J. van Wing, *Études Bakongo,* DDB, (2nd ed., 1959); F. Bontinck,

"La première évangélisation du Zaïre," *Telema*, no. 1 (1980): 25-38, and "La deuxième évangélisation du Zaïre," ibid., no. 2, pp. 35-62.

3. There is also a flourishing congregation of diocesan Sisters, as well as one of diocesan Brothers in need of a bit of a shot in the arm.

4. Vatican II has not eliminated the notion of being "sent to the pagans" (cf. *Ad Gentes*, nos. 27, 32, 20).

5. During the colonial era the mission in Zaire remained, as far as could be managed, a Belgian national monopoly; see Bontinck, "Deuxième évangélisation."

6. Cf. Laveille, *L'évangile au centre,* pp. 278-88.

7. See the meanderings of the Kwango Mission, ibid., pp. 195-226, 264-77. Cf. also R. Agenenau and D. Pryen, *Chemins de la mission aujourd'hui* (Paris, 1972); *Une nouvel âge de la mission* (1973); and *Après la mission* (IDOC-France, 1975).

8. Cf. *Ad Gentes,* no. 16.

9. "Noël, temps de naître, joie de créer, " *Telema,* no. 4 (1975): 52-57; Mbinda Sambu, "Essor liturgique au diocèse de Boma," ibid., no. 4 (1976): 27-29; A. Abega, "La liturgie de Ndzon-Melen, ibid., no. 4 (1978): 41-50.

10. "Libération de l'expression corporelle en liturgie africaine," *Concilium,* no. 152 (1980): 71-80.

11. The singular is *Mukongo,* the plural is *Bakongo.* The meaning is "pertaining to the [ethnic group] Kongo."

12. "Du souvenir de nos morts à la mort des souvenirs," *Telema,* no. 3 (1975: 3-5); R. Mejia, "Communion des saints, communion avec les ancêtres," ibid., pp. 40-46; and (see n. 1, above) "À propos des réligions populaires d'Afrique," pp. 34-36.

13. See especially the dossier of the 44th Semaine de Missiologie de Louvain, 1974, entitled "Qui portera l'évangile aux nations?" See also B. Joinet, "Je parle dans la maison de mes hôtes," *Lumen Vitae,* no. 4 (1974): 525-40; Joinet, *Le soleil de Dieu en Tanzanie* (Paris: Cerf, 1977); W. Bühlmann, *The Coming of the Third Church* (Maryknoll, N.Y.: Orbis Books, 1976); P. Kalilombe, "Un certain type de mission est revolu," *Telema,* no. 4 (1975): 75-84; V. Mertens, "Conditions de présence et d'action des missionnaires," ibid., no. 1 (1976): 61-72.

14. The African Protestant branch that has had the most to suffer is the Kimbanguist church, which today is the flourishing object of the appreciation and respect of all its sister churches of missionary origin. See *Telema,* no. 3 (1979): 39-66; no. 2, pp. 51-60.

15. "Allocution de Paul VI au Symposium de Kampala, no. 2, *Documentation Catholique,* no. 1546, cols. 764-65.

16. It is true that certain objects blessed by the Catholic church also serve this purpose in a confused way. Medals, rosaries, crucifixes, and small blessed crosses are very much in vogue.

17. "Du Dieu sensible au corps au Dieu sensible aux cultures," *Telema,* no. 4 (1978): 3-5.

18. K. Davire, "Communautés Chrétiennes de base," *Telema,* no. 3 (1979): 15-26. See also *Vivant Univers,* no. 318 (1978), especially the remarkable AMECEA study, Aug. 13-16, 1979, "Conclusion of the Study Conference of the AMECEA" (Zomba, Malawi; Eldoret, Kenya). It should be remarked that the pastoral practice of the Diocese of Kisantu is still traditional, centered around the priest and the sacraments. The efforts of the Christian grassroots communities are no match for a ramshackle, old-fashioned clergy sorely in need of *aggiornamento.*

19. A. Cnockaert, "Christ, tradition et nouveauté," *Telema,* no. 4 (1978): 25-40 (see n. 17, above).

20. See "Réligions populaires" (the article cited in n. 1), pp. 30-36.

21. Ibid., pp. 21-22.

22. See n. 12, above.

23. "Réligions populaires," p. 34. It is inaccurate to describe this personage as a diviner. He does not pretend to foresee or foretell the future. He plumbs the invisible and scrutinizes the occult depths where the spirits move.

24. *Kindoki* is a most complex belief and practice. It embraces the moral data of "jealousy," with its malevolent consequences, contains a compendium of malicious practices, and occasionally deals with concepts devoid of all malignity, equivalent to "superman," "extraordinary," or "marvelous power."

25. See the detailed analysis of *kindoki* (sorcery) and *nikisi* (fetish) by Bwakasa Tulu kia Mpansu, *L'impensé du discours en pays kongo* (Kinshasa, 2nd ed., 1980).

26. We have no cause to lull ourselves to sleep with illusions. The family remains the sole institution of viable and solid security in Africa. Even heads of state are aware of their practically unconditional dependence upon their families. Even state institutions tend to bend to the demands of family

and clan—hence a most astute form of "corruption," consisting, when examined very closely, of a siphoning off of public goods and services for the use of the clans and ethnic groups (which from the point of view of the clan is altogether logical); see also n. 2, above.

27. See Belengi Nzileyel, "Le christianisme actuel chez les Bantous: de l'huile flottant sur l'eau?" *Telema*, no. 2 (1977): 9-17; E. Cambron, "Kimvuka ya lutondo à Idiofa," ibid., pp. 19-30; P. Tempels, *La philosophie bantou* (Paris: Présence Africaine, 1948), where the author attacks the same problem, after having had the courage to admit the failure of the "cultural mission/colonization."

28. The whole movement of indigenization, pricked to life by Vatican II, explicitly encouraged by Paul VI in his message *Africae Terrarum* and in *Evangelii Nuntiandi*, and recently reemphasized by John Paul II in Africa, is a frank promotion of inculturation (*Telema*, no. 1 [1979]). As crystallized in the local communities, it narrows the gap between actual cultural life and the Christian faith.

29. It is this terror, which cries for liberation, that ought to constitute the point of departure for a consideration of the role of Christ as Liberator. This terror of the sorcerer is fundamental to the African psychology in general and to that of the Mukongo in particular.

30. Thus the ancestors symbolize the helpful nearness of God, being his mediators of life.

31. For all practical purposes, we, the generation born around 1930, are ignorant of most of the practices here described. For example, I had to go personally to the places where they are maintained and learn everything "from scratch."

32. See Belengi, "Le christianisme actuel chez les Bantous."

33. Comparable to the liturgy of exorcism in Congo-Brazzaville; see "Le mouvement croix-koma," *Vivant Univers*, no. 303 (1977): 42-48; and *Telema*, no. 2 (1979): 43-44.

34. See Massamba ma Mpolo, "Thérapeutique et évangile," *Telema*, no. 2 (1978): 35-48. The author examines the psychological and moral influences on disease, which, from the African point of view, is not to be looked on just in its somatic, or material, aspect.

35. Ibid.

36. Msgr. A. Sanon, "Mission d'évangélisation à l'heure de la pastorale," *Telema*, no. 1 (1975): 23-29.

37. Indeed the country's first bishop, Msgr. Kimbondo, was ordained at Kisantu in 1956. Kisantu was long the diocese with the greatest number of indigenous priests and Sisters. This is no longer the case.

38. The practice of *bureaux* (mistresses, concubines, supplementary wives) tends to encourage free, unregulated unions, and thereby in certain respects it presages a matrimonial irresponsibility with regard to marriage, which will be passed on to succeeding generations. See "En Afrique, le mariage prend le maquis," *Telema*, no. 3 (1978): 3-4, and "Autour de l'inculturation du mariage," ibid., no. 1 (1979): 3-4.

39. An efficacious and enlightened pastoral has not yet appeared. In the Diocese of Kisantu the bishop has seen fit to take penal measures, refusing Christian burial to polygamists. The Lenten Pastoral Letter of 1980, which promulgated this sanction, is at least ambiguous on this point; the clergy will not be happy until polygamy has become a matter of clandestinity. The local church has not yet come to grips with the basis, the actual root, of this admittedly complex problem.

23

TRINIDAD

Anthony Pantin, C.S.Sp.,
and Michel de Verteuil, C.S.Sp.

Introduction

The starting point for a reflection on mission in the local church in relation to other major religious traditions must be a reflection on the meaning of mission today. "Mission" can be used in three senses that are noticeably different: (*a*) a very general sense of the "work" of the church, which is necessarily the mission of Jesus himself; (*b*) a more restricted sense of the work of the church for those outside of itself, those who are not or do not experience themselves as within its fold; (*c*) a still more restricted sense of the preaching of the gospel of Jesus to those who have not heard it or who have not yet put their faith in it. These senses are in descending order of priority, which means that we must reflect on them in that order if we are to understand correctly how to carry out mission in the third sense.

The Mission of the Church

In trying to define the mission of the church in the widest sense we can use as terms of reference the petitions of the Lord's Prayer,

> Hallowed be thy name,
> Thy kingdom come,
> Thy will be done on earth as it is in heaven,

and ask,

> How is God's name hallowed?
> What is his kingdom that we desire should come?
> What is his will?

Anthony Pantin is the Archbishop of Port-of-Spain, Trinidad. Michel de Verteuil, Provincial of the Holy Ghost Fathers in Trinidad, is also involved in leadership training.

On answering these questions (which are really one question) it would be good to use the terminology current among theologians of the third world and say that God's "will" (i.e., his loving purpose) is that all men and women should attain the freedom that he has called them to. The most recent formulation of this kind was the Puebla statement of the Latin American bishops, which describes the mission of the church as follows: "Christ, our hope, is in our midst as the Father's envoy, animating the Church with his Spirit, and offering his word and his life to people today in order to lead them to full and complete liberation" (no. 166).

We could also go back to the terminology used by Paul VI in his encyclical *Populorum Progressio* and say that God's "will" is the fullness of human development for all men and women and for all humanity (no. 17), culminating in the process through which, "By reason of his union with Christ, the source of life, man attains to new fulfilment of himself, a transcendent humanism which gives him his greatest possible perfection" (no. 16).

Or again, following that same encyclical, we may see the mission of the church as bringing people to make the transition "from less human conditions to those which are more human," with conditions that "finally and above all, are more human" being, "faith, a gift of God accepted by the good will of man, and unity in the charity of Christ, Who calls us all to share as sons in the life of the living God, the Father of all men" (nos. 20–21).

The mission of the church, then, is to preach the name of Jesus as the symbol (the effective symbol) of God's will, his plan to hallow his name through the establishment of his kingdom—and this is the full and complete liberation of humanity.

Once we are clear on this concept of mission we must ask ourselves another question: What in the context of the relationship between the Catholic church and other major religious traditions are the major obstacles to the "full and complete liberation" of people? Only by asking that question can we discuss the topic in a down-to-earth way, avoiding vague abstractions that will not help us to find the right solutions for the church in our time. We can find obstacles in two problem areas: (1) the need to foster unity and interdependence in the human family; (2) the need for continuity of spiritual tradition.

Unity and Interdependence

One of the essential elements in the process of human liberation is the experience of all men and women that they form one human family, that they are all limited and dependent, on the one hand, all needing the collaboration of others and receiving it, and on the other hand that they all have a unique contribution to make to the building up of the world and being given the opportunity to make it.

Taking a negative approach we can say that one of the major obstacles to human liberation is the feeling of some that they are independent of their fellow men and women or of any group and (corresponding to this) the feeling of others that they have little or nothing original to contribute.

This twofold feeling of independence and superiority, on the one hand, and of having nothing original to contribute, on the other, is an important reality in our

Caribbean society. Whole groups in our society receive the message that they are industrious, intelligent, creative, and generally superior people, whereas other groups receive the message (a message which they have internalized in a deep way) that they are lazy, unintelligent, and generally inferior. This grouping is made in our society according to well-known criteria, and in particular according to race, social class, and education, with frequent overlapping between the criteria.

It is, then, within this system of grouping and categorization, so harmful to true liberation and so opposed to God's "will," that the church of Jesus Christ exists, having as its mission to proclaim in word and deed his gospel that all men and women are free and creative and at the same time dependent on one another, their relationship with God being the foundation and the clearest expression of this truth. Within the church Jesus wills to do (another way of saying that its mission is to do) what the Gospels narrate he did while on earth, to call the human family back to unity. The manner of doing this remains his manner, which is to welcome those categorized by society as inferior, to assure them that the kingdom is theirs and that he is leading them like lost sheep to the pastures that are theirs by right and from which they have been wrongfully excluded. At the same time he serves notice on society that God does not judge people as people do, that the last will be first and the first last, and that the kingdom will be taken away from the rich and powerful. For the gospel, then, the "good news to the poor" is the dramatic sign of the unity of the human family and the most effective way of bringing it about.

What has all this to do with the relationship between the church and other religious traditions? Simply that in our Caribbean society (as in many others today) religion has been one of the criteria for dividing people. Through their religious affiliations people learn to adopt attitudes of superiority to other groups, looking on them with suspicion and frequently with disdain. In practice, the name of God becomes a source of further division and categorization instead of a source of solidarity and mutual respect. A further complication comes from the fact that almost all Hindus and Muslims in our society are of Indian origin and so the religious categorization overlaps and reinforces the ethnic categorization.

In his talk to the United Nations in October 1979, Pope John Paul II said that "the work of peace is served by constant reflection and activity aimed at discovering the very roots of hatred, destructiveness and contempt." It is certain that one of these "roots of hatred, destructiveness and contempt" is the tendency to categorize groups, and therefore the mission of the church must in some way be concerned with the fight against it.

We can conclude that we must take a new look at our priorities in mission. We must see to it that fostering interdependence and mutuality among different religious traditions (and in particular, respect for those whom society categorizes as inferior) must be at the very center of mission today. We say "at the center" because these things were fostered in the past, but usually in a secondary way, hedged about with qualifications and warnings, a luxury that could be insisted upon when other things had been attended to. For many centuries now it has been the uniqueness of the Christian message that salvation comes through the name of Jesus only. Human solidarity has been fitted in where possible. In this context, and remembering our past history, it is natural that all our Christian (and especially our Catholic) instincts will be sending out warning signals of the dangers of watering down the message, of syncretism, and of indifference. Thus the importance of asking ourselves what the mission of the church is and of being aware that the divisions of our society are an evil so great and so urgent, and at the same time so opposed to the gospel of Jesus, that they clamor for a reexamination of our concept of mission. It is precisely one of the original insights of the teaching of Jesus that we find ourselves by forgetting ourselves, that through selfless service we find our true identity.

In this reexamination of the church's priorities in mission, we must follow two paths, the theological and the practical and pastoral, remembering that the practical is the more urgent as well as the more influential. It remains true that people first live and then philosophize.

Theology. The theological task before us is to redefine the identity of the gospel message in such a way that it includes within itself respect and appreciation for other religions. Church identity and relationship with other religions must be seen not as opposed but as complementary realities, so that if we do not respect other religions we have lost an essential element of our own. We must refuse to have the matter posed as it has been in the Statement of the Question: "Christians' dialogue with persons of other faiths must be related, on the one hand, to respect for what the Spirit is doing in these religious traditions, and on the other hand, to the duty of witnessing to the Christian faith." Posing the question like this gives the impression that "witnessing to the Christian faith" is a reality distinct from and prior to respecting "what the Spirit is doing in these religious traditions." Immediately it sets up an opposition where there is none and immediately it sows the seeds of superiority that have in the past borne fruits of "hatred, destructiveness and contempt."

We must not minimize the importance or the difficulty of conceptualizing a new way of thinking on this issue. Seminaries and other theological centers in our region must work at developing a language for Christianity suitable for challenging the evils of our time. Apologetics must be expressed in a new language that fosters human solidarity rather than undermining it.

To indicate generally what lines will have to be followed, we must develop and lay renewed emphasis on the nature of Christianity as a search for God, on the church as a pilgrim people, and on the Spirit of God filling the whole world. We shall then be able to see that it is of the nature of the church to be in dialogue with other religions and indeed with all manifestations of God's presence, and that the ability to dialogue is not optional but essential to being a Christian today.

Obviously one of the crucial areas of reflection must be the concept of universality. As several theologians (notably Juan Luis Segundo in *The Community Called Church*) have pointed out, our concept of universality has been greatly influenced by our concept of the church as "conquering," and this in turn has been influenced by our concept of greatness as a conquering thing. During his visit to Poland in 1979, Pope John Paul II said, "There is no imperialism of the church, there is only service." We see this as a call to redefine universality in nondominating terms; we see it to mean that "the Christian is the one who understands all history," as Segundo expresses it, or that the church is "the servant of all kingdom values," as others have said. This, of course, is only a start but an important step to understand the concept of universality in a way that is both loyal to our tradition and in accord with the imperative of our mission in today's world.

The findings of some modern philosophers and psychologists on identity in general would also be helpful: when they show, for example, that for persons as well as for cultures identity and relationships are complementary realities and that through selfless relationships we establish identity.

Practice. We can identify three levels at which the church should work to develop attitudes toward other religions that are in tune with its mission.

Liturgy: It is important to recognize that prayer forms are not merely a powerful sign of our deep attitudes but also a powerful force in molding these attitudes. It is this fact that an old Catholic adage expressed by saying that there was a close connection between "the law of praying" and "the law of believing."

In this area the universal church has set the example by changing the forms of the prayers for Jews and for believers of other religions that are prescribed for Good Friday. Instead of praying in a form that reflected our belief that they must become Catholics, we now pray that they come to the fullness of their faith, leaving it to God to interpret our prayer according to his own wise purposes.

The problem, however, is that in the modern church there is plenty of room for individual petitions at the level of either the diocese or the local community. We need therefore to educate Catholics in what we might call the art of praying for people of other religions, using forms that would reflect our commitment to human solidarity and mutual respect. One way in which this could be done would be for the Ordinary to prescribe prayers that could be used as the prayers of the faithful on interreligious occasions or at interreligious prayer services. They could then serve as guidelines for more spontaneous prayers.

Ecumenism: The Catholic church should be known in the region as a religious group that encourages all forms of religion and that is hurt when other religions suffer setbacks or when they are under attack. Officials of the church, such as priests and especially bishops, should be happy (when invited, of course) to offer constructive help: for example (as has happened in Trinidad), to mediate between factions in another religion. Our attitude should be that we offer our help out of fellow-feeling, as a group having its own problems, and this implies that we in turn are willing to receive help from other religions.

Individual Relationships: Catholics should be encouraged to enter into constructive relationships with people of other religions, manifesting attitudes of encouragement and admiration that would serve to build up their own faith. We should keep as the ideal that a person meeting a good Catholic would feel: "Now I have met this person I feel motivated to become a better person according as God is calling me."

Two points should be made here. First, we must be sensitive to the times past when the church was experienced as aggressive and dominating. This does not mean that we should harp on the past or foster guilt feelings among ourselves; it does mean, however, that we relate to others with sensitivity and understanding, being careful to avoid a patronizing attitude, on the one hand, and not being surprised if we meet suspicion and skepticism, on the other.

Second, we must be clear that our attitudes are not part of some strategy, "bending over backwards to please them," as is sometimes said. They should flow from our faith that God is calling us to be servants of solidarity in the modern world and a challenge to the present divisions in society. We are not therefore interested in whether our own attitudes are reciprocated or not. Our own purpose is to carry out as faithfully as.we can the mission of the church today.

Continuity of Spiritual Tradition

In order for men and women to move to "full and complete liberation," it is necessary for them to experience continuity in their lives, continuity at the level of the physical, the psychological, and the spiritual. When people do not experience continuity in their spiritual journey there is always instability or its opposite, rigidity and fanaticism.

Christianity in Europe has developed in continuity with the past, it was grafted onto a pre-Christian spiritual history. Pagan thinkers such as Virgil, Aristotle, Plato, and Socrates, although holding views directly opposed to Christianity, have been seen as "naturally Christian souls" (to use the classical expression), their writings have been "baptized," and in certain schools they have been called "saints." In this way European Christians experience themselves as having a long spiritual history with a pre-Christian as well as a Christian phase. This has been a deeply humanizing ("liberating") experience resulting in extraordinary human and spiritual achievements of which "church art" is only the most striking sign.

This was already the biblical understanding of spiritual growth. The Jews experienced their pagan ancestors, such as Noah, as "fathers in the faith," and the first Christian communities, who were predominantly Gentile, experienced themselves as "of the seed of Abraham" according to the Spirit.

The sad fact, however, is that the peoples of the third world in our time have not been allowed to make a similar spiritual journey. Christianity was preached to them as radically opposing rather than fulfilling their spiritual history. There are still many Catholics today who remember with a certain bitterness that they were taught to look on their parents, not to mention their ancestors, as "damned" and therefore to see their spiritual journey as starting from the time of their commitment to the church. As a result Christianity has been for many an alienating experience; they were not "coming home" to the kingdom.

The religious traditions of any people are the symbols of their spiritual quest. Anthropologists have shown how such factors as climate, terrain, and lifestyle have influenced the way in which all peoples have experienced their relationship with God. When therefore as Catholics we dialogue with religions that are traditional among our people, we are not primarily working to spread the church; we are discovering the roots of our own experience of God, our own spiritual journey. This dialogue is primarily part of the process by which a church becomes truly local, grounded in its own experience of God. It is not an extra-ecclesial but an intra-ecclesial activity.

For us in the Caribbean this dialogue has barely started. We must examine the roots of such religious practices as fasting and vegetarianism, the symbolism of colors among Hindus (contemptuously called "coolie colors" in our society), the marriage rites and the legends, always to try to find out how God has been manifesting to this particular people.

Here again the field of liturgy is important, although almost nothing has been done to develop liturgies that would reflect the ancestral customs of people of African and Indian descent. Marriage is an obvious example of an area where a beginning could be made. In one of the Caribbean territories, Catholics and Hindus prepared a joint marriage service, which could be used when one partner was a Catholic and the other a Hindu; unfortunately the ceremony was divided into the "Catholic ceremony" and the "Hindu ceremony" as if Catholic marriage was a reality apart from some other kind of marriage.

Preaching the Gospel to "Those Far Away"

There has always been in the church two movements, one of concern for members and another of concern for nonmembers. These two movements have traditionally been symbolized by Peter and Paul, Peter's vocation being to care for those within the community and Paul's to reach out to those outside; this latter has been traditionally called the specifically "missionary" vocation. The classical story of the emergence of this vocation is found in chapter 13 of Acts, where the Christian community is described as a thriving community with a great number of "prophets and teachers"; but the following happens: "One day while they were offering worship to the Lord and keeping a fast, the Holy Spirit said, 'I want Barnabas and Saul set apart for the work to which I have called them.' So it was that after fasting and prayer they laid hands on them and sent them off" (13:2-3). It has happened thus in countless Christian communities and still happens today that whereas the majority of the community is content with looking after itself, some feel called to reach to those outside.

We must recognize the special form in which this special missionary vocation exists in every situation. As we have already mentioned, religion in our society is a source of division, and of division into classes. We have "high class" and "low class" religious groups; for example, Catholicism is considered "high" whereas the African religions are considered "low." This does not, of course, mean that there are not poor Catholics, because they are in fact the majority of Catholic membership; it is, however, true that generally speaking you don't find wealthy members of the African religions.

As a result of this situation there are groups in our society who would consider that the Catholic church is not "their thing." Some years ago, at a priests' meeting, the priests were able to identify certain groups that as a general rule would not be found in the church. If we remember the context of the church as a "high-class" religious group we can see the significance of missionary work as bringing the message of God's love to those who experience themselves as "far away." Chapter 2 of the epistle to the Ephesians becomes relevant to our situation: "Now in Christ Jesus, you that used to be so far apart from us have been brought very close" (vs. 13), or again, "He came to bring the good news of peace, peace to you who were far away and peace to those who were near at hand" (vs. 17).

We must remember that this "missionary work" is a delicate enterprise; there are many hurts that remain, memories of rejection and snobbishness. It will be necessary to remember the biblical meaning of "the name" when we speak of the name of Jesus, being aware that the important thing is the "inner meaning" of Jesus, which is as we have seen the message of God's love to those who experience themselves as far away. At times we shall have to keep silent on the church in order precisely to help people become comfortable within it, to reassure them that they can be at home within it and that the kingdom is really theirs. It is in this situation that the story of Acts 13 can be important, since only some people can reach out in this nondominating way, and the rest of the community must content themselves with laying hands on these special members and sending them off.

In this connection we must query the use of the expression "major religious traditions." Precisely what is the meaning of this word "major"? It may merely mean "most numerous" or "spread over large parts of the world"; generally, however, it indicates "superior" and becomes a term of superiority. This is especially important in our context, since African religions are generally not classed as "major" and yet are the ancestral religions of the majority of our people. We must therefore be clear in our own minds and in our preaching that every religion is in some way a manifestation of God's message and a valid path to God. In this sense we need to reflect on Christianity and Hinduism and Islam classing themselves as a sort of club of "major religious traditions."

Preaching the Name of Jesus to Those Who Have Not Yet Heard It

The mandate of the Gospels that the message of Jesus is to be preached to every creature remains in force. Our church here in the Caribbean continues to need its catechumenate program, always bearing in mind that this program must foster human solidarity and mutual respect.

It may be well, however, to state clearly that there is absolutely no evidence to prove that a servant church will draw less adherents than a church with a plan to conquer. It is, on the other hand, to be expected (speaking humanly, of course) that a servant church will attract people of sincerity and true Christian spirituality. We certainly have plenty of experience of people who joined the church from such religions as Hinduism and fell away after a short while, apparently (as far as one can judge these things) because their Christianity was not sufficiently rooted in their own culture. The seed was sown but had not really taken root.

Some years ago the bishops of the Antilles Conference put out a statement to help priests in the work of preparing adults for the sacraments of initiation. They made the following points when speaking of adults who belong to other religions:

In accepting non-Christians into the church, respect should be shown for their cultural heritage. Great emphasis should be laid on the fact that faith in Christ fulfills the highest aspirations of their traditional religions. Instructors should help them to experience this concretely and with specific examples. So too they should be encouraged to maintain religious customs to which they remain attached and which can be given a Christian significance, for instance, dietary customs, traditional dress, and the like. They should be encouraged to maintain traditional names, especially if these have a religious significance. Where possible, aids to this end should be prepared and circulated by the local liturgical commission.

We must say, however, that not much has been done to implement this directive.

Concerning the question whether or not missionaries should have a special role in working out relationships between the church and other religions, we would make two comments:

1. This is not at all our experience; on the contrary, our experience here is that it is local priests (and bishops) as well as laity who have taken the initiative in developing a creative relationship.

2. Why is this possibility even suggested? Does it, perhaps, come from a desire to find something "specific" that missionaries can do and local people cannot? If this is so, then it springs from a false questioning as to the role of missionaries in the local church. We must start from the premise that the local church has the gift per se to be a missionary church, in the widest sense; it is up to the missionaries to fit in where necessary.

24

THE UNIVERSALITY OF SALVATION AND THE DIVERSITY OF RELIGIOUS AIMS

Joseph A. DiNoia, O.P.

An important aspect of the relations of Christians in the United States (and in the West generally) with other religious people is the determination to be respectful of the values enshrined in other traditions and of the upright life of their adherents.

Many factors have converged to encourage this determination. For one thing the outcome of many decades of scholarly study of the religions of humankind has been a widespread and growing appreciation on the part of Christians of the nobility and richness of other religious traditions. Increased travel and communication have heightened contacts among religious people throughout the world. Major world religions like Hinduism, Buddhism, and Islam are enjoying periods of vigorous resurgence, in part stimulated by the need to reassert national, cultural, and religious identities after centuries of Western domination. Representatives of these religious communities actively propagate their doctrines in predominantly Christian and Jewish Western societies. Such reverse missionary activity has intensified public awareness of the diversity of religious beliefs and practices and has compelled Christians to consider the distinctiveness of their own claims in the midst of an enlarged "marketplace" of religious ideas. An emerging world Christianity requires an assessment of other religions that is flexible and affirmative enough to permit the adaptation of Christian institutions and doctrines to a variety of cultural circumstances. Finally, after centuries of dispute with religious skeptics, many Christians welcome the opportunity for deeper study of other religions and for dialogue with their adherents: they hope that such contacts will enhance their understanding of their own as well as other faiths.

Joseph DiNoia, Dominican priest from the United States, is Assistant Professor of Systematic Theology at the Dominican House of Studies in Washington, D.C., with teaching responsibilities in fundamental theology and philosophy. He is book-review editor of *The Thomist*.

A major task for Catholic theology of religions in these circumstances is to articulate a more generally sympathetic and just account of other religions and a more confident view of the state of their adherents than have prevailed in Christian communities in the past. Christians also seek guidance from theology of religions for their study of the doctrines of other traditions, for their collaboration with their adherents in projects of common human concern, for their participation in interreligious dialogue, and for their support of the aims and aspirations of other religious communities.

In present circumstances Christians also expect theology of religions to affirm and legitimate the continuing Christian mission to bear witness to the divine plan of salvation, the unique role of Jesus Christ within it, and the heavy responsibility of the Christian community in advancing its consummation. The object of this paper is to present an argument showing that attitudes of respect and esteem for the distinctiveness and integrity of other religious traditions are fully compatible with a conception of Christian mission that is faithful to the specific content of central Christian doctrines about salvation and about the unique role of the Christian community.

I

The Christian community teaches that the aim of life it fosters is worthy of pursuit by all human beings without exception. Generally speaking it has not taught (and in view of its central doctrines probably could not consistently teach) that salvation constitutes the aim of life only for some limited group of human beings or only during some one segment of the course of world history. On the contrary, as is clear in Catholic teaching, the Christian scheme of doctrines is ordinarily understood to include doctrines about the universality of salvation.

According to these doctrines all human beings who have ever lived—including those who lived before the appearance of the Christian community—are called to participate in a relationship of union with God. Some Christian theologians (for example, Karl Rahner) have construed these doctrines to mean that the very existence of the universe and of humankind within it is to be attributed in the first place to the divine intention to enter into union with human beings. In addition there is the teaching that human beings, both because of their creatureliness and because of their sinfulness, could not attain their true and divinely willed destiny without benefit of divine aid. If such be the universal human condition, then the divine remedy—to be truly effective—must have a universal impact. Hence the doctrines about the universality of salvation culminate in the teaching that Jesus Christ is the universal savior: human beings who attain their true destiny do so only in virtue of the grace of Christ.

It is doubtful whether a Catholic theology of religions could be fully in accord with central Christian doctrines if it taught that the Christian pattern of life and the aim of salvation whose pursuit it fosters were fitted only to particular cultural and social circumstances or only to particular periods in history. A theology of religions that took such a view would presumably be committed to the additional view that the different religious traditions that have emerged in various cultures over the course of history each have a legitimate claim to shape the lives mainly of persons who find themselves sharing the presuppositions prevailing in those particular cultural settings. This account of the matter would in all likelihood include some version of the view that the different aims proposed by various religious communities are each more or less equally worthy of pursuit, depending on historical or social circumstances. It seems clear, however, that a theology of religions that adopted such views could not be consistent with traditional Catholic interpretations of central Christian doctrines and especially of those about the universality of salvation.

In order to study something of the logic of these teachings about the universality of salvation, it is important to examine the connection between this complex set of doctrines and the traditional ascription of a unique value to the Christian community and to membership in it. This connection can usefully be exhibited in terms of an analysis of the logic of religious doctrines, which is suggested by the critical philosophy of religion.[1]

The doctrinal scheme of the Christian community, like the schemes of other religions, may be characterized as fostering an overall pattern of life in its members. In the Christian scheme there is a doctrine that proposes a comprehensive aim for human life: the whole of life should be directed to the attainment of salvation, which consists in a relationship of union with the Blessed Trinity. This practical doctrine recommending a comprehensive course of action is linked with a number of other practical doctrines enjoining a variety of moral and institutional courses of action on the members of the Christian community. In teaching that the aim of life is salvation as union with the Trinity, the Christian scheme can be said to ascribe an inherent value to God (who is good without reference to any further object or existent), since it is only in his presence that an intrinsically valuable state of being (which is good for its own sake as an end in itself) can be attained. Thus, in addition to many practical doctrines, the Christian scheme can be said to possess a doctrine that expresses its basic religious valuation. This valuation can take a variety of forms, which have in common this logical feature: the ascription of unrestricted primacy-ranking predicates to the referent God as applying equally (according to the logic of trinitarian doctrines) to the Father, to Jesus Christ, and to the Holy Spirit. This basic valuation teaches that the trinitarian God is at the center of the pattern of life that Christianity fosters and thus it gives point to the main practical doctrines of the Christian scheme.

In addition to its basic religious valuation and main practical doctrines, the Christian scheme contains many beliefs about the human condition in view of which it is reasonable to seek the goal that Christianity recommends for human life. These existential conditions include the constituents of personal identity and the nature and range of personal agency in human beings, the limitations associated with creatureliness and sin, and the resultant incapacity of human persons to attain the true aim of life without benefit of God's initiative. There are other central Christian beliefs about the manner of the exercise of this divine initiative in the history of the human race culminating in the life and destiny of Jesus Christ, by central doctrines ascribing particular value to the events of his life as reported in Scriptures (and hence to knowledge of these events), and by central practical doctrines recommending a course of life conformed to him. These doctrines converge in the ascription of inherent value to the Christian community (insofar as this is where Jesus Christ abides in his Spirit) and intrinsic value to participation in its life (which constitutes the first stage of a relationship with God). In addition to these valuations, there are other doctrines ascribing contributory value to the Christian community both as providing the means for its members to attain the full measure of union with God (the "beatific vision") and as bearing witness to the rest of the human race about its true end.

If, as the Christian scheme teaches, the true aim of life is salvation as union with God and if membership in the Christian community is the divinely willed means given to attain this aim, then it would not be consistent with the central doctrines of the Christian scheme to ascribe to other religious communities a value equivalent to that ascribed to the Christian community. Thus, although Christian doctrines affirm the universality of salvation, they also assert that the Christian community has privileged public access to knowledge about this aim of life and to the means to attain it. Any ascription of value by theology of religions to the doctrines, institutions, and forms of life of other religious communities must be qualified, it seems clear, by ascriptions of inherent, intrinsic, and contributory value to the Christian community and to membership in it.

This unique valuation of the Christian community entailed by central Christian doctrines is sometimes expressed in terms of the notorious formula *extra ecclesiam nulla salus*. This formula appears to have originated as a way of describing the imperiled state of persons who had broken off communion with the main body of the church by heresy or schism.[2] But its history shows how readily and inevitably it comes to be applied to describe the state of persons who have never been members of any Christian community. To many people today the arrogant exclusivism associated with this extended use of the formula renders it unacceptable on any interpretation of its meaning.

But if our analysis of the logic of the connections between doctrines about salvation and the unique valuation of the Christian community is correct, then it would be puzzling indeed if the Christian community were not prepared to hold some version of the claim expressed by this troublesome formula as a way of describing the state of persons who are the members of other religious communities or of no religious community at all.

Each of the world's major religious traditions seems to claim that the aim of life it proposes is the one most worthy of pursuit by all human beings without exception. A claim of this sort appears to be implied by the respective basic religious valuations that analysis suggests are ingredient in the doctrinal schemes of these traditions. To ascribe an unrestricted inherent or intrinsic value to some existent (as do Christianity and Islam, for example) or to some state of being (as does Theravāda Buddhism, for example) is to propose that something be valued in a certain way not only by the members of a particular religious group but by human beings generally. It would be odd (though naturally not impossible) for a religious community—in view of its definition of that on which its pattern of life is centered—to manifest indifference with regard to the courses of action and particular valuations and beliefs that are understood to foster attainment of the true aim of life. It is perhaps no more strange for a Christian to teach that there is no salvation outside the church and the pattern of life it fosters than it would be for a Theravāda Buddhist to teach that there is no attainment of Nirvana except in the following of the Excellent Eightfold Path. Regrettably such claims are sometimes made in an arrogant tone and with disrespect for other religious people. But no religious community deserves to be accused of arrogant exclusivism for being consistent and serious in its teachings about the aim of life it proposes and the means it regards as necessary to reach it.

II

The seriousness with which a religious community regards the aim of life it recommends imparts considerable urgency to questions about the chances outsiders have of attaining it. In Christianity (as in Buddhism) there are teachings which address these questions.[3] Such questions need not be felt with particular urgency, to be sure, if a religious community were to assume that all religious communities foster identical aims of life, or that the different aims they propose are all worthy of pursuit, or that any of the patterns of life they foster conduce (whether equally or unequally) to the attainment of the true aim of life. Whether rightly or not, the central teachings of the Christian community (and arguably of other major religious communities as well) seem to rule out such assumptions. Hence Christian theology of religions tends to focus prominently on other religious persons' prospects of attaining the aim of salvation despite their persistence in patterns of life that seem to point them in other and possibly wrong directions.

Generally speaking, in current Roman Catholic theology of religions, this issue is addressed in two ways. One trend takes up the traditional line of ascribing to morally upright non-Christians a hidden affiliation with the Christian community. Connected with this view are a variety of formulations allowing for the possession of the dispositions of implicit faith and charity, and a variety of theories explaining the acquisition of the required "revealed" knowledge supporting such dispositions. The second general trend represents a more recent development of traditional notions about the partial possession of truth on the part of other religious traditions. According to this way of accounting for the salvation of non-Christians, their religions may themselves be channels of grace for them. These two approaches are logically distinct: optimism about the salvation of morally upright, implicit believers does not commit one to an ascription of contributory value (by describing other religions as channels of grace) to their religions. Nonetheless, these two strands are often combined in theology of religions (as by the most influential current exponent of this discipline, Karl Rahner). Both these ways of accounting for the salvation of persons who do not have public access to the means of grace provided by the Christian community share an important assumption which needs to be challenged. According to this assumption, the concept of "salvation" successfully designates the aim of life sought by all human beings and religious communities.

This assumption has had a long history in Christian doctrine and theology which it is no part of the purpose of this paper to recount.[4] It is connected with an equally venerable notion according to which Christianity is said to fulfill or supersede all other religions. Contemporary Christianity inherits these notions from the influential literature in which the first comprehensive account of the relationship of Christianity to other religions was first formulated in late antiquity. In this first theology of religions the Christian account of other religions was framed in terms of its relationship to Judaism.[5] In much the same way that Christians could argue that the fundamental aim of Judaism was completely expressed and more reliably fostered by Christianity, they sought to show that the basic ethical and soteriological doctrines of the religions and religious philosophies of late antiquity were fulfilled and superseded by Christian doctrines and life. Indeed, in the continuing debate about these matters between Christians and non-Christians the central soteriological doctrines of the Christian community were decisively reshaped. In any case, Christians could plausibly attribute to the adherents of other religious traditions—partly on the basis of what they themselves might have to say about their doctrines—the pursuit of the aim of life more fully defined and more surely advanced by Christianity.

The notion that other religions are superseded and/or fulfilled by Christianity has always figured prominently in Christian theology of religions in large measure because Christians have generally held some version of the view not only that all human beings would seek the salvation about which Christian doctrines teach if they knew about it, but that they universally do in fact seek this aim, though perhaps under different guises. Moreover, the need to reconcile Christian confidence in the salvation of non-Christians with the unique valuation of the Christian community encouraged Christians to ascribe the pursuit of this aim to all human beings. Salvation is what all of humankind seeks in its deepest or highest aspirations, according to this standard view of the matter.

This view may have had some plausibility in the circumstances in which Christian theology of religions was first developed and in much of subsequent history, but it poses certain difficulties today in view both of the scientific study of religions and of what other religious people might be expected to say in the course of proposing their doctrines.

The view that all religious people are seeking an aim which could be described as "salvation" might at one time have been able to invoke the comparative study of religions in its support. Pursuing a line of inquiry much dependent on the work of S. G. F. Brandon, some comparativists sought to employ the category of "salvation" to identify certain common features in the doctrines about aims of life among existing (and extinct) religious traditions.[6] Christian theologians could then appeal to the apparent universality of certain ranges of soteriological doctrines in order to support the universality of salvation as the aim of life sought in all religions and surpassingly advanced by Christianity.

But more recent comparative work undertaken in this area suggests that earlier studies read a substantial Christian content into the doctrines of other religious traditions.[7] Hence some comparativists are now seeking to construct a definition of the term "salvation" that is more widely applicable and less dependent on the specific meanings it is given in the Christian scheme (or in other religious schemes, for that matter).[8] Given the particularity of the content of the Christian doctrines about salvation, such studies are not likely to lend support to the view that salvation as Christian doctrines define it is what all religions seek. Even when soteriological doctrines are identified in other religious schemes, it does not follow that they possess the kind of central significance that doctrines about salvation possess in the Christian scheme. If appeal to the comparative study of religions is to be appropriate in Christian theology of religions, then it will have to be made with the recognition that the Christian doctrines about salvation are analogous not to any and every teaching in other religions about the amelioration of the human lot but to specific teachings which seek to define and foster the true aim of life which these religions pursue.

A more serious difficulty with the notion that other religious people are seeking and can attain salvation is connected with the self-descriptions of the adherents of other religions (rather than with the empirical study of their doctrines). This difficulty is more serious because Catholic Christians are committed by official policy to enter into dialogue with other religious people, and this policy by definition requires attention to the distinctive claims that other traditions advance in their teachings.[9]

Suppose that a Christian theologian should say that Theravāda Buddhism is fulfilled by Christianity or that Theravāda Buddhists can attain salvation through the practice of their religion. What is argued in support of similar assertions in the literature of late antiquity (in which it is stated, for example, that Judaism is fulfilled by Christianity or that Platonists can attain salvation) is assumed to be demonstrable with regard to Buddhism (and presumably Vedānta, Confucianism, and other religions as well). But in view of what Buddhists might say in the course of proposing their own doctrines, it seems implausible to assert that such doctrines are fulfilled by Christian doctrines or that Buddhists aim to attain salvation through the pattern of life fostered by their doctrines.

Suppose the following to be a plausible statement of some central Theravāda Buddhist doctrines:[10]

Like the schemes of other religions, the doctrinal scheme of Theravāda Buddhism can be characterized as fostering an overall pattern of life in its adherents. In this scheme there is a doctrine that proposes a comprehensive aim for human life: the whole of life should be directed to the attainment of Nirvana. This practical doctrine recommending a comprehensive course of action is connected with a number of other practical doctrines—usually summarized as the Excellent Eightfold Path —enjoining a variety of courses of action whose adoption is meant to advance one along the way to enlightenment. In teaching that the aim of life is the state of enlightenment and the extinction of desire, the Buddhist scheme can be said to ascribe an intrinsic value of an unrestricted sort to the state of being designated as Nirvana: it is good without reference to any further object or state of being. Thus, in addition to many practical doctrines, the Buddhist scheme can be said to possess a doctrine that expresses its basic religious valuation. This valuation can take a variety of forms, which have in common this logical feature: the ascription of unrestricted primacy-ranking predicates to the referent Nirvana as a state of being that is supremely worthy of pursuit and attainment.

In the course of explicating the basic religious valuation and the main practical doctrines of his scheme, a member of the Buddhist community would probably need to appeal to certain important beliefs about the human condition and life in this world in view of which it is reasonable and proper to seek the aim which Theravāda Buddhism recommends for human life. These existential conditions include various human situations that unavoidably involve unhappiness, the dependent origination of unhappiness in desire leading to successive rebirth, and the need for the extinction of the desire for existence or nonexistence if unhappiness is to cease. Divine or supernatural beings—if they exist at all—are subject to the same existential conditions and cannot be counted upon to contribute to the human advance toward enlightenment.

Much current Catholic theology of religions can be understood to suppose that the Theravāda Buddhist doctrine of the extinction of all desire is in some way analogous to some aspects of the Christian doctrine of salvation. The Buddhist account of the attainment of the true aim of life involves the doctrine of the "nonself": that is to say, the point at which a member of the Buddhist community could be said to have attained Nirvana is with the realization that there is no substantial or permanent self. The illusion of the self, or the soul, or the inner core of personal identity must be overcome if true extinction of desire is to be attained. All the practical doctrines of Buddhism are intended to bring its adherents to this goal.

But in Christianity the point at which one of its adherents can be said to have arrived at the true aim of life involves the person's continued personal identity—not to mention its fullest possible realization—and a relationship of intersubjective union with God. The practical doctrines of the Christian community are intended to foster the development and enrichment of personal life in view of this goal.

It seems clear that significant differences (I have not meant to uncover clear-cut oppositions) obtain between Christian and Theravāda Buddhist descriptions of the state of one who has achieved the true aim of life. These differences arise from other ones linked with the basic valuations, the main practical doctrines and the overall patterns of life in the respective schemes of these two traditions. It might be that a Christian theologian or missionary well versed in the doctrines and traditions of Theravāda Buddhism could mount some arguments to show how these differences could be resolved in particular cases. But in the absence of such arguments it would seem implausible to designate as "salvation" the distinctive aims that Christian and Buddhist doctrines recommend, and further to suggest that the practical doctrines of these two communities advance their members to the attainment of aims that are in some hidden way congruent or identical.

For this reason a Catholic theology of religions seems implausible when it yields assertions implying that Buddhist doctrines are fulfilled by Christian doctrines or that members of Buddhist communities can attain salvation through the practice of their religion. This difficulty occurs in especially acute form in formulations that seek to describe other religious people as hiddenly (implicitly or anonymously) Christian.[11] Such assertions seem not to do justice to the distinctive claims at least of Theravāda Buddhism (and arguably of other religions as well).

Suppose that a Buddhist should wish to express confidence about the chances of some Christians' attaining Nirvana. Suppose further that in order to do so the Buddhist should assert that some Christians attain enlightenment and final extinction of desire insofar as they find and follow the Excellent Eightfold Path laid out in a hidden way in Christian doctrines.[12] Such an assertion would be comparable to Christian theological formulations describing particular religions as channels of grace or means of salvation for their adherents, and I introduce it here in order to underline the difficulty posed by such Christian formulations.

To pursue this illustration, suppose that a Christian should accept such a statement as a well-intentioned acknowledgment of the religious and ethical values of Christianity on the part of some Buddhist. The Christian might nonetheless be inclined to regard this Buddhist valuation of Christian as somewhat improbable, since Buddhist doctrines and Christian doctrines do not—at least on the face of things—foster the same comprehensive patterns and aims of life. This would be true even if elements of the Excellent Eightfold Path could be isolated in Christian doctrines, especially practical ones.

The Christian pattern of life is centered on God as the source and term of the fullest possible human self-realization in eternal life. Hence Christians might have some difficulty seeing how the doctrines and life of their community foster an aim of life rather different (and possibly opposed to) the one they expressly commend and support. As Buddhist doctrines can plausibly be construed to teach, the true aim of life consists not in a permanent intersubjective union with any divine being but in the extinction of desire and with this the extinction of the desire for personal identity. A Buddhist who wanted to frame his acknowledgment of the worth of Christianity in terms of an ascription of contributory value would have to show how particular Christian doctrines advance the attainment of an aim other than the one they explicitly commend. In the absence of arguments showing this, the Buddhist valuation might well seem implausible and irrelevant in view of the basic valuation, central beliefs, and main practical doctrines ingredient in the Christian scheme and pattern of life.

Formulations in theology of religions that describe other religions as channels of grace or ways of salvation (in some strict and not simply metaphorical sense) and ascribe the pursuit of salvation to their adherents would in all likelihood pose similar difficulties in view of what Buddhists, Hindus, and others might be expected to say in proposing and developing their doctrines. I have argued that in part the difficulty here lies in the assumption that salvation is what other religions seek for their adherents. Insofar as they convey ascriptions of direct contributory value—"salvific value"—to other religions, formulations in theology of religions fall short of doing full justice to the distinctive doctrinal claims put forward by non-Christian religious traditions.

III

"I once read through a collection of the lives of Roman Catholic saints," wrote the Buddhist scholar Edward Conze, "and there was not one of whom a Buddhist could fully approve. This does not mean that they were unworthy people, but that they were bad Buddhists, though good Christians."[13]

This remark suggests, as I have argued, that the doctrinal standards by which a person would be judged to have attained the true aim of life in Buddhism are rather different from those that would be invoked in appraising Christian values of life. Both a Christian saint and a Theravādin arahant would be regarded by their respective communities as having attained or being on their way to attaining the true aim of life. But the states of mind and being of such persons would be described in rather different terms. Seeking and attaining Nirvana are not the same things as seeking and attaining salvation.

This point could be extended and generalized. As has already been suggested, the world's major religions cannot plausibly be described as proposing different ways to identical goals. "Salvation," "Nirvana," and "Paradise" are not simply different terms designating the single reality sought by Christians, Buddhists, and Muslims under different descriptions. Christianity, Buddhism, and Islam, respectively, employ these terms in ways that are intertwined with specific and distinctive views about what is worth seeking and why. Persons whose lives have been shaped by the particular doctrines of these communities ought not be described as advancing willy-nilly to the same goal by different routes. Such a description of what they are up to will seem implausible and perhaps even impertinent to religious people who are intent on the pursuit of union with the Blessed Trinity, or enlightenment, or the garden of delights. Christianity, Buddhism, and Islam (and other traditions as well) each foster different sorts of dispositions in their adherents, in view of distinctive teachings about the aim of life, the reasons for pursuing it, and the means to attain it. And each can be understood to claim that the aim of life it proposes is the one most worthy of pursuit by all human beings without exception. Adherents of these traditions who took part in an interreligious dialogue would presumably be prepared to advance arguments in support of their claims, showing how they were true, right, or good, connecting them with each other in the overall patterns of life they foster, and linking them with other areas of human knowledge and concern.

My argument up to this point has been in part a "plea for the recognition of differences"[14] on the part of Christian theology of religions, especially when it seeks to take into account the "salvation" of the members of other religious communities. If it is to be respectful and just in its account of other religions—as present circumstances clearly require—then Catholic theology of religions will have to be more circumspect in its employment of the concept of salvation in teaching about other religions and their adherents. I have meant to argue not that the concept be abandoned in theology of religions but, rather, that it not be permitted to obscure the distinctive teachings other traditions propose about the aim of life and with these the overall integrity of their schemes of doctrines and patterns of life. I have argued that it is inappropriate for Catholic theology of religions to assume that salvation is "really" what all religions are seeking for their adherents. An assumption of this sort appears to be embedded in theological formulations in this field that ascribe salvific value to other religions and describe the dispositions of their adherents in primarily Christian terms.

My aim now is briefly to sketch an alternative way of accounting for the place in the plan of salvation of non-Christian religions and their adherents. I shall argue that it is consistent with Christian doctrines about the universality of salvation to develop theological formulations which respect and do justice to the distinctive claims that other religions make about the aim of life. The kind of formulations I have in view would be framed in terms of the concepts of the "providential diversity of religions" and "prospective affiliation with the Christian community."

Instead of ascribing to other religions a present salvific value, the theological formulations envisaged here would assert that other religions play a real but as yet not fully specifiable role in the divine plan to which Christianity bears unique witness. Instead of attributing to non-Christian persons a hidden or implicit association with the Christian community, furthermore, theology of religions should speak of a prospective or future affiliation on the part of the present members of other religious communities.

The unique valuation of the Christian community and of its particular role in the divine plan need not be construed—though it has sometimes in the past—as excluding the attribution of some providential role to other religious communities in the overall plan of God for the salvation of the world. Although this providential role is less concretely specifiable than that of Christianity (and of Judaism), it is nonetheless possible to ascribe such a role to other religions without prejudice to central Christian doctrines or to the unique valuation of the Christian community entailed by these doctrines. The notion that other religions play some part in the divine plan accords with traditional teachings in which it has been affirmed that they contribute to the acceptance of the Christian faith on the part of certain individuals or in certain cultures, or that they foster the development of a social climate supportive of values of which Christians approve, or that they may be instruments of some divine purpose. The complete nature of this providential role will be disclosed only with the consummation of human history, which Christianity longs for and proclaims in its doctrines about the last things.[15]

I have observed in the course of this paper that Christian theology of religions has been—and continues to be—profoundly influenced by formulations in which the Christian community explicates its relationship to Judaism.[16] The Christian conception of this relationship is lately undergoing extensive revision. One important trend in this developing discussion is represented by the effort on the part of some Christians to be more explicit about the permanent providential role of the Jewish community in bringing about the consummation of history. To be sure, the Christian stake in such efforts is considerable: if the promises to Abraham and Moses have lost their validity, then Christian confidence in God's promise in Christ is likely to seem misplaced. But despite the singular importance that Christians attach to ascriptions of providential value to the Jewish community, it is possible that an analogous valuation would be in order with respect to other religious communities as well. The notion of the providential diversity of religions has a valuation of this sort in view: God wills that other religions perform functions in his plan for humankind which are now only dimly perceived and which will be fully disclosed only at the end of time. Other religions are to be valued by Christians not because they are channels of grace or means of salvation for their adherents, but because they play a real but unspecifiable role in the divine plan. One might speak of what has been called "the unsubstitutableness of the God-willed missions" of non-Christian religions.[17]

Paralleling the notion of the providential diversity of religions is the notion of the prospective affiliation of non-Christians with the Christian community. In place of a hidden *present* association, the theology of religions I am sketching here would envisage a prospective or *future* affiliation with the Christian community on the part of persons who are now either explicit members of other religious communities or are not affiliated with any religious community.

Like the valuation implicit in the concept of the providential diversity of religions, the phrase "prospective affiliation" has the eschatological future in view. Just as the providential role of non-Christian religions will be fully revealed only when the divine plan has been consummated, so the participation of non-Christian persons in the salvation to come will be sealed by their visible but future affiliation with the eschatological community of the just. This concept can also be employed to refer, by way of the theology of death and purgatory, to possibilities latent in the individual futures of non-Christian persons.

The ascription of a prospective affiliation with the Christian community to non-Christians does not require the support of any properly Christian valuation of their present religious and moral dispositions and conduct. A theology of religions ruled by this concept could acknowledge the goodness and uprightness of other religious people without ascribing salvific value to these qualities. Such qualities can be esteemed for the role they play in the pursuit of the distinctive aims of life of the communities of which such persons are members and as the outcome of fidelity to the doctrines—especially the practical ones—by which the lives of such persons in religious communities come to be shaped. The specific ways in which the presently observable and assessable conduct and dispositions of non-Christians will conduce to their future affiliation with the Christian community and thus to their "salvation" are now hidden from view and known only to God.

IV

A theology of religions framed in terms of the concepts of the providential diversity of religions and the prospective affiliation with the Christian community would be able to do justice to the distinctive claims put forward by other religious traditions and to support a vigorous and forthright view of the Christian mission.

The theology of religions I have in view expresses the presumption that the members of non-Christian communities could give an adequate description—in terms of the basic valuations, practical doctrines, and central beliefs they profess—of the dispositions that are fostered in their communities and that are exhibited in the conduct of their lives, in their comportment toward others, and in their civil and social intercourse. Such a theology of religions can do justice to other religions by acknowledging and respecting the qualities they engender without describing these qualities in terms that are appropriate only within the Christian scheme of doctrines, namely, as salvific or grace-filled. Though undoubtedly well intentioned, it cannot in the end be truly respectful of the doctrines and life of the members of other religious communities to attribute to them the unwitting pursuit of the aim of life as one defines it in one's own community.

The theology of religions being sketched here also affords a more straightforward affirmation of the distinctiveness of specifically Christian doctrines about the aim of life, or salvation, than is possible in theological formulations that ascribe some salvific value to non-Christian religions. Christian confidence in the universality of salvation rests not on the universal dispersion of vaguely soteriological doctrines in other religious traditions but on a particular set of divine promises and actions about which the Christian community is charged to give faithful witness in its evangelical mission.

Teachings about salvation figure prominently in the overall pattern of life and worship of the Christian community. Indeed, sometimes the most important Christian doctrines get summarized in the form of a narrative aptly designated as the story of salvation. The Christian message in a nutshell is the good news of salvation. This story is complex. The term "salvation" itself can refer to past events already accomplished, to the continuing transformation of Christian believers, and to the final consummation of the history of the human race.

According to the Christian story of salvation God has undertaken to bring the larger story of the world to a happy ending. Christians hope for salvation not because they have learned from experience that things always turn out for the best, nor because they are persuaded that human yearnings for deliverance entail some ultimate satisfaction. The Christian hope for salvation, in all its aspects, rests on convictions about the reliability of the divine undertakings about which the Christian community must bear witness.

The particularity and complexity of specifically Christian teachings about salvation give force and content to the Christian community's hope that the final consummation of salvation will include the broadest possible range of human beings. Religiously serious persons have sometimes found it paradoxical that the happy ending of the human story as a whole—if there is to be one—is expectantly and, in the Christian view, authoritatively sketched in the story of that particular segment of the human family that has come to be known as the Christian community. There may be paradox but there need be no arrogant exclusivism in this claim. It is no part of the Christian story (at least in its mainstream versions) that only the members of the particular Christian community will enjoy the final consummation with which God has promised to end the world's story. It is, however, part of that story that the fulfillment of the divine promise about history's happy ending depends in some largely obscure way on the continued existence of a particular community, limited in duration and extent, within the larger human family. The perseverance of the Christian community in fidelity to its Lord and in persistent narration of its special story is of intrinsic significance for the salvation of the rest of humankind, including that portion of it that existed before the time of Christ.

It is of the essence of the Christian mission to bear witness to this faith and hope in salvation and at the same time to respect the values present in non-Christian religions. The concepts of the providential diversity of religions and the prospective affiliation with the Christian community, because they acknowledge the distinctiveness of non-Christian doctrines about the aim of life (and other crucial matters), also permit a strong affirmation of the distinctiveness of Christian doctrines about salvation. Thus these concepts do not involve a denial or diminution of the Christian doctrine about the universality of salvation. To suppose that religious communities foster distinctive (as opposed to identical or congruent) aims of life is not equivalent to supposing that the different aims commended by particular religious communities are all equally worthy of pursuit. A theology of religions shaped by the concepts I have proposed would permit arguments by Catholic participants in dialogue or by Catholic missionaries to the effect that the aims of life commended by other religions inadequately or erroneously or misguidedly envisage the true aim of life that the Christian community in fact commends and fosters. The theology of religions I have sketched here preserves the unique valuation of the Christian community and respects its doctrines about the universality of salvation without prejudice to its ability to recognize and even learn from the manifest diversity of religious aims and therefore the distinctiveness and integrity of non-Christian religious schemes and patterns of life. Such a theology of religions provides a more adequate and traditional legitimation for Christian mission than does one in which evangelization comes to be viewed primarily as the identification of virtualities already present in other religions or as the explication of inclinations already implicit in the dispositions of their adherents. Theological formulations that imply this view of evangelization and mission do justice neither to the distinctive claims of other religions nor to the particular hope for salvation about which Christians are charged to give witness.

Notes

1. In developing these clarifications of the logic of religious doctrines, I am aided at many points by Joseph M. Bochenski, *The Logic of Religion* (New York: New York University Press, 1965), and by William A. Christian, *Meaning and Truth in Religion* (Princeton: Princeton University Press, 1964); *Oppositions of Religious Doctrines* (New York: Herder and Herder, 1972), and "Bochenski on the Structure of Schemes of Doctrines," *Religious Studies* 13 (1977): 203-19.

2. See Hans Küng, *The Church* (New York: Sheed and Ward, 1967), pp. 313-19, for a brief historical account of this formula.

3. In this paper I consider only some Christian teachings of this sort. For some corresponding Buddhist doctrines see, for example, Phra Khantipālo, *Tolerance: A Study from Buddhist Sources* (London: Rider and Company, 1964) and K. Sri Dhammananda, *Why Religious Tolerance?* (Kuala Lumpur: Buddhist Missionary Society, 1974).

4. See Louis Capéran, *Le problème du salut des infidèles: Essai historique* (Toulouse: Grand Séminaire, 1934).

5. See Jaroslav Pelikan, *The Christian Tradition*, vol. 1: *The Emergence of the Catholic Tradition* (Chicago: University of Chicago Press, 1971), pp. 55-67.

6. See S. G. F. Brandon, *Man and His Destiny in the Great Religions* (Toronto: University of Toronto Press, 1962) and *The Savior God: Comparative Studies in the Concept of Salvation Presented to E. O. James* (Manchester: Manchester University Press, 1963); R. J. Z. Werblowsky and C. J. Bleeker, eds., *Types of Redemption* (Leiden: E. J. Brill, 1970).

7. Willard G. Oxtoby, "Reflections on the Idea of Salvation," *Man and His Salvation: Studies in Memory of S. G. F. Brandon*, ed. E. J. Sharpe and J. R. Hinnells (Manchester: Manchester University Press, 1973), pp. 17-37.

8. Douglas Davies, "The Notion of Salvation in the Comparative Study of Religions," *Religion* 8 (1978): 85-100.

9. I have argued this point at considerable length in "Catholic Theology of Religions and Interreligious Dialogue: A Study in the Logic of Christian Doctrines about Other Religions" (Yale Ph.D. dissertation, 1980).

10. Here I propose what I take to be plausible illustrations of some Theravāda Buddhist doctrines. But it should be noted that nothing in my argument depends logically on the adequacy of my description of Theravāda Buddhism. My argument concerns the construction of theological formulations given the reasonable supposition that Christians will have occasion to, encounter religious communities whose doctrines will manifest distinctive claims about the true aim of life and related matters. The illustrations I offer here are meant to exemplify something of the range of logical

requirements that theology of religions must meet in present circumstances.

11. The concept of implicit faith has its logical home in the Christian scheme where it is employed to designate a feature of the faith of Christians who are not able fully to articulate the content of Christian doctrines but whose faith is nonetheless authentic and complete. The use of this concept to describe the dispositions of non-Christians is an extended one, posing considerable philosophical and theological problems that cannot be treated adequately in a short space. For reasons which will become obvious in the course of this paper, I believe that the concept of implicit faith ought to be abandoned as a way of accounting for the upright dispositions of non-Christian persons.

12. This point was suggested to me by a passage from a Buddhist scripture, the Mahāparinibbāna-sutta (V, 23–30), in which the wanderer Subhadda asks the Buddha about the value of non-Buddhist teachings. For a translation of this text, see *Dialogues of the Buddha,* part 2, trans. T. W. Rhys Davids and C. A. F. Rhys Davids (London: Pali Text Society, 1910), pp. 164–69. I do not mean to imply that the valuation of Christian doctrines suggested to me by this text would indeed be accepted or propounded by official or authoritative teachers in any Buddhist community.

13. Edward Conze, "Buddhist Saviors," *The Savior,* ed. S. G. F. Brandon (Manchester: Manchester University Press, 1962), p. 82.

14. Steven T. Katz, "Language, Epistemdogy and Mysticism," *Mysticism and Philosophical Analysis,* ed. Steven T. Katz (New York: Oxford University Press, 1978), p. 25.

15. See George A. Lindbeck, *The Future of Roman Catholic Theology* (Philadelphia: Fortress Press, 1969), pp. 9–25, 35–38, 56–58.

16. From the extensive literature on contemporary Jewish-Christian relations, see the helpful survey of some significant issues in Harry Siegman, "A Decade of Catholic-Jewish Relations: A Reassessment," *Journal of Ecumenical Studies* 15 (1978):243–60.

17. George A. Lindbeck, "Theories of Religion and 'Method in Theology' " (manuscript, 1979).

25

MELANESIA

James J. Knight, S. V.D.

Melanesia refers to an ethnic rather than a geographical or political reality. It refers primarily to the indigenous populations of the southwestern Pacific islands of New Guinea, including small offshore island groups, the Bismarck Archipelago, the Solomon Islands, Vanuatu, New Caledonia, and Fiji. These populations had their first contacts with Catholic missionaries in the sixteenth century, when Franciscan chaplains accompanied the Spanish ships on their early Pacific voyages.[1] Alvaro de Mendana, who explored the Solomon Islands during 1568, even abducted some islanders, with the intention of eventually returning them to the Solomons as missionaries to their own people. Alas, they died in Peru. But with the decline of imperial Spain and the Catholic missionary movement of Europe in the seventeenth century, it took almost three hundred years before the French Marists, on December 21, 1843, returned a Catholic missionary presence to Melanesia.[2] After several failures, this presence developed into a sturdy missionary movement that has established twenty-six flourishing Catholic dioceses (local churches) across Melanesia. (For the purposes of this paper, and to avoid ambiguity, I shall restrict the use of the term "local church" so that it refers solely to the Catholic communities of a particular diocese, united in faith, sacramental life, and mission around their bishop. By this restriction I do not wish to imply that the term may not be given other meanings.)

The Melanesian populations of today see themselves as different from, yet very identified with, the populations to which those heroic nineteenth-century missionaries addressed their preaching and witness. The political, social, economic, and religious realities with which modern Melanesian populations must come to grips, and to which the local churches of today must direct their mission, are also different from (though often the results of) the forces with which those nineteenth-century Melanesian populations and missionaries struggled. For example, the challenges and crises of nation-building in the newly independent countries of Fiji, Papua New

James J. Knight is presently Dean of the Divine Word Society major seminarians in Papua New Guinea. He is likewise Secretary of the Commission on Ecumenism for the Bishops' Conference of Papua New Guinea, and chaplain to a prison.

Guinea, Solomon Islands, and Vanuatu give new and clear goals for their Melanesian populations, as a new and definite context for the mission of the local churches in those countries. The little-known struggles for an acceptable form of self- determination by the Melanesian populations of New Caledonia and Irian Jaya give the mission of the local churches there another new and more difficult context. Neither France nor Indonesia is likely to give full political independence to these valuable pieces of real estate. And the unevenness of past and present economic and social developments has moved some Melanesians into positions of privilege and wealth, while it has pushed others into dependency and deprivation. No diocese is completely free from the challenges that this kind of social and economic growth produces. All these challenges and contexts, however, have their roots in the beginnings of the colonial era in the closing decades of the last century.

Then there are the challenges and contexts for mission that the millennia-old and enduring non-Christian religious traditions of Melanesia present to the local churches.[3] These religious traditions challenge a local church to embark on an inner dialogue with itself, as much as on an external dialogue with authentic representatives of these traditions. Each local church is forced to carry on its own dialogue, although not in isolation from any other church (one hopes).

Today's context, for the mission of the local church in relation to the religious traditions of Melanesia, is shaped by modern cultural revivals. Cultural revivals in Melanesia take many forms, and have their effect on Christians and non-Christians alike. They come in waves; they grow and decline, but never completely disappear. Local churches ignore, to their own peril, the yearnings and struggles deep within Melanesian souls expressed in these revivals. And the effectiveness of a local church's response to this mission context and challenge will affect, for better or worse, the effectiveness of that church's response to other mission contexts and challenges.

Melanesian Religion before Christianity

The first source to be explored for an understanding of the mission of the local church is Melanesian life and religion as manifested before the arrival of the Christian missionaries.

The Depth of Melanesian Religious Traditions

From their excavations in the Tapini area of Papua New Guinea, archaeologists tell us there were people living in Melanesia 26,000 years ago.[4] Some archaeologists speculate, from the nature of the Ice Age and the probability of migration from Southeast Asia, that there may have been people moving through Melanesia as early as 50,000 years ago. Be that as it may, the date of 26,000 years ago gives us an adequate indication of the depth of human experience in Melanesia. It is impossible for us to guess at the precise kind of life and religious experience those earliest inhabitants had, except that they were hunters and gatherers and probably nomadic; and we know nothing of the kind of religious experience they had.

About 9,000 years ago there is evidence, again from archaeological excavations, that Melanesians began a slow move from hunting and gathering to gardening and animal husbandry, notably of the pig. The pig was brought into Melanesia by immigrants from Southeast Asia during this period as an already domesticated animal. In the Highlands of Papua New Guinea, the move from a predominantly hunting and gathering economy to a predominantly agriculturally based economy was completed by about 6,000 years ago.[5] The changeover probably took longer in areas where the game was more plentiful and the population less dense. A few small Melanesian groups are still primarily nomadic hunters and secondarily slash-and-burn gardeners. The introduction of the ground-edge stone ax in the Highlands and elsewhere, about 7,000 years ago, enabled an easier clearance of forest area, which hastened (where it was so used) the final stages of the agricultural revolution.

If present-day evidence can be a reliable guide for speculating about the past, and I think it can in this instance, we may postulate that with the change of the economies there was an accompanying religious change in the way Melanesians related to their environment, ancestors, and other spirits. For sure, gardening anchors a population to a particular locality much more than hunting and gathering. The particular environment of a horticulturally anchored population would, as a result, have gained a more important place in their cultural and religious heritage. It is likely that the ancestors became more influential as well in their religious heritage. The continuing proximity of the ancestors' graves, and the growth of devotion associated with these graves, would account for the ancestors' new prominence. This localizing of populations was undoubtedly an important factor in the development of the manifold cultural and religious traditions of Melanesia.

Indeed, if we consider that 4.5 million Melanesians speak over one-fourth, or 1,200, of the world's known languages, we are tempted to picture Melanesia as hundreds of small language groups living the past millennia in total isolation from one another. But this is a distorted picture of "Old Melanesia." There was much social, economic, and cultural overlapping from one group to the next, and for all those past millennia trade routes have criss-crossed Melanesia. In archaeological digs in the Eastern Highlands of Papua New Guinea seashells have been uncovered, which, according to the evidence, arrived there 14,000 years ago. The only way these shells could have reached there was by trade. But new technological innovations, myths, rituals, and beliefs, as well as shells, moved along these trade routes.[6]

Localized populations and a flourishing trade between populations seem to be the dynamic and context that shaped the cultural and religious traditions of Melanesia. The traditions established themselves with bewildering variety and richness. Each localized population had a clear cultural and religious identity. This allowed it to select from its trading partners the rituals, myths, and beliefs that were useful to it. It also allowed a localized population to interpret its new rituals, myths, and beliefs to fit its own situation. Contrary to much popular opinion, the religious prehistory of Melanesia can only have been one of extraordinary vigor. From an examination of the evidence, especially the oral traditions of a number of ethnic and cultural populations, Dr. Roderic Lacey of the University of Papua New Guinea concludes "that the historical context and substance of religious life, belief and ritual in precolonial Papua New Guinea was a situation of change, fluidity and movement."[7]

Characteristics of Melanesian Religious Traditions

"Change, fluidity and movement" have been a central feature of the religious traditions of Melanesia before and after their contact with Christianity. But all aspects of the traditions are not equally open to change; some are stubbornly resistant to change and, paradoxically, change in some aspects only reinforces continuity in other aspects. A better understanding of change and continuity in these traditions can be attained only after we have clarified the possibilities of change in the light of other characteristics of Melanesian religious traditions. When one considers the multiplicity and variety of these traditions, the formulating of general characteristics is necessarily a risky business. Still it must be done if we are to make progress in understanding these traditions. And it can be done as long as it is remembered that they are in fact generalizations.

A second general characteristic—the first being change—is the drive to possess an "abundance of life" in all its presently available forms. In the first place, this is cosmic and biological life, but the acquisition of cosmic and biological life must manifest itself by success in every area of human endeavor. In an important paper entitled "A Fundamental Melanesian Religion," Father Ennio Mantovani describes it as the belief

> in what has been called "fertility," but which is much more than biological fertility (and therefore the term "fertility" should be rejected as inadequate), and in a life which has "spiritual" aspects like "big name," success, prestige, luck, beside health, wealth etc. All this is meant by the term *bios*, which is life.
>
> Second, *bios* is not limited to humans, but is cosmic; it refers to every "creature"—humans, animals, vegetables, the whole world.[8]

On the one hand, for traditional Melanesians this ultimate value was a concern for survival. Survival meant a constant and not always successful struggle. A most unpredictable environment, the opposition of one or more hostile spirits, and the powerful sorcery of enemies—all endangered one's very existence. Because survival was such a precarious enterprise, it would seem that one's aim had to be, on the other hand, for an abundance. Abundance first of all in the subsistence economy, which could then be transformed into social and political prestige and power—real proofs of a "Melanesian abundance of life."

What we have termed a "Melanesian abundance of life" is concretized and epitomized in the traditional and modern Melanesian "big-man." In most Melanesian societies, a leader is a man who has demonstrated his ability to marshal his own and his followers' economic resources into exchange partnerships with other important leaders; to lead his followers to victory in battle; and to bring them to consensus on critical issues. Because of his success he will marry many wives, and (he hopes) will have even more children. Above all, his followers and enemies will behold him as a man of wealth, power, and standing. His power, standing, and in some societies his wealth as well, will remain his even through the major disruption of his death; he will remain a "big-man" in the life beyond the grave, which in Melanesia is essentially an extension of life this side of the grave. Hence, although disrupted by death, a "Melanesian abundance of life" continues in the life beyond death.

In some Melanesian languages there is a term that identifies a reality as the source of real abundance and success. Codrington, in his classic *The Melanesians* (1891), identified this term in the New Hebridean languages as the word *mana*. He described it thus:

> It is a power or influence, not physical, and in a way supernatural; but it shows itself in physical force, or in any kind of power or excellence which a man possesses. This *Mana* is not fixed in anything, and can be conveyed in almost anything; but spirits whether disembodied souls or supernatural beings, have it and can impart it; and it essentially belongs to personal beings to originate it, though it may act through the medium of water or a stone, or a bone. All Melanesian religion consists, in fact, in getting this *Mana* for one's self, or getting it used for one's benefit—all religion, that is, as far as religious practices go, prayers and sacrifices.[9]

If we divorce this term from the unfortunate use that Marett and others put it to in their futile search for the origins of religion,[10] we can appreciate it as a Melanesian speculation about a kind of metaphysical source, which, if tapped correctly, would provide a full participation in the abundance of life.[11] This point is borne out by another statement made by Codrington: "Of course, a yam naturally grows when planted, that is well known, but it will not be very large unless *mana* comes in play; a canoe will not be swift unless *mana* be brought to bear upon it, similarly a net will not catch many fish, nor an arrow inflict a mortal wound."[12]

To make a crude paraphase; "without *mana* there can be no salvation"; salvation, of course, being an abundance and success in all the possibilities of human life. Consequently a big-man, who by his visible success demonstrated his possession of *mana,* was naturally deemed to have an ideal relationship with his ancestors and the important spirits of his world.[13]

The third characteristic is the extensiveness and strength of the Melanesian belief in the efficacy of ritual. This results in a great multiplicity of rituals in Melanesian life. If it is performed correctly, a ritual links together two spheres of life and power, so that one sphere is harnessed for the benefit of the other. Or else a ritual, correctly performed, separates two dangerously opposed spheres of life and power, so that one sphere does not damage the other. The one sphere is a visible, empirical object (e.g., a garden, a sick child, a canoe), which is in obvious need or danger. The other sphere is a source of life, energy, power, and fortune. Malinowski claimed that this sphere, or source, was somehow contained in the words of the spell, which usually accompanied the actions of a ritual.[14] Depending on how the life, energy, power, and fortune are directed by the ritual, it will bring good or bad fortune, life-giving or destructive power.

In the myths of Melanesia are many ancestral heroes who, because they possessed the correct ritual knowledge, were able to perform such Herculean feats as shaping the landscape, causing canoes to fly, vanquishing the enemy in war, providing new technological and social innovations. Because much of this knowledge was lost, as it was handed down from one generation to the next, the Melanesians of a later period could not participate in life with the same fullness with which their ancestors had been blessed. If the correct knowledge of each appropriate ritual had been handed down in its complete form, the present generation would be able to perform exactly the same feats as their ancestors performed. This seems a very utilitarian approach to ritual, and no doubt it is. But it is precisely this belief in the effectiveness of ritual correctly performed that allows Melanesians to give themselves so totally to ritual celebration, and to life in all its forms. It also makes them participators in their cosmos, rather than passive receivers.

This leads us to the fourth characteristic of Melanesian religious traditions: secrecy. If a person, family, or clan possesses the know-how of a ritual, it is considered their power and their wealth. Hence, while they may broadcast the fact that they possess the knowledge, the knowledge itself they keep a tightly guarded secret. They might, for an item of equivalent value, exchange a ritual secret with a friendly trading partner. Secrecy, however, is essential, since the value of ritual knowledge depends on others not knowing it.

The fifth characteristic is the central importance of the ancestors. When there is a small misfortune, or good fortune, in a family, the family will normally attribute it to the spirits of a recently dead relative. If the good or bad fortune affects the whole clan, it is normally attributed to the remote ancestors, the spirits of the founders of the clan. In the great majority of cases they possess the means of solving the problems that the clan faces. There is a myth found in many parts of Melanesia that gives the story of a community that is being destroyed by a monster. In some places it is a sea monster, in other places it is a giant boar from the forest. This monster breaks down houses and kills the inhabitants of the village. The survivors decide to abandon their village. In their rush to leave their threatened village they leave behind a woman with her baby son (at times twin sons). The woman takes shelter in a cave or some place secure from the monster. The child miraculously grows up and the mother trains him for battle with the monster. Then one day he faces the monster and, after a desperate battle, kills it. The mother and son bring the remnants of the community back to the village. The son takes a wife and becomes the real ancestor of the clan community.

Certain ancestors, like the one above, have proved themselves capable of protecting the community against forces that threaten to destroy it. Other ancestors have shown that they are the great benefactors of their clan. These ancestors gave the clan their land, their social, economic, and religious institutions, all the technological and ritual innovations they possess and, most of all, the clan's identity as a people.

Often the gift that the ancestor gave to his clan was won at great cost and danger to himself. Edai Siabo, for example, was the founder of the *Hiri* trading system. He was out fishing one day with his clan brothers when he was captured by a *dirava* spirit. The *dirava* spirit drew him down into a cave in the bottom of the sea. His brothers thought he was lost at sea and searched for him. Meanwhile the *dirava* spirit taught Edai Siabo the knowledge necessary for building the seagoing *lakotoi* canoe.

Later he was discovered in the sea and brought back to his village. When he awoke, as if from death, he began to teach his people the knowledge that he had gained while away in the depths of the sea. A traditional Melanesian is greatly indebted to his ancestors.

It is important to make a theoretical distinction between mythical and historical ancestors, even though in practice it is sometimes hard to do so.[15] A historical ancestor can be a great warrior, hunter, fisherman, gardener, feared sorcerer, the one who led his clan onto their land, or a combination of any of these. His fame has kept him alive in the memory of his people. All his extraordinary feats demonstrate that he possessed great power—*mana.*

A mythical ancestor lived in the primordial time, or rather, just at the close of primordial time, and his or her actions initiated historical time. From a religious perspective the important difference is that the historical ancestors enjoyed life in abundance: they possessed *mana,* while the mythical ancestors initiated life as it is lived in historical time. They did this by providing the first men and women with genitals, or the plants and animals essential for their food, or necessary weapons and tools, or by freeing the community from a force that threatened to annihilate it. They are deities, but not nonhuman deities in the Jewish meaning of "the gods." Historical ancestors however, tend to take on the attributes of mythical ancestors, and this makes it difficult at times to draw this distinction between them in practice.

A group of mythical ancestors, important for the purposes of this paper, have become known as *dema*-deities.[16] The word *dema* is taken from the language of the Marind-anim people who live on the southern coast of Irian Jaya. A *dema* is an ancestor who, because of some difficulty or other, is either killed violently or chooses to die; but the body is hardly buried when something miraculously happens. From the body of the dead ancestor grows a coconut tree, a yam, a taro, or some other plant or animal essential for the livelihood of the community. Jawi was the first person to die among the Marind-anim, and from his head grew the first coconut tree. In Simbu Province there are no coconut trees, but there is a *dema* myth. Mondo and Mundua were two brothers. Mondo went out in the bush one day and turned himself into a pig, and began rooting around in the ground for food. Mundua happened to come past the same way and realized that Mondo had turned himself into a pig because he saw Mondo's bird-of-paradise plumage hanging on a tree. Mundua went on home. Later Mondo turned himself back into a man. He went to get his bird-of-paradise plumage from the tree and suddenly realized that Mundua had discovered that he had turned himself into a pig. He went back to their house and told Mundua: "You and I are from the same mother and now I have great shame. I shall die and from my grave will come pigs." Shortly afterward Mondo died and from his grave came a stream of pigs, enough for all of Simbu. The *dema* insight brings to mind the insight that stands behind "Unless a wheat grain falls on the ground and dies, it remains only a single grain; but if it dies, it yields a rich harvest" (Jn. 12:24).

A sixth characteristic of the religious traditions of Melanesia is their lack of concern for the creation of the physical universe and for a main transcendent deity over the multitude of spirit beings. There are many creator deities who have shaped the physical world into its now familiar pattern; but few Melanesian deities have created out of nothing *(ex nihilo)*. The people of Wogeo Island, off the north coast of Papua New Guinea, are an exception. They believed that their deities created the whole world, except for their own island, which always existed. Creation out of nothing was evidently not a serious question for traditional Melanesians. Nor was transcendence or monotheism. The deity who had most to do with giving the physical environment its now familiar shape, and perhaps giving some of the necessities for life as well, is usually "the great deity." Still, he does not preside over the other deities and spirits, much less over the people. Rather, he has graciously removed himself from the day-to-day affairs of the community, leaving the living, the dead, and other minor spirits *(masalais)* to ponder and solve the dilemmas of human existence. Yet he is not a transcendent, totally other being. He is just further away in the universe, and basically still part of it. He can usually be reached in times of extreme necessity. Finally, there are a good number of Melanesian religious traditions that do not have a "great spirit" at all.

The seventh characteristic is a concept about how interpersonal relationships ought to be. This concept is usually given the term "reciprocity," although it has also been termed "retributive logic," "equivalence,"[17] "the liability complex," and the state of *lo*—a Pidgin expression for, although not completely corresponding to, the English word "law."[18]

The clearest evidence of this concept is in the development of an exchange partnership. An exchange partnership grows out of the giving and receiving of gifts. On the surface the concept of reciprocity controls the exchanges so that there is an evenness or equivalence between the value of the goods given and received by each partner. The purpose of the exchanges, however, is not just the free flow of goods. Rather, the purpose is the achievement of a friendly and trusting relationship between the two partners. The two partners must go on exchanging goods until they are satisfied with the parity of their exchanges and the quality of their relationship. Ideally, once this state of parity and satisfaction is achieved, there would be no more exchanges, since further exchanges would only disrupt the relationship. In the Tangu area of Madang Province of Papua New Guinea, this ideal state in an exchange partnership is called *mngwotngwotiki*. K. Burridge says of *mngwotngwotiki:*

> For the Tangu the concrete symbol of true amity in the heart is the exchange which both parties deem to be equivalent, and concerning which neither party is swayed by the malicious gossip and principles of others. In a more absolute sense such an exchange, which no one else questioned or tried to mar, would stand as a model, the exchange *par excellence*. Carried to its logical conclusion the implication is that in the best of all possible worlds, since all exchanges would be equivalent and true amity reign over all, there would be no longer any need to make exchanges.[19]

Naturally, in most exchange partnerships the ideal is yet to be achieved, and so the partners continue to initiate new exchanges.

This concept of reciprocity and the achieving of a satisfying parity between the partners also regulates the relationship between a traditional Melanesian and the spirit beings in the person's universe, and, as we shall see, applies normally to the relationship between a Melanesian Christian and Christ.

One final feature of Melanesian religious traditions is the essentially nonmissionary, or better, nonproselytizing, character of these traditions. A tradition and all it contains is the property of a definite people. The institution of secrecy guards the religious treasures of that people, and outsiders seek them at their risk. An outsider may be incorporated into this people, though rarely will the most treasured secrets be revealed to the outsider. The only news that will be proclaimed abroad is that this people owns powerful rituals, of which other peoples would do well to be afraid.

By way of a conclusion to this section let us consider again the first characteristic: the basic openness of Melanesian religious traditions for change. When we look at this characteristic in the light of the last seven characteristics, the openness of the traditions to changes becomes a much more complex reality then it at first seemed. We can only point out aspects of this complexity; it is not possible to explore those aspects here.

There is an openness to change in each of the last seven characteristics; but a distinction must be made between the expressions of a characteristic and the fundamental belief or attitude which, strictly speaking, constitutes the characteristic itself. This belief or attitude undergirds the expressions, and in the dynamic characteristics—the drive for an abundance of life, belief in ritual correctly performed, the centrality of the ancestors, and "reciprocity" as the way relationships ought to be—it even promotes experimentation in the expressions. A belief in the centrality of the ancestors, for instance, pushes a tradition to accept and interpret, according to its understanding of an ancestor, figures like Adam, Abraham, David, Mary, Christ, and the like or the belief in the effectivenes of ritual correctly performed urges a constant search for new rituals and more correct ways of performing old rituals.

Changes and experimentation in the expressions, however, do not necessarily bring a change in the belief or attitude contained in a characteristic. It could have the opposite effect of reinforcing the belief or attitude. This seems to be the case in times of rapid social and economic changes. Such changes undermine the prestige and authority of the big-men by causing new items of wealth and symbols of power (new expressions of an abundance of life) that are not available to traditional big-men. This causes a loss of community self-worth, since a Melanesian community relies on the reputation of its big-man for its identity and self-confidence. In order to obtain the new wealth and symbols, ritual activity is resorted to, especially when all other means have failed. (A search for effective rituals, rather than reliance on a transcendent, unchangeable being, is the usual Melanesian way of dealing religiously with rapid economic, political, and social changes.) All this, it seems, reinforces, rather than undermines, the belief in the effectiveness of ritual correctly performed, as well as other fundamental beliefs. Unlike their expressions, changes in fundamental beliefs come very slowly; they are modified little by little.

With the essentially nondynamic characteristics—the lack of concern for transcendence and creation, secrecy, and a nonproselytizing attitude—changes, in respect to their fundamental beliefs and attitudes, come as slowly as they do with the dynamic characteristics. But a change in these nondynamic characteristics should bring a modification of the dynamic characteristics. A change from a lack of concern to a real concern for transcendence and creation, let us say, should provoke modifications in a Melanesian understanding of ritual, the way relationships ought to be, the ancestors, and the abundance of life. There will be little change in the nondynamic characteristics, however, as long as there is a general, implicit assumption that the dynamic characteristics, as traditionally understood and accepted, are sufficient to handle all current problems. The evidence of the past hundred years demonstrates that this assumption remains solid, and at times amazingly creative. It has generated hundreds of revivalist and millenarian movements.

Melanesians and Catholic Missionaries

On December 21, 1843, two Marist missionaries, Bishop Douarre and Father Viard, landed at Balade in the north of New Caledonia and established the second Catholic missionary presence in Melanesia. Protestants of the London Missionary Society had been active in Tahiti since 1797 and were extending their influence westward through the Marquesas, Tonga, the Cook Islands, Fiji, and the Loyalty Islands. The landing on New Caledonia was an attempt to establish a Catholic beachhead in the western Pacific before the arrival of the Protestants. The beachhead held until July 1847, when the Melanesians, desperate from a famine, attacked the mission, savagely killing one Brother. The remaining missionaries were fortunately picked up by a French sloop and taken to Sydney. Another attempt to gain a foothold in New Caledonia was made in 1848, and it also failed. But a third attempt in 1851 succeeded.[20]

On July 16, 1844, Pope Gregory XVI founded the Vicariate Apostolic of Melanesia and entrusted it to the Marists, making Father Jean Baptiste Epalle its first bishop. Bishop Epalle landed on San Cristobal in the Solomon Islands on December 2 of the following year and died seventeen days later, after being attacked by hostile Melanesians on the island of Santa Isabel. For ten months the mission of San Cristobal showed signs of promise; but when Bishop Collomb, Epalle's successor, arrived twenty-one months later, one Marist had died from malaria, three had been killed by a hostile neighboring group, and even their relationship with their hosts had deteriorated to a dangerous level. The mission was abandoned and Collomb moved to Woodlark Island off the southeast coast of New Guinea. From Woodlark a further mission was established on Umboi Island (then known as Rooke Island). But less than a year later Umboi was also abandoned, as a result of the deaths of Bishop Collomb and a fellow Marist, as well as the obvious indifference of the inhabitants to the message the missionaries preached.

A longer period of contact between Melanesians and Marists was sustained on Woodlark Island. A schooner had dropped the Marists there on September 15, 1847. The Muruans, as the people of Woodlark are known, gave the missionaries an enthusiastic welcome. The interest of the Muruans was clearly focused on trade, especially for the iron tools that the Marists had brought with them. However, the Marists quickly established large gardens and within three months they were making regular catechetical tours of the villages.[21] Yet after seven months the interest of the Muruans had faded, for they could see no good reason for giving up their traditional beliefs and rituals. Father Thomassin wrote to his family in France on June 24, 1849:

> To reason with our unhappy pagans is not to demonstrate the truth of our holy religion. They will frankly admit "We are ignorant, we are wrong," but will not go any further. They will reply, "We act like that at Murua and our ancestors did the same." They will say "We live like this and we are content. If we abandon our prayers the universe will collapse, famine, plague and the lerous (malevolent spirits) would not leave us any rest." If you reason with them, they will laugh in your face.[22]

Meanwhile, a rift grew between the missionaries and the Muruans because of a famine that had struck. Fearing the Muruans might become too demanding, the superior of the mission decided against providing them with food from the mission's ample garden. Thus an opportunity for building up a trade partnership, plus the basis for a genuine human relationship, was lost. In fact the opposite happened. When the famine ended, the Muruans and missionaries were thoroughly estranged from each other.

A new superior attempted to heal the rift by sending six young men for a visit to Sydney. They returned to Woodlark marveling at the wonders they had seen and wanting to build a "Sydney at Murua." For some months there was a renewed interest in catechetical instructions and the Marists hoped that a conversion movement was under way. These hopes were dashed, however, when a second famine struck at the beginning of 1853. The missionaries aggravated the situation by "ascribing the Muruans' misfortune to divine displeasure at their tardiness in becoming Christians." The Muruans responded by pleading with the missionaries to ask their God to go away and leave them alone. The extent of this new breach can be gauged by the fact that the starving Muruans even refused an offer of food from the Marists.[23]

The Catholic missionary encounters with Melanesians between 1843 and 1855 revealed the sureness and vigor of the pre-Christian religious traditions of Melanesia. Initially these encounters were friendly enough, but in every case the relationship between missionaries and Melanesians deteriorated after some months. This was due in part to the missionaries' lack of appreciation for the role of exchange partnerships in the development of interpersonal relationships, as well as the missionaries' laudable but costly practice of refusing to ally themselves with any one group. But even if the missionaries had possessed a good understanding of "the way relationships ought to be," and had been willing to work at developing such relationships, it is still doubtful whether the Melanesians would have considered the missionaries as anything more than rather useful trading partners.

To Melanesian eyes these nineteenth-century missionaries were a very unimpressive group of men. Left behind by wandering schooners, with few weapons and a severely limited supply of trade goods, they were more an object of ridicule than fear. They soon became sick, died quickly, or were killed easily. While at times the missionaries claimed that their God was punishing the unfortunate Melanesians for not accepting their message, their God in fact seemed to do very little to help his mission-aries. In Melanesian terms there is no way in which it could be said that these missionaries participated in an "abundance of life."

A Second Start

From 1854 the Vicariate Apostolic of Melanesia had neither missionaries nor bishop. The Marists continued to make steady progress among the Malanesian population of New Caledonia, which had been made, together with New Hebrides, a new vicariate apostolic. In 1881, however, a Catholic missionary presence returned to the Bismarck Archipelago in the person of Father Lannuzel, a diocesan priest from France. He had been chaplain to the Marquis de Ray's ill-fated colony, New France, on New Ireland. With the collapse of the colony, Father Lannuzel moved to the Gazelle Peninsula on New Britain and began mission work among the Tolai people.

About the same time the Holy See assigned the task of evangelizing the Vicariate Apostolic of Melanesia to the Congregation of the Missionaries of the Sacred Heart. The pioneer band of three missionaries also set sail for New Britain, and by coincidence were given a festive welcome prepared by the people and some European traders for Father Lannuzel, who was expected to return at that time from a visit to Sydney. After a number of shifts in location (one of which was caused by the people burning the station to the ground at the instigation, it would seem, of the notorious trader Thomas Farrel), Bishop Couppe, the first bishop of New Britain, in 1890 established the permanent headquarters at Miokio, now known as Vunapope.[24]

From New Britain the Missionaries of the Sacred Heart founded the first Catholic mission off the New Guinea mainland on Yule Island on the southern Papuan coast in July 1885. The previous year Germany and England had annexed as colonies the eastern half of New Guinea and the islands of the Bismarck Archipelago. Holland had annexed the western half of New Guinea as well. None of these nations was particularly favorable toward Catholic missionary efforts. Yet by the end of the century Catholic missionaries had established new beachheads in most areas of Melanesia. Dutch missionaries of the Sacred Heart established themselves at Merauke on the south coast of Irian Jaya in 1895. In 1896 missionaries of the Society of the Divine Word landed on Tumleo Island and began the evangelization of the north coast of eastern New Guinea. The Marists returned to the Solomon Islands in 1898. Although in terms of human sacrifice the price continued to be high, the foundations of the local churches were laid. By the close of the nineteenth century the Vicariate Apostolic of Melanesia had divided into a series of vicariates apostolic. This process continued in the twentieth century.

The context for missionary activity in the 1880s and 1890s was different from that of the 1840s and 1850s in two respects. First, by 1880 coastal-dwelling Melanesians had learned that the killing of a white man could bring a fiery retaliation, especially from warships that shelled their villages. The presence of a white man had become a manifestation of power that could not be ignored. Second, Melanesians had become much more dependent on iron tools, beads, cloth, and above all tobacco, for which they traded their copra. These items had become necessary for a true "abundance of life." When Father Lannuzel arrived in the Gazelle Peninsula, a well-organized trading establishment was already doing business there. He was also welcomed by a Tolai big-man named To Litur.

That the military and economic power of the colonial period brought prestige and new possibilities to the missionaries does not mean that they condoned all that the colonial administrations and commercial enterprises did. Bishop Couppe, for instance, protested and finally broke the attempt of the German colonial administration to establish "spheres of influence" for the Catholic and Methodist missions on New Britain. He also protested to the German parliament against the way the German New Guinea Company was exploiting its Melanesian workers. In turn, his founding of schools was opposed by the company, because it wanted only docile laborers.

But it is doubtful that the tension, which normally existed between missionaries and colonial and commercial administrations, was always perceivable to Melanesians. It was more likely that Melanesians saw in missionaries the possibility of gaining access to rituals, which they postulated, according to their basic beliefs, must be associated with the production of European goods. Hence a trade relationship between Melanesians and missionaries, which would lead to "true amity" and the eventual revelation of all secrets, was undoubtedly a desired goal. Nevertheless, this does not deny that many, who first listened to missionaries hoping to have secret rituals revealed to them, instead found in Christ an entirely new meaning for the "abundance of life."

On the other side, Catholic missionaries, beginning with the missionaries of the Sacred Heart in the Gazelle Peninsula, took a very positive stance toward Melanesian cultures. By their attendance at and interest in festivals, they confirmed what they saw as basically good; often preferring to allow what was morally objectionable in these to die out naturally. They felt there was time enough, and generally held the overly optimistic view that objectionable practices in the religious traditions of Melanesia would fade away within a few generations.

After 1900

From the established centers Catholic missionary activity spread over most of Melanesia. However, the first and, particularly, the second world wars set mission work back severely. Even so, a large increase in personnel, much improved medical treatment for tropical sicknesses, modern means of transport, and a far better understanding of Melanesian cultures have more than compensated for the losses caused by the wars. There are now twenty-six dioceses or local churches in Melanesia.

Nevertheless, during this period there has also been a remarkable growth of Melanesian revival movements. The popular name given to these movements is "cargo cults." They have also been called, variously, nativistic, messianic, millenarian, and adjustment movements. John G. Strelan, in his *Search for Salvation*, summarized an early movement as follows:

The 1920s saw the rise of a number of cargo movements throughout Melanesia. Ronovuro, a prophet who lived at Espiritu Santu in the New Hebrides, in
1923 foretold the coming of a great flood, as well as the return of the dead with
white skins. The dead, he said, would land on the island from a ship loaded
with rice and other foods. But, since the Europeans would seek to prevent the
unloading of the goods, one man, representative of the rest, must be offered as
a victim. Consequently, a planter, Mr. R. O. D. Clapcott, was shot, his body
mutilated, and parts of it eaten. The movement came to an abrupt halt when
the government intervened swiftly and powerfully; Ronovuro and two accom-
plices were executed. However, by 1937 the movement had again gathered
momentum. It peaked in 1947 when the so-called "naked" cult spread far and
wide.[25]

Cargo cults are syncretistic movements; but their wellsprings are the religious traditions of Melanesia. The more successful movements usually have jelled around
one charismatic personality. This person offers the hope that the frustrations, which
his followers are experiencing, will end with the coming of an entirely new situation.
The new situation will come about when the ancestors (the dead) either send an
abundance of goods—formerly knives, rice, tinned food, clothes, and these days
radios, cars, ships, and airplanes as well—or else reveal the rituals necessary for
producing these goods. European goods have become essential to a Melanesian
"abundance of life"; the means for obtaining them in a cargo-cult movement are the
generosity of the ancestors and the effectiveness of ritual correctly performed. One
final feature, which shows the creativity of these movements, is the way traditional
myths are elaborated and retold, so that they provide an intellectual explanation of
the present situation.

The emerging churches of Melanesia have over the past sixty years been affected
by cargo-cult movements. At times large sections of local churches have deserted
and joined cargo cults; some have deserted permanently, though for most it has been
a temporary state. At other times, Catholics have maintained a membership in both
a cargo cult and a local church. Consequently, to varying degrees the development of
the local churches of Melanesia has been retarded by the cargo beliefs of many members. While modern pastoral practices in dealing with cargo beliefs and active movements are without doubt more enlightened than they were in the past, there is still
much to be done.

The Context and Challenge to Mission
in Regard to the Religious Traditions of Melanesia

The context of mission is the world, or a particular aspect of the world, in which a
local church happens to find itself. The challenge to mission for the local church
comes from elements within the context that need to be addressed by the saving
gospel of Christ. A missionary of a local church is one who is able to recognize such
elements and to address the saving gospel of Christ to them. Our task here is to
recognize those elements in the religious traditions of Melanesia that are in need of

having the gospel of Christ addressed to them. In order to come to this recognition, we must first clarify the context, that is, the state of the religious traditions of Melanesia today.

John Strelan's description of a modern cargo-cult movement is a useful starting point for this clarification:

> Cargo activity on Bougainville Island in the 1960–1970 period could be said to have taken place on two levels.
>
> On one level, there was traditional cargo cult activity—what is known locally as *longlong lotu:* songs and prayers to the Virgin Mary in cemeteries; magico-religious practices with expectations that the ancestors would produce money, clothing, trucks, and other goods. These activities were, and are, especially prevalent in the Bougainville hinterland. In July 1976, for example, it was reported that cultists at Kopani No. 1 village, about 50 kilometers north of Kieta, had been digging up coffins and stacking them in a house in the hope of attracting cargo. Violence was also a feature of this movement; it was reported that some of the 500 adherents had been torturing villagers who would not join the cult.
>
> On another level, cargo beliefs and expectations found expression not in cults or cargo movements as such; rather cargo hopes focused on certain political figures, chief among whom was Paul (now Sir Paul) Lapun. It seems certain that many of those who voted for Lapun in 1964, and again in 1968, did so in the expectation that Paul Lapun would lead them along the road to cargo. In similar vein, the formation of the political organization known as Kapikadoe Navitu brought with it an upsurge in cargo hopes and expectations, even though the organizers of the association did their best to avert such a thing happening. Cargoism, politics and business have become inextricably interwoven on Bougainville, just as they have in Madang, Lae, the Sepik, and other parts of Melanesia.[26]

A few villages around Kopani No. 1 have been as recently as April 1980 still locked in cargo-cult activities of the traditional type. A large number of Catholics around that area, however, have deserted the cult and returned to the church community. This seems to be fairly common with those cargo cults that flourished in Catholic areas in the late 1960s and early 1970s. Since the gaining of independence by Papua New Guinea in 1975 and the Solomon Islands in 1977, no large-scale cargo cults have managed to take hold. A few small ones have started, and the symbols that are used (e.g., the flag of the former colonial power) suggest a tension with the elites who manage the new nations rather than with the Europeans, their power and wealth.

On the level of cargo beliefs and expectations focusing on political and business personalities and institutions, there is ample evidence of their enduring vigor. Even though at first sight the means appear secular or profane, the actual use made of these personalities and institutions springs more from a belief in the effectiveness of the appropriate ritual correctly performed than from an empirical assessment of what might be the results of the actions taken. But even if the belief in the effectiveness of ritual correctly performed and the power of the ancestors dies, cargo expectations will remain because these expectations spring from Melanesian beliefs about the nature of the abundant life and the way relationships ought to be.

Furthermore, if the notion of the "abundance of life" remains basically materialistic, then the death of the belief in the ancestors and the effectiveness of ritual can only be a loss. It will mean that there will be no more reason to celebrate than the immediate acquisition of those goods and prestige which at that moment make up the abundance of life. As can already be seen in some of the new elite, it is only a small step from this emptying of Melanesian beliefs to the crudest form of Western materialism. Any deeper participation in and celebration of life is impossible.

The nature of one's belief in the abundant life also affects one's conception of how interpersonal relationships ought to be. In traditional Melanesian society the ideal exchange relationship was, as we have already seen, an exchange relationship that needed no more exchanges. In *Mambu*, his classic work on cargo cult, Kenelm Burridge claims that the root cause of cargo cults was frustration. This frustration resulted from the failure of Melanesians to engage Europeans in exchange partnerships that morally bound the Europeans to their Melanesian brothers. The failure came from the inability of Europeans to recognize that, in the Melanesian understanding of relationships, a trade partnership meant the partners became morally committed to each other and, above all, to arriving at a true equivalence in their relationship. If Melanesians could have engaged Europeans in moral partnerships, so that the Europeans would have shared their seemingly unlimited abundance of goods with their Melanesian brothers, true Melanesian equivalence and amity of heart would have been possible. Since this did not happen, Melanesians turned in frustration to the ancestors to provide them with the unlimited abundance of goods they needed. Burridge also claims that with the goods they hoped to receive from the ancestors, Melanesians intended to build up with Europeans exchange partnerships, which would eventually be equivalent, produce amity of heart, and have no need for exchange.

There is evidence enough that this kind of frustration may build up again; only this new wave of frustration will not be with the Europeans so much as with the new elites, who manage the new nations and enjoy the benefits thereof. At present among Melanesians there are still strong ties and exchange partnerships between the elites and their kinfolk in the villages. But as relationships of economic and social advantage expand among the elites, at the expense of less rewarding relationships between the elites and their village partners, frustration is bound to increase in the villages. At the moment this is only a trend. Nevertheless, if the trend continues, the question becomes: How will the frustration express itself? Will it cause a new outbreak of traditional-type cargo cults? Perhaps in more remote villages it will. Yet if the present state of the trend in urban areas is any indication of the future, the expressions could be much more violent. Gangs of young "dropouts" in urban areas are already very angry and lawless.

This concept of amity through equivalence and reciprocity serves Melanesians well when regulating alliances between groups who are either hostile or strangers to each other. It provides a goal to be striven for, even though in practice it is hardly ever reached. But for relationships other than between clan and kinship groups, it proves a very inadequate model. The following quotation from Barry Irwin bears this out. Irwin describes the relationship between Christ and Christians in Simbu Province, Papua New Guinea. However, his remarks are true of what is observable of Christian and Catholic life throughout much of Melanesia. In the Salt-Yui area of Simbu Province, the vernacular words for owing someone a debt are *pring pangwo*.

> In confrontation with Christianity the Simbu react with typical *pring pangwo* philosophy. "Christ died for our sins." This is interpreted as meaning that Christ took away my *pring pangwo*. This initially gives a tremendous sense of relief until the full weight of one's indebtedness to Christ is realized. Then the Simbu begins to "pay off" Christ by attending church services regularly and assisting the mission to whom they are affiliated as much as possible. No demand is too great. But a time comes when each clan feels it has paid enough for Christ's grace and church attendance drops off and there is a gradual decline in following the particular mission's rule for Christians. It is not so much a return to paganism as a completion of obligations.[27]

What missionaries, who become frustrated and negative about this state of affairs, do not realize is that in traditional Melanesian terms this sort of a relationship with one of the spirit world is an ideal relationship. But it is hardly a model for the relationship between Christ and the Christian.

There is another relationship that seems to be a better model for the relationship between Christ and the Christian, that is, the relationship between brothers. Melanesian brothers are totally committed to one another. This relationship demands much more than the equivalence and the amity of heart of an exchange partnership. But still there is need for caution. As a part-time prison chaplain, I have met prisoners who, though unwilling and against their better judgment, had felt obliged to perjure themselves in a vain effort to save a guilty brother from prison. As a result, both brothers ended up in jail. This relationship too needs to be addressed by the saving gospel of Christ, so that the freedom and integrity of the individual is safeguarded.

At the basis of these challenges to the mission of a local church in Melanesia is the meaning given to the "abundance of life." What does an abundant life mean to those who have access to power, wealth, and prestige? What does it mean to those who are denied any real access to such things? What does it mean for the person who wants to be a true brother and preserve his own freedom and integrity? The belief in the effectiveness of ritual correctly performed will eventually give way before the sciences, and the ancestors may lose out to overseas experts and other gurus. But unless the saving Word of Christ is effectively addressed to the Melanesian understanding of the abundant life, and the way relationships ought to be, destructive tensions will permeate the whole context.

Needs That Local Churches Must Look To

A Melanesian local church is the result of an interaction. On the one side of this interaction, there was the missionary, the Word of God that he preached, and the particular form of Catholicism that was his heritage. On the other side, there was a Melanesian community, to whom the missionary preached, and their particular religious heritage. In this interaction some things were creative; others were destructive. Theologically, the Word of God was the most creative element in the interaction: "Men, having been reborn by the word of God (cf. 1 Pet. 1:23), might through baptism, be joined to the church which, as the Body of the Word Incarnate, lives and is nourished by the word of God and the Eucharist (cf. Acts 2:23)" (*Ad Gentes*, no. 6).

Understood in this sense of Vatican II, the Word of God in the above interaction brought into existence a new People of God, which, nevertheless, still must grow to its full stature in Christ. Growing to full stature in Christ means, among other things, that a young church must come to terms with, and integrate into its own life and mission, both the form of Catholicism it inherited from its missionary and the form of religion it inherited from its Melanesian past. Today this coming to terms with and integrating of a double heritage is often called the process of inculturation. In this paper, we confine ourselves to one aspect only in this process: the mission of the local church with regard to the religious traditions of Melanesia.

To understand more precisely not only the missionary challenge, which these religious traditions present to the local churches of Melanesia, but the needs of the churches if they are going to respond creatively to the challenge, a distinction must be drawn between two levels of life in the churches. The first level is the village, or clan-based, congregations, with their own leadership, organization, and concerns. The second level encompasses all those who are involved in the parish, deanery, and diocesanwide life and organization of the local churches. The number of Catholics on this second level is small, and the majority of them are, even today, expatriate missionaries. Melanesian participation at this level is small indeed.

At village and clan level, though, the situation is quite the reverse. There are strung out across Melanesia thousands of small Catholic communities who are committed to Christ and live out that commitment as they see it unfolding in their daily lives. Some communities are fortunate enough to have the help of trained leaders and a catechist, and to receive regular visits from a priest. But the majority of communities are not that fortunate; they make do with much less. Still it is in these communities that the beliefs, prayers, and practices of the pre-Christian religious traditions and the traditions established by the missionaries are evaluated and then integrated or rejected.

In these village and clan-based Catholic communities the most vital dialogue in the local churches of Melanesia is taking place. The dialogue is, first of all, an inner dialogue among Catholics themselves. But in areas where Catholics and Protestants live side by side, it invariably includes Protestants. Finally, on occasions it also includes the representatives of cargo cults and other revivalist movements. It is a dialogue that those working on the parish, deanery, and diocesanwide level cannot afford to ignore.

Let us briefly review the development and content of this dialogue. In the early years of many local churches there was a real convergence of concerns. What Laracy says of early Catholicism in the Solomon Islands is generally true of early Catholicism throughout Melanesia:

The islanders' conversion was made to appear less a break with indigenous custom than adaptation of it by use of overt similarities between Catholicism and traditional religious beliefs: the externalization of spiritual power in material objects such as the Eucharist, blessed medals, Holy Water and rosary beads, the belief in life after death and the practice of honouring the dead.[28]

Although unfortunately phrased, this statement does point to the continuity that Melanesians experienced between their Melanesian traditions and Catholicism. This continuity opened up the possibility of an ongoing transformation of the old in terms of the new. Yet, while Catholic prayer and sacramental life seem to have retained their relevance to the concerns of Melanesians, the transformation of Melanesian Catholic life has, especially in later years, been slow. In clan and village communities it is rarely possible to distinguish Catholics from their non-Christian neighbors on account of their lifestyle alone. The resurgence of cargo-cult beliefs and movements, plus the obvious interest and involvement of Catholics in them, are also evidence of the absence of real transformation in Christ of all aspects of Melanesian life.

Could it be that transformation of Catholic life has been slow because the convergence of concerns between Catholicism and traditional beliefs has been too shallow and superficial? I believe this has been so, and that now urgent attention must be given to deeper problems, particularly the place of transcendence in Melanesian life and what for Melanesian Catholics constitutes the true "abundance of life" in Christ. The answers to these questions cannot be given in advance, for it must be discovered in the continuing dialogue of committed Melanesian Catholics. The pursuit of this dialogue is the responsibility of the thousands of village and clan-based Catholic communities across Melanesia.

The pursuit of the dialogue and transformation of life will mean, I believe, that Catholics and all Melanesian Christians will have to suffer a loss of their Melanesian souls before, as it were, finding their Melanesian souls again. By "soul" I mean that which fires the imagination of Melanesians and gives an existential meaning to life and the world around them. On a more theoretical level, soul is the action of those dynamic characteristics of the Melanesian religious traditions, of which we spoke in the early part of this paper, on the daily lives of individual Melanesians.

Although caution is necessary when suggesting the speed of secularization in Melanesia, modernization does cause old beliefs to be set aside, or at least placed in brackets for long periods of time.[29] In time this will cause a loss of the Melanesian soul, quite apart from the dialogue between Christianity and traditional beliefs. We are reminded of the saying of Christ: "For anyone who wants to save his life will lose it; but anyone who loses his life for my sake . . . will save it" (Mk. 8:35). The Greek word translated by "life" here is *psyche*, soul. "Life" is no doubt the correct translation, as Jesus was referring to life as a totality. But in our present context, and for the sake of finding a theological principle on which the dialogue and transformation of life may rest, we could give *psyche* its stricter meaning of "soul." We can now paraphrase the Lord's maxim as follows: "He who saves his Melanesian soul will lose it, and he who loses his Melanesian soul for my sake will find it." Those who are involved on the parish, deanery, and diocesanwide level have this difficult task of seeing that suitable theological input is given to the dialogue, so that the deeper realities of life and soul will be pondered.

By way of conclusion, I would like to suggest that a starting point for this theological input and pondering of the deeper realities is the transformation of the *dema*-deity. The *dema*-deities of Melanesia were, as we have seen, killed, or died of their own choice, so that a particular food, which was a necessity for the community, could be born from their bodies. The emphasis is on a transformation, which was required for the traditional "abundance of life."

A probing of the death of Jesus is necessary to discover the transformation called for in Melanesian life. But the probing must be wider than just the fact of the death of Jesus, just as the probing of the *dema*-deity must be wider than his or her death if the transformation brought by the *dema*'s death is to be fully appreciated. Catholics must probe the incarnation, life, death, and resurrection of Jesus to discover the extent of the transformation he brings. Above all, a probing of the incarnation is necessary in order to discover the transcendence of the Word, who became like us in everything but sin. For with a growing sense of the transcendence of the Word, the liberating relationship between Jesus and his Father, and the real power of his death to transform every aspect and depth of Melanesian life can be appreciated.

The *discontinuity* between the religious traditions of Melanesia and Catholic faith must be outlined as clearly as that which forms a continuity between the two. It is the perception of a clear discontinuity within a continuity that has the power to transform. In a nutshell, the perception of the mystery of the transcendent, all-powerful, and totally other God, who became close and utterly powerless in the death of Jesus, has the power to transform any and every notion of the abundant life, as well as fulfilling the basic insight that, as in the death of *dema*-deity, life may come from death.

Notes

1. Colin-Jach Hinton, *The Search for the Islands of the Solomon* (Oxford: Clarendon Press, 1969), pp. 28–67. Also, André Gschaedler, O.F.M. "Religious Aspects of the Spanish Voyages in the Pacific during the Sixteenth Century and the Early Part of the Seventeenth," *The Americas— Academy of American Franciscan History* 4 (1948): 302–15.

2. Ralph M. Wiltgen, S.V.D., *The Founding of the Roman Catholic Church in Oceanea 1825–1850* (Canberra: Australian National University Press, 1979), p. 320.

3. Cf. Theodor Ahren, "Christian Syncretism," *Catalyst* 4, no. 1 (1974): 3–40; "Concepts of Power in Melanesian and Biblical Perspectives," *Point* 1 (1977), pp. 61–86; "Local Church and Theology in Melanesia," *Point* 2 (1978): 140–58. Ahrens has given the best analysis so far of these challenges and contexts.

4. J.P. White, K.A.W. Crook, B.P. Ruxton, "Kosipe: A Late Pleistone Site in the Papuan Highlands," *Proceedings of the Prehistorical Society* 36 (1970): 157–70.

5. J. Golson, "No Room at the Top: Agriculture Intensification in the New Guinea Highlands," in Allen, Golson, and Jones, eds. *Sunda and Sahul, Prehistoric Studies in South East Asia, Melanesia and Australia* (London: Academic Press, 1977).

6. Roderic Lacey, "Religious Change in a Precolonial Era: Some Perspectives on Movement and Change in the Precolonial Era," *Point* 2 (1978): 170–76.

7. Ibid., p. 178.

8. Ennio Mantovani, S.V.D., "A Fundamental Melanesian Religion," *Point* 1 (1977): 156.

9. R.H. Codrington, *The Melanesians: Studies in Their Anthropology and Folk-lore* (London: Oxford University Press, 1891), p. 119.

10. Marett, *The Threshold of Religion* (London: Methuen and Co., 1909).

11. Bronislaw Malinowski, *Magic, Science and Religion* (Garden City, N.Y.: Doubleday Anchor Book, 1954).

12. Codrington, *The Melanesians*, p. 120.

13. Many languages in Melanesia do not have a word corresponding to *mana*. These are mostly Papuan (in the technical sense) languages. Even though they do not possess a corresponding word, these Melanesians do have the assumption that the word *mana* implies.

14. Cf. Malinowski, *Magic, Science and Religion*.

15. Mantovani, "Melanesian Religion," p. 161.

16. A.E. Jensen, *Myth and Cult among Primitive Peoples* (Chicago: University of Chicago Press, 1963), pp. 83–146.

17. Cf. Kenelm Burridge, *Mambu* (New York: Harper & Row, 1970).

18. Cf. Theodor Ahren, "Christian Syncretism."

19. Burridge, *Mambu*.

20. Wiltgen, *Oceanea*, pp. 320–21.

21. Hugh Laracy, *Marists and Melanesians: A History of Catholic Missions in the Solomon Islands* (Canberra: Australian National University Press, 1976), p. 23.

22. Ibid., p. 24.

23. Ibid., p. 29.

24. Cf. Reiner Jaspers, M.S.C., "Kolonialismus und Missionstatigkeit—Erlautertan Der Religionsgrenzziehung auf New Britain Nach 1890." Benziger. I am much indebted to Father Jaspers for discussions we were able to have about this period of mission history. Any misinterpretation or distortion of these events, however, is my responsibility alone.

25. John G. Strelan, *Search for Salvation: Studies in the History and Theology of Cargo Cults* (Adelaide: Lutheran Publishing House, 1977), p. 20.

26. Ibid., p. 42.

27. Barry Irwin, "The Liability Complex among the Simbu Peoples of New Guinea," *Practical Anthropology* 19, no. 6 (1972): 282.

28. Laracy, *Marists and Melanesians*, p. 66.

29. Gary Trompf, "Secularization for Melanesia?" in "Christ in Melanesia," *Point* 1 (1977): 208–25.

26

INDIA

Albert Nambiaparambil, C.M.I.

For us Christians in India, the context of the mission of the local church is one of constant relationship with people of other faiths. The same may be said also about all other Asian countries. The late Holy Father, Pope Paul VI, had this call to give to the followers of other faiths, in Bombay, in December 1964: "Therefore we must come closer together, not only through modern means of communication. . . . We must come together with our hearts, in mutual understanding, esteem and love. We must meet not merely as tourists, but as pilgrims who set out to find God, not in buildings of stone but in human hearts."[1]

Can the Christians, the church in India, join others in this pilgrimage "to find God"? What are the demands and the risks involved on the part of the individuals and the communities that are in "place," that is, the Christians who are in a place along with followers of other faiths, but act as if they are out-of-place? How is this search for God touching the lifestyle of those communities that are in the process of becoming "local," of finding their "place" in a place? In what way is this joint pilgrimage, this mutual enrichment in the communion of dialogue among religions affecting the commitment to mission? A community that lives, that celebrates the good news of salvation in Jesus Christ is and should be committed to the task of sharing this good news with everyone, and also invite its fellow pilgrims to this communitarian celebration. Are these double commitments complementary or exclusive? There is no sense in toning down the importance of either of these calls.

We are not making here any attempt to define the term "mission." We take it in the more comprehensive sense, as identified with the whole mission of the church, as inclusive of all forms of activities aimed at promoting and strengthening the ideal of Christ's kingdom as spelled out in the synagogue of Nazareth (cf. Lk. 4:18-19). Evangelization or mission can also be understood in the rather restricted sense of proclaiming or sharing the good news of salvation in Jesus Christ as felt, received,

Albert Nambiaparambil, a member of the Carmelites of Mary Immaculate (Kerala), is the Secretary to the Commission for Dialogue of the Catholic Bishops' Conference of India. He is also Secretary to the Indian chapter of the World Conference of Religion and Peace.

and celebrated in this community, the church, with the intention to call people and to lead them to accept Christ and to express this acceptance by joining this community. Understood in this sense evangelization has this goal—leading others to the membership in the church. Since this study is aimed at relating the task and the call of mission with other religious traditions, let us understand mission here in this restricted sense. Again, let us gather all that comes under "relation with other religious traditions" within the phrase "interreligious dialogue." Here, too, we do not make any effort to define this interreligious dialogue. For our plan and purpose it is enough to accept the findings of the Catholic Bishops' Conference of India, in the effort of a local church to understand dialogue, in the context of preparing for the Synod in Rome on Evangelization: "In view of the fact that India has nurtured several of the world's great religions, the Church in India is called upon to be an earnest pioneer of inter-religious dialogue. It is the *response of Christian faith in God's saving presence in other religious traditions and the expression of the firm hope of their fulfillment in Christ.*"[2] Let us take special note of the italicized words. I was a participant in the workshop that worked for hours to reconcile the twofold commitment of the local church. There was a sense of release of tension once we reached an agreement on the description above. This description of dialogue finds a place for dialogue in itself, and avoids using words like "means" for something else. At the same time the call to dialogue is seen as coming from one's own Christian existence. It may be observed that the report of the workshop has a significantly different version: "the expression of the firm hope *of the fulfillment of all things in Christ.*" The change was made in the document that came out of the Bishops' Conference, referring to the question of dialogue as related to the main theme of the session: evangelization.

One may try to arrive at a theoretical reconciliation of these two or two-in-one tasks, prescinding from all efforts in the actual field of dialogue and evangelization. But to have the warmth of experience we fall back here on some concrete steps in this line.

Recently I saw a confrere of mine, Father Celsus, C.M.I., in the midst of some thirty lepers, from the lepers' colony in Cochin, Kerala. They were discussing their difficulties, the difficulties of these lepers, living in a community but forced to be isolated from the rest of the people. For an outsider like me it was difficult to follow their language that brought out the agony of isolation from those in good health. There was one Mr. Velayudhan—a Hindu, employed in a factory—helping the priest give voice to those who have no "voice" in the so-called healthy society. Shall we call this get-together an example of dialogue, or one of evangelization?

For some years I have been moving up and down the country organizing inter-religious dialogues of different kinds with the aim of getting our communities in touch with other religionists, making them in this very process open to God's saving presence. To mention two steps in this line: We have organized, in twelve centers, multireligious panel sessions, sharing sessions (with no discussions *on* religion), around the theme: "Values in a Fast-changing World," spread out over three evenings. Values touching family, employer-employee relationships, caste as it exists now in its positive and negative aspects, the fate of religion in a scientific age, the right to move from one religion to another, religious roots of exploitation, and so forth came in as topics for deeply personal sharing of experiences and ideas in these sessions. All these dialogue sessions were jointly organized under the auspices of different multireligious units, and invariably ended with some time given for multireligious prayers.

Again, for the last few years we have been organizing, with great joy and benefit for the participants, multireligious "Live-Together" sessions of two to three days. These are days of intensely personal meditations, and sharing sessions with no discussions at all on religion. We conduct these Live-Together sessions, incorporating into them shared meditations, shared reflections on personal topics such as "my prayer-meditation-religious experience," "my religious experience and my discovery of my neighbor," "an event that changed my life," "my religious experience and my approaching death." We spend much time in songs and *bhajans*. Are these expressions of commitment to mission or of dialogue? Or are these attempts in which we have been witnesses to our Hindu friends drawing from the deep waters of their own traditions, blocking the efforts to proclaim the good news of salvation in Jesus Christ? It is enough to mention here that there are tensions in the communities, in the "local" churches that are out-of-place, although in a "place."

There are tensions even in the very participants, perhaps healthy tensions. These tensions may be for them certain shocks, which I called elsewhere by the name "purification shocks."[3] We shall return to this later.

A Church in Search of New "Places"

Let us now focus our searchlight on a few recent attempts (known personally to me) at incarnating the church, the community, trying out new styles of life and new ways of being in a place. In Bareilly, in North India, Father Deenabandhu, O.F.M., has been experimenting for the last few years, in the Franciscan spirit, translating it into a way that will be intelligible to the spirit of India, in a life of spontaneity, utter simplicity, reducing his needs to the minimum.[4] In the same ashram is a young man who is known all around as the *chottabhai,* the little brother. True to the counsel of the gospel, he moved for months from village to village, with nothing in his hand. He was all joy when he recalled to me that during those months of pilgrimage for the proclamation of the gospel he was the guest of all, and that the poor people of other faiths shared with him all that they had. Within a kilometer from this ashram is a small ashram of Sisters, trying out the hard life of the villagers. The Sisters, all from South India, from Kerala, described their apostolate in all joy and spontaneity as an apostolate of "being" there. To the villagers they are "sisters." They are never threatened by anyone in the village, nor is their presence in any way a threat to those of other faiths. For they are too small for that.

In central India, in a village near Narasingpur, Swami Premananda, a Norbertine priest, is launching a new kind of ashram, trying to reconcile the guru tradition of Hinduism with that of a superior of a monastery, along with that of a professor and a director of studies in a seminary.[5] Here, too, simplicity is the keynote of the ashram and the participants. Two kilometers from this ashram is the hut of two medical-mission Sisters. With no walls around, with no gates or "Beware of Dogs" sign, this hut is in no way different from that of the rest of the villagers. In Chanda is Father Prasannnabhai ("joyous brother"), C.M.I., who moves from village to village as a disciple of a Hindu guru for three years, sharing the frugal offerings of the villagers and learning Sanskrit from the guru. In Kulithalai near Tiruchirappalli in South India is an ashram always open to anyone who steps in seeking peace (*shanti*), whether the person is a Christian or a Hindu.[6] The whole atmosphere of the ashram is one of prayer, solitude, and contemplation, the inmates following a very simple lifestyle. Here one meets people especially from the West, uprooted in their own society, who have lost the sense of the divine, of mystery, in their society. In a functional society, caught in the competition, human dignity, a personality, is a casualty. They do not have a sanctuary, a "cave" into which they can withdraw. In this ashram they find their roots again, and return home with a deep sense of peace. In a unique Christian experience expressed in an "Indianized" ashram-context they find their own home.

In the city of Banaras there is a priest, a carpenter, Brother Viswas of the Little Brotherhood. For years he worked in the shade of a tree, with fellow carpenters, learning the art from them. Now he is a master of the art in his own right. Is what he is doing a dialogue or a mission? Recently a Little Sister of Jesus, sharing her experience of "being" in a hut lost among other huts, had these words for us: "When the people are not coming to the church, we the church go to the people." She adds that a Hindu villager who does not even know the alphabet had this to say about the life of these Sisters: "We don't love you for what you give us. We can't make a person happy by giving material things. It is what you all *are* which makes us happy."

Traveling round India as I have gives me this feeling: actual encounter is going on between Christianity and other religions in India. There are over thirty dialogue groups that bring together believers of different religious traditions in the communion of dialogue. This encounter of religions is affecting, slowly but steadily, the prayer and lifestyle of our Christian communities. The singing of *bhajans,* which was limited to the Hindu temples, is becoming a common feature in the Christian institutions. Techniques of concentration such as yoga are finding their place in Christian groups. Many seminarians spend some time in Hindu ashrams, such as Sivananda Ashram, of Rshikesh.

All this should not give the impression that these efforts are representative of the mainstream of the church in India. Nor do we say that these attempts are accepted without questioning by Christians at large. In many cases the opposite is true. Many Christians feel that their self-identity is disturbed, and they are in tension because of these very experiments of relating Christian communities to other religious communities. In the very efforts to become truly "local" in a place, the Christian community is at times polarized into opposing camps. There are many unresolved tensions and problems.

Now our analysis will enter into the context and the nature of these riddles, with a view to picking up a few unresolved issues for the study of the different mission institutes and of other churches. We are moving toward those "elements which are now emerging somewhat consistently from experience and which therefore seem significant for thinking and action in the future," as suggested by the guidelines given for reflection on the topic under study.

Planting Seeds

In our efforts to gather our forces for the evangelization—the mission thrust—we may not overlook the fact that we are doing this with the heavy weight of the past on us in the so-called mission countries. To mention one such burden of the past: there is our colonial heritage. Those of other faiths often look at our mission as remnants of the past colonial adventures. There are a few concerted attempts coming from outside the Christian camps focusing the spotlight on this fact of history.[7] Again the good news was presented and is still being presented clothed in a cultural pattern, in symbols, in linguistic forms, in visions, and in ways of life foreign to the soil where the message is being sown. We are using consciously the word "sow" instead of the word "planting." Without judging the history or the missionaries in their efforts at presenting the Christian message in this or that cultural pattern, let us confess that this prevents the message from becoming "good news" in a "place." The Christian communities, in some part at least of this country from where these thoughts spring, are judged "foreign" by the followers of other faiths. When we say "foreign" there is no attempt to blame anyone. What is of importance in this is not the place of birth of the missionary; rather, the attitudes are in question. True, native-born people can be more easily tuned to the harmony of a particular culture and heritage. But if you are born into a community that is Westernized, birth by itself may not be enough to be in "place" in a territory, in a country. It is often true that "Indians become relatively foreign to their own culture,"[8] feeling like outsiders, assuming thought patterns that are foreign, ignorant of the stories and of the rhythms of a folk of the place where they are immersed or inserted. Their words fail to become real "seeds." Perhaps in a real effort to relate themselves to other religious traditions the Christian communities will be more and more forced to feel themselves in this or that "soil," to make people ask questions that have some meaning in the "place."

Again in this very effort, in giving the message of salvation in Christ, they will learn to forego the language of self-sufficiency, of possession, of the rich man (which, I am afraid, is too materialistic and triumphalistic and hence self-defeating). In this effort at discovering a new relevant language for God's self-disclosure, of his inner life, they will arrive at an experiential perception of the divine self.[9] As a part of this pilgrimage we may have to get over an undue preoccupation with numbers. The attempts described earlier, made in different parts of this country, judged from numbers of conversions made, are all total failures. But are they not, all the same, attempts at "missions," at presenting Christ? Let us not make the mistake of saying we do not need numbers, and that we do not need conversions. If Christian existence is a communitarian one, a visible celebration, we need numbers as the sign of this presence. But numbers should not be the norm of interpreting the success or failure of a mission. In other words, facing other religious traditions, we may not reduce mission or proclamation to making people members of the church.

Local Churches Becoming in "Place"

There was a time when a church was judged indigenous or foreign according to what persons held certain positions or jobs or functions in the particular church in question. There was also a tendency to judge a church "local" by the liturgy used in the community. Hence efforts were made mainly in those two lines to give the communities a "native" look, to make the liturgy "Indian" in India. Here, too, the outer coloring, if it does not point to an inner life rooting within the "place," may prevent the message from becoming incarnate.

The local church is to be the embodiment and manifestation of the entire mystery of the church. Although the vision of Vatican II, of church as the People of God, carries with it a shift of emphasis, in the life of a community with the burden of being associated historically with the colonial expansion, it takes a long time to become truly people in a place. Since Vatican Council II, a shift of focus has taken place from an institution to a group of persons, who are subjects, who live their *own* lives. This is called for precisely here where mission is considered as an attempt at Westernization. In other words, it makes no sense in projecting mission as transplanting something previously constituted. This transplantation is an easy task. But to be a community that feels "in place" in the midst of Hindus, Muslims, Sikhs, Jains, and so forth demands the courage to try the untried.

We have tried, and are still trying, to present Christ and his message through our educational institutions, hospitals, nursing homes, and mass media. These are all useful and greatly needed even now. But what of the image that ordinary Hindus get about the messengers of the good news? If they get the picture of a good administrator, of an efficient organization supported by funding agencies, the purpose is not achieved. It is a great danger to the cause of the gospel if energy is wasted in making the church a carbon copy of a church elsewhere instead of allowing it to become attuned to and expressive of a religious experience as conveyed in the celebrations, symbols, and pilgrimages of the people concerned.

These new, small, Christian, prophetic attempts of the "little ones" to become grassroots communities of persons expressing their mutual relations in terms and gestures that have meaning "right here" are disturbing traditional Christian communities, whose value patterns are being challenged by these grassroots centers.

These little flocks will have to find a new form of unity—not a unity of uniformity but a unity expressed in multiple forms, in multiple solidarities, and thus even becoming different "peoples" in the same "place." To bring out the import of this let us take an instance: in India religious experience almost everywhere seeks and finds connatural expression in and around pilgrimages by pointing to the Holy, to the Beyond in the rivers, in the mountains, through myths and stories that narrate the touch of the divine. Any meaningful presentation of the message of incarnation will have to unfold this cosmic presence of divine. Only a group of people who join the pilgrimage of spirit with co-religionists will be able to find new expressions in the midst of the people here. In this effort we may have to find new organizations other than the dioceses and parishes to let the "seed" sprout and live. A church that does not mix with the laughter and pains of a people cannot be truly local, cannot celebrate fully "This is my body." In the Live-Together sessions referred to above, we had a touching experience of this new life in communion with our fellow pilgrims when we held our Sandhya-Meditation just before the dawn of the day. In one such session held at Cochin, a Hindu layman of the place, Shri Govindavallaba Bharatan, who was helping us in the meditation, initiated the sharing in these spontaneous words:

> Oh, Divine Light of the Universe, wake up in me; let me feel you as the Crescent and the Star which Prophet Mohammed defined as the constant thing, the soul, the Allah. Oh, Divine Master, let me feel in Thee the Supreme Flame of Zoroaster into which all the existence can be consecrated, so that we can arise therefrom charged and purified. Let me feel in Thee the *kālachakra* [the wheel of time] of Buddha, the eternal *chakra* of cause and effect, the *chakra* symbolizing time in creation and destruction. Let me feel in Thee the cross which is the negation of ego, the I when cut across which denotes the ocean in which the Son of God died that humankind may live; And let me shed at Thy sacred feet the sacred *pranava* within and without, which permeated the entire universe and is the cause of the whole creation. Oh, Divine Master, with all these merging at the touch of Thy lotus feet, let Thy touch open the lotus petals of my heart. . . . Let me expand to take in the whole of humankind, which is nothing but Thy creation.

Syncretism

At this point we must stop for a moment at one of the red signals flashed at any attempt to develop a meaningful language of symbols, signs, and rituals for a multireligious context: the red sign of syncretism.

A few observations may not be out of place in understanding the problem. No religious symbol or concept can be understood apart from its religious context. A symbol like "OM" finds meaning within the context of the Hindu religious experience. Are we ready to grant that another "faith," another religious tradition is to be approached as the "other"? You cannot treat another community of believers as objects. You cannot grasp a person as a person, as a subject, except in the communion of interpersonal relations. And this communion is possible only against the background of the transcendence, in the experience of participation in the Being. In this process of "we" formation, of communion of persons, the participants feel that "Man is more."[10]

Similarly a Christian should look at any religious symbol only as a part of the communion of dialogue, in the encounter of religious experiences. We see Saint Paul looking at the "Unknown God" (cf. Acts 17:23), a symbol which came in the flow of the religious experience. If you go around picking up symbols or concepts with the attitude of an objective analyst, of one doing comparative religion, you are doing violence to the reality of religious experiences. Hence no religion should be syncretistic. Again many specialists may be found guilty of the violence against this flow of religious experiences if they introduce a symbol without making sure that the use of this symbol really helps their community in the expression of the faith. It should be a violence to the spontaneous flow of my religious experience, and you will be leaving me sterile and dry, if you as a specialist overlook the evocative, suggestive value of religious symbols and words. A luxury of isolation is to be avoided, once you admit the communitarian dimension of religious experiences and your own insertion into this or that community. This is all the more true in areas where a particular community, because of its history, may feel its identity threatened by the acts of a few specialists. This may result in an unhealthy tension. There is also a tension that is a sign of growth, resulting from the earnest efforts of a community to be open and receptive to the vibrations of another community. Such a tension should be welcomed. We shall come back to this point in the final stage of this study.

In relating the commitment to evangelization in a religiously pluralistic society, the missionary—one who is sent—should not forget that the gospel is not reaching out to the other person in an empty space, in a vacuum. On the other hand, the message, the good news, should be personal to him or her in those depths of religious consciousness or sensitivity. As we have observed above in connection with syncretism, we would be doing violence to the religious phenomenon if we were to stop the religious experience in its flow. In like manner we cannot fossilize it or objectivize it. Religious experience is a vital reality, giving the religionists a wonderful capacity to adapt to new situations, to seek new answers to old problems. The role of a Christian rooted in a local community would be to help one rediscover one's own sources of life. In India the dialogue sessions on values in a fast-changing world, and the series of dialogues on science and belief, have this goal to help each other rediscover the religious roots of values.

True, there are instances wherein resurgences within a religious tradition at times turn out to run off the track. They may take the form of fanaticism, when new offshoots are used for exploitation (especially in the case of those persons uprooted from society and suffering from a religio-cultural vacuum). Christian communities in the West must take urgent steps to help these uprooted persons, through centers of East-West spiritual encounter in the West itself, so that they do not become victims of exploitation by self-styled bogus "gurus" and performers of short-cut experiments to self-realization. Recently visiting one such center I found a guru, or *bhagavan,* surrounded by a thousand seekers of spiritual experience, almost all from outside India. Is this an exodus from Christianity to another experience? Can the local Christian community in India help these pilgrims to make their pilgrimage into the deep sources of their own living waters?

Dialogue and Evangelization

This paper is being written in a mission station in Munnar, South India. This area of hills is always fresh and green with tea plants. The whole area is still fresh with the memories of the colonial period; of the companies, with their base in England, that owned the tea estates. There are around 700 Catholics in this parish, all being local converts in a period of thirty years. The mission belongs to the Carmelites, of the

Oriental Rite. Christians are fervent. They frequent the Sunday liturgy and a few can be seen during the weekdays too participating in the divine liturgy. All are workers. The Catholic community gets some help from the relief services of the parish. All around, indeed at the very bus stop itself, there are small shrines dedicated to different local deities. If you ask the children (Hindus), they will say that their god—Karupu Swami—is there pointing to their shrines and that the God of Christians is up there pointing to the church. They live in peace and harmony. There is a lived dialogue. But can we say that they relate their religious experiences in a communion of mature persons? To a great extent they exist as Hindus and as Christians because they see their faiths or ways of life as distinct. To be a Christian is to be different in the society. This is more or less true of Christian communities all over India. If you ask any ordinary Hindus or Christians whether or not there is anything wrong in this situation, they may even find it difficult to grasp the question. Even after eight years of up-and-down-the-country-life as secretary of the Commission for Dialogue, for bringing about a change in the attitude of Christian communities toward other religions, I feel that a good deal remains to be done. Most ordinary members of the Christian community do not want to be nudged from this state of affairs. Hence we hear from educated laity reactions like: "We don't want Hinduization. We seek Indianization." As we have mentioned, some Christians are troubled by the attempts made here and there to give a different look to the modes of prayer, in the use of symbols, and so on.

Much confusion and tension exists not only in the minds of ordinary Christians but also in the minds of priests and missionaries. They find it difficult to relate in clear terms to this new phenomenon of "dialogue" among religions, to what they are, to their commitment to evangelization. To some this amounts to a withdrawal from the commitment to mission proper. Even among the Hindus there is a good amount of suspicion—also in those who come for the organized dialogues—as to the sincerity of this thrust to interreligious dialogue. A serious attempt was made in the Asian Mission Theology Consultation on Evangelization, Dialogue and Development, held at Nagpur in 1971, to relate evangelization to dialogue.[11] In 1969 a clear call to dialogue was given in the Church in India Seminar,[12] also for a fresh commitment to evangelization.[13] Just as there are many understandings of evangelization, so, too, there are many understandings of dialogue. We have pointed to the need of an incarnational, rooted presentation of the good news. This amounts to saying that the word of the missionary is to be dialogic, a word that cuts through the person to whom it is addressed.

But in one sense at least, as referred to earlier, dialogue is a pilgrimage of "hope in the fulfilment of all things in Christ." In this search all are equals. Between evangelization understood as proclamation leading to conversion, and dialogue seen as a pilgrimage of all the religious traditions, the relation is not that clear or distinct. Any attempt to make dialogue among religions a means for the mission in the restricted sense will be rejected by those who are committed to the call to dialogue as a pilgrimage of hope and love. They see dialogue as an activity fully justified in itself, although they would welcome the present trend to find the proper place of dialogue in the more comprehensive idea of evangelization as identified with the whole mission of the church. The Guidelines of the Catholic Bishops' Conference of India on Inter-Religious Dialogue accepts the situation of tension between the two poles of Christian existence in these words:

It therefore seems better to accept the fact that there is a tension in the Church and in every Christian between these two activities. This tension has to be lived through in life and at the source of diversified vocations and charisms in the Church. It is a tension that corresponds to the tension between the two poles of the Church's existence: she is a pilgrim church, on the way to the Father and therefore imperfect, and at the same time she is somehow a real anticipation of the eschatological renewal operating by the power of the spirit (*Lumen Gentium,* no. 48). In the former aspect of her existence it is always her duty, as it is that of all other groups and of every person, to seek from within brotherhood of men and understanding and the accomplishment of God's design for mankind. This is the justification for dialogue. On the other hand, as the anticipation of the eschatological renewal of all things and as the sign of God's kingdom, it is her duty to invite all men to conversion through the proclamation of the eschatological event of the resurrection of Jesus Christ, a proclamation done with the authority of the risen Lord who lives in her (Mt. 28:18–20; *Ad Gentes,* no. 9).[14] Is the reconciliation that is achieved in this statement satisfactory? Although this document comes from the dialogue commission of the C.B.C.I., in actual situation many are yet struggling for a solution. Perhaps further research by local churches, by local communities carrying on in their life-situations both the commitments and tasks will resolve the tension in their own lives, though they may not be able to give a clear formula that will satisfy all. Perhaps we may have to see this tension as a part of our Christian existence, between the pulls of the "not yet and the now." If experience confirms anything, this can be said that dialogue is no obstacle to evangelization; rather it has helped evangelization as stated by the Consultation on Evangelisation of Patna.[15]

Nonbaptized Christians

In a Consultation on Mission organized by the Gurukul Theological College, Madras, of the Lutheran churches, the question of nonbaptized Christians (people of other religious traditions by birth, but who confess their acceptance of Christ as the one redeemer of humankind, and accept him as the Lord of their lives) who find it practically impossible to become members of this or that church through baptism was discussed. In that very consultation there was a public illustration of this situation when one of the speakers, a young Muslim convert to Christianity, shared with us his story, immediately followed by a Muslim who expressed his decision and option in life to preach Christ to the Muslims as an unbaptized Christian.[16] A survey held in Madras by the same college showed that around 10 percent of the persons interviewed belonged to this category. In a situation wherein becoming a member of a church through baptism amounts—in the judgment of society—to a change of one's culture, this phenomenon can be understood. Such nonbaptized Christians are found in many parts of the country, especially with the mounting pressure from a hard core to show that Indian culture is Hindu culture and that to become a Christian is to swim away from the mainstream of this culture.

What should be the relation of these persons or groups to the community of Christians? Can they be allowed, as a community, to celebrate their existence in a parallel way? Sooner or later this topic will have to be studied in depth and this should be done in the context of the local communities wherein this is felt as an issue to be taken seriously. Again, the ecumenical dimension of this question is to be given due weight when such a study is being planned.

Local Church versus Universal Church

What should be the role of the universal church in the context of the local churches that go through this process of becoming "local" or of finding their "place," within one and the same territory. Will the universal church allow or encourage multiple solidarities?

Perhaps the different regional churches may have to suggest ways and means and norms of encouraging and coordinating these multiple solidarities, these multiple expressions of communities "in such a way that a variety of cultural expressions converge towards a unity of communion."[17] Any temptation to impose uniformity may come in the way of the flow of the Spirit. Universal, national, regional churches will respect the autonomy of these root communities. At the same time these communities will have to be ever conscious of the vibrations that an experiment or expression in this living cell is going to have on the other churches, on the communion of the local churches. In areas wherein the past history is still a heavy weight, where economic and other forms of dependence are added to this, conscious efforts are to be made to make these communities become aware of their freedom, to be "subjects" and not to be carbon copies of any other community.

The Responsibility of a Religion for the Religious Formation of Others

An unresolved question keeps coming up in the gatherings of Christians in India, especially when our relation to the formation of those of other faiths becomes an issue. This was also a subject that was discussed in the seminar of the Federation of Asian Bishops' Conferences that studied our relation with Muslims. The question is, How far are we responsible for the religious formation of students of other religions who pursue their studies in our educational institutions? All seem to agree that we have a responsibility for the moral education of these students. Are we bound to provide—to the extent that it is possible—for the religious instruction of these in their own religion, even to the extent of getting a Hindu or Muslim, accepted by them, for this purpose? In answering this we have to take into consideration the possibility of these students leaving our institutions as agnostics or humanists or atheists, questioning their own roots and values, and at the same time being left without any other supporting value system to fall back on. In India this was an issue of discussion as early as in 1969, during the Church in India Seminar. Whenever the matter was discussed, agreement was found difficult. There are many side issues involved, especially concerning the right of the minorities to run institutions, which in India is guaranteed in the Constitution. The matter becomes delicate in the context of certain demands made by the majority community to conduct even religious worship in the institutions run by the minorities. A theoretical answer alone, it appears, will not meet the different situations. Solution, if any, to these and similar questions, on the relation of minority groups to the majority community can be worked out only on local levels, around concrete issues. This and similar problems wherein rights and duties of the different communities are touched need further study.

The Uniqueness of Christianity

Another question raised repeatedly in the context of Christians encountering other believers is that of the uniqueness of Christianity, especially in light of certain sayings of our Hindu friends such as "All religions are equal, one and the same," and "Religions are different paths leading to the same goal." Along with this we see the preoccupation with the "uniqueness" of their own religion vis-à-vis the openness to other religions. There is no attempt to formulate this uniqueness of Christianity or the role of the church in this uniqueness. Looking at the whole question from the viewpoint of one involved in interreligious dialogue and at the same time feeling the urgency of proclaiming and sharing the good news of salvation in Jesus Christ, one observation may not be out of place: a uniqueness that is expressed in a possessive, triumphalist, conquering, static, closed language, and in which is drawn a picture of the church as the center of the movement in dialogue, will defeat the commitments of both dialogue and mission. The language in which this affirmation of the uniqueness is made is vitally important.

Conclusion

Christian missionary thrust in the nineteenth century took the form of education, of the reform of social and religious evils within Hinduism. The reaction from within Hinduism took two forms—the resurgence of both reformative and conservative forces.[18] This resurgence was occasioned, conditioned, and influenced by the encounter of Hinduism with Christianity. But the leaders of this renewal went back to their own original sources, to a rediscovery of true Hinduism.

Something similar is happening in postindependent India. Recently I visited a Hindu center committed to the training of young Hindus for the propagation of Hinduism, to defend themselves against any attack on their culture, to bring back to the Hindu fold converts to Christianity and other religions. The young recruits are given training in traditional Hinduism. A Christian may see this as the work of a few fanatics, but it is much more than that. Within Hinduism itself there is a reaction against the resurgence of the hard, fundamentalist core.

These lines are being written while I take part in the Fourth National Charismatic Convention in which over 8,000 delegates are going through a renewal with the call: "Let all proclaim Jesus Christ the Lord."

Sitting in the open-air auditorium, I heard a few leaders of the movement remind-ing the delegates of their obligation to proclaim Jesus, to make disciples. What dis-turbed me more than anything was the closed attitude that a few took toward other religions; not a word was said about "God's saving presence in the religious tradi-tions of humankind"; nor did anyone propose dialogue with other religions, even as a preparation for the mission proper. Among Christians, too, there is strong reaction to this fundamentalist thrust. How are these encounters within the Christian com-munities and within other religious traditions going to affect the future efforts at mission proper and at dialogue understood as the pilgrimage to find God? Whatever be the multiple forms that the encounter of Christianity with other religions is going to take, only in an atmosphere of communion, of openness in dialogue is the church in India going to see its own new face and find for mission a new meaning here, as well as in other countries where the church finds itself in the midst of other religious traditions united in the one pilgrimage of Hope.

Notes

1. Cf. *Acta Apostolicae Sedis* 56 (1964), n. 1032.

2. Cf. *Report of the General Body Meeting of the Catholic Bishops' Conference of India* (Calcutta, 1974), p. 140, and Guidelines for Inter-Religious Dialogue of C.B.C.I. (Varanasi: Dia-logue Commission, 1977), p. 4.

3. Albert Nambiaparambil, C.M.I., "Dialogue in India," *Vidya Jyothi,* March 1974, and *Dharma* 1, no. 3 (January 1976).

4. Jyotiniketan Ashram, Kareili, Bareilly, U.P.; Director, Fr. Deenabandhu O.F.M.

5. Saccidananda Ashram, Sanskuari, Narsingpur, M.P.

6. Saccidananda Ashram, Thannirpally, Kulithalai, Tamilnadu; Fr. Bede Griffiths.

7. Cf. "Christianity in India, A Critical Study," *Vivekananda Kendra Patrika,* August 1979 (editorial office: 3 Singarachari St., Triplicane, Madras-5, India).

8. François Houtart, "The Franciscan Missionaries of Mary, of the Province of Madras" (July); cf. Prospective Cards, no. 712/76.

9. J. B. Chethimattam, "Evangelization and Inter-Religious Dialogue" (paper presented at the International Mission Conference of Manila, 1979).

10. Cf. Paulo Freire, *Pedagogy of the Oppressed* (Harmondsworth, England: Penguin Books, 1972).

11. Cf. J. Pathrapankal, ed., *Service and Salvation* (Bangalore, 1973).

12. *The Church in India Today,* pp. 243–44.

13. Cf. "Light and Life We Seek to Share," a report on the All India Consultation on Evangeliza-tion, Patna, 1973.

14. "Guidelines for Inter-Religious Dialogue" (Varanasi: C.B.C.I. Dialogue Commission, 1977).

15. Cf. "Declaration of the Patna Consultation," in J. Pathrapankal, *Service and Salvation,* p. 373: "Dialogue fosters respect and understanding. Far from lessening evangelical zeal it makes the task of evangelization more inspiring and meaningful."

16. Herbert E. Hoefer, ed., *Debate on Mission* (Madras: Gurukul Lutheran Theological College and Research Institute, 1979); "An Introductory Paper on the Relationship of the Church to Non-Baptized Believers in Christ," by Herbert Hoefer, pp. 353ff.

17. Cf. Michael M. Amaladoss, S.J., "Inculturation and Tasks of Mission" (paper presented at the International Mission Conference, Manila, 1979).

18. Anto Karokaran, *Evangelization and Diakonia* (Bangalore: Dharmarerm Publications, 1978), chap. 2.

27

THE NON-SEMITIC RELIGIONS OF ASIA

Aloysius Pieris, S.J.

Perspectives and Clarifications

Perspectives

Today's mission crisis is basically an authority crisis. It is well known that in the heart of the traditional churches that founded the missions, the once all-pervasive authority of the institutional leadership has been increasingly questioned or simply ignored. Those who wielded authority saw it as a crisis of obedience. To the rest it was simply a crisis of credibility. When this crisis matured in the colonial frontiers of the same churches, that is, in the so-called mission lands, it traveled back to the center in the guise of a mission crisis. As we see it, therefore, the mission crisis is neither more nor less than an authority crisis.

In Asia this crisis lay dormant for centuries, like embers, until Vatican II fanned the embers into a conflagration of self-criticism, leaving the church's "missionary claims" in cinders. From these cremated remains we Asians are called upon to resurrect a new, credible symbol of God's saving presence amid our people, an authoritative word from a source of revelation universally recognized as such in Asia. In short, we are summoned to discover the contours of a new missionary community that is truly qualified to announce God's kingdom and mediate the liberative revolution inaugurated by Jesus through his life and death—a community that seeks no other sign of credibility or authority than that which such mediation would bestow upon it. What is asked of us, then, is nothing short of an ecclesiological revolution. Thus the frontier situation in which we live has opened up a new horizon for us. Though our praxis is punctuated by debates and deliberations, we have no hesitation

Aloysius Pieris, Jesuit from Sri Lanka, is the founder and Director of Tulana, a center for dialogue between Christians and non-Christians, more specifically between Christians and Buddhists. The author of several articles, he is the first Christian to obtain a doctorate in Buddhist philosophy from the University of Sri Lanka.

about the direction of our quest. The perspectives are clear and self-evident.

It is these perspectives that I wish to set forth here. They consist of assumptions that require no substantiation but need only to be explicated around the concepts that are the framework of this seminar: mission, local church, and religions.

1. The term "local church" is a tautology, for there is no church that is not local. We hasten to add that the Christian communities in Asia are all truly churches, and therefore authentically local.

2. This, however, does not imply that all local churches *in* Asia are necessarily local churches *of* Asia. Most of them, regrettably, are local churches of another continent struggling for centuries to get acclimatized to the Asian ethos. Obviously our reference is to the so-called Western missions, which are Asian branches of such local churches as those of Rome and England. This applies in a limited way also to the Oriental Rite churches, which can legitimately claim to be local churches *of* Asia—though perhaps not always of *today's* Asia. I confine my observations here to the former category, the Western missions.

3. Nonetheless these observations do not warrant the conclusion that the immediate task of local churches *in* Asia is to become local churches *of* Asia, or that this is an indispensable condition for the evangelization of Asian nations. That is a species of missiology lying beneath the theories of "inculturation" now in vogue. We do not uphold this view. We see the process of "becoming the local church *of* Asia" only as an accompaniment or a corollary to the process of "fulfilling the mission of evangelizing the (Asian) nations." Put conversely, it means that the local churches *in* Asia have not fulfilled their mission and therefore have failed to produce local churches *of* Asia.

4. The mission to the nations is primarily (cf. Medellín, 1968) even if not exclusively (Puebla, 1980) a mission to the poor. He who entrusted this mission to us has defined it so. Since good news to the poor is always bad news to the rich, the liberation of the rich is mediated by the liberation of the poor, not vice versa. Our mission, in other words, is prophetic and has been colored from its inception with a class option. Hence the observation: a local church *in* Asia is usually a rich church working *for* the poor, while the local church *of* Asia could only be a poor church working *with* the poor, a church that has been evangelized, a church that has become good news to Asians.

5. This church, however, is a little flock, a tiny minority in Asia and has no monopoly of this mission. The great (monastic) religions that antedate Christianity also claim to possess a message of liberation for the poor of Asia. That is why the local churches *in* Asia look upon these religions as rival claimants; but in a local church *of* Asia, they will have already become collaborators in a common mission.

6. The moment we associate the Asian poor and the Asian religions with our prophetic mission, we are in the middle of politics. Also, poverty and religiosity are two areas in which confrontation with two political ideologies, capitalism and Marxism, cannot be avoided. These two ideologies are directly involved with the "liberation" of the Asian poor and have some definite

theories about and attitudes toward the Asian religions. The local church in Asia, whether prophetic or not, rich or poor, is a political church: a neutral church is a contradiction in terms, for it would not be local.

7. Since all these religions and ideologies claim to be liberative movements, saviors of the masses, only the poor will decide who is competent to liberate them. Neither textual proofs (our authority is mentioned in our holy books) nor the appeal to tradition (we always claimed this authority and people used to accept it) are adequate today. Authority is the spontaneous manifestation of a church's competence to mediate total liberation for the people of Asia. The ultimate source of this authority is He who entrusted the mission to us. But He has identified himself with the poor as the victim-judge (cf. Matthew 25), and it is in and through the poor that the church or any other religion or ideology will receive his authority in Asia. The authority crisis therefore remains a permanent possibility in the mission of a local church in Asia.

Clarifications

The political implications of this prophetic mission constitute only one source of the conflicts that the local churches experience today. Another major divisive factor, which can be more easily eliminated, is found purely in the area of semantics. The key words "religion" and "poverty," which together describe the Asian ethos, are themselves polysemous words, signifying contradictory realities. Those engaged in missiological debates—especially the liberationists and the inculturationists—are both guilty of oversimplifying this complex question.

It is curious that even the Medellín papers when speaking of the phenomenon of "poverty" take a zigzag path, now deploring it, now counting its blessings. The ambiguity can be traced back to the Gospels. When Jesus invited the young man to sell all things and give (not, of course, to the temple, but) to the poor, he required the rich man not to be rich and the poor not to be poor! The Marian manifesto in Luke announces the messianic intervention whereby the positions of the rich and the poor would be reversed, implying that both riches and poverty be eliminated. The attempt to distinguish economic from evangelical poverty does not help to clear this ambiguity. The only way out would be to admit a distinction between forced poverty, inflicted on some by the hedonism or the indifference of others (Dives and Lazarus) and voluntary poverty embraced as a protest and a precaution against forced poverty. The one is enslaving; the other is liberating. In Eastern religions, voluntary poverty is a spiritual antidote against Mammon working in people psychologically. In liberation theology, it is also a sociological weapon, that is, a political strategy, necessary in the battle against organized selfishness or Mammon's principalities and powers. Mahatma Gandhi is the most outstanding Asian example of voluntary poverty with both its psychological and sociological implications.

A similar clarification is desirable in the understanding of "religion." Under the influence of a Marxist critique of religion, and the biblical hermeneutics of Latin American theologians, some Asian liberationists define religion and poverty as negative forces forming an unholy alliance from which the Asian masses have to be liberated. Poverty for them is an evil in itself. Religion is said to perpetuate it, first, by restricting the area of spiritual liberation to the nonsocial, nonpolitical, noneconomic plane (Does such a plane exist?) and, second, by legitimizing as well as allowing itself to be legitimized by oppressive systems that create and maintain the evils of poverty. The inculturationists, on the other hand, ignore or gloss over this negative aspect of religion and sometimes of poverty, except perhaps when they acknowledge the failure of *other* religions to inspire a Mother Teresa who would alleviate the sufferings of the poor. The demand for radical transformation of society as an indispensable condition for the elimination of sufferings is neutralized by "apostolic works," which turn victims of poverty into perpetual objects of compassion. They would also appreciate the monastic thrust of major Asian religions in that these religions value property as something to be voluntarily embraced in order to combat selfishness and acquisitiveness. They would want the church to absorb these traits of various religions in becoming more "at home" in Asia. But this approach of the inculturationists sounds too accommodative in the minds of liberationists.

The reality is more complex than that. Religion too has an enslaving and a liberating dimension as much as poverty does. After all, has not the same Christian religion produced a theology of domination and a theology of liberation?

Table 27.1 p. 430 shows, in tabulated form, the contradictory realities that the words "religiosity" and "poverty" designate. They show that these words are bipolar, each containing a negative and a positive pole. Besides, each pole has two complementary dimensions: sociological and psychological, or more precisely, sociopolitical and individual. I hope that the ensuing discussion of concrete issues will become clearer in the light of this fourfold distinction.

Concrete Issues

Inculturation, Indigenous Theology, and Oriental Spirituality

Inculturation is something that happens naturally. It can never be artificially induced. A Christian community tends to appropriate the symbols and the mores of the people around it only to the degree it immerses itself in their lives and struggles. That is to say, inculturation is the by-product of an involvement with the people rather than the conscious target of a program of action. For it is the people who create a culture. It is therefore from people with whom one gets involved that one understands and acquires a culture.

The questions that are foremost in the minds of inculturationists are therefore totally irrelevant: namely, whether a particular church is inculturated or not, or why it is not inculturated and how it could be inculturated. Yet it is relevant to know why such irrelevant questions are asked so frequently in our local churches today. Our diagnosis is that the inculturationists are starting off from the observation, valid in itself, that the ecclesiastical culture of the ministerial church in Asia is elitist and stands aloof from the culture of the poor masses. This cultural gap is even more pronounced in former European colonies such as India, Malaysia, and Indochina, where the seminary training and all clerical communication is done in the language

Table 27.1

Dimensions→ Poles ↓	*Psychological* (individual)	*Sociological* (political)
The Enslaving Face of Religiosity	Superstition, ritualism, dogmatism, etc.: transcendentalism (=Manichaeism, Docetism, etc.).	Religion's tendency to legitimize an oppressive status quo = religion's tendency to serve Mammon or Anti-God; commercialism.
The Liberating Face of Religiosity	The interior liberation from Sin (=Mammon, Anti-God, Tanha, etc., or exploitative instincts).	Religion's organizational and motivational potential for radical social change (e.g., independence movements in Asia).
The Enslaving Face of Poverty	Imposed poverty violating the dignity of the human person (alienation).	Poverty as the subjugation of peoples by the slaves of Mammon (= disinheritance, dispossession, etc., through colonization, multinationals, etc.).
The Liberating Face of Poverty	Voluntary poverty as one's interior liberation from Mammon, i.e., a spiritual antidote (emphasized by Eastern religions).	Voluntary poverty a political strategy in the liberation of human society from Mammon or organized Sin (stand of liberation theologians).

of former colonial masters. But what the inculturationists fail to perceive is that the aforesaid cultural gap has an economic base; that the church's twofold culture indicates a sociological process in which the class division of the wider society has been ecclesiologically registered in the life of the believing community—a sin against the body of the Lord, as Saint Paul would have put it; that the culture of the clerics represents the dominant sector of the believing community; and so on.

Moreover, the irrelevance of the above-mentioned questions, which is at the center of the inculturation debate, is rooted in the erroneous presupposition that churches in Asia are not inculturated. Every local church, being itself a people, is essentially an inculturated church. The relevant question to ask, therefore, is: Whose culture does the official church reflect? Which is the same as asking: Which class of people is the church predominantly associated with? Do the poor—the principal addressees of the good news and the special invitees to Christian discipleship—constitute a culturally decisive factor in the local church? Thus the whole inculturation issue derives its significance from the local church's basic mission to bring—and become—the good news to the poor in Asia.

Incidentally, the current discussion on indigenization, if situated in the context of this basic mission, would require that we review critically the instruments of apostolate that most local churches are using for the training of ministers (i.e., the seminaries) and for the education of the laity (schools, colleges, technological institutes). Are these not the institutions that perpetuate the aforesaid cultural gap by maintaining the class division lying beneath it? Did they not originate in an era when evangelization was restricted to mean a quantitative extension of an already stratified ecclesiastical complex with no idea of the ecclesiological revolution that "evangelization" constantly evokes?

In the contemporary church, this ecclesiological revolution seems to have begun with the mushrooming of "basic communities" or "grassroots communities" or *ecclesiolae*. We shall indicate later the specific contribution that Asia offers toward this revolution. Suffice it here merely to record that the growth of such apostolic communes coincides with a reevangelization of the church as a whole, the evolution of new ministries and the formation of new ministers within the cultural ethos of the poor, and the reawakening of the poor themselves to their irreplaceable role in the liberative revolution that Jesus referred to as the kingdom. One bishop in Sri Lanka has to his credit at least four ministers formed outside the traditional seminary. The second batch has begun training. The present writer too is engaged in a similar project. Indeed, there are a few laboratories of hope where the Christ-experience of the less privileged gets spontaneously formulated into an indigenous theology.

If, however, this last observation is valid, namely, that an indigenous theology in our context is an articulation of the Christ-experience of Asia's poor, then neither the clerical leadership of the church nor even the Asian (liberation) theologians who have been educated in an elitist culture can claim to be the engineers of an indigenous theology. In fact, like the hierarchical church, these theologians too speak of the poor in the third person. This is an implicit acknowledgment that they are not really poor. On the other hand, the poor have not yet been truly evangelized and they too are not therefore qualified as yet to spell out an indigenous theology for Asia. No doubt they have received the *seed* of liberation from the gospel and from other religions—the "positive pole" of religiosity as we named it earlier. To evangelize Asia, in other words, is to evoke in the poor this liberative dimension of Asian religiosity, Christian and non-Christian. For the unevangelized poor tend to reduce religion to an opiate, to struggle without hope, and to submit too easily to the religious domination of the elite class.

The Asian dilemma, then, can be summed up as follows: the theologians are not (yet) poor; and the poor are not (yet) theologians. This dilemma can be resolved only in the local churches *of* Asia, that is, in the grassroots communities where the theologians and the poor become culturally reconciled through a process of mutual evangelization. This reciprocal exposure to the gospel means that the theologians are awakened into the liberative dimension of "poverty," and the poor are conscientized into the liberative potentialities of their "religiosity." Thus if there is any model of a local church for Asians, it should be in those Asian communities where the positive poles of religiosity and poverty merge; such communities do exist in Asia outside the Christian churches, and to these we shall soon turn our attention.

This said, I consider it a waste of time even to comment on the efforts of those scholars who employ their knowledge of ancient religious texts to build up conceptual frameworks for an "indigenous theology," which the people have no need for. The present writer, himself a classical Indologist, does not deny that the sacred texts contain the nucleus round which contemporary Asian religiosity has evolved. But to draw an indigenous theology from ancient texts without allowing the actual practice of religion to play its hermeneutical role in the interpretation of those very texts, is to make the cart pull the horse.

It is more profitable, perhaps, to discuss the efforts of those who concentrate on oriental spirituality as the locus of an indigenous theology. This seems to stand for what we have described here as the positive (i.e., liberative) pole of Asian religiosity. It is a whole way of being and seeing, which one acquires when the inner core of one's personality (variously called "mind," "heart," "soul," "consciousness," etc.) is radically transformed by means of an asceticism of renunciation. Its aim is to free the human person of the ego, cleanse it of its innate thirst for power over others, and purify it of its propensity for acquisitiveness. It is a psychological process by which one experiences an interior liberation from Mammon, to use a biblical idiom.

In this matter there are four pitfalls to avoid. The first caveat I wish to offer is that indigenization should not amount in practice to that species of "theological vandalism" by which, all too often, the oriental techniques of introspection are pulled out of the soteriological ethos of Eastern religions and made to "serve" Christian prayer with no reverence for the wholeness of the non-Christian's religious experience. We protested against this insensitiveness at the Asian Theological Conference (1979) and we reiterate it here, offering at the same time an alternate approach (below), which respects the self-understanding of other religions.

The second warning is that any tendency to create or perpetuate a "leisure class" through prayer centers and ashrams, which attract the more affluent to short spells of mental tranquillity rather than to a life of renunciation, is an abuse of oriental spirituality. To turn Asian religious experience into an opiate that deadens the conscience of both the rich and the poor vis-à-vis their respective stations in life is un-evangelical. The positive pole of Asian religiosity has to synchronize with the positive pole of poverty. It is the hallmark of an Asian religion to evoke in its adherents a desire to renounce the ego and abandon the worship of Mammon—indeed a fine complement to Jesus' messianic mission to the poor, which the church claims to continue in Asia.

Commercialism is the third danger on the list. What used to happen to our material resources like tea, copper, wood, and oil is now happening to our spiritual treasures. They go West, thanks to the conspiracy of merchants and missioners, and return attractively processed—to be sold back to us for our own consumption. The local agents of exploitation are most to be blamed. For some of our Maharishis and Roshis from Asia have turned meditation into a veritable dollar-spinner! Transcendental meditation (TM) is an example of how an oriental product has returned to Asia after being processed into a sophisticated article in the West. Such imported goods seem more respectable in the eyes of most clerics and religious of Asian origin. Being of an elitist stock by training, they recoil from consulting the authentic sources of oriental spirituality, which are found at their doorstep. After all, they belong to the local church of another continent, as we explained earlier. Many ecclesiastical superiors quite understandably find these processed goods "safer" for their subjects. The challenge that original religiosity of Asia throws at the church is thus neutralized. Even renewal programs sometimes are so arranged as to keep the participants from being drawn into the spiritual mines of Asia.

Our fourth and final remark is about the conscious and unconscious motives that inspire spiritual dialogues with other religions. I suspect that the spiritual sharing of religious insights is advocated often as a strategy against a common enemy, be it secularism or consumerism, atheism or communism. The Christian obligation to make an open attack on the principalities and powers that build altars to Mammon—for what else are atheism and consumerism?—is carefully replaced by an excessive zeal for intramural sharing of spiritual patrimonies among selected groups of religionists. The emphasis seems to be put on the "negative pole" of Asian religiosity. Regrettably, therefore, the so-called oriental spirituality is endorsed in Christian circles as an apolitical escape from complex human situations, rather than allowed to burst forth as a prophetic movement against the organized sin that keeps Asia poor.

Asian Religions and the Politics of Poverty
in the Context of the Local Church's Mission to the Poor

Poverty is not just a socioeconomic condition of the Asian masses; it is also a political reality. Marxists claim that religion thrives on it. Capitalists teach that Marxism capitalizes on it. Both Marxists and capitalists are busy with the politics of poverty. Religion, which has its own theory of poverty, is caught in between. It is in the midst of these politico-religious ambiguities that the local churches *in* Asia are called to exercise their prophetic mission to the poor. Evangelization takes place always within or against but never outside a given political system.

It is suggested here that in this forest of conflicts we can see a clear path opened before us here in Asia, thanks to its ancient tradition of "religious socialism." Before I describe this phenomenon, let me define the term "socialism." Being a loaded word, I wish to restrict it to mean the theory and praxis of social organization in which the means of production are owned by a whole community and the fruits of labor are distributed among the members equitably. The principle of justice involved here is expressed best in the famous Marxian adage: "To each according to his need; from each according to his ability." In a way this seems to be the norm that an average human family of any culture adheres to. Why we call it "religious" will become evident as we try to describe this phenomenon.

There are actually two clear versions of religious socialism in Asia: namely, the more primitive form practiced by the clannic societies and quasi-clannic societies spread throughout the vast stretches of nonurbanized Asia, and the more sophisticated form represented by the monastic communities of Buddhist (Hindu, Taoist) origin. The clannic society is known to anthropologists as pretechnological (I prefer to say pretechnocratic) and its belief system as "animism"—a word that I prefer to replace with the more appropriate phrase "cosmic religiosity" in order to include also the refined religious expressions such as Shintoism and Confucianism. In this system the order of nature and the order of society overlap; social harmony is ensured by cosmic communion with the elements of nature. The communism of Asian monks, on the other hand, is founded on a meta-cosmic religiosity, which points to a Salvific Beyond attainable within humankind through gnosis; it inculcates, not a negation of cosmic reality as is often erroneously thought, but a "non-addiction to cosmic needs." However, the origin and early development of this system has been historically associated with the feudalism that came to be superimposed on clannic societies.

Note therefore that the two species of socialism belong to two different social systems (clannic and feudal) and to two different religious systems (cosmic and meta-cosmic). The relationship between the two varies according to regions. There could be—and not seldom there are—contradictions between the two. The monastic community may practice perfect communism within its own membership but act as a feudal lord toward the clannic societies. After all, has not history proved that a socialist nation can be exploitative with regard to other countries? The monastic life has often succumbed to this weakness wherever it is maintained by, and therefore made to legitimize, feudal (and now capitalist) regimes. What the monks own in common and share equitably could very well be the property of clannic societies, expropriated by political regimes that seek religious sanction from the monks. Thus contemplative life supposedly based on "voluntary poverty" could be the luxury of a leisure class that is actually maintained by the "really poor."

This, incidentally, is why we warned the oriental-spirituality enthusiasts not to foster a feudal or leisure-class mentality, the indigenizers of theology to become poor, and the inculturationists to get involved with the masses.

This contradiction between the way monks share land and its fruits and the way the rural societies share land and labor seems to fade into a happy symbiosis in some of the least urbanized and the least technocratized areas of Asia. Monks supported by alms live in remote villages in the framework of a religious socialism that knows no cultural or economic gap between the monastic community and the village community. Religion is not made to justify a class division, even if the monk remains a soteriological symbol and spiritual guide set apart and above the common folk.

This phenomenon may not be so widespread or so permanent as we would like it to be, for there are hostile influences eroding it both from within the Asian cultures (e.g., feudalism) and from without (e.g., capitalist technocracy). Nevertheless, in this we have an Asian model of a basic community. Here poverty—even economic poverty—seems to acquire an evangelical flavor because it is practiced "voluntarily" for the good of the community. I seek to be satisfied with what I really *need* but give all I *can* to the community. In rural socialism, the earth is everybody's property and nobody's monopoly. In monastic socialism, cosmic needs are made to serve rather than obsess humankind. This is a religious conviction, a salvific path. It is a system in which poverty and religiosity conspire to liberate humankind from "cosmic obsessions," for which urbanized Asians have learned another name: "consumerism."

Thus reinforcing the conclusions of our previous arguments, we suggest that, if the local church's point of insertion in the Asian ethos is the multiplication of grassroot apostolic communities, then Asia offers fresh motives for creating them and holds up its own indigenous mold to cast them in. Inculturation? This is where it happens. Indigenization? Here is its one and only locus. Oriental spirituality? You have here its finest societal expression. The ecclesiological revolution we so eagerly wait for as a prelude to inculturation and indigenization is none other than an evangelical response to the promises that religious socialism of Asia offers our local churches today.

In fact great political leaders of Asia saw in it a great political and social antidote against capitalism, consumerism, and, of course, feudalism, which is not yet erased out of Asia. The Sarvodaya movement, as originally envisaged by Mahatma Gandhi and organized by Vinobha Bhave, was founded on this conviction. Mao Tse-tung and, more particularly, Ho Chi Minh recognized in the peasant mentality both an ingrained capacity for a socialist reconstruction of society as well as a natural inclination for acquisitiveness. The struggle between Grace and Sin, God and Mammon is never absent in Asia. This is what makes our adoption of rural socialism both a religious imperative and a political option.

If the local church *in* Asia dismisses this idea as utopian, it is precisely because it is not *of* Asia but is a monarchical or feudal establishment of another continent, seeking desperately to be "inculturated" now—after having failed for centuries to strike roots in Asia. It was the church that once linked evangelization with colonization; and it is the church that now offers us a capitalist, technocratic model of "human" development as "pre-evangelization." Even this criticism of ours is severely censured by the church. Recently the European central authority of a local church, which was planted here 400 years ago, reprimanded the Asian theologians for criticizing capitalism! Even in the official documents in which it questions the values of this atheistic system, one does not often hear it "calling the devil by his name," to use an Asian idiom for exorcism. For the church sees a greater threat in Marxism, which is becoming a rival religion in the third world. Marxist states, no doubt, are confessionalist and give no official recognition to any view of life or code of behavior other than their own. Thus when the church faces established Marxism, it sees, as in a mirror, its own authoritarianism and dogmatism, its own reluctance to give autonomy to the local communities in the periphery, and its own manoeuvers to centralize power. What is more, if the church hesitates to challenge capitalism openly because the church is indirectly associated with capitalism's institutions, it cannot also condemn Marxist atrocities in Asia without recalling its own colonial centuries, which have left indelible scars on entire nations. This dilemma of the church in Asia is further accentuated by the fact that the time and energy wasted on theoretical battles against Marxism are not more fruitfully devoted to the practical task of joining Asia's own war against injustice and exploitation. Such a church is not prepared to appreciate or foster Asian socialism because of its political implications. To sum up then: the first and the last word about the local church's mission to the poor of Asia is total identification (or "baptismal immersion," as I am about to call it in the next part of this paper) with monks and peasants who have conserved for us, in their religious socialism, the seed of liberation that religiosity and poverty have combined to produce. It is the one sure path opened for the local church to remove the cross from the steeples, where it has stood for four centuries, and plant it once more on Calvary where the prophetic communities die victims of politics and religion in order to rise again as local churches *of* Asia. It is this death and resurrection that I wish to discuss now.

The Way Toward the Ecclesiological Revolution:
The Double Baptism in Asian Religiosity and Asian Poverty

The Jordan of Asian Religiosity

Schillebeeckx has drawn our attention to the fact that the baptism under John was Jesus' first prophetic gesture, the memory of which became a source of lasting embarrassment to the first generation of Christians. The embarrassment lay in the fact that Jesus, whom his followers had come to worship as the Lord and the Christ, had thought it fit to begin his messianic mission by becoming himself a follower of John the Baptist. The ecclesiological implications of this Christological event have not been sufficiently appreciated in the contemporary church. I wish therefore to draw from it at least four missiological principles for the local churches *in* Asia.

In the first place we observe that Jesus was faced with several streams of traditional religiosity when he answered his prophetic call. Not every kind of religiosity appealed to him. From his later reactions we gather that the narrow ideology of the Zealot movement did not attract him. Nor did the sectarian puritanism of the Essenes have any impact on him. As for the Pharisaic spirituality of self-righteousness, Jesus openly ridiculed it. His constant confrontations with the Sadducees—the chief priests and elders—indicate that he hardly approved their aristocratic "leisure-class" spirituality. Rather, it was in the ancient (Deuteronomic) tradition of prophetic asceticism represented by the Baptizer that Jesus discovered an authentic spirituality and an appropriate point of departure for his own prophetic mission. In opting for this form of liberative religiosity to the exclusion of others, which appeared enslaving, Jesus indulged in a species of "discernment" that we Christians in Asia, confronted with a variety of ideological and religious trends, are continually invited to make.

Second, we can immediately sense in this event, a peculiar reciprocity between John's own personal spirituality and that of his followers. The Baptizer represented a world-renouncing spirituality of an extreme sort. We are told that he lived "with nature" rather than "in society"; his diet and his dress—things picked up from the forest—were symbolic of this brand of hermit asceticism. But the Baptizer did not impose it on the baptized. The latter were the simple and the humble, the "religious poor" of the countryside, the ostracized but repentant sinners, the *anawîm* who were drawn by the Baptizer's preaching and his lifestyle to be ever more receptive to the good news of imminent liberation. Thus the poor too had a spirituality of their own. It was therefore at Jordan, when Jesus stood before the Baptizer and among the baptized, that the two streams of spirituality found their point of confluence. Jesus himself, about to pass through a wilderness experience of hermit asceticism, comes to John not to baptize others, but to be baptized, thus identifying himself with the "religious poor" of the countryside. Once again the ecclesiological implication of this Christological event is too obvious to explain. The Asian local churches have a mission to be at the point of intersection between the meta-cosmic spirituality of the monastic religions and the cosmic religiosity of the simple peasants, to be the locus where the liberative forces of both traditions combine in such a way as to exclude the aristocratic leisure-class mentality of the former and the superstitions of the latter. This is a missionary method we learn from our Master.

The third principle we wish to enunciate here has to do with the "loss of authority" to which we reduced the current crisis of mission. Jesus' first prophetic gesture—like every other prophetic word and deed—is self-authenticating. The prophet speaks and acts in God's name and with God's authority. If an event does not reveal this authority, then it is not prophetic. Jesus' humble submission to John's baptism, embarrassing as it was to early Christians, appeared to them, all the same, as a public manifestation of his authority to preach God's liberating reign about to dawn on the *anawîm*. It was with this act of humility that his credibility was certified by God in the presence of the poor: "*Hear ye him.*" It was a prophetic moment precisely because it was then that both his messianic self-understanding and his missionary credentials before the people were bestowed on him. Would that the local church in Asia be as humble as its spouse and Lord! Would that we Christians seek to be baptized rather than to baptize!

The fulfillment theory of the ancient fathers, now revived by Vatican II—which the present writer has repeatedly criticized in the past—relegates other religions to a pre-Christian category of spirituality to be "fulfilled" through the church's missionary endeavor. It is on the basis of this theory that some (Western) missiologists speak of the need to "baptize" the precursor's religiosity and culture rather than of the prophetic imperative to immerse oneself in the baptismal waters of Asian religions that predate Christianity. The local church *in* Asia needs yet to be "initiated" into the pre-Christian traditions under the tutelage of our ancient gurus, or it will continue to be an ecclesiastical complex full of power but lacking in authority. Only in the Jordan of Asian religiosity will the church be acknowledged as a voice worthy of being heard by all: "Hear ye him." The mission crisis is solved only when the church is baptized in the twofold liberative tradition of monks and peasants of Asia. Like its own Master, let it sit at the feet of Asian gurus not as an *ecclesia docens* but as an *ecclesia discens* lost among the "religious poor" of Asia, among the *anawîm* who go to these gurus in search of the kingdom of holiness, justice, and peace. The many individual attempts made in this direction are but symbolic beginnings. Unless the institutional church takes the plunge itself, it can hardly hope to be for Asians a readable word of revelation or a credible sign of salvation.

The fourth missiological principle comes as a response to the problem of identity that the third principle evokes. There is a phobia both in the West and in the (Western) local churches *in* Asia that there is in Asia a serious threat to the Christian identity of a believing community. A closer look shows that the roots of this phobia lie in the difficult option we have to make between a clear past and an unknown future, between the local churches *in* Asia with a clear Western identity and the local churches *of* Asia that have not yet articulated Asian identity. Further, in the model of the past, the Western identity overlaps the Christian identity, and so in the church of the future, one desires quite rightly that "Asianness" coincide with "Christianness." But Christian identity never exists per se as a neutral quantity from which the Western elements could be deducted and the Asian features added. This difficulty comes from the very nature of a local church, which is at once church and local.

In this, as in everything else, the church must return to its Source: Jesus Christ, who has enunciated for us the principle of losing oneself in order to find oneself. The clearest example is Jesus' baptism in the Jordan. This is precisely the fourth missiological principle. Was it not by losing his identity among the humble but repentant sinners and the "religious poor" of his country that he discovered—for himself and for others around him—his authentic selfhood: the lamb of God who liberates us from sin, the Beloved Son to be listened to, the Messiah who had a new message and a new baptism to offer? John's spirituality was traditional but negative; Jesus' religiosity was positive and entirely new. To John's curses on the self-righteous religious bigots and political leaders, Jesus would add the blessings and promises offered to the marginalized poor and the ostracized sinner. The Baptizer preached bad news about the coming judgment, but Jesus, whom he baptized, had good news to give about the imminent liberation.

The Precursor was conferring the baptism of water on the converts. The beloved Son would have the baptism of the cross conferred on himself for the conversion of the world. The one would question the belief that salvation came simply by membership in the chosen community and ask for individual conversion, but the Other would change the people so converted into a community of love. There would be a radical change also in the lifestyle that Jesus chose in contrast to John's. The Baptizer came without eating and drinking; while the Son of man would go to parties in the company of sinners. Thus plunging himself into the stream of an ancient spirituality, he came out with his own new mission. It is baptism alone that confers on us our Christian identity and the Christian newness we look for in Asia. Is it not the fear of losing its identity that keeps the local church from discovering that identity? Is it not the fear of dying that keeps it from living? The newness of Asian Christianity will appear only as a result of our total participation in the life and aspirations of the "religious poor" of Asia.

The Calvary of Asian Poverty

The trajectory of poverty that links Jordan with Calvary is the other missiological paradigm that we wish our local churches *in* Asia to reflect upon. We have already noted that of all the religious currents of Israel only the Johannine stream of spirituality appeared truly liberative in the judgment of Jesus. John had renounced wealth and power so radically and to such excesses that he had immense authority before the "religious poor" of Israel to speak in God's name. Authority is always associated with poverty, not with power. In fact, at John's preaching those who wielded power lost their authority. They killed him in rage (cf. Mt. 14:1-12). The lesson was clear: only he who is radically poor is qualified to preach the kingdom, and only those who are poor are disposed to receive it. For God and Mammon are enemies.

After being initiated into Johannine asceticism, Jesus is said to have had a decisive confrontation with Wealth, Power, and Prestige: three temptations that he conquered by means of three renunciations (cf. Mt. 4:1-11). Jesus, the laborer's son (cf. Mt.13: 55), who had no place of his own to be born in (cf. Lk. 2:7), would later have no place of his own to lay his head (cf. Mt. 8:20) or even to be buried (cf. Mt. 27:60). Jesus would go much further than John. His poverty was not merely a negative protest, not just a passive solidarity with the "religious poor" of Israel. It was a calculated strategy against Mammon, whom he declared to be God's rival (cf. Mt. 6:24). The kingdom that Jesus announced was certainly not for the rich (cf. Lk. 6:20-26). It requires a miracle for a rich man to give up his wealth and enter the kingdom (cf. Mk. 10:26-27). Jesus' curses on the "haves" (cf. Lk. 6:24-25) and his blessings on the "have-nots" (cf. Lk. 6:20-23) are sharpened by his dictum that it is in and through the poor (the hungry, the naked, etc.) that he would pass his messianic judgment on entire nations (cf. Mt. 25:31-46). No wonder that the very sight of money polluting religion made Jesus resort to physical violence (cf. Jn. 2:13-17). For his mission was a prophetic mission, that is, a mission *of* the poor and a mission *to* the poor; a mission *by* the poor and a mission *for* the poor. This is the truth about evangelization that the local churches *in* Asia find hardest to accept. To awaken the consciousness of the poor to their unique liberative role in the totally new order God is about to usher in (this is how we have already defined evangelization) is the inalienable task of the poor already awakened.

Jesus was the first evangelizer—poor but fully conscious of his part in the war against Mammon with all its principalities and powers. And it was this mission that was consummated on the cross—a cross that the money-polluted religiosity of his day planted on Calvary with the aid of a foreign colonial power (cf. Lk. 23:1-23). This is where the journey, begun at Jordan, ended. When true religion and politics join hands to awaken the poor, then Mammon too makes allies with religion and politics to conspire against the evangelizer. Religion and politics go together, whether *for* God or *against* God.

Not without reason did the evangelists relate Jesus' first prophetic gesture at the

Jordan to his last prophetic gesture on Calvary by using the same word to describe both: baptism (cf. Mt. 3:13–15; Mk. 10:35; Lk. 12:50). Each was a self-effacing act that revealed his prophetic authority. At the first baptism Jesus was acknowledged as the beloved Son. At the second baptism the evangelist heard even the colonial power that killed Jesus proclaim that He was truly the Son of God (cf. Mk. 15:39): indeed a prophetic moment when a humiliation gave birth to an exaltation capable of gathering the prophetic community, as the Fourth Gospel clearly teaches (cf. Jn. 12:32–33). The baptism of the cross, therefore, is not only the price Jesus paid for preaching the good news, but also the basis of all Christian discipleship (cf. Mk. 8:34). Thus the threefold missionary mandate to *preach,* to *baptize,* and to *make disciples*—understood in the past as the juridical extension of one local church's power over other localities through a rite of initiation—must be redeemed of this narrow ecclesiocentric interpretation by tracing it back to the cross: the final proof of authentic *preaching,* the only true *baptism* that gives sense to the sacrament that goes by that name, and the criterion of true Christian *discipleship.*

This cross we have now had for centuries in Asia. It was Fulton J. Sheen, a missiologist of quite another era, who said that the West seeks a Christ without the cross while the East has a cross without Christ. The judgment on the East is not quite exact. If there is no Christ without a cross, as Sheen supposes, could there be a cross without Christ? Can humankind ever put asunder what God has put together: Christ and the cross?

The cross that we speak of—a symbol of shame—is the one that a mercantile Christianity planted with the aid of foreign colonial powers. It is on this cross that the Asian poor are being baptized today! The unholy alliance of the missionary, the military, and the merchants of a previous era now continues with greater subtlety. For the local churches thus planted *in* Asia, being still local churches *of* former colonizing countries, now continue their alliance with neocolonialism in order to survive, thus causing the class division in the church, as we remarked above. Colonial education of the great missionary era has now given way to "development projects," which obviously advocate a theory of development that "developed countries" evolved in the very process of causing underdevelopment in Asia. It is the new form of "pre-evangelization."

New development is giving way to "liberation" in the same climate of Christian megalomania. A small minority church claims to offer "liberation" to Asia without first entering into liberative streams of Asian religiosity, which has its own antidotes against Mammon. A sixteenth-century brand of Latin Christianity—"inculturated," that is "tanned" after being in the oriental climate for four centuries as the one redemptive agent of God—now claims to "liberate" Asia without allowing Asia to liberate it of its Latinity. Hence our final appeal to the local churches *in* Asia: harden not your hearts; enter into the stream at the point where the *religiosity of the Asian poor* (represented by the peasants) and the *poverty of the religious Asians* (reflected in our monks) meet to form the ideal community of total sharing, the "religious socialism" which, like the early Christian communism, can be swallowed up in the jungle of Asian feudalism as well as Western ideologies and theologies. The prophetic communities that have come up as a result of being baptized consciously

or unconsciously into the Asian socialism are now on the trajectory of poverty linking Jordan to Calvary. It is they who speak *with authority* in Asia; it is they who are
the credible words of revelation, the readable signs of salvation, effective instruments of liberation. They are the true local churches *of* Asia, for they have been
baptized in the Jordan of Asian religiosity and on the Calvary of Asian poverty.
Until they are officially recognized as local churches *of* Asia, the authority crisis will
continue in the local churches *in* Asia.

Section 6

RELIGIOUS FREEDOM AND THE LOCAL CHURCH'S RESPONSIBILITY FOR MISSION

Statement of the Question

Religious freedom is a fundamental human right, which *all* persons must respect and foster. At the same time, persecution has always been closely related to the witness of the Christian community. The crucial relation between religious freedom and persecution needs to be examined by a local church in each historical moment as to how it is called to live out explicitly its responsibility for mission—to proclaim Christ as Savior—and to respect the rights of others to religious freedom.

Elements for a Reflection on the Question

- The quality of witness given by Christians who claim their rights in a minority situation
- The intolerance of some Christians
- The implication of state recognition of the church, when the state is either secular or openly associated with a religion other than Christianity
- The resulting discriminations derived from a lack of religious freedom
- Governmental restrictions on the church's witness when that witness is related to matters of social justice
- The kinds of witness possible to members of the local church in restrictive situations: local persons/expatriates; priests/religious/laity
- Constitutional rulings of governments affecting religious freedom
- The witness of the local church in relation to the obligation on the part of other religious groups to witness to their belief
- Situations in which the church, because of its power, assumes responsibility for those matters that are ordinarily the responsibility of the state

Related Questions

- What is the role of the church as an institution in society, and how does this role relate to religious freedom and mission?

- Why is there a lack of religious freedom in a given situation?
- What avenues are open to exploration in an effort to overcome this situation?
- How is the church living its witness and proclamation in this situation?
- Is there another expression of witness that the church would seem to be called to in this situation?
- What is the future of evangelization in this situation?

28

THE SITUATION IN POLAND, WITH SOME REFERENCE TO EASTERN EUROPE

Halina Bortnowska

The Situation of the Roman Catholic Church in Poland

Given our historical background, the concrete situation of the people must be seen within a three-pole reference: state, society, church. In a sense Polish society is married to the church, with a complete separation of church and state. The society, however, is not separate from the church, and hence it is not really a secular society. Thus for us religious freedom in the 1980s has become the test of all freedoms. The extent to which the state will allow this freedom has been taken as a measure of its attitude toward society. Increasingly people who are not believers recognize this test, and see that this measure of freedom is a measure of freedom for themselves. The church has become a kind of house of freedom for others. In the domain of culture, the church sponsors many projects that would not otherwise be possible in a communist state. Here artists find an area where they may search for the truth. In this sense the church is not an oppressive factor, but is a freedom factor for society as such. But, sometimes for its own personnel, there is the interior power of the church that has to be considered: the sheer weight of the social meaning of being a Catholic in Poland.

There is a distinction to be made between society and the state. The state is the equivalent of the structures of government. The national identity of the people transcends the state. The state is seen more in the role of an employer. Identity of the people is situated in a different sphere, for example, in the culture. The government

Halina Bortnowska, laywoman, is Editor of the Roman Catholic monthly review, *Znak,* and is a pastoral worker in the parish of Nowa Huta, near Krakow. She is also consultant to the Vatican Secretariat for Promoting Christian Unity.

must take the church as a partner in its contract with society; it cannot ignore the church, for it needs at least the passive tolerance of the church. The bishops have an information system through their preaching in the pulpit on Sundays; they are thus a source of information and direction, and exercise the power of the media in this special situation. The election of Pope John Paul II helped. His speeches in Poland were not censored; the result was cataclysmic.

The power of the church in Poland is a fact and a historical reality. Until now it has worked on a massive scale for the good of the people. This fact, however, does not preclude that this power can eventually become oppressive. This power survives because of the concern for national unity; there is strict solidarity among bishops, priests, and laity in order not to open the gate to state influence, which would undermine unity and reduce the freedom-giving strength.

This is true of the Roman Catholic church, but it is not true of other denominations. In terms of ecumenism, the Roman Catholic church hardly shares its freedom with others; this is our fault. Over centuries Roman Catholics have created a situation in which others are reluctant to enter and share our freedom. They are aware that closer contacts would endanger their identity. All other independent people lack the shelter that the church provides.

Under the present situation, Catholics in Poland are free to practice as much as they want. There is entire freedom of worship within the church precincts. There is no freedom, however, to build new churches or places of worship. Party members may have difficulty if they attend church, but there is a distinction to be made between those in cities and those in villages. There is no freedom to send children to schools where religious education would be continued, or at least not contradicted; virtually all schools are state schools with a program of antireligious propaganda.

Action that expresses faith, such as all kinds of social action, is limited. We can do works of mercy, but we cannot form independent associations. Therefore much is done individually or through small groups linked to the parish. A Catholic press exists, but is in no way sufficient to meet the demands. The people would produce these things themselves, but they are deprived of the resources and necessary permissions. There are very limited instances of religious subjects in the media.

The General Situation of Eastern Europe

It is not possible to extrapolate from one country to another in Eastern Europe for this question of religious freedom. The historical situation, and particularly that of the nineteenth century, is still present. Hungary and Czechoslovakia have a long tradition of Roman Catholicism identified with Austria, where the church was associated with royalty and the upper classes; contrastingly in Poland, the church has always been associated with the people and, more recently, with the worker. In Moravia there have been examples of Christian witness that have been very positive —priests dying in the mines—and this to some extent has redeemed Roman Catholicism.

In Czechoslovakia and Hungary the hierarchy has a nostalgia to be accepted by the state. Czech culture is permeated by lay, secular trends. East Germany is in a completely different situation. In a generalized way the communist policy is to divide and control. No one is free from the historical context. Freedom is exercised within the historical context with a measure of transcendence. Unless this transcendence exists, freedom is only theoretical.

Freedoms and unfreedoms are differently structured among Eastern European countries. Governments in these countries do not encourage relationships among the countries of Eastern Europe.

The Context of Religious Freedom: Its Relation to Human Rights and the Uses of Freedom

Religious freedom is a fundamental human right, and the statement as such needs no comment. But I would like to add that a kind of self-respect is needed for this right. Religious freedom is a particular instance of fundamental human freedom. Every fight that is only for *religious* freedom is limited and open to dangers. I am not especially concerned for a special privilege to have religious freedom, but I want full rights as a citizen, and within those rights, the right to freedom of conscience. Religious freedom cannot be isolated from other freedoms. Religious freedom flourishes to the extent that other freedoms exist within a society. We need to insist on the totality-of-freedom principle. Consider the example of Jan de Witt when he insisted that the reformed religion would prosper most when people chose it freely.

Freedom depends on how far the people are conscious of the elements of the situation. The more conscious they are of those elements, the more control they can exercise over the situation. If you know what you have chosen and are able to analyze the values, then you are freer. The church in this post-Vatican II period needs to educate the people in this way. Religious freedom is a double notion: the right to be free, which comes from the state and society; the use of the right of freedom by people—for example, within the church. Conscious choice shapes evangelization. If persons have a sufficiently strong inner life, they are not manipulated by the situation. This is a dominant note of *Redemptor Hominis;* it is very important.

The test case of freedom is standing by the truth. In this society (Poland), double-faced compromise as a way of living is very common. The person acting must stand by truth. The relation between persecution and religious freedom is that persecution provides the test case of the supreme standing by truth. *To withstand the boring, humiliating situation of being a second-class citizen over many decades is much more difficult than to withstand a short period of extreme persecution.* Small discriminations are very destructive in the long run.

The Role of the Church in the Future to Open the Way to Religious Freedom

The church will open the way to the future in religious freedom through education, and more than this, it will be the gift of grace. The first mission of the church is to give the people the moral, intellectual, and sacramental background to be free persons. Whatever can be done to foster human rights will include the fostering of religious freedom.

The mission of the church is deeply linked to the style of church life. In the long run the church probably cannot use certain authoritarian measures toward its own teachers. In countries such as ours people are especially allergic to such measures when used by the church. How can we make the church the place where education for freedom happens? How can we make it the school of fair procedure? Unless the situation changes, people will become both allergic and impassive after many years of intimidation by the state; dissent has to be prudent and nuanced so as not to be utilized by those outside.

The Form of Evangelization in the Future

Poland has been more a mission-sending country; people coming in would be a different thing. It is always a cultural shock. However if some Sisters could come who could adapt to the situation, and who would be able to share the experience of another culture, that would be very helpful. We might need some help in bridge-building by persons who would know both Polish culture and other cultures. We need this kind of experience in order to complete the knowledge coming from, for instance, books.

The completion of the faith-experience relates to the whole theory of communication. In order to get some perspective, we need a third dimension: for example, the distant past, the immediate past, and the present. The time-experience can provide this, and it can also be reached through the variety of cultural contacts. This is very important for tradition in order to communicate it to the next generation. Transcultural contacts speed this up. All of this is profoundly related to the question of transmitting the faith; one needs to be properly equipped for this task, in order to make the existing possibilities accessible for the people.

The church in its mission must close the gap between theology and the simple people. In Poland there is the need, within the framework of the existing popular religion, to make it deeper and more Christological, so that it will be sufficiently alive to be transmitted to the next generation.

Witness to those outside the church must be on two levels: (1) the intellectual level, and (2) the witness of the living community, being Christian in the essence. In Poland the God-question is very closely related to the church-question, and in Poland, that means the Roman Catholic church. Other countries (in Eastern Europe) may need preevangelization of a certain sophistication. But also here one must not forget the importance of witness.

The Hope for the Future

History is such a tremendous reality. Church history is not so quick in its happening. It is an illusion to accuse Vatican II for the difficulties happening now. We are still conditioned by the style of Catholicism prior to Vatican II in all countries. All the unresolved questions remain. The future depends on what we do now, but it is difficult to see what we are doing; we have to trust. The prophet is one who can truthfully assess the present situation.

The extent to which the church has been together with the people is of utmost importance: the extent to which the church has been ministering to all their needs with faith motivation. The church in Poland has never been the property of the intellectuals or the rich, and that is where one source of its strength lies.

29

THE PHILIPPINES

Francisco F. Claver, S.J.

Statement of the Question

Religious freedom is a fundamental human right, which *all* persons must respect and foster. At the same time, persecution has always been closely related to the witness of the Christian community. The crucial relation between religious freedom and persecution needs to be examined by a local church in each historical moment as to how it is called to live out explicitly its responsibility for mission—to proclaim Christ as Savior—and to respect the rights of others to religious freedom.

If the foregoing is indeed *the* question with regard to religious freedom and the local church's responsibility for mission (it is how the problem is formulated by SEDOS for this consultation), I believe we should give more than passing attention, first, to religious freedom itself, how it is—or should be—defined, and second, to the history of religious persecutions or the lack of religious freedom to identify the strands that bind the two so closely to each other. I have the feeling that at least in Asia—which will be the geographical and cultural context of this paper—the "crucial relation" noted above is by no means an accident of history.

Religious Freedom

In practice we define religious freedom as the right of a person to decide what form his or her relationship to a personal deity should take, what set of beliefs about that deity to accept, what institutional religion or church to adhere to; and for a group of people who constitute a church, the right to set down the conditions for membership, to have houses of worship, schools, hospitals, such means as they need

Francisco F. Claver, S.J., is Bishop of Malaybalay, Bukidnon, a prelature in the Philippines.

for the practice of their religion. It goes without saying that all this is in the supposition that the individual and communal practice of one's religion does not infringe on
the rights of people of other religions or do positive harm to the common good.

I am aware that the supposition just stated must be explained and specified
further. But it may not be necessary if we accept that supposition to be equally
applicable and pertinent to all other rights and freedoms that we ordinarily call
human. It merely underlines the fact that though human rights are inalienable, they
are not absolute and unlimited taken singly or collectively, neither in the abstract nor
in the concrete.

This brings us to our next point: when we speak of religious freedom, we must
constantly keep in mind that we cannot separate it from other freedoms, other
rights. Human rights make up an integral whole, and one cannot speak of defending
or asserting freedom of religion without at the same time doing the same for freedom
of speech, freedom of association and assembly, freedom of movement, and the like.
The point made here may seem innocuous to people who take human rights for
granted; not to those, however, in situations where totalitarian governments systematically violate human rights and the church does not feel any compulsion to act
unless religious freedom itself is directly attacked. The mentality behind such a stand
seems to assume that religious freedom is absolute and unconnected with other
rights—and is the prime if not the sole concern of the church. This outlook has much
to do, ironically, with the denial of religious freedom and, in its most extreme form,
religious persecution.

Religious Persecution

Sweeping as the statement sounds, religious persecution in Asia—at least of the
Catholic church—is intimately linked with the church's own perception and practice
of human rights. Reviewing the history of persecution of Christians in Asia, I think
we can classify them under two headings: colonial and totalitarian. The terms and
the division itself are arbitrary, but I believe the reasons for them are not, when we
situate them in the general context of Asian cultural pride.

Persecution in Colonial Times. Actually what is called "colonial times" here does
not pertain to a period so much as to the reason for persecution. The paramount one
seems to have been the identification of Christianity with Western culture and power.
Christianity came to Asia with European arms and money, with political and
economic power, and inevitably the fear of and the resentment against intruding
soldiers and merchants were transferred as a matter of corse to the ministers and
priests of their religion. Matters were not helped either by the fact that Christianity
was preached in a distinctively Western form and converting to Christianity also
meant, in practice, embracing a foreign culture and denying one's own.

This seems to have been the case in China, Japan, and India during the four
centuries of Western colonial expansion and hegemony in Asia, in the new
nation-states, too, which came into being after World War II and in which conscious
nationalism was synonymous with adherence to one of the great Asiatic
religio-cultural traditions (Hinduism, Buddhism, Islam).

Persecution under Totalitarian States. The persecution that takes place today under modern totalitarian states is not devoid of the xenophobic characteristics of the type of persecution that we term "colonial"; in fact in many instances it is rooted in them. But there is this added difference: religion is feared and often expressly interdicted as the enemy of state ideologies of varying shades and colors. Such is the case in the Philippines and South Korea (with regard at least to socially conscious churches) and in communist-dominated countries.

Persecution in the Context of Asian Cultural Pride. Earlier we said a church's perception and practice of human rights has had much to do with the kind of persecution inflicted on it. In the first type, the colonial, the church's identification with a foreign power was on the surface sufficient cause for persecution. But the deeper reason, I am afraid, is a cultural one: if becoming a Christian was tantamount to becoming a Westerner, internalizing the culture of foreigners, then the church itself was, unknowingly it is true, guilty of violating a people's basic right to the integrity of their culture. Native Asians did not say so in so many words, nor did missionaries of the type of Ricci and de Nobili, but the unexplicated insight was there—and, more importantly, it was operative. By hindsight, with our more developed sense of culture and faith inculturation, with our more sensitive outlook on human rights and dignity, we can explicate that insight, and so see more clearly why those persecutions were inevitable. Denial of religious freedom (I suspect interpreted in the main as the institutional freedom of the church to preach and convert) was a response to the church's denial of, or at least lack of regard for, people's right to their cultural wholeness and identity.

In the second type of persecution, the totalitarian, the church is persecuted, ironically because it has corrected its faulty perception and practice of human rights: once it accepts that religious freedom cannot be isolated from all other freedoms and rights, it has to be against their violations by totalitarian regimes, and since these regimes cannot brook opposition for whatever reason, persecution is an unavoidable consequence.

This reading of the situation may sound simplistic. Perhaps it is. But I believe its simplicity contains more than just the proverbial grain of salt. Whether it does or not, it will flavor much of what will be said below.

Elements for Reflection: Focus on Witness

If we accept the essential linkage of all human freedoms and rights and, accepting that linkage, view the history of persecutions in Asia in its light, we will necessarily, in our examination of religious freedom and the church's mission, have to focus on the quality of our individual and collective witness. For our purposes, I propose we look at the church—ourselves as Christians—first, as a moral and/or political force, and second, in relation to cultural and social dynamisms. I trust we shall be able, in the process, to touch on the main elements required of our reflection.

The Church as a Moral and/or Political Force

From all we have said so far about the kind of persecutions the church in Asia has undergone through the centuries, I think it is safe to say that the church has suffered persecution because it has been looked at as a force, political in the main, by emperors and kings, by governments both colonial and modern, either by identification (ascribed or real) with foreign political powers, or by the church itself exerting real influence in society. Whether by identification or by possession of real power, the church by and large has been a force to reckon with in the political sphere. This is so even when it vigorously disclaims a purely political role (what are nunciatures for?), whether it is in a minority situation (the usual case in Asia) or in a majority one (as in the Philippines). Again, the bald statement appears to be a gross overgeneralization. To examine the question more closely, then, it will be instructive to attend to *(a)* the area of the church's power, *(b)* the quality of its power, *(c)* its attitude toward other religions, and *(d)* the denial of its freedom because of its use of power and its relations with other religions.

The Area of the Church's Power. If the power of the church, imagined or real, is, as we said, a reason for the persecution it has been subjected to, it must be scrutinized more carefully than we have heretofore done. Nothing will be gained by dismissing it out of hand as nothing more than an easy coverup on the part of persecutors for their real reasons or by simply reiterating our own coverup when we insist that the church is interested only in the things of the spirit or that it does not engage in the game of power politics. The issue of the church and politics is a current one in most of the third world, and we do not intend to get enmeshed in the intricacies of the debate here. But at the same time we must say the debate, as it touches the question of church power, has much to do with our present deliberation, and hence we must honestly face up to its implications.

To minimize controversy on the subject, it may be best to make the distinction that Pope John Paul II is said to have made at Puebla between *lo político* (the political sphere) and *la política* (politics, and indeed, partisan politics). He views the former as the area in which the church, the hierarchical church mainly, can and should play an active role, and the latter as the domain of the lay person. The distinction makes much sense and, as a rule of thumb, has many practical applications. For those who find the distinction too pat, however—and in truth the line between the two areas can be very thin or altogether nonexistent—I suggest recourse be had to Christ's primordial rule of charity; anything that harms people, makes them less human, economics and politics included, falls within the realm of concern of the church (hierarchy and laity), and the only limits one can think of imposing on an area of activity that is as wide as life itself are the possibility of doing greater good or less harm—and common sense. If the church is to have any power at all, the least we can say is that it must be a power for good.

The Quality of the Church's Power. Whether we agree that the church has power and influence or not beyond its strictly institutional membership—and I will not quarrel if we chose to call such power political or moral—the fact is its prophetic role in society at large is a constant task, consonant with, indeed flowing from, Christ's mandate to preach the good news to all the world. The prophetic task is easy enough to describe in societies in which Christian values have become part of the people's cultural traditions, harder where they are peripheral. But it seems to me, whether the cultural milieu is Christian or not, there is always a place for what Archbishop Camara calls "Abrahamic minorities"—communities of believers who try to make the gospel of Christ mean much more than just a set of orthodox beliefs and a code of personal conduct, genuine leavens of society, in other words. Whether their prophetic task, ever pressing, ever active is to express itself in explicit protest or necessary silence, their protest or silence must have an undoubtedly evangelical meaning. If we can say this of the parts, we must say it as well of the whole that is the church; and if we have to talk of church power, we must say that it will have to be none other than the power of the word, spoken clearly and prophetically.

The Church's Attitude toward Other Religions. Defining the church's power as we have done above, needless to say, carries with it a host of other problems, not the least of which is the church's stance, because of its sense of power, toward other religions. Ethnocentricity is a common enough failing when people as *a* people believe themselves superior to others because of their special cultural traditions. The Catholic church has not been untouched by this human fault: "We are the only true church; we have the truth of Christ in its entirety; only we can rightfully and infallibly interpret that truth." Try as we may, if we have indeed tried, we have not in our preaching divested ourselves sufficiently of our (innate?) pharisaism—"the prejudice of the saved." There would be no need to engage here in institutional breast-beating were it not for the palpable harm our bias has done in the church's universal effort to preach the gospel. In a continent as big and as old as Asia, where "face" is a common cultural value, one does not win people over to Christ by first making them lose face—and we do make them lose face in equivalently asking them to deny deeply prized cultural heritages and assume an alien one when they convert to Christianity. Saying this, we should not lose sight of the fact that what we blame ourselves for, our religious ethnocentricity, is just as strong (if not stronger) in people of the great Asian traditions. But this is precisely the point: pharisaism is not to be countered by another form of pharisaism, or there will be no end to our long history of mutual persecutions.

The Denial of the Church's Freedom. What I have sought to show here is that there is, simply put, a clear connection between how the church looks at itself and conducts itself, how its looks at its power and uses it, and the persecution that it has been made to suffer. I do not think more need be added except to stress an obvious conclusion, namely, that in every case of persecution, we have to scrutinize carefully what real reasons lie behind the denial of religious freedom. For I strongly believe those reasons point to some possible future directions and developments in our mission as church. Some such questions as the following can and should be asked: *(a)* Is the denial of religious freedom stemming from strictly political reasons—because the church is indeed enmeshed in real politics (Pope John Paul's *la politica*) and uses its power principally for the protection of its rights and privileges? Or *(b)* from cultural reasons—because the church does in effect ask its converts to renege on their cultural traditions in order to become Christians? Or *(c)* from religious reasons—because the church's faith does demand the defense of the dignity and rights of people, as the Asian bishops in their meeting in Manila in 1970 put it, "whenever, wherever, by whomever" these rights and dignity are violated?

True enough, it is difficult in any given instance to separate the political, the cultural, and the religious, for these are all intimately interconnected, but for a church that is truly church, the only valid and acceptable cause for its persecution should be its faith and the witness it gives that faith in its humble service of people. In other words, if it is to be persecuted at all, let it be for being what it should be, for doing what it should be doing, not from being what it should not be or for doing what it should not be doing.

The Church vis-à-vis Cultural and Social Dynamisms

For the church to be what it should be and do what it should be doing, there is a continual need for it to reexamine and, if need be, redefine its evangelical mission at every historical moment. That sounds presumptuous—as if up till now the church has been on a wrong track. Not really. It is simply an acknowledgment of the fact that our thinking today on religious freedom and human rights, on the one hand, and on the other, on faith and culture, has developed remarkably in recent years, helped not a little by Vatican II and the possibilities it has opened for us to strike out in new directions. Toward that reexamining and redefining, I propose we consider the following tasks of the church in regard to cultural and social forces: (a) consecrating the best in cultural traditions, (b) correcting the worst in those traditions, and (c) cooperating with religious (non-Christian) majorities. The "tasks" are in actuality nothing more than indicative areas of church involvement in the questions raised by this paper's specific subject.

Consecrating the Best. Every people with a definite cultural tradition has what anthropologists call an "ideal culture," namely, what the people themselves believe their culture *should be*. In practice this will be the complex of values, goals, norms, and world-views that spell out for them their ethos as a people. When we look closely at this ethos, we shall find what we can only describe here as the deeply and genuinely human traits of a people, their ideal conception of themselves. There will be differences in those human traits and ideals from culture to culture, in emphases, in nuances, in total configurations (these are what make cultures different), but as expressions of the human, those traits and ideals will be readily understood and recognized by any adult man or woman of whatever culture precisely because of their human character.

This understanding and recognition is the first task of the church in any situation of mission. For it is in the doing of the task that it will discover how it is to go about its evangelizing task—the explicit consecrating (Christifying?) of the best values in any cultural tradition. From the very start, then, the church does away with much of the alienation of its converts from their own culture, and with many of the problems that flow from that alienation: hostility, suspicion, persecution itself.

Correcting the Worst. The real culture of any given people does not always coincide perfectly with the ideal (this is true even of Christians with the practice of their faith). If this fact is accepted, the church's second task is to help correct aberrations from the ideal (in the supposition, that is, that the ideal does in fact correspond with the universally human) by initiating what more and more is becoming acknowledged as primary to the very notion of evangelization: the dialogue between culture and Christian faith.

Cooperating with Non-Christian Majorities. The dialogue I speak of is not to be principally in actual discussions—as most ecumenical conversations are carried out—but at the level of action, of working together toward a mutually acceptable end. Human rights, social justice, the uplifting of the poor—these come readily to mind as areas in which religious groups, Christian and non-Christian, can cooperate easily and with a minimum of theological differences. This cooperation is imperative, especially where Christians are in the minority and initiatives are already being taken by majority religions in the direction we speak of here.

What all this amounts to is the acceptance of the fact that even before the church begins to preach an explicit Christianity, it would do well for it to recognize what is implicit Christianity in prevailing cultural and social forces, to work with these forces, to contribute to them, to enhance them, in the awareness that its primary evangelizing task is not conversion of people to institutional Christianity, nor even simply witnessing to gospel values, but the *doing* of Christianity. True, these three tasks, properly understood, are one and the same thing. We simply wish to underscore Christ's injunction to "fulfill and teach" (Mt. 5:19). I do not think the collocation of the two words is purely fortuitous. The fulfilling before the teaching of his gospel is the strongest witnessing and converting act of which the church is capable.

What of religious freedom and the local church's responsibility for mission? By focusing on the church and cultural-social forces, we have (1) situated religious freedom in the only context that all, Christian and non-Christian alike, will accept as a common ground, that is, their common cultural-social traditions; (2) indicated how the church is to work out its responsibility for mission in regard to the all-important dialogue between faith and culture; (3) highlighted how the church, by placing importance on the cultural context of the faith's preaching, starts straight off in the right direction as far as its being and becoming a local church is concerned; (4) undercut the more common—and to my mind, unnecessary—historical reasons for religious persecution; and (5) made the burden of defending religious freedom and all other human freedoms and rights common to all religions, necessitating dialogue, mutual respect, and cooperation among them. All this is part of that *doing* that we say is of prime importance in the church's mission to the world.

Related Questions: Future Directions

In all that has been said so far, we have, by naming "indicative areas" in which the general problem of religious freedom and the church's mission can be worked out, also outlined the possible directions we could take in the future. At this point, then, by way of résumé and of touching on related questions, we briefly summarize our main points thus:

1. Religious freedom is integral with all other human freedoms. Hence it is inconceivable for a church to be satisfied with guarantees of religious freedom to itself and its adherents while closing its eyes to the denial of other freedoms to people in general.

2. For a church in mission to work effectively for religious freedom, it will have

to push for the entirety of all human freedoms and rights—or it will not escape the accusation of self-interested mission (a frequent cause of persecution).

3. This is tantamount to saying that people's rights and interests must have precedence over, or at least be given equal importance with, those of the church as an institution. The acceptance of this precedence is dictated by the very mission of the church to be at the service of people for the sake of the kingdom.

4. While putting itself wholeheartedly at the service of people, the church must take care not to destroy their culture, their pride in it, the identity they have from it—or it would be guilty of infringing on a people's basic right to the integrity of their culture. This infringing, often unconscious, has been and still is a common reason of antipathy toward the church.

5. To the extent that the sociocultural traditions of a people are expressions and embodiments of genuinely human (and hence fundamentally Christian) values and aspirations (which should include universally accepted human rights and freedoms), the church should be able to cooperate with other religions toward the preservation and enhancement of those values, the attainment and realization of those aspirations.

6. The cooperation envisioned—a positive good in itself—is part of the church's mission of preaching and doing the gospel. In the give-and-take of ideas, the working-out of methods and strategies, the dialogue that is entailed by the idea of cooperation, and the church's perspective on the value of the human person, other specifically gospel values will be made to shine through.

7. The underlying premise of cooperation (or at least its possibility) among different religions is that the obligation to witness to one's religious values is not for Christians alone but for all men and women of faith. A corollary of this is that oppression of people for any unjust reason is a *religious* concern of no little moment.

8. Touching the consciences of people in power (and this includes power-holders in religions that may be closely identified with the state) who violate justice and human rights is a constant task of the church, especially of those groups that we gave special mention to above, namely, "Abrahamic minorities."

9. Since the context of all this, at least as far as the churches in Asia are concerned, is the indigenized and indigenizing local church, ideally the lead must be taken by native-born leaders, expatriates coming in, in supportive roles. However, if the church is truly indigenizing, the distinction between local personnel and expatriates is not one to be unduly stressed: all are or should be members of the local church: all are working for the church to be truly local—and the Spirit will breathe on whom he wills for the building up of the church.

10. Religious persecution and all other questions and problems related to it are thus best left to the discernment of the local church. The practicalities of the general problematic will become more manageable, the pertinent theological and pastoral presuppositions clearer, if that discernment is solidly contextualized in the cultural situation of the local church and focused on its witness to the faith in that same situation. In other words, if the church is to be persecuted at all, it should be for the power of its faith and for this alone, not for any extraneous power it may by acci-

dents of history possess and exercise, and certainly not for its failure to itself respect religious and other human freedoms. Only continuous and honest discernment will show the extent and quality of the power of the church's witnessing to its faith.

The summary statements just made, dogmatic as they sound, are by no means proposed as definitive pronouncements but as tentative hypotheses—hypotheses, that is, to be verified, tested, corrected, even rejected altogether, but only for the generating and developing of further hypotheses, more appropriate, practical, specific, theologically and pastorally sound, and all for this one end: that the church may indeed be free to preach the gospel in all its power. In the final analysis, this kind of preaching is what mission is about.

The very concept of "church power" is open to misunderstanding and misinterpretation (as is abundantly clear from the history of religious persecution in Asia). Should we not, rather, talk of powerlessness, vulnerability, servanthood? But I cannot think of another word to describe adequately the gospel of Christ and the life of the Spirit that it must bring about in those who accept it and live it. However we define "church power"—or try to explain it away to make it sound less political—one thing is clear: real faith, living and lived, will always be a challenge, a power therefore, wherever there is sin, injustice, dehumanization. A rich church, a comfortable and conforming church, practically by definition cannot preach this kind of challenging faith. For like its Lord, the church must ever be a "sign of contradiction," which simply means that its mission is to be persecuted.

30

THE REGIONAL CHURCH OF NORTH AMERICA

Joseph Gremillion

Scope and Setting

The world headquarters (generalates) of forty-five Catholic missionary societies (institutes) have launched this three-year research seminar (1979–81) on "The Future of Mission" through their center for documentation and study, SEDOS, formed in Rome in followup to Vatican Council II. SEDOS is constituted and governed by these generalates themselves, with the knowledge and approval of the Holy See. It is not part of the Roman Curia, and is not directly answerable to the Chair of Peter.

Seminar Structure and Process

After wide consultation with its forty-five constituent member-societies and with many mission specialists from the different regions and cultures, 'the local church' was taken as the focal point for mission, and the questions were reformulated in terms of this context. These subjects for long-term research and reflection are: (1) missionary dimensions of the local church; (2) mission of the local church and the inculturation of the gospel; (3) Christian mission and ecumenical relations in the context of the local church; (4) liberation and justice dimensions of the local church's mission; (5) mission of the local church in secular society; (6) religious freedom and the local church's responsibility for mission; (7) mission of the local church and the missionary institutes (societies, orders, or congregations); (8) mission in the local church in relation to other major religious traditions; (9) mission of the local church in China.

Joseph Gremillion is the Director of Social and Ecumenical Ministry for the Diocese of Alexandria–Shreveport, Louisiana, and Coordinator for the Muslim, Jewish, Christian Conference in Washington, D.C. Monsignor Gremillion was the secretary of the Pontifical Commission for Justice and Peace from 1967 to 1974. He is the author of several books.

Recognizing the diverse religio-cultural, socioeconomic, geopolitical situations in the respective regions of the planet, persons from the local churches of each of the six continents were selected to prepare papers on each of these nine subjects, for a total of at least fifty-four papers.

The Regional Churches

This present paper addresses the subject matter of section 6, "Religious Freedom and the Local Church's Responsibility for Mission." Its assigned focus is the church of the North American continent, in the two nations of Canada and the United States. The term "local church" may also apply to smaller ecclesial bodies, even to each diocese, of which there are over two hundred in the North American region. In this paper, however, the regional or national ecclesial body and presence will dominate, to the exclusion of smaller units.

By reason of my relative ignorance of the Canadian situation, I will devote more attention to the church in the United States, with its particular history, ideologies, and global role. In my judgment, however, the current socioeconomic, political, cultural, and ecclesial situations of the two nations are drawing ever nearer—even closer, for instance, than those of Germany, France, Britain, and Italy as they come together into the community of Western Europe (societal and ecclesial). Consequently I would freely project convergence toward the Christian church of North America, one and plural, local and universal, as a viable possibility in the coming few decades, a goal highly desirable for the next generation of ecumenical and mission endeavor.

In this context the term "North American church" could include all the Christian bodies and traditions of the region—Protestant, Evangelical, Orthodox, and Catholic. I would project comparable convergence among the Christian communities of the ten or twelve other religio-cultural, sociopolitical regions, to form regional churches, for instance, of Latin America, Eastern Europe, Black Africa, North Africa–Mideast, South Asia, Pacifica, and so forth.

The church of Latin America, with its creative theology derived from societal reality and pastoral praxis, has advanced furthest in acquiring its own ecclesial consciousness, expressed through the region's council of bishops (CELAM) and the Medellín and Puebla conferences.[1]

This movement toward the regional church has enormous meaning for "the future of mission" for all Christian bodies. This is clearly perceived through the local-church approach of this SEDOS seminar, with its reflection on the societal and cultural reality specific to each continent and region, as the unit of Christian mission.

Within the Catholic church, regional focus for ecclesial consciousness and identity, organization and pastoral practice are evolving anew from the doctrine of collegiality, providentially restated by Vatican II. This recalls the collegial character of God's people from the tradition of apostolic times and the patriarchates of the early church, to be reapplied after a thousand years of Western European egocentricity and four centuries of nationalist fragmentation.[2]

Religious Freedom in North America

Turning now to my assigned subject, the North American history of religious freedom will be briefly reviewed, together with the acculturation of the "missionary" Catholic church to this original creation of the region's societal matrix, ecclesial and civil. I will trace, very hurriedly, the transplanting of religious freedom as a political ideal to most of the globe's more than 150 nations; and the embrace by the Catholic church of religious freedom as a Christian truth and ecclesial principle during Vatican II—a reversal of church teaching and policy of astonishing dimension after centuries of adamant and oppressive rejection by popes, bishops, and theologians.

The Essential Historical Role of Religious Freedom

Religious freedom was not a mere product of the culture and body politic of North America. Religious freedom played a dominant role in the very conception and shaping of the national characters and constitutions of the United States and Canada. Religious freedom became, therefore, innate to and creative of the two nations, to a degree unknown to any of the other hundred and fifty or so nations of our planet. In many ways, it begot as well a new type of Christianity. This basic process occurred during the region's missionary period, before 1800.

For these reasons the North American experience of religious freedom is of deep significance to the future of mission. Further, as America's foremost historian of Christian mission observes, "In the twentieth century from these two nations came the majority of the personnel and more than half the funds which made possible the remarkable expansion of the Protestant forms of Christianity in that period." The Catholic church of the region, he continues, "while displaying a rapid extension in the United States and Canada, proportionately had only a minor, even though a growing part in the propagation of the Roman Catholic form of Christianity in other portions of the world."[3]

This energetic missionary outreach brought key elements of North American Christianity and culture, including religious freedom, into the young regional churches of Asia and Africa. These in turn, through their educational apostolate and the formation of indigenous leaders, played significant roles in begetting the hundred new nations that have entered the global stage since World War II.

Stages of Development

The evolution of religious freedom in North America can be hurriedly traced through four stages.

1. First Settlements of the 1600s. First, religious freedom was not imported into the United States and Canada; it developed in this new ground. Few if any first settlers had ever experienced it in Europe, where established religions and intolerance of dissidents obtained.

This was especially true of their mother countries, England, France, and Spain. Their first colonies in Virginia and Massachusetts, Canada and Florida were authorized by Anglican and Catholic sovereigns who vigorously persecuted dissent from the one true and established church of the ruler. The Westphalia peace formula of 1648, *Cujus regio ejus religio* (the ruler's religion becomes that of the region), was applied throughout Europe by a hundred Calvinist, Lutheran, and Catholic kings and princes, as well as by the popes and Holy Roman Emperor—until the French Revolution and beyond.

The most creative religious community in the American story, the Pilgrim Puritans of New England, arrived at Plymouth Rock in 1620 as Separatists seeking freedom from the established Anglican church. They "believed that a true church is a body of Christians under the guidance of pastors elected by 'the Lord's godly and free people.' " Their motives were "partly economic . . . partly the desire to keep their children loyal to Christian truth as they saw it and removed from the contaminations which surrounded them . . . and partly 'a great hope . . . of laying some good foundation . . . for the propagating and advancing of the gospel of the Kingdom of Christ' in America."[4]

While seeking religious freedom for their own "covenanted community," the Massachusetts colonists did not tolerate dissenters in their midst, nor other Christian bodies in their area. Catholics were especially feared and Jesuits doubly so: "At the outset their avowed purpose was to 'raise a bulwark against the kingdom of anti-Christ which the Jesuits labour to rear up in all parts of the world' and to escape from the corruptions which afflicted the inhabitants of the Old World."[5]

The Connecticut colony was formed in the 1630s by Massachusetts Puritans who "carried that type of Christianity with them," together with "strict Puritans who had left the mother country for religious convictions." The Rhode Island settlements "were established by religious radicals who had proved obnoxious to the authorities on Massachusetts Bay," led by Roger Williams at Providence in 1636.

Objecting theologically to the union of the ecclesial and civil domains in Plymouth and Boston, Williams pioneered in Rhode Island the "free and independent congregation" and "separation of Church and State" which have begotten fundamental ecclesiologies and political ideologies in the United States, which have affected most "mission regions" of the globe. Under these principles, forms of Christianity other than pure Puritanism "either arose by separation from the Standing Order or were introduced from the outside. They flourished especially in Rhode Island, where from the outset much of religious toleration existed. Such diverse groups as the Church of England, Quakers, and Baptists were present," plus Huguenot refugees from Catholic France.[6]

Maryland and Pennsylvania, founded in 1634 and 1681, were the other colonies most noted for religious liberty. Following his Quaker beliefs, William Penn "made religious toleration part of the cornerstone of the colony." German Lutherans and Brethren began arriving in 1683; also Baptists from Wales and New England (first church in 1684), and Presbyterian Scotch-Irish from Ulster (1701). Even Catholics were allowed resident priests.[7]

Maryland, however, became the Catholic center in colonial days. Its founders, the

Lords Calvert, were English Catholics of some influence at the throne. Jesuit priests came with the first settlers in 1634. "Yet Maryland was not primarily Roman Catholic. Out of expediency or of necessity the founders granted religious toleration. . . . The colony became overwhelmingly Protestant." In 1689 "a local revolution led to the overthrow of the Roman Catholic political control and in 1692 the Church of England was given by law a privileged position. . . . The Calverts became members of the Established (Anglican) Church." While favoring the Church of England with building subsidies and land benefices for the clergy, Maryland authorities allowed other free church groups lacking these advantages. A Methodist preacher arrived from Ulster in the 1770's, to begin the frontier ministry of "riding the circuit" in neighboring areas.[8]

In Virginia, the oldest and most populous colony, "religious motives were either absent or played a subordinate role in its founding and in most of its immigrants." While "law required conformity to the Church of England in public services" and the "General Assembly once offered a bonus of 25 pounds to any one bringing to the colony a clergyman in priest's orders," dissenting groups kept coming in.

Mountainous frontier Virginia, as distinct from the slave-holding coastal plains, became the greenhouse of the Southern Baptists, who began there with two ministers in 1714 to grow into America's most populous and energetic Protestant, or Evangelical, denomination today, with over 13 million members and 35,000 ministers.[9] They gave rise in turn to the separate black Baptist congregations, also most numerous among that race with over 10 million members. Baptists and their Evangelical cousins, often spin-offs from more established bodies, together with the circuit-riding Methodists, played major roles in proclaiming the "free church" gospel across the continent, frontier after frontier, for the next two hundred years.

Virginia also provided major impulse to the other great American current for religious freedom in the person of Thomas Jefferson, the Deist proponent of "the rights of man," much influenced by the Enlightenment philosophers of the French Revolution. He led the campaign to disestablish the Anglican church of Virginia in 1784, and to write "separation of Church and State" into the American Constitution, 1789–91 (see below).

2. Canada and the Quebec Act, 1605–1800. In Canada religious freedom did not develop from indigenous events and ferments comparable to the American evolution. Canada's fate was largely determined by imperial policies and wars of the British and French.

In the United States, as we have sketchily seen, "the desire for religious freedom was prominent as a cause of white settlement and the type of Christianity propagated was primarily Protestant, and of the kinds which were *persecuted in Europe*. In French America the longing for religious liberty was *not a factor* in inducing immigration and the Christianity was entirely Roman Catholic." Also, while in the English colonies, "missions to Indians were incidental. In French North America, Indian missions held the center of the stage."[10]

In 1611 two Jesuits arrived at Port Royal, Nova Scotia, first begun as a fishing settlement in 1605, "and earnestly began efforts to win the Indians. They set about learning the language. Reinforcements arrived. A new settlement was formed (across the Bay of Fundy) in the present Maine. Scarcely had this been done, however, when English from Virginia appeared (1613), killed two of the Jesuits, and carried the other two away captive."

Thus the religio-imperial wars of Europe were transferred to the North American region, where they continued for over two hundred years. On the southern frontier between Spanish Florida and British Georgia, forays between Saint Augustine (1565) and Savannah broke out spasmodically. But the determining conflicts were between French Canada and English America.[11]

The crucial events were: (1) the war of 1756–63, through which Britain took over Canada and the area between the Appalachians and the Mississippi; and (2) the Quebec Act of 1774, under which the British ceded religious freedom to Canadian Catholics and thus assured their loyalty in the War for American Independence.

In the French and Indian War of 1756–63, American Protestants and Canadian Catholics fought each other as soldiers of the British and French armies. The North American scene was but a mini-act in the world wars that raged between these two empires, and the Spanish-Austrian dynasty, for over two centuries, from the storied Spanish Armada of 1570 to Waterloo in 1815.

The religious animus of these struggles reached America as early as 1613, with Virginia's attack on the French settlement and Jesuit mission in Maine, as seen above. For the North American continent's religious freedom and overall history, the British capture of Quebec in 1759 and the peace treaty of 1763 were decisive. Canada with its Catholic settlements and missions up the Saint Lawrence and along the Great Lakes, in the Ohio valley and Louisiana from the Appalachians to the Mississippi, were taken over by Protestant England. Significantly, George Washington, with Putnam and Prescott, heroes of Bunker Hill, and a score of other leaders of the American Revolution were young officers in the war against Canada, French and Catholic.

Under the peace treaty of 1763 the "free exercise of the Roman Catholic faith was guaranteed . . . restricted by the clause, 'so far as the laws of Great Britain permit.' " Restrictions in the mother country were of course very substantial. London's "instruction to the first British Governor was 'not to admit any ecclesiastical jurisdiction of the See of Rome.' At the outset the Bishop of Quebec was forbidden to carry on any correspondence with Rome. Only gradually did the Bishops win concessions. . . . The privilege of jury service was accorded to Canadian Roman Catholics in 1764, twenty-seven years before it was granted in England."[12] The British victory naturally brought an influx of Protestants, many from the nascent United States. Binational and bireligious Canada was born.

It was the Quebec Act of 1774 that assured religious freedom to Canada's Catholics and won their loyalty to Britain in the American War of Independence then two years away. It simultaneously raised the revolutionary temperature of the colonies closer to the boiling point.

By the Quebec Act much of present-day New England and New York, with most of the territory north of the Ohio River from Pennsylvania to the Mississippi, were transferred to Canadian dominion. The act thus sealed off from colonial land speculators and emigrants much of the Northwest Territory (Ohio, Indiana, Illinois, Wisconsin, Michigan), into which the American colonies, and soon-to-be-states, had

already projected their western boundaries. Washington, let us recall, had first attracted attention as a twenty-year-old surveyor in western Virginia. He, Hamilton,
and many other patriots were heavy investors in these lands west of the Appalachians. Now they were suddenly lopped off from Protestant American control and
expansion just as the United States was acquiring its own national consciousness,
identity, and manifest destiny—in favor of Canada, French-speaking and Catholic.

Further, "in a humane and enlightened spirit, (the Quebec Act) guaranteed the
rights of all former Frenchmen 'professing the religion of the Church of Rome.'
Nothing could have alarmed the New England Puritans more than having a sanctioned group of papists on their Northern doorstep. . . . Its provisions, enlightened
as they were, aroused all the historic anxieties of Englishmen on both sides of the
ocean about the threat of Papacy to the Protestant religion." Many Americans became convinced that the Quebec Act was intended by Mother England as a warning
and rebuke to her bumptious colonists, in the wake of the Boston Massacre and Tea
Party.

Such views were not groundless. "One member of Parliament had pointed out in
the debate over the act that if the French-Canadians were promptly reconciled to
British rule by a generous gesture, they might serve as a check to 'those fierce fanatic
spirits in the Protestant colonies.' The Canadians, some Englishmen felt, might be
used at the appropriate time 'to butcher these Puritan Dogs.' "

A wave of revulsion, religious and nationalist, swept the American colonies.
"Alexander Hamilton predicted that the act would leave the colonists surrounded by
'a Nation of Papists and Slaves,' and an indignant Bostonian wrote: 'a superstitious,
bigotted Canadian Papist, though ever so profligate, is now esteemed a better subject to our Gracious Sovereign George the Third, than a liberal, enlightened New
England Dissenter, though ever so virtuous.' . . . The Quebec Act seemed to threaten
what was dearest to many colonists from New Hampshire to Georgia—their sacred
Protestant faith."[13]

The First Continental Congress, meeting in Philadelphia, approved in September
1774 a set of resolutions from Massachusetts, which stated that "The Quebec Act
was 'dangerous in an extreme degree to the Protestant religion and to the civil rights
and liberties of all America,' and the colonists were thus obliged to 'take all proper
measures for our security. . . .' " At the same time, this same Continental Congress
"directed a special plea to the Canadians to join with them in their resistance to
British tyranny."[14]

They did not, in large part because the Quebec Act had granted French Catholics
religious freedom. After the Revolutionary War, tens of thousands of American
Protestants, Tories loyal to England, found refuge and new home in Ontario and
Nova Scotia. About a million Irish joined them in the following century, then
another million Catholics and numerous Orthodox from central and south Europe.
Canada's religious composition became almost equally divided among Protestants
and Catholics, the French predominating among the latter within their Quebec enclave. Religious freedom matured into a Canadian "way of life," comparable in
most aspects to that of the neighboring American states despite differences of history.

3. Christianity and the Enlightenment. This truncated review of two centuries makes clear that religious freedom in North America was hammered out in the hot forge of burning convictions and contests. By no means was religious freedom an import from Europe. It is largely a unique American creation, shaped by the distinctive characters and creeds of many migrating groups, often in tension and conflict—in the name of Jesus Christ.

The Lutheran and Calvinist theologies of individual salvation through personal faith or divine election found fresh new ground in America, uninhibited by Catholic traditions or the new Protestant kingdoms. These "saved individuals" entered into solemn covenants to create their own democratic communities, civic and religious. Before landing at Plymouth in 1620, the Pilgrims set the pattern with their Mayflower Compact, which "formed a 'civic body politic' and promised to obey the laws their own government might pass. In short, the individual Pilgrims invented on the spot a new community, one that would be ruled by laws of its own making."[15]

These self-made laws applied to religious as well as civil affairs, and ranged from Puritan exclusivity in Massachusetts to some degree of toleration of other Christian bodies, as seen above, in Rhode Island, Maryland, and Pennsylvania. But in most cases the practicality of the economic-political situation motivated religious freedom, not theology. The Quaker creed first opened toward full freedom in a serious way, at least among Christian bodies.

It was the Enlightenment, a product in part of Europe's religious wars, which brought religious freedom into the American mind and system as a philosophy and a political principle. Its main exponent was Thomas Jefferson. Through the Declaration of Independence and the Bill of Rights (1776–91), and as president (1801–09), Jefferson was the major architect of the philosophical and juridic form of religious freedom that flourished thereafter in the United States.

In the century that followed, it was to Jeffersonian "Laws of Nature and of Nature's God," and to equality of all humans "endowed by their Creator with certain unalienable Rights," that Catholics, Jews, and others regularly appealed as they swarmed into America during the 1800s—and claimed religious freedom from discrimination for themselves. Today Muslims, Buddhists, Hindus, and other faith communities do the same. Only in this generation have direct appeals to biblical revelation as the basis of human rights and religious freedom become frequent in the United States: among Jews concerning Israel, in the struggle for integration of blacks, in northern applications of the Latins' liberation theology to Spanish-speaking migrants and other groups.

Since 1950 Christian bodies have begun reflecting theologically about religious freedom as a global issue, affecting all faith communities of our interdependent world, in which North America plays for the first time a major role. The freedom of 3 million Jews and 100 million Christians under communist atheist systems has become a prime concern. These new issues affect dramatically the future of mission.

4. John Courtney Murray and Vatican II. By the Declaration on Religious Freedom (*Dignitatis Humanae*) Vatican Council II, the Roman Catholic church proclaimed, for the first time since Constantine, a full and unequivocal teaching on religious liberty, for the individual as a right of conscience, and in the body politic as the civil right of a believing community.[16]

John Courtney Murray, Jesuit professor at Woodstock Seminary, Maryland, and at Yale University, Connecticut, was the principal architect of this declaration. It was his creative thought rooted in the American national experience that prevailed, after two decades of intellectual struggle with curial conservatives in Rome, led by Cardinal Alfred Ottaviani, head of the Holy Office. Murray's "protector" and sponsor was Cardinal Spellman of New York, himself theologically conservative, but thoroughly imbued with "the American way of life" and fully supportive of the first Catholic president, John F. Kennedy. Kennedy had during his electoral campaign of 1960 taken positions on religious freedom sharply opposed to traditional Roman teaching and policy.

Murray was brought into Vatican II as Spellman's personal theologian. His basic book, *We Hold These Truths,* came out in 1960, just in time for use in the numerous quiet soirees and conversations that animated and largely created Vatican II (1962–65). Indicative of Murray's American roots, his book's title is lifted verbatim from the foundational assertion written by the Deist Jefferson in the U.S. Declaration of Independence: "We hold these Truths to be self-evident, that all Men are created equal, that they are endowed by their Creator with certain unalienable Rights, that among these are Life, Liberty, and the Pursuit of Happiness." This appeal to "Nature's God" and "natural law" was made in 1776, fifteen years before similar Rights of Man were proclaimed by the French Revolution.

Murray was strongly supported by Father Pietro Pavan, principal author of Pope John's encyclical *Peace on Earth,* published in 1963. This ground-breaking document accented human dignity as the source of human rights, derived from revelation and reason and "natural law." Therefore, "Every human being has the right to honor God according to the rights of an upright conscience, and the right to profess his religion privately and publicly." Pope John praised the Universal Declaration on Human Rights, of the United Nations, with its assertion of religious freedom and "the right of free movement in the search for truth . . ." (*Pacem in Terris,* nos. 14, 144, and passim).[17]

The UN Declaration on Human Rights, which reflects historical American and French positions, and was promoted mainly by Eleanor Roosevelt and René Cassin, provided basic guidance to the scores of new nations in the mission areas of Africa and Asia as they enacted their own constitutions and laws. By their experience in Vatican II and its declaration, bishops of those regions developed doctrinally and pastorally to support this new Catholic teaching on religious liberty and "separation of Church and State." Most of them, we must recall, had studied in the Roman seminaries where the hard-line Ottaviani doctrine was dominant and usually exclusive.

I must record that I was also taught in favorable fashion the "Murray doctrine," designated by that phrase, at the Gregorian University, Rome, in 1958. A student asked: "But how can Cardinal Ottaviani and the Holy Office put up with this deviation from sound doctrine?" The Jesuit professor, Father Cereceda of Chile, responded acidly: "That's *their* problem. They don't censor my class!"

Most African and Asian seminarians attended, however, the Propaganda Fide seminary, doctrinally safe because directly controlled by the Vatican Curia, and financed in large part from United States dioceses with Spellman's New York in the lead. But upon returning to their homelands many Roman-trained priests exercised their apostolate side by side with many other Christian mission bodies, and amid strong communities of indigenous faiths. So Catholic pastors adapted their ministry to this pluralist society, in ways somewhat familiar to North Americans, but very strange to a solid Catholic nation such as Italy or Poland.

We see then that religious freedom entered the mainstream of the worldwide Catholic church, and its regional bodies, through a tortuous millennial process of doctrinal development, constantly affected by historical events and sociocultural reality. In this process the United States church for pastoral motives played a fundamental role by consciously acculturating itself within the pluralist American experience of Covenant Protestants and Enlightenment Humanists, and then by sharing this American ecclesial consciousness with the worldwide People of God.[18]

Religious Freedom, Regional Churches, and the Future of Mission

In conclusion, it is my conviction that the North American experience of religious freedom has had and will continue to have great significance for future mission in all the societal-ecclesial regions of the world. Its influence in the classic mission fields of Africa and Asia, briefly surveyed, will continue, but under diverse forms according to their evolving societies. Theologies of religious freedom, and ecclesiologies appropriate to each region, become a major mission imperative and pastoral need.

Black Africa, with its numerous Christian population and Western-planted churches, will follow paths quite different from the regions of North Africa, the Mideast, and Southwest Asia, where resurgent Islam is centered and dominant. Over a thousand years ago Islam did develop a type of freedom for Jewish and Christian communities that was quite "liberal" as compared with that of Europe from Charlemagne to Louis XIV (A.D. 800–1700). The forty new Muslim nations of these regions now face the challenge of a more thoroughgoing religious freedom, largely of Western *secular* origin, along with other Western cultural imports. Many view these as grave threats to the Islamic Ummah, along with the Jewish People now returned in Israel, largely under American auspices. The Jews in turn face new decisions about religious discrimination in their own country, for the first time in 1,900 years, after suffering grave oppression in Christian Europe, and especially in Catholic Italy, Spain, and Poland.

Christian influence is negligible in these three Muslim regions, and among the 2,000 million Hindus and Buddhists, Confucianists, Taoists, and Maoists of Asia's other regions. However, Western-style religious freedom presses upon all these religio-cultural geopolitical regions, so that of late even China allows the Christian church to show itself in public again. However, full freedom even for the local church—a fortiori for alien missionaries—is denied in most of Asia, as well as in Eastern Europe. Yet even there, religious freedom is written into Marxist constitutions and treaties, but only grudgingly ceded, for instance, in Poland and the Soviet Union.

North American Catholics, led by scholars such as Jacques Maritain and John Courtney Murray and by bishops such as Gibbons and Ireland, Dearden and

Spellman, faced up to the reality of pluralist democracy. They evolved out of pastoral need the theology of religious freedom that has recently entered into Catholic doctrine worldwide via Vatican II. It was John Courtney Murray who focused the issue, tested his research and theories, and articulated this theology in open Catholic and secular classrooms and seminars, publications, and debate. In many ways Murray is historically the first theologian of the *North American* Catholic church, reflecting on that ecclesial region's unique history and culture, its ethnic, political, and intellectual currents—in the light of faith and evangelization.

Murray's method is applicable to wider probings toward a North American theology embracing many other fields, such as family and social ethics, church unity, and ecclesiology—including freedom, authority, and participation *within* the church.[19]

Such regional theologies are needed in Africa, Asia, and other continents in order to arouse ecclesial consciousness and identity, so that the churches of the respective regions can deal with religious freedom and other mission issues in a manner best suited to their own peoples, histories, and cultures. The church of Latin America, as seen in the first part of this paper, has led all other ecclesial regions in this direction.

Karl Rahner perceives that Vatican II's greatest theological promise is movement toward such regional incarnations of the gospel—toward a *world* church that is truly universal as distinct from one grounded mainly in Greco-Roman culture. In these "great local churches" Rahner foresees "a pluralism of proclamations" and of liturgies, as well as "a significant pluralism with respect to canon law . . . and other ecclesial praxis as well."

Rahner judges that the theology of Vatican II makes a clear break from that of the church implanted by the first great mission of the apostle Paul, in the Greco-Roman culture of the Mediterranean basin—a break as significant as Paul's own rupture from the Jewish theology and pastoral practice of the church of Jerusalem.

Rahner states that "doctrinally the Council did two things which are of fundamental significance for a world-wide missionary effort. . . . A truly positive evaluation of the world's great world religions is initiated for the first time in the doctrinal history of the Church." Second, "the documents on the Church, on the missions, and on the Church in the modern world proclaim a universal and effective salvific will of God which is limited only by the evil decision of human conscience and nothing else."

Consequently "basic presuppositions for the world mission of the world Church are fashioned [by Vatican II] which were not previously available. The Declaration on Religious Liberty can also be seen in this perspective, since for all situations throughout the world the Church expressly renounces all instruments of force for the proclamation of its faith which do not lie in the power of the gospel itself."[20]

Notes

1. See my chapter, "The Significance of Puebla for the Catholic Church in North America," pp. 310–29, in John Eagleson and Philip Scharper, eds., *Puebla and Beyond* (Maryknoll, N.Y.: Orbis Books, 1980); also, my keynote address, "Puebla: Implications for Mission in the 1980s," mimeo-

graphed, 39 pp., Annual Mission Institute of Chicago Cluster of Theological Schools, Lutheran Seminary at Chicago, April 1980.

2. Cf. *Lumen Gentium,* passim, esp. no. 22; also, Karl Rahner, "Towards a Fundamental Theological Interpretation of Vatican II," *Theological Studies* 40 (December 1979), pp. 716–27.

3. Kenneth Scott Latourette, *A History of the Expansion of Christianity* (New York: Harper & Row, 1937–45); quotation from vol. 3, *Three Centuries of Advance, 1500–1800 A.D.,* 7 vols., p. 186.

4. Latourette, *Three Centuries of Advance,* p. 191; source and inner quote from William Bradford, first governor, chap. 2 of his *History of Plymouth Plantation, 1606–1646;* W. Davis, ed. (New York: Scribners, 1908).

5. Ibid.; inner quote from Cotton Mather, *Magnalia Christi Americana,* or the Ecclesiastical History of New England from its First Planting in the Year 1620 unto the Year of Our Lord, 1698; 2 vols. (Hartford: Silas Andrus, 1820).

6. Ibid., pp. 192–93.

7. Ibid., pp. 197–204.

8. Ibid., pp. 205–6.

9. Ibid., pp. 206–9.

10. Ibid., p. 171; italics added.

11. Ibid., pp. 171–72.

12. Ibid., pp. 183–84.

13. Page Smith, *A People's History of the American Revolution* (New York: McGraw-Hill, 1976); quotation from vol. 1, *A New Age Now Begins,* pp. 407ff.

14. Ibid., pp. 435, 585.

15. Ibid., pp. 152–58.

16. Cf. Walter Abbott, ed., *Documents of Vatican II* (New York: America Press, 1966).

17. In Joseph Gremillion, ed., *The Gospel of Peace and Justice* (Maryknoll, N.Y.: Orbis Books, 1976).

18. For a full view of the Protestant and Enlightenment roles in shaping America, see Robert Bellah, *The Broken Covenant* (New York: Seabury Press, 1976).

19. See D. Hollenbach, J. Coleman, R. Lovin, B. Hehir, "Murray's Unfinished Agenda," *Theological Studies* 40 (December 1979), pp. 700–15.

20. Karl Rahner, "Toward a Fundamental Theological Interpretation of Vatican II," *Theological Studies* 40 (December 1979), pp. 716–27.

31

BRAZIL

João Batista Libanio

Introduction

The subject of religious liberty was of deep interest in the Catholic church in the 1960s, chiefly because of the discussion on that topic during the sessions of Vatican Council II.[1] Before the conciliar declaration theologians were trying in heated debates to sort out the complexities of the subject. There was a systematic fear that, under the pretext of religious freedom, camouflaged laicism or religious indifferentism would be promoted. With the encouragement of an official document of the church, however, the study of the subject continued.[2]

With the launching of this SEDOS consultation we shall have a better idea of the situation in respect to religious freedom in the different social contexts at the practical and theoretical levels.

In this brief presentation we shall try to show how, in the Brazilian context, the theoretical side is not the most important. We live in a different situation. Our historical experience will be used to illustrate the present situation and its particular character.

The Theoretical Context of the Problem

The problem of religious freedom in the more precise meaning of the term is not raised explicitly in a society where the religious dimension is a dominant and basic one. It will therefore be in the pluralistic, modern, and European context that the question will be treated. Until the time of Vatican Council II the Catholic church opposed the thesis of religious freedom, insisting on the objective reality of truth rather than on the value of the freedom of conscience. The discovery of modern subjectivity is at the origin of the defense of religious liberty as a fundamental hu-

João B. Libanio, S.J., is Professor of Theology at the Catholic University of Rio de Janeiro, a member of the National Institute for Pastoral Planning of the Brazilian Bishops' Conference, and adviser for pastoral work in several dioceses in Brazil. He is the author of several articles and books.

man right, not because error has rights but because human persons must be respected in their beliefs. The conciliar declaration *Dignitatis Humanae,* concerning religious freedom, was the codification and approval of the results of much reflection and discussion in our Christian milieus on that subject. Its approval meant a great step forward for the consciousness and practice of the church.

It is important to call attention to this theoretical context of religious freedom in order to understand the problem in Brazil's sociocultural situation. It has become proverbial to say that there is not one but many Brazils. If this can be said of the economic field it is naturally true of the cultural area and affects the question of religious freedom.

This problem exists in the fullest sense for only a small sector of the inhabitants of the country, at most 20 percent. They are a small élite who feel the need to defend their autonomy as believers or nonbelievers, struggling against every kind of religious imposition on the part of the state or the dominant religion. This phenomenon was more in evidence during the empire, when the Catholic church was the official religion. At that time a small number of Masons and positivists began the struggle against the church for religious freedom.[3] The reaction of the church was conservative. From the second half of the last century reformed clerical structures ensured the church's presence among the people. Religious freedom, being the demand of an insignificant minority, was rejected. Today the situation is one of perfect religious freedom as this is formally understood from the theoretical point of view. When the republic was established, church and state were legally separated. Because of this, the other religions could claim for themselves the measure of freedom that was formerly reserved for the Catholic church alone. Protestant missionaries, especially from North American sects, arrived in great numbers to win for their religion this traditionally Catholic country. More recently, members of Eastern religions have been arriving in Brazil.

Thus in the theoretical sphere there is no problem of religious freedom in Brazilian society. The social strata who have had their Cartesian-Kantian revolution have all the guarantees they seek, in order to practice, defend, and propagate their faith. It is in the interest of the present regime to encourage this religious pluralism, with the ultimate purpose of weakening the position of the Catholic church. This is not for religious reasons or for the defense of human rights, but for ideologico-political considerations.

This position of openness reflects the situation of the church in our cultural centers in which the modern climate of pluralism is lived and breathed, with its concern for individual autonomy and its consciousness of personal freedom. If we go to the interior of Brazil we shall still meet priests and parish communities where the medieval climate of religious intolerance predominates. There the "believers," as Protestants are popularly known, are marginalized, segregated, and confined. This reflects one of the Brazils to which reference was made earlier.

The responsibility of the local church in this regard is demonstrated by a widening climate of tolerance and understanding with regard to other religions. This ecumenical spirit is now part of the official consciousness of the central church, of the CNBB

(National Conference of Brazilian Bishops) and is propagated by means of publications and symbolic gestures. Only in the traditional Catholic periphery are there still pockets of resistance where there is an atmosphere of orthodox, medieval intolerance. But it is only a matter of time. As the communications media more effectively penetrate these isolated areas, the faithful will open themselves to the pluralistic world and get away from sectarian religious positions.

The Fundamental Problem in Brazil

The question of religious freedom in Brazil concerns only a small (though powerful) minority, the intellectuals. I see three principal problems with regard to religious freedom in Brazil: the domination of the masses by clerical Catholicism, the domination of the blacks by white Catholicism, and the situation of conflict arising from the preaching of social justice. A Catholicism of European-Portuguese origin was implanted in Brazil as the exclusive and dominant religion. At the level of the masses this domination still continues. But the African religions, which came with the blacks from Africa, feel this domination more strongly. Moreover, the church in recent times has demanded its right as a religious body to speak about social matters. Only when we have analyzed those problems can we fully appreciate the importance of religious freedom and of the consequent pastoral responsibility of the church.

Dominant Catholicism

We are concerned here not with Catholic religious intolerance in relation to the intellectual strata of society, but with the mechanisms of the religious domination of the popular masses. Catholicism was planted in Brazil as part of a war of conquest, expressed as a Portuguese colonial project.[4] In the undertaking the greatest victims were the indigenous cultures, reduced today to small enclaves throughout the country. In spite of this policy of colonization and domination, traditional Catholicism in Brazil allowed areas of religious freedom within its borders for the devotees of these religions. Naturally that situation was not assessed from the point of view of Enlightenment criteria of religious freedom. Such a problem was outside the religious framework of the period.

Traditional Catholicism was expressed in popular forms with much vitality, creativity, and participation by the laity through brotherhoods, third orders, processions, pilgrimages, promises, and ex-votos.[5] Of these, the ones of a devotional and protective character were preferred.[6] In other words the religious life of the people was centered fundamentally on devotion to saints, the Virgin, Christ, and God, and in promises made to them with a view to protection, favors, and help in need. Many studies are devoted to the nature of this traditional Catholicism.[7] Here we are concerned with the amount of room for initiative and freedom offered to Christians. The weight of clerical structures did not impede the emergence of religious leaders, charismatics, and hermits, for these structures were not coherent or powerful enough to repress this popular participation. Without putting the question of religious freedom in modern terms, it happened in fact that it existed for lay Catholics in the heart of the church. The most important religious practices and devotions were the creation and contribution of the laity, as suggested above.

From the second half of the nineteenth century a Romanizing process was begun within the church in Brazil.[8] In the expressive words of a sociologist, the tactic of the religious destitution of the laity was introduced.[9] The area of religious freedom was restricted for them; the taking of initiatives and autonomy in their religious practices were gradually taken over by the clergy, thus reducing the laity to the role of religious consumers and not producers of religious symbols.

Here the problem of religious freedom is posed in a different way. These religious activities and initiatives that the Catholic laity had enjoyed for centuries were taken from them in the name of their incapacity, ignorance, and religious backwardness. Popular Catholicism was modified, not so much in its expression and religious forms as in the position of the laity in relation to religious practices. If processions were formerly a ritual truly created and led by the people, with the presence of the priest as officiant, they now became an official parish affair. The initiative was institutionalized. Generally it became attached to some strictly priestly ritual, such as the celebration of Mass or Benediction, so that the clergy were able to keep control of it.

This process gained ground during the course of a century. By the time of Vatican Council II, Brazil had a strongly clericalized church, with little room for the lay masses. Autonomous movements of the laity arose only among small segments of the intellectual class, through Catholic Action. In popular Catholicism an exclusively clerical domination prevailed without room for initiative and creativity on the part of the people. But this religious deprivation was superficial.[10] It was not possible to destroy entirely the centuries-long practice of creative religious freedom. This has remained deep in the consciousness of the people and awaits the social conditions that will allow it to come to the surface once more.

Our reflection is from the point of view of the responsibility of the local church. What then have our churches done in the area of restoring to the laity the rights that they exercised for so long, and which were taken from them because of historico-cultural circumstances? In this context, the basic ecclesial communities appeared. They are the best affirmation of the religious freedom of the popular masses within the church. In that respect we are a long way from the problem of religious freedom in the Enlightenment sense. The fundamental problem for our church is the freedom of the people, of the poor classes within the church, to function as ecclesial agents and not simply as passive recipients of religious benefits.

These grassroots Christian communities give evidence of the practice of religious freedom in several different ways.[11] In the first place the Christians affirm that they are conscious of their own worth. People are changed in these communities as they feel themselves to be more involved in the real problems of their lives, when they get down to their root causes, when they take on commitments with real brothers and sisters for a well-defined objective. The result is a growth in self-confidence and in the recognition of the worth of other persons, whereas formerly fear, and lack of confidence and self-esteem regarding their own possibilities and those of their companions in the community predominated. The dominant classes had succeeded during centuries of indoctrination in instilling into the consciousness of the oppressed classes a generalized self-abasement. "The poor have no confidence in the poor" because both are without means and unable to solve their problems. "The poor confide in the rich" who have the power to solve problems. These assertions were often heard among the popular classes. They inhibited any kind of creative freedom within a popular ecclesial community. It was necessary to overcome such ideological indoctrination by means of concrete experiences of success and advancement. Consequently, one of the first great transformations brought about in the people by belonging to and having experience in a grassroots Christian community was a breaking down of the barrier of self-abasement and fear, so as to become aware of their potential as a popular class.

Obviously, such a transformation was not brought about by a stroke of magic. It came about through well-defined experiences, which brought a change of awareness. These experiences are the expression of a new understanding of religious freedom, outside the context of traditional Enlightenment theory but certainly within the popular concept of religious freedom. Outstanding among these experiences was the reappropriation of the Word of God and, as a result, the development of a particular literature. Up to that time Christians assimilated only the interpretations of Scripture that the clergy communicated to them through their sermons, in catechism classes and biblical courses. The faithful were simply consumers of the theological output of the clergy. A new phenomenon arose in the grassroots communities in the reading of the Bible. Through Bible circles the people began to meet to read the Scriptures in relation to their concrete life. They established a double relationship between the Bible and life. In the first place, they read it from the viewpoint of the oppressive situation in which they lived: housing conditions, exploitation in work, exclusion from participation in political life, and so on. They then saw many elements, nuances, teachings in the Bible that the clergy had never explained because they lived in another social world. Second, they were able to establish another relationship, that is to say, between Scripture as a standard of criticism and the promised reward for their own activity.

Now the Word of God judges their lives. As a result of this double confrontation, that between Scriptures and the oppression, and between Scriptures and the initiatives it challenges them to undertake, people in the grassroots ecclesial communities are developing a new reading, a new popular exegesis of the Scriptures. The people are establishing an intimate relationship between life and the Word of God. A basic ecclesial community wrote in its report that "since we began to learn to read the Bible, the people are discovering in it the facts of life" (District of Itacibà). In technical terms, once a community has become the subject and agent of the interpretation of Scripture, this latter becomes a reality in their lives, an expression of their creative "religious freedom." A backwoodsperson from Ceará, named Antônio, reading the passage about the vocation of Abraham, said: "Now I have understood; the people are just like Abraham, walking like him without quite knowing where the road leads. Outside all is uncertain, but within the people have this certainty: God wants this of us! If Abraham found what he was looking for, we too can find it. We have only to keep on and never lose heart." The exegete Father C. Mesters comments that for Antônio the story of Abraham is no longer past history; it has become as well a mirror that reflects for him the story of his own life.[12]

Analyzing an interecclesial meeting of base ecclesial communities, which took place at João Pessao in 1978, the same Father C. Mesters compares the fact that a people is making its own the Word of God, to the light breeze that the prophet Elijah felt on Mount Horeb as a sign of the presence of God. A gentle breeze blows, the wind changes direction, God manifests his presence in a new way. A new meaning is being given to the Bible by the church, which itself is being renewed by being born of the people. They are transforming themselves into courageous, active-interpreters of the Word of God.[13]

The area of religious freedom in the base ecclesial communities has been further widened by their creative interpretation of the Word of God. It has shown itself in other ways in meetings and liturgical celebrations, in new ministries, in meaningful pastoral decision-making. They are substituting for a Catholicism of external, perfunctory deeds, determined from outside by the clergy, new practices that are simple, born of their lives, by consensus and the decision of the community. There have been cases in which the freedom of the laity has succeeded in bringing members of the clergy to reverse their decisions. Thus, for example, the members of a grassroots Christian community told a priest who had come to celebrate Mass that there would be no Mass because two families in the community were quarreling and only after their reconciliation would they have it. Another community had a "holy card" printed with the photograph of Alberto Torres. He was a simple man, the father of a large family, who left his mark on the path of life. He wrote nothing; only his virtuous life singled him out as a patriarch. For this reason, so the text ended, "the people of the community remember him. We proclaim him our PATRIARCH." This was an ecclesial gesture of freedom, of gospel purity and extremely significant for a popular ecclesial community. The new ministries form another area of that freedom. They vary according to the needs and rhythm of the communities. In general they are a response to very concrete needs or to special charisms. One community has its "spiritual counselor," officially designated by it to comfort families who have passed through some trial. Other services have to do with worship, teaching, social life, economic life, political action, and charitable witness. In all these cases, the creative and free character of the community shows itself. These services are not introduced from outside, but are born of the awareness the faithful have that they are taking that place in the church which corresponds to their faith and vocation.

The grassroots Christian communities recapture in a certain way that freedom which the faithful enjoyed within the church before the Romanization process. Nothing comes from nothing. They are discovering the traditional, deep sources of traditional Catholicism in what is original, popular, autonomous, and free.[14] In new forms, in response to other sociocultural needs and conditions, we see lay leaders emerging who are assuming meaningful roles in popular ecclesial life. At the level of secular activities, the popular classes always kept their institutions, where they enjoyed autonomy and freedom. Since the religious field was closed to them by the increasing clerical authoritarianism, their experiences were confined to barrio groups, samba schools, carnival clubs, and the like. We purposely leave aside the African religious world so as to give it special mention later on.

The dominant, clerical Catholicism, especially after Medellín (1968), for a number of reasons internal to the church and because of heavy political repression, permitted this new area of freedom to exist within it. We are thus living one of the strangest paradoxes. While, outside the church, the heavy cloud of political obstruction, police repression, and an oppressive regime hung over it, an area of freedom within it was opening up for the laity of the popular classes. Or more exactly, the popular classes conquered that area of decision within their communities. A detailed analysis of the sociopolitical and ecclesial conditions that explain this paradox would take much space.[15] For our reflection it suffices to note the fact of the existence of this religious freedom and its originality in relation to the classical European Enlightenment or to the two groups in our country to which reference has been made. It is a religious freedom situated over against the dominant ecclesiastical structures, and not so much the secular forces hostile to religion or the other intransigent religious sects.

Dominant White Catholicism and the Religious Practices of the Blacks

The relation of the dominant Catholicism to the African religions of the blacks who were imported as slaves reflects in the religious field what is happening in the sphere of economics. The problem of the religious autonomy of the slave was never raised. Slaves were slaves in every sense and dimension. Because of this, slaves were baptized en masse before they left their country or on arrival in Brazil. They were taught the religious dogmas and the duties of worship they were to follow. They wore branded on their breast the badge of the royal crown to indicate that they were baptized and that taxes had been paid for them. When they arrived without having been baptized, they were taught certain prayers. For this purpose the teachers were given one year, at the end of which they had to present their neophytes at the parish church.[16]

The Catholic religion was one of the structures that helped to maintain the colonial system of domination. It carried out the task of inculcating in the slaves servile obedience, passive patience, dependence, and the surrender of their dignity.[17] For that reason the blacks were not able to develop a religion of their own, but had to follow the rituals and worship of the dominant religion. They were denied any autonomy whatever within the logical coherence of the slavery system. The very imposition of the Catholic religion was interpreted as a grace for the Africans and a religious obligation for the whites. A. Vieira, in a famous passage addressed to the slaves, said: "I have no doubt now that the captivity resulting from the first migration [from Africa to Brazil] was ordained by His Mercy towards freedom in the second [from earth to heaven]."[18] The same speaker continues: "This is the prayer I have to make for you today: your Confraternity of our Lady of the Rosary promises you all a certificate of emancipation, through which you will enjoy not only eternal freedom in the second migration to the other life, but as well you will be set free [here below] from the greater slavery of your first state [in Africa]."[19]

In another expressive passage A. Vieira points out to the slaves the spiritual superiority of their distressful situation: "Your masters, whom you serve by doing so much work, should be more envious of your sufferings than you are of their pleasures. Imitate the Son and the Mother of God, together with St. Joseph, in their sorrowful mysteries, which you share in your condition and situation, lowly and painful in this life but exalted and glorious in the next. In heaven you will sing the joyful and glorious mysteries with the angels and there you will rejoice to have achieved with such merit, by your continuous suffering, that which they are not capable of doing."[20] Preaching such as this had the effect of domesticating the African religion—taming it, crushing it, and covering it over with Catholic features. The same A. Vieira tells us of a procession of slaves: "I went in procession with them [the slaves], nearly a thousand souls, not counting many who remained on the farm. The whites took no part in it as they would have their own later. The difference between the two was that the whites, with clubs, magistrates, and law officers, were unable to maintain order. They were always talking, while the slaves kept such good order and harmony, walking one behind the other, their hands always raised, and all singing *Ora pro nobis,* that they greatly edified the whites, so much so that the judges threw in their faces the good example of the slaves."[21]

The domination of white Catholicism over the religion of the blacks had a violent beginning. Many blacks, at the time of their baptism, their entry into the church, were fire-branded with the royal seal—a crown or a cross—as proof that the royal tax on each one had been paid.[22] This mark did duty for a baptismal certificate. Imagine the trauma for an uneducated person of associating the sacrament of Christian initiation with the brand of slavery! What this told them was that the freeing of the soul from the slavery of the devil was the beginning of a terrible captivity.

Side by side with that manner of baptizing the blacks, another phenomenon was going on. Gilberto Freyre has observed that in the shadow of European customs and Catholic rites and doctrines, the forms and accessories of African culture and myth "were preserved."[23] In psycho-social terms, the blacks concealed their rites and religions under the legitimating veil of names and ostensibly Catholic rites. The blacks ordered their religion in a manner that was acceptable to the whites, conserving the essential elements. The domination of the white religion had the effect of repressing the religion of the blacks.

Today the problem of religious freedom presents itself as one of allowing enough space for these religions to flourish in their purity and creativity. In part the emergence of the Afro-Brazilian rites can be explained by the lessening of the dominance of white religion. Obviously, the influence of the communications media cannot be forgotten; it serves the advantages of the political interests to lessen the power of the social commitment of the Catholic church at the present time. It also serves for tourist and economic purposes. However, these factors do not wholly explain the phenomenon. There is also the factor of a certain new religious freedom gained by the obscure popular masses, who find themselves in cultural continuity with the slaves.

The internal logic of the nature of religious freedom demands of us a different attitude in face of the phenomenon of the Afro-Brazilian rites. The official attitude of the Catholic church has been marked by the idea that they were the product of pure religious ignorance. One of the more prominent Brazilian bishops of this century, Cardinal Sebastião Leme, said in 1923 in a pastoral letter that has become a model: "The ultimate reason, the final cause of all our evils is, we acknowledge, the ignorance of religion."[24] But in many cases the "religious ignorance" was a defense, a hope for a period of "religious freedom," which would come about only with a lessening of the pressure from the dominant religion of the whites.

The emergence of Afro-Brazilian rites is not unrelated to the phenomenon of the grassroots ecclesial communities. Each consists of the people's recovery of their freedom and creativity in the area of religion. One expresses itself within the Catholic church, the other on the margin, reflecting a cultural-religious resistance of the black to centuries of domination. Religious freedom shows itself in both cases in relation to a type of religious domination not contemplated in the Enlightenment context. It is not, then, a reason deriving from the Enlightenment that is invoked against the imposition of dogmas. It is the popular awareness that resists, and takes advantage of the openings presented by, the dominant systems. The problem of religious freedom for the masses seems bizarre to the Enlightenment mind. For that reason this problem is found only in countries where domination is being contested by the masses. The religious phenomenon of the grassroots ecclesial communities and of the emergence of the Afro-Brazilian rites is part of that resistance and contestation, in spite of many ambiguities and confusions. But there is no escaping the penetrating influx of the dominant ideology through the social communications media. These disturb and confuse consciences. They divert the popular classes from their course. Meanwhile, they do not succeed in destroying the significant, ultimate freedom inherent in these processes. For this reason, it is necessary that there be clear, theoretical reflection to throw light on the ambiguities and confusions of such manifestations of freedom and help them correct their course. Religious freedom must interface with other processes of liberation so that all may be bound together in an inflexible unity. They are not parallel phenomena but, rather, aspects of one and the same integral process. Outside this general frame of reference the particularity of the religious sphere, its relevance, and its autonomy cannot be understood.

Religious Freedom in the Social Field

To the extent that states are consolidating and achieving greater autonomy there is less and less need for religion to justify itself. Because of that, the institutions that were the vehicles of the legitimation of religion are disappearing from the public social scene and are being confined to specifically religious tasks. The political theology of Johannes B. Metz is presented precisely as a protest against this process, in an attempt to recapture the political character and social critique of the faith and of the church.[25] I am not going to delay here to analyze the significance, range, and results of that post-Enlightenment position of political theology in Europe.

In Brazil the phenomenon acquires its originality in the midst of a complexity of factors and conflicting interests. We shall confine our reflection to the period of Brazil's political life that began with the military intervention in 1964. At that juncture of events, the legitimation of religion was made very necessary or at least extremely useful. In fact the coup d'état had been prepared by means of mass mobilization and the wooing of the middle classes through huge religious mass meetings. The "Family Rosary Crusade" was used to prepare the "marches for God, family, and democracy" that mobilized great multitudes against the government of João Goulart.[26] The nation was said to be threatened by the enemies of morality (corruption) and religion (atheistic communism), so that the intervention of force was looked to in order to "save religion and morality." The rosary figured as a catalyzing religious symbol of protest against the Bolshevist peril that threatened. Women had a fundamental role in that movement, since they were more sensitive to the appeal of religion and conservatism.[27] In that way a climate of politico-religious fervor was whipped up so that the Central Commission of the National Conference of Brazilian Bishops declared after the military intervention that

> in answer to the general and anguished expectations of the Brazilian people and in.face of the rapid advance of communism for the conquest of power, the armed forces came to the rescue in time and prevented the implantation of a Bolshevist regime in our country. This would have meant the suppression of the most sacred freedoms beyond imagining, and especially of religious and civil liberty. Immediately after the victorious outcome of the revolutionary action, there was a feeling of relief and hope, especially because in the face of an atmosphere of insecurity and near desperation in which the different classes and social groups found themselves, the divine protection was felt in a perceptible and undeniable way.[28]

This declaration reflects, without doubt, much of the mentality of the average Catholic of that period. And it shows clearly how the prior mobilization achieved its objective, which was to create a climate of insecurity, with religion threatened, so that the military intervention was interpreted as divine protection that brought relief and hope. Precisely at that moment security, relief, and religious freedom began to disappear and the popular social groups and those associated with them suffered the worst misrule.

As things developed, the true significance of the military coup d'état began to be realized as well by those less well versed in political analysis. We entered then into a new phase of church-state relationships in what concerned the pastoral freedom of the church. To understand the situation better we would have to distinguish, in the concept of "church," its theological reality as sacrament of salvation (cf. *Lumen Gentium,* no. 1), or sign of the reign of God, and its sociological dimension as social institution characterized by specific functions in society.[29] We are going to consider it here under the aspect of social institution, with its own specific function that flows from its theological awareness. The two planes intersect, however. As social agent, the church stands over against the state through the visibility of its representatives. However, it does so in the name of theological legitimacy, which flows to it from its awareness of the mission received from Christ. Conflict with the state arises precisely when its action touches on the social area, and it then invokes the gospel to legitimize its intervention in the social sphere.

The church will enter into conflict with the state at two levels after 1964, that is to say, at the level of its official representatives—CNBB, regional groups of bishops, official interventions—and at the level of small individual communities, living, vital groups who, in the name of their ecclesial conscience, act in society. Usually, and in the ideological/institutional sense, the name "church" is used at the first level and not at all at the second. In our reflection we shall see how as a matter of fact the opposite is happening at the practical level of the struggle for religious freedom in the social field. The institutional level tends to lose importance in that conflict to the extent that the official areas of it diminish and the groups and grassroots Christian communities step up their struggles, because the fundamental contradictions remain the same and are becoming ever more acute.

At the level of its official representatives the church of Brazil came into conflict with the state especially in the defense of human rights. Our examination of this will be divided into *three sections*: a quick and systematic overview of the principal conflicts between church and state in recent years; a brief explanation of that phenomenon; and reflections on it in some church writings. The three points are naturally in relation to the church as official institution.

For the *first section* of our examination, we shall use the material organized for the inquiry of the Ecumenical Center for Documentation and Research (CEDI).[30] It divided the subject into different items in conformity with the aggression committed by the state against the church, as follows:

Defamatory Accusations. Following the methods of Hitler, the repression tried to defame as much as possible the Brazilian institutional church in order to diminish its credibility before the people and thereby weaken the impact of its witness and protests against the violations of human rights. Anonymous letters, falsified writings and photographs, involving outstanding members of the hierarchy, were used. At least two famous writers lent themselves to this role of accusers and defamers of the church. Newspapers with a big circulation, notably the *Estado de São Paulo* in the person of one of its editorial writers, continue even now to make insinuating accusations against the CNBB and leaders of the hierarchy. In government itself, various generals repeat the classical refrain of communist infiltration in the church and the involvement of churchpeople in subversive movements. The most famous case was the police frame-up in the imprisonment and death of the communist leader Carlos Marighela, involving the Dominicans. Some bishops, such as Dom Helder Camara, Dom Paulo Evaristo Arns, Dom Antonio Fragoso, Dom Waldyr, and Dom Pedro Casaldáliga, were among those most often attacked by the regime and its organs of repression and information.

Violation of Domicile. We have been present on occasions when churches were violated by police forces in order to arrest some people and beat up others. In the Cathedral of Nova Iguaçú, the diocese of Dom Adriano (a bishop who is very closely watched by the security agents), a bomb exploded, destroying the altar and the tabernacle. Residences of bishops, vicariates, organs of the CNBB, private residences of bishops and high church personalities, offices of pastoral centers and of Christian movements, Catholic universities, pastoral meetings in the most diverse parts of the country—all have been invaded by the police, prisoners taken, people abducted, material confiscated, and furniture smashed.

Prisoners. The number taken already exceeds a hundred, including nine bishops, eighty-four priests, thirteen seminarians and Brothers, and six friars, because of homilies critical of the regime or participation in popular demonstrations or because they were considered subversive, or for helping persecuted or suspected persons, or for having been engaged in pastoral action with workers, students, and peasants, or for having protested against the arbitrary behavior of the forces of repression.

Torture. There are thirty-four verified cases of the torture of priests, religious, and seminarians. The best-known case is that of Brother Tito, the account of which was widely published, especially after his tragic death. Not only was he broken physically but he was destroyed psychologically, his torturers hounding him until he committed suicide.

Deaths. The most tragic case was that of the young priest from Recife who was very close to Dom Helder Camara and who was barbarously tortured to death. Up to now his case has not been legally clarified, thus leaving a serious suspicion that his assassination was the work of the police. Other cases, such as those of the missionaries Fathers R. Lukembein, S.D.B., and João Bosco P. Burnier, S.J., had to do with the defense of Indians or arrested persons. There are other cases, such as those of the seminarian W. Bolzan and Father A. Pierabon, whose deaths seem to have been the responsibility of the forces of order. During a strike in São Paulo a worker, an active member of the Worker Apostolate, was machine-gunned by military police.

Abductions. Abductions have been another method used by the repressive forces, that is to say, night arrest, without judicial warrant, of members of church organizations, especially of Catholic Action workers, pastoral workers, priests, Sisters, and so forth.

Trials. The list would be a long one if we were to mention the innumerable trials initiated against members of the church. Several bishops, such as Dom Waldyr, Dom Alano, and Dom Estêvão, were charged with criminal offenses. Up to now none of these have been brought to trial. Other trials were instituted against priests. The best-known trial is that of the Dominicans, which resulted in the condemnation of three of them to four years' imprisonment.

Expulsions. In the case of foreigners the juridical procedure was to order their expulsion from the country. At least ten priests or pastors have been expelled. There have been instances in which visas were not renewed; others in which pastoral agents were molested; others again in which superiors judged it more prudent that they should leave Brazil.

Prohibitions or Censorship. Frequently the conflict took the form of direct prohibitions, by the government, of meetings or of some report or publication of news concerning the church. Dom Helder Camara was forbidden access to radio and television and neither his name nor his picture could be published in any medium of social communication in the country.

This is a short, incomplete sketch by way of illustration of the repressive actions of the regime against the institutional church in the persons of its official figures.

Regarding the *second section* of our examination, it does not require much mental acuity to discover the causes and the reasons for such illegalities by the regime. The security forces themselves had to produce some justification at least before the courts. The accusation heard most often was that of "communist infiltration," or "subversion." In concrete terms this meant that those accused persons or organizations of the church did not approve of the economic and political model that was being forcibly implanted in the country. Objectively it was a question of reinforcing the implantation of a savage capitalism at the cost of the exploitation and oppression of the ordinary people. Consequently the repression fell on the popular movements and on all those who were connected with such interests. The ultimate reason, therefore, for the persecutions is to be found in the fact that the church put itself on the side of the oppressed, defending their fundamental right to organize, to struggle, and to protest against the illegalities committed against the masses and against middle-class people who were in solidarity with them.

The moment the church understood and then began to preach seriously the social dimension of the gospel, it showed itself as being in opposition to, and at the same time the object of repression by, the regime. It continued to have full freedom and total support wherever it confined itself solely to matters of religion and cult. For this reason, in some churches in which bishops, priests, and pastoral workers did not get involved in the social field but stayed strictly in the area of religion, there has been no friction. The "religious freedom" called in question by the regime would refer only to the social and political sector. The church was denied the right to make pronouncements in this field as being outside its competence. But for its part the church claims this competence, as deriving clearly from the gospel. The defense of fundamental human rights and, in a special way, of the oppressed is a basic element of gospel preaching.

For the *third section* on this topic, we shall indicate some of the important stages in this awakened conscience of the church as revealed in explicit documents.

In May 1970 the eleventh General Assembly of the National Conference of Brazilian Bishops met. Reports of frequent cases of torture were heard persistently in the country and abroad. Until then the bishops had not, as a national conference, made any public pronouncement on such a subject. In the General Assembly many bishops presented concrete, irrefutable cases. The minister of justice attended for a while to refute the charges, but he was not convincing. On the contrary, he confirmed the bishops in their belief that the reports were true. For this reason, at the end of the meeting they made their first joint protest in incisive terms: "As pastors, responsible for the gospel mission, we should be failing in our duty if we did not pronounce upon the fundamental aspects of our present reality which certainly concern the HUMAN PERSON." It is obvious that the meaning of "religious freedom" goes far beyond the strictly religious field and includes the sphere of the fundamental rights of the human being. The bishops continued:

We are thinking in the first place of the administration of JUSTICE, regulated indeed and protected by our laws, but which we sincerely believe is being frequently violated by proceedings that are subject to delay and uncertainty, by detentions effected on the basis of suspicions or hasty accusations, by inquiries begun and prolonged over many months, with persons held incommunicado or deprived not infrequently of the fundamental right of defense. On the other hand, it is notorious that, in spite of denials, there is a vivid awareness in our people and it is widely accepted by international public opinion, there is a notable incidence of cases of torture in Brazil. . . . Thus, in virtue of our apostolic mission, we should be seriously remiss in our duty if we did not point out at this time our firm opposition to all and every kind of torture, physical or psychological, wherever it shows itself in Brazil or in any other country in the world. . . . We are witnesses of the tragic situation in which a large part of the population is living, especially in the interior, in country places and in the periphery of large cities, due to the ridiculous salary scales and the low purchasing power of money.[31]

The Representative Commission of the CNBB published one of the most telling documents charging violations of human rights and defending explicitly and especially the masses of the country.

Having given some facts about the deaths of the missionaries Fathers Rudolfo and Burnier, the kidnaping of Bishop Adriano, and other acts of violence committed by the regime, the bishops asked about the interpretation of these facts, and suggested some answers. They pointed out some grave reasons: the denial of justice to the poor, for whom the church is interceding; the impunity of criminal policemen; the maldistribution of land; the situation of Indians; national security as the ruling ideology.[32] Once again we find the church pronouncing its prophetic word over the social situation and meeting with opposition and repression on the part of the state.

Three other documents of the episcopate are worthy of mention. In one of these, "Christian Requirements for a Christian Order,"[33] the bishops elaborate a kind of Magna Carta with a view to the creation of a sociopolitical order in which basic Christian values would be respected and in which there would be social relationships compatible with the Gospels. The text is rather technical, well structured, and of universal import, due to its formal character. Coming to more concrete matters concerning the national situation, "Aids to Social Planning" points out the basic anomalies of the system in operation up to now and which is showing signs of corruption and decay.[34] On the other hand, it draws attention to the fundamental demands of justice, beginning with the needs and aspirations of the majority group, the masses. Of still greater relevance and urgency is the document published in February 1980 by the CNBB, the result of discussions in their last General Assembly: "The Church and Land Problems."[35] In that document they look at the very serious land problem in the rural areas. This is one of the constant causes of conflict between church and state, whether with capitalist interests in the countryside or with the repressive forces at their service. The bishops address their teaching on the social aspects of private property to their "brethren in the faith and to all responsible persons of good will," emphasizing the demands of justice and the motivation of the Gospels and the grace of God. Again there is a clear awareness that religious freedom demands prophetic words concerning such concrete subjects as private property.

Recently the conflict has been modified in its external forms. It does not now seem to concern so directly the government as the forces of capitalism, represented by the landowners and the proprietors of communications media. The high-circulation newspapers representing the interests of capitalism have become the biggest opponents. In certain remote places the local political authorities still continue to protect the landowners in their repressive acts, in the conflict with the pastoral workers of the church. Thus it seems that the struggle between the government and the church is tending to diminish in the sense that other groups are taking over, of their own accord, the interests of the capitalists. If the government is not keen to give the church its rights, neither does it wish to be in conflict with it. It leaves to the press and other sectors of society the task of opposing the social stance of the institutional church.

At the level of small, concrete communities scattered throughout the national territory, whether in rural or urban areas, the conflicts with the state will continue. The regime will see them as a peripheral and regional problem, but in reality there will be a continuation of the same clash between a living evangelical community announcing social justice and an oppressive system that is crushing, exclusivist, and arbitrary. Rather, the regime will go on acting through local forces and by means of the publications media. These have already begun to suppress facts that would point to the continuation of the same situation of exploitation or to the defensive action by the church and the reprisals that follow.

To the extent that the members of the base ecclesial communities belong to the popular classes, they will be continually subject to the illegalities of the regime: expulsion from their lands, imprisonment, processes, and so forth. Nothing suggests that this struggle will ease off. On the one hand, capitalism is being brutally imposed, especially in the rural areas and, on the other, the masses are growing in awareness and bettering their organization, in great part through the base ecclesial communities. For that reason, the communities will clash with the interests of capitalism. And the fundamental awareness of the base community is its awareness of the integration there is between a life of faith and social commitment. The way in which the base ecclesial communities read the Gospels and live the ecclesial life urges them to commit themselves to the process of transforming social reality. The conservative forces are already reacting and will go on reacting against the grassroots communities. There the conflict between a "religious freedom," understood as the living of a committed faith in the social field, and the capitalist system, dependent, marginal, and ruthless, will go on. Thus the grassroots communities see these activities as deriving from their faith, and the regime will understand the faith as a merely religious function, personal and domestic.

Conclusion

This brief investigation of religious freedom and the responsibility of the local church brings us to various conclusions.

1. The Enlightenment theory of religious freedom, as a defense of a pluralist society in which each individual could practice his or her own religion without hindrance or imposition by the state, was a reality in Brazil in the time of the empire and concerned only a small stratum of society. Even today there are the more critical groups who protest against a modality of the church reminiscent of times when dogma and morals were dictated by the clergy.

2. There was, during our religious formation, a time when a good deal of popular religious freedom existed. This was curtailed by the process of Romanization, which began in the second half of the last century and whose effects are felt even yet. Besides, there are symptoms of a reappearance of that phenomenon. On the other hand, the phenomenon of the base ecclesial communities is now increasing, and in these the area of religious freedom is being widened.

3. With regard to the religion of the blacks, the blacks lived through centuries of domination. During that time the blacks conserved their practices under the guise of Catholic rites as a defense against cultural domination. Actually, with the lessening of white Catholic cultural pressure, the Afro-Brazilian rites are blooming and occupy a place in the religious sphere that formerly they were unable to do.

4. The area of greatest conflict and in which the responsibility of the church is most explicit is the social. Because of the demands of the gospel, the churches began to defend the rights of the poor, promoting respect for life while condemning the violations of the fundamental rights of the human being. At that time the repressive forces of the state, in their defense of the interests of capitalism, attacked the church in the person of its representatives, workers, and communities.

In the light of the faith the church of Latin America sees the fact that many of its children should give their lives in defense of religious freedom as a sign of the Lord's grace and a pledge of hope. As this study was concluding our continent was shocked by the terrible event of the death of Archbishop Romero. He symbolizes in a significant way evangelical courage carried to the extreme of the gift of life. Romero, who was assassinated in a church as he was in the act of celebrating the Eucharist, incarnates the highest expression of religious freedom in conflict with the interests of capitalism, defended by the armed hand of the state.[36]

—Translated by William Halliden

Notes

1. Cf. P. Delhaye, "Liberté Religieuse," *Catholicisme Hier, Aujourd' hui, Demain* 6 (Paris, 1975), cols. 676–89.
2. Cf. K. Hörmann, "Religionsfreiheit," in K. Hörmann, ed., *Lexikon der Christlichen Moral* (Innsbruck/Vienna/Munich: Tyrolia, 1976), cols. 1375–83.
3. Cf. Brasil Gérson, *O Regalismo Brasileiro* (Rio-Brasilia: Catedra, 1978).
4. Eduardo Hoornaert, *Formação do Catolicismo Brasileiro, 1550–1800* (Petrópolis: Vozes, 1974), pp. 31ff.
5. Pedro A. Ribeiro de Oliveira, "Catolicismo Popular e romanização do Catolicismo Brasileiro," *REB* 36 (1976): 133–37.
6. Ribeiro, "Religiosidade Popular na A. Latina," *REB* 32 (1972): 354–64; "Catolicismo Popular com base religiosa," *CEI,* Supplement 12 (September 1975), pp. 3–11.
7. At the instance of the CNBB, E. Samain has compiled an extensive bibliography on popular religion, which was published in *INP* (Rio de Janeiro, 1975).
8. The notion of the Romanization of Brazilian Catholicism was suggested by R. Bastide and developed by R. della Cava in *Miraclet et Joaseiro* (New York/London, 1970), according to Pedro A. Ribeiro de Oliveira in his article, "Catolicismo Popular e romanização do Catolicismo Brasileiro," *REB* 36 (1976): 131, n. 1.

9. Ribeiro and C. Medina, *Autoridade e Participação* (Petrópolis: Vozes/CERIS, 1973); Ribeiro, "A posição do leigo nas comunidades de Base," *SEDOC* 9 (1976), cols. 286-95; "Catolicismo Popular," pp. 137-40.

10. For methodological reasons, I postpone for a few paragraphs the repercussions of this phenomenon of the African origins and religions of the blacks on the masses.

11. See the experts' findings on and analyses of the interchurch encounters of the grassroots Christian communities: *SEDOC* 7 (1974/5), cols. 1057ff.; *SEDOC* 9 (1976), cols. 257ff.; *SEDOC* 11 (1979), cols. 705-850.

12. C. Mesters, "Flor sem defesa," *SEDOC* 9 (1976), col. 336;

13. Ibid., "A brisa leve, uma nova leitura da Biblia," *SEDOC* 11 (1979), col. 733ff.

14. Eduardo Hoornaert, "Comunidades de Base: Dez anos de experiância," *SEDOS* 11 (1979), col. 719.

15. See the excellent work by Luiz Gonzaga de Souza Lima, *Evolução Política dos Católicos e da Igreja no Brasil* (Petrópolis: Vozes, 1979).

16. H. Koster, *Travels in Brazil* (London, 1816), p. 409, cited by Gilberto Freyre, *Casa-Grande & Senzala* (Rio de Janeiro, 1975), pp. 352-53.

17. E. Hoornaert, ed., *História Geral da Igreja na A. Latina;* vol. 2, *História da Igreja no Brasil* (Petrópolis: Vozes, 1977), p. 257.

18. Ibid., p. 329.

19. Ibid.

20. Ibid., p. 349.

21. Ibid., p. 384.

22. Ibid., p. 302ff.

23. Freyre, *Casa-Grande,* p. 355.

24. Quoted, in Jóse Comblin, "Prolegômenos da Catequese no Brasil," *REB* 27 (1967): 846.

25. Johannes B. Metz, "Politische Theologie," *Sacramentum Mundi, Theologisches Lexikon für die Praxis* 3 (Freiburg/Basel/Vienna, 1969), cols. 1232-40; "Les rapports entre l'Eglise et le monde à la lumière d'une théologie politique," *La Théologie du Renouveau* 2 (Paris, 1968): 33-47.

26. M. Moreira Alves, *A Igreja e a Política no Brasil* (São Paulo: Brasiliense, 1979), p. 111.

27. Ch. Antoine, "L'Église et le Pouvoir au Brésil, naissance du militarisme" (Paris: DDB, 1971), p. 33; in English see *The Church and Power in Brazil* (Maryknoll, N.Y.: Orbis Books, 1973).

28. "Declaração da CNBB sobre a Situação Nacional," *REB* 24 (1964): 49.

29. J. B. Libanio, "Conflito Igreja-Estado," *Encontros com a Civilização Brasileira* 4 (Rio de Janeiro, 1978):29-40.

30. *Repressão na Igreja no Brasil: Reflexo de uma situação de opressão* (document published by the Archdiocesan Commission for Pastoral Ministry in Human Rights and of the Marginalized; São Paulo, 1978).

31. "XI Assembléia do Episcopado Brasileiro," *SEDOC* 3 (1970), cols. 85-86.

32. "Comunicação Pastoral ao Povo de Deus," *SEDOC* 9 (1977), cols. 786-96.

33. *Documentos da CNBB, Exigências de uma ordem política* (São Paulo: Paulinas, 1977).

34. *Estudos da CNBB, Subsídios para uma política social* (São Paulo: Paulinas, 1979).

35. National Conference of Brazilian Bishops, *Igreja e problemas da Terra* (São Paulo: Paulinas, 1980).

36. L. A. Gomes de Souza, "A fé imersa no conflito político. O testemunho pastoral do Arcebispo de San Salvador," *CEI Supplement* 26 (March 1980), pp. 44-53.

Section 7

THE MISSION OF THE LOCAL CHURCH AND THE INCULTURATION OF THE GOSPEL

Statement of the Question

Through the process of inculturation the church is born anew in different societies and cultures each time the Word of God is sown in good soil; and from its seed, a new Christian community springs up. Inculturation is a means of bringing the Word of God to different human groups with the idea of establishing a relationship of them with God. In every local church an ongoing inculturation/evangelization process is needed for a continual purification and deepening of the faith-experience so that cultural/historical encrustations will not limit the effectiveness of the Word of God.

Elements for a Reflection on the Question

- The interaction between traditional culture and influences coming from techno-logical and other developments in the modern world
- The influences of this interaction on the spirituality of the local church and the way the people understand the gospel message
- The dynamism emerging in the local church as witness to, preacher and proclaimer of the gospel
- The effect of the witness of the local church on the surrounding community
- The process of discerning what culture is
- The extent to which distinctions can be made between religion and culture
- Inculturation as it concerns persons who live in complex situations that cannot be separated from culture

Related Questions

- What are the problems of inculturation in a situation where the church has been to some extent imported from another culture?
- What are the tasks needed if inculturation is to be effective?
- What is the role of the small Christian community in this process?
- What is the place of mutual responsibility among local churches in this task of inculturation?
- How would you define the process of inculturation that will lead your local church to a new level of maturity?

489

32

DENMARK

Oluf Bohn

Whether in Asia or in Europe, the kernel of inculturation will always be the same: the bursting open of a given culture to the liberating and reconciling particularity of Christ in such a way that the same culture does not lose its identity.[1] In "post-Christian" Western Europe inculturation therefore is, on the one hand, the process by which the local church renews itself by a deliberate return to the liberating and reconciling particularity of Christ. On the other hand, the same local church has to learn to face the new experiences and/or changes made in the culture where it is placed, with such a loving respect that the experiences and changes, without losing their cultural and historical identity, may open their own particularity to the particularity of Christ. In consequence thereof, the church would renew its life also in that part of the history of humankind (cf. "in hostorium hominum intrat," *Lumen Gentium,* no. 9).

My Diocese

My "local" church is the diocese of Copenhagen, which is the whole of Denmark. The Catholics are around 30,000 in number, that is, about .5 percent of the total population, and the number has not increased for almost thirty years. The Catholic community consists of converts, of people whose family has been Catholic for some generations, and of an increasing number of Catholic immigrants (mostly refugees and workers from abroad). This means that many of the Catholics have no intimate contact with Danish culture; they even have serious problems accustoming themselves to the plain Danish way of living. Many of the Catholics of the old stock as well as converts are feeling very uncomfortable in our present cultural situation.

The great majority of Danes (about 93 percent of the population), belong to the Evangelical-Lutheran church because infant baptism is still a widespread habit, and the Evangelical-Lutheran church until now has been the church of almost all Danes. For several reasons the ecumenical movement is not strong among either Catholics

Oluf Bohn, layman, is a high school teacher in history, religion, and Greek culture in Aarhus, Denmark. He takes an active part in in ecumenical work and is presently editing a new edition of the documents of Vatican II.

or Lutherans. The Catholic church in Denmark, therefore, is confronted with the choice between alternatives: either to try to fulfill the mission in Denmark alone or to combine its missionary activities with those of the Lutherans, who are positive toward ecumenism. The latter alternative would allow the church to further both its own activities and the ecumenical movement.

Because the church wants to strengthen ecumenical endeavors, missionary action on its own will hamper or even endanger ecumenism, because it will make Lutherans believe that we Catholics have returned to the old way of proselytism. We cannot, therefore, fulfill our missionary task without also furthering ecumenism.

The Lutheran Church

In spite of the high percentage of infant baptisms in the Lutheran church, Christianity has very little impact on everyday life. The percentage of regular churchgoers is rather low, perhaps between 150,000 and 200,000 persons on Sunday. But these figures do not tell how many go every second Sunday, or more irregularly. The percentage varies very much from parish to parish, depending more or less on the influence of the pastors or on the cultural surroundings. On the west coast of Denmark, Christian traditions are held in much higher esteem and a high percentage of the population take part in church activities, but it is also there that we find the most widespread prejudices on the part of Lutherans toward the Catholic church.

A Secularized Culture

All this implies that the Danish cultural life in many aspects is a secularized culture. Christian thinking has no influence on social or cultural life in general. Even if a belief in God and perhaps in Christ exists outside the circles of practicing Lutherans, such believers keep their belief as a private resort without any wish to bear witness to their faith.

Since Vatican II there has been a relatively increasing comprehension of secularization as something positive among Catholic theologians. In *Evangelii Nuntiandi* (no. 55), Pope Paul VI wrote that secularization, which is not to be confounded with secularism, "is the effort, in itself just and legitimate and in no way incompatible with faith or religion, to discover in creation, in each thing or each happening in the universe, the laws which regulate them with a certain autonomy. . . ."

But even if secularization is recognized as something positive, this teaching of the universal church has not, until now, been applied in practice, and has had very little influence upon the ideas that govern the mission of the church. It is, however, of utmost importance for the understanding and the process of inculturation that secularization be better understood. This point will be taken up again later.

Mission: Liberation

Evangelization is the proclaiming of Jesus Christ, of his life, his death, and his resurrection. As Pope Paul VI expressed it in *Evangelii Nuntiandi* (no. 9), "Christ proclaims salvation, this great gift of God which is liberation from everything that oppresses man but which is above all liberation from sin." Evangelization is the commemorating of Jesus Christ not only as a doctrine, but above all as an EVENT. "Christianity. . . is a concrete particularity which ought to be universalized by the proclaiming of the gospel of Jesus Christ. Christianity is the singular particularity of the man, Jesus Christus from Nazareth."[2] It is of such tremendous importance that it therefore can be of universal value to every person in his or her concrete time and place.[3] Through the anamnesis, the church, by proclaiming the gospel and by administering the sacraments, is making this event, Jesus Christ, present to us.[4]

The whole life of Jesus Christ was a very concrete one, in a given culture, at a certain time, and it was therefore through this definite particularity that he revealed God, his Father, to us. He did so especially by rejecting several elements in the Jewish belief, and by being rejected for the same reason. Through his life, through the rejection by some of the Jews, through his death and resurrection, he made agape the all-prevailing theme of his particularity. This agape is the liberating and redeeming force in the particular life of Jesus Christ, and the church and the sacraments have their origin in this agape; they are expressions of it.

> A situation in the life of Jesus Christ must not be regarded as a closed, finite thing, delimited by other historical situations. . . . Since it is the *manifestation* in this world of the eternal life of God, it always has a dimension open to that which is above. . . . Its meaning, the number of its possible applications, is even at its own historical level, something limitless, even before we come to the forms in which it is universalised in the Church and in individuals.[5]

"The eternal life of God" is another word for agape and it is this particularity in the life of Jesus Christ that *is to be inculturated*.

It was always thus. Take as an example the transmission of the Christian faith to the Hellenistic world by the Christian-Jewish community, which was firmly rooted in a Jewish cultural setting. The letters to the Colossians and the Ephesians bear witness to how the particularity of Jesus Christ through the Christian-Jewish culture created a Christian-Hellenistic culture. The inculturation of the gospel was not only a creation of new language and a new religious comprehension for people in the Hellenistic world. It was a *liberation* of the Hellenistic people from its divinized universe, and a reconciling of the Jewish-Christian and the Hellenistic-Christian people in Christ (cf. Eph. 1:21 ff.; 2:14).

Because the life, death, and resurrection of Jesus Christ is something particular, it has a liberating and redeeming effect for all people in all cultures if they are willing to receive it as a reconciling of all men in Christ (cf. Eph. 2:14). The mystery of our salvation is so great that every aspect of it may have its own "name": liberty, agape, forgiveness, liberation, and so forth. But for our purpose it seems to me most adequate to use "agape" as a common denominator for the particularity of Jesus Christ in the following considerations.

Eros—Agape—Culture

The concept "eros" is, to me, the most useful concept for expressing the kernel of all activity in every culture, and "agape" therefore is the best one to express God's offer to humankind of salvation and liberation that does not suppress eros, but liberates and surpasses it (cf. Eph. 1:10).[6]

Jesus Christ lived his particularity in a certain culture, and this particularity was "spread" through the mission of the church to many cultures. You cannot live your Christian life "outside" a culture. But what is a culture? The question is raised because of the undisguised hesitation to define culture found among Catholic scholars.[7] It is not sufficient to define culture as an economic, political, and one or more religious systems having as its kernel the values that express the foundation of human life. The definition confirms that human activity in all spheres of life belongs to culture, but it does not pay sufficient attention to the fact that all these spheres exist in a very complex interaction. Changes in one sphere have repercussions in other spheres.

Culture may therefore be defined as a complex system of economic, political, social and, often, religious spheres, which intend to satisfy the need of a people for a safe and secure life. This definition should suffice whether the culture exists under stable conditions, or is trying to overcome different challenges. This need for a safe and secure life I shall identify with the eros mentioned above.[8]

Eros—not to be understood as eroticism or sexuality—is humankind's instinct and urge to secure one's own life, that of one's family, of one's group, and so forth. This eros manifests itself in the very different cultures people have created and continue to create according to the varying conditions in the world. Eros has its great values without which no human life could exist, but it has its obvious limitations also. It cannot conquer death, and in times of crisis, it will make people inclined to devour everything that threatens their security, even other people. There is no real reconciling force in eros, and no real forgiveness because of one's fear of destroying oneself thereby.

The only answer to all that is the all-prevailing agape of Jesus Christ. Agape is liberating; it has conquered death and sin, and sets human beings free to love God and their neighbour without fear of being destroyed, even when this love is demanding a complete giving-up of themselves.

Secularization and Mission

Secularization is not only a stage in the cultural development of Europe. It is to a large degree a result of the demythologizing of the world that began with the inculturation of Christianity in the Hellenistic world.[9] This is not a fact that we reluctantly have to acknowledge, but something we have to praise. Secularization does not only refer to Europe, but expresses *theologically* that every culture exists by its own right,[10] and that it therefore shall preserve its cultural identity when it receives

God's liberating and reconciling agape through the missionary activities of the church. Every culture, of course, will have to pass a stage of purification, when people become reconciled in Christ. Its "eros" must be purified in order to be integrated into agape, but it must not be destroyed; otherwise the given culture will be dissolved with a disastrous result for the people concerned.

The Secularized Culture in Denmark

The mission of the local church has to take place in a society that for generations was Christian, but where the development in culture in general has been so fast that it has left most of the Christian groups, including the Catholic one, far behind. It is a very pluralistic culture, so whatever one states in general can be disproved by pointing to this or that phenomenon, but on the whole it is true.

In order to avoid misunderstandings I am here using the term "secularization" as a cultural stage where one understands the world not only according to the laws of nature, but just as much according to the "laws" of history, of social science, psychology, and so forth, and where people perceive themselves as agents of history. This, in short, is obvious in Danish culture. The development of culture among the farmers in the cooperative movements, often inspired by the most valuable theology of N.F.S. Grundtvig (d.1872) the Christian folk-high-schools, and among the workers in the cooperative movements and the trade unions has created an intimate understanding of the possibilities life offers to people, and that people have the right to form their own lives.

Even though the culture of many farmers is still influenced, often rather vaguely, by Christian ideals, they, together with the workers under social-democratic inspiration, are responsible for an educational system that has the idea of furthering social equality for all citizens, enabling them toward *self-realization* in their own lives.

The emancipation of women has a long tradition in Denmark and the idea of self-realization in life has supported the wish of many women to receive educations that could enable them to provide for themselves. This development, together with a general trend in society, has created great changes in family life, at least in the realm of ideas.

Especially in the 1970s and on, a growing criticism of the liberal competitive spirit, and a greater concern for society because of the increasing pollution of the environment, is easily observed. The inability of the nuclear family to solve the many rising problems has created a movement toward living together in larger groups.

To conclude: the inhabitants of Denmark are very conscious of their right to judge for themselves and of the right to self-realization in their own lives. These trends have led to a comprehension of liberty as independence, and have created a new underlying philosophy. This philosophy is revealed in many ways by the language in current use in Denmark.

Language in general is influenced by technological, scientific development perhaps not so much in actual vocabulary as in its general spiritual thrust. Problem-solving often means the creation of new or better institutions or organizations to handle problems professionally with material support. These institutions are administered by professional employees, using all scientific knowledge available. This development is supported by the experience that problems in earlier days also had their roots in bad material conditions.

Three examples may help to illustrate the problem. For the nursing and care of old people, nursing homes were built in the endeavor to make their living as materially comfortable as possible, but very few have really understood that old people also need someone to care for their spiritual life. Families with social problems or with educational problems will be supported materially with new and better homes, situated in better surroundings, but few are caring for the underlying spiritual problems of these families. Drug addicts are supported materially and treated with nerve pills and the like, but few persons will commit themselves personally to help these addicts.

Of course, there is a reaction against this way of acting, especially among younger persons today. These are persons who are inspired by the events of May 1968. They understand to a certain degree that the problems cannot be solved without a human and personal commitment on the part of the people who surround the three groups mentioned above. Especially among younger persons one finds an understanding of human conditions based on a psychological-sociological comprehension, namely, of the emancipation of women and of sexuality, to mention two important spheres. Their language will also often be marked by different kinds of Marxist expression.

In the secularized language there is no trace of traditional Christian concepts or attitudes. There is not so much talk about "my responsibility," "my guilt," or "fault," or "my problem," but of the guilt of society, the responsibility of society. Love is no longer understood in Christian terms, but only as "eros," which means that personal commitment for another is diminished in favor of emphasizing personal need for another. There is, of course, a traditional middle-class understanding of love, but as far as I can see, it is losing ground.

All this raises the question whether or not the traditional Christian vocabulary on the whole permits a dialogue with representatives from these new cultures. The "churches" are often speaking in a language that they are not sure is understood by others, even by all churchgoers, for example, words such as "love," "forgiveness," "sin," "guilt," and "God."

There are no rules without exceptions. Even if it is true that most of the nonpracticing people have no comprehension of the Christian vocabulary, one sometimes meets nonpractitioners with the same old-fashioned, rather sentimental vocabulary used by Christian conservatives or fundamentalists.

The Christian Community

What is the possibility for the church in Denmark to meet all these challenges? It is no longer a problem that many of our priests and Sisters come from Germany or the Netherlands. The real problem is that the Catholic community on the whole has no adequate missionary concepts. As already mentioned in the introduction, many are refugees, immigrants, or people who for very personal and/or private reasons have converted to the Catholic church. But even among the Catholics from traditional Catholic families, one seldom finds people who are worried about traditional Catholic culture having lost connection with the secularized culture. They simply do not understand what has happened. Catholics are often sheltering themselves behind the walls of a "spiritual" ghetto, or have erected a "catholic" culture for themselves, made up of components from Irish, Italian, or Bavarian Catholicism.

For many of these Catholics the reforms of Vatican II offer no inspiration or motive for a remodeling of the lay apostolate or community life, or for a better understanding of the world. They therefore also stand totally aloof from all ecumenism, and cannot see why Lutherans and Catholics should cooperate in the proclaiming of the gospel. Consequently they have no comprehension of what it means to mission that the world is secular.

The Way of Furthering Inculturation

The local church in Denmark is standing at a cross-roads: will it reject the post-Christian culture in Denmark, or does it want to begin a dialogue with it? Vatican II states in *Gaudium et Spes,* no. 36, that the autonomy of the world not only is a fact furthered by humankind today, but that it also corresponds to the will of God. That means that the local church has to understand that it must recognize the main trend of the culture in Denmark. Secularization is legitimate (cf. *Evangelii Nuntiandi,* no. 55), and we must draw the conclusions from that statement by realizing it in our own lives.

First of all we have to return to the liberating and reconciling particularity of Christ. Christ's coming to the world had the character of an event. The New Testament tells us about this event by telling us about the acts and words of Jesus Christ. The event is a life lived with God. We have to understand the life of the Son of God better and better, so that it "becomes a part" of our life, so to speak, so that his liberating and reconciling particularity bursts our particularity open to the particularity of other people.

We also have to understand our own experiences better. Experiences are new or forgotten dimensions in our own lives and in the lives of others, and these experiences should be measured by the particularity of the event of Christ, first and foremost his agape.

Christ's liberating agape would overcome the fear, the feeling of powerlessness, and the ghetto mentality of the Danish Catholics. Among other things, it would make us understand the teaching of the church about the autonomy of the world, and give us courage to enter into the necessary dialogue with our fellow citizens. Christ's liberating agape would also let us enter into ecumenical work, which is so highly recommended by Vatican II (cf. *De Oecumenismo,* nos. 9, 12).

The Dialogue

Dialogue in the understanding of Pope Paul VI (cf. *Ecclesiam Suam,* 1964), means an indefatigable, affectionate, and kind will to conversation: the will to explain the gospel. But at the Synod in Rome in 1974, many cardinals and bishops widened the scope of dialogue so that it also meant to listen *and* to learn from the experience of other people.

All that is prominent in Danish culture, the political tradition, the emancipation of women, the right to realize one's own life, the new trends in family life, etc.—deserve our full attention. But that is not enough. The human experience of suppression, of alienation must also draw our attention. What does it mean when it is asserted that "structures" may hinder one's self-realization? Have the results of psychoanalysis any bearing on our understanding of society and mission? Is abolition of oppressive structures liberation? Through dialogue we not only can bring forward a will to listen and to learn, we must commit ourselves to all the problems.

First, when this whole process has ended, or at least is going on, we shall be able to offer the particularity of Christ, his agape, correctly, because only now shall we be able to accept humankind and make the person understand what the liberating particularity of Christ means to one and to one's culture.[11] Dialoguing with others, therefore, means to make people understand that that "eros" with which they try to realize culture is not liberating or saving humanity, but tends to destroy it if eros is not integrated into agape. Second, it may call the human being to a reconciliation in Christ, and make him or her a practicing Christian, perhaps not a Catholic but an active Lutheran—hence ecumenism would be promoted.

How to Carry It Out?

This effort of inculturation will, in my opinion, not be accomplished so much by preaching as by living this Christian life in Danish culture. Even if many Catholics in Denmark, for different reasons, are living on the outskirts of Danish culture, they are nevertheless much more part of it than European missionaries are part of the culture in Africa, for example, at the beginning of their missionary work. That means that inculturation is not so much the bursting open of two different cultures to the reconciling particularity of Christ as it is the bursting open of a more old-fashioned Catholic, Danish culture to the dominant Danish culture.

But it has to be done by *living* this liberating Christian life amid everything that is going on in Denmark. By taking part in the formation of the Danish culture we are giving witness to God, and we still can refuse to take part in what we understand as being against the agape of Christ. We cannot do this in isolation. I propose that, besides working with Lutherans, we have to form smaller basic groups for mutual support in this inculturation project, and perhaps even more in order to let that community life bear witness in itself to Christ.

It is, of course, impossible theoretically to explain what kind of task such basic groups would have to undertake. The reason is that the life and activities of such Christian basic groups would depend entirely on their own experiences. Nevertheless, I venture to propose what I myself could imagine as their task.

For the time being a feeling of resignation and despair seems to spread among people partly because of the economic crisis, and partly because the belief in political solutions is vanishing. A basic group that would try to realize its life, inspired by the particularity of Christ, his agape, would or should be full of Christian hope: hope, not only that the kingdom of God shall break through once, but a hope full of dynamism because the kingdom of God is already present among Christians who are trying to realize the agape (cf. Lk. 17:21). In other words, a basic group should be anticipating the kingdom of God through its activities.

Such basic groups could help old people in their isolation, families with social problems, drug addicts. All that would require an enormous effort, but it might be possible for a basic group of a usual size to help a few persons. By their attempt to integrate people such as those mentioned above, they would offer them the possibility of participating not only in a social life with more meaning, but also of participating in the liberating and reconciling particularity of Christ. Resignation and despair could wither away, and a real hope could take its place.

Conclusion

I am not proposing or suggesting that all Catholics should live in basic groups, take part in ecumenism, or commit themselves to politics, or work against pollution. Danish culture is, as I mentioned earlier, very pluralistic and no one can know which of the many ideas will have a future or is "truth" itself. That would mean that different Catholic groups may have access to different non-Christian groups, but inculturation is not achieved by allowing one group, for example, conservatives, to teach others to become conservative Catholics "in Danish," staying apart from all other groups. If inculturation is to be realized, it must carry with it a bursting open of all "culture groups," that all may be reconciled in Christ. Genuine pluralism means mutual respect and unity in love.

Notes

1. Cf. my article in *SEDOS Bulletin,* no. 7 (1980).
2. Théoneste Nkeramihigo, S.J., *Telema* (no. 4 (1977), p. 23; or *SEDOS Bulletin,* no. 6 (1979).
3. Cf. H.U.v. Balthasar, *A Theology of History* (London: 1963), p. 67.
4. W. Kasper, *Glaube und Geschichte* Mainz, 1970), pp. 98ff.; J. B. Metz, *Zur Theologie der Welt* (Mainz, 1968), p. 19 and n. 13; in Eng. see *Theology of the World* (New York: Seabury, 1979).
5. H. U. v. Balthasar, *Theology,* p. 67.
6. The use of the concept "eros" in this paper does not do justice to the concept of eros as a whole. Eros is a love that may be the expression of my will to do good, of my will to "create" existence. Eros may be my will to approve and affirm that another person exists and that this same person is in need of my help. But eros is at the same time also claiming an approval from the person whom I am helping. This is so because eros is also an expression of my need for self-affirmation and of my urge to realize myself. Meanwhile this self-affirmation and self-realization cannot come into my consciousness with the approval of other persons. Eros, therefore, is a dynamic force in the human being; it erects culture, it creates societies, but it has certain limits. Agape, God's love to us, is a love rendered by grace, and it has no need of "returning to God" as his self-affirmation. Agape does not destroy eros; it liberates it. The idea is developed further in the text.
7. Cf. David Power, "Kulturelle Begenung und Religiöser Ausdruck," *Concilium* 13, no. 2 (1977), p. 114. In Eng. see "Cultural Encounter and Religious Expression," in Herman Schmidt and David Power, eds., Liturgy and Cultural Religious Traditions, Concilium 102 (New York: Seabury, 1977), pp. 100-112.
8. Cf. David Tracy, "Ethnischer Pluralismus und systematische Theologie," *Concilium* 13, no. 1

(1977), p. 60.In Eng. see "Ethnic Pluralism and Systematic Theology: Reflections," in Andrew M. Greeley and Gregory Baum, eds., *Ethnicity*, Concilium 101 (New York: Seabury, 1977), pp. 91–99.

9. Cf. Metz, *Zur Theologie der Welt,* pp. 16 ff.

10. "The world is set free" (Metz, ibid., p. 16).

11. Cf. T. Nkeramihigo, S.J., "A propos l'inculturation," *Telema,* no. 4 (1977), p. 26; or *SEDOS Bulletin,* May 1979.

33

CHRISTIANITY AND THE AYMARA—A CASE STUDY

Curtis R. Cadorette, M.M.

Christianity has been part and parcel of Peruvian life for over four centuries. When Francisco Pizarro landed on the coast of Peru in 1532 he was accompanied by clerics whose express purpose was the conversion of any and all peoples of Christianity or, more accurately, the Catholicism of the Spanish Crown. Judging from the vast number of churches, chapels, and Christian symbols that appear in modern Peru and especially the altiplano, one can only surmise that the task of evangelization was effectively carried out. The community without a chapel, minute as it may seem, is a rarity. In the mountainous areas of the country where Quechua and Aymara are still the language of the vast majority, it is difficult to find a hill without a shrine and cross on its summit. In the small Peruvian town where this essay is being written a huge Catholic church dominates the plaza with its sundry monuments—all topped with crosses. Only the sundial seems to have avoided Christianization. Judging from appearances, it would seem that the town of Chucuito is as thoroughly Christian as it is Aymara. High above the town, which borders Lake Titicaca, one can see an imposing hill whose cross and patron saint, Bartholomew, are said to control the fortunes of this tiny Andean village. In times of drought or social tribulation the Aymara *campesinos* will climb the treacherous paths to offer their petitions to the hill's cross and patron in the hope that their suffering will be alleviated. This is the time-tested way of the Aymara, which they and their ancestors have utilized for centuries. They have no doubt about the efficacy of the cross that watches over the town of Chucuito. They believe in its efficacy because they are Christians. They also believe because they are Aymara *campesinos* whose very existence is profoundly tied up with the land and its produce over which the cross of Saint Bartholomew gazes. There is no doubt that these people are Christian and even less that they are Aymara. They have been for many centuries and it appears that they will be such for many more to come.

Curtis R. Cadorette, a Maryknoll priest, is the Director of the Aymara Institute, a research center located in the Peruvian altiplano, the purpose of which is to provide basic cultural information on the Aymara people. He is also engaged in the Aymara zone south of Puno.

As obvious as the equation of the Aymara and Christianity may be, one is ulti-mately forced to ask what such a situation means. What does it mean for the Aymara *campesino* to be a believing Catholic in this high, Andean world that offers spectacu-lar beauty and almost insurmountable challenges to existence? What does it mean for Christianity that a people as oppressed, hard, and pragmatic as the Aymara would accept its faith and values as their own? Neither question can be answered easily because neither question has ever been seriously asked. Little attention has ever been paid to the faith of the Aymara or what such a faith means on a larger scale. The history of this neglect is the history of Peru itself. The Aymara and their world are of no value because they are not Spanish, because their values and language are Andean, because they are nonwhite and resistant, because to the embarrassment of the dominant culture of the oppressor they have managed to survive. No one pays much attention to the beliefs of an exploitable base. There is another reason, more benign and less incriminating, which explains the lack of understanding of the Aymara's religious world—its phenomenal complexity. Rather naturally the Catho-lic faith of the Spanish became intricately mixed with the Andean culture of the Aymara, both of which are exceedingly complex in themselves. To pull apart the components of this compound so completely mixed together is now nearly impossi-ble. One can only see the result of a long process of cultural fusion, which defies the most adept anthropologist or theologian to break apart. The amalgamation of Christianity and Aymara culture is a fact and, as such, it speaks for itself. The fol-lowing paragraphs propose to do just that—let the Christianity of the Aymara state its own case. After an explanation of the methodology of observation we shall use and a few helpful hints for the reader, we propose to explain an Aymara *fiesta* step by step with all its convoluted symbolism. We feel that this is the best way to grasp what Christianity really means for the Aymara and how its symbols function in their lives. Perhaps a brief caveat is in order before we actually begin. What follows may seem extraordinarily complex and symbolic. In fact, it is. To understand the Aymara and their Christian faith requires patience and an ability to deal with the infinite nuances. What we are about to see is a confusing mixture of Aymara social values, religious beliefs, and Spanish Catholicism being blended into the cauldron of a feast that is vital for the sustenance of the people involved.

The Generous Patroness: The Feast of the Assumption in Chucuito

If by some quirk of fate one were to arrive in the town of Chucuito in mid-August, a whirlwind of social and religious activities connected with the Feast of the Assump-tion would confront the casual visitor. Undoubtedly all the activity would seem a bit incoherent—processions, dances in the streets, cases of beer, and seemingly unlim-ited numbers of intoxicated people gesticulating wildly—the basic components of any Aymara fiesta. For the person unfamiliar with the indigenous cultures of the Andes, things would seem rather mysterious. There would be every reason to doubt that all these activities are tied up with the Feast of the Assumption, at least that associated with European Catholicism. It proves nearly impossible to divine the real meaning behind all the frenetic merrymaking, religious gestures, and strange symbols that pervade the atmosphere. In one moment people are in a procession with marked devotion, and in the next they are drinking immense quantities of beer with equal fervor. Watching all this as a spectator one is bound to become a bit confused before a cultural puzzle which, at least according to the outsider's sensibilities, does not display much meaning. It all might seem interesting and exotic, but there appears little possibility of making sense out of such a chaotic scene. The chaos, however, is nothing more than a mask that hides a very rich and invigorating ritual for the Aymara. Once the spectator realizes this the fiesta begins to take on a certain meaning.

What is perfectly clear is that the Feast of the Assumption in Chucuito is a tremendously symbolic event, which influences every mode of the participant's being. This does not mean, however, that the poor outsider is doomed never to understand. As human beings we all use similar symbols, albeit with different shades of meaning. For this very reason we feel that an analysis of a feast like that of the Assumption is doubly helpful; it makes the world of the Aymara a bit more understandable, as well as our own. The analysis must be made step by step so that the rich but complex meaning of the fiesta will become clearer to us, as well as the sensibilities with which we ourselves perceive the phenomenon. We could perhaps have chosen an event in the social and religious life of the Aymara with a bit less complexity, but we would have been forced to sacrifice a good deal of richness. This particular fiesta is a microcosm of the Aymara's social and religious world. What it all means dawns on the spectator bit by bit. We have been observing this fiesta for nearly five years and its real meaning is just beginning to come to the fore. This observation has proved to be the key that has opened up the inner meaning of the Aymara for us with their rich and varied religious, social, and economic values. What we want to communicate to the reader is this very richness of the Aymara as a people and as believing Christians. The Feast of the Assumption has proved to be an ideal tool in opening up the meaning of this world with its special religiosity, social structure, and history. What one sees upon pulling apart a fiesta bit by bit and day by day are the values that underlie and vitalize the events. The task is occasionally tedious, but it seems to be the only viable method that takes into proper account the values of the Aymara and our way of perceiving them.

Methodological Considerations

Before we begin the actual analysis of the fiesta in Chucuito, it might prove beneficial if we clarify our own perceptual framework in dealing with the complex cultural factors involved in the study. Basically we are trying to note the components of the fiesta in a structural and empirical way, that is, with a minimum of judgment. It is best to focus our attention on the components for the simple reason that they give us the best picture when they are properly assembled at a later point. Although a cultural event such as an Aymara feast gives the impression that it is a solid, unitary event, such a perception is rather superficial and has more to do with the observer's own biases. What we intend to do with the Feast of the Assumption is look at the various colors that make up the painting before we view it as a totality. Following this metaphorical turn, this particular fiesta strikes us as a set of symbols, delicately arranged, which helps to develop and maintain the Aymara culture in a vital and understandable way. The fiesta is really a pedagogical process that offers the necessary information for a cultural identity to be forged. Although the event is clearly religious in tone, its impact is not exclusively religious. In other words, we are dealing with a symbolic totality, a mosaic composed of many pieces, each of which provides a special impact. This very totality is sacred for the simple reason that it is symbolic. One might say, then, that the fiesta is super-religious. Religion in the fiesta is one symbol among many that play a role in the total process. The religious atmosphere that we see is the end product of symbols working together, and not the exclusive result of the specifically religious. In the Feast of the Assumption in Chucuito there are social, economic, religious, and spatio-temporal symbols in various gradations and combinations. The position and intensity of each one varies during the total process but, in the final analysis, they all work to make the fiesta meaningful for the participants. When we perceive the symbols functioning as a whole it becomes obvious that they together transmit a central message, which in this particular case is that the totality of Aymara culture in Chucuito is sacred, and that its unity and sacrality must be preserved through symbolic enactment. As we shall see in the events themselves, what the fiesta communicates to its devotees is a very particular message: "Our culture and life here are valid and in these very acts we express our consent to what they mean." As one dances or participates in a religious act the subtle pedagogy of the feast makes its influence felt, with the participant feeling the sacred influence of the feast and reaffirming his or her identity as a citizen of the religious and civic reality that is the town of Chucuito and its Aymara inhabitants. Of course, no one articulates the lesson learned in such explicit or rational terms. The process is tacit and almost unconscious. After all, we don't articulate who we are; we live who we are.

In a certain sense it would seem correct to say that the very fiesta is a symbol that diffuses a central message. The feast and its message become the primary symbol in an elaborate process in which secondary symbols, be they religious, social, or economic, function as supports in the total process. Before we pass to the actual events in the festivities, it might prove beneficial if we briefly look at the actual scheme of symbols involved. What we must keep constantly in mind is that this feast has a predetermined message or primary symbol that does not vary. The secondary symbols utilized are nuanced and shifted in such a way that they make the primary symbol's impact more poignant. These secondary symbols are utilized in the diverse religious and social events in the process; their arrangement may vary but their purpose and number do not. They have an elaborate history of use based on the history and identity of the town itself. If they shift it is because Chucuito's self-perception has changed. In fact, there is a negligible shift because of the very conservatism of a fiesta as a social phenomenon. After all, its central message is one of eternal value and the necessity for continuity.

Although we are forced to be simplistic, we have selected four types of secondary symbols that seem to us the more obvious in this fiesta and the most important in conveying the central message that we have already mentioned. We allude to them only because we wish the reader to have some conceptual model before we go into the convoluted events themselves. We can clearly see four types of symbols at work: *(a) religious symbols* tied up with Roman Catholicism, *(b) spatio-temporal symbols* related to the geographic nature of Chucuito, *(c) fertility symbols* related to human sexuality and agricultural productivity as a unit, and *(d) symbols of historic relatedness*. When we go through the fiesta step by step it will be obvious that these four categories are too global, but they may help us to sort out the ways in which the fiesta transmits its meaning. Even within a given symbolic category there are many ways in which it functions; for example, the religious symbolism rotates between a certain statue used in the feast and a banner of the Virgin of the Assumption. At one moment spatio-temporal symbols may be more obvious than religious ones, although we must understand that all the symbols are ultimately related to each other. None is independent because all are being utilized to communicate the already determined message or central symbol. For this reason the components of this symbolic equation never really change. This is not surprising because what is looked for is cultural status and not change.

What should be no surprise is that this fiesta has little to do with its title. It is a far more complex phenomenon than the assumption of Mary celebrated as a Catholic feast day. It is, rather, a rite of identification and renewal sponsored by a female principal. Whether one wants to identify this female principal with Mary is a moot point. What is certain is that this fiesta has virtually nothing to do with the Roman Catholic dogma or its celebration—something the Aymara have exceedingly little interest in or understanding of.

The Fiesta: What People Say

According to the common wisdom of the Aymara *campesino* of Chucuito, the Feast of the Assumption is the key event as far as the town's vitality and future are concerned. This is the feast in which the collectivity obtains the necessary force to continue on as a living entity. The people who sponsor the feast on a yearly basis in the typical Aymara and Andean way, that is, the *alferados,* are seen as people of great prestige who have vitalized the town through their generosity and interest in the well-being of Chucuito. Assuming the responsibility as *alferado* of the fiesta is something one does with the utmost seriousness, not only because being an *alferado* is tremendously expensive, but because it permanently alters and elevates one's social situation in such a way that great prestige is obtained, which demands solid maturity on the part of the *alferado* and respect for the position from the people. To be an *alferado* one must volunteer for the position, have a certain standing and respect already established by the passage of time, possess economic resources, and, most importantly, be accepted by the populace in such a role. During the fiesta every action of the *alferado* is observed as a symbol. The spirit of the town becomes entrusted and incarnated in the *alferado* whose actions are oracles that determine the course of things to come. The *alferado,* then, embodies civic sacredness. (It should be understood that when we use the term *alferado* we are referring to a married couple—the husband and wife form a unity in accord with Aymara culture.)

Another factor that people are quick to note is that the Feast of the Assumption is a *campesino* fiesta. In other words, those who participate are from the culturally marginated and economically oppressed sector of Peruvian society. They speak Aymara as their first language and are racially Native Americans. The *mestizos,* those who speak Spanish and normally are of mixed blood, do not participate in this fiesta in any real way. Their feast, Nuestra Señora del Rosario, takes place in October with very different dynamics much in accord with the racial and symbolic bifurcation of contemporary Peru. When we asked various *campesinos* in Chucuito if it were possible that a *mestizo* participate in the feast or be an *alferado,* everyone rather quickly and emphatically denied the possibility. As we shall shortly see, this feast is Andean in every sense of the word—its roots are Aymara and it has little to do with the world of the Spanish. As a matter of fact, it does everything possible to block out the world of the conqueror.

The Fiesta

August 14: The Vigil

1. In the afternoon of August 14 the *alferado* designated a year earlier for the *fiesta* (husband and wife) begins to prepare the necessary items for the coming events, namely, candles, incense, ritual cloths, etc. The *alferado* is helped by *devotos,* former *alferados,* devotees of the fiesta, relatives, and friends.

2. When the necessary materials are ready all proceed to the main church in Chucuito, Nuestra Señora de la Asunción. Entering through the main door they formally ask the sacristan permission to remove the statue of Mary, *la Virgen de la Asunción,* from the retable of the main altar and place it in the sacristy where certain women arrange and dress the statue in ornate vestments. Once ready it is taken to the main altar again where it is placed on an *anda,* or portable platform used in processions. When the statue has been arranged on the *anda* and properly secured with rope, those present offer prayers for the successful outcome of the fiesta and for themselves. It is felt that this is an especially propitious time for prayer to the Virgin of the Assumption.

3. Next, a series of wide ribbons is hung from the roof of the church to the floor. The ribbons are in groups of four and form a type of tent. Normally there are four such "tents."

4. Candles are placed on the steps of the main altar leading to the *anda* of the Virgin of the Assumption. Again, prayers are offered.

5. Everyone now enters the sacristy again. In a carved wooden chest placed on a shelf there is a banner of the Virgin of the Assumption. (This is the only time in the year in which the chest and its sacred content will be touched. Also inside the chest are six sticks, which will form a pole on which the banner will be hung, and a small crown, which will be placed on top of the banner. The banner is referred to in Aymara as *Yiwuna.*) The *alferado* approaches the shelf on which the chest reposes and makes the sign of the cross before taking it down and opening it slightly as he (the *alferado*) kneels down.

6. The entire party now leaves the sacristy, but without turning around; that is,

they walk backwards so as not to change the orientation in which they entered the sacristy. Arriving at the altar with the *anda,* all kneel down and make the sign of the cross. With all walking backwards, the same procedure is repeated in the middle of the church; namely, kneeling and making the sign of the cross.

7. Arriving at the atrium of the church, all repeat the procedure above for the third time. Certain *devotos* now place a reed mat *(k'esana)* on the floor along with shawls. The *alferado,* who has been carrying the chest, places it on these materials.

8. The *alferado* offers prayers and incense, making these ritual gestures toward the east. (The atrium of the church lies in that direction.) By this action it is understood that permission is being sought to open the chest and touch its sacred contents.

9. The *alferado* (husband and wife) now remove the chest's top, and all those present examine the contents to see if they have been touched in any way in the past year. As we have mentioned, the chest contains six sticks, a crown, and the banner of the Virgin. The banner is wrapped in silk, which is sewn with a special stitch by the *alferado* of the previous year. If there is any alteration of the contents, especially of the stitches in the silk cover, it would be considered a catastrophic sign. If the covered banner lies to the east it is a good sign, to the west a bad one. The *alferado* now examines the stitch in the silk to ascertain if the stitch made by last year's *alferado* was done toward the left or toward the right. The *alferado* undoes the stitch with the same hand and in the same direction of the previous year. The banner is now removed by the *alferado* while the *devotos* put together the pole on which the banner is hung along with the crown on top. The assembled standard is carried to the house of the *alferado.*

10. The standard is placed in the house of the *alferado* where it will reside until the end of the feast with the exception of a few brief excursions for processions. In the house a series of prayers is offered along with numerous libations poured on the earth known in Aymara as *ch'allas.* This activity goes on for several hours.

11. The *alferado* now leaves the house and goes to the church to pray. As the *alferado* is walking to the church, dances and fireworks begin in the main plaza. After praying, the *alferado* returns home, usually quite late.

August 15

1. On the morning of August 15 the *alferado* offers incense to the standard in his house and then leaves for the church to attend Mass. (This is the first time and one of the few times, in which a priest in any way participates in the feast. It would appear that the priest is perceived much like the *mestizo*—extrinsic to the process.) When the Mass is over there is a procession with the *anda* of the Virgin of the Assumption. The procession goes around the main plaza of the town accompanied by the priest and *alferado*. The procession terminates at the main door of the church.

2. At this moment the selection of the new *alferado* for the coming year takes place. Obviously a process of selection goes on previously, but at this moment the new *alferado* steps forth and is acclaimed by the people. The priest ratifies the choice by giving a blessing to the new *alferado* and then departs. The *anda* is put back in the church and all present go to the house of the current *alferado for a banquet that he*

provides. The new alferado accompanies the current *alferado* in this meal. When all have eaten, the current *alferado* leaves the house, followed by the entire group of people. They begin a dance in the plaza, which will go around the perimeter of the plaza three times.

3. At roughly 4:00 P.M. nearly everyone in the town of Chucuito begins to head to the main church to wait outside for one of the principal acts of the fiesta, called *wajcha*. (The term defies translation.) Three or four men appear in the tower of the church and everyone presses together below. The men begin to throw *q'ispiña,* a type of candy made with sugar and *quinua* flour. They also periodically throw animal heads, two of llama and four of sheep. The scene below is utterly wild as everyone tries to grab a piece of *q'ispiña* or a head. If one manages to obtain *q'ispiña* a certain amount is eaten, while some is saved and later placed in the family larder where it is thought to preserve the harvested barley and *quinua* from decay. The pandemonium is incredible, especially when the heads are thrown. There is something strange about the six heads—nobody from Chucuito itself ever captures them, despite the furious competition. In a ritual fight that is friendly in nature, the residents of Ichu, a town about six kilometers to the north, always end up with the heads. They have come to Chucuito with the express purpose of capturing the llama and sheep heads. Capturing these heads is a portent that the crops and cattle of Ichu will grow well in the coming year. Once they have all six heads, the people from Ichu head off to a nearby *cantina* in Chucuito where they offer libations of alcohol to the animal heads. Once this rite is concluded and everyone is sufficiently intoxicated, they all return to Ichu with their booty. On the following day, August 16, there is a special feast in Ichu and the heads are cooked in a soup. Everyone who participated in the *wajcha* in Chucuito eats the soup. The bones left over from this soup are then divided among the participants who guard them in their houses. It is said that the bones have a special spirit who protects cattle from any harm.

4. *Licencioya*: Once the *wajcha* has been completed, the *alferados,* current, new, and old, kneel down in front of the church's main door where they make the sign of the cross and ask the Virgin permission to depart *(licencioya)*. After leaving they go to the main plaza to begin a dance, which will again go around three times. What is unusual about this event is that women dance with women and men with men. Each time they pass by the church dancing in this manner they ask permission of the Virgin of the Assumption to depart. Once this dance is completed all go to the house of the current *alferado* where prayers and incense are offered to the standard.

August 16: Khephant uru

1. On the morning of the 16th several men prepare a *ramada* in the house of the current *alferado* in the same fashion as it would be arranged for a newly married couple. The *ramada* is a type of booth or small house made of branches and flowers, and is adorned with carrying cloths *(llicllias),* which are multicolored. Benches are placed around the *ramada,* or matrimonial booth, much as they would be in any wedding ceremony. Once everything is ready the *alferado* (the couple) sits in the *ramada* where the rite of *arcu* is performed. In this rite people approach the *alferado*

one by one and offer food on a plate. This completely voluntary gesture indicates a social and economic relationship between the person who has presented the food and the *alferado*.

2. Once the rite of *arcu* is completed all leave the house and dance in the main plaza. Once the dance is over the *alferado* returns home and places the standard in the *ramada*. At this point there is a ritual of pardon in which all present ask forgiveness mutually for any offense they may have committed. (The asking of pardon is the first and characteristic gesture carried out by the Aymara prior to any religious undertaking. It is felt that it is impossible to have truly effective ritual without a fraternal atmosphere.) Once the standard is placed in the *ramada* there is a series of alcohol libations offered to the standard and the earth.

3. The *alferado* ramada again sits in the *ramada* in the customary manner— the wife on the left and the husband on the right. The *ramada* always faces east. At this point another rite, called *asjjata,* is carried out. It is similar to *arcu* in style, but is less binding socially. Again people approach the *alferado* with gifts as a recognition of prestige or as a token of gratitude for past favors received. The gifts, which can be food or money, are placed in a dish by the *alferado*.

4. After *asjjata* there is a customary meal of *mondonguito,* a type of tripe soup. The soup's content is from the llamas and sheep that were butchered the previous day for the *wajcha,* except for the heads, which are being eaten in Ichu. All partake of the soup as a gesture of fraternity.

5. Once the meal is over the *alferado* takes the standard and, accompanied by all, goes to the main plaza where a dance begins in honor of the Virgin, whose image is on the standard.

6. Once this dance is over everyone returns to the house of the current *alferado* where the standard is put back in its place. For all intents and purposes the fiesta now stops until the Octave of the Assumption.

The Octave

1. A few days before the Feast of the Assumption begins in Chucuito, the neighboring villages name auxiliary *alferados* whose task it is officially to represent these villages in the festivities. Their selection is a voluntary procedure and normally it is a question of picking known devotees of the Virgin of the Assumption. Their work begins on the evening of the octave when they leave their respective villages bound for Chucuito and the *alferado*'s house with alcohol and punch. When they arrive in the town they immediately go to the *alferado*'s residence to present their drinks.

2. In the morning of the octave the *alferado* carries the standard to the church where a Mass is celebrated in the presence of the new and old *alferados,* as well as sundry devotees.

3. Once the Mass is over there is a procession around the town in which the old *alferados* carry the *anda* of the Virgin of the Assumption and the *alferado* of the current year bears the standard. Just before returning to the church the current *alferado* gives the standard to the new *alferado,* who was nominated on August 15. Everyone enters the church and prays. The *anda* is left on the altar and the new

alferado departs with the standard, which will remain in his house for two days.

The Day after the Octave. 1. The auxiliary *alferados* from the surrounding villages now return home where they construct *ramadas* just as we described previously. Similar voluntary offerings are made to these individuals.

Two Days after the Octave: *Ch'ucuñ uru* **"Sewing Day."** 1. Around noon the new *alferado* goes to the main plaza where he initiates a series of dances, with or without the *alferados* of the previous years. These dances usually go on until 4:00 P.M. when the new *alferado* goes home for a quick meal.

2. After eating, the new *alferado* carries out the standard from his house and meets the *alferado* of the year, who has just passed in front of the church. They enter the church and upon arriving at the main altar make a reverence to the *anda* of the Virgin, which has resided there since the last procession. Prayers and incense are offered. Now all enter the sacristy where the chest in which the banner is placed is taken down from its shelf by the new *alferado*. The same gestures of August 14 are utilized. Everyone walks backwards to the atrium, kneeling and making the sign of the cross three times.

3. Once in the atrium the same reed mats and shawls are placed on the floor, facing the east. Again there are libations of alcohol and incense offered just as they were on the 14th. The *alferado* of the year that has passed asks permission of all present and begins to disassemble the standard. Once it is taken apart it is folded and wrapped in silk. The husband and wife begin to sew up the cloth banner in the silk, each on either side. Once the silk is half sewn, the new *alferado,* husband and wife, begin to sew in the same fashion. Once the banner is completely sewn up it is placed in the chest with the six sticks and crown. The chest is carried back to the sacristy by the new *alferado* and the same procedure is followed: all kneel down and make the sign of the cross three times before entering the sacristy where the chest is left in its traditional place. This concludes the rite of *Mamit ch'ucuña,* or "Sewing the Virgin."

4. Upon arriving at the atrium, all the *alferados* offer libations *(ch'allas)* and prayers to the Virgin of the Assumption. Then the new *alferado* leaves the church while a band stationed outside begins to play a special melody. The *alferado* begins a very rapid dance, as if it were a race between the new and old *alferados*. Again the dance goes around the plaza three times and each time the dancers pass the church they kneel and, making the sign of the cross, ask permission of the Virgin to depart.

5. After the third round there is a period of merrymaking in the plaza. Afterward a goodly number of people go to the house of the new *alferado* for a toast. The fiesta is now concluded.

Analysis of the Fiesta

What we have described is, in fact, a very superficial account of what transpires in the Feast of the Assumption in Chucuito. There is an infinity of details that was not mentioned. For example, the whole question of economic relationships established in the fiesta was mentioned only obliquely. If nothing else, the reader should be convinced by now that the Aymara are a highly complex people and masters of the symbolic. As we saw, every gesture is laden with meaning and is measured to produce a specific effect. But what does all this mean vis-à-vis the inculturation of the gospel in such a culture? What does such a long narration say about Christianity's past and future in the altiplano? Clearly there are no facile answers.

It would appear that Catholicism is a basic part of Chucuito's symbolic world and that its influence is extremely pervasive. But precisely how is that influence functioning in such a complex phenomenon as the fiesta we have just described? Our suspicion is that Catholicism, in some strange way, has become the mechanism par excellence of cultural expression. This is a strange irony of history in view of the fact that Spanish Catholicism deliberately tried to disrupt and even destroy the symbolic world of the Aymara. The ironic end-product of this struggle seems to be a type of Aymara Catholicism that developed an immunity to change or real assimilation to the Spanish world by using its religious and social symbols as shells filled with an entirely different symbolic content, much like a hermit crab. A good example of this phenomenon is the Virgin of the Assumption. She really has nothing to do with the Mary of European Catholicism. She is never even referred to by that name. Rather, she is the *Mamita* or "Little Mother." In other words, the Virgin of the Assumption is none other than the *Pachamama*, or Earth Mother, of Aymara and Andean popular religiosity. The *anda* and its statue are Spanish, but its meaning most certainly is not. It should come as no surprise then that, in a world so culturally bifurcated as this, there would be two fiestas of two Virgins in Chucuito, one for *campesinos* and one for *mestizos*. What that says is that there are two symbol worlds living side by side. When the *anda* of the Virgin of the Assumption is taken out, those who participate are affirming the religious world of the Andes, which now uses a Catholic format with an Aymara content. When the *anda* of the Virgin of the Rosary is carried about, the *mestizos* who participate are engaged in the symbolic expression of their mixed world whose principal symbols are derived from Spanish Catholicism. In no way do they coalesce into a single person called Mary. There are two distinct persons with little in common. Both groups are using symbols to express their legitimacy and neither recognizes the other group as valid. At this point in Peruvian history there seems little chance that the two groups will ever blend into a truly Catholic or, even less, Christian body. As an aside, we should mention that one of the tragic consequences of this situation is that Catholicism has become a vehicle of cultural competition and domination, which on occasion is patently anti-evangelical. After all, there is the whole question of oppression, which is a very palpable factor behind the *mestizo* carrying his *anda*. He wants it known by all that his world is the dominant one and that his religion bears that fact out. At the same time, Catholicism in its Aymara form has provided a mechanism for cultural survival. Clearly the gospel brought by the Spanish has been a mixed blessing.

Let us return to our feast to see exactly how the symbols we have been observing are used and what the implication of their use is. Previously we mentioned what we consider to be the central message or symbol of this particular event and alluded to four categories of secondary symbols that brought across the message of the fiesta. It might prove beneficial to look briefly at each group, keeping in mind that the categories are generic and that there is a good deal of interplay between the four groups.

Religious Symbols. To try to classify the religious symbols in a feast like that of the Assumption is a frustrating task. After all, there are so many activities that seem religious. For the sake of much-needed simplicity we shall fix our attention on those symbols that have some connection with the specifically cultic, be it the *anda* or the act of making the sign of the cross. The two most powerful symbols are clearly the *anda* and the standard of the Virgin of the Assumption. From the beginning of the fiesta until its conclusion, one or the other is with the *alferado* as a symbol of the Virgin's participation in the entire process and her affinity with those involved in the activities. (It is interesting to note that both images are feminine. As far as we know Jesus is never referred to, nor are any masculine religious symbols utilized in the fiesta.) One image or the other presides over the festivities as they diffuse a sacredness to the entire phenomenon. They are obviously numinous and living objects as far as the *campesinos* of Chucuito are concerned. This may be difficult for the rational Westerner to appreciate, but the two images embody a true holiness. To touch either image without sufficient reason or respect is equivalent to sacrilege. People are really convinced that what they do is being viewed and judged by the Virgin in the most literal sense. She determines each act that the *alferado* and *devotos* carry out, and not the reverse. If the Aymara culture of Chucuito is legitimate in its varied forms of expression, it is because she makes such a pronouncement. Of course, the adept anthropologist would say just the opposite, and rightly so, but the Aymara are not known to put much stock in such views. At many points in the fiesta people stop, kneel, make the sign of the cross, or in some way attempt to connect their being with that of the Virgin. In other words, there is an identification process going on. All the elaborate symbolic gestures are meant to convey a connection or identity with the Virgin. Why else the intricate process of walking backwards with eyes fixed on the *anda*? What one comes to understand is that the people who participate in this fiesta consider themselves the sons and daughters of the Virgin of the Assumption and, as such, people with a legitimate identity in Chucuito. To be a *devoto* is to belong to a reality; it is to have dignity and value provided by the very religious symbols of the fiesta, along with others.

Spatio-Temporal Symbols. Once this identity has been established between the Virgin and the *campesino* of Chucuito, a process of delineation must be set up. It must be shown in some way exactly who belongs to this reality and who does not. The fact that processions go around the town plaza three times in a very fixed and traditional pattern is meant to do just that: declare the boundaries of the identity in question. The *anda* of the Virgin stakes out her territory in the process. In a sense that is less metaphorical than we might imagine: the Virgin's *anda* declares who can be a true citizen of Chucuito and who cannot. She sets out the time and place for inscription, which is the fiesta itself. The spatio-temporal symbols are extremely important in limiting the power of the Virgin in a positive way. The influence cannot be overly diffuse without running the risk of dissipating her power. A person from Puno simply cannot obtain legitimate citizenship in Chucuito because he comes from another space and time in which the Virgin of Chucuito does not exercise any real power. The influence of the Virgin has a very specific sphere of power indeed. Judging from the surrounding communities that participate in the fiesta, the influence extends six kilometers north and south. Spatio-temporal symbols are also necessary to keep a sense of order and purpose in the entire process. By following rigid time and space norms one's need for order is assuaged. For that reason the sequence of events in the fiesta is virtually invariable.

Fertility Symbols. To discuss fertility symbols is to run the risk of being declared an unrepentant Freudian—something we most certainly are not! Be that as it may, there seems ample proof that there are some very powerful fertility symbols in this particular fiesta. The most obvious is the *ramada* that is set up in the *alferado*'s house. In Aymara culture the *ramada* represents the productivity of the couple as generative and supportive. It is the fundamental symbol of marriage and all that term means in such an earth-oriented culture. The fact that the Virgin's banner is solemnly placed in the *ramada* by the *alferado* is all too obvious a gesture. It is a declaration that the ultimate fertility of the *ramada* derives from the Virgin of the Assumption. She is the patroness who makes all things possible by providing growth and produce. Anyone who knows Andean cultures will immediately recognize that the patroness, despite her Spanish title, is really the *Pachamama*. Mary has simply become the principle of fertility that she is in so many other cultures that have assumed Catholicism. But this is not some type of crass equation between Mary and fertility. Placing the standard in the *ramada* is a very symbolic, even poetic way of saying that, at least in the area of fertility and sustenance, all things are channeled through the female principal. The Virgin of the Assumption thus represents wholeness and totality in this particular symbolic mode. Because the fiesta uses fertility symbols it is that much more real to the participants who, as Aymaras, see the family as a sacred entity. One thing the Aymara will never subscribe to is Christian Platonism.

The fertility symbols also have influence in the animal and plant kingdoms if the use of *q'ispiña* and the animals' heads is any index. Exactly what such symbols mean and where they come from is a profound question. The connection of *q'ispiña* and animal heads with the Virgin is tenuous at best. Their symbolic etiology seems to be distinct and perhaps they are examples of pre-Christian symbols being transferred into a new context without entirely losing their prior significance. One can only speculate, but it seems possible that the whole episode of *wajcha* has some connection with animal sacrifice and tribute that were carried on long before the arrival of the Spanish. Is it just possible that the Feast of the Assumption had an Andean predecessor?

Historical Symbols. The last symbolic category is the most difficult to speculate on for the simple reason that there is exceedingly little history about the *campesino* community of Chucuito, either before or after the Conquest. The one fact that does seem fairly certain is that Chucuito was once an important Aymara city and the center of the Lupaca people. This fact might explain the visit of the people from Ichu, who are not Lupaca. (Linguistically their Aymara is quite distinct, although Ichu is only six kilometers to the north. Oral legend has it that they are not even Aymara but from a group, possibly from Ecuador, that was transferred to the area during the Inca empire to form a buffer zone to the Lupaca who were in the process of being dominated by Cuzco when the Spanish arrived.) Do we have the residue of some former tributary process being symbolized in the *wajcha*? One can only guess as no one in Chucuito can provide an explanation for the phenomenon. Also we have the whole question of auxiliary *alferados* from the neighboring villages. Do they perceive the Virgin of the Assumption as a powerful patroness to whom they are paying tribute by offering beverages to her *alferado*? There certainly is an aspect of reciprocity involved as their gesture of tribute allows them to set up *ramadas* in their communities, thereby maintaining the spiritual and economic network that pertains to the Virgin. We have never really determined what lies behind their motivation. Perhaps what these historical symbols are trying to communicate is that the *campesino* community of Chucuito has a long and venerable history and that the Virgin of the Assumption is responsible for this very continuity. There really is something remarkably powerful about the historical symbols we have mentioned. They keep alive relationships that existed before the Spanish set foot in the altiplano in a subtle, almost unconscious way.

If our speculations about the use of symbols in the fiesta are correct, particularly in terms of the historical symbols, then one has to give considerable thought to the whole question of popular religiosity and cultural resistance. It seem fair to state that the Virgin of the Assumption is the key instrument in giving an identity, limits, fertility, and history to the Aymara of this area. Rather than causing them to assimilate into the Spanish world, the devotion to the Virgin has helped them keep their culture and social structures intact. Perhaps we should be a bit more conscious of decrying the alienating influence of *campesino* religiosity. It just might be that our denunciation is nothing more than an expression of ignorance about a real cultural dynamism operative among the Aymara. Certainly pastoral planning must be a bit more adept and dig into the reality before it makes too many decisions. At least at times it seems that an expression of popular religiosity like the one we have seen is the most holistic and healing phenomenon available for an oppressed people. It is strange irony of history that symbols that were forcefully imposed by the Spanish with the hope that they would break apart the culture have proved to be the very instruments in keeping the culture vital. What the Spanish apparently never realized was that the Aymara would use their very symbols but almost entirely change their semiotic value. By doing that they transformed Catholicism into a conservative force in the literal sense—a force that favored their own culture's preservation. We suspect that as long as the Aymara world is threatened, and it still is, then Catholicism will continue to function as the primary symbol of resistance. Whether such a situation is good or bad, evangelical or not, is not ours to judge. We are a long way from having enough data to judge the validity of the Feast of the Assumption as a cultural or a Christian phenomenon. It is rather doubtful if we ever will.

Conclusion

When we began this paper our purpose was to describe how the gospel has inculturated itself into Aymara society. At least in explicit, detailed terms we have not achieved our goal. We have, rather, described an apparently religious event for the reader, who can judge to what degree the gospel has penetrated this world. We have raised many questions and provided few answers. What does seem certain, however, is that a vital and distinctive form of native Catholicism has evolved from the evangelization that took place here four centuries ago. This Andean Catholicism is now basic to almost every aspect of the culture, in religious, social, and even economic terms. The question remains, however, as to how Christian this cultural Catholicism is. We would be the last to say that the terms are in any way synonymous. Cultural Catholicism can be the most efficient instrument for blocking out the gospel. Its resistance to change borders on the taciturn at times. It cares little about exterior reality beyond its provincial sphere of influence and is absolutely loathe to engage in any type of self-articulation that it does not even consider to be a value. At the same time it has provided people with a religious framework within which to live their lives and preserve their culture despite often fierce opposition. It is a mechanism that works and has kept this and other cultures alive in their own peculiar, convoluted ways. It is clearly not all bad.

Perhaps the only thing we can conclude is that Catholicism is an inevitable result of evangelization. More often than not it is neutral morally and unavoidably cultural. The challenge is to utilize it in an informed, respectful way that produces evangelical results. To do that requires a good deal of information about the culture, which can only be gathered slowly. At least in terms of the Aymara, most of the information is still missing. At the same time, to judge a culture evangelically demands an even more replete knowledge of what the gospel is and how it works in society. The answers lie a long way down the road.

34

INDIA

Pearl Drego

The split between the Gospel and culture is without a doubt the drama of our time, just as it was of other times [*Evangelii Nuntiandi*, no. 20].

Introduction

Long before the concept of "local church" emerged in contemporary theology, pastoral thinking in non-Western societies became acutely aware of the gaps between the local culture and the witness of the church as expressed in the liturgy, in theological language, and in forms of spirituality. In India cries of distress from missionaries about the distance between a Western-cloaked Christianity and indigenous cultural realities have been heard since the seventeenth century.

One example in India was the work of Robert de Nobili, who said:

> . . . in this part of India . . . the whole work of conversion has been fruitless precisely because there was no adaption to the customs of the country. . . . They will be blinded to all reasoning if the preacher is alien to their culture. . . . Together with personal holiness and soundness of doctrine, adaptation to local customs is of absolute necessity for the preacher of the Gospel; we have deemed it our duty to prescribe this adaptation with a view to render conversion possible.[1]

The word "adaptation" is a twentieth-century translation but de Nobili spoke of adopting, taking on, embracing local customs, being consistent with the culture of the people, being all things to all people, being Indian to the Indians.

Pearl Drego, a member of the International Grail Movement, is the Director of the Transactional Analytic Centre for Education and Training, New Delhi. She is also engaged in running a women's development project, counseling, formation, and retreat work.

Some Approaches

In tracing the history of the concept of inculturation I find several related concepts in use: adaptation, Indianization, and indigenization. These terms mark the development from a theology of spiritual colonialism to an incarnational theology. By studying the documents, articles, and conference papers of the last thirty years concerning this area, one can discover a great change in the use of these terms (though some people use them interchangeably even today). Each has a nuance that the other does not have and marks a certain phase of church history that in turn is shaped by international secular history.

Ecclesial Colonialism

As Western scholars in the 1920s began to be aware of the rich heritage of the world religions, as the rise of the nations gave birth to a new world consciousness in which nations and cultures previously regarded as "inferior" or "pagan" began to take their rightful place on an equal footing with the big world powers, as anthropology and sociology showed up the relativity of Western culture among the host of specific "cultures" that filled the earth's islands and continents, theologians and missionaries (maybe theologians before missionaries) began to separate the content of the Christian message, the core of Christian life, from the cultural forms, symbols, and concepts in which they were expressed and communicated.

But it was not long ago that the very European act of genuflection was seen as the best way to respect the Blessed Sacrament, that the Gothic spire was an essential indication of the parish church, that Gregorian chant was the finest expression of liturgical song, and the Anglo-Saxon face of Christ or an Italian madonna were the most evocative symbols of Christian piety.

Neocolonialism

There are thousands of Catholics, lay, religious, and clerical, for whom this is still true, for whom the foreign cultural form in which they were nurtured is the only valid form of Christian witness and Christian mission. This is because of centuries of missionary history in which the process of cultural and political colonization went hand in hand with Christian conversion. However, the long-standing Christian communities of India have historically developed cultural forms of their own, related to the history of their conversion by a particular nationality of foreign missionaries, and by the particular cultural forms in which the gospel was expressed in the recent centuries.

These Christian communities already have well-developed cultural systems that can be called the cultures of Indian Christians. To speak of inculturating these Christian communities seems, first, to imply that they have no culture and, second, to impose on them another layer of culture to which centuries of colonization have made them feel a stranger. This is cultural neocolonialism, or a supraculturation. We need to see the actual lived reality of a people to foster a genuine inculturation that involves an unlearning of past colonial history, and a relearning of present reality.

Adaptation

The first attempts in this direction took the form of "adaptation" by which in the 1950s in India attempts were made in a public way to bring Indian dance and music into gospel plays and into the liturgy, Hindi hymns were being composed, Christ and Our Lady were being represented in Indian garb, and tribal songs replaced Latin chants. In spite of recurring waves of protest this process continued into the 1960s and priests took to kurta-pyjamas, saffron robes, and chappals; nuns to sarees; church artisans to Indian styles of painting, sculpture, and design. Intensive studies began on symbols and gestures used in Hindu worship, and parallel to these movements was a serious study of Indian religions, their theologies and scriptures, in a search for concepts, for schemas, for terminology in which the emotional difficulties felt toward "pagan" things were ironed out, so that what was "shocking" in the 1960s had become commonplace in the 1980s. But resistance to change dies hard and often the old system continues to exist under changed patterns and traditions.

Change of Attitude

What is significant in the process is the change in terminology and the change in attitude that went along with it. "Adaptation" implied a change of outward forms, almost a kind of local disguise through which to proclaim the mission of the church. It implied an adjustment on the part of the evangelizer, the adoption of another's cultural forms from a position of security and certitude. It also implied a new tactic for converting non-Christians by using symbols with which they were familiar.

Indianization and Indigenization

Gradually the more specific term "Indianization" came into vogue, emphasizing the need to identify with what was *Indian* and not merely to make a few adaptations. Indianization demanded a more radical stance in which "foreign" or "Western" influence had to be disowned in favor of what was typical to the country. While adaptation meant a certain "adding" and "modifying," the term "Indianization" meant a "divesting" and "canceling." Indianization also implied a change in identity and belonging on the part of Indian Christians. Sometimes it included the removal of foreign authority structures and putting Indian personnel at the helm of church institutions.

Yet even this word seemed inadequate. Precisely because of the latter meaning, that is, change to Indian personnel, "Indianization" did not convey the depth of the cultural process required. Besides, while it seemed suitable to ask foreign missionaries to Indianize, it seemed strange to ask the Indian church to Indianize. In fact this was highly resented.

At the same time, especially in the late 1960s, it was obvious that there was no one

Indian culture and that when people spoke of Indianization they were often referring only to Hindu cultural forms and Hindu religious traditions. The realization of the need to adapt to Islam, to Buddhism, and to the wealth of tribal religions and cultures led to the use of the term "indigenization." This allowed for a broad spectrum of movements in keeping with the local situations. However, even this term began to be used mainly for liturgical change, and for changes in dress, art, music, and customs. In fact, as late as 1975 I find articles in theological journals that equate indigenization with Hindu ashram life.[2] With the development of a more incarnational theology and a liberation theology that focused on the church's mission in relation to sociocultural and socioeconomic structures, the term "inculturation" came onto the scene in the late 1970s.

At the First Bishops' Institute of Missionary Activities (Manila, August 1978), I heard inculturation discussed not as

> a means but an ingredient of evangelization. It is to make the Lord present in a recognizable form. . . . Inculturation is the process by which every moment of our lives, every aspiration and talent of our culture, is synthesised into a unity that will one day be the total glorification of Christ. The paschal mystery is the law of all inculturation. Here inculturation is not just a way of witnessing to Christ but of accomplishing and fulfilling his work of Redemption.

But inculturation and indigenization continue to be associated.

Inculturation vs. Indigenization

> Inculturation, which is the consequence of the incarnational economy of salvation, is part and parcel of the mission of the Church. . . . Every aspect of the life and activity of the Church should be incultured or indigenous: indigenous life-style, indigenous arts, liturgy, spirituality, indigenous forms of religious life, indigenous organisations and institutions. Theology, to be authentic and pastoral . . . must be a reflection in faith on the Church's Christian experience in the contemporary world and history.[3]

Although the terms "inculturation" and "indigenization" continue to be used together, the term "inculturation" removes the antiforeign and anticolonial sting from the word "indigenization." Like the latter, it drew attention to nonreligious aspects and focused on the need to incarnate the church not only in traditional religious symbolism but also in the particular customs, rituals, values, and myths of a particular local community. The term "inculturation" had far-reaching consequences in view of an anthropological concept of culture. It can be readily applied to a local theology, a local language, a local liturgy, a local pattern of priestly and religious formation, a local spirituality, the use of local media of communication, and so forth. Besides, it also takes into consideration the cultural patterns of contemporary India that are very much part of current Indian reality and yet cannot be called indigenous, for example, the integration of theology and mission and church structures with modernization, urbanization, mass media, technical culture, and socioeconomic movements. In this sense a guitar Mass, a meditation with slides, a *Progoff Journal* retreat, a blue-jeaned pastor, an apostolate for rights against slum eviction may well be inculturating the Gospel while not exactly indigenizing it. Therefore inculturation is more all-inclusive and has less sectarian overtones than indigenization.

It is more in tune with the incarnation theology of *Gaudium et Spes*:

> There are many links between the message of salvation and human culture. For God, revealing Himself in His Incarnate Son, has spoken according to the culture proper to different ages. . . . The Church, sent to all peoples of every time and place, is not bound exclusively and indissolubly to any race or nation, nor to any particular way of life or any customary pattern of living, ancient or recent. Faithful to her own tradition and at the same time conscious of her universal mission, she can enter into communion with various cultural modes, to her own enrichment and theirs too. By riches coming from above, it makes fruitful, as it were from within, the spiritual qualities and gifts of every people and of every age. It strengthens, perfects and restores them in Christ. Thus by the very fulfilment of her own mission the Church stimulates and advances human and civic culture. By her action, even in its liturgical form, she leads men toward interior liberty.

The historical development of terms is not just a matter of language but expresses the process of clarification and experimentation within the church over the past decades. A change in term coincides with a change in attitude and orientation, and outlines the changing *context* of mission and evangelization.

I find the nuances of all the terms mentioned above contained in writings on evangelization and inculturation. For example, in *Evangelii Nuntiandi* Pope Paul VI says that "evangelization involves an explicit message, *adapted* to the different situations constantly being realized" (no. 29). A similar expression is his statement that "the building of the Kingdom cannot avoid *borrowing* the elements of human culture or cultures" (no. 20) and that "individual Churches . . . have the task of assimilating the essence of the Gospel message and of *transposing* it . . . into the language that these particular people understand" (no. 63). However, he also has more radical aspects of inculturation in the following expressions: "For the Church evangelizing means bringing the Good News into all strata of humanity, and through its influence *transforming* humanity from within and making it new" (no. 18). And "strata of humanity which are *transformed*: for the Church it is a question . . . also of *affecting and as it were* upsetting through the power of the Gospel, mankind's criteria of judgment, determining values, points of interest, lines of thought, sources of inspiration and models of life, which are in contrast with the World of God and the plan of salvation" (no. 19).

Guidelines for Inculturation

In these statements we have guidelines toward a vital social and cultural critiquing, a transformation process affecting social structures and lifestyles and not a mere adaptation or transposition. Theories of inculturation can be roughly divided into those that favor transformation and those that favor transposition. Transformation is a way of inspiring and challenging social realities; transposition is transplanting the same content in different forms just as one puts the same tune into different keys. However, while transformation is dynamic and unique to each local context, transposition is universalizing, applying general principles to particular situations. Both processes have their relevance in the processes of inculturation.

From the Classical Concept of Culture to an Anthropology of Culture

The move from "transposition" to "transformation" is also indicative of the move away from a classical concept of culture to an anthropological concept. In fact these two concepts of culture are still confused in pastoral writings. It is the classical concept that is meant by "the field of evangelizing activity is the vast and complicated world of politics, society and economics, but also the world of culture, of the sciences and the arts . . ." (*Evangelii Nuntiandi,* no. 70). In this sense culture implies the highest civilized forms of intellectual and artistic achievement. Such a concept restricts culture to a very small segment of the earth's population and a small segment of human achievements. Many attempts at "inculturation" in India have therefore been influenced by the old concepts and focused only on the classical Indian theologies and philosophies, classical literature, art, poetry, music, and dance.

Historically, culture first referred to cultivation of the soil, and later referred to cultivation of the mind. It first appears in Bacon's *Advancement of Learning* (1605), in which it came close to the idea of perfection, and the idea of perfection was identified with the idealist concept of ethical and spiritual perfection as embodied in the classical and Christian heritage of Europe. At times culture referred to the general state of intellectual and moral development in society as a whole; at times it referred in a narrower sense to the general body of arts and intellectual work. With the discovery of non-European cultures the distinction was made between national culture and a "cultured" person. Samuel Taylor Coleridge in 1830, and later Matthew Arnold, distinguished between external civilization and intellectual phenomena. But the tribal cultures had still not received due recognition for their worth, and culture was still connected with a highly developed civilization.

In the English language, it was Tylor in 1871 who in his book *Primitive Cultures* gave one of the earliest definitions of culture that implied all human societies have a culture. He said it is that "complex whole which includes knowledge, belief, art, morals, law, customs and any other capabilities and habits acquired by man as a member of human society."

Thus it was only toward the late nineteenth century that *culture* was separated from *a culture,* that the anthropological and sociological "cultures" emerged as relative and comparative, indicating what different peoples of the earth do, and think, and make, how they organize their life and interactions, their faith, worship, family life, and politics. In this concept of culture there was no fixed link to artistic and intellectual merit. It was clear too that these world cultures could not be evaluated by any one given value system originating in European tradition. The new trend removed ethnocentric and ideological prejudices.

A European-based Christianity was suddenly faced with a world of national and local cultures that had a value and integrity in themselves. The missionary was less and less the bringer of culture and more and more the bringer of a message. But even this spiritual message was cast in a given cultural form, the Christian life was taught in a given cultural framework, it was the child of a particular Western historical epoch. Only in the 1940s as the cries of secularization and national independence of colonies hit Western civilization did the church become keenly aware of the way in which the missionary processes had alienated the local Christian communities from their cultural surroundings. As these cultural surroundings became more and more respected as entities in their own rights, the process of making links to the immediate cultural milieu began, not only as a means of spreading the gospel but also as a means to integrate the local church communities with their cultural past and cultural present. Vatican II further hallowed this process and gave it a third dimension by seeing it as essential for the task of evangelization: of proclaiming the action of God in history by preserving and promoting the values of other traditions and cultures, so that they may find their fulfillment in Christ.

Discovering Culture

However, even with the new emphasis on culture of the world and the identity of each culture as an integral whole, there is much confusion as to how to approach the study of a culture, what constitutes its substance, and therefore what is inculturation of the gospel. This will depend on whether we see a culture as being static or dynamic, as an accumulation of cultural traits or a network of feelings, as a collection of customs or a system of interaction, as a historical process or a hierarchy of relationships. For this we need a model for analyzing culture and criteria for evaluating human freedom and human justice. If our concept of culture is limited, then our concept of inculturation will be limited.

I speak of a model of culture because science and epistemology today are very conscious of the ways in which we perceive reality. Empirically we cannot know reality "as it is." All we can talk about is how we perceive it. So no one can claim to know what culture is. I can only say what I mean when I use the term, how I organize data into a pattern or model that I call "culture." Ian Barbour writes: "Theoretical models are novel mental constructions. They originate in a combination of analogy to the familiar, and creative imagination in inventing the new. They are open-ended, extensible, and suggestive of new hypotheses. Such models are taken seriously but not literally. They are neither pictures of reality nor useful fictions, they are partial and inadequate ways of imagining what is not observable."[4]

The Psycho-Social Model of Culture

The model for analyzing culture that I offer for your use is a relatively unknown one. It is derived from the social psychiatry of Dr. Eric Berne. In his analyses of organizations and cultures he was influenced by the discoveries in psycho-social dynamics made by experts such as J. L. Moreno, W. R. Bion, and Le Bon. My purpose in presenting this model is to get a holistic picture of culture on which to build a total picture of inculturation of the gospel.

Three Areas of Culture

Berne distinguishes three modes of group behavior: etiquette, technicalities, character.

Applied to a culture, this psycho-social model reveals three categories: (1) transmitted designs for thinking, behaving, and valuing in a particular society; (2) the actual organization of material and social life of a particular human group; (3) socially programmed ways of feeling, handling biological needs, emotional expressions (especially compliance and rebellion). A simplified version of the same can be made with a diagram of three elipses stacked one over the other:

(1)   Beliefs and values of a culture

(2)   Technicalities and communication systems

(3)   Emotional patterns and responses

The Psycho-Social Model and Classical Anthropology

Kroeber and Kluckhohn found 164 definitions of culture. Anthropologists continue to define culture according to their assumptions and methodology. By using the psycho-social model that I have presented, we can see how every definition or description of culture relates to one of the three categories in the model and how inculturation has so far emphasized only one or two of three categories:

1. Ralph Linton: "The sum total of knowledge, attitudes and habitual behaviour patterns shared and transmitted by the members of a particular society."

(1)   Knowledge (in relation to beliefs)

(2)   Knowledge (as know-how)

(3)   Attitudes and habitual behavior patterns

2. Kluckhohn and Kelly: "All historically created designs for living, explicit and implicit, rational and irrational and nonrational, which exist at any given time as potential guides for the behavior of man."

(1)   Designs for living (nonrational)

(2)   Designs for living (rational)

(3)   Designs for living (irrational)

3. Kroeber: "The mass of learned and transmitted motor reactions, habits, techniques, ideas and values and behaviour they induce."

(1)   Ideas and values

(2)   Techniques

(3)   Motor reactions, habits, behavior

Explanation of the Three Categories

Category 1 focuses on culture as an organized system of thinking and symbolizing by which a particular society gives meaning to its experience of the world, governs the relationships among its members, makes choices on how to use natural and human resources, structures the use of time, makes sacred the cosmic universe, and supports the emotional experiences of its members with a consistent frame of reference.

Category 2 focuses on the realm of observable phenomena, the artifacts, the events, the structures and institutions, means of production, the work-life, and so forth that concretize and also shape the symbolizing process of a particular society. It is what people do and make because of the conceptual framework of category 1. It also includes the options taken in the real world for which the society later builds up the belief-system of category 1 to reinforce these options, stabilize them, and even enforce them.

Category 3 focuses on the psycho-motor and -feeling responses that are current in the society: the psychic realms of mythic experience, the reservoirs of social energy, and the dark underworld of instinctual life as expressed *(a)* in the songs, dances, legends, forms of intimacy and creativity, forms of celebration and mourning; *(b)* in the depth of ritual and custom; *(c)* in the felt compulsion to conform to the society's patterns; and *(d)* in the legitimate ways of defying categories 1 and 2. Experiences of being satisfied or deprived, of succeeding or failing, being worthwhile or useless, being blessed or cursed, of being a hero or a traitor, insofar as these are programmed by the family and society, are all part of category 3.

The Categories Form a System

The three categories are interrelated. For example, if we take the dowry as an institution we find that *(a)* in category 1 there are beliefs about woman, about her worth and function in the family, her status in the original family and the new ownership of her person, about mutual exchange between families, and so forth; *(b)* in category 2 there is a pattern and procedure for accomplishing the bargain, there are options for negotiation of price, a system of communication by which the arrangement is made, the sequence of events related to the handing over of the money or assets, options for keeping it that the society allows and the system of material possessions, preservation, and supply that is kept up, the actual giving of the dowry, for instance the bridegroom's family acquires wealth, or the newlyweds acquire wealth, or the bridegroom's sister acquires a dowry. The options available within the society form part of category 2; *(c)* in category 3 there are feelings of obligation, of anticipation, of deprivation or satisfaction, feelings of worth or worthlessness on the part of the bride, feelings of power on the part of the husband's family, feelings of resistance, of bondage, of frustration.

Any process of social transformation, for example, in the dowry system, will require a change in the whole system of beliefs-options-feelings and will affect the power structures of the society. It will upset those members of the society who maintain the power system and therefore requires to take into consideration the psycho-dynamics of power shifts and to protect those who stand to gain by the transformation.

In the process of modernization that is sweeping traditional cultures, what happens in terms of the model I have given is that changes on the level of category 2, that is, of mechanized industry, science, and trade, are rapidly increasing, while category 1 and category 3 are not changing to match the advances. This is why industrial society in Japan is so different from industrial society in India or the United States. The integration of their own specific belief systems with category 2 makes for the unique differences between them. Each forms a network that is specific to its own inherited patterns of acting and feeling.

Culture as Configuration

Therefore, in the analysis and evaluation of cultural realities the process of inculturating the gospel needs to take into account the fact that each culture is not just an accumulation of items but forms a consistent whole. The three categories mentioned above form an interrelated complexity. Ruth Benedict brought out this significant perception of human cultures. According to her, a culture is like an individual in having "a more or less consistent pattern of thought and action." She says that each culture comes to have its own characteristic "purposes" and "goals" (category 1), and its own "emotional mainsprings" (category 3). According to her view, cultures differ not only because one trait is present in one while it is absent in another but still more because they are "oriented as whole" in a particular direction. Each society has to make a few choices from the "arc of potential human purposes and motivations" that are theoretically within its reach. And out of a million possibilities, a culture forms its own world-picture, its own unique "configuration" of the three categories. By becoming aware of this quality of a culture we realize that by merely inculturating the gospel in one or other cultural traits, for example, in a particular local custom, or a particular indigenous gesture, in a local dress or local songs, we may be touching on a few items and missing the core of the whole configuration, the "ethos" of the culture. On the other hand, we do need to look at the elements of the configuration as well.

Elements of the Categories

In order to get a comprehensive picture of the task of inculturation I developed the model as given below.

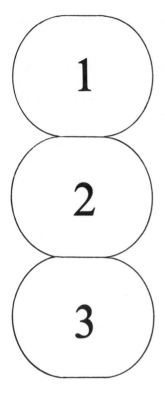

Religious and philosophical beliefs; ideologies; values; rules; moral codes; beliefs about life and death, good and evil; beliefs about being male and female; beliefs about wealth and poverty, fertility and entropy; superstitions; customs; rituals; social hierarchies and prejudices; expectations of the ideal man, the ideal woman; methods of reward and punishment; etc.

Factual knowledge; skills; techniques; methods of production and distribution; economic processes; science and research; planning and organization; distribution of political power; etc.

Ways of experiencing and of acting out love, hatred, pleasure, pain, acceptance, rejection, obedience, resistance, hungers, needs, drives, friendship, jealousy, birth, death, freedom, identity, fear, hope, fulfillment, etc.

Inculturation Today

What we see happening today in India under the banner of inculturation can be understood using the three categories. Inculturation on the level of category 1 involves recognizing the seeds of the gospel present in the sacred schemas of non-Christian cultures, allowing the Christ experience to shine through the prism of the indigenous spirituality, finding new methods of approaching the highest Trinitarian mysteries in the simplest forms of religiosity no less than in the sophisticated clarification of classical sages. Much work is being done in this line through dialogue with the mythic and mystical traditions of Islam, Hinduism, Buddhism, Taoism, and so forth. A special harvest of riches is also emerging from the mystical world-views of tribal societies. However, the gospel has also a response to make to superstitions and magical beliefs in culture. It is significant that modern industrialized societies are as rife with magic and esoteric psychic phenomena as the so-called traditional societies. Also traditional beliefs that support social discrimination and harden levels of social status are present in both modern and traditional cultures and need to be confronted by Christ's good news of freedom. Beliefs about man, woman, suffering, joy, sacrifice, equality, poverty need to be challenged by the values of the gospel.

The process of inculturating the gospel is a process of entering into the freedom movements by which a particular society is overhauling the values in its current life. First among these are the struggles for justice among the poor, which challenge the belief systems in category 1 that perpetuate exploitation on the part of the rich and passivity on the part of the poor: for example beliefs that emphasize the innate differences between different economic strata, that ascribe political power to a few, that squash any challenge of the status quo as a disruption of peace and order. Second among the freedom movements of today are the struggles of peoples to shape their own political destiny without being tortured, imprisoned, or put at a disadvantage in any way. A third movement of freedom is the struggle for the dignity and rights of women. Unless the total and local church makes its mark on the position and role of women in the surrounding culture, it is bypassing a major responsibility in inculturating the gospel.

Inculturation in category 2 involves a socioeconomic analysis of class, of the distribution and exercise of political power, the exploitation of labor, the balance between science and human welfare. Here the incarnation of the gospel means the application of Christ's values of justice and equality to the ways in which the culture manipulates and controls material resources, acquired knowledge, skills, and social opportunities.

It requires resistance to the unchecked buildup of industrial technology as it is being imported from the West and a fostering of local technology that benefits the local masses. So far the church has communicated technology, skills, and education through its schools. But these have not always served the poor. Now new movements of nonformal education, education to the realities of the environment, are sweeping mission stations and local Christian communities. Through these processes of learning people are becoming aware of facts, statistics, and resources that are connected with their material and social rights. Many Christian priests and religious are also changing their designs of living on the material plane to harmonize with the designs of living of rural communities, for example, simple food, clothing, and housing. Local raw materials, local medicine, and local handcrafts are given new recognition as against those rapid trends in Westernization and modernization that are damaging to the local culture. In fact it is a modern reaction to technical civilization that is also built into the Westernization process. There is a world-over movement toward intermediate technology and rural development. The Marxist trends within India and within the church have put much-needed attention on the relationship between the gospel and socioeconomic reality, and on the impact of this reality on the ideologies and belief-systems of the particular society. What they often fail to support their efforts with is the harnessing of energies of category 3. There are dynamos of construction and destruction on this level of community process, and the workers for justice have often been surprised when a whiplash of reaction sweeps over their work like an unexpected and deadly tidal wave.

The inculturation of the gospel is incomplete if we stick only to categories 1 and 2 without touching the rhythms of living of category 3. The closed-circuit mentality of many Marxist Christians is the result of blocking out the unknown terrain of category 3. Inculturation in category 3 involves moving into the depths of psychological experience within the community and recognizing the action of Christ in moments of misery and distress as well as in moments of healing and rejoicing. Many of these feeling-level experiences are also programmed and conditioned by culture and need to be freed from the limitations of categories 1 and 2.

It is important to recognize that the salvific gift of Christ is ultimately a freeing from bondage to culture, though it is through culture itself that life and grace manifest themselves. Here the mystery of the incarnation can help us to see Christ within culture, transforming culture, taking us beyond culture, and as it were almost de-culturing us.

Spiritual Experience and Culture

Though I have included religious beliefs, rituals, and theological world-views in category 1 of culture, I place spiritual experience on a level of its own, called Dimension 4, because it is not a category of the same caliber as the thought patterns and behavior patterns of category 1. Yet the configurations formed by categories 1, 2, and 3 will certainly shape this dimension, namely, the spiritual experiences of a particular society, conditioning them to have certain forms instead of others. If the core patterns are more extrovert in character, then religious experience will have an emphasis on historical salvation, on divine intervention in human life, on sacramental ritual. If the core patterns are more introvert, then religious experience will tend to be highly personal, contemplative, and mystical. The visions of the Beyond and of God will be affected by the belief systems of category 1, and vice versa. The religious experience of the people will also in turn shape the configurations of their culture; the forms of prayer and worship will *emerge from* as well as carve their patterns on other parts of social life.

The differences between culture are wider in category 1 and come nearer to each other in categories 2 and 3. They come even closer in Dimension 4, which is the spiritual. Studies in comparative religion and religious phenomenology continue to highlight the amazing similarities in structure and expression of religious experiences in different cultures. It is important to remember these universal trends in each culture because if we are too busy inculturating in what is particular to each group we may miss the universal aspects that spring from the basic humanity of each person and each cultural grouping—aspects that are highlighted by their spiritual experiences.

While categories 1, 2, 3 are integrated with Dimension 4 (spiritual experience), there is an individual spiritual experience that is *beyond the cultural circumference,* though it will be influenced by it. Some of the deepest spiritual struggles are those in which the individual person strives to be free from the three cultural categories and to flow with the movements of the Spirit into uncharted regions for which the culture has no name and perhaps no signpost either.

This recalls to us that the primary call of the gospel of Christ is to a personal conversion or metanoia, and not to a cultural conversion: "As the kernel and centre of his Good News, Christ proclaims salvation, this great gift of God which is liberation from everything that oppresses man but which is above all liberation from sin and the Evil One, in the joy of knowing God and being known by him, of seeing him, and of being given over to him" (*Evangelii Nuntiandi,* no. 9).

A unique aspect of this message is that it takes shape within the concrete history of an individual or within the cultural categories of a particular group. The variety of cultures and human experience is a reminder of the variety of ways in which the Lord creates and redeems the peoples of the earth. We need to recognize that in the past the church has limited the Christ experience to particular Western forms, based on Western belief-feeling systems. Now we can look for new forms within Eastern, African, Latin American, ethnic, and even international forms.

Indeed, on the level of spiritual experience there is more than inculturation taking place in the church. A new integrated spirituality that borrows from the spiritual traditions of East and West, from the myths, dreams, and rituals of American Indians, African peoples, and Indian villages, as well as from modern techniques in psychotherapy and psychodynamics is becoming increasingly popular.

Interestingly enough those who have popularized in Asia and in the West the modes of praying that have originated in Hinduism and Buddhism do not themselves belong to these cultural and religious traditions. Yet they are inculturating the gospel in the latter. Zen techniques of meditation, Taoist practices, transcendental meditation from India, yogic awareness of the self, the Advaitic experience of the Ultimate, Chinese philosophy, and Indian methods of contemplation are influencing Christian prayer and worship the world over. I find that many local Christians, urban, rural, and ethnic, find these experiences relevant and should not be denied these riches by being told to stay within their own cultural boundaries. In fact it is precisely the individual's capacity to go beyond the programming of his or her culture that is one instance of the exercise of "interior liberty" that Christ offers to each person.

Culture as Limitation

While an individual will be shaped by culture, the experience and options he or she has will go beyond culture. In fact the more a person exercises inner freedom the less he or she will be bound by culture. When the integrated person does follow the values and patterns of culture it will be because of choice and not because of compulsion. In order to exercise new options the individual needs to be challenged and inspired by the world-pictures of *other* cultures. Fortunately this is happening more and more in the modern world. Lawrence LeShan writes:

> No one world-picture works completely. . . . We live in a perceived-reacted to universe that is incomplete by its very nature. We are held in this invented-discovered reality by the fact that it is a premise of every world-picture that it is the *only* picture of truth. [By increasing] the number of world-pictures we can perceive-react to . . . we may then *choose* which conception of reality fits the needs we have predominant at the moment. We cannot do this, of course, until we are clear that none of the valid systems of organizing reality is closer to truth than the others; that each is a different way of perceiving and reacting to what *is*.[5]

Confrontation and cross-fertilization with other cultures are therefore enriching to any given culture. Christian missionaries have provided ample opportunities for this to happen. Inculturation needs to be matched with this counterprocess in a sensitive way, as any challenge to a culture is inevitably felt by its people as a threat to their very existence, because category 1 is usually transmitted with the belief that "our way is the only and best way for our people." And yet the gospel has to challenge the culture at various points, especially its claim to be absolute. So while inculturation may be relevant to new Christian communities, the counterprocess may be more relevant to the old Christian communities.

Discernment and Openness

If the process of inculturation stays only as *in*culturation, then it adapts the individual more securely to the environmental programming, instead of freeing the individual from the slaveries of his or her culture and letting what is best in culture unite with what is best in the self. Understanding the various elements of culture and their impact on the person is therefore vital in any task of inculturating the gospel. If a local church is not conscious of its cultural riches as distinct from its cultural limitations, then it cannot even begin to inculturate the gospel in a truly Christlike way. A genuine inculturation will bring the individual Christian *(a)* openness to the programming of cultures, both one's own as well as others; *(b)* ability to discern those values that are healthy, and to reject those that are destructive; and *(c)* a desire to be enriched by other cultures and a readiness to share one's own.

Christ in Culture and beyond Culture

Every culture forms a configuration and shapes the consciousness of its members as a society and as a network of relationships. The individual shares in an environment of intellectual and emotional nutrients that feed both personal and interpersonal life, gives norms for acting, and induces certain behavior patterns. At the same time as the environment fosters growth in personhood it sets boundaries, which are the very boundaries of the culture. Just as Christ expressed himself in the language and symbol of his day, yet challenged those forms and symbols that kept persons in bondage, so also the task of inculturating his message involves transforming the heritage of the people and yet leading them to critical points beyond the fixed boundaries. The gospel of Christ takes us through culture, beyond culture, through the particular in its depth, to what is most universal in the human person. In this way inculturation of today is not the inverse of colonial deculturation but restores a local community to their rightful traditions, helps them to purify these as well as point the way beyond their limitations, to *new* experiences of inner and outer consciousness that are not present in the local cultural configurations.

International Matrix

The process of inculturation in modern times also needs to take note of the unique existence of situations that are multicultural or are marginal to a given culture. Besides, more and more people from many cultures are showing great flexibility moving in and out of their own cultural milieus, taking on alien cultural systems, and forming new cultural configurations. The acculturation process of the East by the

West and the West by the East, the presence of Indian scientists in American and European *sannyasis* in Asia, the "foreign" experts on Hindu experience and Buddhist meditations are further evidence that a person from one culture can move with much flexibility into another. An increasing number of people in the church, at local, national, and international levels, are integrating the best in many cultures and in the world religions. This integration should not be denied the local Christian communities at village and ethnic levels. While charged with the task of inculturating the gospel in their own cultural categories and in their own day-to-day history, they have a right to share in a growing international culture. In this way, while there is a particularizing trend through inculturating the gospel, there is a universalizing trend reculturating the local community.

The Condition of the Westernized Christian

It is the international matrix of contemporary cultures that will help the "Westernized Christians" to come out of their ambiguous cultural position. In order to see what the history of colonial Christianity has done to the individual personality of the Christian and to see how paradoxical it is to speak of indigenizing local Christian communities who have lived through decades, perhaps centuries, of having to adopt foreign ways to be Christian, we need to look at culture in the context of personality.

Often from the way in which inculturation is spoken about in theology, one gets the impression that culture encompasses the whole of an individual's life. But in speaking about the whole gamut of culture we need to keep in mind that it is only part of the total experience of the individual person. Not everything he or she thinks, feels, and does is determined by culture, although a large portion is. However, the following diagram is a reminder that culture shapes only one-third of a person's behavior and self-awareness:

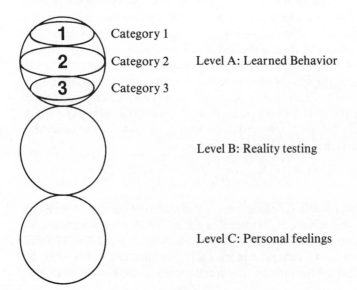

Category 1

Category 2   Level A: Learned Behavior

Category 3

Level B: Reality testing

Level C: Personal feelings

Supraculturation

The history of missionary activity often canceled out the categories of the local culture and imposed a new set of categories in which the Christ experience and the Christian lifestyle were unmistakably Western. The diagram of the individual Christian who was converted in this way in colonial times was inadvertently designed to look like this:

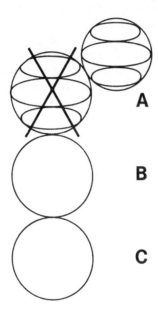

Here the traditional cultural categories of belief, reality operations, and feeling reactions are substituted by a foreign set of categories because the missionaries did not distinguish between the essence of the Christian message and the cultural media in which they themselves were born. Everything relating to the "pagan" culture was seen as dangerous and therefore whatever could be discarded was discarded. There are examples where the missionaries even prescribed a particular style of dress for Christian women to wear. (The Capuchins made the Catholic women in Bettiah wear a dress distinctively different from their non-Catholic counterparts—a dress the good fathers probably saw in Rajasthan and admired for its wide skirts and similarity with European gowns.) Often too the economic survival of local converts demanded that the missionaries set up a parallel structure of economy in category 2, buying land and helping the local Christian community to form its own patterns of income through outside help.

The Compartmentalized Christian

As time went on and the antagonism of missionaries to local culture turned to a patronizing benevolence, the "level A" of the individual Christian began to change. Some of the old beliefs crept back, as did some old social systems. The third category returned with full force because not much attention was put on Christianizing the emotional systems, the hinterlands of consciousness, and the more intimate areas of human relationships. Emphasis was, rather, put on the theologies and doctrines of category 1 because the safeguard of Christians was seen to lie in the beliefs they professed and in their loyalty to the scheme of life they were given. But in fact customs surrounding caste, class, and dowry, for example, continued side by side with the Christian belief-system as did family patterns, child-rearing practices, and demonic seizures carried over from pre-Christian days.

So the diagram of the individual Christian in non-Western societies looks like this:

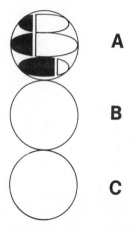

The darkened areas are the untouched remnants of local culture, local behavior patterns, and feeling responses. There is no flow of interaction between the two sections. The individual Christian carries an in-built conflict in level A of personality. There are two designs for living that have not yet encountered each other in depth. Yet over the centuries they have coexisted side by side and formed unique configurations that can be called cultures in their own right, even though the conflicts between them have not been resolved. However, the energy absorbed in defensiveness and protection of identity as a result of supraculturation is one of the reasons why such local Christian communities are not missionary in zeal or outlook. They are so busy defending their internal boundaries that the gap between them and the surrounding cultures becomes greater still. This gap makes conversion to the church exceedingly difficult, as this involves entering another cultural grouping.

Supraculturation by Inculturation

But the problems arising from this gap cannot be solved by now demanding that such local-church groupings return to their indigenous patterns of culture. When this demand is called inculturation and is imposed on the old Christian communities that have already adjusted to the two-world syndrome of local culture and foreign Christian culture, a deeper alienation is created for the individual personality. His or her diagram then looks like this:

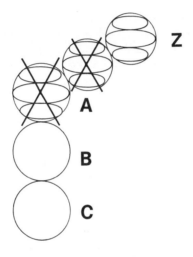

Even though Z is made to look as A once looked in the past, it is still a reality outside the immediate social experience of the person. There is an even heavier alienation when Z is designed by so-called experts who take items from non-Christian cultures and treat these as authentic expressions of the indigenous cultures. Any inculturation of the gospel has to be experienced by the people themselves as relevant to the social and psychic roots of their *contemporary* experience.

A vital element of the model of culture I have presented is its empirical existence. It is not inferred from obsolete texts, from ancient literature, or from academic history, but is constituted by the lived reality of the present, the beliefs, technics, and behaviors that are operative and alive in a particular society. Sometimes these may be implicit, even hidden, or they may lie dormant and can be revived; however, they are all locatable in the present-day reality. In this sense every social grouping, every clan has its own culture or subculture and can have the gospel related to its own unique history and cultural realities. So too the local Christian communities have a right to their own cultural identity however much they may have "borrowed" or "added" in the past.

A Hothouse Approach

And so in countries like India it is mostly in seminaries, religious houses, and formation centers that one finds signs of inculturating the gospel—not in the midst of local Christian communities. So "inculturation" as a cultural pattern in the church is still more of an "outside" import. When local Christian communities hear of inculturation as quoted by present-day theologians, they regard it with distaste, as though their cultural identity is being threatened, as though they are being pushed backwards into traditions that do not have a value in their present-day life. For them inculturation feels like the bed of Procrustes. In fact it is the Western churches that have benefited more from inculturation than local non-Western churches, as can be seen from Western theological studies. However, if inculturation of the gospel is to become a genuine process among the people, they need to be conscious of their cultural history and their present cultural realities. Tools and methods of analysis need to be designed as instruments for making a people culturally self-conscious and therefore able to monitor their future cultural history.

Women to Change Culture

Here the role of women can be very special. Women are important communicators of culture as they teach children through the family. Children imbibe their cultural categories basically through their parents, especially mothers. If the education of children in the house could be controlled, the whole cultural system of that society would be controlled. Is the church ready to make a daring cultural change through engaging the energies of the women? If women take up this challenge, every cultural system will be shaken to its foundations. Then inculturation will become reculturation and the truth of the good news will be heard from the housetops and the housewives.

Conclusion

Inculturation of the gospel today includes the following processes:

1. Removing the trappings of a Westernized colonial Christianity. Many local-church communities are still carrying cultural items that were once transported from Europe, even though these have been long discarded by Western churches, so they need to be educated to new options.

2. Realizing that there is no universal Christian culture, no one standard Christian lifestyle, no one ideal of Christian family life, and so forth. What is Christian in a culture has to be discovered within the terms of that culture.

3. A new respect for the myths, world-views, social values, customs, and so forth, and a search for what is Christian in them.

4. A search for the Christ experience and the trinitarian experience through the spirituality of the world religions and of ethnic religions.

5. Development of Indian theologies deriving from the charismatic insights of Indian sages, Indian sects, and Indian tribes.

6. Using traditional dress, dance, greeting forms, adoration postures, color, customs, and prayers found in local cultures, for the development of an inculturated liturgy connected to the daily life of the worshiping community.

7. Realizing that merely sitting crosslegged, singing *bhajans,* and doing *arati* is a thin veneer of inculturation in cultural values. Attitudes to life are not penetrated and shaken up by the spirit of the gospel.

8. Changing those attitudes and actions transmitted by the family system that tarnish the quality of human life and suppress equality and justice.

9. A conscious reflection on the assumptions and beliefs of a society, discerning what is life-giving from what is life-destroying and therefore evil.

10. An insertion into the struggles of the poor and oppressed; a fight against the people who perpetuate exploitation, discrimination, and a building up of just systems of work, production, and power.

11. Cross-cultural interaction whereby the Western and Westernized churches begin to learn and assimilate cultural values like those of silence, interiorization, cosmic harmony, the meaningfulness of dreams, the spirituality of fantasy life, simplicity of lifestyles, closeness to nature, the value of unconscious processes, methods of psychic healing, and so forth.

12. Raising the quality of human life and human relationships so that the Spirit has a fertile soil in which to complete the work of God's kingdom on earth.

I believe that we need to approach culture with the attitude that Nikos Kazantzakis approached the almond tree when he wrote:

> I said to the almond tree,
> "Sister, speak to me of God."
> And the almond tree blossomed.

Notes

1. Translated from the Latin of "Robert de Nobili on Adaptation," by S. Rajamanickam, S.J., De Nobili Research Institute, Palayamkottai (1971).

2. Sr. Shraddha, "The Indigenization of Religious Life," *Vidyajoti* (November 1975), p. 463.

3. Archbishop D. S. Lourdusamy, "On Theological Formation," *Vidyajoti* (October 1979), p. 400.

4. Ian G. Barbour, *Myths, Models and Paradigms* (London: SCM Press, 1974).

5. Lawrence LeShan, *Alternative Realities* (New York: Ballantine Books, 1976).

35

GHANA

Peter Kwasi Sarpong

As a church leader, I have often pondered over my role and the role of the church in my society. There was a time when the Christian religion was unknown among my people. During that time, my people were *very* religious. They had a clear idea of a Supreme Being, superlatively great, incomparable, unsurpassable, unique, creator of the universe, everything and all human beings. They regarded this Being as the final explanation of all phenomena. If they did not always seek direct contact with him through the liturgy, this was less because they doubted his accessibility, power, or mercy than simply because, reflecting over their own deferential attitude toward their political leaders, they considered it irreverent to approach this Supreme Being personally.

The idea of the Supreme Being was not restricted to some impersonal force. God was a personal spirit very much interested in the affairs of human beings. The final appeal in every dispute, he was thought to be a just, if patient, judge who would even out matters in the end, rewarding the good and meting out appropriate penalties to malicious people. Because of his exalted nature, he had left the supervision of the affairs of the world in the hands of his superintendents, the lesser deities. These were his sons, created by him, who manifested his qualities in one form or other. They were supposed to do his will and they could act only when and inasmuch as he allowed them to. While one of them represented his creative capabilities, another would manifest his wisdom, and yet another would be symbolic of his anger. He was not to be confused with these divinities in any way; neither, indeed, was he one of the pantheon of divinities. They wielded much power, but that was all in the interests, and on behalf, of God.

Next we had the ancestral spirits. These were human beings who had died, fulfilling certain conditions such as an irreproachable life and a good death. Having been

Peter Kwasi Sarpong is the Bishop of Kumasi, Ghana.

537

admitted into the place of bliss, they entertained a great interest in the affairs of the living and were concerned that their laws and regulations be meticulously kept.

Besides these three great categories of spirits, my people believed in other spiritual powers, potencies, and agencies, such as witchcraft, magic, totemism, and so forth.

These then formed the body of belief of my people. They still form the basis of my people's religious belief. The point to note is that, in those days, religion was part of life. It was not just something that one learned—a kind of fashion that one took after. It molded one's character. Indeed, so natural was religion to my people that there were no formal religious classes except for a few specialists like chiefs, priests, and war leaders. A child grew up in a religious environment and atmosphere. He or she took up the traditional religion through imitation, participation in religious celebrations, trial and error, punishment, observation, and the like. From cradle to grave there was no major turning point in a person's life that was not marked by one ritual or another. Religion was not, in the first place, a matter of belief. It was principally a matter of behavior. One had *to do* the will of the spiritual overlords. It was not a question of whether one was seen or not. The religious character of my people was such that they would not do anything forbidden just because nobody would see them. The spirits were watching, and that was what mattered.

The ancestors were a source of morality in the sense that most of the laws of society were said to have emanated from them, and they were keen on seeing that these laws were kept to the letter. Through periodic ceremonies, the fidelity to the ancestors was renewed, but at the same time it was believed that the ancestors had power only over their own kith and kin. There was, for instance, nothing like "the ancestors of the Ashanti nation." Ancestors were invoked with reference to particular clans or lineages. So the influence of the ancestors was restricted.

So also was the influence of the divinities. The divinities had sectional interests catering for those who put themselves under them, except in the case of great tribal divinities who were supposed to be concerned about the plight of the whole tribe. As a matter of fact, what devotees of one divinity were supposed to be to one another was not what they were supposed to be to those outside their fraternity. One might be obliged to speak the truth always to one's co-devotee without being in any way compelled to be truthful to others.

But when it came to the Supreme Being, the story was different. He was the undisputed source of all morality, universally acknowledged, with power over everybody. He had implanted in humans his conscience, a kind of "inner voice" by which he talked to us. He would judge human beings according to whether or not they listened to this inner voice in all that they did. He had created something called "character," and character was what distinguished humankind from any other living creature on earth. Persons with no character were not human beings. They were only clothed in the skin of a human being. The marks of character were many. Among the most important were kindliness, truthfulness, gratitude, faithfulness to promises, hospitality, friendliness, and courage.

I am not saying that among my people there were no crimes or sins. There were. What I have described was the ideal situation, but, in the words of Saint Paul, people do not always do what they know to be right and they do not always refrain from doing what they know to be wrong, so that I find myself doing precisely what I know I should not do!

Motivation, I think, is a powerful instrument in this whole area of morality. Something that the religion and the culture of my people lacked was the concept of enabling grace, helping one to do the right thing and urging one to abstain from doing the wrong thing. But by and large the religion of my people had a grip on them. Aberrant behavior was the exception and it was severely punished with unfailing consistency.

It is true that the religion of my people was this-worldly. It concentrated too much on the affairs of this world. A religion, if it was to be of any use, was to help one here and now. It had to help people overcome the thousand and one problems that they came across during the course of their lives. They were confronted with barrenness, poverty, sickness, the ever-present danger of death, shame, short life, and so forth. To these problems, people wanted an effective answer, and they found the remedy in their religion. Another area of conflict between the religion of my people and the Christian religion is that the former was dominated by fear instead of the love that Christ preached. Then, of course, there are some doctrines that could not possibly have been known by my people. If one talks about such mysteries as the Trinity, the Incarnation, the Holy Eucharist, the Virgin Birth, the Ascension, the Assumption, then one goes completely from the realm of primitive revelation to the realm of true revelation. These apart, it is a fact that my people, in the past, were honest. It is a fact that they were morally good. Crimes that have become so common in our day and age were simply unheard of in those good old days.

Induced abortion was an abomination. There was no prostitution. Contraception was unknown. Broad-day robberies, exploitation of the weak and the powerless could never take place. These are only a few examples. The tragic fact is that nowadays if you hear that a girl has had an abortion, then she must be either a Christian or educated or both.

What is wrong? This, for me, is what indigenization or inculturation is about. It is about *relevance*. It is about *influence*. It is about *effect*. The situation I have described is still what obtains among at least 60 percent of my people. They are simple. They believe in God, the ancestors, the divinities, and the rest of the potencies. Their religion has an impact on them. The function of religion for them is to produce the kind of good citizens who bring material blessings not only upon themselves and their relatives but also upon the whole community. Hence a person of wicked character is socially unworthy and unacceptable. The religion that my people practice has a salvific value—even if it is a salvific value with a difference in the sense that the accent is on the present life.

One must be "saved" in order that one may enjoy one's existence here and now. One must be "saved" so that others may be "saved" in like manner. One must be "saved" so that God may be pleased. The religion of my people has a humanizing effect on them in two distinct ways: it enables them to develop character and thus live in accordance with their conscience and their dignity as persons. It also enables them to live in union with God, the source and sustainer of humanity and of true salvation.

The gospel of Christ is a liberating gospel. It saves. It employs the most powerful weapon ever discovered—love. "Love" is a word that comes easily to our mouths but it has implications that are far-reaching, implications that are, indeed, terrifying. Lenin is once alleged to have said: "Give me a few men like Saint Francis and I can change the world without recourse to violence." This is what all people want. This is what peace is about. This is what Christ brought—peace on earth, peace through love. If then in the wake of the preaching of the gospel of peace, the gospel of liberation, the gospel of love, the gospel of unity, I see around me nothing but slavery, dissension, violence, and exploitation, and if casting my mind back I realize that this was not the case in the past, then it becomes not just a right but an obligation for me to find out what has gone wrong.

It cannot be the message itself that is to be blamed. It must be something connected with *the way* the message has reached us. The message itself is universal, it is sublime. It knows no racial or geographical barriers or boundaries. If it had been made *relevant* to my situation, things would not have taken the turn they have. If, when the seed was brought it had been realized that God had already prepared the Ghanaian soil for it and if, therefore, the message had come without the soil, it would have developed roots quickly, germinated, and borne fruit. The message of Christ is totally different from the cultural modalities in which it is preached and heard. Indeed, if the message of Christ is universal, then it must be at home in every culture. It must be adaptable to the needs and interests of all people. When Christ said, "Go and preach to all nations," this is what he meant. "Nations" implies peoples with their sensitivities and sensibilities, peoples with their peculiarities and idiosyncrasies.

Inculturation means indigenization. I understand by indigenization the process through which something originating outside a culture is made to take root in that culture and become native to it. Christianity becomes indigenous to us as the Christian message and its institutional form enter our cultural unit and undergo definition, explanation, adaptation, adoption, reinterpretation, and new discovery so that the people of my cultural unit can recognize that it belongs to them. Inculturation has nothing to do with the color of the person. It is an attitude of mind. It is a conviction that the gospel of the Lord is a saving gospel, which must be adopted by all humankind.

Inculturation, therefore, goes much deeper than the superficial use of drums or African or Ghanaian materials. Inculturation requires us to make a comprehensive examination of the forms and the practices of Christian worship and also of the cultural forms of Ghanaian life so that by the use of whatever is selected, adapted, arranged, or rejected, whether from the visual arts, the performing arts, crafts, architecture, clothing, concepts, or language, the Christian people of Ghana can, in their worship, know that God has entered in a decisive way and is continually entering into all of life and that they may have as rich a fellowship with him as is possible. The process of indigenization or inculturation is only one facet in the ever present experience of discovery and living the Christian life in changing circumstances. Our hope and aim is that Christianity may become truly indigenous to Ghana so that the universal and eternal gospel may be proclaimed with power in the Ghana of today and tomorrow.

Alas, for some mysterious reasons, this has not been the case. The gospel of the Lord takes a stand: it is not neutral. It takes a stand for the victims of poverty and oppression. It is against domination of whatever type. Yet so far, all around me, I see people in abject poverty, powerless, voiceless, outcast, helpless. The question is all too evident: *Where is the power of the gospel?* We have been able to do away with white imperialism, but the black imperialism substituted for it appears to be worse. Where is the power of the gospel in the political, social, and cultural life of my people? Indeed, does not the church appear to be like a foreign institution, something alien to us, something that should have flown on the same plane as the last governor-general? Why must this be so? These are some of the questions posed by the enlightened sections of my people.

In the light of what we know about traditional Ghanaian religion, why shouldn't we make use of our past and of our present background in order to make the Word of the Lord meaningful to our people? Nobody wants to preach syncretism. Much less do we want to preach heresy. We know that there are eternal and universal laws that cannot be tampered with. But surrounding these laws are elements that are clearly peripheral. Even with regard to what forms the central core of the Christian religion, we may easily shift the axis too much to one side. I like the answer that Bishop Zwani of Swaziland is reported to have given to a questioner who asked about the Mass: "Is not Holy Mass the most important thing in the Catholic church? How can you relate to your neighbor if you don't go to Mass?" The bishop's answer was that he wished that in countries like South Africa, the churches would be closed for a month so that people could not go to Mass for a month and would be forced to look at the justice aspect and to ask the Holy Father to say: "You have committed no sin if you don't go to Mass next month; go and do justice in the community." Scripturally, there are two poles in the worship of God: the *vertical relationship* to God, which cannot be divorced from the *horizontal relationship* with one's neighbor. Some of the prophets have said in angry terms: "God says, 'Now your prayers, now your sacrifices are stinking because you have forgotten the poor of Yahweh. You have forgotten the widows, you have forgotten the orphans, you have forgotten the aliens.' " One can never be true to God if one is not true to one's neighbor. Mass should never be used superstitiously, as though you need only go to Mass and things will happen.

It is an ideal of the Christian community that Holy Mass should signify the unity of the community. Any liturgy that does not reflect the community's life is a lie. For people to go to Mass and think that they are a community when they are not a community is a lie, because the Eucharist is a sacrament of unity that also expresses the unity of the community. If there is no unity in that community, it is a lie, and therefore this is one of the sacrifices that God would say he does not want because it no longer reflects the life of the Christian community. The eucharistic community must be a sign to the world that the building up of the community of humankind is the raw material of the kingdom preached by Christ in the gospel. The church invites the world, so to speak, to look to its eucharistic assemblies and to see the final destiny of all humankind foreshadowed therein.

In the end the Eucharist is to be the pattern and ideal for the life of the church as a community. The church in Ghana, as indeed anywhere else, will be an effective sign of the kingdom so much propagated by the gospel if it lives a eucharistic life, which is a life of solidarity and fellowship, of healing and of service.

Does not all this dictate the policy whereby the liturgy is made to reflect the life of the community? Does not this call for a policy whereby the liturgy speaks directly to the people so that the community idea expressed by the liturgy is lived outside the liturgical setting? And how can this be said to have been achieved when my people, who are lively, joyful, and by nature participate actively and fully in their traditional liturgical celebrations, are made to be passive onlookers when the Mass is being celebrated? Even after all the avenues opened by Vatican Council II, the Mass remains essentially the act of the priest celebrant and not of the community. What effect can prayers that are composed even before the actual situation is foreseen have on a people who are used to liturgical spontaneity? Not only are the prayers not relevant to their situation, beautiful as they are, they are composed with a mentality totally different from theirs. To think that these prayers are supposed to be *their* prayers! One could go on multiplying the examples, but what is the point?

Honestly, I do not know whether I am talking sense. But I am convinced that I am confronted daily with a situation that must be altered, a situation that I know requires a profound transformation. How to alter it and how to transform it, I do not know. I am not gifted in analyzing situations with lucidity. But like most of my people, I am practical. The gospel of the Lord has minimal effect on my people. Given the least excuse, when they want children, when they seek success in their business, or when they wish to be restored to their former bodily state of health, they have no qualms in joining newly founded African churches, or falling back on the worship of their traditional divinities.

The influences coming from outside, as a result of the tremendous social changes that are taking place, are eroding traditional values mercilessly. In the urban surroundings respect for authority is disappearing. Sexual morality is being frowned upon. Religion is being derided. There is no guarantee that, sooner or later, these influences will not invade or spread to other parts of the society. The consequences of the interaction between cultures are enormous. It breeds indifferentism, sometimes even cynicism. Hence the relevance of Christ and of his church is being questioned radically.

The church is definitely in a minority position. It is one hundred years old in Ghana. To mark this momentous landmark, the bishops of Ghana have chosen as the theme for reflection: Let Your Light Shine. Has the light of the church shone? The church, as an institution, has indeed done a lot in primary evangelization, in education, in health care, in agriculture, in social welfare, and so on. But what has the church done to produce Christians who shine out and are different from others? What has the church done by way of witnessing to Christ and to the efficacy and credibility of his word? As has been hinted at, in the church that I know now, the emphasis is placed on irrelevant matters: paying dues, buying choir robes, joining associations and organizations, wearing veils (by women) in church, and so on and so forth. This trend of affairs was not possible in a culture that was predominately religious.

To my mind, religion that is divorced from culture can never be effective, and the

Christian religion is gradually being divorced from the culture of the Ghanaian. The Ghanaian church must take up the issue of inculturation with the seriousness it deserves. For this, we need experts in every field: in such major areas as culture, liturgy, theology, and biblical scholarship. However, the church should not just be African. It should also be and remain Christian. Without the *sensus Christianus* we shall be creating a new religion but the *sensus Christianus* is not incompatible with openness. On the contrary, it calls for the *sensus Ghaniensis* as well.

We have also to take into account, of course, the heterogenous nature of our society. It is a pluralistic one, and even in a single community like Kumasi the pluralism may show itself very distinctly. What does one do about those whose ethnic origins are different from that of the local community—and they may form a significant minority? The problems of inculturation, therefore, are many.

Some people have come to regard the status quo as the orthodox situation to be retained by all means. In many cases, converting bishops and priests to a novel way of looking at reality is a gigantic task. Often, convincing Rome that one is as concerned about the purity of doctrine as anybody else is not an easy undertaking. If inculturation is to be effective, one has to be bold, original, sometimes even radical. These terms are not mine. They are old terms used by Vatican Council II. The task calls for imagination and, above all, perseverance and determination. It should start with small Christian communities in which, we hope, love may reign. It is not a task to be undertaken solely by one church. In most cases it demands the concerted action of several local churches and even action on the ecumenical level. For some ecclesiastical jurisdictions within the same province or conference, to go in for inculturation while others leave it out, can easily result in comparisons that may not be too Christian.

Finally, I would like to point out that the process of inculturation should aim at full and meaningful participation of the faithful, not just in liturgical functions (which is extremely important), but in the Christian life as a whole. The liturgy must be adaptable. People must be allowed to show spontaneity. They must be given the chance to participate fully in the mystery that is being enacted. Above all, the liturgy must be such that it speaks to the people just as the traditional religion did. Any truth that the gospel of the Lord expresses, especially in the liturgy, must not only be relevant, which it always objectively is, but must be *seen clearly* to be relevant to the Ghanaian, whether a university professor, or a taxi driver, or a farmer, or a hospital nurse.

36

A FRAMEWORK FOR A DISCUSSION OF INCULTURATION

Robert J. Schreiter, C.P.P.S.

Certainly one of the major tasks facing the local churches today is understanding what it means to have the gospel take deep root in the full life of their communities, and what this entails for their own senses of mission. There is a strong feeling in many local churches that there is a disparity between the experience of the saving power of Jesus Christ in their lives and the modes of expression now available for living, proclaiming, and celebrating that reality.

The reasons for this disparity are many. They have to do with the convergence of different cultural and religious traditions upon the local community, with the sweep of rapid social change, and with the ability of the larger church to come to grips with local problems and issues.

The purpose of this presentation is to provide a framework for looking at some of the questions surrounding the inculturation of the gospel; that is, the process whereby the Word takes root in the community and grows into its full stature. Since this presentation is for discussion, and hence heuristic in nature, it will try to present some guiding principles that are broad enough to encompass many of the problems that are arising, yet specific enough to be applied to concrete issues.

These principles are grouped around four headings: (1) the task of inculturation as part of the mission of the local church; (2) criteria for effective inculturation; (3) analyzing the relation between religion and culture; (4) responsibilities of the local church growing out of the task of inculturation.

Robert Schreiter, priest of the Society of the Precious Blood, is the Dean of the Catholic Theological Union at Chicago, and teacher of systematic theology and history of religions. He is also the Co-director of the Chicago Institute of Theology and Culture.

The Task of Inculturation as Part of
the Mission of the Local Church

To understand what inculturation is, and what role it plays in the development of the local church, one needs to begin by looking at how the Word of God becomes present to a local community.

The Word of God is not an abstraction to be reduced to a printed text. The experience of the West since the Gutenberg revolution has been to consider a word as something that can be stored and retrieved in a written text, as in the Bible or in a church document. However, the Word of God needs to be conceived of in a more dynamic fashion. The good news of God is not news unless there are not only speakers and message, but also hearers as well. The gospel is an event, encompassing speakers, a message, and the hearers. It is meant to be an act of performance, encompassing all three of these factors. Only then can the Word be the Word, fully alive.

If all three are to be fully engaged, the event of the Word must be performed within a circle of comprehension that allows speakers to speak and hearers to hear. This circle can be constituted in two different ways.

In the first way, the hearers are conformed to what the speakers perceive as the inner structure of the message. In this approach, the hearers are drawn out of their own culture into a reality somewhat similar to their own where they then receive the Word and carry it back to their home culture. An example of this is to be found in Orthodox Christianity, where the performance of the Divine Liturgy is the reality par excellence. All other realities are conformed to it and within it. The vision of church that underlies this approach understands the church as coextensive with the kingdom of God; hence it is the task of the world (and the culture) to fit into the church, rather than the church making its way within the world. Culture is attended to insofar as it helps with the transmission of the message as the speaker understands it. However, if the culture does not prove to be helpful, it needs to be put aside in the event of the Word.

A second approach sees the relationships in a different pattern. The message can be heard only if spoken in the accents of the hearers. Hence the speakers must first conform themselves to the contours of the hearers' world before enacting the event of the Word. From an ecclesiological standpoint, the vision here is that the church is not yet coextensive with the kingdom of God. While it may be the vanguard of the kingdom, the reality of the kingdom is a still larger, more encompassing, and yet to be realized phenomenon. The act of evangelization is essential to the church's growth into that fuller reality. But the church grows toward the larger reality of the fulfillment of the kingdom of God on earth, rather than the earth growing toward the fuller reality of the church. Hence the church (the speakers) needs to conform its understanding of the message to the reality in which the hearers (the culture) find themselves. In this approach inculturation is not just a step that might be helpful in a deeper understanding of the gospel; it is imperative in order that the event of the Word might take place at all.

This second approach is grounded in an even deeper guiding principle, which lies at the heart of the Christian experience, namely, the incarnation. God did not first conform us to his reality in the full revelation of himself to us in Jesus. Rather, Jesus appeared as the revelation of God under the concrete historical circumstances of a people in the Mediterranean basin. None of the cultural rules was suspended to make this revelation possible; yet within the limitations (and possibilities) of that culture the kingdom of God could be announced—and inaugurated—effectively.

The great paradox lying at the heart of the Christian message is that the universality of God makes itself manifest in the radical particularity of the concrete human condition. Jesus did not assume generic humanity and hover above our condition; he grasped it in all its concreteness and individuality. What this means is that God has chosen to reveal himself fully to us only when his Word is incarnated in concrete historical and social circumstances. When we try to escape that reality in our evangelization, we are like a message full of static noise, not yet tuned exactly on a cultural receiver.

What does this mean for the local church? It means, first of all, that the event of the Word is only fully enacted when the triad of speakers, message, and hearers is all in place. Hearers enjoy primacy over speakers because of the missionary nature of the message—it is meant to be heard. Thus within its own life the local church can be truly alive only when that Word is allowed to address the concrete realities of the immediate world in which the local church finds itself.

Second, when the local church evangelizes, it must allow the Word to be enacted within that same ambience of hearer, speaker, message. Or to put it another way, to the extent that inculturation takes place, to that extent the mission of the local church can be achieved.

But this respect for the primacy of the hearer brings with it a paradox. In the inculturation of the gospel we take special pains to respect the cultural pattern, yet at the same time proclaim the gospel, which, if effective, will bring about change in the culture. In fact, preaching the good news could be defined as the transformation of the human and social situation toward the kingdom of God. Are we proclaiming respect for the structure of a culture, on the one hand, and then setting about changing it, on the other? The paradox starts to look more like a dilemma for the local church.

This problem requires that we look more closely at the dynamics of transformation, which is part of the good news. I would like to suggest that, according to my reading of the preaching of Jesus, there are three guiding principles involved in that transformation: inclusion, judgment, and service. Only when these three principles are active together in the event of the Word does the paradox of respect and transformation not turn into an insoluble dilemma.

The principle of inclusion grows out of Jesus' invitation to all to become part of the kingdom. In contrast to competing notions of chosenness in that period, Jesus' conception of membership included not only those traditionally considered faithful, but also the terrorist (Zealot) and the collaborator (tax collector), the intellectual (scribe) and the social outcast (prostitute), the rich and the poor, the handicapped —indeed, all were invited to become part of the kingdom. While some might not respond positively to the invitation, the invitation was nonetheless there.

What this means for the local church's task of inculturation and evangelization is that all people and cultures, in principle, can become part of the kingdom and, a fortiori, the church. If God's creation is good, as the book of Genesis so boldly affirms, then all of it can be part of his saving reality. Hence a local church cannot too quickly exclude persons (e.g., oppressors), customs (e.g., polygamy), or social relationships (e.g., socialism) in the task of inculturation. God accepted in Jesus and Israel the full range of limitation of a concrete culture; the full enactment of the Word demands as much from us.

The principle of judgment grows out of Jesus' call to repentance and conversion as part of the entry into the kingdom of God. He is presented as speaking harshly to those situations where people insist on bondage to their sins or to their possessions. He calls upon the handicapped to give up relations of dependence that bind them to less than a full human reality.

To understand the force of the principle of judgment, one must pair it with the principle of inclusion. For effective inclusion in the kingdom of God, relationships that of their nature exclude from the fullness of participation by all need to be eradicated. Any relationships that cause restrictive bondage need to be identified and changed. Without these, inclusion is superficial or even hypocritical. Thus relations of domination and oppression, relations that foster dependence (as those which keep a local church a "mission church" for decades or centuries) need the word of judgment.

What this means for the local church's task of inculturation and evangelization is, first of all, that its sense of inclusion is not based on a cultural romanticism. Human cultures, while good, are skewed by sin. Second, the criteria by which judgment is undertaken are not drawn from the speaker's culture, but from what would constitute criteria of greater or lesser participatory inclusion within the hearer's culture. Thus, polygyny may seem to result in exclusion for some women according to the speaker's perspective; but it may mean the best way of inclusion of women in the fullness of life in the hearer's culture.

The principle of service grows out of Jesus' frequent words to the disciples as to how they should relate to the reality of the kingdom of God. In service *(diakonia)* one does the truth. One centers upon the other and so is able to listen and enter the other's reality. Just as the Father sent the Son to serve, so we in turn are commissioned to be servants.

What this means for the local church's task of inculturation and evangelization is that the posture of the local church in the enactment of the Word is a posture of service. Only within that attitude can the principles of inclusion and judgment be developed properly. Without service, inclusion can become a paternalistic gesture that patronizes rather than frees. Without service, judgment can become self-righteous. Service takes place within the network of relationships of the hearer's culture. In other words, service happens in areas where the hearer's culture needs service, not where the speaker's culture either thinks service is needed, or where it feels more comfortable serving.

When these three principles are held together, the transformation that the gospel brings changes the culture, but in an organic way. It helps the culture to become more truly itself, more truly alive, more redolent of the image of God, which, as a creation of God, it is meant to be. In so doing, the culture grows into a fuller realization of the kingdom of God and explicit manifestation of the saving grace of God in Jesus Christ. It becomes a dwelling place of God.

Criteria for Effective Inculturation

While we may agree that inculturation is the path to be followed in building up the local church, those who have been involved in this process know how difficult it can be. How does one avoid the pitfalls of paternalism or other forms of domination? How does one know when one has been successful in the inculturation process?

I would suggest considering an assumption and two criteria for evaluating the relative effectiveness of the inculturation of the gospel in a local-church situation.

The assumption flows from the definition of preaching the good news proposed above: the transformation of the human and social situation toward the kingdom of God. In view of this definition and what has been said about the operations of the inculturation process, we need to assume that the inculturated Word of God always addresses the central values that give form to a culture. An enactment of the Word that does not include these values within its purview falls short of inculturation. It is for this reason that the issue of transformation is an issue at all.

Given this assumption, and what has been said about the inculturation process above, the two criteria I would propose have to do with affirming the identity of the culture and locating the need for social change.

The criterion of affirmation of identity flows out of a theology of creation. If God created the world as his own, and found it good, then there must be much to affirm in a local situation. If God saw fit to reveal himself fully in the person of Jesus, who was a member of a concrete culture, and that message was meant to be spread to all cultures, then any cultural setting has more positive than negative qualities. This theology of creation and incarnation, well within the mainstream of Catholic Christian theology, forms the basis for implementing this criterion of affirmation of identity.

How would such a criterion affect the decisions of the local church as regards the inculturation process? First of all, it should slow the pace by which value and identity forms found in the culture are changed. The need to change values and identity forms often grows out of an inability of the speaker to comprehend rather than any inner need of the hearer.

Second, it should help keep in mind the crucial role of a sense of identity for a community. Key aspects of identity are inner consistency and continuity. These help a community to maintain a point of reference in the face of innovation. Without a sense of identity as consistency and continuity, humanity withers. We have instances of whole peoples disappearing when their identities are removed or suppressed, as among the Amerindians in the Americas. We also see what happens when individuals and families from rural and village situations are transplanted to urban settings. Thus this criterion requires not only an eye for what is changing, but also the speed with which that happens. Thus conversion is a gradual process, which occurs over a longer period of time than we had previously suspected. An insistence on rapid change usually has one of two consequences: either a veneer of Christianity will mask an untouched cultural identity, or that cultural identity is swept away and people die as a people.

Third, the criterion of affirmation of identity is linked with the idea of the inclusive character of the kingdom of God. Indeed, one could say that the kingdom of God cannot come to full flower until it has been the leaven of transformation in each human culture and situation, until every human culture has been included in its embrace. It is only then that the Word of God will have been fully enacted.

Questions one can ask in each local church about affirmation of identity would include: Do the decisions we make together in the local church enhance or detract from the peculiar identity of this community? Do these decisions more clearly indicate what kind of people we are and have been? Do these decisions more clearly indicate our possibilities and make us more alive in our current situation?

Using this criterion with these kinds of questions can help resolve debates about the so-called ethnographic approaches to contextualization, where there is a difference of opinion about incorporating old customs, rites, and myths in Christian praxis. If these retrievals enhance self-understanding in the present, they lead to positive inculturation. If, on the other hand, they are experienced as archaisms or restrictive of current social relationships (i.e., if they alienate the younger segment of the population or make them feel unduly controlled by the older segment of the population), then effective inculturation has not taken place.

The criterion of locating the need for social change flows out of a theology of redemption. If God found the world to be good, he also found it in need of redemption. In fact, the Christian experience of God is most clearly understood in the movement of salvation. The key to understanding God is to be found in the death and resurrection of Jesus. In other words, local situations are in need of varying degrees of transformation in order to come to their full realization in the kingdom of God. Death stalks our world in many forms, and the power of God is needed to overcome them. The good news of Jesus is that death can be overcome. Change shares in the ambivalence of death and resurrection—actualities dying and new possibilities being born in the ashes of the old actualities. Hence the cycle of death and resurrection, which God wrought in Jesus, offers us the hope of coping with the varying kinds of change either needed or forced upon a local community.

Because the message of the death and resurrection of Jesus is central to the gospel message, the enactment of the gospel, in addressing the central values of a culture, also highlights the incomplete realization of those values. It points out the need for repair in human relationships, for resolution of conflict, for facing rearrangement of social relationships as outside forces impinge upon the local community. Put theologically, the gospel highlights the need for salvation and redemption in the local church.

What does the inculturation process look like when this criterion is implemented? First of all, how previous self-understandings of the community relate to its current situation become more clear. One should be able to see more clearly how the accumulated popular religion of a community—be that Christian, non-Christian, or a combination of the two—has been developed to respond to needs of the local community in coping with its environment. By looking at points of social change, and the previous response of religious activity to them, one can find both what would constitute the deeper needs for change in the community and the paths toward resolution ordinarily taken. One thus discovers the range and flexibility of response within that community in the face of change. This is particularly important because what the speaker sometimes may identify as a need for social change would not be considered as such by the hearer. Trying to change the wrong things can retard or even impede the inculturation of the gospel.

Second, locating the need for social change can open up a local community more effectively to its neighbors, however proximate or global these may be construed. The intrusion of larger social, economic, and political realities is often a major area where the adequacy of a community's response is tested. Effective inculturation would mean that these needs are identified and that at least some process is brought forward for coming to terms with the realities engendered by these intrusions. As a minimum, this would mean that the local community does not try to seal itself off from the unavoidable realities.

Third, effective inculturation means not only identifying points of stress or ill in the local community, but also identifying pseudo-resolutions of those problems. Pseudo-resolutions are attempts at cheap grace, which do not really address the root of the problem. They either stop at mollifying the impact (an anaesthetic) or try to obscure the problem by addressing something else (mystification). Thus legislating against abortion, rather than addressing the problem of why people are seeking abortions, would be an example of mystification. Some problems become perennial because of the pseudo-resolutions applied. They work at closing the doors on possibilities that might lead to deeper transformations. Often pseudo-resolutions become enshrined in a culture out of a sense of helplessness in dealing with the enormousness of the problems at hand. That helplessness often can lead to a deeper experience of the power of God, who can save us precisely in those areas where we are least capable of helping ourselves.

When the criteria of affirming identity and locating the need for social change are used simultaneously, one can ascertain the relative effectiveness of the inculturation process. They are mutually related. Identity is not a static reality; change is part of living. Social change without some point of reference leads to alienation and inner death. Without identity, a community loses its soul; without facing change, it loses contact with the larger world of which it is a part. Theologically they represent the two dimensions by which we experience God: creation and redemption.

Analyzing the Relation between Religion and Culture

Understanding relations between religion and culture are difficult and subject very much to the local circumstances. Rural and urban situations, situations with competing religious systems, relatively stable and rapidly changing situations—all these circumstances affect how one goes about addressing the relations between religion and culture.

I would like to take but one perspective here; namely, what to keep in mind when analyzing the relation between religion and culture in the inculturation process. The suggestion is a simple one: do not use one set of analytic tools to study religious activity, and a second set of tools to study cultural patterns. In the question of inculturation, of how the gospel can take root in a local church, one cannot afford to separate out religion from culture in the analytic process.

To make this separation, as though religious activity can be clearly differentiated from cultural patterns and so translated from one culture to another, presumes that religion has to do only with the ideational, or world-view, dimension of culture. While religion certainly has an ideational component (it is a system of beliefs), the inculturation process requires closer attention to religion as an activity. Religious belief and language cannot be understood in abstraction from religious practice. In fact, I would suggest that it is far more important to look to religious practice than to religious belief in the inculturation process. Why would this be the case?

First of all, to start with explicit religious beliefs and then to look for corresponding religious practice means that the inculturation process might overlook major aspects of religious activity. Some religious activity may not be correlated with a religious belief (noninstitutional religion), and other religious activity might be seemingly opposed to stated beliefs (as in the case of the use of magic and witchcraft in Christian communities). To look for this correlation of belief and practice results primarily from experience in the last four centuries of Christianity, since the time of the Reformation. Prior to that time *religio* referred ordinarily to a special living-out of the gospel in a monastic or mendicant order (what we still call "religious life"). The Reformation insistence upon the Word of Scripture as the sole norm of faith and life, rather than a living tradition as the norm of faith and life, led to seeing Christianity primarily as a system of beliefs. Prior to that period, plurality in belief tended to be branded as heresy only when it led to heteropraxis, as in the denial of the authority in the community or refusal to participate in community and sacramental life. After the beginning of the Reformation, beliefs could be excoriated regardless of concomitant practice. To see religion primarily as a system of beliefs is certainly a minority view among religious systems even today.

If one insists upon using the same mode of analysis in studying both culture and religion, the inculturation process is aided in a number of ways.

First of all, less violence is done to the identity of the culture when religious change takes place. One of the things that religion is about is how to live in a given culture. If a local church is serious about inculturation, the inculturation of the gospel will mean that one can live in this culture better than before. Too often the introduction of Christianity has meant an alienating influence (as, for instance, in Japan or many parts of Asia).

Second, since practices tend to be more multivalent in meaning than ideational formulations, there is less danger of missing what is actually going on in a culture when one attends to practices.

Third, with the exception of democracies where religions are voluntary associations, religion is usually almost inextricably woven into the cultural fabric. Thus in parts of southern Asia, to be Thai (for example) is to be Buddhist. To forsake Buddhism is to denounce citizenship for all practical purposes. Using the same tools for cultural and religious analysis will allow development of concepts of "double belonging," that is, being a Buddhist Christian.

Fourth, the problem of syncretism becomes more manageable. When one applies this same principle to cultures long associated with Christianity, one realizes that a fusion of Christianity and culture is not only common, it is absolutely necessary. The real issue in most syncretism debates, it seems to me, is not whether such a fusion of religion and culture will take place, but who will control the process. Our insistence on setting up ideational standards for religion and religious inculturation, and using a different set of standards for cultural analysis, has led to unfortunate results in many instances. By not including healing, medicine, magic, and witchcraft as "religious" concepts, we have contributed to the development of the thousands of independent churches in Africa. If we were not willing to be total in our religious inculturation, others were.

In summary, using different methods of analysis for religion and culture reflects a bias about their relation coming out of particular North Atlantic circumstances. Both have to do with values, both have to do with coping with life, both have verbal expressions that incorporate those values with the experience of life.

Responsibilities of the Local Church
Growing Out of the Task of Inculturation

It would be my hope that the discussion in the previous three sections would indicate that inculturation is not merely an option for the local church, but an imperative. The local church cannot be true to its Lord or to its mission without attending to the dynamics of what constitutes the enactment of the Word of God, the questions of identity and social change, of understanding religion in its cultural setting.

The question of the local church's responsibility, however, is often phrased in terms of its responsibility in the task of inculturation toward the larger church. Coming as Catholic Christians from a history of some centuries of centralization, and the need to impose uniform standards to ensure reform of decadent situations, the challenge of inculturation is often obscured by an overriding sense of control. Catholicity and unity have always formed a major part of the Roman Catholic experience of church. How does this square with the imperative of inculturation as sketched out here for the local church?

There will be an inevitable tension, both in the areas of inclusion (How can this be included and contribute to the sense of unity?) and in judgment (What does a new practice say about the historic experience of Christianity?). But this tension should be a healthy dialectic, based upon the same principle of incarnation outlined above for the patterns of inculturation in the local church.

The church can be itself only when it is deeply rooted in its immediate contexts. Without this, the universal church becomes a form of mystification, floating above the human reality where God is at work. Thus the universal church needs the local church to call it to task, to keep it faithful, to remind it of the multiplicity of forms of human existence and need.

At the same time, the local church needs the community of other local churches which make up the universal church to provide it perspective in complex issues, which might be lost because of the nearness and intensity of those issues. The local church needs the challenge of the larger church to test its experience against that heritage of Christian faith shared by local churches past and present. And it needs the solidarity of other local churches in times of persecution. A sense of trust, a sense of patience, and a willingness not to try to solve everything all at once need to prevail.

Hence the local church's responsibility extends not only to the task of inculturation in its own context, but also to being accountable to other local churches who together share the responsibility for the transmission of the gospel.

Section 8

THE LIBERATION AND JUSTICE DIMENSION OF THE MISSION OF THE LOCAL CHURCH

Statement of the Question

In each local church the tasks of evangelization and, consequently, of liberation have specific characteristics, but the elements common to all local churches are: the essential relation of justice to the gospel message; the place/role of the poor in relation to the coming of the kingdom; and the prophetic role of those who call others to awareness of injustice.

Elements for a Reflection on the Question

- In fidelity to the gospel message, changes in sociopolitical and ecclesiastical conditions in one part of the world must be prepared, supported, and accompanied by correlating measures in other parts of the world
- Evangelization with respect to justice is a mutual and shared responsibility of the local churches everywhere
- The reluctance on the part of a local-church authority to face up to justice issues is a source of conflict at times
- The criteria needed for discerning the prophetic role among those who call others to an awareness of injustice
- The part played by multinationals in situations of injustice
- The meaning of working for justice from other than a North Atlantic viewpoint
- The consequences of the tendency in the North Atlantic regions for churches and aid agencies to measure missionary effectiveness by the input of personnel and material resources in other parts of the world
- The question of the right of those who are in situations of injustice because of institutional violence to have recourse to physical violence
- The distinction of roles among members of the local church: local/expatriate personnel
- The implication of Christian witness in situations of injustice
- The process of enabling persons to seek justice and peace without imposing outside or foreign aims
- The relation of the church to international organizations working for justice

Related Questions

- Within your local church, how is the relation of justice and liberation to the proclamation of the gospel message understood concretely?
- How does the church relate to the poor in your situation?
- What are the situations that seem to call for prophetic witness?
- What happens when the church consciously chooses to be a church *of* the poor?
- From past experience, how should problems of injustice be handled in the future in the context of the gospel?

37

NEW ZEALAND

Brian Ashby, D.D.

Statement of the Question

The local church, for the purposes of this paper, is the Catholic church of New Zealand. It consisted of four dioceses up to March 1980 and now has six, the two new dioceses being formed by dividing the Archdiocese of Wellington and the Diocese of Auckland.

Catholic Profile

There are 478,530 Catholics (1976 census), mostly of Irish extraction. Evangelized originally by the newly formed Society of Mary from 1838, the church has depended heavily on Irish diocesan clergy from the missionary colleges, especially All Hallows in Dublin. Likewise, religious congregations came mostly from Ireland, their task being, in the main, to teach in Catholic schools and to nurse in hospitals and in institutes for the aged. New Zealand has had a national seminary since 1900. Indigenous personnel in both clergy and religious are now the vast majority. In the 1950s we counted one priest for every five hundred Catholics. Now I use a rule of thumb of one priest for every five hundred families.

In general, the New Zealand church has all the attributes and facilities of a developed church. In the last decade it has produced its own set of catechetical texts based on its directory, *We Live and Teach Christ Jesus.* I believe that this is a magnificent effort for a comparatively small Catholic community.

Geography and Population

New Zealand is a long, narrow country the size of Italy, consisting of two main islands and extending from the subtropical north to the temperate south. There is a drift to the north, so that Auckland, the northernmost city, ranks as a modern me-

Brian Ashby is the Archbishop of the Roman Catholic Archdiocese of Christchurch, New Zealand.

tropolis with its 600,000 people. In fact, two-thirds of the total population of about 3 million reside in the northernmost provinces.

Auckland is said to be the largest Polynesian city in the world, the local Maoris and the post-World War II immigrant Pacific islanders being concentrated in that city and its environs. There are some 270,000 Maoris and some 61,354 Pacific islanders in New Zealand.

Having been an English colony, and now an independent member of the British Commonwealth of Nations, New Zealand was colonized by English, Irish, and Scots. A sparing immigration policy has meant that this mixture has remained constant, except for a significant and beneficial immigration of Dutch in the period 1950–70. Government, legislation, social institutions, and spread of churches reflect the United Kingdom parentage, though New Zealand pioneered many aspects of welfare-state policy.

Economic Development

A capitalist society in the free-enterprise model, New Zealand is a cheap source of electrical energy, which is attractive to foreign investors, for example, the Australian-based Comalco (aluminum smelter). It has the faults of this system: social tension based on the widening gap between rich and poor, liquidation of businesses (mostly small) that become the victims of efficiency, unemployment and disillusion of workers, with the profit motive resulting in industrial strife.

For this study, it is important to note that (1) the geography and the compactness allow for relatively easy communication; what is done in one diocese will be quickly known in the others, and imitated or spurned according to their assessment of the worth of the initiatives; and (2) Auckland's size and the concentration of Polynesians pose special problems for the civil and church community there.

Ecumenism

New Zealand is almost wholly Christian—Anglicans (29.2 percent), Presbyterians (18.17 percent), Catholics (15.3 percent) heading the mainline churches and the American-type sects. While apathy and clerical unwillingness impede the growth of ecumenism, there have been great advances. New Zealand figures prominently in the Secretariat for Unity booklet "Ecumenical Collaboration at the Local, National and International Level" (1975), and even more strikingly in the composite report on world ecumenical activity for its November 1979 meeting of delegates of ecumenical commissions. Probably the fact that Catholics are a minority has given some urgency to the ecumenical task.

Certainly in the liberation and justice dimension of the mission of the church, the New Delhi principle is fully adhered to, our Ecumenical Secretariat on Development (ESOD 1975–) being a structured expression of this collaboration. While church courts other than the Catholic have probably shown greater courage in addressing themselves to topical issues of injustice, for example, racism, I believe that the greater unity of the Catholic church has meant that awareness-raising on the subject of this paper has had a deeper and wider spread than in the other churches. A few years ago ESOD convened a meeting of church funding and mission agencies. The philosophy of most of those represented was antediluvian in terms of modern development theory as compared with the Catholic stance. However, it can safely be said that in the liberation and justice dimension the mission of the Catholic church in New Zealand has an ecumenical counterpart and indeed, in some initiatives, is organically united with the agencies of the National Council of Churches (NCC).

Elements for a Reflection on the Question

General Orientation to the Pacific

In several ecumenical forums, the question has arisen as to whether the New Zealand church should relate exclusively to Southwest Oceania or be more broadly based in its orientation. In fact, we believe that we should relate in a special way to Asia, and especially Southeast Asia as well as to Oceania. Project funding has reflected this belief. It reflects the political reality, New Zealand having been linked with Asia particularly through SEATO (South-East Asia Treaty Organization). Politically and commercially, it has strong ties with the United States, even to the extent of being thought of as a puppet on the American string (e.g., Vietnam war). Its heaviest commercial concentration remains with England, as the recipient of its agricultural products still by far the main export, though the Middle East and Japan are increasing in importance as trading partners.

As regards the Catholic church, however, our mission effort is directed especially to Southwest Oceania. The 1980 *New Zealand Catholic Directory* lists fifty-three priests serving in this area. They are matched by religious Sisters, especially Missionary Sisters of the Society of Mary and the Marist Brothers of the Schools. To all intents and purposes, the Pacific sphere of influence coincides with the territories entrusted to the Society of Mary in the creation of the Vicariate Apostolic of Western Oceania. It is noteworthy that the religious congregations cited are of the Marist family. Other religious congregations are also active, and the same area has been the site of post-World War II foundations of New Zealand-based orders in their zeal for a missionary foundation. Southwest Oceania, in return, especially Tonga and Samoa, has been a good recruiting ground for vocations. In latter years, too, New Zealand missionary personnel can take much credit for such developments as the booming Pacific Regional Seminary in Suva and the rapid indigenization of church personnel in the Pacific islands. While the apostolic pro-nunciature in Wellington also embraces Tahiti and the Maquesas, only the Cook Islands of the traditional Picpus territory comes markedly within the New Zealand sphere of influence.

For many years the New Zealand Catholic Women's League has, through its branches, adopted a "mission station" in the Pacific. Secondhand clothes, books, and food, have given way to cash donations to these missions, the result being an impressive $65,000 in the past twelve months.

Following the resolution of a combined meeting of the episcopal conferences of Australia, New Zealand, Papua New Guinea and the Pacific (CEPAC) on the occasion of the visit of Pope Paul VI to Sydney in 1970, a far-reaching development conference was held in Suva, Fiji, in 1972. Its theme was "The Catholic Church and the Peoples of the South Pacific." Its aim was to site a conference in the Pacific, rather than a metropolitan country, to hear local voices and to promote regionalization. Their message was clear: "We have problems like the evolution from a subsistence economy and land tenure; you go home and solve yours." A further aim—to encourage the formation of justice and peace commissions or other human development agencies—has not been immediately successful. However, the conference, inspired initially by the New Zealand Justice and Peace Commission, was a trailblazer. Further conferences in Tonga (1975), Suva (1978), and Noumea, New Caledonia (November 1979), have considerably advanced all the aims of that original conference.

It is hoped that at a combined meeting of the same bishops conferences in Sydney, May 28–31, 1980 *(a)* final approval will be given to the Pacific Partnership for Human Development (see below) and *(b)* a confederation of Oceanian Bishops' Conferences will be approved for further investigation and establishment. As regards this latter, besides the concept of episcopal collegiality, such arguments as help to the Tahiti church in protesting against nuclear testing (Mururoa Atoll) have been advanced.

Mutual and Shared Responsibility

The New Zealand church has shared the world development of aid and development philosophy, from relief and emergency funding, to donor-recipient project-funding, to the present partnership concept, with its emphasis on full human development and reformation of structures of social injustice.

In the last decade, there have been significant developments.

1. Australia and New Zealand agreed to share project funding in Oceania, Australia (Australian Catholic Relief—ACR) to fund Papua New Guinea and Asian projects, New Zealand (Catholic Overseas Aid—NZCOA) to fund Pacific projects, monies for these purposes being transferred to the respective agencies.

2. Southeast Asian countries (India then excepted), Australia, Canada, and New Zealand joined together in the Asia Fund, which has become the Asia Partnership for Human Development (APHD), which I understand is fast becoming a model for other parts of the world, with seven "donor" countries in it.

3. The evolution of the Pacific Partnership for Human Development (PPHD) has been described above. The statement of goals and criteria describes the essence of such a partnership. In 1979 $100,000 of New Zealand Lenten Campaign's $120,000 went to the partnerships: ecumenically and civicly the New Zealand church is a close collaborator.

4. Ecumenically, the Commission for Evangelization, Justice and Development (CEJD) works closely with Christian World Service (CWS) of the National Council of Churches. Joint funding occurs often; the executive secretary of the commission, the Reverend E. J. Curnow, is a board member of CWS, and from March 1980 the commission has invited the director of CWS to join its development committee.

One of the resolutions of the Suva Conference (1972), at which there were ecumenical observers, was to hold an ecumenical consultation on development. For New Zealand this took place in 1973, resulting in 1975 in the formation of ESOD. Headed by a full-time executive officer, the Reverend M. Elliott (Anglican), the secretariat has four members each from the Catholic church and the National Council of Churches. Described as a low-profile, grassroots agency, ESOD has been a useful tool in awareness-raising on human development problems overseas and in New Zealand.

The postwar governmental and community based CORSO has worked in close liaison. It has in the main been staffed and stimulated by Christian activists, and has leaned heavily on church support. In 1973 CORSO tried to divest itself of its image as a relief organization, losing much of its status-quo support in the process. In 1979 government withdrew its financial support on the grounds that it was too "political," the word being defined by a high court judge in another case as "the aim to indoctrinate to one particular point of view." This, the judge saw, as being incompatible with "charitable," the usual umbrella under which government supports voluntary agencies.

Writing in protest on CORSO to the minister of external affairs I noted that government had chosen to come down on one side of the worldwide debate regarding accountability for the way in which "donor" money is spent.

CORSO remains a force for conscientization. Even the bad publicity it attracted in 1975 and 1979 has done much to raise awareness of the issues involved.

Overall, the bishops remain tolerant. In a spirit of Christian charity and genuine concern for justice, they allow the debate to go on in the New Zealand church. The debate certainly goes on. Currently every aspect of the church's activity in the justice and development field is under fire, though a courageous decision of the New Zealand Bishops' Conference at its Low Week 1980 meeting will probably silence some of the critics and give new heart to the social justice activists. The decision was to confirm the permanence of its Commission for Evangelization, Justice and Development, its membership, and members' mode of appointment for a period of three years.

The elements seem to be these: (1) New Zealand Catholic Overseas Aid (1968–78) was born in the wake of Vatican Council II and *Populorum Progressio*, with their stress on human development; (2) the Christchurch Diocese had already laid the foundation of an aid and development policy from 1960; (3) all the bishops had been schooled in the ideals and emphasis of Vatican II; (4) NZCOA was led by an able and far-seeing bishop, the late Cardinal Delargey; (5) the churches and secular activists were caught up in the vision of 1 percent aid with all its implications, especially of the causes of injustice.

Then came the seeming reversal: (1) economic recession with the government aid vote being an easy one to slash, especially as the electorate was not very vocal in its support; (2) the growing strength of the right-wing voice in the church; (3) the lessening of emphasis from the universal church, especially in the change of direction of the Pontifical Commission for Justice and Peace in the past five years; (4) undoubtedly, the greater awareness of the social justice activists in the real causes of poverty and their stress on the need for domestic education.

"Give a man a fish and he has a meal; teach a man to fish and he has a livelihood" was a beautiful concept in 1973, when we had our first nationwide promotion of "Action for World Development" (used in Australia in 1972 in preparation for the International Eucharistic Congress at Melbourne). Now such a slogan has overtones of political dynamite.

Liberal capitalism, the multinationals, and so on are not popular windmills to tilt at. Much less popular is to support a domestic issue like Bastion Point (Maori—indigenous people—land) or HART (Halt All Racist Tours, in connection with sporting contacts with Southern Africa).

These issues have been supported by the Christchurch Commission and ESOD with vociferous national reaction. Last year in one diocese twenty parishes refused to send the Lenten Campaign collection to their commission. The Lenten Campaign itself was in jeopardy, and in the last few years has been under suspicion, though it too has been confirmed by the bishops at their Low Week 1980 meeting.

Naturally any talk of using the tools of social analysis has an immediate reaction of neo-Marxism with scant regard for the prophetic and meticulous tracing of the way in *Octogesimo Adveniens*.

The reaction of one bishop to the newly born Pacific Partnership for Human Development (Suva, 1978) nearly saw its strangulation. In fairness, the reexamination at Noumea (1979) has probably put it on a sounder basis, and the controversy over it has probably been a better catalyst for local development committees in the Pacific than years of patient sweet-talk.

Probably, however, the block does not lie at the episcopal level. Unease there has been among them, misunderstanding also. However, as noted regarding the 1980 Low Week meeting, the bishops see justice as an integral part of evangelization. It was music to hear one bishop, who hates confrontation, say at the meeting, "It is inevitable that in the justice and liberation field there will be areas of tension."

So, at the hierarchical level, blame lies with some priests, as in every aspect of the renewing church. Lack of reading and reflection has meant that they do not relate liberation and justice as integral to the proclamation of the Word. Moreover, by temperament and traditional ministry they do not feel free to encourage or even permit laity to exercise their competence in this field.

At the lay level the principles are professed by many. Application of the principles to concrete issues is something else again. In the Diocese of Christchurch, it can almost be guaranteed that forums such as the Diocesan Pastoral Council will be split down the middle on justice issues such as anti-apartheid, nuclear testing, visits of nuclear warships, and so forth. At least, I take some pride that 50 percent have been conscientized to some extent.

Finally, our ecumenical involvement in ESOD is currently under review by the bishops, though a decision to withdraw from it has not yet been made. As chairman, I am encouraging the executive officer and the secretariat to raise the low-profile grassroots approach. One problem is the question "What does it do?" "We do not know it." The other is that, with relatively strong commissions for evangelization, justice, and development in three dioceses, Catholic agencies do not need to call on its resources as much as the other churches do. However, in regard to the first problem, the National Council of Churches has examined it closely and has not, at this time, found it wanting.

I have proposed to the bishops that from September 1980 three-quarters of the cost of ESOD be borne by our commission as an educational project rather than as a direct and escalating cost on conference funds. CWS, the aid agency of the NCC, has been responsible for ESOD costs from its establishment. This makes it much easier for the NCC executive to be approving.

As a reflection, education to justice and liberation has been a major element in the whole question of reluctance and opposition. Is not the intention of the donor that all money go to overseas projects and emergency relief? New Zealand is finding some of the answers. The national and diocesan commissions are, in fact, funding domestic educational projects; some donors are giving specifically for these; as noted, it could be assumed that 50 percent of Christchurch donors, at least, are giving with a clear or vague idea that justice, and not just charity, is involved. However, accountability for the spending of donors' money remains a live issue.

In defending our social-justice activists against the accusation of being neo-Marxist, especially leveled by one Catholic weekly, *The Tablet*, I wrote a guest editorial for the other, *Zealandia*. In other forums I have used the checklist given by Pope John Paul II at Puebla for their orthodoxy (part 3, nos. 33–34).

It is probably inevitable that some activists, faithful to the church and well grounded in its teaching, attract followers who do not understand the theology so well. Thus the justice and liberation theme is involving a considerable number who have ceased to be practicing Catholics, but whose motivation for their involvement is undoubtedly Christian. *Octogesimo Adveniens* warns that such people could become identified as groups holding a philosophy alien to Catholic teaching. There are a possibly growing number of extremists. They do not seem to have emerged as a group holding an opposing ideology.

My belief is that a strengthening of existing diocesan commissions, and the establishment of new ones, by a process of education and activity will reabsorb some of the extremists and attract potential activists into their circle. For the rest, it is regrettable but true that the process of "open church" must lead to some casualties as people mistake humanism for Christian humanism in this field. We have already seen it in the defections of priests and religious who have misunderstood selfhood for personhood and real maturity.

Multinationals

Our National party government has recommitted itself to the doctrine of free enterprise. This seems to include massive investment in our country by multinationals, particularly in the fields of ore refinery and synthetic petroleum production. The multinational comes under fire by the activists for all the usual reasons. It is probably not discerned as an evil as keenly as it would be in an international third world forum (e.g., BISAV, Baguio City, Philippines, 1979).

The Joint Working Committee has had three meetings (nine days) on the nature of corporate morality, with particular reference to multinationals. It has also participated with the governmental New Zealand Planning Council and Commission for the Future in reflecting on the same and allied subjects.

I am personally torn between wanting to see our country find an economic base more stable than our predominantly agricultural one and realizing the dangers of massive foreign investment.

The North Atlantic Mentality

In the late 1960s the Christchurch Diocese investigated the possibility of sending a "mission team" to a missionary diocese. The project was abandoned when the Senate of Priests agreed with the expression that it would be "pouring priests and resources down the institutional hole." This remark was leveled particularly at the Pacific nations, which have tended to adopt Western models.

Self-reliance, as a concept of human development, with the mutual interdependence that follows, is gaining some credence in Pacific political and economic evolution, but is less evident in church affairs. We hope that PPHD will be a genuine two-way process with all partners sharing in the giving and learning experience.

The partnership concept already explained points to some understanding that the measure of missionary effectiveness does not lie in providing personnel and material resources alone. What of the Catholic Women's League branches that have "adopted" mission stations? Are they purely paternalistic or indulging in ecclesial colonialism? For the Catholic Women's League (CWL) the question is pertinent. Would they do better to fund through PPHD? At the partnership level we are agreed that now is not the time to press the point. Let PPHD prove itself. At CWL level it is fair to say that the dichotomy between paternalism (maternalism?) and partnership has created considerable tension within their ranks, and that there is an acute awareness of that dichotomy.

The Society of Mary, the Missionary Sisters of the Society of Mary, the Sisters of Saint Joseph of Cluny, the Marist Sisters, and the Marist Brothers are the religious institutes with the greatest stake in the missionary enterprise of the Pacific. It is hard to judge their conscientization in the justice and liberation aspects of their apostolate.

In 1976 an abortive attempt was made to establish a National Mission Council consisting of representatives of the mission-sending institutes as well as social-justice elements of the local church. The aim of the late Cardinal Delargey was to ensure that the mission-sending philosophy was consonant with the justice and liberation philosophy of the local church, as well as to widen the base of the Pontifical Mission Aid Societies. The council has never been reconvened.

At a different stage of the evolution of development philosophy, many parishes "adopted" mission parishes with largely paternalistic aims. For these, continued adoption has become a matter of routine parish sentiment and loyalty. Parishes, recently dissenting from the more radical issues of justice and liberation, have tended to find some missionary project as the object of their Lenten or other collections—a protest in the paternalistic model.

Probably the greatest problem in this section lies in the missions themselves. This essay already reveals the reluctance of local churches in the missions to set up consultative procedures and to trust lay competence. The aid agency as a money-club still predominates.

The PPHD controversy was centered on the alleged unwillingness of ACR and NZCOA to fund institutional projects, for example, churches, seminaries, schools. It was, in fact, agreed at Noumea that such institutional purposes could be included in genuine human advancement. This has expression in the criteria agreed on at Noumea. With the funding mechanism unlocked at the Noumea meeting, the Pacific Regional Seminary immediately received a grant of $100,000.

Pacific watchers believe that its development is being inhibited by the amount of development money available both from government sources, including the superpowers, and from voluntary agencies. Such an assertion would need, were space available, to be documented by an incursion into the world strategic value of the area. PPHD is presently initiating a research project on this very subject.

Even at church level, however, it does seem that both Papua New Guinea and the Pacific are in no way fully dependent on PPHD, nor indeed on the Sacred Congregation for the Evangelization of Peoples. The worldwide religious institutes that staff the missions and the major European and American funding agencies seem to lend a ready ear to the pleas of enterprising bishops and their cooperators.

Hence, as a reflection, it seems necessary that massive education on the liberation and justice dimension of the mission of the local church needs to be pursued at the very level of the missions themselves among both indigenous and expatriate personnel.

The Question of Violence or Nonviolence

Nonviolent strategies have been preferred, and have been the subject of a variety of seminars for small numbers of participants over the past decade. The Hawaiian peace-activist, Jim Albertini, has recently concluded a national lecture tour advocating this view. Several Quakers and a Taizé Brother have been among his predecessors.

Local Expatriate Personnel

The question has little significance in our milieu.

The Implication of Christian Witness

The standard accusations of politicians stung by criticism, of businessmen hurt by statements on capitalism or free enterprise, and so forth is that church people are meddling in politics, or abetting Marxism.

The normal counsel to Christian activists is "Be prudent," that is, in many contexts, "Do nothing." One takes heart from Pope John Paul II's words in his address to members of the Secretariat for Christian Unity (February 1980): "Is not courage an essential ingredient of prudence?" After hearing, within the space of a few days, Jim Albertini and Senator Diockno of the Philippines, both jailed (repeatedly in the former case, and for two years in the latter), I encouraged participants by suggesting that we could suffer a lot more than we were doing in our Christian cause.

We live in a democracy where free speech is a right, where assembly is mostly lawful, and where our greatest boast is our egalitarianism. Stepping out of line is probably a greater sin than the reason for it.

Outside Aims

As noted, the partnership concept is a genuine attempt at enablement. In both PPHD and APHD the project choice and the funding are made in partnership. One of the remaining criticisms of PPHD is the idea of a Pacific-based executive committee meeting *twice* a year in a different Pacific nation after a period of exposure in that locality. Yet that practical consequence is at the heart of the partnership concept. With our own Maoris, too, there is a growing desire to make their own decisions about their future.

Relationship to International Organizations

The New Zealand Commission for Evangelisation, Justice and Development is a member of Caritas Internationalis, its executive secretary, the Reverend E. J. Curnow, presently serving on two of its committees. He and Jocelyn Franklin of the National and Auckland commissions have regularly attended meetings of Caritas. As well as APHD we have a lively contact with the Asian churches through the office for Human Development of the Federation of Asian Bishops' Conferences. Bishops have attended BISA meetings on three occasions. New Zealand has long since had a network of relationships with the various development agencies of the church in many countries. Our commission will send two delegates to an Asian consultation in Indonesia to help in the organization of Lenten campaigns in the region. Among other influences, the personal work of Father E. J. Curnow at the international level has attracted into the Pacific partnerships the agencies of Canada, Ireland, and France, with others also seeking membership. Catholic Relief Services of the United States of America seems to operate on a different basis.

Related Questions

Justice, Liberation, and the Gospel Message

The name "Commission for Evangelisation, Justice and Development" is clumsy. At our Low Week 1980 meeting, the bishops recommended a more suitable title. It, however, answers the query in this section very clearly.

In 1973 the first meeting was held to group the existing Justice and Peace Commission, New Zealand Catholic Overseas Aid, and missionary interests in the traditional sense under one umbrella. This followed the logic of the message of Pope Paul VI from Samoa in 1970 and the 1971 Synod of Bishops statement on Justice in the World; it predated the more striking affirmations of the essential relationship between the proclamation of the Word and the liberation from social sin in the deliberations of the 1974 Synod with their magisterial expression in *Evangelii Nuntiandi*. The preamble of the commission's charter quotes opposite passages from *Evangelii Nuntiandi*. In the changes the commission has faced during its evolution and establishment that preamble has not been challenged. The changes have included the writing of several constitutions, challenging at bishops' conference and diocesan commission level of the model and its mode of operation. This has included reversal of some conference resolutions during the gestatory period 1976–79.

Of interest has been a significant interplay of national and diocesan thrusts. Both the Justice and Peace Commission and New Zealand Catholic Overseas Aid were established as national bodies. Three dioceses had or developed a titular Catholic overseas aid committee to arrange for the funding of the NZCOA from the diocesan Lenten campaign and to manage the one-third of the Lenten collection and other local donations retained by them.

Auckland had the framework of a commission as part of the overall pastorale mandated by its bishop, the then Bishop Delargey.

In the six years of evolution of the commission, Auckland, Wellington, and Christchurch set about establishing more authentic commissions for evangelization, justice, and development ("peace" having lost favor in the title as not expressing the full reality). They also moved significantly to include a mission thrust, that is, one based on proclamation of the Word. These evangelization or mission committees are still in a fledgling state, but I believe they will do much to revitalize appreciation of the missionary apostolate of the church in the sense of primary evangelization.

Paradoxically, members of the national CEJD have at their three meetings voted by a majority not to have national committees for evangelization and justice. The Development Committee is the project-funding one and was set up at the first meeting in July 1979 as a necessary adjunct for the commission's funding operation.

"Evangelisation" in the title of the national commission therefore remains at present rather empty. It must be said that the national director of PMAS is a member ex-officio with full voting rights. It can also be said that the Mission Sunday collection has not suffered through the Lenten Campaign but has risen significantly. The unwillingness to have a national committee is the basic reason for the National Mission Council being in recess, as noted above.

"Justice" in the title is in the same position, though our collaboration with ESOD and CORSO assures that there are national agencies speaking on topical issues of injustice.

In declining to set up at this time national committees of CEJD, members see the need to preserve diocesan autonomy and to strengthen or establish diocesan commissions.

In summary: (1) sociologists could make much of the initial national bodies stimulating the formation of diocesan bodies; and diocesan bodies, as they have grown, seeking a new relationship with the national commission; (2) the commission's establishment and operation clearly illustrates the relatively easy communication throughout New Zealand; (3) within the official church, therefore, and in diocesan structures the relation of justice and liberation to the proclamation of the gospel message has concrete structural expression.

At our March 1980 meeting members of CEJD, while again by majority declining to set up national committees, agreed on a national consultation on a justice theme, namely, the use of energy, and one on evangelization in the light of justice and liberation. This latter, as the bishops noted, at their Low Week 1980 meeting, bids fair to assume maximum importance: *(a)* come to grips with differences in ideology and method within the commission; *(b)* be an educative process for the whole New Zealand church; *(c)* highlight that justice and liberation are a constitutive element of the gospel task; *(d)* clarify the direction CEJD should take in the future.

The Relation of the Church to the Poor

In the welfare state who are the poor? Are they the relatively poor economically or the spiritually impoverished affluent? Where does power lie and where are the marginalized? Social activists address themselves to these questions helped by a variety of secular studies such as those coming from the government-sponsored Commission for the Family and the New Zealand Social Services Association.

The church's traditional charitable outreach is well developed, through specific religious institutes, Catholic Social Services of each diocese, Vincent de Paul Society, and so forth. In general this outreach must be considered one of welfare rather than questioning of the structures, of working for the poor rather than with them, so that they can have a say in deciding on issues.

For over a century, Catholic schools have dominated the pastorale of the New Zealand church. They number 304 and enroll some 64,000 children. They have been the prime object of resources of parishes, religious institutes, clergy, and bishops.

They suffer the limitations ascribed to them in *Justice in the World*, but have also been the spine of New Zealand Catholicism. Currently some 50 percent of Catholic children are not in our schools, but the commitment of those parents using them has never been higher.

In the context of the question of the church as a church *of* the poor, it would seem necessary for the church to divest itself of its schools if it is to be free enough to be a poor church *of* the poor. Current negotiations with the state to integrate our schools with the state system may eventually allow for a less-distorted pastorale where personnel and resources can be devoted to the genuine poor in a more balanced way.

Analysis for Prophetic Witness

1. The general problems of a capitalist welfare state organization.
2. Need for critical oversight of the consequences of free-enterprise policy.
3. The promotion of a genuine multicultural society, especially in relation to Polynesians, including indigenous Maoris, these latter being the center of a cultural revival. In 1977 the bishops commissioned a study by the anthropologist G. A. Arbuckle, S.M. His survey *The Church in a Multi-cultural Society* is highly regarded.

The survey involved a wide cross-section of the New Zealand church, but its findings and recommendations have not yet penetrated at depth.

4. Conscientization within the church. The official catechetical directory *We Live and Teach Christ Jesus* gives prominent space to the justice theme.

5. Cooperation with the poor elsewhere, discernment of New Zealand projects for funding, spread of the partnership philosophy.

6. Critical appraisal of racism, unemployment, treatment of welfare-state beneficiaries, use of energy resources and finance on defense rather than on welfare.

The Future

1. The remarks above regarding integration of Catholic schools may well point the way to the future. Assured of their "special character" by the 1975 Private Schools Conditional Integration Act, Catholic schools should be able to continue their vital apostolate with state salary and maintenance funding, and rather less absorption of the resources of the Catholic community.

2. Among the social activists, lay people are in the vast majority, as church documents recommend.

3. "Lay ministries" has been a constant topic in the past few years. In fact, Christchurch Diocese has a lay prison chaplain and a lay head of Catholic Social Services, both paid by the diocese. This laicization of the justice apostolate should increase.

4. It has been noted that such a process must be seriously initiated and encouraged by the local churches overseas, especially in our context, in the Pacific.

5. UNDA New Zealand and UNDA Oceania already exist as members of the worldwide radio and television UNDA. They must both be taken more seriously, strengthened and attuned to the Catholic voice in other means of social communication.

6. An accurate analysis of the New Zealand social structure should help the church to find a place in it that expresses the values of the kingdom, especially in regard to the poor and the weak.

7. There must be continuous awareness-raising or conscientization, and the reform of selfish structures, which breed social sin and oppression. It is hard to see the victory being won this side of the Parousia, but then we are Christian humanists and the Parousia must remain an integral part of our vision.

38

LIBERATION FOR FREEDOM: REFLECTIONS ON THE TASK OF THE CHURCH

Giancarlo Collet

Introduction

Theological reflection on freedom, if it is not to miss its point, must start with an analysis of real freedom, that is, it must be in a context of social and political and—last but not least—ecclesiastical freedom or liberation.[1] Even if in this article this analysis itself is not entirely achieved, but rather suggested, at least its implications will have been indicated. The *social conditions* under which the church is to undertake its mission in the world can be defined in the following way:

1. Since the beginning of the modern period, the world has been on its way to unity. The growing interdependence in the social, political, and economic spheres as well as in the field of communications technology has brought about an increasing mutual interdependence. Structures and institutions have been increasing their power decisively while, at the same time, the immediate dependence of human beings disappears more and more into anonymity.

2. The growing unity of the world we are now witnessing is happening under the pressure of circumstances. The influence of European and American ways of life and interests on the non-Western world imperils other peoples' opportunities for developing freely and creatively, insofar as they are still able to do so and have not already become fascinated or blinded by Western modes of living.

3. The world is threatened by poverty, hunger, disease, unemployment, war, and an exploited and destroyed environment, on the one hand, and by growing resignation, apathy, and cynicism about coming to terms with any given situation, on the other. All this creates a kind of "communion in fate," an "ecumenism of suffering,"

Giancarlo Collet, layman from Switzerland, is Theology Assistant at the Catholic Faculty, the University of Tübingen, Germany.

in which freedom is threatened everywhere and in many ways, even while it is still being sought.

The church's words and actions on freedom have to reckon with these same social conditions. Moreover, there are *ecclesial conditions* that need to be considered:

1. Since the voyages of discovery and the period of colonialization, the church has through its missionary activity entered into this global unity. The Western church became a world-circling presence at the end of the nineteenth century. This is not merely the result of imperialism. Even though the church has not always come to its full realization, the Western church, by its missionary activities, has become a world body, and Christianity has become a factor to be reckoned with in world history.

2. The one church, now a world church, undertakes its task in various socio-cultural and sociopolitical circumstances. The undertaking task is done by the individual local churches, and they succeed to the extent that they discover their own identity. The latter is achieved by overcoming the alienation caused by the hegemony of a single uniform ecclesiastical culture, and an awareness of diversity within the church.[2] The "glory" of the Western church is its universality in world history; its "sorrow," however, lies in misunderstanding particularity.

3. Historical accretions and social expectations have produced in the church a need for legitimation. This need is the reverse of the church's "identity problem," namely: "The more theology and church try to become relevant in the context of modern problems, the deeper they are drawn into their own Christian identity crisis. The more they try to assert their identity in traditional dogmas, rites, and moral notions, the more they become irrelevant and unreliable."[3]

The mission of the church (or its right to speak of the God of Jesus Christ) also depends on its basing its own identity on identifying with the "least of (its) brothers" (Mt. 25:40) and with those who "have no one" (Jn. 5:7), on whether it contributes its share toward a humanization of the world.[4] This means, however, that the church can contribute to the history of human freedom only if its "gesture of freedom" is an inviting one and if it becomes a "place of freedom."

If we are to build "a world where every man, no matter what his race, religion or nationality, can live a fully human life, freed from servitude imposed on him by other men or by natural forces over which he has not sufficient control; a world where freedom is not an empty word," then the solidarity of the church with the history of human freedom must not be made to depend on the "opportunities for evangelization" of Christianity. The "suffering person" is in itself reason for commitment to human liberation. Conversely, however, the church does not do justice to its mandate when it foregoes witness to the kingdom of God begun in Jesus Christ and to its freedom (*Populorum Progressio*, no. 47, and *Evangelii Nuntiandi*, no. 14).

The Gesture of Freedom

Christian faith wants human beings to come to the experience that, through the mediation of others, they are unconditionally accepted by God and, on the basis of this, can also accept others.

What is special about this truth, that is, God's accepting us in unconditional love, is that it needs to be communicated freely and to be accepted in freedom. Love reveals itself only in its realization. Therefore God's acceptance of us is realized when we trust the promise of such a love and share it with one another.[5]

What God in his acceptance of us intended with the freedom revealed in Jesus Christ is essential. Only the experience of being unconditionally accepted liberates freedom from the need to guarantee its significance by means of self-assertion and self-achievement. Freedom, itself substantiated by love, is able to define its action through love. "Christian freedom, by claiming to make man's true freedom accessible to him, is the epitome of a self-substantiation that is given to man, not achieved by him; created man, by virtue of his createdness, would be unable to achieve such freedom."[6]

Freedom must be understood as being communicative; we are not here concerned with a human potential in the sense of self-realization, where the "other" comes into the picture merely as a limitation of one's own freedom. Rather, communicative freedom means realization of a common freedom, a freedom where individual freedom owes its existence to the freedom of others. "Communicative freedom means that another person is not experienced as limitation but as a condition for the possibility of one's own self-realization."[7] Where such freedom is to become a reality and where it is to be successful, its absolute postulate is that its intent and purpose must be anticipated if freedom is to be established.[8] Love is successful only where its absoluteness is believed in and its realization hoped for.

Human freedom cannot confer on itself the absolute significance that men and women have no command over. Therefore this intent and purpose of freedom must also be communicated to them. The experience of absolute meaning is given to human freedom only by means of the historical reality of other freedom. Christian faith, therefore, keeps pointing to Jesus: because, in him, the intent and purpose of freedom is made explicit as unconditional love; because, in him, the absolute precondition of a new history of human freedom is given, "When Christ freed us, he meant us to remain free" (Gal. 5:1), which once again teaches Christians how to give; they become, for one another, the unconditional grounds for and the goal of human freedom. Through Jesus, God's acceptance is promised every person, and those who trust this promise maintain communion with God on condition that they share in his acceptance of all (cf. 1 Jn. 4:7-14). "God's love aims . . . at a universal communion of all men and women, in union with himself. This eschatological communion is now represented and symbolized by the communion of the faithful."[9]

Christian freedom therefore does not create its own meaning, but receives it as a gift. This opens up an area of reality for human freedom where it can perdure, is acknowledged, and learns that it may and must exist. God's acceptance of humankind is enjoined on people themselves, as a task, so that they may give one another meaning and joy. That is why the circumstances wherein people mutually acknowledge and accept one another must be made humane. Inhuman structures must be changed and behavior altered. For the unconditional acceptance of men and women concerns, on the one hand, the social conditions they have to live in; but, on the other hand, freedom in conditions is no guarantee for freedom in attitudes.[10] An "ethos of freedom" is called for, concerned for the freedom of all.

In order to learn how relationships are to be shaped concretely as condition for and in recognition of human freedom, an analysis of the specific situation, of its ideas concerning freedom, and of its concepts of alienation is indispensable. A truly analytical rationality will necessarily also have to be shaped into political postulates for the realization of freedom and justice.[11] Neither the misunderstanding of practical implementation nor the inhuman misuse of rationality are precluded by this.[12] As M. Honecker writes:

> There is no other way toward the discovery of a more just and a more humane society than the use of reason. In this context, we must speak comparatively of a more just and a more humane society. What justice and humanity are in concrete circumstances has to be defined in the realm of what can be achieved. In a society whose members are threatened with famine, nutrition is more important than education. In a society where the majority have become objects of manipulation by a few who lord it over them, it is not enough to refer to the fact that these puppets are economically quite well off. In this case, reason cannot be content with demanding material security; it ought to insist on spiritual emancipation as well as material security. Reason, therefore, can only become active within a process of discovering truth and justice. Truth and justice are not definite and fixed values that have been determined once and for all. They are goals toward which social behavior is oriented; society can only approach them in a process of communication and interaction. Since society itself is not a completed structure but a continuing process, the society that is both just and worthy of human beings is not a condition achieved once and for all, but a task that must be continually realized.[13]

What reason opens our eyes to, even when we do not know how to implement it, is love of neighbor, which does not permit the heart the neutrality of the disinterested bystander (cf. Lk. 10:25-37).

Challenged by the "pain of negation," Christians protest against those circumstances which are the cause of suffering—injustice, oppression, exploitation, poverty, hunger—because they cannot remain unbeholden to their fellow human beings. They will dare to change inhuman conditions; they will not fail to recognize all who suffer for the sake of their commitment to freedom. Christians will also be prepared to suffer the same privations, for they know that there is a kind of distress that cannot be removed by changing structures but must be accepted and suffered, in order to alter circumstances, namely, the constant inability of living up to the Christian challenge, suffering in the solitude of one's own nonidentity, the pain of unrealizable love, the sting of finiteness and death.

A Place of Freedom

In actual life, the church is the established scene where the unconditional definition of human freedom is anticipated and realized. The church is a community of human beings who trust in the promise of God in Jesus, who allow him to give his love to them and, by passing this love on to others, mediate it in history. The gesture of freedom must therefore define both the church's existence and its activity. As a "creature of the spirit" (cf. Eph. 2:17ff.), the church anticipates the future kingdom of God that is the destiny of all men and women. Where the spirit of freedom is alive, the kingdom already begun in Jesus takes shape. This makes the church the beginning of a "new creation" and the herald of that toward which humankind proceeds in its history.

The church, in anticipation of communion with God under his rule, thus represents the destiny of human society. "In the church we are concerned with the anticipatory presence of human destiny within society," writes Pannenberg.[14] It is symbolic of the promised universality of the kingdom of God that people from all countries and all nations belong to it—"Jews and Gentiles." The only advantage the church has over the rest of humanity is that there has been granted it to receive and recognize God's acceptance in Jesus and thus to begin a life of freedom in unfree conditions. Its unique and specific task, the meaning of its mission, is that all may arrive at the knowledge of this truth, and trust the church in turn.

The church must, already now, represent God's kingdom in its life, the kingdom that is the future of all people and of the whole world. The kingdom of God makes freedom and justice possible among human beings. Freedom and justice appear among them by liberating them from the necessity of asserting and vindicating themselves, thus placing them into a new interrelation of mutual acceptance.

The church therefore is to be understood as the place of eschatological freedom; it is not subject to the "powers of the world" nor to their law, but committed solely to the "law of Christ" (1 Cor. 9:21) and the "law of freedom" (Jas. 1:25). Between the concrete church and its destiny, the kingdom of God, there is a difference that cannot be taken away. Hence the church, "if rightly understood, always lives by the proclamation of its own transience and its historically progressive absorption into the future kingdom of God, which is the goal of its pilgrimage."[15] The more the promised kingdom of God is realized within the life of the church, the more it becomes evident as being the destiny of humankind as well. For that reason all evangelization and every action of the church must be in accordance with its presence as symbol. The witness for the kingdom of God begun in Jesus must be at the core.

Where this is successful, the church bears witness to

> the acceptance by God against the complicity of human involvement in guilt and against the temptation of using political and social power to dispose of people's humanity. The church thus represents the cause of justification and consequently of freedom. It bears witness to God's partiality for the weak against all aspects of oppression; it therefore represents the cause of justice. It gives evidence of the presence of Jesus for others even to death on the cross; it therefore represents the cause of selfless love. The church manifests the transcendent power of the Risen Christ—which encompasses heaven and earth —against worldly powers that set limits and are always entangled in internecine strife. The church represents therefore the cause of peace.[16]

The fact that the one church is divided into several communities distorts and obscures its charge of representing the kingdom of God among men and women. As long as Christ's church is divided, it will be able to realize the promise given men and women by God and the unconditional definition of the meaning of freedom as love only imperfectly and not without guilt.

> The church maintains its sanctity, its bond with the one God and Lord of all only if it is united. Indeed, it can find the way back to unity only by reflecting on its sanctity: Only if one has become aware of the provisional character of the church's organization and teaching regulations as compared to the future of the kingdom of God and of the one Lord Jesus Christ, and as compared to the bond in the spirit of divine love and all this implies for the self-assessment of the churches—only then will the differences of the Christian communities lose their divisive meaning.[17]

Real unity is therefore a basic condition for enabling the church to attend to its mission in the world. An ecclesiological monoculture's dogmatic intolerance as well as fanatic sectarianism must be overcome by church unity, if a pluriform liturgical life, ecclesiastical order, and theological reflection are to be made viable. This would imply the realization of communicative freedom among the churches themselves and within the church; it would make identity possible for others and grant it to them; it would also make it possible to find one's own identity in promoting and recognizing the identity of others. As long as the church is unable to realize freedom within its own confines, it will find it next to impossible to legitimate its mandate for the liberation of all.

It remains the specific task of the church to mediate God's unconditional acceptance of men and women. However, the church can represent the claim of Christian freedom only as a community of liberated individuals. For that reason, the church must become the "place of freedom"; this calls for internal reforms.[18] Christian freedom, to be sure, first proves itself within the community of the faithful. Pesch writes:

> According to New Testament understanding, this community is marked by freedom of speech, by a free renunciation, by generosity and care; by promoting lively spontaneity and by banishing legalistic ways that have a paralyzing effect; by a release from selfishness, from enslaving "vital interests," even from fear; by granting peace and joy (cf. Rom. 14:7); by breaking through constricting conventions, by a stimulus toward an ever new unanimity.[19]

The Politics of Freedom

To be sure, the kingdom of God that is promised to men and women does not consist of a program for shaping social reality. Like eschatological reality, it cannot be identified either with a church order or with certain political forms. Yet those who trust the word attested to by the church and the promise of that word anticipate their goal—communion with God—and find therein the freedom of action which influences the organization of human association and of the relationship with nature. "The Church, founded on the Redeemer's love, contributes to the wider application of justice and charity within and between nations. By preaching the truth of the gospel . . . [the Church] shows respect for . . . political freedom . . . and fosters these values" (*Gaudium et Spes*, no. 76). Because God is mindful of the humanity of people, Christians seek to promote this by resisting inhumanity and by seeking better forms for realizing freedom. The

> productive and critical impulse of Christian belief in God for the purpose of restorative action benefiting humankind and a purposeful political application for a better future of humankind does not neutralize the eschatological reservation. This reservation remains critical and productive even there, because humanity is not the subject of a "universal providence.". . . God's reservation is shown in that humanity itself is not the universal subject of history and that its temporal providence is surpassed by the Lord of history.[20]

Political freedom is a necessary actualization of the freedom that Christians declare. Where the concretization of God's acceptance of humanity is relinquished, it cannot become historically mediated. But where Christian freedom is consciously realized, this realization occurs in the historical arena of politics and the legal order as well; for these have been instituted by human beings themselves as requisites for shaping society. Politics and law, however, are not given once and for all; they are quantities conditioned by history and need therefore to be shaped. An attitude that is open to new and better possibilities of human association, and averse to being satisfied with the status quo, is required if law and politics are to be human and not merely arbitrary.

Herein lies an opportunity for Christian freedom to indicate and expose in the first instance the limits of realizing individual freedom, while drawing attention to the inhibition and suppression of human freedom and to outline new possibilities of communicative freedom. We cannot be concerned with safeguarding individual freedom alone. Such freedom is always due to some other freedom; realization of freedom therefore implies a view of society as a whole, without however "functionalizing" the individual. Rather, the issue here is to keep alert an interest in the freedom of all and to realize it. For only the mutual recognition and legal safeguard of the current realization of freedom makes a free and just society feasible.

This touches upon another opportunity for Christian freedom: the possibility of overcoming sectarian interests that more or less define politics, and of being aware of its responsibility for others and not letting responsibility end where they suffer contradiction and opposition.[21] In order to realize their mission for the liberation of men and women, and on the basis of God's unconditional acceptance of all, Christians will stand up for the realization of freedom and justice politically as well, even if this means giving up traditional privileges or not laying claim to them.

The "distance" between church and state could provide the church an opportunity to create "models" of free attitudes and to experiment to see which of them would be conducive to a more humane life for the entire society. "The specificity of a Christian approach can only be a praxis of human communication and interaction, which is paradigmatic for society, or, in the word of the New Testament: the doing, the *poiein* of truth, of justice, of God's redemptive will."[22] Only where political freedom is realized (and this holds for the church as well) does it not remain an "empty word." Only then does the "pathos of talk about freedom" not fall into the danger of merely compensating for the absence of practical realization.

Notes

1. Cf. L. Dullaart, *Kirche und Ekklesiologie* (Munich-Mainz, 1975), pp. 97ff.; F. v. d. Oudenrijn, *Kritische Teologie als Kritik der Theologie* (Munich-Mainz, 1972), pp. 203ff.

2. J. Amstutz et al., *Kirche und Dritte Welt im Jahr 2000* (Einsiedeln-Zurich-Cologne, 1947), pp. 90–104, 170–84.

3. Jürgen Moltmann, *Der gekreuzigte Gott: Das Kreuz Christi als Grund und Kritik christlicher Theologie* (Munich, 1972), p. 12; Eng., *The Crucified God* (New York: Harper & Row, 1974), p. 7.

4. M. Hofmann, *Identifikation mit dem Anderen: Theologische Themen und ihr hermeneutischer Ort bei lateinamerikanischen Theologen der Befreiung* (Stockholm-Gottingen, 1978), pp. 94ff., 163ff.

5. Karl Rahner, "Ueber die Einheit von Nachsten- und Gottesliebe," *Schriften zur Theologie* 6 (Einsiedeln-Zurich-Cologne: Benziger, 1968), pp. 277–98; Eng., "Reflection on the Unity of the Love of God and Neighbour," *Theological Investigations* 6 (Baltimore: Helicon, 1969), pp. 231–249; idem, "Der eine Mittler und die Vielfalt der Vermittlingen," *Shriften zur Theologie* 8 (Einsiedeln-Zurich-Cologne: Benziger, 1967), pp. 218–35; Eng., "One Mediator and Many Mediations," *Theological Investigations* 9 (New York: Herder and Herder, 1972), pp. 169–84. Edward Schillebeeckx, *Christus und die Christen: Die Geschichte einer neuen Lebenspraxis* (Freiburg-Basel-Vienna, 1977), pp. 792ff.

6. J. Baur, *Freiheit und Emanzipation: Ein philosophisch-theologischer Traktat* (Stuttgart, 1974), p. 40.

7. M. Theunissen, *Sein und Schein: Die kritische Funktion der Hegelschen Logik* (Frankfurt a. M., 1980), p. 46; cf. H. Krings, *System und Freiheit: Gesammelte Aufsätze* (Freiburg-Munich, 1980), pp. 125ff.; J. Heinrichs, *Freiheit-Sozilismus-Christentum: Um eine kommunikative Gesellschaft* (Bonn, 1978), pp. 16ff.; H. Peukert, *Wissenschaftstheorie-Handlungstheorie-Fundamentale Theologie: Analysen zu Ansatz und Status* theologischer Theoriebildung (Düsseldorf, 1976), pp. 273ff.

8. Paul Ricoeur, *Hermeneutik und Strukturalismus: Der Konflikt der Interpretationen,* 1 (Munich, 1973), pp. 199–226; orig. Fr., *Le Conflit des interpretations: Essais d'hermeneutique* (Paris: Seuil, 1969); Eng., *The Conflict of Interpretations: Essays in Hermeneutics,* ed., Don Ihde (Evanston, Ill.: Northwestern University Press, 1974).

9. W. Pannenberg, *Die Bestimmung der Menschen: Menschsein, Erwählung und Geschichte* (Göttingen, 1978), p. 26; Eng., *Human Nature, Election, and History* (Philadelphia: Westminster, 1977).

10. Gerhard Ebeling, "Frei aus Glauben," *Lutherstudien* 1 (Tübingen, 1971): 308–29; quotation from p. 328.

11. Cf. M. Horkeimer, *Zur Kritik der instrumentellen Vernunft: Aus den Vorträgen und Aufzeichnungen seit Kriegsende* (Frankfurt a. M.: A. Schmidt, 1974), pp. 335ff.

12. Ibid.

13. M. Honecker, *Konzept einer sozialethischen Theorie: Grundfragen evangelischer Sozialethik* (Tubingen, 1971), p. 50.

14. W. Pannenberg, *Thesen zur Theologie der Kirche* (Munich, 1974); cf. idem., *Grundzüge der Christologie* (Gütersloh: Mohn, 1969), p. 390; Eng., *Jesus, God and Man,* trans. Lewis Picke, 2nd

ed. (Philadelphia: Westminster, 1977); idem. *Theologie und Reich Gottes* (Gütersloh: Mohn, 1971), pp. 31ff; Eng., *Theology and the Kingdom of God* (Philadelphia: Westminster, 1969).

15. K. Rahner, "Kirche und Parusie Christi," *Schriften zur Theologie* 6 (Einsiedeln-Zurich-Cologne, 1968): 348-67; quotation from p. 351; Eng., "The Church and the Parousia of Christ," *Theological Investigations* 6 (Baltimore: Helicon, 1969), pp. 295-312.

16. W. Huber, *Kirche* (Stuttgart-Berlin, 1979), p. 144; cf. pp. 177f.

17. W. Pannenberg, *Das Glaubensbekenntnis ausgelegt und verantwortet vor den Fragen der Gegenwart,* 3rd ed. (Gütersloh, 1979), p. 165; cf. idem "Einheit der Kirche als Glaubenswirklichkeit und als ökumenisches Zeit," *Ethik und Ekklesiologie:* Gesammelte Aufsätze (Göttingen, 1977), pp. 200-210.

18. Cf. K. Rahner, *Strukturwandel der Kirche als Aufgabe und Chance* (Freiburg-Basel-Vienna, 1972); idem., *Schriften zur Theologie* 14 (Einsiedeln-Zurich-Cologne; Benziger, 1980).

19. R. Pesch, "Die erinnerte Freiheit Jesu," *Freiheit in Gesellschaft* (Freiburg-Basel-Vienna, 1971), pp. 21-38; quotation from p. 27.

20. E. Schillebeeckx, *Christus und die Christen,* p. 761.

21. Cf. T. Koch, "Selbstregulation des Politischen? Von der Notwendigkeit kollektiver Handlungsziele," *Stimmen der Zeit* 194 (1976): 105-16.

22. M. Honecker, *Konzept einer sozialethischen Theorie,* p. 65; cf. idem, *Sozialethik zwischen Tradition und Vernunft* (Tübingen, 1977), pp. 9 ff.

39

A UNITED STATES EXPERIENCE

Marjorie Keenan, R.S.H.M.

Introduction

The United States is an enigmatic presence on the world scene at present. Barely recovering from Vietnam and Watergate, struck by the energy crisis, the taking of United States hostages in Iran, and the Soviet invasion of Afghanistan, the United States appears to itself and to others to be troubled, unsure. The United States church is part of this picture, and shares profoundly in the present difficulties. Yet springing out of these recent crises is a church that speaks increasingly in favor of the poor, that acts with strength in favor of the marginalized. This action is at times confused, divided, ambiguous. Yet it is there. What is that presence? What are the implications and modalities of the church's action? The following paper attempts to address these questions in part by considering justice and liberation within the local church on three levels: (1) the local United States church, with emphasis on the National Conferei ce of Catholic Bishops and religious men and women; (2) the local diocesan church in Brooklyn, New York, as an example of a third world diocese in the first world; and (3) the local church in a nonterritorial parish within the diocese seeking to promote human dignity within a strong faith community.

I

To speak of justice and liberation within the United States context is to wander through a maze of questions and to gaze into a kaleidoscope of rapidly changing situations. The complexity of the subject can lead only to generalizations without universal application and particularizations that cannot be taken as typical of the

Marjorie Keenan, a member of the Religious of the Sacred Heart of Mary, is research coordinator in the United States for Prospective, an international center for research and communication. She is also a member of the Pontifical Commission for Justice and Peace.

Special gratitude is due to Monsignor Anthony Bevilacqua, Chancellor of the Diocese of Brooklyn, for his help, and acknowledgment must be made to him for the use of material concerning the immigrants in the diocese. Gratitude must also be extended to the members of other diocesan offices and to the Reverend James Hinchey of Saint James Cathedral. —M.K.

American scene. Yet this in itself is an index of what justice and liberation mean to the American church and explain, if only in part, the variety of responses to any one problem, as well as the hesitations, the gropings, the contradictions.

One of the questions that might be asked would be: Is the United States the oppressor, the oppressed, or both? From a world perspective, the answer might be "the oppressor," while many of the American people might see themselves as the liberators, the defenders of human rights and freedom. From the domestic viewpoint, the so-called minority groups, such as Native Americans, blacks, Hispanics (a catch-all phrase for widely varying Spanish-speaking groups), and women, would consider themselves oppressed, while another segment of the population would see the United States as receiving the oppressed: the Soviet dissident, the Vietnamese refugee, the thousands of Cubans fleeing Castro's regime. From the point of view of action in favor of justice, each one of these perceptions can lead to a valid position. The actions, however, may be in opposition and lead to misunderstanding and division within the church and other groups in society.

In addition to the extreme complexity of the United States situation, due in part to its very size and varied population, certain aspects of the American political self-understanding need to be underscored. The form of government in the United States is, in principle, participatory, with government accountability to the people through various elective processes. Even if it can be validly argued that presently this system has or is breaking down, the concept marks the American people deeply. Individuals and groups express their opinions on a wide variety of social and political issues; government officials, elected or appointed, are subject to pressure groups or officially registered lobbying bodies, each trying to promote a particular issue or to preserve a particular self-interest. "Write to your congressperson and ask that . . . " is certainly the most frequently urged action by socially oriented groups. This political context explains, but again only in part, the political tonality that work for justice takes on in the United States. In the vast majority of cases, such political action is not ideologically oriented, but rather pragmatic.

Also basic to the American system is a carefully protected concept of the separation of church and state. Originally meant to assure freedom for both bodies, in the present situation it leads to myriad difficulties of cross-interests and litigations. The principle, however, has preserved the United States from a certain anticlericalism and allows the organized churches to present their views to the government as independent bodies. Because the Catholic church, for historical reasons, developed its own welfare system, it can also lead to real and apparent conflicts of interest.

What Local Church?

Equally complex in the United States is an existential definition of the local church. One might say that there are different agents of justice within the church acting out of the same contextual framework and using as a basis the same social teachings of the church, yet drawing fundamentally different conclusions from these same givens. This distinction can be made when considering either the institutional church on a national and diocesan level or when speaking of the various groups within the Christian community. There is no national program for justice within the church, no unified efforts for liberation within the Christian community. There are as many agendas as groups, as perceived injustices. Is this because there is no commonly perceived threat? Is it because of the lack of education to the justice dimension of the gospel message? This dispersion of efforts is a weakness, but the variety of efforts, on the other hand, makes the church present in many areas, with many people.

The National Conference of Catholic Bishops and Work for Justice

Within recent years, the American bishops have, as a body, made continuous efforts to bring the Christian community as a whole to see that working for justice is integral to the evangelizing mission of the church. This is evident in the revised catechetical directory, in diocesan pastoral letters as well as collective statements and direct involvement in action for justice. Historically this is a significant development because of the immigrant nature of the United States church.

During the early periods of immigration, the main effort of the church was directed toward helping the newly arrived population adapt to strange and sometimes hostile surroundings. The church aided greatly in the assimilation process but, by this very fact, could not at the same time influence public policy. On the contrary, the church withdrew, as it were, from the social arena and created its own schools, hospitals, and other welfare agencies. In the schools, however, great emphasis was placed on patriotism and on socialization to the surrounding culture.

After World War I, the forerunner of the Episcopal Conference did draw up a program for social reconstruction, which dealt with the problems of society as a whole, but until the 1930s there was little social consciousness in the church, and, in general, the American bishops continued to follow loyally the policy of the United States government until the time of the Vietnam war. Since that time, the National Conference of Catholic Bishops (NCCB) has developed a more critical stance, supporting or opposing the government on a variety of social issues. Often these stances may appear to be overly nuanced. This is inevitable because of the size and composition of the American hierarchy.

Structurally the principal organs for the promotion of justice within the NCCB are found within its civilly incorporated body, the United States Catholic Conference (USCC). Within this conference is a department of Social Development and World Peace, subdivided into two sections, Domestic Social Development and International Justice and Peace. The structure itself is indicative of how justice questions are situated within the United States church. The church is conscious of the United States role on the international scene and of the Catholic church as a transnational actor. Many of the bishops' stances concern the international arena. Care is taken, however, to discern the moral, as opposed to political, issue involved and to consult the local church before acting. An example of this would be the recent efforts of the American hierarchy to support the transfer of the Panama Canal to the Panamanian government.

The bishops' collective efforts for justice generally find expression in one of two ways: pressure put on one or another governmental body and pastoral statements. The first type might be considered that of advocacy. For example, various members of the hierarchy or of USCC staff offices testify before congressional committees, in the name of the USCC, when legislation is being prepared. For instance, Cardinal Krol spoke in favor of the ratification of SALT II to the Senate Foreign Relations Committee, pointing out, however, the moral implications of the present arms policy of the United States. (Interestingly enough, another member of the hierarchy testified before the same committee as a representative of Pax Christi, speaking against the ratification of SALT II as an immoral escalation of the arms race, thus pointing out the varying positions within the American church on any one issue.) Another form of this advocacy work would be the filing of a friend-of-the court brief with the Supreme Court. Recently such a brief was filed on an abortion ruling by a Chicago court and will be heard by the Supreme Court.

Pastoral statements can take two forms: a declaration of the Administrative Board of the NCCB/USCC and Pastoral Letters of the entire conference. Within the past few years, the bishops have issued pastorals on abortion, arms control and disarmament, capital punishment, the economy, education as a right, family life, food and agricultural policy, health care, housing, human rights, South Africa, the Middle East, the aged, and many other social issues.

Even the scope of the list above points out one of the weaknesses of the bishops' efforts to educate the Christian community. A pastoral statement does not have within it normally any further educative process. This is left to the local bishop. So, while the statements are rich, they often pass unnoticed.

Finally, since many of the bishops' efforts are directly or indirectly political, the question arises of the church, as a power, meeting with the government, a power of a different nature. What will be the ultimate effects of the increasing relationships between the church and the government? Will the church, the body of bishops, be seen as one more political group to be curried or rejected? What is the role of the church in the political context of the United States? Is a diminution of freedom inherent to the present type of relationship? Is, on the contrary, the church thus able to speak for the voiceless?

A Unique Effort on the Part of the Bishops to Promote Justice

As part of the bicentennial celebrations of the founding of the United States, the NCCB developed a two-year process, entitled *Liberty and Justice for All*, which culminated in a three-day Call to Action Conference in October 1976. As often, the process was certainly as important as the product, and it stands as a unique effort to listen to the concerns of the entire Christian community. It was likewise conceived as a practical implementation of *Octogesima Adveniens*, no. 4, in which Pope Paul VI asks the Christian community to apply the teaching of the church to its concrete situation, in the light of the gospel. It is interesting to note that the encyclical is entitled *A Call to Action* in its English translation.

As one phase of the preparation, the bishops organized seven three-day "hearings" in various parts of the country during which a group of bishops and other church leaders listened to invited experts and concerned local people on a series of issues. This was coupled with a nationwide program of grassroots discussions in an effort to identify the justice concerns of the church. While over 800,000 people participated in this process, many of the dioceses did not seek to do so. In some cases, it was distrust of the methodology or opposition to dealing with such questions. In others, it was a simple conflict of commitments and an overcrowded calendar.

While participation in the preparatory phase of the conference was varied, over 150 dioceses sent delegations to the conference itself. The 1,350 official delegates and the 1,000 accredited observers had previously received abundant documentation, including a theological reflection on each main topic, a report on the various consultations, and draft recommendations. These recommendations were grouped under the general headings of church, family, person, neighborhood, humankind, nation, ethnicity/race, and work. In brief, a meeting specifically devoted to justice touched upon almost every aspect of the life of the Christian community. While the notion of liberation may have many connotations in the United States, that of justice is broadly understood and deeply felt.

The conference formulated 180 recommendations to be submitted to the bishops as the basis of a five-year pastoral plan on the promotion of justice. Obviously, to seek theological consistency, or even solid theological thought, from a group of this size and composition would be impossible. Likewise, certain overlapping in the recommendations was inevitable. The representivity of the participants has likewise been questioned. Since the majority were part of diocesan delegations, this remark, if true, does not indicate an inherent imperfection in the conference process.

Any concentration or the weaknesses of the Call to Action Conference masks its overwhelming strength. The hurts and pains of many were heard as never before. An immense sea of suffering was revealed. Still more, tentative solutions were offered. The bishops were challenged, that is certain, but so was the entire Christian community. The bishops seemed at first to be overwhelmed by the outcome. This apparent first negative reaction was in part diffused, however, in the Bishops' Assembly, which took place almost immediately afterward. Careful consideration was given to the recommendations and the validity of the vast majority of them recognized. At the end of this meeting, the bishops issued a pastoral statement intended as an initial response to the Call to Action. It likewise addressed some of the more controversial issues concerning priestly celibacy, married priests, and the ordination of women, simply reiterating the church's present discipline on these and similar questions. This raises the interesting dilemma of a sharp separation in the manner of treating issues, which seem to many to spring from a common root. This same pastoral points out that the Call to Action Conference could not be the sole factor in determining the social agenda of the church. The NCCB/USCC has its own social priorities and likewise recognizes the existence of other issues that need to be addressed by various groups. It likewise states that the more specific a proposal in the social area, the more room there is for disagreement.

At their next assembly, in May 1978, the bishops issued a five-year pastoral plan, with a monitoring process built into it to assure implementation. The plan is a bishops' statement outlining what they intend to do. It is not a plan for the church as a whole. The emphasis is strongly on education for justice, but the bishops do commit themselves to work for justice in specific areas such as economic justice, disarmament, world hunger, and the church as community. They collectively pledge to seek justice and to live justice, and end by saying:

> We pray and we trust that God's love, alive in the hearts of our people, will fire their imaginations and enkindle in them a desire for a more simple way of life, free from dependency on luxuries mistaken for necessities; that it will liberate them from pre-judgements about others which are an obstacle to sharing the faith with them; and will enable them to view with an objective eye the deleterious effects on human beings of unjust social structures and to strive with courageous hearts to change these for the better. That it will intensify their commitment to service out of love for the one who loved us first. So also we pray and trust the same for ourselves.

The stress is on change: personal change, social change, structural change. The Christian community as a whole is called to this. The sense of mutual responsibility, so strong during the preparation and the conference, is continued in the bishops' response.

It is difficult, if not impossible, to evaluate the ultimate effect of the Call to Action Conference on the United States church. There have been various implementation meetings and plans; one or another diocese has chosen to concentrate on certain sections of the recommendations; a pastoral on racism as a social sin has been issued by the NCCB. These are the measureable results, and perhaps no more can be said. The Call to Action Conference was, in any case, an extremely important initiative on the part of the bishops and one particularly reflective of the approach, within the United States, to questions of justice.

Religious Men and Women—And Work for Justice

The Call to Action Conference involved the laity in its process from beginning to end. Many lay persons in the United States have devoted their lives to promoting social change. This is particularly true among minority groups where religious and priests are few. However, within the American church certainly among the most active agents in work for justice are the religious men and women. Religious are found in all aspects of work for justice. Returned missioners are making reverse mission a reality. "We have left all" finds concrete expression in a sharing in the life of the very poor. Individuals, communities, congregations, and the Conferences of Major Superiors of both men and women are actively promoting justice, educating to justice. This is certainly not without difficulty and painful polarization and occasional serious error.

For the American religious, their very citizenship leads to their involvement in the political process. Much work for justice is done through coalitions seeking to influence local, state, and federal governments. A directory of justice and peace groups working in the United States and of Catholic origin would list several hundred organizations directly or indirectly related to religious congregations. This characteristic of work for justice reaches out far beyond those men and women religious working directly in justice causes to many hundreds more through such organizations as Bread for the World, Pax Christi, and Network—all urging pressure on legislators as one extremely important component of working for systemic change.

The involvement of religious in work for justice has not been easy and has involved a profound shift in self-understanding. What is the role of religious within the church of *Lumen Gentium*, within that of *Gaudium et Spes* and *Evangelii Nuntiandi*, within the understanding of the church's commitment to justice as expressed in the 1971 Synod? American religious have taken these questions to heart. The responses have led to polarization at times, to errors at others, but overall to an increasingly confident commitment to justice within an evangelical perspective.

One field within which American religious have been typically active is with multinational corporations. By buying stock in certain companies and grouping together in coalition with other religious groups, orders and congregations have been able to bring stockholder suits against various multinationals acting in third world countries. Occasionally these suits have been won and policies changed. Even when such suits are not won, the boards of directors of the corporations are now very much aware of this other voice in their midst. Such action always has a certain amount of ambiguity about it, but it has taken its place alongside direct identification with the poor, advocacy, community organizing, justice education, and many other forms of work.

In the Conferences of Major Superiors, the commitment to justice is especially marked. In 1976 the Leadership Conference of Women Religious added a member to its staff to work particularly in questions of justice in an international light. This is simply a visible sign of the long-standing and often pioneering commitment of women religious to justice. Several recent events have given focus to the efforts of major superiors both men and women.

In November 1977 representatives of the Conferences of Major Superiors of North and South America met in Montreal to attempt to articulate a preferred future for religious life. While no common stance could be taken, justice concerns ran throughout the sharing. Each conference drew its own conclusions. The men's delegation from the United States asked their conference to consider the religious vocation anew in the face of today's poverty and injustice, to help the major superiors to take a stance with and for the poor of the world. The women's conference, after prayer to become a just people, pledged to be in greater solidarity with the poor even if not all of their Sisters would be in direct service. They promised to continue their efforts for education toward systemic change and to work with others to promote political efforts to ease the social and economic struggles of others. They also linked their consciousness, as women, of oppression to that of the struggle of women throughout the world who feel oppression in many forms.

In August 1978 both conferences met together to continue reflection on justice. Three commitments resulted from five days of prayer, social analysis, and sharing.

1. Knowing that we must begin with ourselves, we resolve to live more simply, to be sparing in our use of goods, and to search out ways to divest ourselves of affluence for the sake of a more just world.

2. Realizing that we lack full understanding of our social, economic and political life, we commit ourselves to structural analysis and theological reflection. We pledge ourselves to initiate national and regional programs in the fields of education and mass communication in order to deepen awareness and stimulate efforts for global justice.

3. Recognizing the need for effective action, we promise to use more of our energies for solidarity with oppressed peoples in the United States, as well as in other parts of the world.

Each conference continues to seek ways to implement the commitment to justice. It is interesting to note that both the bishops and the Conferences of Major Superiors stress structural change. Both also consider justice as a way of life. The religious men and women are perhaps better placed at times to enunciate the personal and communitarian needs of others, the bishops to trace the theoretical background out of which both must work. The efforts are usually collaborative and mutual on the national level.

How effective is this thrust toward justice among religious? It has given rise to painful divisions within and among congregations, to a certain separation of "prayers" and "doers." While major superiors may take stands, it is questionable that they are able to bring their orders and congregations with them easily. There is a certain confusion between a basic evangelical commitment to justice and an identification with one or another social issue. Efforts have been made in several religious congregations to divest themselves of superfluous property. A report was prepared on this subject at the request of one of the bishops' committees. Also there is a slow redistribution of personnel from heavily populated areas to regions of the country where religious are few. Efforts have been made to explore a spirituality of justice and the notion of social and political ministry. All these efforts are still at their beginning, however. With all the uncertainties, it is widely recognized that religious men and women, and particularly the women religious, are an active and often a leadership group in work for justice.

II

How many, even within the United States church, realize that there are two dioceses in New York City? Overshadowed by the Archdiocese of New York, the Brooklyn Diocese nevertheless embraces two of the six boroughs of the city. When it was established in 1853, the Brooklyn Diocese covered nearly 5,000 square miles, the whole of Long Island, New York. With the creation in 1957 of the Diocese of Rockville Center, the diocese became unique in the United States. It is now the smallest in area with only 179.25 square miles of territory. It is the only totally urban diocese in the United States and possibly in the world. Despite its smallness, the Diocese of

Brooklyn has the largest Catholic population of any diocese in the United States. Of its more than 2 million Catholics, half the total population, nearly half are new immigrants. At least 50,000 enter the diocese annually, overwhelmingly poor, speaking twenty-three different languages, often black, competing for diminishing numbers of jobs. Half the children born in the area covered by the diocese are baptized Catholics. Fifty-four percent of these children are on public assistance.

Brooklyn has been characterized as a third world diocese in a first world country, with the immense difference that the third world came to Brooklyn at a time when the church was not ready to receive it. What does justice and liberation mean within such a context? How can the church attempt to meet the many needs of the newly arrived people, of the old immigrants at a time when assimilation is no longer the aim of the newly arrived populations? How can the "other diocese" help alleviate the social situation of New York City, which relegates whole sections of the population to misery. How does one stop the flight of the white population from the diocese? Is it possible to minister to groups of widely differing ethnic and cultural backgrounds and still maintain any semblance of unity in the diocese? A financial crisis is the logical outcome of a poor population. Many parishes must be totally subsidized or cease to exist. And all of this in a time of decreasing vocations, increasing median age among clergy and religious.

Within the diocese are the usual social service and welfare agencies found in most of the dioceses in the United States. In view of the situation described above, advocacy and direct service are equally important and extremely complex. In the following remarks, however, special attention will be paid to how the diocese is attempting to meet the needs of its new peoples, how it has become a "diocese on the move."

Diocesan Goals and Priorities: The Context of Work for Justice

In 1976 Bishop Francis Mugavero, the ordinary of the diocese, established a task force of priests, religious, and lay persons to set goals and priorities for the diocese so that there could be a unified approach to its essential problems. As a basis for their work, the task force drew up a mission statement for the diocese, which stresses the proclaiming of the gospel and the establishing of the kingdom in the very concrete situation of Brooklyn/Queens, the two boroughs of New York City within the Diocese of Brooklyn. The church is seen as community. This community must strive above all to know God in faith. Diversity in language, culture, and customs is stressed in the liturgical life of the church. There is no hint of assimilation of differences within this faith community.

The task force then set various goals, the first of which related to growth in living faith. An explicit connection is made with the works of justice as an expression of faith. Among the weaknesses pointed out is that the particular exigencies of the different cultural groups were not being adequately met within the context of the church. It was also apparent that there was little emphasis on adult religious development. Education is child-oriented.

A lack of priests has led to a broader comprehension of ministry within the Brooklyn church, and the task force urged that the pastoral ministries be broadened and more people trained to work among the various cultural groups who, unlike the earlier immigrants, do not usually bring their clergy with them. The clergy and religious in the diocese, in addition, are not reflective of the new demographics of Brooklyn/Queens. Because of the immense needs of the new immigrants, this cultural sensitivity that must characterize the pastoral minister necessarily embraces an understanding of the real needs of those with whom they minister and whom they serve. Specific training is therefore necessary.

In developing the goal concerning an increased awareness and response to the human service needs of the people of the diocese, the task force saw the importance of the church's being "a strong advocate for the fulfillment of unmet human service needs and for social justice." In particular the church should become "an advocate before government and corporate entities so as to enable local communities to meet their own needs and, where necessary, provide services directly." Again, as with the bishops and religious, working for justice within the United States context almost necessarily implies an advocacy role with various levels of government and legislative pressure. It is likewise interesting to note that the approach to meeting needs is on a local, neighborhood level. This is particularly important for the development and maintenance of a sense of identity in a city as large as New York. The human person must find community support. In addition the various ethnic and cultural groups tend to cluster in certain areas. Differing cultures and customs make it particularly important to approach the people where they are.

Flowing from this is another objective with strong implications for justice. The diocese is to "develop within the context of human service the goal of neighborhood stabilization." Since an extremely large proportion of the Catholics in the Brooklyn diocese are immigrants, either new immigrants or older ones maintaining a strong ethnic tie, some of the older groups feel particularly menaced by the new arrivals. The former group have perhaps purchased small homes in working-class neighborhoods. They have, as it were, begun to rise and do not want to see what they have worked hard to get shared with others. In addition to economic reasons, there are also strong racial overtones to the refusal to allow people from a different background to move into the neighborhood. A hate-filled atmosphere can quickly develop, with outbreaks of violence. In some cases the presence of the church has been the only stabilizing influence in the area, as precarious as this stability may be. The groups in conflict may both be predominantly Catholic. A NCCB Pastoral Letter on Racism neither reaches nor touches these groups, as important as a statement of principle may be.

From goals and objectives to actual programs and results is a long distance. The diocese, however, does have an articulated overall program of what the church should be: a person-oriented community of faith, allowing for diversity, seeking to be a voice for the voiceless. What will the future hold as these goals are worked out? In projections made for 1990, the trend toward a poverty population will continue. Brooklyn and Queens will have to contend with large unemployment, a shrinking job market, and dramatic cutbacks in the city's services. The number of immigrants will continue to rise. (In fact, a new Cuban Center was opened in June 1980 to help resettle the influx of Cubans now beginning to reach the diocese in increasing numbers.) If these predictions come to pass, there will probably be increasing competition among the various ethnic groups within the diocese. Housing, health care, and crime will be major problems. Efforts must be made to stop neighborhood decay, difficult at a time when banks and other lending institutions are reluctant to invest in New York City. Education will become increasingly important in poverty areas where, at present, 40 percent of all persons over twenty-five years of age have less than eight years of schooling and where approximately 63 percent of the youth sixteen to twenty-one do not have a secondary school diploma. Justice and liberation take on added urgency in such a situation. A new model of church mission appears to be a necessity, concludes one report on the topic. Efforts are certainly being made in this direction but encounter major difficulties of lack of preparation on the part of the clergy and religious.

Major Concerns of Some Bodies of Priests and Religious within the Diocese

In this respect it might be interesting to examine briefly the priorities and agendas of some of the structures that group together priests and/or religious.

A Senate of Priests meets nine times a year. During the past five years, the subject of how best to work with various ethnic groups has been a topic of discussion. Each year, likewise, the subject of adequate preparation is stressed, including the problem of the priests, however few in number they may be, coming to the diocese without any background in English. Social issues dealt with are mainly those directly touching the people: housing and education, for example. One year, however, the question of world hunger was addressed. The majority of the topics discussed pertain directly to priestly life.

The Sisters' Senate, on the contrary, apparently does not deal with internal concerns at all, these being met within their own congregations. A review of their recent annual goals shows an interesting progression. In 1974 the senate committed the Sisters to "unify and further individual and inter-congregational efforts toward Gospel justice." The following year they identified themselves as "the Sisters of the Brooklyn Diocese" and narrowed their justice focus by pledging "to work for liberty and justice for all by searching out means to help women achieve their basic rights and by empowering them to affect society." For the following years, the goal became "ministry for Gospel justice to an urban people." All the programs developed by the Sisters' Senate flow directly from this conception of ministry. Collaboration with priests and laity is likewise stressed. This emphasis on justice does not mean that the Sisters have taken on totally new ministries. The majority continue in education and health-related ministries. Neither can one conclude that the Sisters of the diocese have internalized this justice priority. It is, however, a stated and motivating goal.

A Diocesan Justice Priority: Ministry with the New Immigrants

At the beginning of the 1970s it became obvious to some priests within the diocese that Brooklyn was once again becoming an immigrant diocese. To begin to elaborate a pastoral response to this new and urgent situation, a Catholic Migration Office was founded in 1971 under the leadership of Monsignor Anthony Bevilacqua, also chancellor of the diocese. The emphasis of the office was to meet the real needs of the new peoples in the diocese, and therefore it was important to know who these peoples were. Basic questions were asked, first of all from the viewpoint of the newcomers:

1. Who are the newcomers? In certain language groups, such as the Spanish speaking, it is important to know what particular country they come from. In other instances (e.g., Italy, Yugoslavia, Czechoslovakia), even though they come from the same country, it is important to know from what part of the country they originate.
2. How many are there? Why did they come? Where are they located? Are they located in concentrated groups or scattered throughout the diocese?
3. How recently have they arrived? What is their median age level? Their customary occupations, skills, professions, educational level?
4. What is their religious education and practice background?
5. What is their predominant economic status?
6. Are there deep-seated political or other traditional rivalries between groups from different nations or even between certain groups within the same country?
7. Are they legal residents or illegal aliens? Is it their intention to remain in the United States permanently or to return to their native land as soon as feasible? Are they here with or without their family?
8. What are the highlights of their culture and customs, including important religious festivals and patriotic holidays?
9. What are the special needs and problems of the newcomers in general and of certain groups in particular?

After having determined who the people are and their special needs, it becomes equally important to look at the problem from the point of view of the host church. How many priests and religious in the diocese speak their language? Are there any from the country of origin or from a country whose native tongue is the same? What is the attitude toward the newcomers on the part of the clergy, religious, and laity? Are any willing to work with them? What are the financial implications? The approach therefore is directed toward the person who is to find a place within a particular faith community. Assimilation is not emphasized but, rather, a sense of mission with and among the newcomers.

These newcomers fall into at least twenty-four separate groups. Examples from some of the main ones will highlight the problems. There are 600,000 and more Spanish-speaking Catholics in the diocese. Puerto Ricans, who are American citizens, form the largest single group, but there are significant numbers from the Dominican Republic, Cuba, Central and South America. The number of Mexicans is increasing. Large numbers of them are illegal aliens (undocumented workers). There are only forty-six native Spanish-speaking priests to work with this entire group, while sixty-five American-born priests also are included in the Spanish apostolate. The Haitians number 130,000 but fall into two distinct groups. Some are educated and speak French. The majority are uneducated and speak Creole, and the majority of these are illegal aliens. Seven priests work with the Creole group, while two are native French speakers. Two Americans help out in the French-speaking work. There is only one priest, native-born, to work with the 40,000 Croatians, an appellation they prefer to Yugoslavs. Of the 30,000 Koreans in the diocese, 4,000 are Catholic. This is one of the fastest-growing communities in the diocese. One priest works with them.

In face of such a situation, pastoral planning is difficult and must necessarily be multifaceted. Priority would have to be put on a person-to-person-contact with the newcomers, and no effort made to force acculturation. The newcomers must determine the pace at which they wish to adapt. In addition, assistance is to be extended to all newcomers, including non-Catholics. For this, close ecumenical collaboration becomes essential. The activities of the church per force have to exclude any involvement in nationalistic tendencies or movements that are devoid of any religious dimension. It would seem that to act otherwise with such a mixed population could jeopardize the pastoral work of the church.

One of the serious problems that immediately presents itself is the unity of the diocese. With separate language ministries, how does one preserve a sense of unity? With little stress on acculturation, how does one assist the newcomers to become part of any parish grouping? Should a priest, even a native-born one, necessarily be assigned to one of these specialized apostolates simply because he speaks the language? What image of church does it give if the American clergy is absent from the various ethnic groups? In view of all this, it seems important within the diocese to train the priests to speak the various languages of the newcomers as, among many other things, a sign of the commitment of the church to the welfare of the immigrants. This is a reversal from an earlier model of the immigrant church. Priests now being ordained are expected to speak an additional language, usually Spanish. How well they know the culture is another question, especially for some of the ethnic groups.

One of the major problems facing the immigrants is their very status as immigrants. Uncertain and frightened, the immigrants are often reluctant to approach government agencies for assistance. They do, however, trust the church. The Diocesan Catholic Immigration Office has therefore established neighborhood offices staffed by legal counselors. These offices assist all immigrants and have a very heavy case load. Lack of funds seriously hampers this work. Immigrants also need help with jobs, welfare payments, food stamps. They need to be able to find doctors who speak their language. It would be impossible to separate this ministry into a spiritual and service aspect. The needs intertwine; the approach must be one. Direct service must be coupled with advocacy. The office has been able to influence immigration legislation on the federal, state, and municipal levels.

A Particular Case: The Illegal Alien

While work with legal immigrants presents problems, that with and for the undocumented migrant is of a special nature. These people are the voiceless, the defenseless, the marginalized. As such they claim the special attention and concern of the church.

The Diocese of Brooklyn has one of the largest concentrations of undocumented workers in the northeastern United States. They are here illegally and are therefore wrongly tagged as criminal. In the Brooklyn area many of these undocumented entered the country legally, usually as visitors or students, and overstayed or took jobs without authorization. This subjects them to deportation, not criminal prosecution. It is evident that no accurate figures can be given as to the number of undocumented immigrants. There may be well over a million in New York City. Many fear their presence and oppose efforts to help them. Monsignor Bevilacqua estimated that 95 percent of the local population are opposed to the church's leadership position of amnesty for these aliens. This opposition can turn into active hostility and threats of violence. Continuous efforts on the part of church leaders to educate the Christian community to its obligations to these people are an absolute necessity. It is especially difficult to attempt this in poverty areas.

What are the special difficulties of these undocumented? Since they can be deported at any time, they try to make as much money as they can as quickly as they can, often taking two jobs and being paid below the legal rate. There is no legal recourse for poor working conditions, and it is difficult to obtain hospital or medical care. The psychological strain of fear of arrest and subsequent deportation is intense and has harmful effects on family relationships. Many undocumented families move from place to place lest the immigration agents discover them. This means that the children change schools frequently and do not make friends.

Why is the church especially concerned with this group of people? First of all, a large percentage are at least nominally Catholic. Because of their cultural background, they look to the church for help. It is their only link with a strange world. The transnational character of the church makes them feel at home in it. Finally, the church does not consider primarily their undocumented status but, rather, their needs as persons, as strangers to be received in Christ's name.

So the church becomes the advocate of these people who dare not raise their voice. Legislative influence is extremely important. Amnesty must be promoted, various repressive measures defeated. Abuses of immigration services must be denounced. Every opportunity must be seized to bring the issue up in various forms: television, newspapers, talks, and conferences.

These people need spiritual and psychological support. They must be helped to find medical aid and bail money when necessary. Still more important, they must be given adequate legal assistance in an effort to regularize their status.

Church leadership within the diocese is strong but, as previously noted, the majority of the Catholic population cannot follow this lead. Brooklyn has been called a third world diocese. This is its fourth world.

The Diocese of Brooklyn has effectively and publicly recognized that justice and liberation are integral to its evangelizing mission. Frustrations, divisions among clergy, religious, and lay remain. Various groups vie for extremely limited funds. The socioeconomic situation of New York City is declining. Violence is rising, jobs falling. The "other diocese" is seeking out new ways, is trying to develop an attitude of flexibility, to evolve a new model of church, to live out plurality in unity. First world solutions are being applied to this third world within it. This is a diocese on the move. It is too soon to evaluate the outcome, but we are grateful for the movement.

III

Saint James Cathedral is an anomaly. Situated on a concrete island formed by the Brooklyn exits of two major bridges, it yet has a strangely country air because of its adjoining cemetery. Founded in 1822 as the first Catholic parish on Long Island, named the pro-cathedral of the Brooklyn Diocese in 1853 until, perhaps, something more appropriate could be built, it was not until 1972 that Bishop Mugavero made Saint James the permanent cathedral of the diocese.

As a cathedral parish, Saint James has no territorial boundaries. Actually the residential population of the surrounding area is extremely small. The church seems to have been passed by, or left behind, in the midst of warehouses, factories, and educational institutions. The area is generally poor, although a group of apartments backing onto the cathedral are middle class. Since the vast majority of the members of the parish travel there by choice, they do not reflect the economic and racial condition of the area. While there is a Spanish-speaking priest on the ministry team and one of the three Sunday Masses is in Spanish, Saint James could not be considered an ethnic parish. By definition almost, as a cathedral it could not be. The church belongs to all the people of the diocese.

What is a mission to justice in such atypical circumstances? What common orientation can prevail? What form should, or even could, a parish life take?

For a number of years, Saint James seemed to be on the margin of diocesan life: a large plant including a school and convent but no children, the bishop's seat but not his residence. Despite this, in 1976 a plan was approved by the bishop for the revitalization of the cathedral. A team-ministry approach was basic to the plan: many needs could best be met by a sharing, collaborative, varied group of pastoral ministers.

The cathedral goals as then traced out indicate what factors would be considered important in the future life of the church. Saint James was to be an alternative-parish model based on the concept of a voluntary community. Most parishes cannot allow themselves to make this statement. The principle would not, however, be selectivity but, rather, outreach to the increasing number of urban and inner-city Catholics who are lost to the church because of a certain anonymity inevitable in a large city parish. The parish was to be a community of believers; all else would flow from this. This community would try to be particularly responsive to the needs of the many marginalized and alienated Catholics. Hence a sense of compassion, spiritual poverty, and openness would have to be inherent to the spiritual life of the community. Finally, this community of believers was to be characterized by "a commitment to responsible service on behalf of other alienated or dispossessed peoples—victims of every kind of violence and injustice—as a means of spreading the Kingdom of God on earth among the human family." This is a sharing model of work for justice. The ideal presented is a church of the poor, be its members economically favored or disadvantaged.

Saint James is just beginning to find new life. The efforts are many and seem, in general, to indicate organic growth. Its mission is not seen to be solely, nor even perhaps consciously, primarily one of justice. Its goals and subsequent programs, however, indicate how a mission to justice and liberation is inevitably part of the mission of any community of believers.

The liturgical life at Saint James is rich, characterized by a solemn eucharistic celebration on Sunday. The homily, in this context, is a powerful pastoral force, consciously linking the Christian message and sensitivity to the needs of others. The source and strength of this concern for others is clearly the eucharistic community. Another element of education for justice is the weekly celebration of Vespers. During Advent and Lent, this corporate liturgical prayer takes on added importance by a careful choice of speakers who, within a basically prayerful context, relate prayer and life. The topics chosen are directly related to social questions; the speakers are prominent Catholics or Christians of other denominations. Each Sunday different parishes from throughout the diocese are specially invited to participate in Vespers. Parish members are also urged to invite Catholic or non-Catholic friends to a prayer in which all can share.

Efforts at outreach and concern for others take on a more directly educational form in lecture series. An example of this would be the eight-week "Our Shepherds Speak" series during which bishops from around the country spoke on such questions as capital punishment, land use, nuclear disarmament, and racism. This gave witness to the individual bishop's concrete commitment to teaching justice and living justice. The talks were based on Catholic teaching but also represented the personal views of the bishop. The question period that followed each talk brought out a variety of responses, some intellectual challenging of statements made, some further exploring of the question, some seeking to know how the bishop reached this personal stance. An informal gathering followed each session, giving people an opportunity to meet the bishop personally and to continue the exchange. This series reached people from various parts of the diocese and from other parts of New York City. Plans for another, similar series are already under way.

Other educational programs are being planned, including general and particular justice questions within the context of the social teaching of the church. Such programs are intended as a service for the entire diocese and meet the wishes of the bishop to have the cathedral become a symbolic center of unity for the diocese.

Various cultural programs are an integral part of the life of the cathedral. Music and art are seen as powerful means of promoting human dignity. They are universal forms, in a language accessible to all. The concerts, the art exhibits, the liturgical music all manifest a humanizing element of Christian community, one of celebration and unity in sharing a common experience. This is, in itself, liberating.

Finally, mention has already been made of the large plant no longer in use. The empty buildings will soon be put to new use, giving witness to a commitment to community needs and to the marginalized. A large state mental institution is closing. Some of the mentally handicapped children will be rehoused in the former parish convent. The abandoned school building will be transformed into inexpensive housing and an expanded diocesan center belonging, as it were, to all.

Many of these initiatives are only at their beginning or have not yet been realized, as in the case of plant use. Evaluation is therefore difficult. It is clear that the cathedral is fulfilling a mission of education for justice and calling for a commitment springing from belief in Christ's redeeming love. It could be questioned as to whether opportunities are given to express this commitment in concrete terms. Is this possible, however, in a parish of this type? Is it desirable? Should the members of such a community, which is of a voluntary, nonterritorial nature, be helped, rather, to integrate a commitment to justice into their spiritual life, finding expression for this within their local and professional communities? Can the cathedral parish reach more than a limited number of people and become a force within the entire diocese? Is it somewhat on the periphery still, not coming to grips with the socioeconomic and demographic situation of the diocese? Should it even try to do so? Should it, rather, be a place for all, an alternative?

Saint James is not a typical parish, nor does it carry out its mission to justice in the usual way. It would seem, however, to be a viable model of the church's role in education for justice. Its undeniable strength is in the depth of the life of prayer and worship to which it gives witness.

Conclusion

The justice and liberation mission of the local church in the United States has been briefly examined from three aspects: national, diocesan, and parish. For each level an effort has been made to isolate those aspects that are more peculiar to the American church. This has meant omission of many aspects. The difficulties of this mission have been pointed out at each level. They are closely linked to the history of the United States, to that of the church within the United States. The United States is one of the major actors on the world scene; the church is conscious of this. It is a rich country with masses of poverty within it. It is struggling theologically with this. New peoples are starting to reshape the country, to alter its cultural composition. The church, as well as the country, are equally unprepared for this. The present expression of the justice mission of the church is therefore uncertain, struggling, perhaps failing, perhaps unclear. This is perhaps its greatest strength, leading it closer to becoming a church of the poor, the weak, the uncertain of all but God's power and love.

40

AN AFRICAN VIEW

Gabriel Ojo

I have deliberately chosen to consider this topic from a local point of view, since it deals in essence with the local church. Hence the account that follows relates to the experience, as viewed by a lay person, of the mission of the local church in Nigeria in particular, and in Africa in general, to which the generalizations made can be so widely extended. In looking at the dimensions of liberation and justice, I have also attempted to adopt a historical perspective by dividing the account into three phases. These are, first, the evolution of the mission of the local church; second, the mission of the local church today; and third, the mission of the local church in the future. Furthermore, I have considered liberation and justice in common-day terms. In other words, the legalistic and canonical views have been left aside for the consideration of qualified experts. In any case, issues of liberation and justice are yet at a practical and down-to-earth level within the local church in Africa.

The Evolution of the Mission of the Local Church

In many parts of Africa the local church has existed for a little more than one hundred years. Strictly speaking, only the oldest church communities are that old. In the interior of each of the countries, especially in the remote and relatively inaccessible countryside, the local church is many years, if not decades, younger. In spite of their varying ages, they all share some common origins traceable to the presence of visiting priests who resided at first in the more accessible parts of the country, usually in coastal locations. Laity, coming in touch with the priests, relayed the message (Word of God) farther into the interior, which could be reached at that time only by trekking along bush paths. Such patterns of contact went on until about the third or

Gabriel Ojo, layman, is Professor of Geography at the University of Ife, Ile-Ife, Nigeria. He is also National Secretary of the National Laity Council of Nigeria.

fourth decade of this century when the visits became more frequent. It was only in the 1940s that priests in African countries started using bicycles, and much later in the 1950s that they were able to use automobiles. The type of vehicle used was an important factor in how far and fast the message of God could be spread.

Most of the local churches in the early days relied on the assistance of catechists. Being laity, normally more knowledgeable than the local parishioners and next in rank in this and many other respects to the priests, catechists were highly regarded by the people. On the other hand, they were treated like glorified domestic servants by the priests. From the point of view of the evolution of the early local church, they were an important link between the priests and the other People of God. The catechists assumed the primary role of instructing other lay persons in the Word of God, using as their *vade mecum* the catechism and Bible stories.

In spite of the role of indigenous catechists who were present most of the time and who intervened between the priests and the parishioners, the local church was for all practical purposes regarded in its early years as a foreign institution. For one thing, the early missionaries were all foreigners. They were conspicuously racially different, being Europeans. They were unable to communicate directly with the people, because of language differences. A few of them, however, made gallant efforts to learn and use the rather complex local languages. Even then, the accent was never the same and betrayed them as not truly belonging to the local environment.

The priests had strong economic ties with the world outside the local church. They were dependent on gifts and donations from outside, mainly Europe, to run the local churches. They distributed holy pictures, rosaries, and prayer books, and in some cases performed the role of local dispensers in giving not only first aid but also treatment for common ailments. The local inhabitants had the impression that the priests' resources were bountiful and probably inexhaustible.

In those early days of the local church, the priests existed in a world of their own, with only strictly official contact with other categories of the People of God. The parishioners treated them as being distinctly holy persons who had nothing in common with their poor parishioners. In other words, there was a sharp dichotomy among the People of God of the time, that is between the clergy and the laity, whose respective spheres of influence never overlapped. The separation was not based on the distinction of religious roles alone. It rested also on the gaps caused by the levels of education that the two classes acquired, the priests being the "learned men" and the parishioners being the uninformed and untutored. In general welfare terms, the priests belonged to the elite and upper class of the society while their parishioners were of the lowly struggling class.

In those early days the liberation and justice dimensions of the mission of the local church were related and directed to the pressing issues of the time and determined by the structure of the human relationship just sketched. The local church was the beacon of light that grappled with the darkness of ignorance, superstition, and diseases. The schools, which were in essence missionary schools, became the front of the assault unleashed on the forces of conservatism and traditionalism. The silent war of liberation waged on the shackles of poverty by those who had the rare opportunity then of school education was led by the local church.

Justice took on new dimensions as the authority of the old order was being questioned and reexamined. No longer was an action proper because the elders said so, but because it was espoused by the local church. A new economic order, which did not rest on exploitation and servitude, emerged and was being defended in the open. Might was not necessarily right any longer. Those who would have suffered in silence under the pre-local-church order had understanding and a sympathetic refuge in the local church. The author remembers vividly how in 1947 the local church stood resolutely on the side of a parishioner in one local church community who defied a long-standing custom of the land by not allowing the corpse of his father to be cast away into a reserved forest simply because he was struck dead by lightning. It was a grim battle, so to say, which the local church won out of sheer doggedness. Before the arrival of the local church, the culprit would have been ruthlessly liquidated and ostracized for even daring to challenge traditional practices. Examples of such liberation and justice, which the local church procured, can be multiplied at numerous levels.

The Mission of the Local Church Today

Many transformations have taken place in the local church even though it is, for all practical purposes, a relatively young institution, as previously indicated. It is no longer the only institution that fosters educational development through the running of schools. The governments of these countries have not only participated in the educational enterprise but have in some cases taken over mission schools. Today's local priests are no longer foreigners. In most cases, they are indigenous inhabitants, generally referred to as "sons of the soil." They are no longer the most educated persons in their communities. Many of the parishioners of the local church today are lawyers, engineers, doctors, and university professors, to mention a few among those who can claim similar educational achievements in their own fields. There are fewer full-time catechists than in the early days. By contrast they cannot effectively perform any longer the role of contact persons between the priests and the parishioners. Furthermore, the local church has been moving toward being independent in respect to its financial resources. The days when priests were dispensers of material and religious objects were gone; other specialists in various fields had taken their place, medical doctors for instance.

It is necessary to grasp this reformed image and status of the local church, as it is today, to be able to appreciate its involvement in liberation and justice. It is also significant to note that the consequences of its changed image and status have been felt more internally than otherwise in recent years. The local church has fought for liberation and justice first and foremost within itself. More than ever before, every class of the People of God is participating or struggling to participate more actively in the decision-making processes affecting the local church. Unlike in the early years, all members are asking questions on role and participation of themselves and others. Priests can no longer constitute themselves alone into a class that hardly communicates with the others. In fact they are being called upon from time to time to give regular accounts of their stewardship directly to the people.

The parishioners continue to press for further involvement in the work of the church on an equitable and just basis. They want to know how church projects are being executed, by whom, and at what costs. They want to plan the raising of funds and support for the local church, along with the parish priests. In some cases they want to be involved in running the seminaries to the extent of knowing why particular students have to be asked to withdraw. In short, the liberation and justice dimensions of the local church have a deep-rooted implication for dismantling barriers that existed in previous years among the People of God, who now want to see themselves as different parts of the same body that must work together in a systems fashion for the welfare of that united body and all its parts.

It is pertinent to call attention to the rapidly growing involvement of women in this trend toward liberation and justice. Although it is often thought that women in Africa have more or less been confined to a secondary role in the society as a whole, there is every indication that within the local church they have through their own contributions vied for positions not inferior to those of men. The differentiation of roles, which makes the women tackle specified assignments (for example, church cleaning and decoration), portrays them as specialists rather than as subordinates. The same can be said of the men in the performance of their own specialized roles.

The liberation and justice dimensions of the mission of the local church seem to be less consequential in the wider society today than some decades ago. By and large the local church has been dwarfed by some other modern institutions. For example, governments have taken over not only the schools but also the hospitals, welfare centers, and related economic enterprises that the local church provided and operated years back. In a few countries the resistance that the local church has put up against these trespasses and takeover bids by the governments has brought the church and the state into close confrontation. Currently the local church in Nigeria is fighting tooth and nail to preserve the right of parents to send their children to schools of their choice, including private schools. On the other hand, some state governments are attempting to abolish private schools. Although the issue has been taken to court for constitutional interpretation, it is a reflection of the challenges to what was previously regarded as the privileged position of the local church, which used to have the last say on such matters.

In many other ways the views of the local church on nonspiritual matters have lost the weight attached to them some years ago. During the civil war in Nigeria, for instance, the opinions of church leaders on how to reconcile the combatants were openly derided and ignored as good enough for the pulpit but unacceptable and impracticable within the context of the cold realities of politics of national survival. Such attempts to draw a distinction between what is often called the church view and the common experience of the people have set limits to the dimensions of the mission of the church in the areas of liberation and justice. However, this is not to say that deaf ears have been turned completely to the admonitions of the local church.

It must be emphasized that in many parts of Africa the church continues to exert its presence and influence in a variety of sociopolitical matters. The local church has come up from time to time, especially through the various episcopal conferences, to make its views unambiguously known on certain issues of the moment, such as contraceptives and abortion, educational and political rights, as well as just wages and the dignity of labor. Similarly the laity councils and various lay apostolates have become much more than the mere watchdogs of the interests of the local church; they are real catalysts in the public sector where they are, by virtue of their calling in life, active participants and protagonists. At the parish, diocesan, and national levels the voice of the laity is loud and clear on the constitutional rights of the citizens as well as the responsibility of the governments to guarantee these rights.

The Mission of the Local Church in the Future

The extent to which the local church can continue to animate the society in the future for liberation and justice will depend on how committed it is, in the face of many odds, to identify itself with the totality of the expectations and aspirations of the people. Perhaps it is a well-known fact that the true test of the church can be determined at the grassroots level where the problems of liberation pinch most and are therefore best articulated. It is at this level that solutions, if they can be found, will be immediately felt and become most reassuring and comforting. Hence the local church has a unique opportunity of grappling with the totality of the expectations and aspirations of the people, which cannot now be defined in too precise a manner because, by nature and character, they are wide-ranging and dynamic.

Broadly speaking, however, they can be subdivided into material and spiritual expectations and aspirations. Certainly the local church, not unlike the universal church, can be said to be already fulfilling its role with regard to the spiritual aspects of life. It is in relation to the material aspects that fears may be expressed about the inadequacy of the current efforts being made by the local church. By projection into the future, one's fears can become proportionately magnified, since increasing material needs have to be satisfied.

The local church needs to step up its activities for the total liberation of Africa and its diverse and multiple inhabitants. The local church must be seen as helping people to obtain and preserve the acknowledged human rights for life (especially for self- and group-preservation), education, and welfare. The right of people to justice and fair play should be a concern of the local church. Anything that would detract from these rights should be seen as an enemy of the People of God, and it should not be given breathing space for survival.

In conclusion, the local church should be the soul of each nation, the bulwark against corruption and oppression, and the antidote against people's inhumanity. For it to succeed in this onerous task, the local church will require the cooperation of all People of God at all times. Such cooperation must be based on at least three principles or lines of action. The first concerns the form of administration to be adopted by the local church, which should follow the principle of local church democracy. To be effective and to be in conformity with recent socioeconomic and political experiences of the area, the local church must from now on be administered by consensus rather than by autocracy. Because of the importance of this point on the African continent, it is necessary to repeat many times that the days of priestly autocracy are already behind us. Every effort should now be made to practice local church democracy as the government of the People of God by the People of God for the People of God at the local church level.

The second principle, which is closely related to the first, is that of local church management by acceptance. All those who are involved in the management of the local church must see themselves as being accountable and responsible to God through the People of God. They must manage the local church in a way and manner acceptable to the People of God, that is, of course, to the majority of the people. At one time a priest was charged with the responsibility of managing a parish as long as his administration was acceptable to the bishop. Today the scope of acceptance must be expanded to include the People of God acting through pastoral and laity councils, among others, who assist the bishop in the administration of the church. In general, once the principle of local church democracy is adopted, that of management by acceptance will follow naturally.

The third principle deals with the necessity to communicate. All the People of God will be able to work together as interdependent parts of a body only when they are linked together by adequate information on what they are doing or are to do, both as individuals and as groups. To strengthen the local church, the Word must be in constant circulation. The responsibility to spread the Word must be shared by all so that it can speedily reach all those who are not yet in the fold.

Although these principles or lines of action for reinvigorating the local church may sound revolutionary, they can be implemented as long as there is goodwill without upsetting the growth and development of the church. In fact their implementation will enable the local church to fit smoothly into a world of rapid social and structural change. One more point should be made as the final implication of this contribution. Although most of the points made in the foregoing paragraphs are couched in general terms, in order to render them applicable to a continent of considerable diversities, it is hoped that the reader will be able to adapt the generalized statements to the local church under consideration at any time. Obviously there should be as many approaches as there are local churches.

41

THE AUSTRALIAN CHURCH

Christopher Sidoti

This paper is not a thesis, carefully footnoted, nor a research document. It offers a "general overview" and is a personal reflection based on my experience as a twenty-nine-year-old Catholic and as an employee of a church justice agency for over two years. If the paper seems to give undue prominence to the Catholic Commission for Justice and Peace, that is because I know more about that agency and its work than I do about other agencies and their work.

The demand of Christian discipleship, the mission bequeathed by Jesus Christ, is to follow him. Liberation is integral to this mission. Jesus identified himself totally with our humanity (cf. Phil. 2:6–7). He fulfilled the prophets whose constant call was for justice (cf. Mt. 5:48). He clearly acknowledged those who were blessed in God's eyes and those who were cursed (cf. Lk. 6:20–26). He announced the coming of the kingdom where justice will dwell (cf. 2 Pet. 3:13). He established the commandment of love (cf. Jn. 13:34) and the model of service (cf. Jn. 13:15), which are inseparable from the justice of God (cf. *Justice in the World*). He showed the lifestyle that accords with God's will (cf. Mt. 25:35–37).

The mission of Jesus Christ continues in the communities that form themselves around his name. Drawing from the words of the prophet Isaiah, he clearly described this mission:

> He has sent me to bring the good news to the poor,
> to proclaim liberty to captives
> and to the blind new sight,
> to set the downtrodden free,
> to proclaim the Lord's year of favour [Lk. 4:18].

This mission is also the mission of his church, the mission for which his disciples were sent out (cf. Acts 1:8).

Christopher Sidoti, layman, is the Associate Secretary for the Australian Catholic Commission for Justice and Peace. He is also a member of the national executive of the National Youth Council of Australia.

Jesus lived and acted in a concrete situation, in a particular moment in history in a particular society—Palestine, during the first third of the first century A.D. His life and his actions had political and religious implications.

The task for the church today is to examine "the signs of the times" in an attempt to discern the Christian response appropriate to our particular moment in history and our particular society. This examination draws the church back to the Scriptures, to the message of the life, death, and resurrection of Jesus Christ. That message is the reality of the kingdom of God, already in the world and yet to come.

Jesus Christ died once for all (cf. 1 Pet. 3:18). His mission is universal, for all people in all times and all societies. But it is for the church in each time and each society to rediscover the mission and the message in the contemporary world. This task falls to the church at all levels—universal, regional, national, and local.

Thus a necessary part of the mission of the Australian church is analysis of the society in which it is located, reflection on the analysis in the light of the Scriptures and magisterium, and action on behalf of justice.

Situating the Australian Church

The Australian church is situated in a predominantly European society on the edge of the largest and most populous continent, Asia. It is located in a society that has traditionally been dominated by myths of general well-being, equality, and independence ("lucky Australia") and by an ideology of free enterprise.

The myth of general well-being holds that there are no poor in Australia, that all are able to live comfortable lives. There is ample evidence to the contrary. The Royal Commission of Enquiry into Poverty, in an extensive official investigation, revealed the widespread incidence of poverty throughout the nation. A recent study indicated that there are almost 2 million poor—one person in seven. These people experience life as a continuing search for adequate food and clothing, shelter, medical care, education, and employment.

The incidence of poverty is particularly high among certain identifiable groups: aged persons, single-parent families and families whose sole breadwinner receives a low income, sick and handicapped persons, the unemployed, single women, recently arrived migrants and refugees, Aboriginal Australians. In most cases, the poor are those who, because of race or status or some disability, have no regular income and no power in society.

Poor Australians face the particular hardship of being poor in a predominantly rich society. It is in fact a society that largely denies the presence of extreme poverty in its midst. So, in addition to the physical effects of poverty, poor Australians must also endure the psychological suffering of being ignored, of having their very existence denied, of having no access to the conspicuous wealth all around them, of being personally blamed for their own condition. Being poor in a rich society involves unique hardship.

Despite the present and growing wealth of the country as a whole, poverty in Australia is increasing. Rapid social change is occurring. It is associated with the introduction of new technology and the transfer of capital from manufacturing to mining sectors. These changes result in rising unemployment, greater numbers of poor, the allocation of wealth away from the poor and toward the rich, and the increasing powerlessness of individuals and communities before the entrenched interests of power and capital.

The myth of equality holds that, not only are there no poor in Australia, but there are also no rich; all are equal in a great middle-class society. But Australians in fact are not all equal. Far from being in a land of equal opportunity, the vast majority of Australians encounter inequality as a daily fact of life. Attempts by reform governments to guarantee more equal access to education and health care have been short-lived, repealed by succeeding conservative governments, so that the parliamentary path to social change has been discredited.

The myth of equality is evident, too, in Australian democracy. The national political process is structured on the Westminster system of representative parliamentary democracy. But equality is more theoretical than actual. Inequality is entrenched even at the most basic level of voting: electorates are weighted in favor of rural (and more conservative) voters. The principle of "one-vote, one-value" is implemented in only two of the nine political divisions in the nation.

Inequality is a fact in much more serious ways. In Australian society, power definitely lies with the rich. They have better access to the political process and more power in their own lives, in their interest areas, and in the nation as a whole.

The myth of independence holds that Australia is an autonomous, sovereign state with full control over its present and its future. But Australian society is entwined in the web that is the modern world. It is increasingly dependent, politically and economically, on what happens elsewhere in the world.

Politically, Australia has been tied by successive national governments into close alliance with the United States. Because of this alliance, Australia became involved militarily in the Korean war and the Vietnam war and in the "emergency" in Malaya in the 1950s. It has become the site of several United States communications stations, which greatly increase Australia's vulnerability to nuclear attack.

Economically, Australia is dependent on the economies of the United States, Japan and, to a lesser extent, Western Europe. Like many other nations, it is subject to the capricious movement of international capital. Australia has been unable to insulate itself from the international economic recession of the past decade. On the contrary, it has suffered long-term damage from it, as multinational companies have withdrawn from Australia's manufacturing sector in favor of the greater profits found in manufacturing in East and Southeast Asia and in resource exploitation in Australia. Both trends mean the loss of hundreds of thousands of jobs in Australia. The future may see Australia as the world's quarry, with great wealth for the local elite and their multinational partners and poverty for the majority of Australians.

The myth of independence reinforces the isolation of Australians. Tucked away at the end of the world, supposedly independent of the winds of history around, Australians generally remain ignorant of events in the wider world. They show little understanding and sympathy for the struggles of other peoples for liberation and development. They have a poor experience of solidarity with other peoples, of common action for justice.

The ideology of free enterprise underpins Australian society. It is *not* an ideology of "capitalism"—even use of that term implies a social analysis that is considered Marxist! It is an ideology of "free enterprise": the individual is supreme, not the community; competition is the fundamental rule, not cooperation, and the marketplace the sole arbiter; government should encourage "free enterprise" in all fields, including those of such basic human needs as health, legal rights, and housing.

The ideology of free enterprise, with its associated myths of general well-being, equality, and independence, makes for a society that is highly competitive and individualistic, that has poor awareness of social issues and poor social analysis, that largely ignores its own injustices. The greatest injustice is perhaps the very fact that in Australia there need be no poverty and oppression. It has sufficient wealth both to guarantee the basic human needs of all its citizens and to provide for a positive role in supporting the full human development of other peoples.

The Australian Church Responds

Action on behalf of justice is an essential part of the mission of each part of the Christian community, from the universal church through to the individual Christian.

The Australian Episcopal Conference

The Australian Episcopal Conference (AEC) is the collective assembly of the forty-three Australian bishops. It meets twice yearly in plenary sessions and in committees. The committee principally concerned with issues of justice is the Episcopal Committee for Development and Peace.

The AEC's commitment to action for justice is not particularly strong. It has a good record in areas of traditional Catholic morality, such as abortion, and in certain less controversial areas, generally removed from Australia, such as the situation of refugees and the detention of political prisoners. But it has failed to speak and act in its own name on many of the most serious social issues in Australia.

The AEC has established a number of agencies at the national level, whose work concerns areas of social injustice in Australia. The Catholic Commission for Justice and Peace, Australian Catholic Relief, and Action for World Development are responsible to the Episcopal Committee for Development and Peace. The Australian Catholic Social Welfare Commission is responsible to the Episcopal Committee for Social and Charitable Works. The National Missionary Council is responsible to the Episcopal Committee for Missions. The work of these agencies and their relationships with the AEC are important components of the Australian church's justice ministry.

Catholic Commission for Justice and Peace. The Catholic Commission for Justice and Peace (CCJP) was established by the AEC in 1968, following the establishment of the Pontifical Commission for Justice and Peace in the Vatican and the request by Paul VI that national episcopal conferences consider establishing similar bodies. The Australian CCJP was restructured in 1972 and given its own charter in 1978.

The CCJP is a body of twelve persons, from all over Australia, appointed by various groups of bishops. Its chairman is the Episcopal Deputy appointed by the AEC as a whole. The remaining eleven are priests, nuns, and lay people.

The CCJP receives an annual grant from the AEC (A$115,000 in 1980), with which it manages a national office, employs a full-time staff of five, and conducts programs. In recent years the CCJP's priority areas of work have included Aboriginal Land Rights, unemployment, human rights, refugees, and issues of justice in the church.

There has been considerable public discussion of the status and work of the CCJP during its short life. In 1977, for example, a prominent Catholic layman, B. A. Santamaria (of whom more later), presented to the AEC an extensive brief arguing for the abolition of the commission. He fought his case in the secular and religious press for six months before the AEC reaffirmed its continued sponsorship of the commission.

This sort of attack on the CCJP intensified again late in 1979, following publication of the Social Justice Statement. This annual statement is one of its most important tasks each year. The 1979 statement dealt with unemployment, which it described as the "most serious social problem in Australia today." The statement not only described the unemployment situation but made positive proposals that were contrary to the policy of the Australian government. Following publication of this statement, political and media attention was focused on the commission. There was public disagreement between the prime minister and the commission's national secretary. The secretary of the AEC intervened in the dispute by releasing a statement that supported the prime minister, debased the status of the statement (and by implication the CCJP), and contradicted the CCJP's national secretary. This statement was released without prior consultation with (or even notification to) the CCJP.

This incident has brought to a head a persistent question of attribution of CCJP statements to the AEC. The AEC has always been concerned to distance itself from the CCJP and its statements. In spite of this, CCJP statements are frequently attributed to the bishops. In years gone by, no doubt this error arose out of a misunderstanding of the relationship between the two bodies. But both bodies have often explained the relationship so that innocent attribution must now be rare. Still, the attribution continues, generally coming from critics of the CCJP, especially from clergy and laity associated with B. A. Santamaria's National Civic Council.

Attribution, then, is no longer innocent but deliberately intended to embarrass the bishops and damage the CCJP. And it is successful in doing this. There have been several developments that give rise to fears for the commission's future position. Certain bishops have sought to give the one bishop on the CCJP a power of veto over all decisions—the bishop, they say, should not simply be "one among equals." Further, strong attempts were made, almost successfully, to prevent publication of the 1980 Social Justice Statement on the social and political responsibilities of Christians. Moves to stop another CCJP program have been more successful: the AEC has twice refused to endorse a proposed educational program in support of Aboriginal Land Rights.

The CCJP's current position then is ambiguous. It is well supported by many sections of the Catholic church and of other Christian churches. But it has encountered continuing opposition from reactionary groups, both inside and outside the AEC. The result is that a considerable proportion of the commission's limited resources is diverted to internal questions of survival rather than to the wider demands of Christian service.

Australian Catholic Relief. Australian Catholic Relief (ACR) was established in 1964 as the Australian church's agency for international aid and development. It receives its funds by way of donations from Catholics, especially through Project Compassion, the annual Lenten appeal.

Like the CCJP, ACR is a national body whose National Committee members come from all parts of Australia. The AEC appoints one of its number to be episcopal deputy and chairman. Other members are appointed by groups of bishops and by other church bodies. These members are priests, religious, and lay people.

For many years, ACR led the field among Australian aid agencies. Very early in its history, its principal focus changed from relief to development. This meant that it sought to use its funds to change situations, to encourage the development and independence of communities, and not simply to give aid that maintained the basic status quo.

Parallel to this emphasis on development was a commitment to justice education. ACR realized that development in the third world would come about only if there were change in the first world. The interdependence of human societies caused this. So it decided to commit some of its resources to justice education in Australia.

These concerns for development and justice education caused the same reaction against ACR as the CCJP had experienced, if not quite as intense. More conservative elements within the church objected to funds going for education and opposed, on an ideological basis, many of the development projects assisted. Pressure on ACR became apparent in reduced contributions from some areas and actual withdrawal from Project Compassion by one diocese.

A change of executive leadership in ACR in 1977 has produced noticeable changes in the agency. The commitment to development and to justice education is still acknowledged but the practice of the agency has altered. ACR now has no staff with development-education qualifications working nationally. It has become reluctant to fund activist Aboriginal organizations, as the bishops most concerned with Aboriginal areas are quite opposed to Aboriginal initiatives for self-determination. Decisions to fund controversial projects are generally kept hidden rather than used as catalysts for education and change.

Many of ACR's problems are similar to those faced by the World Council of Churches because of the Program to Combat Racism. Unlike the World Council of Churches, however, the opposition has left ACR rather directionless and no longer playing a leadership role in Australia.

Action for World Development. Action for World Development (AWD) is jointly funded by AEC and the Australian Council of Churches. It had its genesis in an ecumenical study program on world development in 1972. Following that study program, both sponsoring agencies agreed to continue to fund AWD to enable it to service the work of many local groups that continued after the study program.

Today AWD is a network of local groups concerned about justice and development. It has groups and offices in all states and a national coordinating structure. AWD's programs are primarily group-based and state-based. Even the sorts of activities undertaken vary from place to place. In Queensland, for example, AWD has played a prominent political role in support of Aboriginal Land Rights and in opposition to restrictions on civil rights by the state government. New South Wales groups, by contrast, have been more concerned with issues of personal lifestyle than with particular national social issues.

The broad focus of AWD is education and action. It seems, however, that the network in general has turned away from prominent involvement in national political issues in favor of more localized and more personal activity.

Although CCJP and AWD would share a common theological perspective, the two agencies are opposites in operation: (1) CCJP is primarily a national agency with some local contacts; AWD is primarily localized, although with a national office and national staff; (2) CCJP focuses on major national and international issues; AWD's primary focus is local; (3) CCJP sees political lobbying as an important part of its role; AWD is more concerned with network-building. The two agencies, then, frequently complement each other. Together they provide a strong force for social change.

AWD was the center of considerable controversy in the past, when its activities were more public. For example, it was the target of B. A. Santamaria's attack in 1977 along with the CCJP. In more recent times, however, controversy has lessened and the AEC agreed to guarantee AWD's grant for a three-year period.

Australian Catholic Social Welfare Commission. The Australian Catholic Social Welfare Commission is the bishops' advisory body on social welfare. It consists primarily of the directors of church counseling and welfare bureaus. In addition, there are several persons co-opted because of particular expertise: The commission's members are predominantly clerical, predominantly male, and predominantly welfare administrators. There are no representatives of consumers or even of the St. Vincent de Paul Society, the largest Catholic welfare-delivery organization in Australia.

The commission sees its role very narrowly. It is concerned with social welfare, not social justice, and many of its members openly express the view that there is no connection between the two. It sees its role principally as advising the bishops—in 1979, for example, it conducted a consultation on the family to prepare a report to the AEC. It also plays a limited public role: it has made public statements on such matters as family law and the National Commission of Inquiry on Human Relationships. But it has said and done almost nothing on the questions of poverty and unemployment, and avoids any consideration at all of Aboriginal issues.

Attempts have been made to give the commission a wider vision. In particular, a national Catholic Conference on the Church in Social Welfare was sponsored by the commission in May 1980. This conference saw a strong call from all sections of the church for greater cooperation between welfare and justice ministries because of the complementary nature of the two. The Australian Catholic Social Welfare Commission, however, has dismissed the conference's recommendations and has disowned the entire process of the conference.

National Missionary Council. The National Missionary Council (NMC) brings together representatives of mission societies and missionary orders in the Australian church. It has therefore had a strong representation from those associated with fund-raising for missions and those operating from a theology of mission as "out there." Equally, there have been strong advocates of a wider view of mission as the mission of each local church and each individual Christian at the local level. This second group has placed greater emphasis on the close relationship among mission, justice, and development.

The tension between these views of mission continues within the NMC and within the Australian church in general. Increasingly, however, the wider justice-oriented view of mission has found expression in the work of the NMC. This is evident in the greater orientation toward justice education. So, for example, the NMC is conducting a program (with the assistance of Australian Catholic Relief) to devise guidelines for the integration of justice-mission-development issues and perspectives into school curriculae in all subjects. The Catholic Missions Office of the Sydney Archdiocese is also sponsoring a program (again with Australian Catholic Relief assistance) for conscientization of teachers, education officials, and students on justice issues.

Religious Orders

Many religious orders, and groups within religious orders, have responded to the gospel command to justice. It is impossible to provide a comprehensive list of developments in this area, but three examples may provide some indication of the direction.

Sisters of Mercy. The Sisters of Mercy devoted their first national assembly in 1977 to the theme "Mercy and Justice." The conference was open to any interested people and made a particular attempt to involve poor and disadvantaged people. The conference sought to provide a new direction for the order's ministry that was appropriate to the contemporary Australian context.

The official documents of the order, including those coming from this conference, reflect a concern for justice and a call to individual communities to implement that concern in their own activities. The order has established a national justice committee to monitor and encourage the development of this ministry.

In response to these moves, one province of the order is convening a consultation between Sisters and Aboriginal people. The consultation will take the Sisters to the Aborigines (not the reverse) and will involve bias in favor of Aboriginal participants in numbers and program.

Marist Brothers. The Marist Brothers have also shown concern for justice issues at the national level. Like the Sisters of Mercy, the Marist Brothers have developed a policy that incorporates a strong justice dimension and a commitment to justice education in schools. A committee of the order has sought to assist schools in taking up justice education by preparing programs and resource material for use by teachers and students.

De La Salle Brothers. The De La Salle Brothers were established to be of service first to the poor. As happens very often, however, the order came to acquire property and schools that cater more to middle-class churchgoers than to the poor. The order has been carefully reviewing its activities and its use of resources and personnel in recent years in an attempt to reassert its traditional priority. The consequences of this reassessment are apparent in Sydney. Several communities have pooled funds to employ a lay woman to coordinate, encourage, and resource justice education in schools and to conduct in-service training in this for teachers. Three Brothers in Sydney have also been withdrawn from more traditional apostolates in favor of work with disadvantaged groups. Two work with young people in an inner-city area with a high incidence of crime and drugs. The third works with Aboriginal people.

Local Action

Much of the "action on behalf of justice" in Australia is taking place at the local level in a largely uncoordinated manner.

There has already been reference to Action for World Development, a national network of local groups concerned about justice and development. The Young Christian Workers and the Young Christian Students are other national organizations with their primary focus on local groups and local action. Both groups have had a difficult history in Australia—periods of opposition from certain bishops have seen the organizations barred in some dioceses and have generally hindered the development of large mass movements. Apart from these national groups at the local level, local action is generally uncoordinated and frequently unseen.

Local Justice Groups. The development of parish and diocesan pastoral councils in Australia has been very slow. So, too, has the development of local justice groups. Both CCJP and ACR have established links with a number of these groups, but they are entirely independent in their structure and program.

In most instances these groups operate on a diocesan or regional basis. They seek to work with the support of the local bishop, but generally they have little or no regular contact with him. Some are established by the local bishop and the members appointed by him, but equally the groups can simply be a number of interested people who want to act on justice issues from a Christian perspective and so either establish themselves or approach the local bishop for approval.

The programs for these groups are generally oriented toward justice education. Many conduct programs on important social issues or on the ministry for justice generally. Most assist the CCJP in promoting the annual Social Justice Statement and ACR in promoting Project Compassion. One or two have been more active in actually pursuing issues both by means of public statements and by means of direct approaches to politicians.

Parishes. The gospel demand for action for justice has not, in general, reached the vast majority of churchgoing Catholics at the parish level. Here both clergy and laity have retained an individualistic, pietistic Catholicism. So social issues and Christian responsibility are rarely the subject of homilies. Parish activities almost exclusively relate to worship, to parish administration, and to the Catholic education system.

To take an example, parishes constitute the primary vehicle for distribution of the annual Social Justice Statement on Social Justice Sunday. Priests are urged to preach on the theme of the statement and to orient the Sunday's liturgy around the call to act for justice. But barely a third of parish priests even order copies of the statement for their parishes. It is not possible to ascertain the proportion who preach on social justice but from personal experience I would say that the proportion is probably very small. These simple observances of Social Justice Sunday are not important in themselves but they can contribute to an assessment of the acceptance of justice as integral to evangelization. Unfortunately, among the Australian clergy and most of the laity even a nominal acceptance is lacking.

Education

The Catholic church in Australia has an extensive education system, at primary, secondary, and, more recently, tertiary levels. Today there are over a half-million children in Catholic schools—about one-sixth of all school children.

Much of the history of Catholic schools has involved an attempt to gain community acceptance and government funds. For this reason, Catholic schools have increasingly tended to be not an alternative system of education but almost a mirror image of the state system with the addition of a distinct course in religious education ("Christian Doctrine" as it used to be known). This situation has drawn criticism from theological conservatives who challenge contemporary catechetics and argue for the teaching of dogma at every available opportunity.

The situation is also criticized by those who see Catholic schools as necessarily countercultural if they are to be true to the gospel. Gospel values cannot simply be dogma, nor can they be isolated to a distinct area of study. They must underlie the whole curriculum and methodology of education. So justice issues must surface in a critical understanding of economics, history, literature, science—in short, all subjects. And the mode of instruction must reflect these values—learning should not be simply classroom-based but must take students to the poor to hear their voices and views. And the organizational structure of the school must not be based on relationships of dominance and subservience but only on service and respect.

In the past, Catholic education in Australia has failed to meet gospel demands. Catholic schools were noted for their harsh discipline, the brutal treatment of students. They sought to produce model citizens of the dominant culture rather than critical activists for social change. They increasingly became the preserve of the rich rather than existing for service of the poor.

There has been a healthy awakening of conscience more recently, however. Many religious orders, individual teachers, and even whole schools are reorienting their work toward justice. There are many genuine attempts to change. The National Missionary Council's program to develop integrated justice curriculae already mentioned is an example of this. But change is slow in coming. Changes in Catholic schools reflect more the changes in society rather than a heightened awareness of the demands of the gospel.

Ecumenism

If action for justice is to be a true reflection of the kingdom, it must be ecumenical action. For the kingdom of God is a kingdom of communion and fellowship, and not one of division.

The Australian Catholic church's record in the area of ecumenism has not been good at the level of joint action. Theological discussions and interchurch statements on dogmatic issues have been significant, but there is little evidence of active cooperation. The Australian Episcopal Conference and the Australian Council of Churches rarely meet as such. With the exception of Action for World Development, discussed above, they have no joint programs.

Some church agencies, on the other hand, show greater commitment to ecumenism. The Catholic Commission for Justice and Peace, for example, has a policy of acting ecumenically. Its charter contains an objective of performing its work "in an ecumenical perspective." In pursuance of this objective, the CCJP and the Australian Council of Churches have established a joint task force to promote church support for Aboriginal Land Rights. The CCJP has also conducted joint conferences with the Australian Council of Churches and with agencies of the Uniting Church of Australia. It meets annually with the equivalent agencies of other churches and involves them in the preparation of the Social Justice Statement.

National Civic Council

No discussion of the social and political work of the Catholic church in Australia can ignore the National Civic Council (NCC) and its president, B. A. Santamaria. The NCC is a secular, predominantly lay organization that has a strong continuing influence on the church.

The NCC has its origin in Catholic Action in the 1940s. At that time, B. A. Santamaria combined his leadership of Catholic Action with the leadership of the Catholic Social Studies Movement ("the Movement"), which infiltrated the Australian Labour party and trade unions in an anticommunist crusade. The Movement used all the tactics of its communist opponents: secrecy, manipulation, authoritarian control. It sought power for itself, not for people. Its initial concern for the well-being of ordinary people was combined with an anticommunism that came to dominate everything else.

The Movement divided the Australian Labour party, the unions, and the Catholic church. It was supported by the Australian bishops who declared that Catholics were bound in conscience to accept the social "teaching" of B. A. Santamaria. This support extended to the Democratic Labour party, the new political party formed after the Australian Labour party split. The Democratic Labour party was modeled on European Christian democratic parties. It became a minority Catholic party in Australian politics but was successful in keeping the conservative parties in office for sixteen years. It collapsed in 1974.

The split in the church eventually resulted in appeals to Rome by the opposing factions. One sought a declaration that the church should not give official backing to an organization that played a party political role; the other faction opposed such a ruling. Eventually in 1958 the decision from Rome favored the former. When official church sponsorship was withdrawn, the Movement was restructured as the National Civic Council. It was constituted as a secular organization but was in fact solidly Catholic. It retained most of the Movement's clerical and lay membership and continued (and continues) to have a major influence within the church.

The NCC is solidly founded on the theology of the 1930s. It therefore stands totally opposed to the theology that underpins the work of such agencies as the Catholic Commission for Justice and Peace. Its world-view is based on a cold-war perspective that divides the world into two camps and sees the West as pitted against the advancing forces of monolithic atheistic communism. It therefore has no understanding of or sympathy for the struggles of oppressed peoples.

The NCC campaigns strongly against the CCJP and other church agencies that seek to respond to the gospel demand for justice. This has consequences for these agencies at the national level, since the influence of the NCC on the Australian Episcopal Conference is such as to make the very survival of the agencies uncertain at times. It also has consequences for the effectiveness of these agencies at the local, parish level: NCC members and supporters (clerical and lay) occupy important positions in most Catholic organizations and in a very large number of parishes.

The history of the church and the NCC also causes difficulties to such agencies as the CCJP in another way. The divisions of the 1950s were deep and lasting. They cause many Catholics to want to avoid involving the church in any public controversy or internal disagreement. Many or even most bishops would be remembered among these. Others, who opposed the Movement, see the new agencies in the same light and so seek to apply the Vatican decision of 1958 to them. But there are clear distinctions between the Movement and the Catholic Commission for Justice and Peace, for example. The Movement was party-political and sought to influence public policy by active infiltration of a political party and trade unions; the CCJP is totally nonpartisan and rejects on theological grounds the tactics of infiltrating other organizations. The Movement operated in total secrecy; the CCJP is completely open. The Movement attempted to bind people in conscience; the CCJP appeals to people in a prophetic rather than a dogmatic way. The Movement sought to control; the CCJP to serve. The Movement pursued power for itself; the CCJP aims to empower people.

General Comments

From an overview of the ministry for justice in the Australian church, many general aspects become apparent. A few of these are especially significant and so worthy of brief comment.

Gaps: Implementation and Credibility

There have been many fine documents produced by the universal church and the Australian church, which speak of the church's commitment to action for justice.

But in this country, at least, the fine words are not matched by action. At almost all levels of the church, lip service is given to the justice ministry; the social teaching of Vatican Council II, the synods, and the popes are praised and the vocabulary of liberation is mouthed, but there is little evidence of implementation.

The justice message of Scripture is largely unknown to most Catholics. It has no obvious effect on the program of parishes and dioceses or on the daily lives of good, churchgoing Christians. To some extent agencies such as the Catholic Commission for Justice and Peace indirectly promote the implementation gap. They are pointed to as examples of the church's active concern for justice and used to excuse inaction by other parts of the church. They are thus an effective, if disliked, means of diverting criticism away from the Australian Episcopal Conference, for example.

The implementation gap is closely associated with a credibility gap. When the church is seen to be inactive in its professed concern for justice, its prophetic voice is easily discredited. It then loses its position of witness for the gospel. In fact its apparent hypocrisy becomes a scandal to the world and a disillusionment to the poor and oppressed.

Collective Irresponsibility

The church as an institution seems unwilling to accept the necessary consequences of the gospel call to justice. Individual bishops and individual Christians profess commitment to this ministry and support for agencies active in this area. But such individual support is not translated into institutional support. The institution seems different from the sum of its individual members. The result is collective irresponsibility, coexisting with individual, personal commitment.

To take the Catholic Commission for Justice and Peace as an example once again, individual bishops profess their support for the CCJP and its work. But the Australian Episcopal Conference is another matter. The AEC has continued to sponsor and fund the CCJP in spite of considerable opposition, but it constantly seeks to restrict and control the work of the commission and to distance itself from the commission. These two aims are in fact contradictory: the more control the AEC exercises over the CCJP, the less it is able to distance itself from the CCJP. Those active for justice thus face a difficulty in dealing with opposition from an impersonal institution whose individual members profess support.

Australia's Isolation

Australia is literally at the end of the world—only New Zealand could compete with it for that title. It is isolated from the main currents of intellectual and theological debate in the world. It is insular and largely introspective.

The result of this isolation is a general ignorance of what is happening overseas. For the Australian church this means a poor understanding of the post-Vatican II insights into mission and the intimate relationship between evangelization and liberation (cf. *Evangelii Nuntiandi*). It also means a reluctance to evaluate critically the continuing practices of past decades. Many recent developments are reducing this isolation. In 1974 Australian Catholic Relief joined other Catholic relief and development agencies in a Partnership for Development in Asia. The Australian Episcopal Conference is considering the formation of a federation with the episcopal conferences of New Guinea, New Zealand, and the Pacific.

For the Catholic Commission for Justice and Peace, there have been close links for many years with the Office for Human Development of the Federation of Asian Bishops' Conferences. International contact was greatly enhanced in 1979 when a consultation of church justice and peace agencies in Asia and the Pacific was held in Tokyo. This consultation led to commitments for closer regional cooperation and to the establishment of a network to respond quickly to human rights violations in the region.

Divisions within the Church

There are deep divisions within the Australian church. The justice ministry does not produce these divisions; it merely reveals the divisions that already exist. The little research that is available indicates that a large number of different issues (theology, ecclesiology, attitudes toward ecumenism, views on catechetics, commitment to the justice ministry) produce a division along the same lines.

These divisions are not causes for concern in themselves. Differences of opinion can lead to healthy debate and the development of new and deeper insights. This is not happening in Australia, however. The divisions are ignored, papered over, denied behind a façade of unity. The result is an unhealthy situation where the image conflicts with the reality and where the church's leadership is increasingly removed from the actual situation.

Conclusion

The Australian church, then, is halfhearted in its commitment to the call to action for justice. There are many groups genuinely concerned for social issues and very active in response to the message of Jesus Christ. But the wider social dimensions of the gospel and the magisterium are largely unknown to Australian Catholics or, where known, largely unaccepted or ignored.

42

THE PHILIPPINES

Christine Tan, R.G.S.

Introduction

These are reflections from men and women, religious and lay workers, immersed in the struggle for liberation and justice. We submit these thoughts as coming from a sector of the church steeped in service to the world, yet in anguish over its mutilated condition.

The following pages are the fruit of our direct ministry toward the deprived. We do not intend to give the impression that all the church has done has been worthless, or that its sins of omission far outweigh its deeds of compassion. We are not the judge. This is only how we have felt the burden of injustice, and how we are disturbed by the feeble response toward justice. In this spirit we ask the reader to share our lives.

Where Is the Church?

The dimension of liberation and justice in the mission of the church has not been wanting if we are to glean through ecclesial pronouncements such as the synodal document *Justice in the World* (1971), and our Asian counterpart, that of the Federation of Asian Bishops' Conference (1974). Justice and peace committees and commissions have mushroomed throughout the globe. Religious congregations of both women and men, through the general chapters and similar venues, have articulated their new thrust as a commitment to justice and the marginalized.

Yet how have these words translated themselves to the person in the street, the farmer or factory worker, in the cities of Jakarta, Bangkok, Colombo, Bombay, Manila?

After almost eight years under a regime of repression, the Philippine experience has been dismal, and perhaps this experience is akin to that of Asian countries under

Christine Tan, a Religious of the Good Shepherd, is the chairperson for the Ecumenical Movement for Justice and Peace and also for the Central Implementing Task Force of the Association of Major Religious Superiors of the Philippines. She is also currently a community worker in Leveriza Slums, Manila.

totalitarian rule. With our controlled media, systematized brainwashing, with the rape of our natural resources, the eviction of our poor, and the suppression of conscience, with our massacres and salvaging, our arrests and tortures, where has the church presence been?

Here follows a description of torture, not uncommon to our ears. Why do such tragedies not evoke strong ecclesial censure?

I was made to lie down on a wide object (it felt like a flat iron sheet). This was cold against my back. Someone removed my briefs. I heard them move an object closer to me which seemed to have rollers and grated against the cement floor. . . . A hook was attached to my hogtied hands. Next I heard the grating of steel which must have been some kind of a pulley. They pulled up the hook, pulling my hogtied hands and raising the upper portion of my body, suspended, while my feet remained attached to the edge of the iron sheet. How it hurt—stretching the flesh and bones on my arms. In this hanging position a towel was placed over my nose and mouth, and again the water from the hose commenced and the interrogation. The same questions over and over again, while the pulley pulled me higher, bit by bit. The steel creaked. Tighter still became the handcuffs, stretching my flesh and bones. . . .[1]

Our Asian countries have been and are gravely abused by the mighty transnational corporations. This is a reality as stark as it is insurmountable. Efforts have been made to penetrate labor unions, to organize and conscientize laborers, and to demand the least of human rights from management. How cautious business enterprises would have been if these efforts were supported by vast church resources, and strengthened by official voices from the church hierarchy. But why is such support so seldom offered, such voices so muffled, if heard at all?

Let us not overlook the crimes of developing nations—eviction, prostitution, controlled media, exploitation, to name a few. Why does the church remain silent? Does its silence make this injustice right?

Alexander Solzhenitsyn writes:

The universal suppression of thought leads not to its extinction but to its distortion, ignorance and the mutual incomprehension of compatriots and contemporaries. For the voices destined to express what was known at the appropriate time fell prematurely silent, the documents perished, and the gaze of the outside researcher could not penetrate into those dark depths, beneath the piles of unsorted rubbish. If we wait for history to present us with freedom and other precious gifts, we risk waiting in vain. History is us, and there is no alternative but to shoulder the burden of what we so passionately desire and bear it out of the depths.[2]

For Whom Is the Church?

The mission of liberation is a cultural task. We define "culture" as a pattern of life, created by people, precisely to cope with life. We define "liberation" as the elimination of that which threatens life, and the building of that which enhances it.

To be a church of liberation, we must treat with great care the beliefs and customs of our people. If we do not take their beliefs seriously, we shall force them to move, not according to their culture, but according to ours.

In Asia, during the past centuries, we brown people have been the victims of so-called missionary activity. With appreciation for the missionaries' efforts and good intentions, and for countless heroic lives freely given, we cannot help but today, in retrospect, speak the truth, so as to avoid the mistakes of the past. In the name of the cross, missionaries have not only transposed and imposed their structure, lifestyle, theologies, material wealth, and created needs into our virgin land, but have generally failed to listen to our *sa-ak*, our cries, and consequently have bypassed the chance to walk side by side with the native-born, in building a kingdom recognizable to the Asian soul.

Rare has been the missionary who came like Jesus—poor, patient, free—and, like Jesus, incarnated himself in the commonness of the masses, and from this vantage point worked together toward the liberation of the undefended.

With this species of evangelization, compounded by political and socioeconomic powers, what image of the church has evolved? From the millions of oppressed, we view a proud church, insulated and isolated, moneyed, preoccupied with the powered elite. It is far too distant from the farmer, the slum-dweller, the factory worker. For them, this church is not one from whom to expect succor.

If Jesus had become man to redeem all humanity, is it not injustice in itself for our church today to concentrate on the upper crust of society rather than be at the service of all the sectors? Is the church not to be held accountable for the implementation of its words?

A fisherwoman, Aling Miling (in reality Emelina de Leon, a local leader in Navotas, Philippines, 1980), from the fishport in Manila, exclaims: "The church people—the nuns, priests, bishops—will never come down to our level. They cannot leave their comfort. They are afraid to leave their security. They will never come down to us. That is why they should not talk so much because they do not know what they are saying."

The Church Within

The structure and policies of our institutional church, sad to say, in our experience in the work for liberation, are such that most of the time church workers find it more difficult to contend with ecclesial bureaucracy than with the military itself.

Within our own church, scrutinize our practices, our freedom of speech, right to due process, freedom of conscience, right to be heard, to dissent, to appeal. Review our system of appointments and assignments, from bishops to local superiors of women religious. Most key positions are filled by keepers of the status quo. If one rocks the boat, particularly in matters of justice, is there room for that person within the "higher" places of the institutional church?

In many instances, from His Holiness John Paul II to our local bishops and papal nuncios, we hear the cry for separation between church and state. Persons engaged in political action have been looked on as illegitimate sons and daughters.

But then we observe bishops and priests mingling with dictators, blessing aircraft carriers, celebrating Mass for well-known torturers. Is this not also political action on the macro level? In the mind of the ordinary person, this act of lending ecclesial presence to confirmed oppressors, commends the action of the oppressor and legitimizes it. This is our culture. This is how we interpret deeds.

If we church persons continue to live our particular lifestyles of comfort and opulence, when 80 percent of our compatriots are hungry; if we continue circulating among the upper sectors, be this in our mold of thinking or in our content of prayer, if we continue talking to ourselves instead of unleashing our resources and ourselves in the service of the world, the time will come, if it has not already come, when we shall not understand our people, and they will turn away from us.

From the World Council of Churches, we quote:

> In following Jesus, there is always the danger of detour, of falling aside from the correct road, of being unfaithful and betraying Him. That was the danger confronted by many of the churches to whom the New Testament letters were addressed. This detour occurs when ecclesiastical institutions and believers are caught in the web woven by the principalities and powers of this world.

Outside the Church

Consequently, in the movement for liberation, be this a peaceful revolution or an armed struggle, our church has abdicated its role as teacher in favor of that of a spectator. Save for a few instances, it has failed to speak, to condemn, to lead, to immerse itself in suffering humanity, particularly when this oppression is caused by structured societal sin.

Communism, within the past three years in the Asian scene, has escalated to a frightening degree, depending on which side of the fence we stand. During the past century, we have been brainwashed on the evils of communism, more from hearsay than from direct experience. We are continually reacting and afraid, pointing a finger as at an enemy, protecting ourselves by covering our eyes. We ask: Is this the church of dialogue, of unity, is this the Good Shepherd? We have already lost the worker to Marx. Will we lose the student to Mao?

So often have we been warned and alarmed about the evils of the left, but why do the evils of the right continue, unexposed and unopposed? Are we millions in the third world not suffering from the violence of hunger caused by the avarice of transnational corporations, with the cooperation of repressive regimes? We feel the anguish of not owning a hut and a piece of land, of failing to provide food for our family, of witnessing our children starve and die from sickness and malnutrition. The right has its own breed of violence, insidiously deceptive.

From the heart of a Filipino farmer in a remote village, we hear:

> Our forefathers were here centuries ago. Together, we cleared this land and flattened the mountain. But until today, we do not even own the land under

our huts. Prices keep rising, but we receive the same pay. We are getting more and more destitute. Look at our children's faces. They eat only once or twice a day. They are sick. We have no medicine. We have no more hope.[3]

So often we hear of priests and religious being warned about engaging in activities with the left, yet no priest or religious is cautioned about becoming involved with rightist regimes. No church person has been asked to withdraw his or her investments from transnational corporations.

The Plight of the Local Church

We have, all these years, tried with our mind and strength to be loyal to our institutional church. Had there been no Vatican II, perhaps this blind loyalty would have been sustained. Had the world not undergone such a rapid pace of change, perhaps this loyalty would have been lasting.

But as we stand now, here in Asia, side by side with 70 percent of the world's population, during the darkest era of our political, social, cultural, and economic struggle, we workers for justice, together with our sisters and brothers, look to the institutional church for succor.

Instead we find it unreachable, un-understandable, unfeeling. It is no longer credible. Its voice no longer resonates. Even its faith we hold in question. We see a massive organization frantically trying to preserve itself. For us, this monolithic church, as life-giver, has already died.

To whom then shall we turn?

A Local Answer

There are forces that for many years have been working toward social transformation. They have been sympathetic to our aspirations and ideals. These forces have given hope to our people. Their actions, unlike ours, have been generally congruent with their words. Their dedication often surpasses ours, their commitment to people stuns even the doubtful mind. Should we now turn to them in cooperative effort? Should we allow our institutional church to die out.

Our Hope: The Genuine Local Church

While we lament over the lethargy of our institutional church, we are resolute in our love and are determined more than ever, as its militant minority, never to abandon it.

We must instead devote our time and consume ourselves to bring about true and lasting change within the institution. This could be done with deep prayer, patience, organization, uniting our church to the masses through dynamic integration, and most important of all, the credibility of our personal lives. If we succeed, our church, chastened and radicalized, will still be valid to our people in our time.

Simultaneously with this, a new church has to be born—if it is not already born. It shall not be found in basilicas or theological treatises, but deep within the stream of humanity. Its members, like Jesus, have to be poor, ordinary, and living messages of the gospel.

Shorn of pomp and power, this will have to be a poor church, for ecclesial, social, economic, and political powers will work against it. This will have to be a brave church, for it will not be too different from the revolutionary Christianity of the early believers. This will have to be a faith-filled church, for its future will be as dark as its present is perilous. From the institutional church, it could never expect recognition.

Its tasks will be multiple. It will have to evolve a coherent theology of contemporary social realities. Its spirituality must be vivifying, that it may give life to its members and life to the world. There will be little room for internal and external contradictions. It will have to prove that there is no incompatibility between genuine Christian movements and genuine movements for liberation. Finally, this church should be immersed in the cries, the anguish, the pain, culture, aspirations, the hopes and struggle of our people.

To us, this kind of church is what we would like to call *the genuine local church, the church of the incarnation*, for only through it can Jesus continue his saving mission of the world.

May this church of the incarnation, and the institutional church, chastened and radicalized, be—after much struggle, pain, and dying—ONE.

"God so loved the world as to give his only begotten Son." Incarnation as mystery and as spirituality is not a mystery of method but a mystery of unlimited love, the love and concern (prophetic and messianic) for a suffering and wandering humanity. Incarnation is the partner of mission; love and concern are made concrete in sharing of life and service with the rest of society. . . . It is love leading to identification.[4]

Conclusion

Silence has its limits.
There are moments when, without any tangible utility,
Something has to be said
    for no other reason than that it is true.
If it is not said, the moral order of the world
    suffers a blow
    that is hard to overcome, harder than its
    violation by brute force.
And this principle is valid also for the silence
    "to prevent something worse happening."
For ultimately the worse that could happen is that
    truth and justice
    would no longer find spokesmen
      and martyrs
      on the earth.[5]

Notes

1. Task Force on Detainees of the Association of Major Religious Superiors of the Philippines, *Sixto Carlos, Jr.*, February 1980.

2. Alexander Solzhenitsyn, *From under the Rubble.*

3. Mang Pedro, a sugarcane worker in a remote village in an island in the Philippines, 1980.

4. Adolfo Nicolas, S.J., "Formation and Spirituality for Mission," East Asian Pastoral Institute, 1979.

5. By a German priest, 1934.

Part II

PERSPECTIVES OF THE MISSION OF THE LOCAL CHURCH: AN ANALYSIS OF THE REFLECTION/STUDY PAPERS

Mary Motte, F.M.M.

An analysis of the reflection/study papers presented in the preceding part yielded four major clusters of variables, which may be seen as the different elements that constitute the living expression of mission in the local church today. Each of these clusters is described below.

First Cluster: The Variables That Give Specific Shape to the Mission of the Local Church

This cluster is the strongest from the perspective of the number of variables that constitute it. Since the authors of the papers were requested to stress the way in which mission is concretely realized in the context of a local church, this result was predictable.

The general focus of the cluster is the inner dynamic, which makes it possible for the church to carry out the mission confided to it. This inner dynamic may be described as the task of the Christian community to deepen continually its inculturation of the good news of Jesus Christ, which it has received and which it is called to communicate and share with others.

The papers offer a clear affirmation of the fundamental importance of the role of community, and of the small Christian community specifically, in this task of inculturation. Within the community the faith that binds its members together is continually strengthened and confirmed by the ongoing process of evangelization. The encounter between life situations and the Word of God is at the heart of this ongoing evangelization.[1]

As experiences deepen and increase the awareness of the significance of the church as community, there is likewise a growing consciousness, noted in the papers, of the necessary contribution being made and still to be made by the laity in co-responsibility for the Christian community. It is in this area, precisely, that the continued dominance of clerical control is recognized as an impediment to the full realization of Christian community.[2] This fact is true especially in the development of the ministerial functions of the church.[3] There is also some indication of the need to relate ministries to the cultural requirements of a given milieu.[4] Also, in relation to ministries, the discernment of charisms is seen as an important service to be performed within the Christian community.[5]

A number of examples from the reflection/study papers point out that the deeper levels of inculturation or assimilation of the gospel within a given community or local church can be realized only from within that community. These deeper levels of assimilation are achieved through a continuous process by which the community renews itself and confronts the different aspects of its cultural and historical heritage with the gospel in such a way that these values are transformed.[6] This transformation involves a certain rupture with one's heritage through a process of *kenosis*.[7] It is important to note that neither culture nor history are static, but are changing, though constant, realities found in every milieu.[8]

Freedom is another element that contributes to the inculturation process. In fact, freedom is understood to be constitutive of the Christian community in mission. The examples drawn from the papers point to the fact that religious freedom, an aspect of freedom that is often the object of concern today, can be properly understood only in relation to the other aspects of freedom. The whole area of human rights is included here. The reflections from the papers on religious freedom illustrate, either implicitly or explicitly, that the other aspects of freedom are more fundamental to the existence of the Christian community, or local church, as Christian and in mission.[9]

A number of examples point to the fact that there are various negative realities present within the Christian community today, which hinder the more complete assimilation and inculturation of the gospel message and therefore limit the carrying out of mission. The first of these negative realities is an inadequate evangelization. The principal examples are the following:

1. Catholic or Christian symbols have become a means by which a conquered people, who were baptized in relation to their being conquered, have managed to defend themselves and preserve their cultural identity as a people. These symbols, which convey the traditional Catholic or Christian meaning to those outside the community or group, have taken on a different meaning for the people who use them. This meaning preserves their traditional religious beliefs and values.[10]

2. Traditional religions are part of the cultural fiber of a people, and their values to the people do not automatically disappear with baptism, nor are they automatically transformed into gospel values. Consequently, in moments of crisis, people have recourse to these more traditional forms of religion, when the evangelization process has not been sufficiently transforming. Every Christian community needs continually to deepen its inculturation of the gospel by confronting these traditional values with the gospel and transforming them. This task cannot be done by an outsider, but must be assumed by the community itself. This task could be understood as

a second phase of evangelization, the first phase having been the introduction of the good news to the community by someone from outside.[11]

3. Another example is found in more highly technological societies, where there is often a disparity among the way the gospel is transmitted, the language used in communicating the message, and the actual experience of the people. It is as though there were two levels of language and, consequently, of understanding: one related to technology and everyday life, the other related to the expression of the faith-experience. When this disparity exists, people often do not understand the gospel, nor can they apply it to their everyday, secular experience in a meaningful and trans-forming way.[12]

Another negative reality is the loss of missionary awareness by a Christian com-munity. There is some evidence suggested in the papers concerning a gradual de-crease or loss in missionary awareness, that is, the need to communicate the good news to others who are outside the church. While the examples are few, they do seem to point to a definite reality that has crept into the life of some local churches, either because of outside impositions or from some weakness within the community.[13] The latter is generally rooted in a failure to enter into dialogue with others due to an incapacity to express the faith in concepts that can be understood, that can transmit the message in such a way that the hearers can accept or reject it.[14]

This last example, the loss of missionary awareness, leads to the consideration of another group of variables that make up this cluster, namely, those that express the responsible service of the Christian community, or local church, in its relationship with others through evangelization and dialogue in carrying out its mission of mak-ing known the gospel of Jesus Christ.

However, before the Christian community can focus in a more concentrated way on its service and relation to those persons and communities outside its communion of faith, it has to reflect on its own division—the division among Christians. The reality of divided Christianity needs to be more effectively communicated to the grassroots by church leadership, since Christian unity is essential for effective mis-sion. The papers point out that divided Christianity has been responsible for bring-ing a divided proclamation of the gospel to many places in the past.[15] Examples are also given of a number of efforts made recently in order to heal these divisions.[16]

The responsible service of the Christian community in its relation to the larger, pluralistic society finds expression in two major spheres. The first of these concerns its relationships with persons and communities of other religious traditions. A num-ber of the authors, either implicitly or explicitly, explain religious dialogue as a form of evangelization.[17] It is noted also that no credible and genuine mission can remain indifferent to the presence of other religious traditions.[18] The service of the Christian community in the partnership of dialogue is drastically shaped by the attitudes and objectives understood by those who carry out this service.[19] It should not be forgot-ten that religions have and do at times foster division and divisive attitudes in so-ciety.[20]

The second sphere of relationships concerns secular society, and in a special way its political and socioeconomic aspects. The secularization of society is a phenome-non that continues to emerge in a global way, having unique characteristics dependent upon the society from which it emerges.[21] This phenomenon of secularization has often proved a stumbling block to the Christian community. The church has at times failed to deal effectively with secularization; at times it has seen itself as quite apart from the process.[22] Yet the prophetic function of the church is precisely part of its secularity.[23]

The various trends that emerge in any given society, and which today are often closely associated with the secularization of society, interact profoundly with the members of the Christian community in specific places and at specific times. These trends, which are generally of a political, economic, and/or social nature, are frequently marked with injustice.[24] Peace, liberation from oppression and misery, and justice are or need to be deep concerns of Christians today.[25] The poor, who are frequently caught up in these sufferings and struggles, call all Christians to a deeper understanding of the mission of Christ.[26] The engagement and service of the church must be characterized, and are increasingly so, by a continual process of involvement and discovery of how to be liberative and creative in the face of opposition, injustice, and oppression.

Second Cluster: The Variables, Drawn from Scripture and Theology, That Attempt to Describe the Source and Nature of the Church's Mission, Thereby Constituting the Motivational Basis for Mission Today

The variables that appear in this cluster point to a consideration of the essential relation between mission and the nature of the church. For the church to be church it must be in mission.[27] This mission of the church is introduced into history in a specific way through the incarnation of Christ. The consequence is that the mission of the church must be an incarnated reality.[28]

This mission, which is essentially the mission of Christ continued in time through the church, is concerned with the kingdom of God.[29] The gospel indicates certain concrete signs of the kingdom.[30] The dynamic reality in the continuity of Christ's mission through his followers in the church is his disciples' understanding of the Word of God as an event.[31]

The different reflections in the papers point out certain main characteristics of mission: (1) the mission of the church is one, and this implies a unity among those carrying out that mission;[32] (2) the mission of the church is incarnated and universal, and the church, as the sign of salvation, must convey these two realities if it is to be an authentic sign;[33] (3) the poor are central to the understanding of the mission of the church and to its realization.[34]

Each of these characteristics is being clarified to a greater or less extent through the following concrete experiences: (1) ecumenism among Christians;[35] (2) inculturation, especially in the development and understanding of the local church;[36] (3) in concrete options for the poor, the oppressed, and marginalized peoples.[37]

These experiences are not necessarily separated in their various realizations; in fact, the particular stress on the option for the poor, which exists in various local churches today, appears closely related to the process of inculturation.[38] There are likewise difficulties in the clarification process, which pose deep questions to the understanding of mission.[39]

There are two dynamic processes that translate the mission of the church into concrete reality: transformation and dialogue. Examples given in the papers point out that the first of these processes, transformation, must be continually operative within the Christian community, which is, as it were, its starting point. At this point it is also called ongoing evangelization, renewal, metanoia, conversion.[40]

The second process, dialogue, is that process by which the Christian community is called to relate to those outside its communion of faith. The significant presence of other religious traditions, especially in certain parts of the world, pose profound questions to the church, particularly in terms of the understanding it has of the universality of salvation and the uniqueness of Christianity.[41]

The papers note that present experiences as well as attitudes question the relationship between these two processes: transformation or evangelization and dialogue. There is some tendency to see them related by a positive and necessary tension, but there are still needs for clarification.[42] Also there is an underlying assumption present to some extent in the reflections, namely, that the Christian community in dialogue needs to both affirm its own beliefs and leave them open to be further shaped by the Spirit, whose action is not limited to the Christian community.[43] The increasing secularization of modern society also raises questions for the church in this respect.[44]

Third Cluster: The Variables that Underlie Reflections about the Kinds of Structures and Sharing that are Needed in View of Effective Mission in the Church Today and Tomorrow

Several of the papers stress the communion of faith that is shared among and witnessed to by different local churches throughout the world. This communion of faith is often pointed to as an important factor in expressing the universality of the church today.[45] From this stress emerges a call to a deeper reflection on the meaning of universality/particularity as it is being lived in the church today. The different elements describing the basis of this reflection, in outline form, are (1) the universality of salvation; salvation is intended for all;[46] (2) the church as the sign of salvation;[47] (3) the relation of salvation to concrete, historical experiences;[48] (4) the responsibility of bishops in local churches for mission;[49] (5) the common elements shared among Christians every place, which are derived from a common humanity and a common salvation;[50] (6) the varieties of actual interchurch sharing taking place today, especially at regional levels;[51] (7) the identification of areas that call for more effective interchurch sharing.[52]

Other examples from the papers indicate the inadequacy of certain structures and functions in the present organizational setup of the church. The various experiences of becoming local that the church has had in recent years have been the greatest contributors in pointing up these inadequacies. The main areas of inadequacies appear as certain forms of centralization in decision-making;[53] the role of foreign missionaries in the local church as understood until now;[54] the relation between missionary institutes of different kinds, which see themselves at the service of the church's mission, and the local churches;[55] financial dependency on the part of some local churches and aid coming from other local churches.[56] A number of authors suggest alternative structures and some new ways of understanding these relationships in the context of universality/particularity.[57]

Fourth Cluster: The Variables that Have Emerged in the Evolution of Mission, and that Have Effected both Negative and Positive Transformation in the Course of History

The papers point to a growing consensus about the evaluation of mission as it was realized in the past. This consensus appears to move toward (1) an awareness of a generalized ineffectiveness of mission from several perspectives; (2) the indication of specific realities that have limited the realization of the church's mission, which come from within itself; (3) the indication of elements that have contributed to a positive transformation in mission.

The reflection presented in some of the papers shows how mission has evolved in various places over the years.[58] This reflection generally indicates that amid the sociocultural and political transformations, the traditional notion of mission and traditional missionary methods, which had once been taken for granted, now are being seriously questioned.[59] The question generally asked is to what extent have these methods succeeded in getting the message of salvation across to the very hearts of the people; how far has the preaching of the gospel been relevant in the life situations of a given society, so that the Christian faith has taken deep root in the daily lives of a people.[60]

The realities that are indicated as the source of ineffective mission are: (1) the division of Christianity; in particular the Protestant/Catholic rivalry in mission in the past century;[61] (2) the lack of sensitivity to cultural differences;[62] (3) the continued structures, practices, and attitudes of former ages within certain church institutions and authorities that tend to jeopardize the credibility of the church's mission.[63]

At the same time the papers point out certain realities that have been at the source of effective transformation in mission during the course of its historical evolution. These various dimensions of the church's mission were related to and directed by the pressing needs and issues of specific times, and, insofar as possible, were determined in given contexts by the structures of human relationships. In a positive way, these expressions of the church's mission have led to an evolution in its understanding of that mission and a further transformation in the way in which it is carried out.[64]

Notes

1. Affirmation of the role of community in the inculturation of the gospel: Bien-Aimé, 12; Hardawiryana, 69; Sasaki, 101–02; Herrara, 127–28, 129–33; Boseto, 184; Hally, 262; Wijngaards/ Dirven, 345; Claver, 453–54; Nambiaparambil, 418–19; Pieris, 431–32; Sarpong, 542; Keenan, 593–94.

2. Need for declericalization in order to increase co-responsibility of laity: Bien-Aimé, 9–21; Sasaki, 101; Libanio, 474–75; Ojo, 598–99.

3. Development of new ministries among the laity: Bien-Aimé, 10, 12; Hardawiryana, 44–45; Boberg, 238–39.

4. Need to relate ministries to cultural milieu: Boka, 362–65; Bohn, 490–98.

5. Discernment of charisms is important service in view of ministries: Hally, 261.

6. Ongoing self-evangelization of renewal within the Christian community is the foundation of mission: Bien-Aimé, 11–12; D'Souza, 27; Hardawiryana, 54; Sasaki, 101; Reilly, 206; Winter, 216, 221–22; Pieris, 438–39; Bohn, 490; Schreiter, 549–50.

7. The transformation effected through ongoing evangelization involves a certain rupture through a process of *kenosis*: Boka, 357–60; Knight, 392–411.

8. Culture and history are changing yet constant realities: Drego, 533–34; Schreiter, 548–49.

9. Freedom is constitutive of the community of the church in mission: D'Souza, 29; Hardawiryana, 38, 65; Bortnowska, 447–48; Claver, 451–52, 455; Gremillion, 461, 465–69; Libanio, 485–86; Collet, 570–77.

10. Catholic symbols used by enslaved people to preserve identity: Libanio, 479; Cadorette, 500–14.

11. Recourse to traditional religious rituals on the part of Christians: Bien-Aimé, 11–12; Oduyoye, 146; Boka, 357, 362–65; Sarpong, 542.

12. Disparity between language used for transmission of the gospel and the actual experience of the people: Pieris, 427, 431–32; Bohn, 490; Schreiter, 544, 552–53.

13. Loss of missionary awareness: This idea was presented principally in two privately circulated papers that were used as part of the preparatory material for the seminar, concerning the situation in the Near/Middle East, and written by Farid Jabre, C.M. and David Jaeger. Also Bortnowska, 448.

14. Incapacity to express the faith in concepts that can be understood: Bortnowska, 448; Bohn, 495.

15. Christian unity is essential to effective mission: Motanyane, 74; Oduyoye, 147; Boseto, 171–85; Mutiso-Mbinda, 186–99; Reilly, 202–09; Winter, 225; Bortnowska, 446; Bohn, 490–91; Collet, 575; Sidoti, 612.

16. Efforts to heal divisions among Christians: Sasaki, 105–06; Boseto, 175–85; Mutiso-Mbinda, 191–95; Reilly, 203–09; Winter, 216–27; Nkiere, 294–95; Wijngaards/Dirven, 330–31; Boka, 356–57; Sarpong, 542; Ashby, 558–60.

17. Religious dialogue explained as a form of evangelization: D'Souza, 24, 27; Hardawiryana, 43, 61; Sasaki, 106; Nkiere, 294–95; Knight, 393–401; Nambiaparambil, 415–16; Pieris, 427.

18. No genuine and credible mission can remain indifferent to the presence of other religious traditions: D'Souza, 25; Oduyoye, 144–48; Mutiso-Mbinda, 190–92; Rossignol, 312–13; DiNoia, 377–78; Nambiaparambil, 421; Libanio, 472–73; Sarpong, 539.

19. The service of Christians in dialogue is drastically shaped by their attitudes and objectives: Bien-Aimé, 11; D'Souza, 27; Nambiaparambil, 413–25.

20. Religions have and do at times foster divisions in societies: Pantin/de Verteuil, 370–74.

21. Secularization is a phenomenon that continues to emerge in a global way: Hardawiryana, 36; Oduyoye, 148–54; Reilly, 209–10; Bohn, 491, 493–94.

22. Secularization has often proved a stumbling block to the Christian community: Hardawiryana, 37; Sasaki, 107; Hally, 246–47; Sarpong, 542; Schreiter, 550.

23. The prophetic function of the church is precisely part of its secularity: Balasuriya, 113–14, 119; Rivera/Ramos, 162, 165–68.

24. Trends in society often associated with secularization interact with Christians; these trends are generally of political, economic, and/or social nature and are frequently marked with injustice: Motanyane, 79–80; Herrara, 121–38; Rivera/Ramos, 155–68; Nkiere, 291–92; Wijngaards/Dirven, 331, 337, 345; Tan, 618–21.

25. Peace, liberation from oppression and misery, and justice are or need to be deep concerns of the Christian today: Oduyoye, 152–54; Winter, 226; Ashby, 561–63, 568–69; Collet, 574–77; Keenan, 579–95; Ojo, 598–600; Sidoti, 613–15.

26. The poor call all Christians to the deeper understanding of Christ's mission: Rivera/Ramos, 166–67; Pieris, 427–28.

27. The church is essentially missionary: Hardawiryana, 34–35; Sasaki, 100, 103; Reilly, 203; Rossignol, 305; Wijngaards/Dirven, 317; Boka, 356; Pieris, 427.

28. Mission of the church must be an incarnated reality: Bien-Aimé, 4; Boseto, 172, 174; Mutiso-Mbinda, 187–88; Boberg, 232–33; Nkiere, 291.

29. Mission is the mission of Christ continued in time through the church and is concerned with the kingdom of God: Hardawiryana, 34; Pantin/de Verteuil, 368; Sidoti, 602–3.

30. The gospel indicates certain concrete signs of the kingdom: Pieris, 436–38; Sidoti, 602–3.

31. The dynamic reality of the continuity of Christ's mission by his disciples is understanding the word of God as an event: Sasaki, 103; Herrara, 136–37; Nkiere, 290–91; Boka, 358–60; Sarpong, 543; Schreiter, 545–47.

32. The mission of the church is one and implies a unity among those carrying out that mission: Boseto, 173; Mutiso-Mbinda, 186–87; Reilly, 204–6; Boberg, 232; Nambiaparambil, 418–19; Sarpong, 541.

33. The church is incarnated and universal and as sign of salvation must convey these two realities in its mission: Hardawiryana, 35; Navarro, 83; Sasaki, 100; Nambiaparambil, 418; Sarpong, 540–41; Schreiter, 552–53.

34. The poor are central to the understanding and realization of mission: Hardawiryana, 37; Sasaki, 101; Herrara, 136–38; Rivera/Ramos, 156–58; Mutiso-Mbinda, 188; Nkiere, 293–94; Pantin/de Verteuil, 369; Pieris, 429–31.

35. Ecumenism among Christians: papers 11–14.

36. Inculturation in the development and understanding of the local church: D'Souza, 31; Rivera/Ramos, 155–56, 158–68; Claver, 456–57; papers 32–36.

37. Concrete options for the poor, the oppressed, and the marginalized peoples: Balasuriya, 113–19; Herrara, 120–38; Rivera/Ramos, 155–68; Pieris, 426–41.

38. Option for the poor appears closely related to the process of inculturation in some localities: Rivera/Ramos, 155–68; Pieris, 426–41.

39. The process of clarifying the characteristics of mission through concrete options presents some difficulties which pose deep questions to the understanding of mission. These difficulties are discussed in many of the papers from different perspectives.

40. Transformation (ongoing evangelization, renewal, metanoia, conversion) must be continually operative in the Christian community: Hardawiryana, 34; Sasaki, 104; Herrara, 136–38; Boberg, 234; Boka, 357–60; Knight, 410–11; Bohn, 491–92; Drego, 520, 527–29; Schreiter, 546–48.

41. The significant presence of other religious traditions questions the church about its understanding of the universality of salvation and the uniqueness of Christianity: D'Souza, 28–29; Hardawiryana, 34; Mutiso-Mbinda, 193; Di Noia, 378, 382, 385–90; Pieris, 433.

42. The relation between transformation or evangelization and dialogue: Nambiaparambil, 421–22.

43. In dialogue the Christian community needs to affirm its own belief and at the same time leave itself open to be further shaped by the spirit whose action is not confined to the Christian community: See especially the perspective of dialogue presented in D'Souza, 22–33; Pantin/de Verteuil, 368–76; Nambiaparambil, 413–25; Pieris, 426–41.

44. Increasing secularization questions the church in its affirmation of belief and its openness to change: Balasuriya, 113–19.

45. The importance of the communion of faith for expressing the universality of the church: Bien-Aimé, 9; D'Souza, 25; Hardawiryana, 35, 45, 61–62; Balasuriya, 115–16; Oduyoye, 150–51; Boseto, 184; Boberg, 240; Hally, 245–47, 259–60; Pantin/de Verteuil, 370–71; Nambiaparambil, 423; Gremillion, 469; Sidoti, 602–3.

46. Salvation is intended for all. This theme is evident in most of the papers.

47. The church is the sign of salvation: D'Souza, 22–33.

48. Relation of salvation to concrete historical experience. This theme is evident in most of the papers.

49. Responsibility of bishops for mission in local church: Hardawiryana, 55–56; Motanyane, 77.

50. Common elements shared by Christians are derived from common humanity and common salvation: Hardawiryana, 34–72.

51. Varieties of interchurch sharing taking place today: Hardawiryana, 46–51; Navarro, 83–84; Reilly, 210–11; Labayen, 282–87; Gremillion, 460, 469; Ashby, 559–63; Keenan, 584–85.

52. Identification of areas that call for more effective interchurch sharing: Hardawiryana, 46–51, 56; Motanyane, 75; Balasuriya, 116–18; Herrara, 137–38; Oduyoye, 150–54; Boseto, 179–84; Boberg, 238–39; Joinet, 264–80; Rossignol, 310–12; Bortnowska, 447–48.

53. Centralized decision-making: Hardawiryana, 51–54.

54. Role of foreign mission in local church as understood until now: Bien-Aimé, 13; D'Souza, 27–28; Hardawiryana, 55–60; Herrara, 137–38; Wijngaards/Dirven, 317–50.

55. Relation between missionary institutes and local church: Hardawiryana, 34–72; Navarro, 83–99; papers 15–21.

56. Financial dependency of some local churches on others: Bien-Aimé, 14; D'Souza, 31; Hardawiryana, 45, 47, 51; Motanyane, 75–76; Boseto, 178–79; Labayen, 286.

57. Suggestions for alternative structures and new ways of understanding relationships in the context of universal/particular: D'Souza, 26–28; Boseto, 175–76; Boberg, 241–43; Hally, 250; Joinet, 277–80; Rossignol, 305, 309, 315; Wijngaards/Dirven, 323–24, 327, 332, 334, 338, 346; Pieris, 426–27, 431, 435; Ojo, 600–01; Tan, 618, 620–21.

58. How mission has evolved in various places over the years: Motanyane, 73–82; Navarro, 83–99; Wijngaards/Dirven, 317–52.

59. Amid the sociocultural and political transformations in society, the traditional understandings of mission are being questioned: Boberg, 231–44; Wijngaards/Dirven, 317–52.

60. It is generally asked to what extent the preaching of the gospel has brought about a deep faith rooted in the lives of the peoples: Bien-Aimé, 10; Oduyoye, 146; Boka, 357, 362–65; Libanio, 471–87; Cadorette, 500–14; Sarpong, 542.

61. Divisions in Christianity as the source of ineffective mission: Oduyoye, 140–54; Mutiso-Mbinda, 186–200.

62. Lack of sensitivity to cultural differences at the source of ineffective mission: Bien-Aimé, 9–21; D'Souza, 22–33; Motanyane, 73–82; Balasuriya, 113–19; Oduyoye, 140–54; Boka, 355–67; Pieris, 426–41; Libanio, 471–87; Sarpong, 537–43.

63. Continued structures, practices, and attitudes of former times tend to jeopardize the credibility of the church's mission: Hardawiryana, 51–54.

64. Realities at the source of effective mission in the past: Bien-Aimé, 9–21; Navarro, 83–99.

Part III

AGENDA FOR FUTURE PLANNING, STUDY, AND RESEARCH IN MISSION

General Introduction to the Agenda

This Agenda contains those issues which surfaced during the SEDOS Research Seminar on the Future of Mission. It is not a statement of agreed facts or priorities, but rather notes what has emerged from our reflection and study in the ten groups which were an integral part of the seminar process. This recorded syllabus contains those elements that emerged as a more general consensus, as well as those that remained as divergencies, both of which call us to develop and deepen our understanding, experience, and perspective of mission.

We, therefore, offer this Agenda so that the points it contains may be taken up and explored further in planning, study, and research in view of choices and actions to be taken in the service of mission in the future.

As we now enlarge the horizon of our prayer, reflection, and enquiry by inviting you to join us in the continuation of this process, we hope that we may move toward an ever fuller realization of the Kingdom.

RESULTS OF THE SEDOS SEMINAR ON THE FUTURE OF MISSION, ROME, MARCH 1981

This Agenda is being compiled at the end of ten days of a lived experience shared together by more than one hundred persons from all parts of the world, priests, religious and laity of the Catholic Church, along with some participants invited from the other Churches. Some were persons involved in central administration of missionary institutes and religious congregations, others were in various pastoral activities of the Church, while some others were "experts" who had been asked to write preliminary papers for the Seminar. This report is not intended to be a blueprint for the future of mission, but it is offered humbly as one attempt by some tired drafters working under a time constraint to catch the spirit of the Seminar by sharing some of the results of much discussion, sharing and praying together in small groups, in plenary sessions, in prayer groups, in the corridors, in the diningroom, in the beautiful grounds of Villa Cavalletti, situated in the Alban Hills outside Rome, and in the various groups which formed around particular fields of interest as the Seminar progressed.

We feel that it is best to arrange the results of the Seminar under three broad headings:

A. *THE DIRECTIONS IN MISSION TODAY*
B. *THE CENTRAL ROLE OF THE LOCAL CHURCH*
C. *THE TASK FOR MISSIONARY INSTITUTES*

There appears to have been a convergence in the Seminar taken as a whole around these three key areas, as new and enriched understandings of them developed. The Seminar seems to have entered upon a journey which is far from ended. It may only be just commencing.

A. THE DIRECTIONS IN MISSION TODAY

1. The Seminar has not been directly concerned with the reasons *why* the Church is missionary. It is presupposed that the established teaching in the Catholic Church, at least since the apostolic constitution on Evangelization in the Modern World *(Evangelii Nuntiandi)* published in 1975, is that the whole Church is missionary at all levels. She is missionary by that nature intended for her by her founder, Jesus Christ, and in view of which she is given the gift of the Holy Spirit. The concern of the Seminar has been rather for the manner in which mission is being undertaken today, the *how* of mission.

2. Four main activities stand out:

I. PROCLAMATION
II. DIALOGUE
III. INCULTURATION
IV. LIBERATION OF THE POOR

The results of the discussions concerned with these four principal activities in the missionary action of the Church will be reported separately. However, the close links existing among them in the actual missionary practice of the Church need to be kept always in mind. In each activity, considerations emerging from the Seminar upon which there appeared to be some kind of consensus are first reported, and then questions are listed to be explored further in the future.

I. Proclamation

Considerations which have emerged:

3. The authentic proclamation of the Gospel is a witness by Word, by the silent witness of action, or by the even more silent presence of a Gospel life lived faithfully

among others. At the same time it is a listening to life, discovering the presence of God's Word and Spirit among a people, a presence which has preceded the missionary. In this way the light of the Gospel can continually illuminate the signs of the times to manifest the language which is to be used by the one who proclaims the Gospel here and now (*Gaudium et Spes,* no. 4).

4. The goal of proclamation can therefore be understood according to two models different but complementary:

a) Extending the Visible Communion of the Church

Proclamation here has a "centripetal" purpose, leading people directly into the Church, which in this way becomes a visible communion, implanted within a people in a way that it is capable of growing into a full institutional reality.

b) Recognizing and Furthering the Values of the Kingdom

Proclamation in this model has a "centrifugal" purpose, allowing the power of the Gospel to move out and encounter humanity in its struggles and diversity. It entails in the one who proclaims a readiness to seek the Christ he or she announces. This kind of proclamation of the Gospel is fruitful when it promotes and furthers the values of the Kingdom within a culture and denounces and inhibits what is not of the Kingdom of Christ.

5. This second model is achieving more prominence today and may be directing us to what will become the priority in much future missionary proclamation.

---

6. There remains a need for "full-time" missionaries who are prepared to leave their own country in order to proclaim the Gospel in a foreign land. The "ongoing" evangelization of Churches already evangelized should not curtail this need for the primary proclamation of the Gospel in places where it has never been heard.

7. Statistics indicate that this kind of "full-time" missionary who goes to proclaim the Gospel for the first time in a foreign land is coming increasingly from the young Churches.

8. The proclamation of the Gospel within a Church is an ongoing task which is never completed.

9. The courageous defence of the rights of the poor and oppressed, wherever these are violated, directly or indirectly is a constitutive element in the proclamation made by the Church.

10. An authentic proclamation of the Gospel is particularly necessary in our times among immigrants and refugees around the world.

11. Questions to be explored for the future:

a) What are the implications for the proclamation of the Gospel when we speak today of mission in six continents?

b) Have religious and lay persons in the Church a way of proclaiming the Gospel that is specifically their own? Prayer and contemplation? Political and social action for justice?

c) What are the criteria to use in order to evaluate an authentic proclamation of the Gospel in different regions of the world today, whether it be by word, action or silent presence?

d) How does one proclaim the Gospel to the rich, the powerful, the privileged classes in a culture? By witness of a commitment to Gospel values? By making efforts to enlighten them on the need for transformation of existing institutions and accepted attitudes?

e) How can the proclamation of the Gospel by different missionary institutes and by different Christian Churches be better coordinated to diminish the scandal of divisions?

f) How can listening, learning and discovering become more a part of the missionary proclamation of the Gospel?

g) Are missionaries sufficiently aware of the two models for the proclamation of the Gospel and the criteria for deciding which model is to be employed in a particular situation?

II. Dialogue

Considerations which have emerged:

12. If proclamation is concerned chiefly with presenting Christ, dialogue seeks also to find Him already present in a given situation. Dialogue involves the humble discernment of the Word of God in other persons, in the institutionalized forms of other faiths, in various ideologies and in secular realities. Dialogue can take place on many different levels: chance personal encounters, meetings organized at local or regional levels, in national and international conventions.

13. Dialogue is not a diminished form of mission, an expedient to be used only because direct proclamation of the Gospel is impossible. It is missionary action and is implied in all genuinely missionary activity. The immediate goal of dialogue is the deeper *recognition* of Christ in the other through honest and respectful conversion, which involves risks on both sides.

14. Dialogue is an entry into the true mystery of the other person, fostering a kind of "conscientization" in a "dialogue of life." Authentic dialogue effects a kind of conversion by a deeper *submissiveness* in both parties to the truth, and brings about a kind of mutual "incorporation" with one another in an experience of growing into closer communion (a kind of non-sacramental "baptism"?).

15. Dialogue is a genuine form of Christian *witness*. Dialogue transforms persons and through them becomes transformative of society and culture. Authentic dialogue with those of other faiths, and even with those who claim to be of no faith, will be a self-evangelization for Christians. Dialogue with other faiths calls for an accompanying dialogue within the Christian community.

---

16. Concrete situations should be the focus of dialogue, not merely principles and abstract presentations of positions.

17. Dialogue, when carried on in a spirit of faith, readily becomes a prayer dialogue.

18. It is acceptance by Catholics of the "relativization" of the "Catholic Absolute" that the Catholic Church is also a "searching" Church. This becomes possible only by understanding the life and mission of the Church in terms of the larger realities of the Risen Christ, the Holy Spirit and the Kingdom, all of which, of course, though *distinct* from the Church are *inseparable* from her total reality.

19. Dialogue always presupposes a desire for the total liberation of one's partner in dialogue and a concrete involvement, wherever possible, in effecting this liberation. Any form of imposition is destructive of authentic dialogue. The "tactical" dialogue or the refusal to dialogue "without conditions" prevents an authentic dialogue.

20. Interior silence, modesty, a recognition of the value of little gestures, no anxiety for quick results, a willingness to be present for the other, a person-oriented rather than a results-oriented approach—all these are qualities which greatly assist dialogue.

21. Dialogue is greatly helped by a knowledge of the prejudices in the other, especially the image that is held of us as Church, as Christians and as missionaries.

22. Dialogue often calls for some practical follow-up, e.g., Paulo Freire's method in Brazil developed after his dialogue with the poor.

23. As a positive response to China's opening to the world, Christians should foster and participate in dialogue and exchanges in economic, scientific, educational, cultural, religious and other fields.

24. Christians need to be sensitive to the seeds of a future liberation of the poor growing within a culture, and seek to link these with the first flowering of the Kingdom already present in the Church.

25. Dialogue presupposes faith in the interior action of the Holy Spirit within human hearts.

26. Christian monks and nuns have a privileged place in the Church's dialogue with the great religions of Asia.

27. A "dialogue of life" is implied in any real sharing of life and calls for a willingness to give and receive and to take part in life together.

28. *Questions to be explored in the future:*

a) How can structures within the Christian community be better organized so that the fruits of dialogue with those of other faiths or ideologies can become an effective means of animating the ongoing dialogue within the Christian community at all levels?

b) Can we better structure our missionary institutions, buildings, work and lifestyle so that there is an atmosphere more conducive to dialogue?

c) Can the polarizing tendencies often occurring between the methods of *analysis* and *dialogue* be satisfactorily reconciled in practice?

d) Is the dialogue between missionaries of different Christian Churches, often occasioned and stimulated by a shared missionary concern, given sufficient time and attention by missionaries? Are they sufficiently aware of the strengths and weaknesses in the classically catholic, evangelical and reformed traditions?

e) Is education for the missionary task of dialogue with those of other faiths and of various ideologies receiving sufficient attention in the formation planned for their members by missionary institutes? What formation for dialogue should be given to all? To future specialists in dialogue? (cf. Asian Theological Conference of 1979. V. Fabella, ed., *Asia's Struggle for Full Humanity,* Orbis, 1980.)

f) Are missionaries sufficiently convinced that dialogue has a solid spiritual basis? That it can be an experience that is genuinely kenotic? That it can become for persons a first entry into the *mysterium tremendum* of God and into the basic experience of all faith, "I am not alone in the world"?

g) Can we accept that the first source and supreme model for all dialogue, understood as a facing of the other in total honesty and truth, are to be located in the great mysteries of Christian faith: the Trinity (Jn. 1:1), the Incarnation (Jn. 1:18) and the Holy Spirit (Jn. 20:22)?

III. Inculturation

Considerations which have emerged:

29. Inculturation has its source and inspiration in the mystery of the Incarnation. The Word was made flesh. Here flesh means the fully concrete, human and created reality that Jesus was. Inculturation, therefore, becomes another way of describing Christian mission. If proclamation sees mission in the perspective of the *Word* to be proclaimed, inculturation sees mission in the perspective of the *flesh,* or concrete embodiment, which the Word assumes in a particular individual, community, institution or culture.

30. What is inculturated is the Gospel, or more correctly, faith in the Gospel. In this sense, inculturation is essential to all authentic missionary action. It cannot, however, be artificially induced, but needs to flow spontaneously from the personal faith of people, expressed within the symbols and institutions of their own particular culture.

---

31. Inculturation cannot be artificially induced but occurs naturally when the liberating message of the Gospel is joined to the liberative struggles of the local communities.

32. Inculturation of faith in the Gospel by Christians of a different culture will mean for the Church a new discovery of the Gospel which she proclaims authoritatively to all people, and therefore a new enrichment for the life of the Church.

33. Inculturation will bring always a new healing, purification and transformation of a culture.

34. Through authentic inculturation of a people's faith in the Gospel, Christ becomes concretely alive in that culture.

35. The importance of basic communities in the process of inculturation is

stressed, whether these be *Ecclesial Communities* confessing and celebrating the Gospel, *Communities of Faith* socially involved, or *Communities of Solidarity* between peoples of different faiths or differing opinions.

36. Inculturation of the Gospel remains always the responsibility of the Christian community, of which the missionary is part.

37. With regard to the great heritage of Chinese culture, Christians are encouraged to deepen their appreciation and understanding of its values, in the spirit of Matteo Ricci. A thorough inculturation of the Gospel with the Chinese ways of thinking and living will enrich the whole Church.

38. Inculturation calls for a special *kenosis* in the missionary who disposes himself or herself for change and participation in the creative inculturation undertaken by the whole Christian community in a particular place. The missionary is called to be a catalyst of inculturation rather than its agent.

39. Questions to be explored in the future:

a) Some believe that inculturation as a process of missionary action should be subordinated to liberation. They argue that inculturation is a by-product of involvement with the less privileged people in their struggles. Inculturation without involvement in liberation results in the institutional Church identifying with an elitist culture —which is the situation in many Third World countries.

b) Inculturation implies local responsibility. In what way is this compatible with a centralized organization with common doctrines and a uniform discipline?

c) What are the implications for the universal Church of inculturation as a basic missionary principle? For the local Church? For the missionary?

d) Is inculturation of the Gospel among a particular people possible without its assuming at the same time social and political dimensions?

e) What are the particular implications of the process of inculturation within an Islamic culture?

f) How can the Gospel continue to be a challenge to people after it has become inculturated?

g) To what extent should a missionary leave behind his or her own culture?

h) Will the process of inculturation in the young Churches inevitably mean successive stages of declericalization, deromanization and decentralization of the Church?

i) Will inculturation increase the participation of the laity within the Church?

j) How can missionaries best prepare themselves to identify, use and enhance the symbols already existing within a particular culture?

k) Are the ecumenical possibilities of the inculturation of the Gospel at a local level sufficiently explored?

l) Are missionaries sufficiently prepared to re-examine their own understanding of truth in the light of inculturation experiences in the young Churches?

IV. Liberation

40. Liberation as a dynamic of mission today is a thread which has woven itself through discussions of all the challenges we face in mission. To capture the range of

discussion and debate on what has become a central concern in missionary activity in many parts of the world is difficult, if not impossible.

While there was not a clear consensus on an exact meaning of "liberation," "poor," "class," yet all the members recognized their importance.

The considerations which follow here from the discussions are grouped roughly into three areas: liberation and the Gospel, issues in liberation, and the response of Christians to the struggle for liberation.

Considerations which have emerged:

41. The message which Jesus preached was Good News to the poor, freedom for captives. Jesus' own direction of His message of liberation in a special way to the poor is the basis for liberation theology. Puebla reaffirms this in its preferential option for the poor.

42. The process of evangelization can be seen as the process of liberation of the poor.

43. The Gospel as liberation of the poor emphasizes the prophetic aspect of evangelization. It calls for an *analysis* of the anti-Kingdom values in a situation and a *witness* to Kingdom values, recognizing the seeds of liberation present.

44. The poor should not be understood as objects of our evangelization. Rather, since the Gospel is meant for them in a special, even primary way, they understand the Gospel message of liberation better than others. Because of this, they are the agents of evangelization.

45. "The poor" refers to those who are deprived in a systematic fashion, of the means for the fullness of life, by another group. Most commonly, this means deprivation of material means of subsistence and deprivation of basic human rights. It is sometimes used in an extended sense to mean a group of people deprived in some non-material fashion (e.g., women—as the poor.)

46. Overcoming the deprivation, or oppression, of the poor, will ordinarily involve conflict. This overcoming of the oppressive situation involves:

i) analysis of the situation,

ii) struggle between the opposing forces (poor and rich), and

iii) resolution of the struggle.

47. Many forms of social analysis are used. Analysis drawn from a Marxist critique of oppressive patterns in society is commonly used, although by no means exclusively. A clear set of tools is needed, since patterns of oppression tend to be interlocked from a local to a global scale.

48. Liberation theology can be understood as a form of theological reflection which is part of the analysis in the process of ending oppression.

49. The struggle between poor and rich usually follows lines of class (as in much of Latin America), race (as in South Africa), or sex (in many parts of the world). The struggle is marked by violent confrontation—either a violence from the side of the oppressor to maintain the oppressive situation, or from the side of the oppressed to counter and overcome the oppressor's violence.

50. Social analysis reveals the widespread, even global character of oppression. For this reason, commitment to the saving message of Jesus Christ entails commit-

ment to the liberation of the oppressed. This commitment means engagement in the struggle for justice and an end to oppressive structures.

51. The struggle for justice reveals in a special way the relation between liberation and other dynamics of mission. Genuine dialogue in a situation leads to a commitment to the oppressed partner and so to justice. Genuine inculturation happens best when it involves first immersing oneself in the liberative streams of the people. Proclamation of the Gospel involves a genuine enactment of the liberative message for the poor.

52. More than one pattern of social analysis is needed. Latin America has developed its theology of liberation in responding to the Marxist critique. Asia is developing its liberation theology also by identifying the liberative stream in religions and cultures, and joining the Christian experience to this stream. Asia has also noted the power of voluntary poverty, as practiced in the great monastic traditions, for the transformation of Society. The Asian bishops have also urged the "dialogue of life" as part of the solidarity of the struggle for liberation:

—which involves working with the learning from the poor;
—in the process of participation in the transformation of unjust social structures;
—this being a "constitutive dimension of the preaching of the Gospel, i.e., the mission of the Church" (Asian Bishops are quoting the Synod of Bishops, Rome, 1971.)

The tools of social analysis must fit the concrete circumstances of a situation.

53. Even in situations where liberation is proclaimed, as in socialist regimes, new forms of oppression often occur. These need to be criticized and struggled against in socialist regimes as much as in capitalist regimes.

54. In the conflict between poor and rich, both poor and rich need to be liberated from the relations of oppression. Christians insist upon liberation of both. How the rich are liberated is a matter of dispute. Some say through conscientization; others say through the liberation first of the poor.

55. If Christians are to be true to the liberative message of the Gospel, they must align themselves with the oppressed in the struggle to bring justice and love. They must take care not to consider themselves the sole liberators; often solidarity with the oppressed means aligning oneself with liberation movements already alive among the people.

56. Just as the net of oppression tends to be global, so must Christians bring their own international networks to bear upon the struggle for justice.

57. Social analysis is an integral part of Christian spirituality. The commitment to justice is part of the response to the Gospel.

58. In solidarity with the struggle of oppressed people, the Christian is faced with the possibility of engaging in various forms of violence, including armed violence, against the oppressive forces. How to decide about this is a much controverted question. There is a tradition of non-violence as the response to oppressive power in the Gospel. There is also a tradition that permits violence in some circumstances. Depending upon circumstances, Christians may be called to engage in violence in some instances.

59. On responses of missionary institutes to the pursuit of justice, see part C.

60. Questions to be explored in the future:

a) What has been the effect of our responses to injustice?

b) How consistent are we in our commitments to justice? How is it reflected in our policies and use of resources?

c) Many of our home bases for our missionary institutes are in First World countries, which are often the oppressors of Third World countries. How have we responded to that situation? Has there been an analysis?

d) What role does justice play in our formation programs?

e) What are the elements of a *new missionary spirituality* that responds to this mission to the poor?

B. THE CENTRAL ROLE OF THE LOCAL CHURCH

Considerations which have emerged:

61. The Church is a communion directed towards mission, a mission whose goal is communion in Christ, among all people. It is a people gathered to be sent, and sent to be gathered. In this perspective the classical description of communion as the planting of the Church remains valid. The Church is called and sent to be the sign and the instrument of communion and solidarity among all people, a foretaste of the coming Kingdom. It fosters and deepens communion together with its constitutive dimensions of justice and peace, wherever they occur already, and seeks to create them where they are not. A "worthy" participation in the Eucharist, source and summit of the Church, presupposes a lived communion among people (1 Cor. 11: 29). The Church must be ready to recognize true freedom wherever it is emerging and proclaim the reality of this freedom given already in Christ.

62. Not only a conversion of hearts is needed for new Churches, but a conversion to new structures which encourage the recognition of the *charisms present in the people,* foster *new ministries* in accord with these charisms, and stimulate *co-responsibility* at the grassroots level of the Church. Communion requires firstly interdependence, not dependence. Catholic communion is meant to be a pluriform unity, and such a unity in diversity can only be achieved from below. How can we form "Churches of the People," places of human solidarity and Christian communion?

63. In the Catholic understanding it is this communion of all these local Churches that forms the Universal Church—the *ecclesia ecclesiarum*—having as its bond of unity the local Church of Rome. It is this Universal Church which is endowed with the missionary mandate of Jesus. However, for certain historical reasons, the local Church of Rome has for some centuries reserved this mission to herself and has through her agency, the *Propaganda Fide* (now called the Sacred Congregation for the Evangelization of Peoples—SCEP), extended herself to many territories and has established many Churches under her jurisdiction. Thanks to Vatican II, these local Churches now recognize their "right and duty" for self-government (Vatican II,

Decree on Ecumenism and Decree on Eastern Rite Churches). They believe they have an equal share in the mission of the Church and they have a right and duty to initiate new missions without thereby being accused of encroaching on any "exclusive" rights of the Roman Church with which they are in communion.

However, the present structures geared to excessive centralism do not help such missionary initiatives to flower in local Churches.

64. This observation in no way implies a disregard for the special charism of Rome as the bond of communion. In fact, it was with pain that we participated in the several sessions on the fate of the Chinese Church in this regard. We admire and support with our prayers those Chinese Christians who suffered and still suffer for their allegiance to the Faith and the Papacy, and we pray that communion be established between all Chinese Catholics so that they may once more become a self-governing local Church of China, in communion with Rome and in the service of the Chinese people.

65. The other point we make is that the old distinction between mission-sending and mission-receiving Churches is becoming blurred. This is partly because of the vitality of the young Churches which generates vocations and a parallel dimension of the number of missionaries in the older Churches. This situation should help strengthen the conviction that all are mission-sending as well as mission-receiving Churches. The mutual mission to one another thus becomes a further reinforcement of the communion of local Churches. One, of course, immediately senses the need for structures that should help exchange of missionaries among the Churches, structures that complement the SCEP. It is hoped that each local Church will, according to its specific charism, produce the type of specialized missionary that other local Churches require. Mission Institutes have a role to play in this.

66. Besides the exchange of personnel, there is a great urgency for an exchange of *information*. First of all, in the matter of justice, a communication system between the poorer Churches that are most concerned with it and the Churches of the affluent countries, would facilitate global conscientization on various issues. A similar network of information on the researches, surveys, analyses done in so many centres of Theological and Pastoral Reflection would be useful.

67. Sharing of Funds is already in vogue. Organizations like *Misereor, Missio, Caritas,* are splendid examples. It is normally the receiving Church that determines the needs and the modes of spending. Massive development projects in local Churches which are found amidst non-Christians can be construed as a form of colonialism if such projects turn the Christian community into an island of wealth and power amidst poverty. Expansion of institutes with no visible improvement among the poor is a clear sign of this. Care should be taken not to compromise the missionary witness and prophetic call to simplicity and poverty in the Third World by indiscriminate use of funds coming from richer Churches. The local Church must involve the *people* in the decision-making process if she wants to avoid such mistakes.

68. The fundamental revitalization of local Churches takes place through a process of evangelization at the grassroots, through a *kenosis* by which they shed elitist cultures of dominant classes and appropriate the culture of the poor, the pri-

mary addressees of the Good News. It is with such self-liberative acts of *kenosis* that young local Churches can acquire missionary efficacy towards those in their immediate environment and towards other older Churches.

69. Coming now to the internal life of the local Churches, we realize that it exists at various levels of communion: domestic, parochial and diocesan. Besides these accepted forms, there has evolved the structure known as *basic communities,* the ultimate constituents of local Church. In our reflections, we have assigned to them a primary role in the formation of *leaders* (missionaries). The following observations have been made:

a) the basic communities are the origin of missionary vocations as well as the locus of their formation (cf. Part II and Part IV below);

b) it is vital for basic communities to preserve the principle of subsidiarity whereby what can be decided or executed at the grassroots level is not to be decided or executed at a higher level. Rather than delegate powers from above, the Central Authority of the local Church should discern, catalyze, coordinate what takes place below in these basic communities (cf. Bishop Claver's model: procedure from People's Forums to Analysis to Common Vision to Catalyzing Leadership).

c) It is then in basic communities that new leadership is formed and, possibly, that new ministries are born. The restoration of the laity to their missionary role is easier in such new communities. It is there that the lay person becomes a missionary to his/her own people.

70. *Questions to be explored in the future:*

a) What structures would you envisage as means for furthering missionary exchanges among the local Churches? How would such structures relate to the SCEP?

b) With the increasing cultural pluralism and diversification of local Churches what new means should we adopt for maintaining communion among them? What role does the exchange of missionaries play in this?

c) What ways are open to members of local Churches to venture out across new missionary frontiers? (e.g., among a particular class of people, religious group, culture, etc., outside the Churches?) Are lay initiatives subject to canon law and episcopal jurisdiction? What relationship does a missionary have towards the local Church?

d) For questions on Ecumenism, Inculturation and dialogue in the local Church, cf. A, above.

C. THE TASK FOR MISSIONARY INSTITUTES

71. While the future of mission has been the overall concern of this SEDOS Research Seminar, the issue of what this future means for missionary institutes is a focal concern. The kind of future which missionary institutes have, and how to meet the challenges of that future, have shaped many of the discussions during the Seminar.

The considerations which have emerged and the questions for further exploration in the future are presented here in four sections:

I. MISSIONARY INSTITUTES IN THE CHURCH'S MISSION
II. FORMATION FOR THE FUTURE
III. COMMUNICATION BETWEEN MISSIONARY INSTITUTES
IV. BUILDING COMMUNICATION BETWEEN MISSIONARY INSTITUTES AND THE LOCAL CHURCH

I. Missionary Institutes in the Church's Mission

72. This section deals with the specific role of the missionary institutes in the Church's mission, both as to the nature and purpose of such institutes, and specific areas with which missionary institutes should be concerned.

Considerations which have emerged:

73. There are persons in local Churches called to missionary vocations, and missionary institutes provide a vehicle for them to respond to God's call.

74. That vocation often entails leaving one's home Church and culture to engage in proclamation of the Gospel, dialogue, participation in the life of other local Churches, struggle for liberation with the poor.

75. For this reason, some missionary institutes should be international in character.

76. Many missionaries are now coming from countries which were themselves considered until recently as "mission countries"; hence the need for international missionary institutes to mediate these vocations.

77. Evangelization in Churches previously evangelized can also be a task for missionary institutes.

78. The aspect of evangelization stressed in the charism of the institute (e.g., proclamation, dialogue, struggle for liberation, communion, etc.) may give a special character to the missionary institute.

79. The missionary institutes fosters dialogue between local Churches.

80. The presence of missionaries from another Church and culture in a local Church can create a positive tension to stimulate response to the call of the Gospel.

81. International missionary institutes can witness to multi-cultural values within their structures and membership.

82. Missionary institutes can serve as a link in the total network of allowances for the liberation of persons and societies.

83. Missionary institutes can oppose global oppression on the international level and serve as advocates for the poor.

84. Missionary institutes can foster dialogue between the rich and the poor.

85. Missionary institutes should embrace the preferential option for the poor.

86. Questions to be explored in the future:

a) Are our current structures adequate for the future task we face?

b) What role do contemplative institutes play in the future of mission?

c) Will decline in numbers lead to amalgamation of some missionary institutes, especially those originating in countries where few or no vocations are forthcoming?

II. Formation for the Future

87. Formation policies and programmes commensurate with the future task of mission will need to be decided upon.

Considerations which have emerged:

88. More effort needs to be directed toward locating those persons who may have missionary vocations.

89. Formation programmes should not alienate candidates from the people with whom they are to work, especially the poor, by accommodating them to a more affluent class.

90. Local Churches have a large part in forming missionary vocations and in their training for work.

91. New centres for spirituality and social concern, as well as local communities, should be as much a part of formation as traditional structures such as seminaries and novitiates.

92. Formation for leadership of communities should stress skills which facilitate communion, inaugurate social analysis, and empower people in the local Church.

93. A new spirituality for mission will be needed to meet the challenges of the future. This spirituality includes not only traditional individual practices of spirituality (private prayer and asceticism, combat of sin and temptations; discernment, etc.), but also the societal dimension of all these practices, particularly as they relate to justice.

94. The new spirituality will need to deal in a special way with formation to justice and to intercultural sensitivity.

95. In the intervening time until such a new spirituality can be worked out, missionary institutes should be especially sensitive to those charismatic persons opting out of current structures and struggling to find new forms of missionary life. They need the protection and support of the missionary institutes.

96. Questions to be explored in the future:

a) A kind of checklist needs to be developed of the attitudes and skills necessary in the missionary candidate for the future.

b) Revision of programmes may be necessary to ensure proper areas of study regarding aspects for mission.

c) Revision of training may be necessary to include training of candidates in the local community, in a situation outside the candidate's home culture, etc.

III. Communication Between Missionary Institutes

97. This section deals with structures already used and others envisioned to promote communication between missionary institutes. It is also concerned with how these communication networks might promote more effective work in achieving the goals of mission.

Considerations which have emerged:

98. Many structures have emerged since Vatican II to promote contact between religious institutes in general and missionary institutes in particular (e.g., UISG, USG, SEDOS). These structures need to be evaluated in light of their effectiveness for mission.

99. The kinds of Justice and Peace Commissions found within religious institutes need to be extended to a network between religious institutes, e.g., the Justice and Peace Commissions of the UISG and USG working together with SEDOS.

100. Such new networks for global solidarity in justice should also work with other international networks, such as Amnesty International and that of the World Council of Churches.

101. Such new networks for justice should be concerned with the gathering of information, with the ability to mobilize quick response to pressing situations, and with providing solidarity and support to local communities that are struggling for justice.

102. Networks for other kinds of information exchange, e.g., about needs for specific kinds of personnel, and their availability, should be developed.

103. Where possible, structures for communication already existing should serve as the base for expanding these networks of communication.

104. Questions to be explored in the future:

a) Are there other needs for relations, particularly in view of the challenges of mission for the future, which need to be identified?

b) Who will take the initiative in beginning discussions which will lead to the new or expanded networks needed?

IV. Building Communication
Between Missionary Institutes and the Local Churches

105. This section deals with special activities of missionary institutes in local Churches, lines of communication and decision-making between missionary institutes and local Churches, and the issue of financial assistance.

Considerations which have emerged:

106. Missionaries can serve as catalysts for dialogue and for inculturation.

107. Missionary institutes' commitment to justice must be manifest in local Churches by engagement in the struggles for liberation of the people.

108. The structures of missionary institutes should provide for contact at the level of local Churches, especially to provide information pertinent to discernment of future directions for the institute.

109. The issues of flexibility and mobility for missionary institutes is most real in the institute's relation to the local community.

110. The work of the missionary institute in a given area is guided also by the discernment of the local Church.

111. The greater part of evangelization may be carried on by the local Church since it is already inculturated. There may be instances, however, where it is better done by missionary institutes.

112. Financial assistance from missionary institutes should be used in local Churches to enable local people to achieve their genuine objectives.

113. Funding should occur only after thorough consultation with local communities. This consultation often involves helping local communities unlearn patterns of expectation about funding inherited the past.

114. An important criterion for dispersal of funds is how funded projects will be sustained over a longer period of time.

115. Funding should always have in mind the progressive achievement of self-sufficiency of the local Church in the area of finance.

116. Patterns of funding should not result in priests and religious living on different levels and being able to carry out their work with differing levels of resources within the same local area. Moreover, all should be living at the same level as the people with whom they work.

117. Consideration should be given to missionary institutes' sources of funding, i.e., contributors in home countries. Conscientization about how their money is used is important, as well as awareness of injustice in their own home countries.

118. Questions to be explored in the future:

a) How will these understandings of missionary institutes' relations to local Churches affect relations with local leaders, especially bishops?

b) Can there be cooperation between missionary institutes in a given area to equalize the kind of funding provided by their respective members?

c) What will flexibility and mobility mean in this understanding of the relations between missionary institutes and local Churches? How will it be achieved?

CONCLUSION

119. In addition to the general themes of the Seminar, which were discussed in all the groups and have been listed in this Report, a number of groups met sponta-

neously during the Seminar to discuss particular questions. They were the Asian group, the African group, the group on Islam, the group which discussed Missionary Institutes, and the group on Justice and Peace. Each of these groups presented separate reports to the Plenary Assembly, which are not included in this general report.

Also, each day consolidated reports on the discussions which took place in all the groups were prepared by the Drafting Committee and circulated to all. These contain further material on the themes which is not completely incorporated into this final Report.

Finally, the drafters would like once again to confess their limitations and beg forgiveness in advance for contributions that were distorted by us or omitted. In a Seminar of such variety, divergences of opinion were plentiful. While presenting what we saw as the main lines of the themes discussed in the Seminar, we have tried to respect minority views, although we know that we have not fully succeeded. We trust that the Holy Spirit will further, in all of us, the work begun during this Seminar.

Part IV

CAVALLETTI '81: THE SEMINAR EXPERIENCE

Maria-José Tresch, S.S.N.D.

After two years of dreaming, talking, planning, discussing, meeting, and working together on topics of concern to the universal church as well as on such nitty-gritty as hospitality and secretarial services, *the day* had arrived. March 8, 1981, found the "planning" committee all in readiness awaiting the arrival of the first participants at Villa Cavalletti, a retreat house belonging to the Jesuits in the Frascati area of Rome.

Much had gone into the preparation of this ten-day seminar to be held March 8 to March 19, 1981. Besides the choice of topics and the careful selection of "experts" to present the material that was to be the subject of reflection and study during the seminar itself, much preparation had gone into the planning of the actual process to be used and the methodology to be employed during the time to be spent together in the beautiful Alban hills in early springtime. New Life . . . New Hope . . . symbols of what were projected as possible results of this gathering of enthusiastic, searching, committed Christians, lay and religious, women and men. Present in this diverse group were priests and pastors, a bishop, theologians and ecumenists, active missionaries and those in administrative positions, superior generals, vicar generals, councilors, and mission secretaries of missionary and mission-sending institutes. There were experts from all over the globe: directors of pastoral centers, secretaries of episcopal commissions, professors at universities, advisers to bishops' conferences, and leaders with different kinds of apostolic responsibility.

There were those whose interest lay in the educational preparation of missionaries and those who were "out there" struggling with the application of Christian concepts and values to difficult religious and sociopolitical life situations. There were those who were concerned with the problems of dialogue with peoples of other faiths, particularly with those faiths that stem from the ancient traditions of Buddhism, Hinduism, and Islam. At the same time there were others whose concerns were mainly of a pastoral nature, that is, with the *re*evangelization of the Western world or with the ongoing evangelization of the members of the younger churches. Then there were those whose concerns had to do with the theological problems and difficulties arising from today's realities on the six continents who worked together with those

651

whose concerns tended toward the praxis that flowed from radical discipleship and the application of gospel values and principles to today's society with its multifaceted, conflictual life situations.

In all there were 101 delegates from all over the world who assembled at Villa Cavalletti to study the "future" of the mission of the church. SEDOS, the organization in Rome that links missionary congregations and societies, had convoked the group. It was an ad-hoc consultation of a private rather than of an official nature. Questions that had plagued missionary societies since Vatican Council II, practical questions regarding personnel and their placement, questions stemming from the political problems arising from the birth of new nations since World War II, questions springing from new mission theology, questions flowing from the difficulties presented by new socioeconomic structures within older nations as well as within younger ones—all of these were the subject of reflection and discussion. Less concrete but no less important questions were also asked and probed: questions relating to new ministries, new approaches to evangelization, the methodology to be employed in preaching the gospel today, the development and growth of local churches and their relationship with the universal church, along with questions that dealt with the concerns of today's peoples and societies and the application of new ecclesiology to existing "mission" structure. Inculturation, liberation of the poor, and dialogue particularly with those of other faiths, other religious traditions, new cults and sects—all of these concerns entered into the content of each day's work. Hence the emphasis on the title "SEDOS Mission *Research* Seminar."

In order to channel the riches of the varied and valuable experiences presented by the cultural and ethnic groups represented at the seminar along with the wealth of their academic and spiritual preparation, a unique methodology was developed and followed. The particular plan and methodology was used with a hope that it would promote creative reflection and discussion while aiding the participants to work together in some type of ordered fashion that would not place constraints upon the work of the Spirit among them. It was developed to lead the participants to produce a "final" statement or document which would adequately reflect the spirit as well as the concrete "conclusions" of these ten days of working together. It was hoped that these final statements or conclusions would in some way point to the future of mission as well as mirror back with a certain fidelity what was actually taking place on the "mission" scene in the world today. The reflection/study papers, which had been presented by the "experts," had been prepared by them in the context of their own realities, their own unique experiences.

In the preparatory papers for the seminar, the plan and methodology was described as follows:

[It] is designed from elements which have been indicated during the two-year preparation as significant hopes for the seminar. These elements point to a concern for the following:
  —an interaction between life experience and theory
  —an interaction between concreteness and abstraction
  —an interaction between pastoral practice and theology

—an ambiance that will foster enriching relationships among persons from different cultural environments

—an ambiance that will allow for a sufficient balance between work and rest

—an ambiance that will have sufficient structure to enable the group to articulate their sharing in a meaningful way for the future, and which at the same time will be open to the action of the Holy Spirit working among us.

The underlying structure for the ten days, which went into the overall plan designed from the elements and concerns above, included: (1) a ten-day live-in: all participants were asked to commit themselves to this even though they might have resided within commuting distance; (2) days that were envisaged as a series of moments, phases, or spaces of time; (3) days with spaces for prayer, quiet time, meals, sharing reflection study, recreation or free time, rest; (4) these spaces were interrelated and formed a whole; they were spelled out or defined within the constraint of time, but spaces of free time were inserted so as to remove, insofar as possible, constraint and unnecessary pressure; (5) the specific moments of research/work/ study during the session were also envisaged as a series of spaces and followed the basic structure.

The specific moments of research/work/study during the seminar were described in the following manner:

Plenary session: At the beginning of the study of a specific subject there will be time in plenary session of about 1½ hours. The purpose of this time will be—

to hear explanations or clarifications of certain points by some of those who wrote reflection/study papers in preparation for the seminar;
to ask questions about matters arising from the working papers which were studied before coming to the seminar;
to allow for further comments about the subject.

In order to achieve the purpose of this time in plenary, namely *explanations, clarifications, questions, comments,* the interventions by authors of papers will be limited to a *maximum of five minutes.*

The moderator may shorten the plenary if there are not many clarifications, questions, etc.; the group will simply move into the next phase of the day.

Group Meetings: All will meet in small groups following the plenary and coffee/tea break. The purpose of this time will be *to exchange, to share* our reflections, experiences, views about the subject being studied, in order *to deepen* their understandings and visions, and *to move towards* a new level of insight about the subject.

In order to achieve the purpose of this time in groups, *no notes will be taken during the group meetings.* It is a time for sharing and listening.

Personal Reflection: The first working period in the afternoon is set aside for personal reflection on all that has been absorbed by the participants from the study of the working papers before coming to the seminar and from the study and exchange of reflections in the morning. The purpose of this time will be *to try to discover what is emerging* from all this material that seems to be of importance *for the future of mission.*

Group Meeting: The final working period for the day will be in our small groups. The purpose of this time will be for the members of the group *to indicate what is emerging* from the experiences reflected upon during the day *that seems significant for the future of mission.*

In order to achieve the purpose of this time, the secretary of each group will *note* the orientations, the points, etc. made by the members of the group. *It is important that these notes or notations be very concise, to the point, brief and in as few words as possible* (if possible not more than one sentence for each notation, in view of an effective consolidation of the thinking of all the groups).

The secretaries of each group should hand the notations into the secretariat *before 19:00* each day. It is suggested that a black felt-tip pen be used for the notations to facilitate photocopying.

Consolidation, Review, Revision: The notations from the ten groups will be consolidated by the drafters and returned to each participant for review.

A time in plenary on a subsequent day will allow for comments, suggestions, reactions.

This time will be followed by a time in groups, to modify the consolidated notes in view of a final plenary. These modifications of the consolidated notations will be compiled by the drafters and returned to the participants for review before the plenary sessions for final consolidations. It is important that both consensus and divergencies be presented.

Now that we have the actors and the logistics that were prepared to facilitate their participation in the seminar, let's see what really did happen during the ten days which this group of 101 people from all over the world (thirty-six nations from the six continents were represented) lived and interacted with each other. The best way to describe what took place is to call it a faith-experience. It was the coming together of 101 committed Christian people who lived, prayed, shared, and searched with each other on the level of their own faith in and commitment to sharing the good news, the presence of Jesus among all peoples of goodwill.

In order to capture the atmosphere that pervaded Villa Cavalletti during those ten days in March, it is necessary to step back two years and glance quickly over those twenty-four or more months preceding the seminar. This grandiose project would never have been realized had it not been for the willing cooperation of the forty-four congregations that comprise the membership of SEDOS and that also assume the responsibility for its direction and its activities. From the first moment when the executive committee asked for the formation of a volunteer group to do a feasibility study on the seminar on through the afternoon of March 19 when overseas participants, along with superior generals dismantled displays, took down banners, replaced displaced furniture, packed vans that took typewriters, copying machines, and leftover work materials back to Rome, and swept floors, there was a spirit of generous collaboration in an activity that was "ours," which belonged to *us*, the church in microcosm, an activity that was of vital importance to what we all believed in—the mission of the church *now* and into the next millennium. Those two years were filled with the activities of a task force who planned and dreamed and organized, wrote letters and answered questions, and a planning committee that studied, reflected, collected ideas for topics to be studied, made decisions, and encouraged all involved to volunteer their services, which included the searching out of "experts" from the six continents and then the reading of their papers. As the time of the seminar drew closer, liturgy, hospitality, and secretarial services committees were formed. More than half of the funds, all of the housing and transportation, as well as the secretaries and translators for the four languages used during the seminar (French, Spanish, Italian, English) were all volunteered by the member groups of SEDOS. This spirit begun in December 1978 grew, matured, and pervaded the days at Villa Cavalletti in March 1981. The seeds for a faith community had been sown. Even the "experts" had been brought into this sharing atmosphere. Letters had been sent and received, research was done, and papers were submitted to be used in whatever way the task force and planning committee felt would be of most use to the dynamics of the seminar group. Time was given and all in response to only a promise of the possibility of participation in the seminar, with no other remuneration, aside from the travel and hospitality expenses for the ten days in Rome.

As a result only a day or two was needed at the actual seminar for the birth of a palpable faith community, which grew and bore fruit in the "Agenda for Future Planning, Study, and Research in Mission" as the final statement, or document, of the seminar was entitled. This faith community flowed, evolved, grew, and matured through the interaction of all present, at times in small groups, at times in plenary sessions, in animated conversations at meals, in French, English, Spanish liturgical celebrations in small and large groups, along with shared prayer morning and evening. Not to be minimized were the corridor "meetings," the walks in the gardens, the bedroom huddles, and the social-hour groups after the work of the day was finished.

The faith community suffered and grew strong in the small discussion groups, which met twice a day for over an hour and a half each time. These ten groups comprised of approximately ten members each had been formed on the basis of language facility in Spanish, English, Italian, or French. Care was given to provide each group with a variety of participants, some of whom had written papers and others who represented the administration of different institutes. In addition, attention was given to providing a relatively even distribution among cultures and for the presence of women in each group. These concerns resulted in placing some persons in language groups other than that of their first language. Special-interest groups, which touched upon the problems of Asia, Africa, Latin America, Muslim-Christian dialogue, and the "missionaries" themselves, were formed spontaneously. These groups shared their concerns with the larger groups through papers written or presented at Plenary Assembly time.

"Dialogue" emerged as *the word* of the seminar. It was the subject of study, reflection, and discussion. Its use was even attempted during large and small group sessions. Participants grappled with putting the basic principles for real dialogue into practice. We dialogued, we talked at each other, we tried to listen, we became frustrated, we stopped talking, and again attempted dialogue. Much was learned, much was experienced, much effort was made accompanied by much pain, and not all was success, but all left convinced of the values and importance of true dialogue in the mission of today . . . and tomorrow. The experience of learning to *listen* was perhaps among the most painful experiences of the ten days. Some groups experienced this more poignantly than others.

At times there were evident signs of the constant debate on some of the principles of proclamation. This was couched in terms of the demand for our involvement in social analysis if we are to respond to the call for the liberation of the poor as one of the expressions of radical discipleship today, and an apparent opposing emphasis on the urgency that all take part in the "dialogue of life" if we are to share our experience of the Lord with others. Subtle tones turned into strident cries, and vice versa, from day to day. But all were in earnest, and all made efforts to accept the other. The principles of dialogue were the reason we were there—for whom and for what.

As had been planned, the days moved forward in this rhythm of prayer, reflection, discussion, meals, and relaxation. The days were grouped in units of three: two days were dedicated to each topic and the third was given to plenary assemblies on it. At the end of the last session of the day, the reporter of each group rushed up to the secretariat to present the statements that were the result of that day's work. Recommendations for brevity but accuracy in reflecting the thinking of the group were given. Much effort was made to include all important ideas presented, even conflicting positions. A group of drafters—two, or more often three—spent the next hours of the evening and often went on into the night bringing together the work of all the groups into what was called a consolidated report. The input from the groups was organized in such a way that it would help the participants see where there was a convergence of ideas on the topic in question and where there was not. The secretariat collaborated most efficiently, having these reports ready for distribution by the following morning before the participants gathered in their small groups for the work of the day. For the plenary session on the third day, the drafters prepared a draft report from the two consolidated reports on the subject in question.

Each topic was treated in this way. The discussions were rich and varied. Questions, problems, difficulties, dreams, visions were being voiced and discussed. Many of these questions and problems would require much research and time for study and reflection. Some could have various responses depending upon the focus of the institute involved, or on the actual life situation being considered. As the seminar time was drawing to a close it was seen that a document that would be of value would be one reflecting the rich input gathered from all the seminar participants, while giving direction to future study and research on the part of the participants, the "experts," and the religious institutes, as well as to anyone who would be interested in the topics studied during these special days in March 1981 in Rome. And so the title "An Agenda for Future Planning, Study, and Research in Mission" was born. When the first draft appeared for study and discussion by the Plenary Assembly on March 18, there was a general atmosphere of acceptance on the part of the group. The assembly felt comfortable with its general orientation and presentation. A number of ideas were clarified and hammered out at this time. The document was in a very rough state. There had not been sufficient time to reflect upon the whole and to see with clarity the important themes that were emerging. However, that day's work in the Plenary Assembly and in the small groups gave a definite form and direction to the final draft, which was worked on by the drafters and the secretaries during the entire night. The finished paper was at each one's place in the assembly hall by 6 A.M. on March 19. The morning session began at 9 A.M.

This session was marked by an ambiance of comraderie and satisfaction that the ten days had borne fruit. The participants had come for a purpose and good work had been done. There were still questions and unfulfilled dreams on the part of some, but the "Agenda" did not close a door on an event; on the contrary it opened many doors into the future. Some dreams and visions were modified and adapted as a result, and there was a comfortableness with that. The Spirit had been invoked much during those days together and it is not His way to rubber-stamp our personal projects, proposals, dreams, and visions. He moves us to dream only to reform, redo, and reorient those dreams as He inspires us to interact with each other. It is the potter at work. Both are necessary for the building up of the kingdom: the clay and the Potter.

The liturgy of that morning gathered up the hopes and expectations of all together with the days of study, listening, thinking, creating, giving birth, and dying that marked March 8–March 19 for all of us. The theme of the liturgy expressed most adequately what we wanted to be during those days of *search* and *research* and what was the fruit of this unique experience of working together with brothers and sisters from the four corners of the globe. The people made the difference. They converted an ordinary seminar into a faith community. The recessional hymn captured the spirit of the group and its work—the "Veni Sancte Spiritus." We had not finished something, we were going forth to begin again, to create, to search for new ways to preach the good news, to share our faith experience, our experience of Jesus, to be one with the people of our particular corner of the globe, to serve, to love, to hope in Christian joy and faith.

The communion psalm of thanksgiving read by Charles Davignon, parish priest, missionary, participant, and translator, was his personal expression of his and our lived experience at Villa Cavalletti. It caught the lights and shadows of this memorable seminar in a very special way.

A Sedos Psalm of Thanks

Bless the Lord, all you works of the Lord.
Praise and exalt him above all forever.

Moulded hedges and princely pines
Sculptured walks with Villa Cavalletti's blossoming vines, bless the Lord.

You singing, songing, smiling white bird
from kitchen corner on canary perch,
Come, praise and thank your God
    for Him alone we also search.

All you marbled halls, praise the Lord.
All you Italian clouds and sunny skies, bless the Lord.
You soup, you salad, you Frascati wine and crunchy bread, bless the Lord.

You Sisters of Spain and brothers of Ignatius
      on Castelli hills,
      thank our Lord and God with us as we pay our bills.

Groups One thru Ten, bless the Lord.
All you assembly of SEDOS '81, bless the Lord.
Planners and organizers, bless the Lord.
Secretaries and translators, bless the Lord.

Sons of India, France, and America's doors,
      Daughters of Sri Lanka, Africa, England, and Philippine shores,
All thank the Lord that these children,
      each one of us, is called in faith and love,
      in varied hues of cultured trust,
      to dialogue, to witness, to suffer,
      to love, to embody MISSION as our must.

Ten days of grace, bless the Lord.
Thirty-three nations of Adam's race, bless the Lord.
All you paying, praying rich of the earth, bless the Lord.
All you Poor, Oppressed, and Persecuted, bless the Lord.

Everything growing from the reports and drafts
      and finally approved Agenda, bless the Lord.
You selfless writers, bless the Lord.

All you Sinners from world's ends
      united to pray and listen and grow, near Peter's Roman See,
Come now, you Saints of SEDOS
      to preach Christ's Word, to live and love and be.

Typewriters and mimeographs, bless the Lord.
All you loving missionaries, bless the Lord.

Let us bless the Father and the Son and the Holy Spirit.
Let us praise and thank and exalt Him above all forever.

Part V

SIGNPOSTS OF THE FUTURE

Willie Jenkinson, C.S.Sp.

This is an attempt to delineate some future directions of mission in the aftermath of the SEDOS Seminar. An underlying tension at the seminar was how to proclaim the unchanging Jesus Christ, "yesterday, today, and the same forever," in a world of rapid, even phenomenal change. This tension will be at the heart of mission in the years to come, for the paradigms of life, to which men and women have been accustomed, are breaking both in the world and in the church today.

A new world is emerging, a world of shuttles and space satellites, of computers and microchips, of biological breakthroughs and instant communications, a world in which peoples are developing close contacts through growing and diversified patterns of relationships and being bonded together by networks of interdependent commitments.

The effect of these relationships and mutual commitments can be seen, for example, in the global dimensions of multinational corporations. It can be seen in the problems created by permanent groups, be they minorities or majorities, who have no foreseeable realistic access to representation and resort to terrorism or counter-violence. It can be seen in the recognition of the disparity of wealth and consumption of resources between North and South and the growing worldwide recognition of the cry of the poor.

Another element of major significance in this emerging world is the phenomenal development of communications, which make it possible now to focus world attention instantaneously on an event or topic, on an assassination or the death of a hunger striker, the suffering caused by an earthquake or a drought. This is the world in which mission will take place and it must not be considered apart from it.

The other pole of tension is how to proclaim Jesus Christ, the changeless one, the unique revelation of the God of love and the love of God. This task is and will remain the raison d'être of the church's existence. The church is universal and Catholic and continually in mission, but it will be increasingly involved in the changing conditions of the contextual environment in which the message is proclaimed. The paradigm of the church is also breaking. Pluralism is a reality, and not only within the churches of

659

the Christian tradition. It is also emerging within the multiple faiths that have nourished men and women for centuries and whose numbers now amount to two-thirds of the world's population and continue to increase.

Cultures and religions other than those prevailing in Europe are now penetrating and will continue to penetrate Europe and North America without the force of arms for the first time in history. The demands of true dialogue will need to be faced, for they are still only dimly appreciated. Attempts by Christians to enter into dialogue, albeit sincere, are seen all too often by members of other faiths as a tactical change on the part of those who, for centuries, subjected them to condescension and to violent or stealthy opposition.

The Seminar was aware of these situations. Walbert Bühlmann's "third church" and Karl Rahner's "world church" were part of the generally accepted thinking, but the implications of this general acceptance will only be applied in the coming years. Mission in all continents; mission "from everywhere to everywhere" and among all categories of people; the end of purely mission-sending churches and the development of new relationships between interdependent sister churches; the growth of local churches and their relationship to the universal church—all these were accepted, but the implementation of the consequences has be worked out painfully in the future. It is no longer sufficient to say that the missionary brings salvation or grace or God. These are already to be found where the missionary goes. What the missionary brings is a hope embedded in the meaning of the life, death, and resurrection of Jesus.

How will Jesus "yesterday, today, and the same forever" be proclaimed? The answer to the tension between the changing and the changeless may lie in a new appreciation of Christology and of the humanness of Jesus. We touch in him the humanness of men and women with all their hopes and desires; their dreams and visions, and in the humanness of men and women we touch the humanness of Jesus the bringer of hope. He is not changeless or static. The mystery of his incarnation starts with creation, reaches a high point in his life, death, and resurrection, and goes on to our own resurrection. To say something about Jesus is to say something about the missionary, to say something about the "other" wherever he or she may be, across boundaries of race, color, culture, and time. In this understanding of relationship, Jesus is "becoming" rather than static, God is a "changing God." The creed has to be continually re-presented. The missionary will have to confront continually the uniqueness of Christ among the gods of human believing, for the redemption applies to Buddhists and Hindus, to Muslims and Jains and to atheists. Every man and woman has been touched by the humanness of Jesus. Many will continue to be called to proclaim Jesus in a special way, to commit themselves, even for life, to this work. They will be conscious that while there is no salvation outside the kingdom, there is plenty of salvation outside the church. Coping with these challenges will shape much of the mission of the future.

Mission will not escape but will reflect the growing tension within the Catholic church. Participants at the seminar were very conscious of decrease in vocations to the clerical and to missionary religious life. This is not a cause, but rather, one of the symptoms of the tension. The real problem arises from the broken paradigm of a certain security, continuity, and identity, which was shattered by the conciliar decrees and their aftermath. Change was inevitable and disturbing, but at a deep level many have not accepted change. They are sincerely committed to containing it, even opposing it. Rejecting and opposing pluralism, they aim at recovering the lost identity of the preconciliar period. In this tension will lie perhaps the real crisis within the church in the coming decade and mission will not escape it. A renewed emphasis on authority tends to promote submissiveness and conformity as the highest virtues. Emerging local churches will be particularly exposed to pressures urging conformity to a traditional Western institutional model of ecclesiology. Those involved in mission, whether they are indigenous to the local church or are moving across cultural and national boundaries, will be in the vanguard of this potential conflict. Incarnating the faith in different cultures is already a challenge to which will be added an honest awareness of genuine problems in presenting certain traditional formulations of Christian faith and moral teachings. An example of this occurred at the recent Synod on the Family when the bishops of many African dioceses indicated the difficulty of accepting the unique Western cultural models of marriage.

Interpretation of relevant parts of the Dogmatic Constitution on the Church, the Decree on Ecumenism, the Declaration on the Relation of the Church to Non-Christian Religions, the Declaration on Religious Liberty, the Decree on the Church's Missionary Activity, and the Pastoral Constitution on the Church in the Modern World will have particular importance for emerging mission policies. The dignity of the human person is a basic teaching running through all these documents, as it is the central theme also of Pope John Paul II's pastoral and missionary approach. What effect will the coming promulgation of the revised Code of Canon Law have on this fundamental orientation? The dignity of the human person will require of the missionary that he or she be respectful of deeply rooted cultural patterns, and of the richness of others faiths that are salvific. In the years ahead missionaries will need to ask the question whether it is still possible to lay down the theological, verbal, and conceptual categories, "to theologize" for whole continents or for an extended era of time. The significance of diversity of location and time will challenge those engaged in mission to theologize and reflect on the basic simple message of Jesus about the God of love and the love of God across boundaries of space and time, culture and race.

Another paradigm has broken, the traditional and inevitable dichotomy of rich and poor. The quest for fullness of life, integral development, and liberation is better informed and is becoming the focus of the church's mission to an ever increasing degree. The promotion of justice is accepted as a constitutive part of mission. No authentic mission of the future is possible without involvement in the social, political, and economic circumstances of the local and global situation. Paul VI in *Evangelii Nuntiandi* reminds us that "there is no true evangelization if the name, the teaching, the life, the promises, the kingdom and the mystery of Jesus of Nazareth are not proclaimed." When the values of the kingdom are proclaimed they inevitably challenge the forces of injustice and may lead to persecution and to death. There is a continuous relationship and interplay between the gospel and human concrete life at the personal, social, economic, communitarian level, and the missionary will be called to become involved in this. Helder Camara deplored desecration of the Hosts in a parish church of his diocese and maltreatment of and injustice toward the poor. The church, and the missionary whose activity is made up of ecclesial acts, can no longer restrict his or her vision to the religious field and be dissociated from the world's temporal problems.

But the question arises today as to the extent to which a foreign missionary can identify himself or herself with the struggle for justice. How authentic will the voice raised in protest seem to be when it is identified by color, race, culture, or historical background with the very peoples and countries associated with systems of oppression or exploitation? It may well be that a more effectual protest can be made by challenging the social, economic, and political philosophies and programs of governments in the "developed" world where these injustices frequently have their origins. There is a deceptive sense of achievement in going to tilt at windmills that are far away, while at the same time collaborating with the builders of those same windmills at home. It is a sign of the times that injustice can be detected and unmasked but also that the mass media and the powerful interested structures can manipulate its concealment. A greater responsibility will devolve on the prophetic voice of those in mission to make it known and to challenge it.

What of the missionary institutes—of those who give a special place in their lives to making Christ known across boundaries of race and culture or in specially difficult circumstances? It is less than adequate to reaffirm enthusiastically the continuing need for missionary institutes and to undertake renewed programs of recruiting members to prop up or give new life to these institutes. The question of their existence goes deep and is radical. New members will not be attracted by appeals unless they can see clearly the validity of the objectives. There is still an assumption on the part of missionary bodies of Europe and North America that foreign missionaries should be "out there," overseas, regardless almost of the particular circumstances of the situation to which they are going. The question needs to be asked repeatedly whether or not churches in the West express concern about mission tasks on their own doorsteps and whether or not they identify with oppressed and deprived people in their own society. Without such concern their interest in faraway situations is susceptible of misunderstanding. The attitudes of mission supporters and promoters in the "home" churches will need to be set free of paternalism and condescension. Within the institutes, precipitate transfers of personnel from one situation to another, following withdrawal or expulsion, need to be seriously examined in the light of inculturation and the question frankly asked as to whose interests are really being served, those of the missionary institute faced with redundant personnel or the interests of the local church to which they are reassigned?

Perhaps the most difficult challenge facing those who take on a special responsibility for proclaiming Jesus Christ in mission in the years ahead will be the challenge of death. There is no longer a question of "Why mission?" but there is a huge question of "How mission?" The missionary era of the past century is ended. It is finished. The paradigms are broken. The relationships that bind the world together call for new commitments for creativity and the birth of new societies. Mission will involve new births, new growths, and also deaths. An age of persecution may well

SIGNPOSTS OF THE FUTURE

have begun. But even apart from this death there is the death of withdrawal, of not being needed, dare we say it, of being unwanted. Missionaries will be called upon to empty themselves, as Paul said of Christ—and one form of this may be readiness to go away from the location where one is engaged in mission. All religious missionary institutes will be faced with the effects of the change. Many of their members will be simply too advanced in years to readapt to new situations. Expulsion or withdrawal from a previous mission situation will be an added disability to insertion in a new one. They may experience infidelity to a permanent commitment if they leave and they may be only too aware of the immensity of the task still to be performed. But they should not be worried by either. It is not for them to decide when the work will be finished; it is the Lord's and they should go promptly and joyously when this is required. There is considerable force in the argument that they should go even while they are still needed, otherwise their departure may have little effect in such important areas as building self-reliance, encouraging new ministries, and involvement of the local community in its responsibility for mission.

At the institutional level there is need for a positive approach to withdrawal. It is a pretension that it is always the "Western" churches that are sending and going on missions. More internationalization of missionary institutes that are now confined mainly to European or North American membership will help this positive approach. The temptation to go on romanticizing about the past century of missionary expansion needs to be resisted. In a way the myth has to be purified and exorcised if a new era is to begin. Even the terms "foreign missionary " and "foreign missions" will have a doubtful value as a clarion call to service. They are often resented by members of the new churches, who see in them continuing inferences of immaturity and dependence.

Institutes need to plan realistically for the future to make information available to those of their members who will withdraw; to plan their "reentry" into new situations where they can continue their ministry of service; to help them to retrain for these new situations; to undertake programs of training and formation of members for special ministries in the new churches; to elaborate and implement policies of exchange of personnel between the churches of North and South; to set in process a planned devolution of the role of leadership from members of their societies to local churches and their members; to concentrate on new patterns of relationships which may lead to an exchange of personnel surpassing the "missionary" relationships of the past.

The missionary paradigm has changed irrevocably, and adaption, which is often the untimely result of pressures, is not an adequate answer. The changed conditions of the world and church call for new breakthroughs in the years ahead, for a fantastic hope, for creativity that goes beyond adaptation, for a conversion on the part of all those engaged in mission. There is need to reject a tendency to possess Christ and to distort him by confining understanding of him to Western philosophical conceptualizations, to abandon the hidden agenda in dialogue and an attitude of superiority, which derives from power and wealth and connection, to identity with a church recognizable readily as poor and holy rather than as rich, foreign, and well organized.

It is possible that the person committed to mission in these coming decades will be challenged more by the Johannine model of mission than by the traditional mandate of Matthew. John orients the call to mission around the Father. As the Father sends the Son, so the Son sends the disciples—and in this relationship lies the mission of the disciples. They are sent to be the presence of the Father in the world after the resurrection. The manner of their presence in the world will be that of servants doing to others what Jesus has done to them—the menial humble service of washing their feet. Just as Jesus was dynamically one with the Father and was sent into the world by the Father, so the dynamic union between the disciples and Jesus, both in being and in doing, is the mission of the disciples.

The indwelling of Jesus is then the principle of activity in mission for John, and this incorporation into Jesus is the gift of the Spirit. He sees mission not so much as constituted by "sending"; rather, all fruitfulness flows from contemplative union with the Son. No matter how "authenticated" the disciple is, the "sent" missionary has no meaning, if she or he is not doing the works of the Father. The works will be known by John's litmus test, "love for one another."

In the years to come this love for one another as the sign of discipleship may well be seen in a humble service requiring the missionary to decrease, a service of "being with," "accompanying," "sharing," rather than one of leading, guiding, directing, organizing, and managing, which has characterized much of the work of the past. It may be seen also as the fundamental characteristic of the basic communities, which are clearly emerging as one of the most significant developments of future mission in all continents.

At the seminar the significance of centers of contemplation for mission was remarked on with special reference to Asia, but the place of contemplation may well be increasingly significant for the future of all mission. There are signs that it responds to a movement of the Spirit.

The basic challenge for mission in the years ahead is to cope with the phenomenon of rapid change; to undertake mission in an environment that is pluri-religious, pluri-cultural, pluri-ethnic; to recognize the emergence of new paradigms of interdependence, mutuality, collegiality, reciprocity, and relationship. There is still, and always will be, a blessed place for the "bearers of good tidings." Whether they will be called "missionaries" or not, they will come from, and build up, "laboratories of hope" in all parts of the world. They will need to be unafraid of the breaking paradigms, prepared to seek out new interpretations, new imaginative ways of telling the story of the God of love and the love of God, as revealed to us in Jesus Christ, and committed to furthering the values of his kingdom with the potential for conflict and suffering that this will entail for them personally.

Appendix: The Personnel of the SEDOS Research Seminar on the Future of Mission, March 1981

Seminar Services

Steering Committee

Parmananda Divarkar, S.J.
Marie Josee Dor, S.A.
Gabriele Ferrari, S.X.
Robert Gay, W.F.
William Halliden, S.S.C.
Joseph Hardy, S.M.A.
Willie Jenkinson, C.S.Sp.

Joseph Lang, M.M.
Margaret Frances Loftus,
S.N.D.-N.
Mary Motte, F.M.M.
Leo-Paul Nobert, O.M.I.
Godelieve Prove, S.C.M.M.-M
Maria-José Tresch, S.N.N.D.

Specific Services

Parmananda Divarkar Margaret Frances Loftus	Liturgy
Gabriele Ferràri	Co-chairperson for plenaries
William Halliden	Hospitality
Willie Jenkinson	Moderator for plenaries
Joseph Lang Mary Motte	Task force Coordination/drafting
Leo-Paul Nobert Thomas Kretz	Finances and general management
Godelieve Prove	Co-chairperson for plenaries
Maria-José Tresch	Coordinator for secretarial services

665

Secretarial and Interpreter Services

Irene Bonsens, F.M.M.
Josephine Bushell, S.N.D.-N.
Gemma d'Sa, S.C.M.M.-M
Manuela Martinez, I.C.M.
Mercedes Aizpuru, C.M.

Mary John Berchmans, R.J.M.
Charles Davignon
Jeanette Dastous, S.A.
Marie Ivonne Duclos, R.S.C.J.
Helene Miniares, C.M.

Participants

1. Josef Amstutz
   Superior General
   Bethlehem Missionary Society
   CH-6405 Immensee (SZ)
   Switzerland

2. Maria Helena Arns
   General Councilor
   School Sisters of Notre Dame
   Via della Stazione Aurelia, 95
   I-00163 Rome, Italy

3. Tissa Balasuriya, O.M.I.
   Director
   Center for Society and Religion
   281 Denas Road
   Colombo 10, Sri Lanka

4. Antonio Bayter-Abud
   Superior General
   Yarumal Missionary Society
   Carrera 81 N. 52B-120, Medellín
   Apartado aereo 3309
   Medellín, Colombia

5. Jean-Paul Bayzelon
   Superior General
   Paris Foreign Mission Society
   Rue du Bac, 128
   75007 Paris, France

6. Paul-Antoine Bien-Aimé, O.P.
   Pastoral worker
   BP 1746
   Port-au-Prince, Haiti

7. John Boberg, S.V.D.
   Director of World Mission
   Program
   Catholic Theological Union
   5401 S. Cornell Avenue
   Chicago, Illinois 60615
   United States

8. Martin Boelens
   General Councilor
   Congregation of Marianhill
   Via S. Giovanni Eudes, 91
   I-00163 Rome, Italy

9. Oluf Bohn
   High School Teacher
   Marselis Boulevard 3212
   DK-8000 Aarhus C.
   Denmark

10. Boka di Mpasi Londi
    Director/Editor of *Telema*
    Scolasticat S.J.—Kimwenza
    BP 3277 Kinshasa—Gombe Zaire

11. Leslie Boseto
    Pastor, United Church
    Sasamuga
    Choiseul Island
    Solomon Islands

12. Paul Boyle
    Superior General
    Congregation of the Passion
    Piazza SS Giovanni e Paolo, 13
    I-00184 Rome, Italy

13. Mel Brady
    Mission Secretary
    Order of Friars Minor
    Via S. Maria Mediatrice, 25
    I-00165 Rome, Italy

14. Walbert Bühlmann
    Mission Secretary
    Friars Minor Capuchin
    Via Piemonte, 70
    I-00187 Rome, Italy

15. Curtis Cadorette, M.M.
    Director
    Instituto de Estudios Aymaras
    Casilla 295
    Puno, Peru

16. Jean Charbonnier, M.E.P.
    Pastoral Worker/China Research
    Cathedral of the Good Shepherd
    "A" Queen Street
    Singapore 7

17. Michael Chu, S.J.
    General Councilor
    Borgo S. Spirito, 5
    I-00193 Rome, Italy

18. Francisco Claver, S.J.
    Bishop
    Bishop's Residence
    Malaybalay 8201
    Bukidnon, Philippines

19. Giancarlo Collet
    Theology Professor
    Catholic Faculty-Tübingen
    Christophstrasse, 1
    D-74 Tübingen, West Germany

20. Filippo Commissari
    General Councilor, P.I.M.E.
    Via F.D. Guerrazzi, 11
    I-00152 Rome, Italy

21. Ignatius Dekkers
    General Councilor, Redemptorists
    Via Merulana, 31
    CP 2458
    I-0010 Rome, Italy

22. Joan Delaney, M.M.
    Former Exec. Secretary/SEDOS
    Maryknoll Sisters
    Maryknoll, New York 10545

23. Michel de Verteuil, C.S.Sp.
    Training of Lay Leaders
    Archdioc. Pastoral Centre
    2, Carmody Road
    St. Augustine, Trinidad

24. Joseph Di Noia, O.P.
    Ass't. Prof., Systematic Theology
    487 Michigan Avenue, NE
    Washington, DC 20017

25. Therese Disseux
    General Councilor
    Marist Missionary Sisters
    Via Cassia, 1243
    I-00189 Rome, Italy

26. Marie Josee Dor
    Superior General,
    Sisters of Our Lady of Africa
    Villa Vecchia, Via Frascati, 45
    I-00020 Monteporzio Catone
    (Roma), Italy

27. Benitius Egberink
    General Councilor
    Carmelite Order
    Via Giovanni Lanza, 138
    I-00184 Rome, Italy

28. Rose Fernando
    General Councilor
    Franciscan Missionaries of Mary
    Via Giusti, 12
    I-00185 Rome, Italy

29. Gabriele Ferrari
    President of SEDOS
    Superior General
    Xaverian Missionaries
    Via Francesco Nullo, 6
    I-00165 Rome, Italy

30. Michael Fitzgerald, W.F.
    General Councilor
    Via Aurelia, 269
    I-00165 Rome, Italy

31. Robert Gay
    Superior General
    Missionaries of Africa
    Via Aurelia, 269
    I-00165 Rome, Italy

32. Pierre Gordijn, O.F.M.
    Director, Dept. of International/
    Extraordinary Affairs
    Misereor e.V.
    Postfach 1450
    D-5100 Aachen, West Germany

33. Joseph Gremillion
    Director
    Social/Ecumenical Ministry
    P.O. Box 7213
    Shreveport, Louisiana 71107
    United States

34. Joseph Gross
    General Councilor
    Congregation of the Holy Spirit
    195 Clivo Di Cinna
    00136, Rome, Italy

35. William Halliden, S.S.C.
    Seminar Services/Proc. General
    Colomban Fathers
    Corso Trieste, 57
    I-00198 Rome, Italy

36. Cyril Hally, S.S.C.
    Director
    Pacific Mission Institute
    420 Bobbin Head Road
    N. Turramurra, NSW 2074
    Australia

37. Noel Hanrahan
    Superior General
    Mill Hill Fathers
    Lawrence Street
    Mill Hill, London NW7 4JX
    England

38. Robert Hardawiryana, S.J.
    Rector/Theo. Adv.—
    Bishops' Conference
    Pusat Kateketik
    Jalan Abubakar Ali, 1
    Teromolpos 75
    Indonesia

39. Joseph Hardy
    Superior General
    Society for African Missions
    Via della Nocetta, 111
    I-00164 Rome, Italy

40. Hector Herrara Herrara, O.P.
    Radio/Youth Work
    Parroquia San Jose Obrero
    Apartado 241
    Chimbote, Peru

41. Henry Hoeben
    African Desk, Pro Mundi Vita
    Rue de la Limite, 6
    B-1030 Brussels, Belgium

42. Farid Jabre, C.M.
    Professor of Islamic Studies
    BP 624
    Beirut, Lebanon

43. David-Maria Jaeger
Director
Christianity in the Holy Land
Ecumenical Institute—TANTUR
P.B. 19556
Jerusalem, Israel

44. Rafael Janin-Orradre
Secretary General
Spanish Missionary Society
Ferrer del Rio, 17
Madrid—28, Spain

45. Willie Jenkinson, C.S.Sp.
Executive Secretary, SEDOS
CP 5080
I-00100 Rome, Italy

46. Bernard-Antoine Joinet, W.F.
University Chaplain/Economic
Adviser—Bishops' Conference
P.O. Box 280
Dar-es-Salaam, Tanzania

47. Marjorie Keenan, R.S.H.M.
Research Coordinator/
Prospective
106 W. 56 Street
New York, New York 10019
United States

48. Josephine Kollmer
General Councilor
Maryknoll Sisters
Maryknoll, New York 10545
United States

49. Joseph Lang, M.M.
Seminar Task Force/
Proc. General
Collegio Maryknoll
Via Sardegna, 83
I-00187 Rome, Italy

50. Angelo Lazzarotto, P.I.M.E.
Religious Research—Southeast
Asia
Lot 315
Clear Water Bay Road, NT,
Hong Kong

51. João Batista Libanio, S.J.
Theology Professor/
Pastoral Institute—CNBB
Rua Bambina, 115
22 251 Rio de Janeiro
Brazil

52. Margaret Frances Loftus,
S.N.D.-N.
General Councilor
Sisters of Notre Dame de Namur
Via della Giustiniana, 1200
I-00189 Rome, Italy

53. Kenneth MacAulay
Superior General
Scarboro Mission Society
2685 Kingston Road
Scarborough (Ont.) M1M-1M4,
Canada

54. Jean-Louis Martin
Superior General
Quebec Missionary Society
60 rue Desneyers, Pont-Viau
Ville de Laval, H7G LA4
Quebec, Canada

55. John McGrath
General Councilor,
Colomban Fathers
St. Columban's, Grange Rd.
Donaghmede, Raheny
Dublin 13, Ireland

56. Helen McLaughlin
    Assistant General for Africa
    Religious of the Sacred Heart
    Via A. Gandiglio, 27
    Interno 1, Villino 'C,' Scala B
    I-00151 Rome, Italy

57. Ramona Mendiola
    Superior General
    Sisters of the Immaculate Heart of
    Mary
    Via di Villa Troili, 30
    I-00165 Rome, Italy

58. Mauraid Moran
    Directress of Communications
    Religious of the Good Shepherd
    Via Raffaello Sardiello, 20
    I-00165 Rome, Italy

59. Alexander Motanyane, O.M.I.
    Secretary General—Lesotho
    Bishops' Conference
    P.O. Box 78
    Maseru, Lesotho

60. Mary Motte, F.M.M.
    Seminar Task Force/Resource Person
    Via Giusti, 12
    I-00185 Rome, Italy

61. Karl Mueller,
    Mission Secretary
    Society of the Divine Word
    CP 5080/Via dei Verbiti, 1
    I-00100 Rome, Italy

62. Albert Nambiaparambil, C.M.I.
    Secretary—Dialogue Commission
    Indian Bishops' Conference
    Prior General's House
    Cochin 682011
    Kerala, India

63. Rodolfo Navarro Guerra
    Superior General
    Missionaries of Guadalupe
    Córdoba, 17
    Mexico 7, DF, Mexico

64. Leo-Paul Nobert, O.M.I.
    Seminar Services/
    Treasurer of SEDOS
    Via Aurelia, 290
    I-00165 Rome, Italy

65. James P. Noonan
    Superior General
    Maryknoll Fathers
    Maryknoll, New York 10545
    United States

66. Mercy Amba Oduyoye
    Lecturer in Religious Studies
    University of Ibadan
    P.O. Box 1261
    Ibadan, Nigeria

67. Gabriel Ojo
    Professor of Geography/
    National Secretary Council of
    Laity
    University of IFE
    ILE—IFE
    Nigeria

68. Bernard Olivier
    General Councilor for Apostolate
    Dominican Fathers
    Piazza Pietro d'Illiria, 1
    I-00153 Rome, Italy

69. Aloysius Pieris, S.J.
    Director, TULANA
    Dialogue Centre for
    Buddhists/Christians
    435/29 St. Joseph's Estate
    Nungamugoda-Kelaniya
    Sri Lanka

70. Francesco Pierli
    General Councilor
    Comboniani Missionaries
    Via Luigi Lilio, 80
    I-00143 Rome, Italy

71. Godelieve Prove
    Superior General/
    Vice President, SEDOS
    Via di Villa Troili, 32
    I-00163 Rome, Italy

72. Vincent Rabemahafaly
    General Councilor
    Christian Brothers
    Via Aurelia, 476
    I-00165 Rome, Italy

73. Anthony Ramanattu
    General Councilor
    Third Order Regular/Franciscan
    Via dei Fori Imperiali, 1
    I-00186 Rome, Italy

74. Philibert Randriambololona
    Assistant General for Africa
    and Madagascar
    Society of Jesus
    Borgo S. Spirito, 5
    I-00193 Rome, Italy

75. Dirk Rapol
    Study Group
    Missionaries of Scheut
    Via S. Giovanni Eudes, 95
    I-00163 Rome, Italy

76. John Reilly, S.J.
    Retreat Director/
    Theology Lecturer
    Aquinas College
    Palmer Place
    North Adelaide, 5006
    Australia

77. Gabriel Robin
    General Councilor
    Cannonesses of S. Augustine
    Via Camilluccia, 567
    I-00135 Rome, Italy

78. Raymond Rossignol, M.E.P.
    Vicar General
    Rue du Bac, 128
    75007 Paris, France

79. Joseph Hiroshi Sasaki
    Director
    Japanese Mission and Pastoral
    Centre
    28-5 Matsubara 2 chome
    Setagayaku, Tokyo 156
    Japan

80. Robert J. Schreiter, C. P P.S.
    Dean, Chicago Theological Union
    5401 South Cornell Avenue
    Chicago, Illinois 60615
    United States

81. Anthony Smit
    Mission Secretariat
    Salesians
    Via della Pisana, 1111
    I-00163 Rome, Italy

82. Ortrud Stegmaier
    Congregational Research
    Missionary Sisters Servants of the
    Holy Spirit
    Via Camilluccia, 591
    I-00135 Rome, Italy

83. Christine Tan, R.G.S.
    Community Worker in Slums/
    Chairperson: Ecumenical
    Movement for Justice and Peace
    214 N. Domingo
    Quezon City, Philippines

84. Manuel Tavares
    Vicar General
    Consolata Fathers
    Viale delle Mura Aurelia, 11
    I-00165 Rome, Italy

85. Maria-José Tresch, S.S.N.D.
    Seminar Services/Mission Secretary
    Via della Stazione Aurelia, 95
    I-00163 Rome, Italy

86. Josephine Tresoldi
    General Councilor
    Missionarie Comboniane
    Via Boccea, 50
    00166, Rome, Italy

87. Manuel Augusto Trinidade
    Superior General
    Portuguese Missionary Society
    Rua Bernardo Lima, 33
    Lisbon 1, Portugal

88. Jan N. M. Wijngaards, M.H.M.
    Vicar General
    Lawrence Street
    Mill Hill, London NW7 4JX
    England

89. Piet Winnubst
    Director of Foreign Department
    MISSIO, Hermanstrasse, 14
    Aachen, West Germany

90. Harry Winter, O.M.I.
    Pastor/Editor—Ecumenical News
    Holy Family Church
    Box 336
    Pearisburg, Virginia 24134
    United States

91. Francis George
    Vicar General
    Oblates of Mary Immaculate
    Via Aurelia, 290
    I-00165 Rome, Italy

Special Services

92. Mary John Berchmans, R.J.M.
    Interpreter
    Via Nomentana, 325
    I-00162 Rome, Italy

93. Jeannette Dastous, S.A.
    Interpretor
    Villa Vecchia
    Via Frascati, 45
    I-00020 Monteporzio Catone
    (Rome)
    Italy

94. Charles Davignon
    Interpreter
    Pastor—St. Mary Star of the Sea
    Newport, Vermont 05855
    United States

95. Marie Yvonne Duclos, R.S.C.J.
    Interpreter
    Piazza Trinita dei Monti, 3
    I-00187 Rome, Italy

96. Helene Miniaries, C.M.
    Interpreter
    Via Nomentana, 333
    I-00162 Rome, Italy

97. Irene Bonsens, F.M.M.
    Secretary
    Via Giusti, 12
    I-00185 Rome, Italy

98. Josephine Bushell, S.N.D.-N.
    Secretary
    Via della Guistiniana, 1200
    I-00198 Rome, Italy

99. Gemm D'Sa, S.C.M.M.-M.
    Secretary
    Via di Villa Troili, 32
    I-00163 Rome, Italy

100. Manuela Martinez, I.C.M.
    172 Haverstock Hill
    London NW3 2AT
    England

101. Thomas Kretz, S.J.
    Liaison for House Management
    Vatican Observatory
    Palazzo Apostolico
    Castelgandolfo 00040 (Rome)
    Italy

INDEX

Compiled by James Sullivan

675

national security, principle of: in Brazil, 484; in Latin America, 161; in Peru, 129
NATO. *See* North Atlantic Treaty Organization
natural resources: in Asia, 41, 433; in Australia, 211, 563-64, 604; in France, 268; in New Zealand, 569; in Philippines, 617; use of, by rich countries, 336-37, 642. *See also* colonialism
Nauru, 249
Navant, M., 316
Navarro Guerra, Rodolfo, M.G., 83, 630, 631, 670
Neill, Stephen, 109
neocolonialism. *See* colonialism
Nestorians, 22
Netherlands, 325; colonizing by, 403; decline of missionary vocations in, 322; emigration from, 558; missionaries from, 275, 283, 495
Network, 585
New Caledonia, 249, 560; document on, 392-412
New Guinea. *See* Papua New Guinea
New Hebrides, 249, 405
Newman, John Henry, 27
Newton, Isaac, 344
New Zealand: Australian missionaries in, 249; Catholic Overseas aid of, 560-61, 565, 566-67; Catholic Social Services of dioceses in, 568, 569; Catholic Women's League of, 559, 564; Christchurch Commission of, 562; Christian World Service of National Council of Churches of, 560, 563; Commission for Evangelization, Justice and Peace Development of, 560, 561, 566, 567, 568; Commission for the Family of, 568; CORSO of, 561, 567; Diocesan Pastoral Council of, 562; document on, 557-69; Ecumenical Secretariat on Development of, 558, 561, 562, 563, 567; Justice and Peace Commission of, 560, 566, 567; National Council of Churches in, 559, 561, 563; National Mission Council of, 564, 567; Planning Council and Commission of, 564; Social Services Association of, 568; UNDA in, 569; Vincent dePaul Society of, 568
New Zealand Bishops' Conference, 559, 561, 615
Nicaragua, 163, 226
Nichols, James Hastings, 217, 218
Nicolas, Adolfo, S.J., 622
Nicolás del Puerto, Don, 88
Nida, Eugene, 241, 351
Niebuhr, H. Richard, 219, 227
Niebuhr, Reinhold, 219, 223
Nigeria, 288; Australian missionaries in, 249; Christian Association of, 146; Church Missionary Society of, 148; document on, 140-54; National Congress on Evangelism in, 146; National Laity Council of, 596; and Lesotho, 76
Niles, D.T., 222
Nisbet, R., 351
Nkeramihigo, Théoneste, S.J., 498, 499
Nkiere Kena, Philippe, C.I.C.M., 288, 629, 630
Nobert, Leo-Paul, O.M.I., 665, 670
de Nobili, Robert, 452, 515
non-violence, tradition of, 641
Noonan, James P., 670
Norbertine Fathers, 415
Noritake, Suzuki, 108
North Atlantic Treaty Organization, 268
Nostra Aetate, 27, 661
Noumea Conference, 562
nuclear testing, 560, 562
nuclear warfare, 115, 562, 594, 604
nuncios, apostolic, 118, 618
nutrition. *See* malnutrition
Nyerere, Julius, 193, 277, 278
Nzileyel, Belengi, 367

Obadare, 150
Obasanjo, Olusegun, 142
Oblate Fathers of St. Joseph, 121, 138
Oblates of Mary Immaculate, 74, 270
Oceania, 559; missionary activity in, 246, 249, 271; UNDA in, 569

Oceanian Bishops' Conference, 560
Octogesima Adveniens, 562, 582
Oduyoye, Mercy Amba, 140, 629, 630, 631, 670
Ogot, B.A., 192
Ojo, Gabriel, 596, 629, 631, 670
Okullu, 198
Oliver, Roland, 199
Olivier, Bernard, 670
O'Malley, William, 226
Order of Friars. *See* Franciscans
Order of Preachers. *See* Dominicans
Orientalium Ecclesiarum, 642
Orthodox church, interreligious dialogue with, 38
Otárola, Bertino, 121
Ottaviani, Alfredo, 467
Oudenrijn, F.V.D., 577
Oxtoby, Willard G., 390

Pacem in Terris, 467
Pachai, B., 199
Pacific Mission Institute, 245, 250, 257
Pacific Partnership for Human Development, 560, 562, 564, 565, 566
Pacific Regional Seminary, 559, 565
Pacific Region Bishop's Conference, 559, 615
Pakistan, 46; Australian missionaries in, 249; government influence of church in, 37; major religious superiors in, 50; population of, 336
Palestine, 269
Pallotine Fathers, 248
Panama, 161; Canal Treaty of, 226, 581
Pannenberg, W., 574, 577, 578
Pantin, Anthony, C.S.Sp., 368, 629, 630
Papua New Guinea, 198; aid to, 560; Australian missionaries in, 249, 250, 252, 259; as colony of Australia, 248; documents on, 171-85; 392-412; and Pacific Partnership for Human Development, 565
Papua New Guinea Bishops' Conference, 392, 559, 615
Paraguay, 161, 249
Paris Evangelical Missionary Society, 74
Parkinson, C.N., 318, 350
Parrinder, G., 190-91, 199
Partnership for Development in Asia. *See* Asia Partnership for Human Development
Pastor, Alfredo, 139
Pathrapankal, J., 425
Paton, D.M., 351
dePaul, Saint Vincent, 264
Paul VI: address of, in India, 413; advice on justice and peace commissions of, 605; in Australia, 560; condemnation of capitalist system by, 164; example of, 164; statement of, in Samoa, 566-67; and Synod of Bishops, 313; in Uganda, 79; writings of, 287, 345, 351, 366
Paulu, Luis, 218
Pavan, Pietro, 467
Pax Christi, 582, 585
Pedro, Mang, 622
Pedro de Ayala, Fra, 87
Pedro Gómez Maraver, Don, 87
Pedro of Ghent, Fra, 85-86
Pelikan, Jaroslav, 390
Pelletier, Maria Euphrasia, 264
Peña, Raymond, 225, 228
Penn, William, 462
Pentecostal movement. *See* charismatics
People's Republic of China. *See* China
Perfectae Caritatis, 322
Perrin-Jassy, Marie-France, 192
Peru: Association of Exporters in, 123; colonizing of, 500-01; document on, 120-39; JEC youth movement in, 132; JOC workers in, 132; missionaries in, 94, 249
Peruvian Bishops' Conference, 135, 137
Pesch, R., 575, 578
Peter, Saint, 27
Peukert, H., 577
Philip II, King of Spain, 90

DATE DUE

FEB 24 90			

HIGHSMITH   #LO-45220